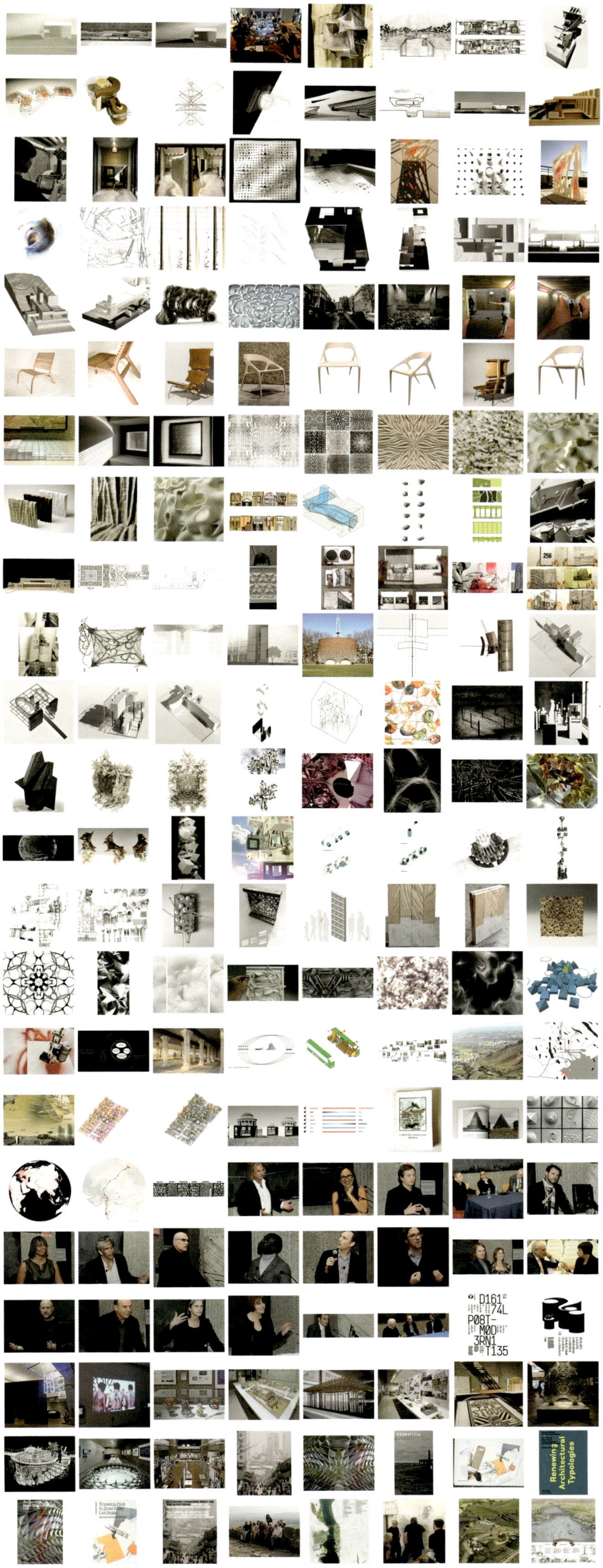

RETROSPECTA

37

Retrospecta 37
Yale School of Architecture
2013–2014

Letter From The Dean

Architecture shapes and is shaped by the wider forces of society. The built environment must adapt to the demands of new industries and economies—ours is a functional art—therefore core aspects of the discipline are immune to shifting styles. Processes of making may change and evolve, but fundamental tenets of space and physical form are timeless. New art climbs on the shoulders of what went before.

At the Yale School of Architecture, we believe in the primacy of building. We embrace new technologies not for their own sake, but as one of many tools to interrogate ideas about building. Students must navigate a multitude of perspectives and ideologies, in the process honing their own voice and preparing to lead the profession. Leadership and collaboration complement one another, and we engage fellow architects and others across disciplines to pursue open questions of place and purpose. We are energized by spirited debate.

Retrospecta documents the work and life of a year in Paul Rudolph Hall. Contained within is inspiration for career-long design pursuits. Guided by history, equipped with core skills, and receptive to outside approaches, our students set forth to construct the future.

Robert A.M. Stern
Dean and J.M. Hoppin
Professor of Architecture

RETROSPECTA 36 2012 2013

RETROSPECTA 2011.2012 YALE SCHOOL OF ARCHITECTURE

RETROSPECTA YALE SCHOOL OF ARCHITECTURE 2010/201

RETROSPECTA 2009 2010 Yale School of Architecture

RETROSPECTA 08–09 THE YALE SCHOOL OF ARCHITECTURE 

TROSPECTA 2007–2008 Yale School of Architecture

RETROSPECTA 2006/2007 Yale School of Architecture

Yale School of Architecture RETROSPECTA 2005/2006

RETROSPECTA 2004 – 2005 YALE SCHOOL OF ARCHITECTURE

RETROSPECTA YALE SCHOOL OF ARCHITECTURE 2003–04

rospecta '02–'03 Yale School of Architecture

RETROSPECTA / Yale School of Architecture 01_02

YALE SCHOOL OF ARCHITECTURE RETROSPECTA 2000—2001

Retrospecta Yale School of Architecture | 1999-2000

Yale School of Architecture Retrospecta 98_99

Letter From The Editors

As a set, the volumes of Retrospecta catalog decades of activity at the Yale School of Architecture. Standing alone, each volume is a snapshot of evolving architectural and graphic design trends. Retrospecta 37 takes progress as its theme, and attempts to mark more than the passage of another year. This volume is organized to record our ongoing growth as a student body, as a class, and as individuals.

This growth builds on our collective traditions—the lecture series and its celebrated receptions, the roster of returning and visiting critics and courses—and charts new ground through our development as designers among a community of scholars. In this Retrospecta, academic work is interspersed with moments that embody the culture and camaraderie of the school. For the first time, mid-term documentation is included for many student projects to show progress on a more intimate scale, giving a glimpse of the process behind the product. Although completed projects and papers suggest finality, the Retrospecta lineage serves as a reminder that our education continues beyond these pages. In that sense, this volume captures our work in progress.

We extend our sincere gratitude to our graphic design partners from the Yale School of Art, Yotam Hadar and Jiyoni Kim, for their invaluable ability to transform concept into physical reality. We thank Dean Stern for clear vision and critical feedback. Richard Kaplan of Allied Printing and Michael Bierut of Pentagram guided us through the complex publishing process. Richard DeFlumeri, John Jacobson, and Nina Rappaport gave us their constant support. Finally, we thank the donors who enable this publication, and the faculty and students who have shared their experiments and inspirations this year.

Dov Feinmesser
Anthony Gagliardi
Jenny (Eunhyung) Kim
Andrew Sternad

Students

MASTER OF ARCHITECTURE I THIRD YEAR

Ali John Pierre Artemel
B.S. Univ. Virginia 2011
Alexandria, VA

Jasdeep Singh Bhalla
B.S. Univ. College (London) 2007, Hayes, United Kingdom

Mary Franklin Burr
B.A. Williams Coll. 2008, Boston, MA

David Burt
B.S. Ohio State Univ. (Columbus) 2010, Mount Vernon, OH

Robert Anthony Cannavino
B.S. Arizona State Univ. 2009, Wilton, CT

Chun Henry Chan
B.A. Yale Univ., New York, NY

Tyler Seth Collins
B.A. Univ. Texas (Austin) 2011, Austin, TX

Ryan Shannon Connolly
B.S. Ohio State Univ. (Columbus) 2011, Sylvania, OH

Carl David Cornilsen **
B.S. Univ. Michigan (Ann Arbor) 2005, Houghton, MI

Danielle Davis
B.E.D. Texas A&M Univ. (College Station) 2011, Garland, TX

Thomas Aaron Day
B.F.A. Univ. Massachusetts (Amherst) 2011, New Haven, CT

Violette Constance de La Selle
B.S. Univ. Virginia 2008, New York, NY

Evan Michael Dobson
B.S. Ohio State Univ. (Columbus) 2009, Springfield, OH

Ivan Farr
B.E.D. Texas A&M Univ. (College Station) 2009, College Station, TX

Clark Chessin Gertler
M.A. Stanford Univ., Weston, MA

Brandon David Hall
B.S. Washington Univ. (St. Louis) 2010, Long Grove, IL

Jing Han
B.A. Univ. Pennsylvania 2010, Beijing, China

Charles Hickox
B.A. Brown Univ. 2008, Boston, MA

Brian S. Hong **
B.A. Univ. California (Berkeley) 2007, Berkeley, CA

Elisa Iturbe *
B.A. Yale Univ. 2008, Bonita, CA

Daniel Peter Jacobs
B.S. Washington Univ. (Missouri) 2010, Urbana, IL

Ann Morrow Johnson **
B.A. Washington Univ. (Missouri) 2009, Houston, TX

Constantine Kiratzidis
B.S. Univ. Pretoria 2006, Phalaborwa, South Africa graduated February 2014

Jacqueline Kow
B.S. Univ. Michigan (Ann Arbor) 2011, Troy, MI

Kyeong Jae Lee
B.E. Seoul National Univ. 2008, Jeonju, Republic of Korea

Russell Campbell LeStourgeon
B.A. Yale Univ. 2010, Nashville, TN

Bryan Andrew Maddock
B.S. Arizona State Univ. 2009, Lyons, NY

Nicholas Cravens McAdoo
B.S. Princeton Univ. 2009, San Francisco, CA

Leeland Thomas McPhail
B.S. Georgia Inst. of Technology 2010, Atlanta, GA

Thomas Michael Medek
B.S. Catholic Univ. of America 2007, Washington, D.C.

Jonathon Robert Meier
B.A. Ball State Univ. 2010, Avon, IN

Christian Thomas Mueller
B.F.A. Rhode Island School of Design 2005, Washington, D.C.

Mohamed Aly Nazmy
B.S. Ohio State Univ. (Columbus) 2009, Orono, ME

Justin Nguyen
B.S. McGill Univ. 2010, Saint-Lambert, Quebec, Canada

Cristian Alexandru Oncescu
B.A. Yale Univ. 2009, Plano, TX

Alexander Osei-Bonsu
B.F.A. Univ. Oxford 2007, London, United Kingdom

Scott Michael Parks
B.A., B.B.A. Univ. Texas (Austin) 2011, Carrollton, TX

Talia Pinto-Handler
B.S. Univ. Michigan (Ann Arbor) 2010, Pittsburgh, PA

Allen Plasencia
B.A. Florida International Univ. 2010, Miami Springs, FL

Jason Dean Roberts
B.A. Judson College (Illinois) 2009, Yorkville, IL

Alexander Julian Sassaroli
B.A. Yale Univ. 2008, New Providence, NJ

William James Sheridan
M.A. Univ. College (London) 2011, Bedford, Nova Scotia, Canada

Kathleen Bridget Stranix
B.S. Univ. Virginia 2009, Vienna, VA

Kailun Sun
B.S. Univ. Virginia 2011, Shanghai, China

Xiaodi Sun
B.A. Franklin & Marshall Coll. 2011, Suzhou, Jiangsu, China

Ian Svilokos
B.Des. Univ. Florida 2011, Ponte Vedra Beach, FL

Jonathan Vincent Swendris
B.S. Univ. Michigan (Ann Arbor) 2011, Ann Arbor, MI

Alice Winn Tai
B.A. Yale Univ. 2008, Forest Hills, NY

Nika Taubinsky
B.A. Brown Univ. 2010, Santa Rosa, CA

Mark Robert Tumiski
B.A. Brown Univ. 2008, Brooklyn, NY

Brittany Lane Utting
B.S. Georgia Inst. of Technology 2011, Peachtree City, GA

Constance Marie Vale
B.F.A. Parsons The New School of Design 2007, Latrobe, PA

Caroline Marie VanAcker
B.S. Univ. Illinois (Urbana-Champaign) 2011, Palatine, IL

Kate Megan Warren
B.A. New York Univ. 2009, Gilford, N.H.

Matthew Hastings White **
B.S. Washington Univ. (Missouri) 2006, Lake Forest, IL

Evan Jon Wiskup
B.S. Washington Univ. (Missouri) 2011, Tampa, FL

Ru-Shyan Yen *
B.A. Wheaton Coll. (Mass.) 2008, Pittsburgh, PA

Sheena Shiyi Zhang *
B.S. Univ. Georgia (Athens) 2011, Watkinsville, GA

MASTER OF ARCHITECTURE I SECOND YEAR

Leah Jaclyn Abrams
B.A. Univ. Pennsylvania 2011, Wall Township, NJ

Maya Catherine Alexander
B.I.D. Louisiana State Univ. (Baton Rouge) 2007, Brooklyn, NY

Elena Rachel Baranes
B.A. Boston Univ. 2011, Washington, D.C.

Emily D. Bell
B.A. Colgate Univ. 2012, Southbury, CT

Hiba Javed Bhatty
B.S. Univ. Illinois (Urbana-Champaign) 2011, Glenview, IL

Kara Marie Biczykowski
B.S. Ohio State Univ. (Columbus) 2012, Amherst, OH

Amanda Nicole Bridges
A.B. Harvard Univ. 2010, Villanova, PA

Alissa Yen Chastain
B.A. Wellesley Coll. 2010, Lafayette, CA

Dionysus Roy Cho
B.A.S. Waterloo Univ. 2011, Edmonton, Canada

Stanley Minsoo Cho
B.A. Univ. California (Los Angeles) 2001, Tujunga, CA

Sungwoo Matthew Choi
B.A. Washington Univ. (Missouri) 2012, Gwangju, Republic of Korea

Suhni Chung
B.S. Massachusetts Inst. of Technology 2009, Seoul, Republic of Korea

Michael Robinson Cohen
A.B. Brown Univ. 2008, Chappaqua, NY

Thomas Rush Friddle
B.A. Ball State Univ. 2012, Muncie, IN

Tamrat Tesfaye Gebremichael
B.S. Univ. Virginia 2012, Alexandria, VA

Bruce David Hancock
A.B. Princeton Univ. 2003, Costa Mesa, CA

Kirk McFadden Henderson
B.A. Yale Univ. 2005, Washington, D.C.

Zachary Dillon Huelsing
M.A. Eastern Illinois Univ. 2007, Chicago, IL

Tyson Jang
B.A. Boston College 2009, Seoul, Republic of Korea

Haelee Jung
B.F.A. Seoul National Univ. 2009, Daejeon, Republic of Korea

John-Thaddeus Keeley
A.B. Harvard Univ. 2007, Morristown, NJ

Julie Kim
B.F.A. Cooper Union 2009, Port Washington, NY

Peter K. Le
B.A. Amherst College 2010, Garden Grove, CA

Belinda Lee
B.S. Washington Univ. (Missouri) 2012, New Haven, CT

Hyeun Jason Lee
B.S. Ohio State Univ. (Columbus) 2011, Falls Church, VA

Minu Lee
M.S. Seoul National Univ. 2012, Seoul, Republic of Korea

Mun Hee Lee
B.A. Tufts Univ. 2010, Seoul, Republic of Korea

Meghan Lewis *
B.S. Washington Univ. (Missouri) 2011, Denver, CO

Meghan Baker McAllister
B.A. Haverford Coll. 2010, Jenkintown, PA

William Ross McClellan
B.Des. Univ. Florida 2012, Tallahassee, FL

Henry Thomas Mezza
B.S. Ball State Univ. 2012, Arlington Heights, IL

Michael Christopher Miller
B.S. Georgia Inst. of Technology 2012, Kennesaw, GA

Nicholas Muraglia
B.A. Columbia Univ. 2008, Los Angeles, CA

Phillip Josh Takeshi Nakamura
B.S. Univ. Utah 2012, Cottonwood Heights, UT

Hui Zhen Ng
B.S. Univ. College London 2012, Singapore

Daniel Huy Nguyen
B.A. Univ. California (Los Angeles) 2011, Torrance, CA

Junpei Okai
B.A. Univ. California (Los Angeles) 2011, Murrieta, CA

Aisha Kiku Pasha
B.A. Brown Univ. 2010, Seattle, WA

Jeannette Kittredge Penniman
B.A. Yale Univ. 2012, Essex, CT

Tyler Benjamin Pertman
B.S. Univ. Alberta 2010, Edmonton, Canada

Mark Wendell Peterson
M.B.A. Univ. Michigan (Ann Arbor) 2009, Brooklyn, NY

Lauren Elizabeth Raab
B.S. Cornell Univ. 2011, Crown Point, IN

Mahdi Sabbagh
B.A. Yale Univ. 2010, Jerusalem, Israel

Robert K. Scott
B.S. Ohio State Univ. (Columbus) 2011, Columbus, OH

Benjamin Lucas Smith
B.S. Georgia Inst. of Technology 2012, Hartford, WI

Sarah Elaine Smith
B.S. Univ. Cincinnati 2010, Cincinnati, OH

Melody J. Song
B.A. New York Univ. 2011, Seoul, Republic of Korea

Amy J. Su
B.F.A. Rhode Island School Design 2009, Portland, OR

Jonathan Feng Sun
B.E. Univ. Toronto 2012, Ontario, Canada

Zachary Adam Veach
B.A. Washington Univ. 2012, Teaneck, NJ

Emau Vega
B.E.D. Texas A&M Univ. (College Station) 2011, Waco, TX

Perry S. Wexelberg
B.A. Univ. California (Santa Cruz) 2008, El Cerrito, CA

John Blakely Wolfe
B.S. Univ. Virginia 2009, Annandale, VA

* Joint degree program, M.E.M., School of Forestry & Environmental Studies

** Joint-degree program, M.B.A., School of Management

MASTER OF ARCHITECTURE I FIRST YEAR

Lisa Ning Albaugh
B.S. United States Naval Academy 2006, College Park, MD
Mohammad Abdulatif Alothman
B.S. King Fahd Univ. of Petroleum and Minerals 2008, Dhahran, Saudi Arabia
Luke Alan Anderson
B.S. Ohio State Univ. (Columbus) 2013, Cincinnati, OH
Jessica Flore Angel
B.S. École Polytechnique Fédérale de Lausanne 2011, Paris, France
Li De Jack Bian
B.S. McGill Univ. 2013, Toronto, Canada
Dorian Ascher Booth
B.A. Univ. Pennsylvania 2012, Ogunquit, ME
Benjamin Stuart Harlan Bourgoin
B.A. Univ. Washington 2012, Lake Forest Park, WA
Ling Jun Chen
A.B. Princeton Univ. 2012, Huntsville, Canada
Tianhui Chen
B.A., B.F.A. Cornell Univ. 2013, Gaithersburg, MD
Andrew Eric Dadds
B.A.S. Univ. Waterloo 2012, Oakville, Canada
Shayari Hiranya De Silva
B.A. Yale Univ. 2011, Colombo, Sri Lanka
Jessica Lynn Elliott
B.Des. Univ. Florida 2013, Casselberry, FL
Dov Feinmesser
B.A.S. Ryerson Univ. 2011, Jerusalem, Israel
Hugo Gregory Fenaux
B.S. Univ. Virginia 2012, Dillwyn, VA
Dante T.H. Furioso
B.A. Wesleyan Univ. (Conn.) 2007, Washington, D.C.
Anthony Vincent Gagliardi
B.S. Ohio State Univ. (Columbus) 2013, Parma, OH
Michelle Jennifer Gonzalez
B.S. Univ. Michigan (Ann Arbor) 2013, West Orange, NJ
Michael Edward Harrison
B.S. Univ. Michigan (Ann Arbor) 2013, Grosse Pointe Park, MI
Ting Ting Pearl Ho
B.S. Univ. Virginia 2011, Hong Kong
Seyedeh Kiana Hosseini
B.A. Tehran Univ. 2013, Karaj, Iran
Anne Lawren Householder
B.A.S. Univ. Illinois (Urbana-Champaign) 2013, Park Ridge, IL
Cynthia Hsu
B.A. Univ. California (San Diego) 2012, Yorba Linda, CA
Samantha Leigh Jaff
B.A. Colby College 2011, Newton, MA
Lila Jiang Chen
B.S. McGill Univ. 2011, Panama City, Panama
Charles Anderson Kane
B.A. Clemson Univ. 2011, Lake Wylie, SC
Sarah Elizabeth Kasper
B.S. Univ. Illinois (Urbana-Champaign) 2013, Crete, IL
James E. Kehl
B.S. Univ. Cincinnati 2010, Newark, OH
Nicolas Thornton Kemper
B.A. Yale Univ. 2011, Kansas City, MO
Eunhyung Kim
B.A.S. Univ. Waterloo 2012, Calgary, Canada
John Walker Kleinschmidt
B.A. Washington Univ. (St. Louis) 2008, Fort Atkinson, WI
Elizabeth Ann LeBlanc
B.A.S. Univ. Texas (Austin) 2013, San Antonio, TX
Vittorio F. Lovato
B.S. Univ. Michigan (Ann Arbor) 2012, Berkley, MI
Clarissa Astrid Luwia
B.Des. Univ. Sydney 2012, New South Wales, Australia
Anne Wing Yan Ma
B.A.S. Univ. Waterloo 2011, Toronto, Canada
Richard David Mandimika
B.A. Univ. Miami (Ohio) 2012, Harare, Zimbabwe
Megan Elizabeth McDonough
B.S. Georgia Inst. of Technology 2013, Ambler, PA
Anna Meloyan
B.A. Univ. Calif. (Los Angeles) 2013, Glendale, CA
Seokim Min
B.S. Korea Advanced Inst. of Science and Technology 2013, Seoul, Republic of Korea
Boris Morin-Defoy
B.S. McGill Univ. 2011, Montreal, Canada
Kristin Louise Nothwehr
B.A. Yale Univ. 2006, Brooklyn, NY
Justin David Oh
B.A.S. Ryerson Univ. 2013, Calgary, Canada
Xiaoyi Pu
B.S. McGill Univ. 2012, Beijing, China
Feng Qian
B.E. Southeast Univ. (Nanjing) 2013, Nanjing, China
Madelynn Christine Ringo
B.A. Univ. Kentucky (Lexington) 2012, Bloomfield, KY
Luis Enrique Salas Porras
B.A. Rice Univ. 2011, Chihuahua, Mexico
Dima Ramzi Srouji
B.A. Kingston Univ. 2012, New Haven, CT
Katherine Rose Stege
B.E.D. Univ. Colorado (Boulder) 2012, Leadville, CO
Andrew John釘Sternad
B.A. Washington Univ. (St. Louis) 2009, Norcross, GA
Winny Windasari Tan
B.A. Carnegie Mellon Univ. 2012, Singapore
You Zhi Eugene Tan
B.A. National Univ. Singapore 2012, Singapore
Caitlin Mory Thissen
B.S. Univ. Utah 2013, Salt Lake City, UT
Chengqi John Wan
B.S. Univ. College London 2013, Singapore
Shuo Wang
B.A.S. Univ. Waterloo 2013, Kitchener, Canada
Xinyi Wang
B.Arch. Tsinghua Univ. 2013, Beijing, China
Xiao Wu
B.S. Univ. Virginia 2012, Hangzhou, China

MASTER OF ARCHITECTURE II SECOND YEAR

John Vincent Farrace
B.Arch. Univ. Southern California 2012, Sacramento, CA
Swarnabh Ghosh
B.Arch. Sushant School Art and Architecture 2012, Gurgaon, India
Daniel Greenfield
B.Arch. Pratt Institute 2006, New York, NY
Yoojin Han
B.Arch. Seoul National Univ. 2012, Seoul, Republic of Korea
Alisa Kay Hintz
B.Arch. Univ. Arizona 2006, Avondale, AZ
Hochung Kim
B.Arch. California Polytechnic State Univ. (San Luis Obispo) 2011, Fullerton, CA
Stephanie Lee
B.Arch. Virginia Polytechnic Inst. and State Univ. 2012, Gaithersburg, MD
Mansi Maheshwari
B.Arch. School of Planning and Architecture 2010, Gurgaon, India
Michael R. McGrattan
B.Arch. Miami Univ. 2006, Silver Spring, MD
Eleanor Kate Measham
B.Arch. Univ. Cambridge 2010, Stockbridge, United Kingdom
Miron M. Nawratil
B.Arch. Virginia Polytechnic Inst. and State Univ. 2007, White Plains, NY
James Morgan Petty
B.Arch. Houston Univ. (University Park) 2008, Schulenburg, TX
Matthew Robert Rauch
B.Arch. Virginia Polytechnic Inst. and State Univ. 2012, Simpsonville, SC
Craig Matthew Rosman
B.Arch. Carnegie Mellon Univ. 2010, Egg Harbor Township, NJ
Jonathan Grant Scott
B.Arch. Boston Architectural Center 2011, Boston, MA
Jie Tian
B.Arch. Iowa State Univ. 2011, Cincinnati, OH
Jay Tsai
B.Arch. New Jersey Inst. of Technology 2010, Hillsborough, NJ
Mengyao Yu
M.Arch. Tsinghua Univ. 2012, Beijing, China

MASTER OF ARCHITECTURE II FIRST YEAR

Karolina Maria Czeczek
M.Arch. Cracow Univ. of Technology 2010, Krosno, Poland
Raphael de la Fontaine
B.Arch. Pratt Institute 2011, New Haven, CT
Julia Futo
B.Arch. Univ. of Applied Arts Vienna 2009, Brooklyn, NY
Elvira Hoxha
B.Arch. New Jersey Inst. of Technology 2013, Tirana, Albania
Stephanie Anne Arrienda Jazmines
B.Arch. Univ. Notre Dame (Indiana) 2011, Glendale, CA
Amir A. Karimpour
B.Arch. Pratt Institute 2013, Moraga, CA
Read James Langworthy
B.Arch. Carnegie Mellon Univ. 2007, Seattle, WA
Mengran Li
B.Arch. Tsinghua Univ. 2012, Daqing, China
Yifan Li
M.Arch. Univ. Adelaide 2010, Chongqing, China
Kate Alexandra Lisi
B.Arch. Rensselaer Polytechnic Inst. 2013, Orange, CT
Laurence Peter Esmond Lumley
B.Arch. Univ. Cambridge 2011, London, United Kingdom
Daniel James Luster
B.Arch. Univ. Tennessee (Knoxville) 2010, Philadelphia, PA
Peter Allen McInish
B.Arch. Auburn Univ. 2013, Dothan, Ala.
Olen Snow Milholland
B.Arch. Univ. Southern California 2009, Boise, Idaho
Katarzyna Magdalena Pozniak
B.Arch. Cornell Univ. 2013, Gdansk, Poland
Ian Stewart Spencer
B.S., B.Arch. Univ. Houston 2013, Spring Branch, TX
Adam Ramsey Wagoner
M.Arch. Kansas State Univ. 2009, McPherson, Kans.
Kin Tak Yu
B.A. Southern California Inst. of Architcture 2012, Hong Kong
Boyuan Zhang
B.Arch. Tsinghua Univ. 2013, Zhuhai, China

MASTER OF ENVIRONMENTAL DESIGN SECOND YEAR

Anuj Daudayal Daga
B.Arch. Academy Architecture 2008, Mumbai, India
Ayeza Rahat Qureshi
B.S. Univ. College London 2008, Karachi, Pakistan
Britton Edward Rogers
B.Arch. Univ. Texas (Austin) 1998, New Haven, CT
Daniel Edward Snyder
B.Arch. Drexel Univ. 1980, Savannah, GA
Jessica Ann Varner
M.Arch. Yale Univ. 2008, Guilford, CT

MASTER OF ENVIRONMENTAL DESIGN FIRST YEAR

Benyameen A B Y Ghareeb
B.Arch. 2008, M.Arch. 2009 Univ. Miami, Kuwait City, Kuwait
Eric D. Peterson
B.A. Hampshire Coll. 2010, New Haven, CT
Eric Wycoff Rogers
B.F.A. California Coll. of Arts and Crafts 2013, San Francisco, CA
Andrew David Ruff
B.Arch. Univ. Tennessee (Knoxville) 2011, New Haven, CT
Brent Sturlaugson
B.Arch. Univ. Oregon 2008, Rapid City, SD

DOCTOR OF PHILOSOPHY FIFTH YEAR

Joseph Lawrence Clarke
M.Arch. Univ. Cincinnati 2006, New York, NY
Kyle Andrew Dugdale
M.Arch. Harvard Univ. 2002, New Haven, CT

DOCTOR OF PHILOSOPHY THIRD YEAR

Anna Bokov
M.Arch. Harvard Univ. 2004, Calverton, NY
Surry Schlabs
M.Arch. Yale Univ. 2003, New Haven, CT

DOCTOR OF PHILOSOPHY SECOND YEAR

Timothy Steffen Altenhof
M.Arch. Acad. of Fine Arts Vienna 2009, Vienna, Austria
Ioanna Angelidou
M.Arch. Columbia Univ. 2009, New York, NY

DOCTOR OF PHILOSOPHY FIRST YEAR

Theodossios Issaias
M.Arch. Massachusetts Inst. of Technology 2011, Athens, Greece
Skender Luarasi
M.Arch. Massachusetts Inst. of Technology 2005, Somerville, MA

EXIT

EXIT

Faculty

OFFICE OF ADMINISTRATION

Deamer, Peggy
Assistant Dean of Student and Academic Affairs and Professor
Forster, Kurt W.
Professor Emeritus and Director, PhD Doctoral Program
Gage, Mark F.
Assistant Dean for Admissions & External Communications and Associate Professor
Hsiang, Joyce
Acting Assistant Dean of Student and Academic Affairs
Jacobson, John D.
Associate Dean and Professor (Adjunct)
Mendis, Bimal
Assistant Dean and Assistant Professor (Adjunct), Director of Undergraduate Studies and Career Development
Stern, Robert A.M.
Dean and J.M. Hoppin Professor

REGULAR FACULTY

Addington, Michelle D.
Hines Professor of Sustainable Architectural Design
Bald, Sunil
Assistant Professor (Adjunct)
Beeby, Thomas H.
Professor (Adjunct)
Berke, Deborah
Professor (Adjunct)
Bloomer, Kent C.
Professor (Adjunct)
Brooks, Turner
Professor (Adjunct)
Easterling, Keller A.
Professor
Felson, Alexander
Assistant Professor / School of Forestry
Garvin, Alexander
Professor (Adjunct)
Gehner, Martin D.
Professor Emeritus
Harris, Steven
Professor (Adjunct)
Hayden, Dolores
Professor / American Studies
Koetter, Fred
Professor (Adjunct)
Mitchell, Edward
Associate Professor
Moon, Kyoung Sun
Assistant Professor
Pelkonen, Eeva-Liisa
Associate Professor
Petit, Emmanuel
Associate Professor
Plattus, Alan
Professor
Purves, Alexander
Professor Emeritus
Rubin, Elihu
Assistant Professor
Sanders, Joel
Professor (Adjunct)

CHAIRS

Adjaye, David
Norman R. Foster Visiting Professor
Aureli, Pier Vittorio
William B. and Charlotte Shepherd Davenport II Visiting Professor
Bellew, Patrick
Eero Saarinen Visiting Professor
Berke, Deborah
William Henry Bishop Visiting Professor
Bow, Andrew
Eero Saarinen Visiting Professor
Carpo, Mario
Vincent Scully Visiting Professor
Eisenman, Peter
Charles Gwathmey Professor in Practice
Gehry, Frank O.
Louis I. Kahn Visiting Professor
Huljich, Georgina
Louis I. Kahn Visiting Assistant Professor
Jain, Bijoy
Norman R. Foster Visiting Professor
Lynn, Greg
William B. and Charlotte Shepherd Davenport Visiting Professor
Porphyrios, Demetri
Louis I. Kahn Visiting Professor
Shim, Brigitte
Eero Saarinen Visiting Professor
Spence, John
Edward P. Bass Distinguished Visiting Fellow
Spina, Marcelo
Louis I. Kahn Visiting Assistant Professor
von Moos, Stanislaus
Vincent Scully Visiting Professor
Wood, Daniel
Louis I. Kahn Visiting Assistant Professor
Zenghelis, Elia
William B. and Charlotte Shepherd Davenport Visiting Professor of Architecture

VISITING FACULTY AND LIBRARIANS

Harries, Karsten
Professor of Philosophy, Department of Philosophy, Yale University
Townsend, Allen
Director, Arts Library, Yale University
Scully, Vincent J., Jr.
Sterling Professor Emeritus, History of Art Department, Yale University

CRITICS AND LECTURERS

Agran, Victor
Apicella, John
Atkin, Rebecca
Bellomio, Anibal
Benner, Andrew
Bernstein, Phillip G.
Biklen, Noah
Blood, John
Bond, Jason
Britton, Karla
Brouard, Paul B.
Buck, Brennan
Buckley, Eric
Bulman, Luke
Caldeira, Marta Justo
Chadwick, Aran
Cowell, Christopher
Davies, Trattie
de Bretteville, Peter
DeDonato, Amy
DiBlasi, Thomas
Doyle, Aidan
Eberhart, John
Finio, Martin
Forman, Avram
Fuermann, Bryan
Gibble, Kenneth
Gray, Kevin
Harby, Stephen
Harrison, Ariane Lourie
Harwell, Andrei
Haughney, Robert
Hawkins, Kristin
Highfill, Brantley
Hsiang, Joyce
Hume, Nathan
Kawai, Yoko
Kenet, Brian
Knight, George
Lauritano, Steven
Lelyveld, Amy
Leung, Jennifer
Long, M.J.
Marchesin, Andrew
Moore, Joeb
Newman, Herbert S.
Newton, Timothy
Organschi, Alan W.
Pell, Ben
Pirie, Laura
Ponce de Leon, Victoria
Puurunen, Eero
Razza, Craig
Rotheroe, Kevin
Sabatelli, Evan
Shahane, Aniket
Sherer, Daniel
Stanley, Edward
Steiner, Philip
Trojanowski, Adam
Wiseman, Carter
Young, Michael
Zook, Tom

Butterfield, Brian
Director of Exhibitions
Hopfner, Adam
Critic, Building Project Director
Reisz, Todd
Daniel Rose Visiting Professor

INSTRUCTORS

Curts, Darin
Instructor in Practice
Pilo, Amrit
Instructor in Practice
Pollack, Jeffrey
Instructor
Salvatore, Ryan
Instructor

Awards

FACULTY AWARDS

Kyoung Sun Moon
2014 Yale University Provost's Prize
Emmanuel Petit
Professor King-lui Wu Teaching Award

STUDENT FELLOWSHIPS

Kathleen Bridget Stranix
William Wirt Winchester Traveling Fellowship
Robert Anthony Cannavino
Gertraud A. Wood Traveling Fellowship, awarded 2013
Ivan Farr
George Nelson Scholarship, awarded 2013
William James Sheridan IV
David M. Schwarz/ Architectural Services Good Times Award

STUDENT MEDALS AND PRIZES

Robert Anthony Cannavino
American Institute of Architects Henry Adams Medal
Daniel Peter Jacobs
Alpha Rho Chi Medal
Jessica Ann Varner
American Institute of Architects Henry Adams Certificate
Craig Matthew Rosman
William Edward Parsons Memorial Medal
Kathleen Bridget Stranix
Wendy Elizabeth Blanning Prize, awarded 2013
Brittany Lane Utting
Sonia Albert Schimberg Prize
Alice Winn Tai
Janet Cain Sielaff Alumni Award
Constance Marie Vale
Moulton Andrus Award
Eleanor Kate Measham
The Drawing Prize
Thomas Michael Medek
Gene Lewis Book Prize
Ayeza Rahat Qureshi
David Taylor Memorial Prize

STUDENT INTERNSHIPS

Bryan Andrew Maddock
Takenaka Corporation Summer Internship, awarded 2013
Evan Jon Wiskup
David M. Schwarz Architectural Services Summer Internship and Traveling Fellowship, awarded 2013

H.I. FELDMAN PRIZE WINNER

Bryan Andrew Maddock
Fall 2013

H.I. FELDMAN PRIZE NOMINEES

Tyler Seth Collins
Fall 2013
Karolina Maria Czeczek
Fall 2013
Ivan Farr
Fall 2013, Spring 2014
Brandon David Hall
Fall 2013
Daniel Peter Jacobs
Fall 2013, Spring 2014
Ann Morrow Johnson
Fall 2013
Kate Alexandra Lisi
Fall 2013
Bryan Andrew Maddock
Fall 2013
Thomas Michael Medek
Spring 2014
Olen Snow Milholland
Spring 2014
Miron M. Nawratil
Fall 2012
Allen Plasencia
Spring 2014
Matthew Robert Rauch
Spring 2014
William James Sheridan IV
Spring 2014
Kathleen Bridget Stranix
Fall 2013
Jay Tsai
Fall 2012
Brittany Lane Utting
Spring 2014
Constance Marie Vale
Fall 2013, Spring 2014
Kate Megan Warren
Spring 2014
Evan Jon Wiskup
Fall 2013

YEAR SEMESTER THEME COURSE NAME CODE

FIRST YEAR

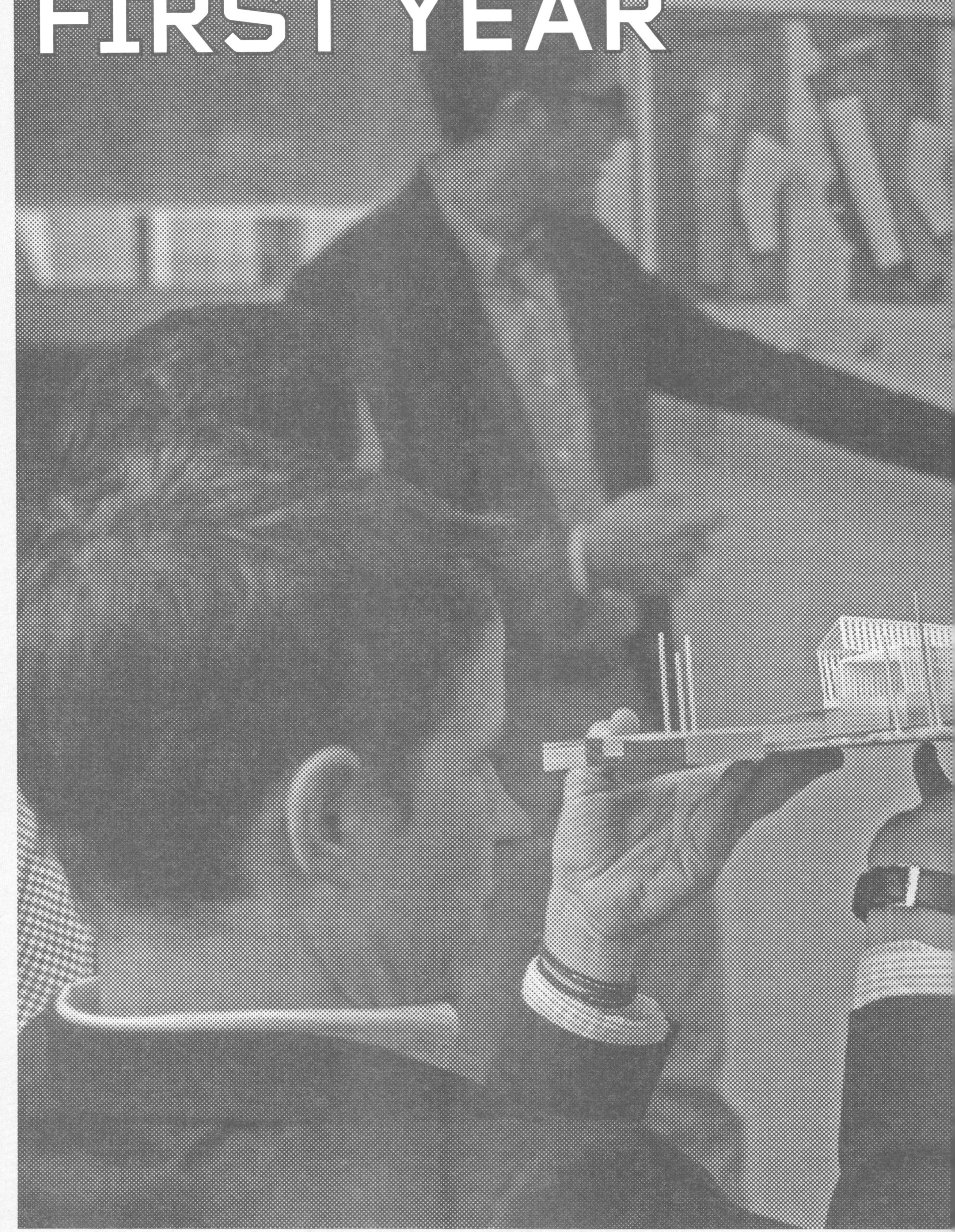

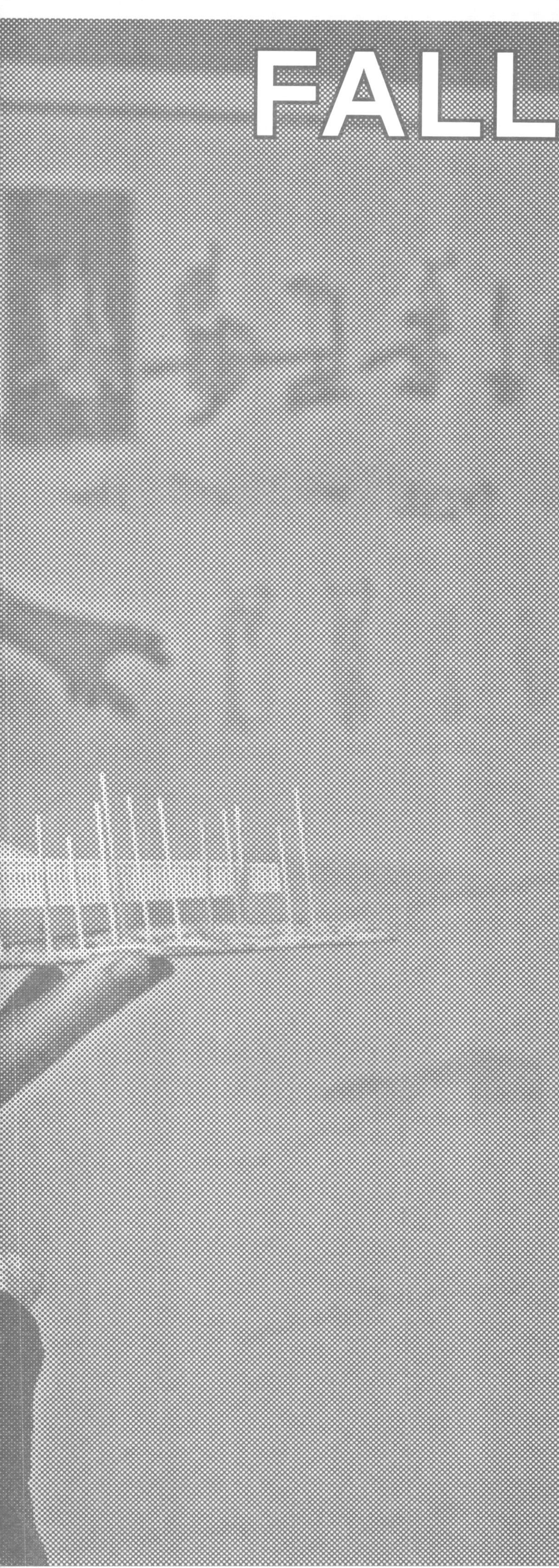

DESIGN STUDIO

This studio is the first of four core design studios where beginning students bring to the school a wide range of experience and background. Exercises introduce the complexity of architectural design by engaging problems that are limited in scale but not in the issues they provoke. Experiential, social, and material concerns are introduced together with formal and conceptual issues.

COORDINATING FACULTY

Ben Pell

FACULTY

Brennan Buck
Peggy Deamer
Joyce Hsiang
Eeva-Liisa Pelkonen

PROJECT ONE: UNDER PRESSURE

For the first project of the semester, you are asked to consider the relationship between architecture and the ground it inhabits through the design and configuration of 4000 cubic feet of space. Working with an abstract topography, this total volume must be distributed as two independent yet related spaces: one defined as interior, the other as exterior to your proposal.

While there is no specific program to accommodate, the nature and scale of these spaces should be distinct and reflect the possibility for inhabitation by one or more people. To that end, the two spaces should be designed and situated to be in dialogue—pressurized by their proximity to one another and to the site, and modulated through the careful control of visibility, communication, and access between them. Thus your proposal must operate as both boundary, delimiting the extents of each space, and threshold, variously mediating their relationship. The site for your proposal is a given topography with basic provisions regarding dimension and orientation (N/S/E/W).

Despite the abstract nature of the site, you are encouraged to consider how manipulating the shape of the ground can produce an armature for specific relationships between your two spaces. In this sense the ground itself should be thought of as providing a third spatial figure, similarly dynamic and engaged with the volume(s) of your proposal.

PROJECT TWO: HIGHER GROUND

The second project of the semester asks students to design a small pavilion to be located directly north of the Eli Whitney Museum, at the current location of the Water Learning Lab. While the students are asked to propose a single, unified structure, the required program consists of two distinct exhibit areas and an information / café area for visitors. Additionally, students are required to address the adjacent Mill River through manipulations of the landscape which would prompt an engagement—physical, visual, or otherwise—with the water. Lastly, students are asked to articulate a clear idea about structure: both in terms of physical support, and the development of particular site metrics which organize relationships between architecture and landscape, intervention and context.

PROJECT THREE: DANCE MACHINE

The final project of the semester entails the design of a small dance rehearsal and performance center in Manhattan, on a site located adjacent to the High Line. The building will be comprised of both a public, cultural dimension and a private function, hosting a performance stage and small rehearsal studios for a residence dance company. To that end, students' proposals will need to address ideas about individual versus collective spaces, sequence, and spatial and programmatic hierarchy. Thus this project asks students to synthesize many of the considerations of the semester—from questions of tectonics and materiality and the shared sensibilities of architecture and landscape, to the explorations of form, program, and structure—into a comprehensive proposal which engages the unique urban character of the site.

JURORS

Kim Ackert
Tobias Armborst
Sandra Arndt
Sunil Bald
Kadambari Baxi
Andrew Benner
Andy Bernheimer
Anna Bokov
Megan Born
Laura Briggs
Marta Justo Caldeira
Angela Co
Kyle Dugdale
Keller Easterling
Karen Fairbanks
Duks Koschitz
Jesse LeCavalier
Chris Leong
Jennifer Leung
David Leven
Jonathan Massey
Bimal Mendis
Joeb Moore
Alan Organschi
Chris Perry
Nicholas Pevzner
Linda Pollak
Dagmar Richter
Shawn Rickenbacker
Nicole Robertson
Karla Rothstein
Surry Schlabs
Michael Tower
Marc Tsurumaki
Michael Young
Elia Zenghelis

CORE CLASSES

1018a Formal Analysis
1015a Visualization II

Shayari De Silva
Ben Pell

PROJECT ONE: UNDER PRESSURE
The inherent geometry of the 'site', which is twice as long as it is wide, was used as a starting point, with triangulated folds made along the sides to the midpoints of their diagonals. These folds create both an exterior slope and an interior space, where in each space the occupant is made aware of the other through a system of perforations. These perforations condition the entry of light and sound from interior to exterior and vice versa, and subtle changes in scale of the apertures accommodate a range of activity.

Pell The appropriation of the primary site geometry as a generator for form is really interesting—the project is at once on the site and of the site, and the effects of this are very provocative. Varying the size of the triangular folds produces a range of spatial conditions and different degrees of enclosure, some of which are inhabitable in familiar ways, and others of which seem to be unoccupiable yet clearly articulated—and all of which are the result of a natural unfolding of the geometric and operational logic of the project.

Pell The triangle motif has a funny relationship to the circular perforations on the surface of these panels. One could argue the triangles work spatially, while the circles work graphically, and ultimately optically, in the ways they play with light and shadow. However, this clear delineation of roles becomes somewhat muddied when the circles become portals—at which point they too become spatial. This could be seen as a lapse in the fundamental logic described before, a good lapse or bad lapse, but the intention behind that moment isn't entirely clear.

Michelle Chen
Joyce Hsiang

PROJECT ONE: UNDER PRESSURE
The premise of this abstract exercise was to create a dialogue between inside and outside along an inclined plane. Drawing inspiration from the Mobius strip—a single twisted surface that in turn creates a continuous path along both sides of the strip—the inclined plane is manipulated in such a way that it generates its own self-contained path. A series of sloping translucent surfaces act simultaneously as shelter and ground; within the interior, spaces are softly lit by the translucent roof, which from the outside appears as solid ground. Any potential monotony of a continually looping path within a contained environment is defeated by traversing this path through varying pockets of enclosure, openness, elevation and descent. Though solid in its physicality, the design is nevertheless experientially precarious.

Pell These are really beautiful. There are some things that seem to be a little bit gratuitous. Like the pattern surface, just because I think that everything else seem to be operating at critical register where we can say, it's about geometry, it's about mass versus plane, it's about form. The other stuff is a little bit decorative. Which is not a bad word but it reads a little bit as an applique rather than something that is intrinsic to the underlying concept of the project.

Deamer So it's like your bag of tricks is all on display and it might be interesting to not have all your bag of tricks on display.

Moore: I think the models are beautifully made by the way, I think there are some really elegant moves; I want to flip them. There's a mixing between an arabesque kind of pattern making, two-dimensional, and an origami, three-dimensional kind of practice which I think you could further and more systematically build from the first insights to the first cuts.

Jessica Flore Angel
Brennan Buck

PROJECT ONE: UNDER PRESSURE
This project for two inhabitable spaces starts with a simple geometric gesture that cuts the site in half diagonally in order to generate two inextricably linked volumes. The interplay between the initial geometry of the site and the new geometry triggered by the diagonal is utilized to instill an affect of repetition. As a result, a new rhythm between solid and void is created that reinforces the ambiguous definition of interior and exterior spaces.

Pell You said the experience is different throughout, but there is also a sameness as you move through. All this seems to be generated by an internal logic of structure, geometry, and sequence. But there might be external forces, such as program or a larger site strategy, that would create difference at a different scale.

Koschitz This is like Studio Bow Wow is doing a computational aggregation a la Paul Rudolph. You're adding lots of little elements, trying to make sense of them to create a whole. This shouldn't be two similar spaces, but really one that is the intersection of the two forms. These are the decisions you make when you take a pen and you redraw what's there. You will not draw the deflated pentagons; what you would do is outline the spaces you want to occupy.

Buck This issue about variation and repetition is a common one with digital production. Just copy and paste. It produces real effects, but variation does not always produce significant difference.

Deamer It's true there's not enough payoff, but you could make more space from within, taking advantage of the poché because the exterior shape is not the same as the interior shape. You're indicating that you know that can happen.

Jenny Kim
Eeva-Liisa Pelkonen

PROJECT ONE: UNDER PRESSURE
Using the simplicity of the sloping plane as a point of departure, the project challenges the stability of the ground and its surroundings by creating a three dimensional matrix on top of the slope. This matrix is then manipulated to play with perspective and scale to create an illusionary space on top of an actual space. To distort the perception of the space even further, mirrored planes are introduced into the lattice to extend the grid into infinite space. The experience of the constructed space is meant to be unique for each viewer depending on their position and movement through the space.

Pelkonen The techniques you used were simple: a grid, a tilted plane, and mirrors. With them she managed not only to imagine a spatial idea but also a spatial experience by pushing the stability of Cartesian space towards instability and not-knowing. A viewer can no longer rely on the predictable order but is invited to navigate space based on physical sensation instead.

Jack Bian
Ben Pell

PROJECT TWO: HIGHER GROUND
The idea of the project is to uncover the artifacts of the past and link them with present conditions. The aggregation of varying morphological layers is a fictional reconstruction of the artifacts, evoking the character of the site that was once used for industrial purposes. A major component of the project is to revitalize the water wheel, once used as a power generator, into a water clock that functionally and symbolically serves as a teaching tool. The new museum proposal is a skeletal reflection of the existing Eli Whitney Museum, constructing a dialogue with the vernacular method of pole barn construction. The layers reveal the distinction between man-made and natural, old and new, while the notational language of representation serves to suggest a continuous relationship between landscape, structure, and skin.

Zenghelis So the solid form in the model is your new museum? Why are you taking away the envelope of the existing, but showing it in the proposed one?

Mendis The grid itself for me could be an entire project. Then the skin, the structure, the scaffold becomes another exploration that deals with ideas of memory. Part of the challenge for me is seeing the overlap of three or four potentially very strong ideas mashing together, but in their mashing up they don't have a clear resonance or cohesion.

Tsurumaki I'm struck by your comment about the grid being both conceptual and real. The model becomes a representation of your working methodology, in some cases about a conceptual logic, in other places a literal representation of things you're proposing to be built. The slippage between those categories is something you need to be more precise about.

Pell It's like the morphine dream. It is suspended in a way in a beautiful state of delirium. There is a mythical quality to it, and I agree to a certain point these are studies that lead to something more concrete as a proposal. The materialization of the ideas is the next step.

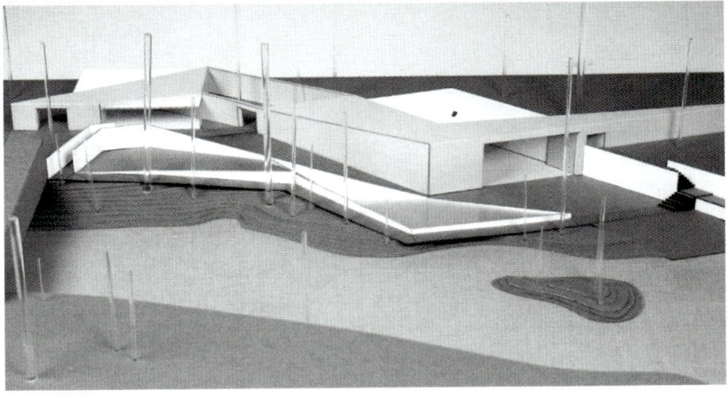

Sarah Kasper
Brennan Buck

PROJECT TWO: HIGHER GROUND
Challenging the basic purpose of the stacked stone walls proliferating the northeast, this project transforms the stripped down stone wall from a simple barrier between the cacophony of the road and the Mill River to a form defining internal spaces. Diverting focus away from the street, the concept of the stone wall as both barrier and volume encompasses the program of a supplementary exhibition and workshop space for the adjacent Eli Whitney Museum. Cutting along the major diagonal axis leading from the entry of the Eli Whitney Museum to the river, the wall is inflected, signaling entry, and expanded, allowing the programmatic spaces to negotiate place within the wall. Their degree of interaction with the wall defines the degree of intimacy of the various programmatic spaces, inclining either towards the public street or the river. Layers of circulation gradually break down in formality as one approaches the final destination, the natural and changing river. One enters the site through a puncture in the thinnest end of the stone wall, marking entry into the sequence of experiencing the site, yet remaining outdoors. From there, one can either move into the wall through the café—the most public space—and follow the internal sequence of enclosed spaces, or one can move directly down the slope on axis towards the river and waterfall beyond. At the river's edge, a meandering and narrow wooden path leads through the trees, marking the most minimal form of landscape manipulation. Breaking down manipulations of the landscape at the site's most natural edge choreographs a sequential experience that gradually immerses visitors into the haptic nature of the site.

Deamer This project makes a seemingly random set of geometries make total sense. The wall becomes a useful strategy to organize movement across the site—parallel to the river—and down from the high bank to the river in addition to organizing the static spaces as well. While some of the static spaces/ volumes are too "dumb" and the wall could have had a more consistent narrative, the project is not just formally elegant but programmatically smart.

Caitlin Thissen
Eeva-Liisa Pelkonen

PROJECT TWO: HIGHER GROUND
The second project of first year design studio explored the role of the pavilion in mediating various site conditions, including water, the surrounding flora, and existing structure, near the Eli Whitney Museum in New Haven, Connecticut. The pavilion is a series of three follies, penetrating the fence line that marks the border between cultivated land and the built structure of the recreational water basins preexisting on the site. A delicate, open air wooden frame allows a fluid visual and sensorial connection between the loosely defined spaces of the pavilion and the surrounding vegetation. The first of the follies represents the gallery space, extruded and nestled between the trees, where children can exhibit their wares made in concurrence with Eli Whitney workshops. The second folly unfolds out toward the water, with a partially enclosed area for the café. The final folly opens directly onto the water, forming a platform where children and families can enjoy direct access to the river.

Tsurumaki We're seeing these as autonomous sculptural forms, but the intention you state is quite the opposite. It's all about these things being embedded in this dense mass of trees, and they're much more about how they're perceived as interior spaces from within, and how the lattice work and the play of light presumably interacts with the trees, branches, and patterns of leaves.

Zenghelis Consequently I find the idea of unfolding contradictory to the essence of that concept. I see them as really fitting in within the forest, but the unfolding is forcing them to relate to the water. It would have been nice to have a model with just tree trunks and trees, the before, and a model after.

Pell You've given new meaning to the expression 'tree hugger.' These things really do squeeze the trees. It's not about getting to the water, but occupying that liminal space between land and water. There's a third landscape between the two that you are giving voice to, simply by framing it, by giving it a scaffold that we can read it against.

Lila Jiang Chen
Joyce Hsiang

PROJECT TWO: HIGHER GROUND
The project arises from the desire to maintain the character of the site by keeping the balance of building volume to outdoors green space unchanged. The design approach is therefore one that merges the new addition into the landscape, generating a playful outdoors space and an underground pocket for workshop classes. The locations of existing trees were used as attractor points in the generation of the undulating landscape, with some of the trees on their original location perforating through the surface. A series of parametric openings creates an ethereal space with natural light, and also provides direct entry points into the underground spaces through a gradually ramping surface. The set of ramps and openings form part of a circulation network that allow the users to seamlessly weave in and out of the landscape and in contact with the river.

Baxi To me it is also the edges. Do you still need that edge? When you see a site plan, this wouldn't read as a line.

Tsurumaki Everything has mysteriously become homogenously and immaterially white. But the success of this project would be all about the materiality of this thing. I'm imaging water running in under this thing and the whole surface being coated with a reflective thin sheet of water, and the light bouncing off of that. That makes me think the edge of your building is like the edge of that island. It is a product of two conditions coming together, and there is a resultant that comes out.

Mendis You can imagine high tide being a boundary that goes into your building and back out again. Then you do get that confluence of reflectivity under the roof surface, and the water having a much more dynamic relationship with the land.

Pell I also wonder if there would be something unique about going to the bathroom in this building.

Mendis You could cut a hole around you... [laugher]... it's immersive.

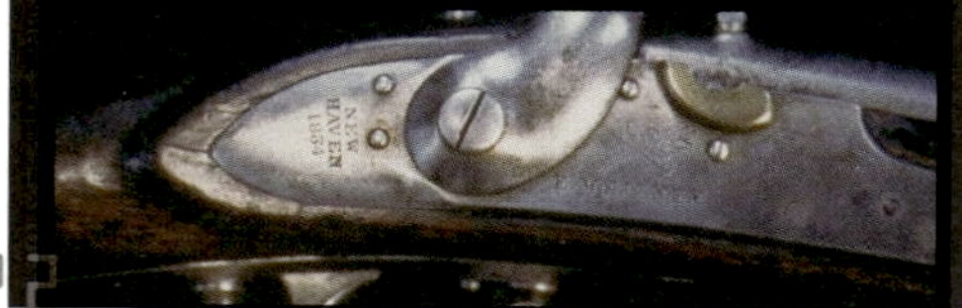

Dante Furioso
Peggy Deamer

PROJECT TWO: HIGHER GROUND
This project questions the benign image of industry that the Eli Whitney Museum presents its students and visitors. The project insists that we must first come to terms with industry and war, northern textiles and southern slaves, guns and violence. It is within the framework of these historical-economic binaries that the project takes shape. The design follows a simple logic of the upper and the lower, the clear and the obscure, and the familiar and the underrepresented. Three simple, stark, rectangular structures, which recall ubiquitous New England gable roof homes, are a foil for an underground space that follows a beguiling logic. The three structures present a concerted blankness to the approaching visitor. Yet upon closer inspection, the visitor is drawn around the buildings, which have multiple points of entry. The project, which appears solid and blank, is in fact perforated, split, cut and open to the river and sky. Below, the visitor finds a labyrinthine underworld.

Deamer This project avoids the issue of appropriate style and forgoes the issue of the man/nature that the majority of students took as starting points and instead addresses the history that the Eli Whitney Museum presents us with. In this vein, a de Chirico-esque or even Rossi-like approach using iconic, vernacular building silhouettes that are divorced from functional readings force the visitor to think about the past and history in a manner that challenges the holdings of the museum itself. The project could be stronger if, at the lower level, it more pointedly proposed an alternate mode of display challenging stereotypical museumology. But the attempt to address a problematic program not through spatial complexity but through ambiguous imagery sets this project apart.

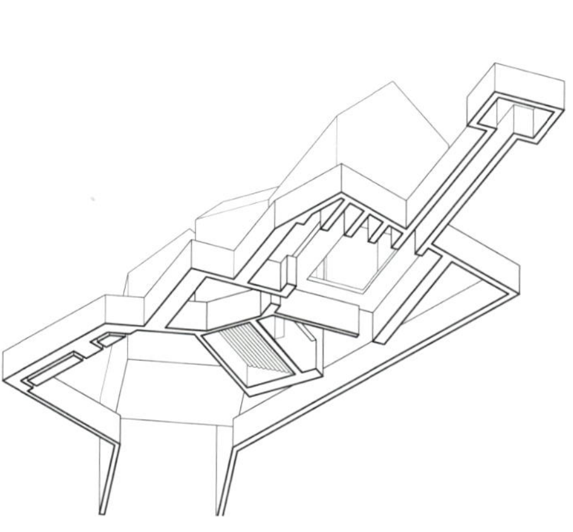

John Kleinschmidt
Peggy Deamer

PROJECT TWO: HIGHER GROUND
The site, at the base of the Lake Whitney dam, was interpreted as a series of thresholds between key land and water forms, all differentiated in section. Ridge, field, shore, inlet, river, dam, lake, forest, hill all unfold in a short but intense sequence as one moves toward the water. Using this as a clue, I sought to intensify existing transitions and layer new thresholds onto the site. A simple glass building veiled in a screen welcomes visitors with a large, flexible exhibition space, inflected against the river's curve. A series of workshops, sheltered and linked by a similar screen, are arranged along the river. These small work spaces are accessible to artists from the water's edge and on display for visitors via a path that rises gently toward an inlet at the base of the dam. Between the exhibition space and workshops, the landscape peels up to admit visitors to a café below. Ramps mediate between levels, extending thresholds between programs.

Deamer This project tries to balance movement with statis; the primary generator of the scheme is addressing a visitor's movement from the parking lot to the river's edge, discovering the museum and the workshops, almost incidentally, along the way. In this, the path is always meant to move the visitor in a zig-zag fashion, walking primarily parallel to the water's edge, with the end/turning points being special viewing opportunities. Many different study models were made to establish both the most provocative path and the manner in which the museum and workshops could be placed and tectonically articulated along it. The final solution here might put too much emphasis on the volume and enclosure of those functions, but the experience of the museum goer would still emphasize movement through the site and down play the hegemony of the museum.

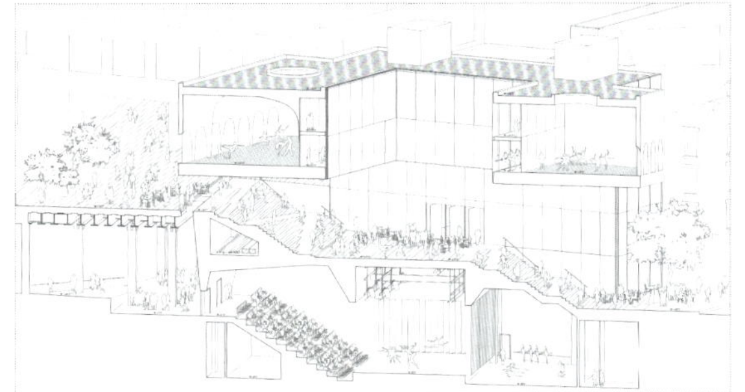

Justin Oh
Ben Pell

PROJECT THREE: DANCE MACHINE
The Meatpacking District coexists with two pieces of great New York City infrastructure: the High Line, and the Manhattan grid. This dance studio presents itself as two buildings to address this infrastructure. A subterranean theater mass connects the grid of street-life and activity to the High Line, while a rectilinear torus contains dance studio program above. At the heart of the torus is an open void, a stage for public performance, a patio for an evening dinner, a viewing point to witness dancers rehearse, and a stage of programmatic cross-pollination.

Pell There seem to be a number of dichotomous conditions in the project: the closed upper doughnut juxtaposed with the open lower plaza, or the orthogonal 'building' and the torqued 'column', for instance. These gestures, while provocative and formally powerful, could benefit from a clearer narrative. Not just the origin story that you start with, which is smart, and funny, but perhaps a clearer narrative about how this split personality relates to the city, to the immediate context of the site and/or perhaps to the cultural context of dance and performance in an urban environment.

Pell Despite the imagery, which is of course very well produced and seductive, you've designed a building that is somewhat of a reluctant icon—or at least an awkward one. The dichotomies of form mentioned before have yet to produce a 'both/and' product, in the Venturian sense of a complex whole, and remain unresolved. The scale is monumental—but a monument to what? The primary urban gesture—the cut through, connecting the High Line to the street—is powerful and convincing, but it allows people to flow through your building without ever really interacting with it, which seems like a mistake rather than an act of selfless urbanism.

Pell Overall, the posture of the project feels right on the site. Some of the great ideas are languishing on their own, and need to be better orchestrated together.

Anne Ma
Joyce Hsiang

PROJECT THREE: DANCE MACHINE
The project looks at performance to activate the site not only being contained to the interior, but also experienced from the exterior. Essentially a 'Vertical Highline,' program and activity is extended upwards in a series of interlacing circulation and occupiable spaces. The 'scaffold' extrudes upwards with the building, inherently producing voids in the structural lattice. The single anomaly is the theatre, a beacon that highlights the two primary features of the design, serving both interior performances as well as providing a surface for external projection. Finally, the accent color represents the public corridor, weaving its way from bottom up.

Young I am just going to jump in. I think this project is fantastic. I love the drawings, I love the model too. The energy and recreation of it is wonderful. So I am going to give you a negative comment here, and you have to take it within those lengths. I think it is a mistake to make only one of them the red whale [laughter]. You have to choose a direction. Either they all become different versions of red whales or they all become different versions of red boxes.

LeCavalier Why?

Young Because it normalizes the project. I think right now you walk by and say, did you see that construction going on over there? Oh, what is it? Well look at the red thing, all the other stuff is just backdrop for the big event; the big event is the red whale. If all of them are some kind of species of porpoise or other kinds of mammals...

Deamer Squids, sharks, whales...

Young The bull nose ones, the manatees; there are a lot of friends in this family. Then, you would see them all floating in the scaffolding of this system. The whole thing becomes a radical reinvention of performance in the city.

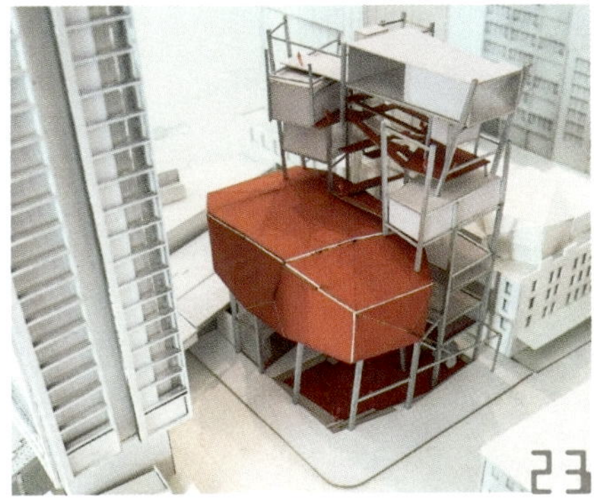

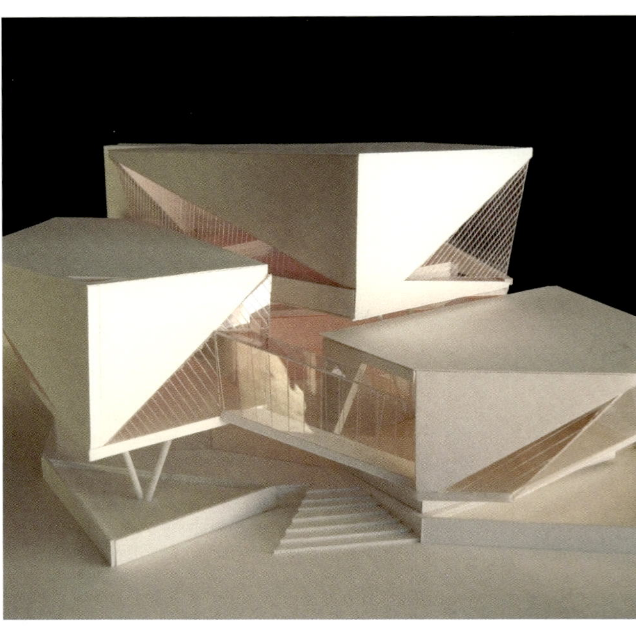

Andrew Dadds
Brennan Buck

PROJECT THREE: DANCE MACHINE
The project explores the dance studio through the lens of simultaneity. Three dance studios array themselves around a central lobby that envelopes the inhabitants within a performance. The dance studios spiral sectionally until meeting at the central auditorium volume that defines the roof of the lobby. The multifaceted volumes are defined by view corridors placed at key contextual approaches to the site.

Arndt You framed this project as a building that is also a performance for the city. I think that is very exciting as a proposal. What you created in the end is some sort of an urban room.

Young When I look at your plans, I don't know if you need to enclose that center piece—talking about the ground floor. It seems like that could be exterior. The strange facets of glass that you need to introduce to mind all the gaps do not strengthen your project. What if all of these half levels, mezzanine levels, slipped levels, from the plinth to the High Line to the building next to it gave you just enough overlap to get you from one to the other.

Richter For me the question is the multiplication of these things. Once you have these three self-similar objects, and then you have a fourth one, why not six, seven, or eight.

Young That argument works if you are doing a tiling pattern, but you are not doing a tiling pattern. These things are slipping over, under, and next to each other.

Buck Right now, it is your attempt to take the original objects and aggregate them into a building. I like the idea that it could be a very humble institution. You can see these three dance studios, small scale, and small infiltrations.

Deamer The High Line becomes incidental. I appreciate that. I wish there was a stronger ideology of the ground.

Winny Tan
Eeva-Liisa Pelkonen

PROJECT THREE: DANCE MACHINE
The project is based on viewing pedestrian traffic flow as a force that pushes into the site from the ground level as well as from the High Line. The design proposes to connect the circulation disjuncture by creating a throughway which cuts the site into two separate programs: a formal theater and a dance school. The path identifies different spatial boundaries and thus circulatory experiences specific to different users: performers, audience, the general public and the dance students. The building appears as two separate entities that reunite at its crowning outdoor performance green roof.

Massey This thing is so excessively internally differentiated I'm starting to get a headache just imagining it. There's a scale misjudgment, in the sense that this massive theater you're trying to break down is actually not massive at all.

Pelkonen But she loves the franticness of the line, and she wants to inscribe it in the façade, so I actually buy it in this case. There's frenzy, it needs to be there.

Pell If there was a reason behind the rhyme, then I would buy it. If the line is really just about bringing the rainwater down to the ground or giving us a broken edge, it's not very powerful. What you're lacking is true synthesis. You're pecking away at it by using a similar material at the same dimension, but that only produces motif.

Massey It's like tying up a hostage with a really short piece of string.

Bernheimer There is a reasonable question to be asked about whether you need all these different wall systems to explain your concept. Instead, the beauty comes from a finely calibrated sense of volume and composition.

Massey Today we have seen very few minimalist approaches toward form, that try to use as little form as possible to create the maximum social dynamism or experiential richness. Formal complexity can crowd out other agencies beyond that of the architect.

Pelkonen Minimalism is so last decade. I think they just drink too much coffee.

Clarissa Luwia
Peggy Deamer

PROJECT THREE: DANCE MACHINE
This theatre does not enclose itself within protective layers to separate it from the outside world; rather, it allows both its program and the activity of its surroundings to shape its form. It peels up a corner of the street to both call attention and create a public space above; it pushes itself into the High Line and pulls the public down to the entrance of the theatre; and as it moves into the interior, the walls peel to redirect paths for the performers and viewers. In doing so, compelling spaces are generated as one moves underneath the High Line, through the Lobby and finally into the theatre itself.

Bald I really like the roof [laughter]. Just this really simple, but unusually articulated object that has a very domestic scale in the way it meets the ground and flies up.

Richter It seems like one of the things you rarely see in Manhattan is a roof because you are always at the ground looking up at things. The potential of this project is exciting.

Young I think the project is incredibly elegant and incredibly precise. This is going to sound like I am nitpicking, but things levitate at around seventeen to eighteen inches—three feet not so much. You can walk around and see 42 inches all over the place. Eighteen inches—that is where the edge of your roof needs to be at. At a certain level, those sorts of really tight dimensions make this project.

Richter It's really exciting to think about this huge surface. What happens when it rains? All those things you have the opportunity to think about.

Young One scupper at the end [laughter].

Buck I feel like there are a lot of beautiful things about the project. However, I find the single volume of the hall at the center a little too dominant and static. There is so much potential to move around it in so many different ways.

FORMAL ANALYSIS

Peter Eisenman

ADDITONAL INSTRUCTOR: AMY DEDONATO

It wasn't until the fifteenth century that two of the most important ideas for the discipline of architecture were defined: the human subject and his or her space of occupation. The course will attempt to outline through lectures, readings, drawings, and critiques the evolution of these two terms in the period of time from 1450–1750, the time of the rise and fall of Western Humanism and the advent of the Enlightenment.

The course will attempt to familiarize the student with the theoretical implications for today's architect as they appeared in Italy in this time period. The purpose of the drawing each week will be to see if studetns can conceptualize in drawing what has been presented in the readings and the lecture. Seeing, therefore, becomes a way of thinking, and drawing as a way of reading.

Anne Householder

CONTEST DRAWING—FIRST PLACE

Xiao Wu

SANTA MARIA DELLA PACE AND PALAZZO DUCALE
Bramante and Laurana

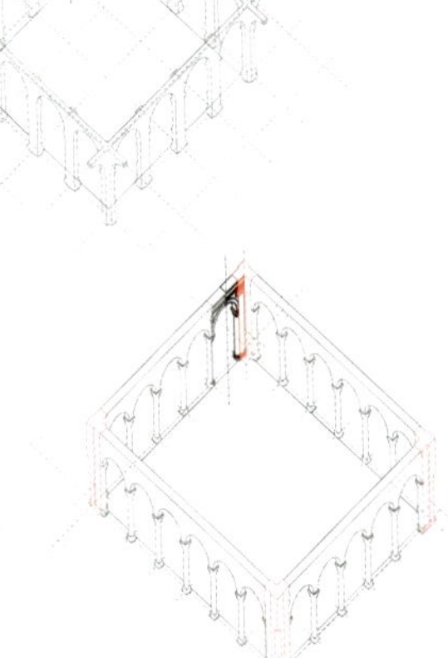

Vittorio Lovato

SFORZA CHAPEL AND CHIGI CHAPEL
Michelangelo and Raffaello

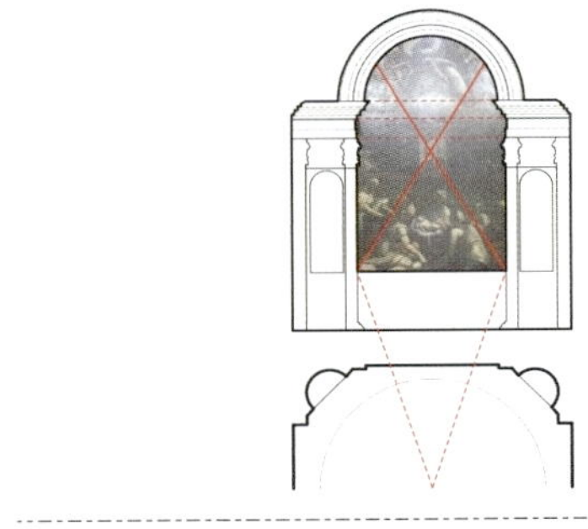

Pearl Ho

CONTEST DRAWING—SECOND PLACE

Justin Oh

CHIESA DI SAN LORENZO AND CAPPELLA S.S. SINDONE
Guarino Guarini

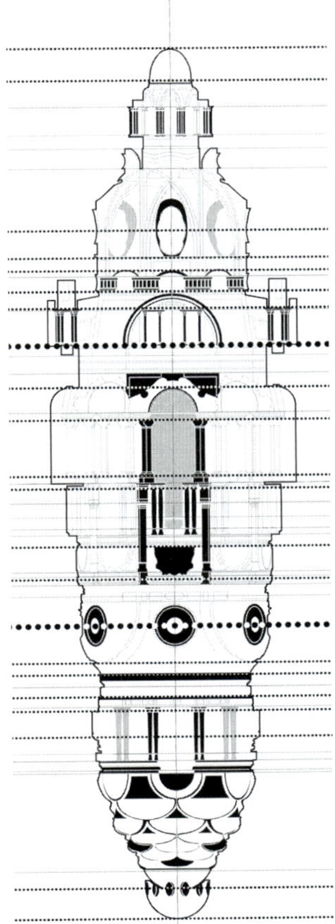

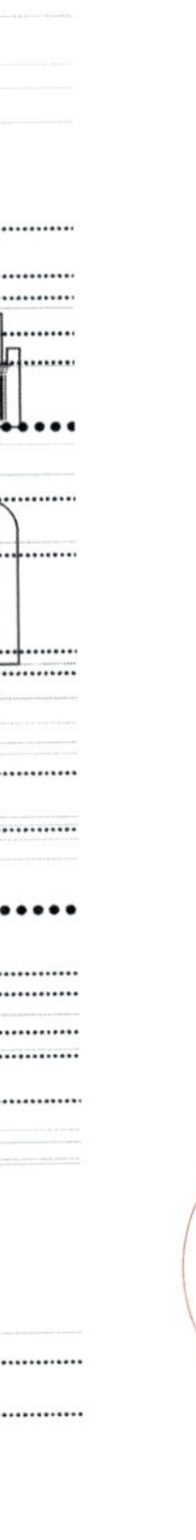

Madelynn Ringo

CHIESA DI SAN LORENZO AND CAPPELLA S.S. SINDONE
Guarino Guarini

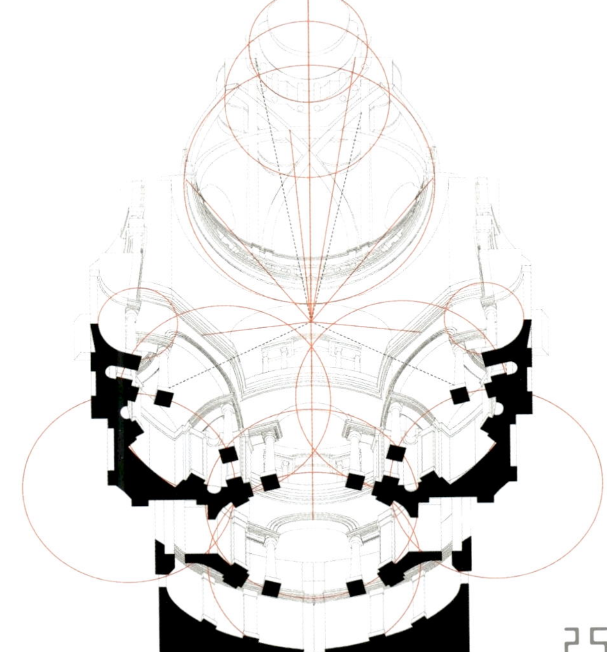

Michelle Gonzalez

NOLLI MAP AND CAMPO MARZIO
Giambattista Nolli and Giovanni Piranesi

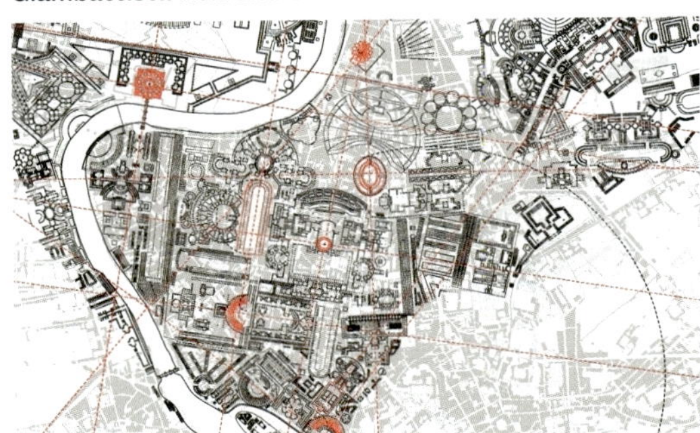

VISUALIZATION II

Kent Bloomer & Sunil Bald

This course investigates drawing as a means of architectural communication and as a generative instrument of formal, spatial, and tectonic discovery. Principles of two—and three-dimensional geometry are extensively studied through a series of exercises that employ freehand and constructive techniques. Students work fluidly between manual drawing, computer drawing, and material construction. All exercises are designed to enhance the ability to visualize architectural form and volume three-dimensionally, understand its structural foundations, and provide tools that reinforce and inform the design process.

Dorian Booth
MINIMAL SURFACE SYMMETRY OPERATIONS

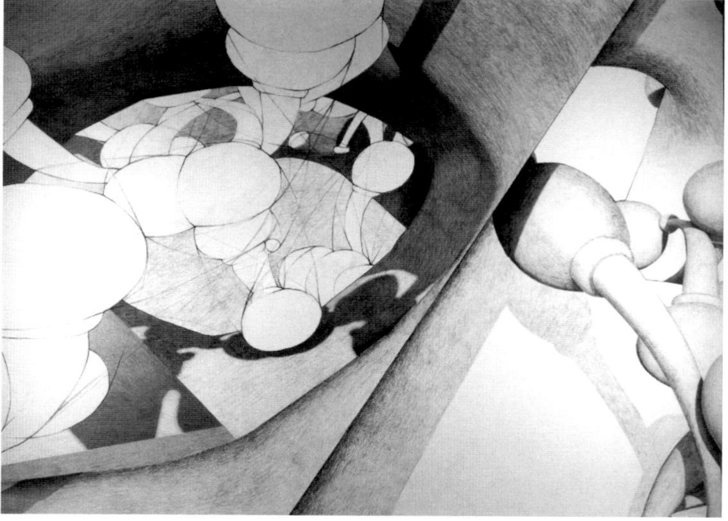

Eugene Tan
COMBINED PERSPECTIVE

Vittorio Lovato
COMBINED PERSPECTIVE

Anne Ma
LATTICE EXPLODED

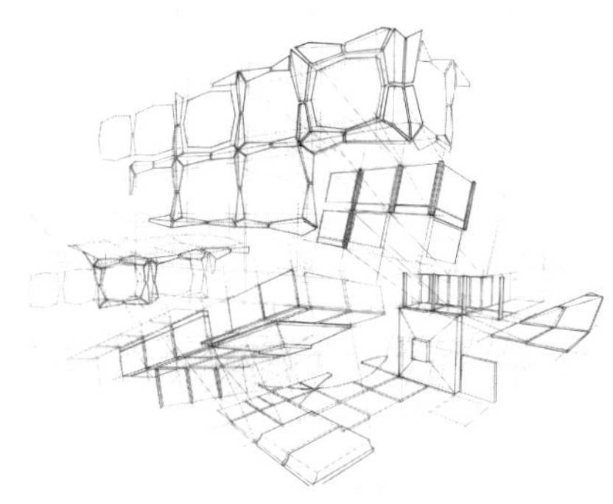

Jessica Flore Angel
COMBINED PERSPECTIVE

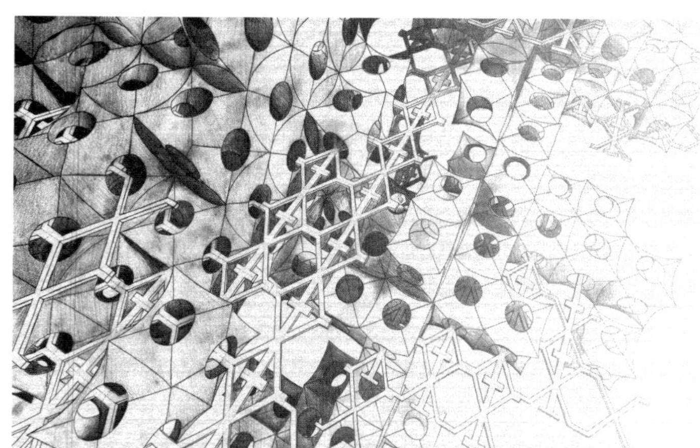

John Kleinschmidt
COMBINED PERSPECTIVE

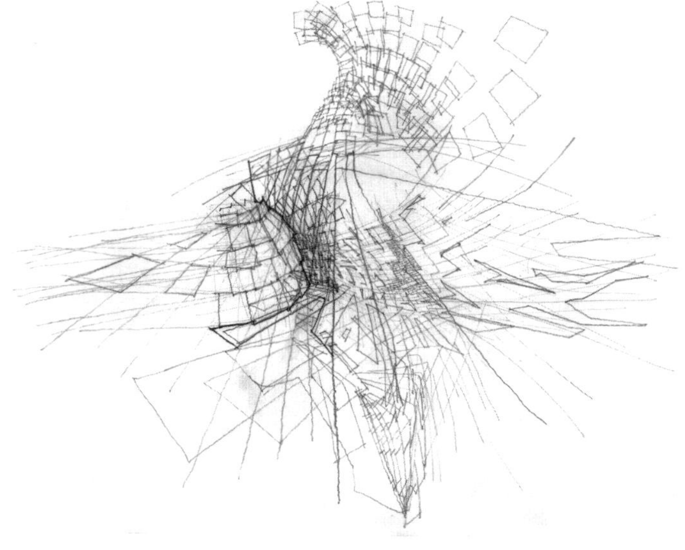

DESIGN STUDIO

This second core studio explores inhabitation through the design of the architecture and detail of enclosure, structure, circulation, and the habitable space it produces. The work of the term focuses on the simultaneous relationship of a body to both interior and exterior environments, and their mediation by the material assemblies of building. With an initial focus on the conception and production of a singular interior space, a sequence of projects gives way to increasing physical and spatial complexity by requiring students to investigate—at close range and in intimate detail—issues of structure and enclosure, organization and circulation, urban site and climate. This work forms the conceptual background for the work in the latter half of the term—the collaborative design and construction of the Building Project, an affordable house for a nonprofit developer in New Haven.

COORDINATING FACULTY

Alan Organschi

FACULTY

Joeb Moore
Andrew Benner
Amy Lelyveld
Peter de Bretteville

PROJECT ONE: DWELLING CODE

Each student, working individually, will encode through measured drawing a set of basic requirements considered essential to inhabitation. Like Meyer's list of 'motives', the code will reflect biological need, technical function, environmental stress, and—perhaps most difficult to measure and therefore most subjective—emotional or psychological tolerance. Implicit in this exercise is the definition of a set of anthropometric and ergonomic dimensions derived from an inhabiting body and calibrated to the technical fixtures and services provided in the minimum dwelling. These dimensions should be carefully recorded, organized, and represented, using clear and persuasive graphic techniques.

PROJECT TWO: REDUCTION AND RECOMBINATION—A MINIMAL DWELLING

For the second assignment, students will have to speculate further on the nature of dwelling and construction by applying the principles of your dwelling 'code.' Through this necessarily awkward confabulation of code and artifact, students will produce, in a sense, a kind of extreme (perhaps even monstrous) phenotype of the minimal dwelling genotype. Although students may be tempted to understand this exercise as the application of a generalized program to a peculiar site, it may also be useful to approach it as an interaction of Debord's 'impinging environments,' ones that will inevitably act to transform (or transmogrify) one another through your design process. We ask that students consider the specific technical means with which the functional demands deemed essential to human inhabitation are answered: a building envelope with aperture (as they might relate to the climate and solar orientation of the stair in its original context) interior surfaces, fixtures, fittings; means or systems of environmental control.

PROJECT THREE: THE NEW HAVEN TEST

For the remainder of the semester and into the summer, students will work—first individually and then collaboratively—to develop a new type of dwelling for New Haven. The assignment is the design of a house. The house will be home to as many as three inhabitants distributed within up to two separate households. It must be physically and dimensionally compact while spatially expansive. The research undertaken undertook at the outset of the semester explored the architecture of the 'minimal' dwelling. We now ask students to deploy and manage limited material, spatial, financial, and human resources in the design of an 'optimal' dwelling, drawing maximal utility, economy, comfort, and spatial richness from conditions of constraint.

JURORS

Jason Bond
Turner Brooks
Marta Justo Caldeira
Rena Cheskis-Gold
Anthony Fieldman
Deborah Gans
Lisa Gray
Celia Imrey
Seila Mosquera
Thach Pham
Laura Pirie
Kurt Roeloffs
Julie Savin
Beka Sturges

Justin Oh
Alan Organschi

PROJECT ONE: DWELLING CODE
The Minimum Dwelling Code is represented as a collection of standard household appliances required to support a family of three. Its 212 square foot footprint is determined by the minimum amount of space required to operate these appliances—no more, no less. As a statement of our material excess, it exists within the ghosted volume of the 2,492 square foot typical United States household.

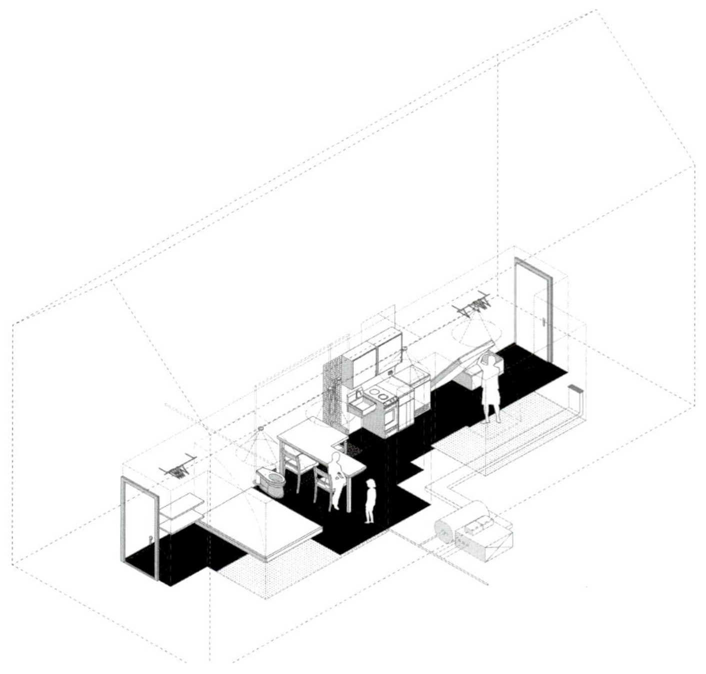

Madelynn Ringo
Joeb Moore

PROJECT ONE: DWELLING CODE
This graphic presents itself as a physiological game that provokes a journey of decision making. Each selection helps define the user's thresholds of privacy, minimalism and survival requirements while also considering external factors such as context, environment, and growth.
These observations build the code of your dwelling phenotype; allowing you to become who you are and encode who you become. The game charts your data on a scale of extremes of living as truly nominal or rather just the affectation of minimalism.

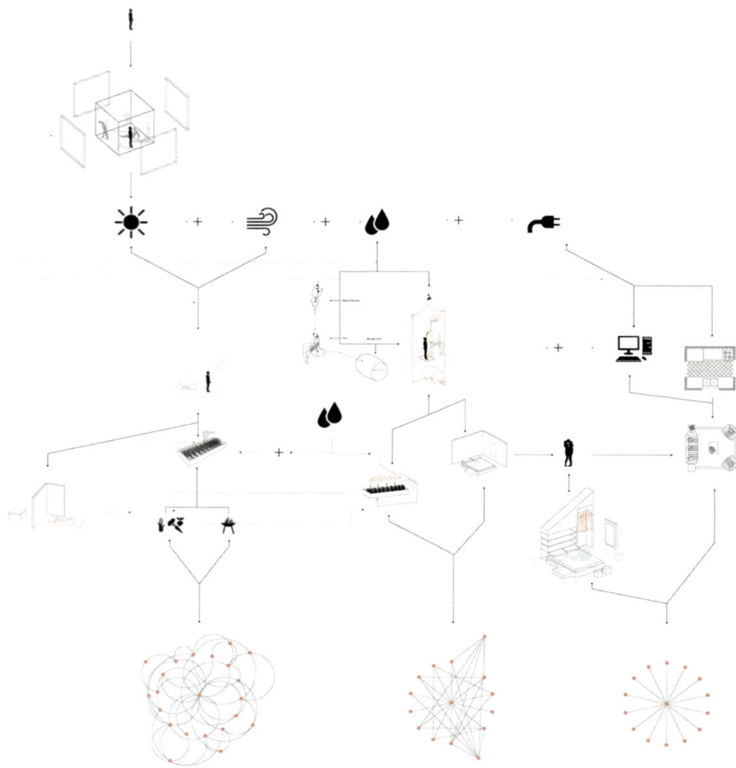

Anne Householder
Andrew Benner

PROJECT ONE: DWELLING CODE
Infrastructure in a home is akin to a computer's operating system. A collection of hardware—water supply, waste removal, heating and cooling, ventilation, lighting, network connections, and sound barriers—service the resident's biological needs and psychological well-being. Applications of the home—producing, connecting, eating, sleeping, and cleaning—draw on these technical systems in order to function. In other words, the dwelling code does not solely depend on spatial relationships, but also the relationship between spaces and their hardware. Applications can then be multiplied or adapted according to family structure and environmental conditions. A minimal dwelling condenses its hardware into a single unit to support the surrounding rooms and activities.

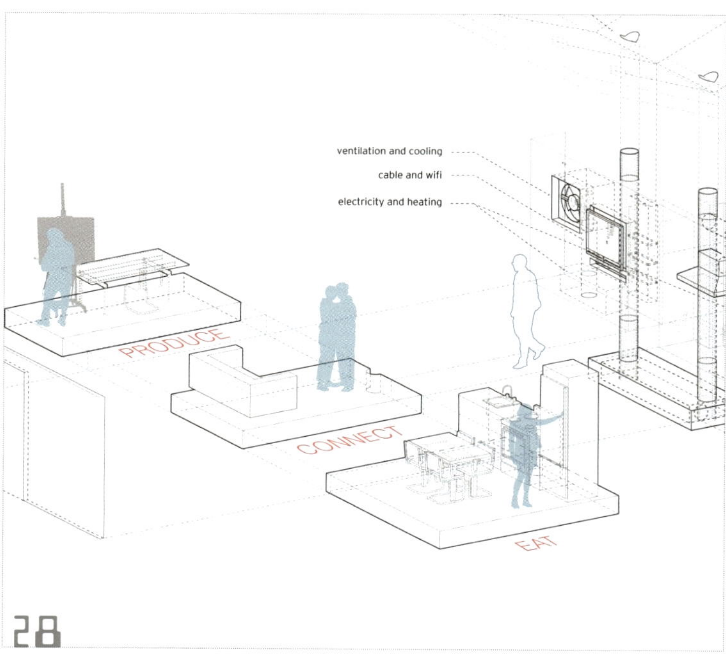

Kristin Nothwehr
Joeb Moore

PROJECT ONE: DWELLING CODE
This project began with an exploration of the role of building systems in supporting the minimal performances of the dwelling. The resultant series of drawings reveals an inhabited poché, in which the thickness of the walls conceals an arterial web of building services. Space is arranged to prioritize an economy of infrastructure, which in turn established a base series of programmatic relationships that would inform the housing prototype.

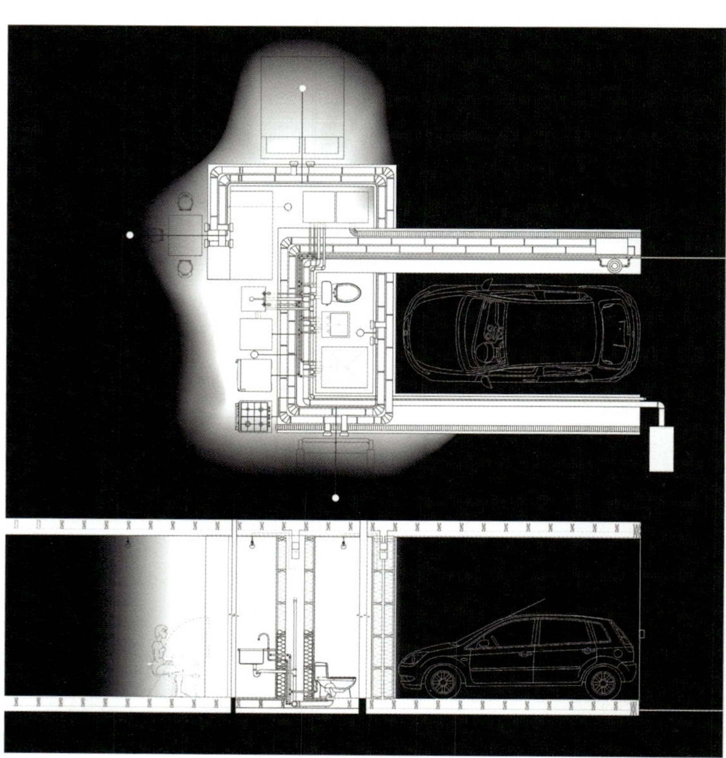

Caitlin Thissen
Alan Organschi

PROJECT TWO: REDUCTION AND RECOMBINATION
By definition, dwelling is the act of existing in a place for an extended period of time. While the duration of a built structure can be generations, the personal items we surround ourselves with—such as books, lamps, shoes, or clothing—eventually become the sole evidence of our existence. The Minimum Dwelling Code expresses the ephemeral notion of dwelling. It articulates the structure of the house as the form to which personal items conform, and then removes the structure to allow for an unrestricted arrangement of possessions. The floating elements in the Stair Conflation represent items essential to living that establish the feeling of home, regardless of the supporting structure.

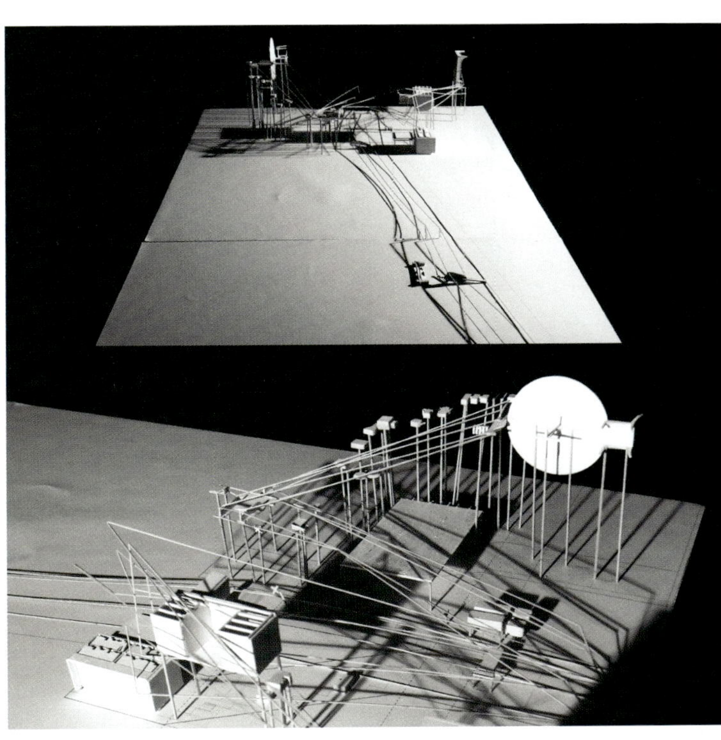

Dorian Booth
Alan Organschi

PROJECT TWO: REDUCTION AND RECOMBINATION
Inhabiting the stair of Le Corbusier's Mill Owners Association becomes an exercise in the mediation between the inherent agoraphobic and claustrophobic conditions of its spaces. The stairs and ramps become points of unprotected exposure. The mass of the stair itself is carved away, creating inhabitable spaces precisely calibrated to their individual tasks. Ultimately, a suppression of the inherent binary of interiority and exteriority in the stair as a dwelling is achieved through the threshold. The monumental door and frame is a point of coalescence between the interior and exterior, creating a field of living conditions within a continuous gradient of spaces.

Justin Oh
Alan Organschi

PROJECT TWO: REDUCTION AND RECOMBINATION
This experiment combines the Minimum Dwelling Code to Corbusier's Mill Owner's Association Building exterior staircase. The durability of the Minimum Dwelling Code is tested with the incline of Corbusier's staircase, carved out of a concrete monolith of the typical United States household to further demonstrate our gluttonous attitude to space and material.

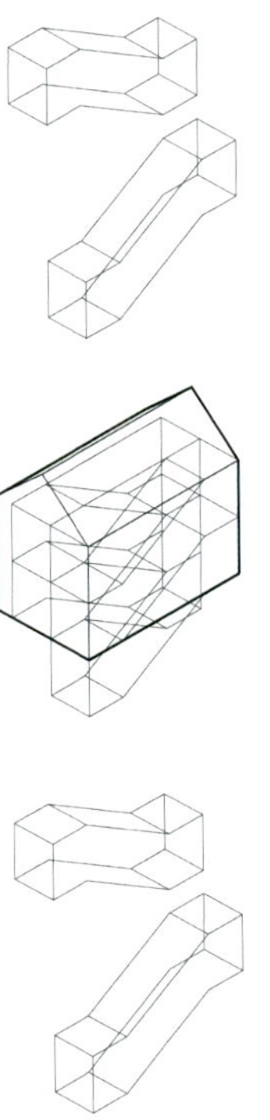

Vittorio Lovato
Andrew Benner

PROJECT TWO: REDUCTION AND RECOMBINATION
Constructed as a hand-held viewing device, this proto-architectural construct arrays all aspects of domestic life around an absent core allowing for a series of concentric informational layers. This viewing device attempts to combine, through a series of contemporary viewing frames (ipad, iphone, thumbnail), the fragments of identities that make up an individual and their domestic spaces Each frame captures an instance of domestic life that helps define one's identity. Like an inverted panopticon, the frames can capture all aspects of domestic life, filtered, framed and layered with information both relevant and frivolous; defining ones identity.

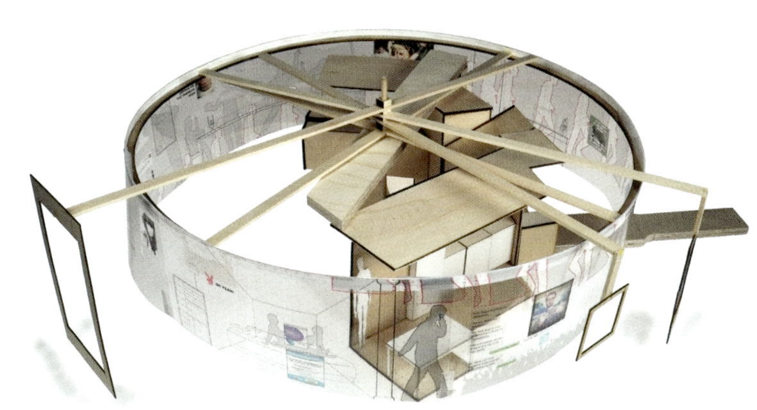

Kiana Hosseini
Andrew Benner

PROJECT TWO: REDUCTION AND RECOMBINATION
The Minimal Dwelling Code generates a spatial configuration of activities by using three key parameters that define the quality of a living space: light, temperature and privacy. The parametric definition of the dwelling allows for it to respond to not only the individual/cultural preferences of the user, but also the specific climatic/ physical dimensions of the site. A user defines a set of activities and the ideal point within a spectrum of light, temperature and privacy for each. Three grids are then identified according to the conditions of the site; each corresponding to one of the said parameters.

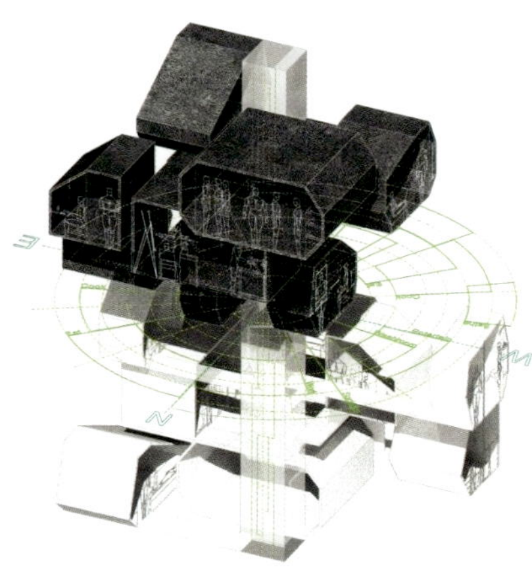

Andrew Sternad
Joeb Moore

PROJECT TWO: REDUCTION AND RECOMBINATION
The minimal dwelling, or the essence of home, is carried within. Psychological needs arising from past memories and future aspirations are projected into built forms. In a mind unbound by gravity, circulation is both a fixed reference and impossible link between spaces that obscure true up and down. The stair insertion forms the center and periphery, revealing and concealing, a liminal structure from which all spaces expand.

Michael Harrison
Joeb Moore

PROJECT THREE: NEW HAVEN TEST
Stereotomic House attempts to make the minimal dwelling large, stealing space from its surrounding through repetitive subtraction. The home uses calibrated voids to produce semi-private exterior spaces for both owner and tenant. Each operation uses the negative to answer concerns relating to space, program and environment.

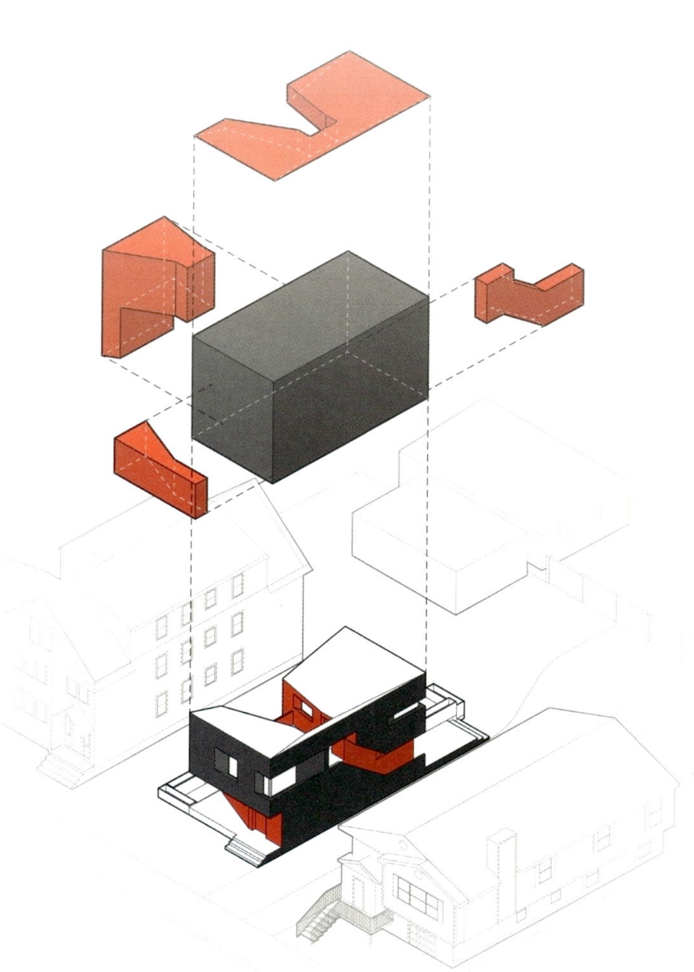

Kristin Nothwehr
Joeb Moore

PROJECT THREE: NEW HAVEN TEST
This project responds to the problem of the minimal dwelling through a bifurcated architectural language that juxtaposes density and openness. The design process began by categorizing the functions and metafunctions of the dwelling—what the house does and what it allows one to do. By packing the functions of the home into a compact, reproducible unit, living spaces are freed. The result is a scheme in which the biological operations of the house take place in a single unit, while two light frame living units emerge parasitically from its mass.

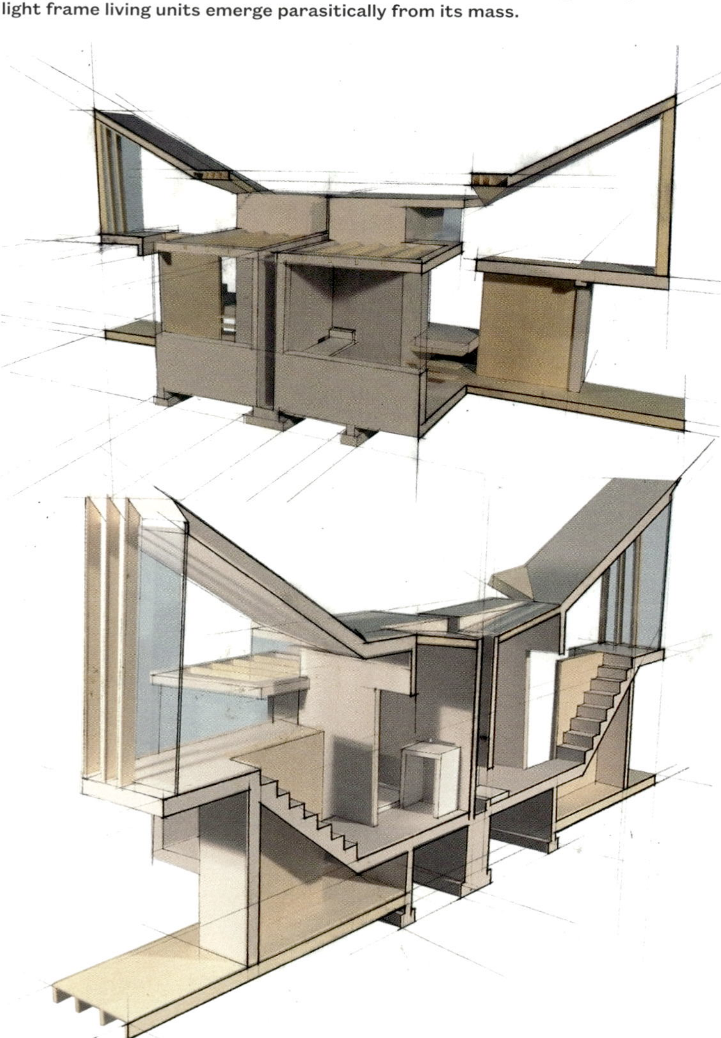

Vittorio Lovato
Andrew Benner

PROJECT THREE: NEW HAVEN TEST
The Domestic Hearth as the symbol and identity of the domestic life is in a state of transition. The ubiquity of mass social media has created a condition where the digital identity of the individual is gaining dominance over the physical collective engagement. The daily routine of getting ready and getting un-ready has also created a condition where the hearth, once a point of convergence for the family and community, must now be challenged to engage a more global context through our new state of individuality. The minimal dwelling attempts to unite the functional, social and spiritual necessities into a modern day domestic space that looks toward itself as it seeks a larger global digitally connected context.

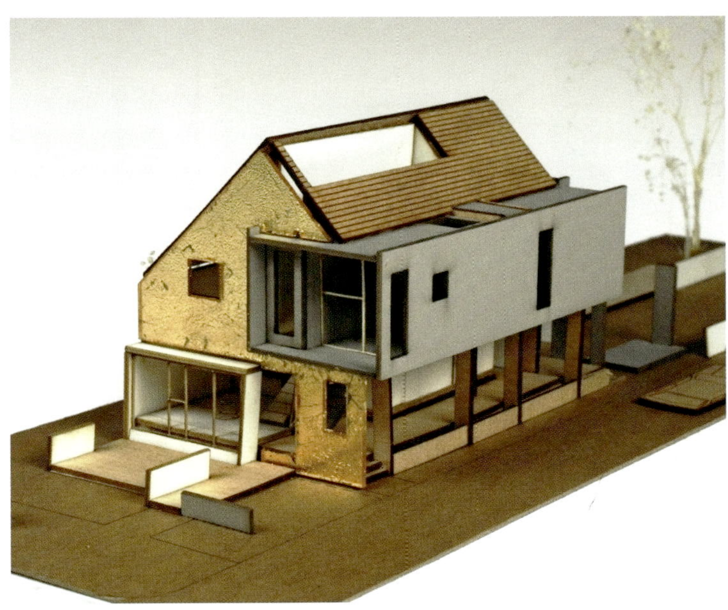

James Kehl
Amy Lelyveld

PROJECT THREE: NEW HAVEN TEST
The courtyard house is a minimal-dwelling model designed to provide a dynamic and relational living experience. It imagines two dwellings framing a semi-indoor court—the primary element of the proposal—wherein the owner and tenant can experience a range of private and shared activities. Especially suited for multi-generational families, this model affords a sense of connectedness between the lives and activities of the house's residents through the medium of the courtyard—instead of the stark separation that would result from a 'party wall'.

Xinyi Wang
Amy Lelyveld

PROJECT THREE: NEW HAVEN TEST
This tiny house claims the ownership of the whole site. The concept of the house is to organize the activities of daily life on an invisible spiral, placing toilet, shower and bed in the middle, while dining and recreation go along the outer surface. There are two rules organizing the form that define the dimensions of each layer: on plan and section. Yards and rooms are equal to this rule and are arranged in this lot as a whole system of living space. Still the layers help to diminish all the rules and shape the experience of the space as an ever-changing process.

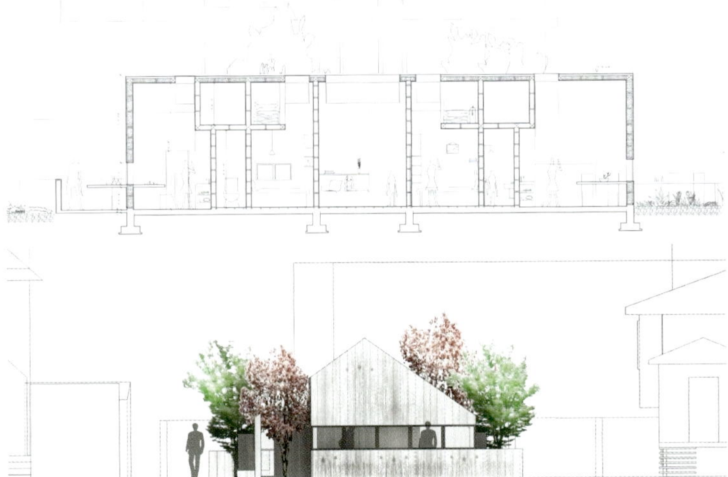

Xiao Wu
Amy Lelyveld

PROJECT THREE: NEW HAVEN TEST
The SMALL HOUSE is shaped into an almost-perfect box, generating an intimate interior space. Although compact, the owner's unit on the first two floors offers a generous atrium space above the dining area. The procession, from living space to the bedroom, is a spatially playful experience. Each window is carefully designed to address a particular relationship to outside. The third floor has separate circulation and can become a rental unit it could also be easily converted into a single family house by simply opening up the interior door near the second floor north-west corner. The house sits far back on the lot, creating a very private backyard and a dynamic front yard which allows for different levels of interaction with the street and neighborhood.

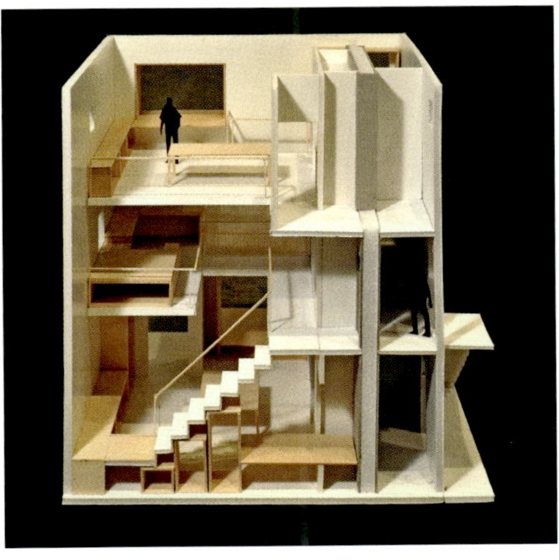

Justin Oh
Alan Organschi

PROJECT THREE: NEW HAVEN TEST
The Minimum Dwelling was designed in response to the client's request for a two unit micro-home prototype with a 500 square foot owner unit and a 300 square foot tenant unit. This requirement was manipulated to accommodate 3 equal units stacked up to 3 stories to better fit into New Haven's large housing stock. An efficient plan allows for prefabrication and customization, while its slender profile permits this prototype constructability on a variety of neglected narrow sites. The additional third unit not only increases the scale of the micro-home, but increases 'eyes-on-the-street', neighborhood densit and return for the developer, while being mindful to the spatial needs of a growing family.

Elizabeth LeBlanc
Peter de Bretteville

PROJECT THREE: NEW HAVEN TEST
Faced with a design prompt akin to micro-housing, the primary goal was to increase the occupant's spatial experience. The manipulation of light, view, and height maintain both privacy and a sense of openness within the tenant and owner space. The east and western walls bring light across the walls in subtle ways while still maintaining privacy from the neighboring windows. The north and southern walls are open to allow views out, visually expanding the space. Rather than having interior partition walls, level changes define public spaces such as kitchen and the living room.

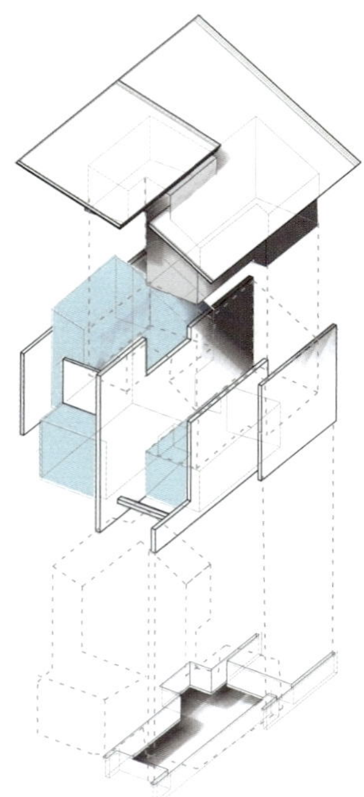

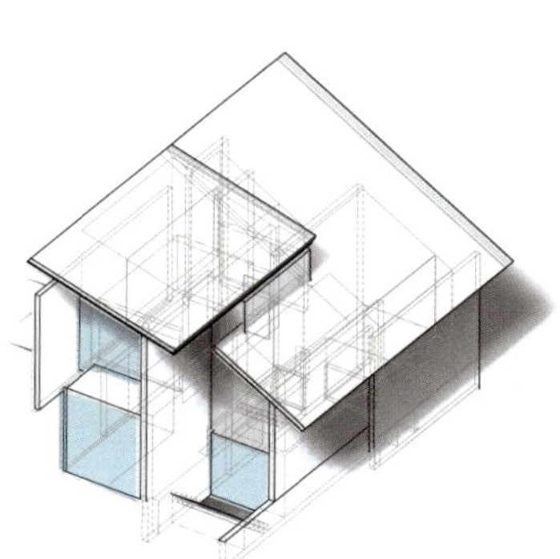

Jessica Flore Angel
Peter de Bretteville

PROJECT THREE: NEW HAVEN TEST
In order to fully address the elongated lot, the project starts with the introduction of a diagonal axis to the rectangular geometry of the site, thus dividing it in two parts. This trace becomes an environmental wall, the boundary that defines two clear entities but also the connecting spine of the whole. The servant apparatus of the house is accommodated along this feature, serving the diurnal spaces on the ground floor and the bedrooms on the upper floors. These units function according to common principles, both on the outside with the scenography of garden, hardscape and transitional spaces, as well as on the inside with a play of natural light coming from skylights attached to the central wall.

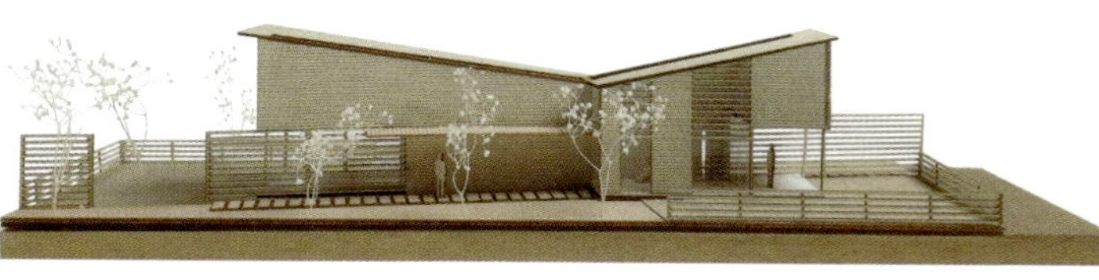

Charles Kane
Peter de Bretteville

PROJECT THREE: NEW HAVEN TEST
During the study of the minimum dwelling, I investigated the problem of maximization within the constraints of a minimal footprint. In the initial minimum dwelling exercise, elements of the house slide and reconfigure to allow the building to adapt to the small size of the dwelling. This initial idea of maximization was carried into the design of the house at 179 Scranton Street. The house, a deceptively simple cube from the street, was derived from two initial moves. The building's central core is occupied by a large sculpted light well that provides a mode to organize circulation, provide natural light and erode the cube's initial simplicity.

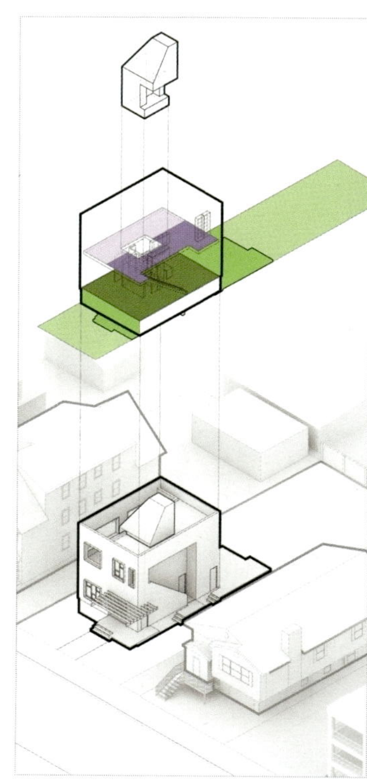

SPRING/ SUMMER

THE JIM VLOCK FIRST-YEAR BUILDING PROJECT

This course examines the materialization of a building, whereby students are required to physically participate in the construction of a structure that they have designed. By engaging in the act of making, students are exposed to the material, procedural, and technical demands that shape architecture. Construction documents are generated and subsequently put to the test in the field. Students engage in collaboration with each other, and with a client, as they reconcile budgetary, scheduling, and labor constraints, and negotiate myriad regulatory, political, and community agencies. The course seeks to demonstrate the multiplicity of forces that come to influence the execution of an architectural intention, all the while fostering an architecture of social responsibility, providing structures for an underserved and marginalized segment of the community.

Since 1967, the Yale School of Architecture has offered its students the opportunity to design and build a structure as an integral part of their graduate education. Unique among architecture schools, the Jim Vlock First-Year Building Project is mandatory for all first-year graduate students.

This year, we are partnering with Neighbor Works New Horizons of New Haven, an organization committed to develop and operate affordable quality housing, and HTP Ventures LLC, a private equity firm interested in mass producing micro dwelling units. Our design work this semester is part of a continuing, long-term collaboration with the New Haven Livable City Initiative to develop the city's 100+ vacant sliver lots. A primary criterion of the selected design proposal will be its ability to be replicated across New Haven as a solution to the longstanding challenge of small, difficult-to-develop urban spaces. The City of New Haven has begun to develop a financial mechanism to fund this endeavor.

This year's house is an approximately 800 square foot dwelling at 179 Scranton Street in the West River neighborhood of New Haven. The house is divided into one 500 square foot unit for the homeowner and one 300 square foot unit for a tenant. Students worked independently during the first half of the semester and then worked in teams to develop seven design proposals. During the summer semester, the entire class of 54 first-year graduate students worked together as a studio to finalize the design of and build the selected house.

COORDINATING FACULTY

Alan Organschi (Studio)
Adam Hopfner (Project Director)

FACULTY

Andrew Benner
Peter de Bretteville
Amy Lelyveld
Joeb Moore
Avram Forman

STUDENT LEADERSHIP

Project Managers: Katie Stege, John Kleinschmidt
Fundraising Directors: Pearl Ho, Nicolas Kemper
Budget Coordinators: Michelle Gonzalez, Richard Mandimika
Photographer: Xiao Wu / Website Manager: Anne Ma
Construction Document Coordinators: James Kehl, Kristin Nothwehr
Detail Coordinator: John Wan / Engineering Coordinator: Eugene Tan

JURORS

Andrew Bernheimer
Stella Betts
Hansjörg Göritz
Seila Mosquera
Herbert Newman
Thach Pham
Lyn Rice
Kurt Roeloffs
Julie Savin
Brigitte Shim
Mark Simon
Robert A.M. Stern

CORE CLASSES

1015b Building Technology
4011b Intro to Urban Design
1016b Visualization III
1017c Visualization IV

Team A

Jessica Elliott, John Kleinschmidt, Clarissa Luwia, Richard Mandimika, Anna Meloyan, Chloe Pu, Shayari De Silva, Dima Srouji

Three essential tenets of dwelling—services for biological needs, storage for mental and physical clutter, and a strong connection to site—are distilled into three distinct elements: prefabricated kitchens and bathrooms, a modular structural storage system, and a series of outdoor garden walls. Service walls and storage walls are delivered to the site for rapid installation; floors and roof are built on site, supported by those prefabricated units.

By packing all essential equipment and storage into the perimeter of the house, generous and flexible living spaces are created with open corners to views beyond. Garden walls and strategic plantings gather the landscape into outdoor rooms in order to conceptually and physically expand the house's volume.

The spatial qualities and organizational logic of this prototype hold true for other potential sites: Prefabricated elements set boundaries; living spaces fit between, and garden walls and outdoor rooms tie the house to its site.

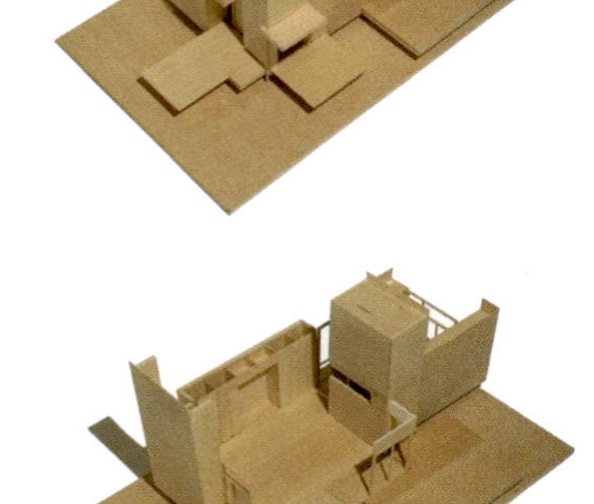

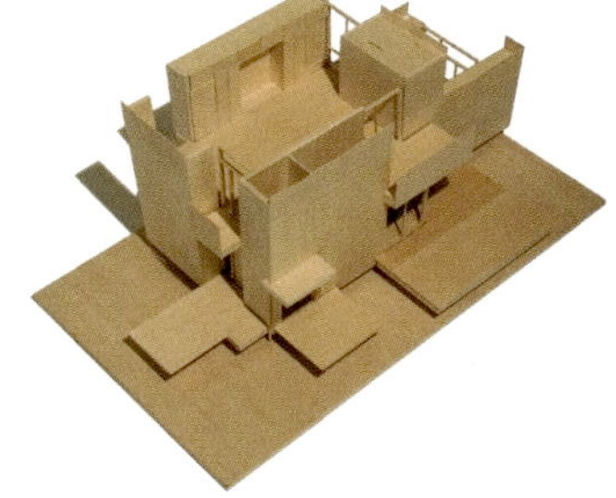

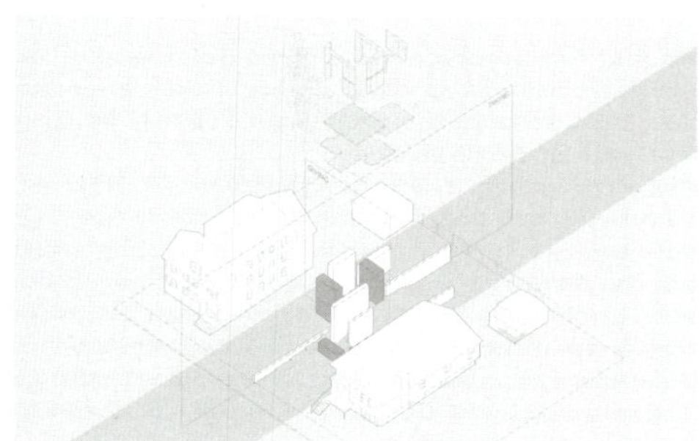

Initial prototype developed by Anne Householder

PROTOTYPE REVIEW

What is interesting about this approach is it presents questions about what is dwelling, what is habitation and what is it to build a house. I think you want to address that a bit more forcefully and conceptually, not only as a logic of the systems but as a system that questions the appearance of a traditional house. —Herbert Newman

TEAM REVIEW

Organschi One of the issues that we have is that 54 students get on the site over the course of a month and a half, so the logistics of this is somewhat of a hybrid. Because of space we'll probably build off site this year, so we're investigating that as part of the process.

Pham I love this project. I've loved it for a long time now, okay just a couple weeks [laughter]. Just a couple of ways to make it better. If I look at the site and the flow, the front door and the side door require you to go around that wall. Could you think about a site layout where the cars are on the right-hand side so that people can just get out of their cars and straight into entrance?

Stern How about the context of the street? We live in a society where there are two cultures — there are highbrow educated people like our Yale students, and the rest of the world who just don't think that flat roof houses fit their perception of what a house is.

Rice I can see your commitment to the interior experience. You can really get a sense of how these volumes start shaping these corners and the kind of illusion that there's more around the bend. But I find that the exterior doesn't go far enough in contrasting with the neighboring projects. I don't think mimicking the siding is the right move.

Bernheimer I actually question the interior. I think that the introduction is really compelling, the psychological aspect and the biological aspect, but other than a couple of places with open shelves, everything must be put away. These panels which close off the interior actually close the project off from the psychological component that makes the house what it is for the person or a family. The inside needs to delaminate to make it a home.

Betts There's a very uniform treatment, whether it's to a bedroom or a living room, where there are these beautifully considered openings for light and view but it feels like a treatment for larger scale housing. There's a uniformity that isn't required here.

Simon I was really surprised by your answer to Bob about flat roofs because you've got immediate neighbors that have flat roofs. Why didn't you mention that. I mean seriously! He's talking about context, you've got a context.

Shim I appreciate the way you presented it with such choreography. The inside dictated so much of your thinking, whereas I see experiments that would lead you to other ways of imagining the exterior. It bugs me that the kitchen doesn't have an outdoor space right next to it so you can barbeque and do all those things. You have room to do it, there's a lot of space, a lot of rhetoric about landscape, but I don't see it being as instrumental as I think it could be in the project.

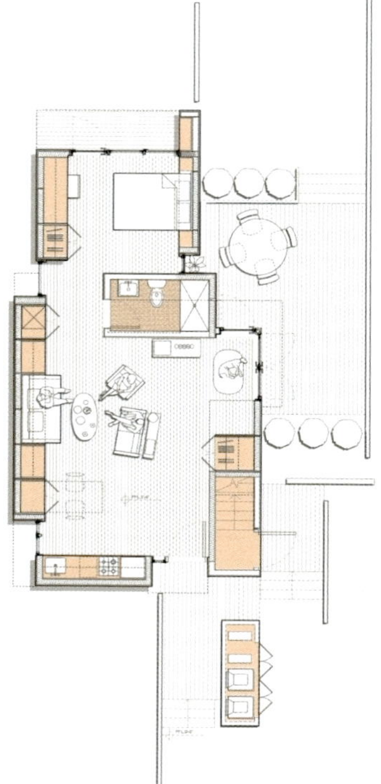

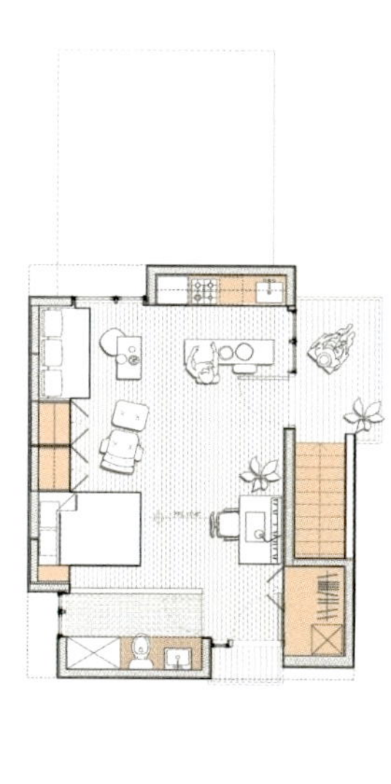

Team B

Dorian Booth, Dante Furioso, Pearl Ho, Samantha Jaff, Sarah Kasper, Nicolas Kemper, Jenny Kim, Xinyi Wang

Our proposal improves on a time tested model, the row house. By delivering street access and private yards to each unit, the row house strikes an ingenious balance between the demand for economical and efficient dwelling and the need for dignity and privacy.

Our house activates the partition, placing it at an angle. Thus skewed, the partition creates dwellings which become alive to the needs of the inhabitant. Substructures form bands which organize the internal rooms. The narrowest band holds functions which require little space, while using ready access to the exterior to create a feeling of spaciousness. The kitchens span the middle of each unit, naturally bringing the inhabitant into their main living spaces, their extraordinary width spilling out onto balconies and then into the site itself.

For larger units a loft over the wide end of the house further augments the flow of the dwelling. Our proposal for 179 Scranton Street demonstrates a small single story unit as well as a larger unit with a loft. The activated partition not only makes more efficient and effective use of narrow lots like that at 179 Scranton Street, but also allows for easy adaptation onto a wide variety of irregularly shaped sites.

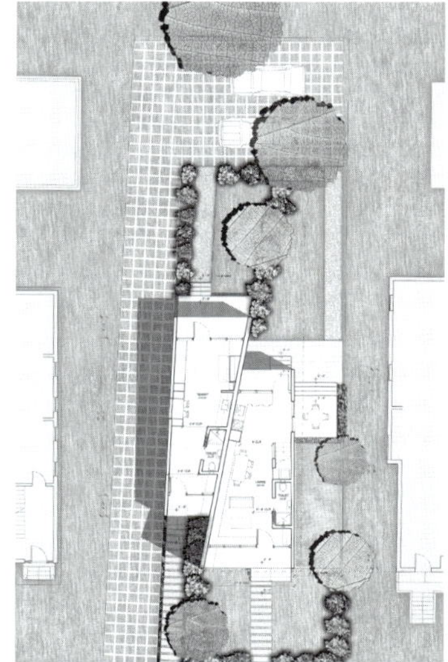

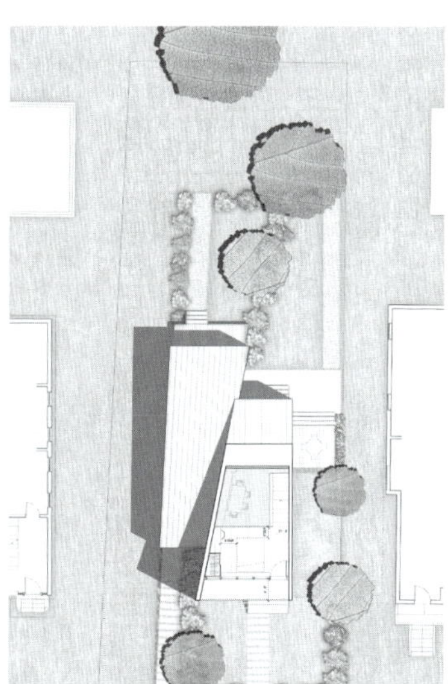

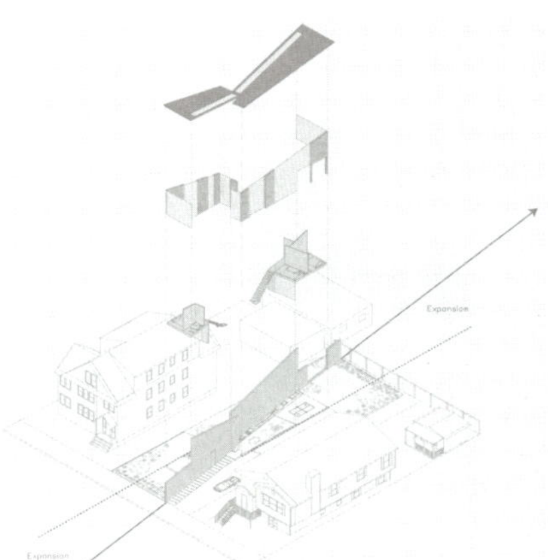

Initial prototype developed by Jessica Flore Angel

PROTOTYPE REVIEW

I think what you're looking for here is the generic and replicable aspect of two houses sitting in situ on either side of the wall. The strong architectural move is to say I've got a long narrow site, instead of dividing it front to back; I'm going to divide it side by side. I think it's a big bold move and it produces hyper skinny units, which you have to make people fall in love with. —Ben Pell

TEAM REVIEW

Stern This is a very interesting scheme and I think a lot of people probably agree. The idea of the row house as a model and the skewering is very intelligent as a thoughtful approach, but I think on a practical level, the bathroom, if you can only have one bathroom has to be adjacent to the bedroom. And who needs all that glass facing the street? But that's another conversation. It really does seem to work. I would compliment you on that.

Rice You're going to have Christmas trees in the window there. I think its right to have owner's presence to the side walk.

Bernheimer I would argue for a much more radical scheme than this. What I really want to see is a real play of this diagonal line. I'm sure you iterated throughout this process, what is the angle, how is it biased, but I wonder if you can look at this as two separate houses and say, what is the narrowest this house can be? And one of these houses becomes the narrowest it can be and the other house can be as wide as it can be. Rethink what the house can be, proportionally.

Göritz I totally agree you can do more with that partition wall if you turned it into a kind of media wall, where all the support and all the services would go. Both bathrooms would be behind each other or in a row and storage and everything would be included in that wall.

Betts To keep up on where the project could be more radical, I too want to take this party wall, which then extends into the landscape, and pack everything into it. Perhaps both tenants are kind of shifting over from one side, so that in fact there is this thickened dividing wall. Then you can put your boiler and other systems in there, and you can be very compact.

Shim The starting point with the angle is really the bright spark of rethinking the site plan. I think it's a really strong site plan. I total agree with Bob that this street elevation is such a wonderful drawing to see because it actually talks about context. It tests the idea of scale and we totally get it, and we understand the wholeness of it in the contribution of landscape and architecture together.

Team C

Luke Anderson, Jessica Flore Angel Michael Harrison, Megan McDonough, Justin Oh, Luis Salas Porras, Katie Stege, Andrew Sternad

Our project consists of two volumes, one suspended within the other, pinned together with an efficient stem of bundled utility connections. From the street, the building is scaled to its context and the tenant unit is clearly articulated within the owner's larger frame. The owner occupies the first floor with ample access to sheltered outdoor areas that expand the perception of interior volume. Inside, a long double height space links front, side and rear porches and reflects light down into the kitchen and living areas. The tenant unit upstairs features two generous porches and is visually distinguished from the owner's space by a lighter material palette. As the owner's family grows, the upstairs unit easily reconfigures into two bedrooms and the owner can occupy the entire house.

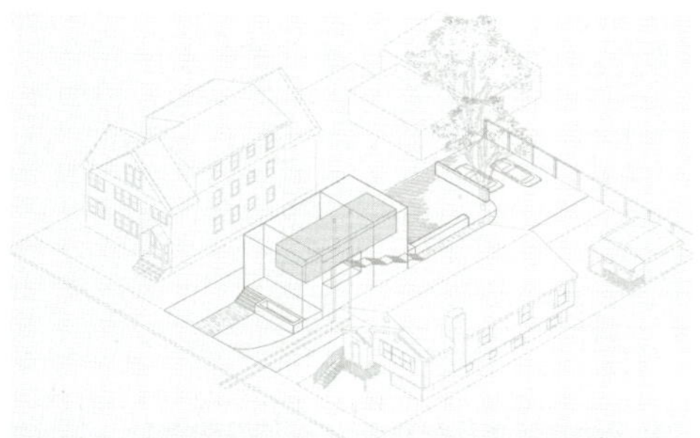

Initial prototype developed by Samantha Jaff

PROTOTYPE REVIEW

The brilliance of the design is the screening of the two side houses and this infinite movement in and out sliding the other way, which opens up a sense of having more space than what is there. The plan is very successful but I can't help but thinking of it as a lobster trap, with the ends sliding in and out. —Turner Brooks

TEAM REVIEW

Rice I still don't buy the discontinuity between the floor and the exterior if the bar above is continuous. I think there's a disjunctive character, it's this object that's sitting on the site, not well integrated into the landscape. There could be a more synthesized idea about the design of the house and the concepts that you're working on there. Seeing the core all there seems like a no brainer, it just makes so much sense for economy and organization but it seems like somehow the landscape concept got left out of the game. I think an integrated landscape would be a big help.

Göritz I would also like to commend you on the fact that you integrate landscape with trees in the back, so it's not just adding trees. You can solve the problem of getting back out with your car by making the whole thing maybe a square that becomes an orchard and you can actually park in that orchard. This is a wonderful feature to the backside, this is the first project that shows this and it also makes a wonderful vista out to the back.

Organschi It is interesting that you raise that concept because the building behind is not so great, so it does handle that.

Stern I think next year we have to take the guest jurors to the site before the jury.

Roeloffs The decision to be humble about the narrowness of the site, and therefore to respond by making the house as wide as you could with the core in the center, it made it very simple, very elegant, and very economical. It allowed you to go to a second floor without a lot of circulation confusion which solves some of the height problems that we saw with other schemes. I also like these simple ideas of pop-outs. You can subtract those and it still has integrity, you can do one less and it would still be convincing.

Shim I think there's something really weird about the front elevation. You see it in that rendering: the piece that is meant for privacy, whether it's concrete or whatever this L-shaped piece is, looks like it's holding up the bar. It doesn't need to do that. What's happening on the back side is actually expressed as something more flowing, as opposed to the panel which looks like it is for privacy, is supporting something that doesn't need to be supported. I think there's a nuance of the elevation and the grammar is a part of the evolution of the project. I think the model at this scale answers a lot of your questions, because you get the continuity of the material from inside to outside.

Simon It seems a bit like you've dropped back to two clichés that we see in all the magazines. If you're going to use a cliché, just stick to one. I really like the idea of the perforated sides which is a modern approach to the porch. The whole scheme is just fabulous.

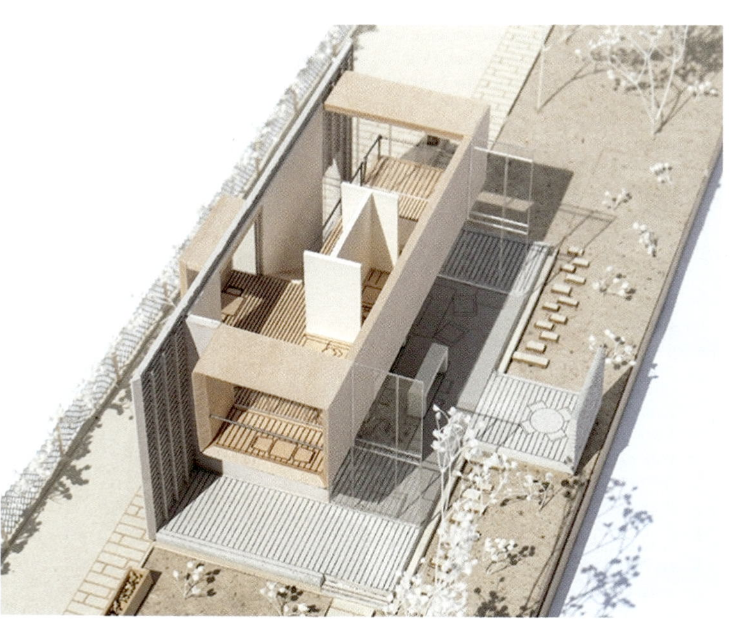

Team D—Winning Proposal
Anthony Gagliardi, Cynthia Hsu, Lila Jiang Chen, Charles Kane, Anne Ma, Seokim Min, Madelynn Ringo, Caitlin Thissen

The faceted cube pushes the limits of residential convention by maximizing internal efficiency and compactness while allowing internal spatial constraints to find their release in the landscape. This allows the importance of landscape to come to the fore, lending a greener and lusher feel to the very dense housing stock of New Haven's urban-scape. As proposed, the tenant occupies the 3rd floor, allowing the owner's space on the first and second floor to spill out onto the land in the form of interior furnishings such as dining tables and pop-out window seats. These elements push and pull on the building's envelope, establishing a unique dialogue between the interior and exterior. As a result, the site becomes an extension of the owner's interior living room that can be visually enjoyed by neighboring sites. Depending on the owner's level of involvement in the up keep of his/her land, landscape possibilities may vary. One can imagine it to be as simple as a flat landscape planted with tall, wild grasses to something more programed such as a planted vegetable garden, thriving because of its direct access to the southern sun.

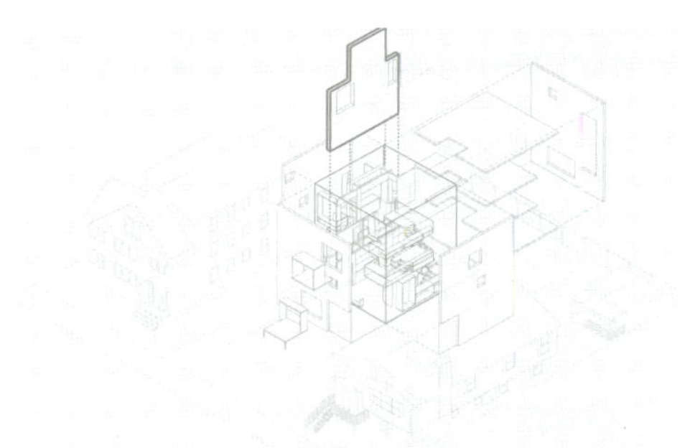

Initial prototype developed by Xiao Wu

PROTOTYPE REVIEW

I think the siting of this thing is really great. It looks right on the site and it's different from the other buildings; its tininess is sort of monumental. It's very clear. —Turner Brooks

TEAM REVIEW

Rice I think this is very smart design. I like the argument of pushing it to the back of the lot to give transverse views to anchor the more intimate space in the back. The faceting that's alluding to a gabled roof keeps a contemporary sensibility. I think all of those things are super smart and very well explained. I think all of that is genius.

Stern Ooh, be careful what you say.

Rice Well there's a but, don't worry [laughter], and it's a big but, a real big but. One of the big attributes is this huge front yard which is then completely undeveloped. Do you leave it in the tenant's hand or the owner's? You should take more responsibility for what that is. The little wall at the front may be operating at the scale of the tiny house; it should be operating at the scale of the lot. I think it has to be like five times more because it's a critical thing. Is it transparent or translucent? What can it do to claim and control that space? Frame it a little more intentionally. The building is so well conceived but the landscape through all the studies hasn't really emerged with the same kind of clarity.

Simon It has to be a part of the composition conceptually. It really feels like the only gesture you've made is that little half wall in the front, and the rest, meh, we're not quite sure what to do with the site. We're architects, we don't deal with site, but you have to with this kind of scheme, you absolutely have to. It's part of your composition. Just like a classic Japanese garden, like a Noguchi piece, he's thinking very carefully about the space around as much as the pieces themselves.

Stern On the one hand this house is slightly wacko, but I kind of like it. It has a little romantic viewing, it has a little character. If I saw one more house from dwell magazine this afternoon, I was going to flip out, so I commend you. I think Lyn said it already, but the interior spaces are really nice.

Betts For me, what's most successful about the project is how it's urban in its concept and developed at the scale of the furniture and the interiors. For me actually the weakest is the architecture. I would say in general I want this project to be more aggressive and more ambitious. I think that the radical move is potentially the way that you've treated the suburban site and the sensitivity to the interior where you started to integrate all of the furniture in the way you're thinking about it.

Team E
Mohammad Alothman, Jack Bian, Benjamin Bourgoin, James Kehl, Vittorio Lovato, Feng Qian, Xiao Wu

This three-story house can adapt to a variety of living situations and sites due to its modular construction and flexible plan. Each living space is continuous and open. Windows at each end of these rooms welcome north and south light, connecting livable spaces on the interior back to the community street-front and private backyard. Utilities, services, and furniture are densely aligned along the west edge of each room. Opposite these working zones, the rooms are clear—opening to the east side-yard gardens, in addition to views down the street. These distinct zones help simplify daily routines and activities. Stairs extending from the utility wall connect each level, enabling convenient reconfiguration of dwelling units.

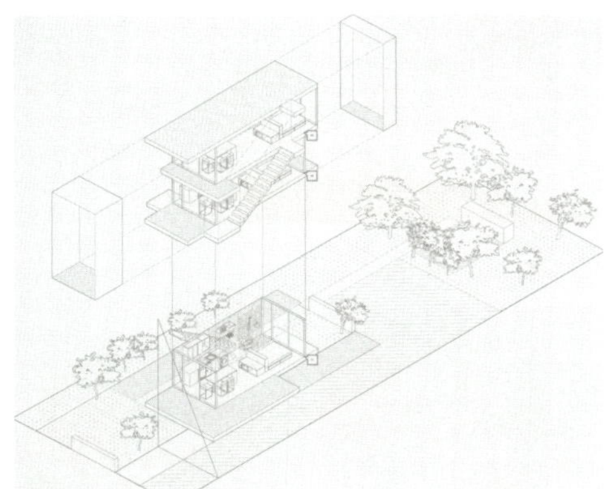

Initial prototype developed by Justin Oh

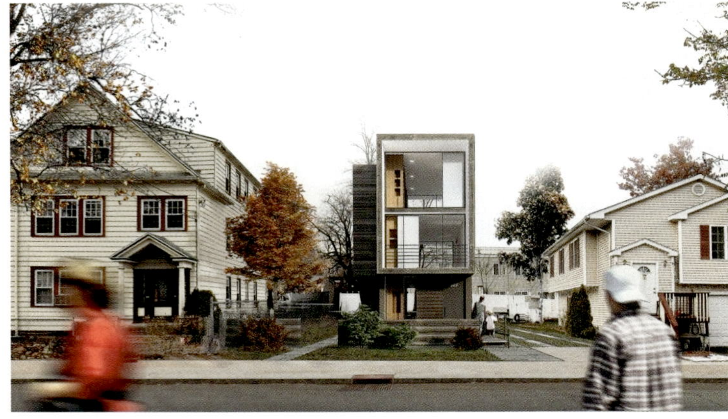

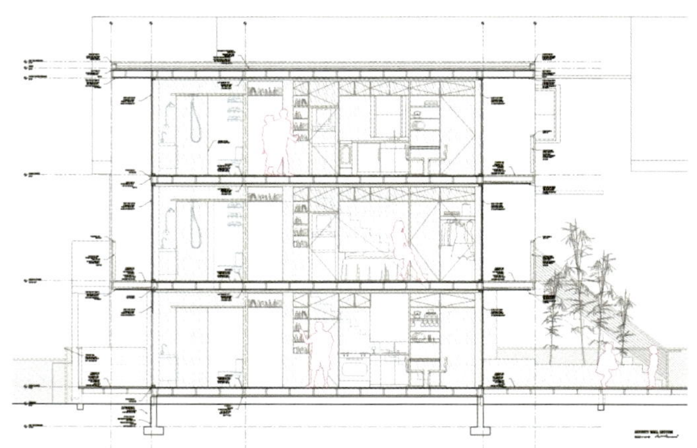

PROTOTYPE REVIEW

As much as I love the axonometric quality of your object on the landscape, I think there's more you can do with the site plan with different strategies to activate these views. It becomes less about the object and more about situating the object to create these relational spaces front and back, left and right. —Joeb Moore

TEAM REVIEW

Simon It needs more domesticity.

Stern Put a gabled roof on it.

Organschi Bob, I thought we had you.

Stern People want more in architecture; they don't want to live in a flat box.

Bourgoin Can a flat box not be architecture? Does architecture have to have a gabled roof?

Stern It has to have things that address the neighbors and it has to engage the street.

Shim I really love your presentation because you talked about the scenario of adaptability and I would probably take it further. If you start off as someone who is single that gets married and then you can imagine that couple aging. Once their kids move away, it might become a live work space or you might have another renter come in, but this question of life cycle and adaptability is really the strength of this project. Where I'm from the issue of intergenerational families living in one dwelling unit is such a big deal. With the grandparents looking after the grandchildren with parents that are working, a house like this could totally accommodate that.

Stern You maximized your envelope with a building but you didn't maximize the site. You talked about engaging with the street but you haven't talked at all about how the residents of this engage with the site, except going in and out of the building.

Rice I think that's the clarity of the diagram, it's so directional. It's hard to imagine occupying these spaces comfortably. I think there's a missed opportunity with the thickened wall of stuff. I think the one diagram I would like to see is if it was to maximize the width of the space, what configuration would make a really comfortable living room.

Bernheimer I think it's diagrammatically linear but there are sub-versions too which are really great. So the whole idea of domesticity actually exists specifically in this moment right here where the shelf becomes the stair. I think that's a total moment of brilliance that this scheme allows despite its linear diagram.

Betts I find the project to be very successful. I was wondering if you extend out this way, and if you can't, can you carve in? There could be a less rigid side yard. One of these becomes a completely solid façade, with windows on this side with an in-board balcony. Maybe it happens on the third floor where you've actually cleared the view of the roof of your neighbor, and then it becomes very site specific. As everyone said you have beautiful diagrams that structurally and infrastructurally set you up in terms of circulation, but then I would start to think about the perpendicular experience so that you get a full width. The one criticism I would have is that it ends up being a lot of the same type of space. I think it can start to belly out in the middle in a way, to create larger spaces.

Stern It needs a little more detail, even forgetting the flat roof, it's just too much of a stark shoe-box. It looks like a manufactured home.

Team F

Lisa Albaugh, Andrew Dadds, Hugo Fenaux, Michelle Gonzalez, Elizabeth LeBlanc, Kristin Nothwehr, Susan Wang

Our project responds to the problem of the minimal dwelling through a pinwheel organizational strategy, in which spaces expand sequentially from a dense central core. Beginning with a primitive rectangular volume, four programmatic arms spiral from the stacked core to generate interior and exterior spaces. Our scheme deploys the utility core to its traditional functional purpose, while also expanding this volume outward as a plastic composition of planar projections. The result is a spatial layering of owner and tenant, in which each unit experiences the core as a knot that both unifies the whole and defines the part.

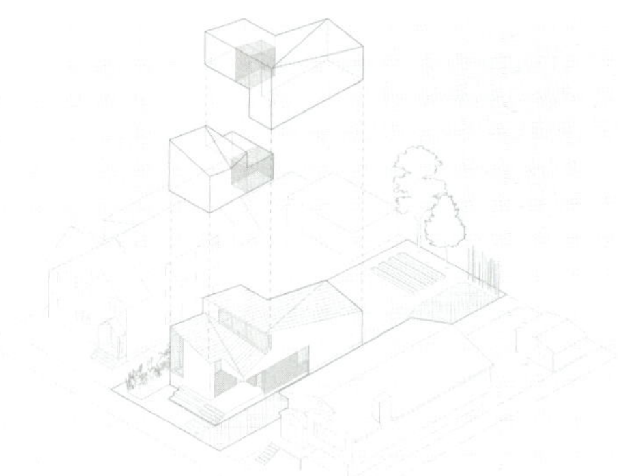

Initial prototype developed by Andrew Sternad

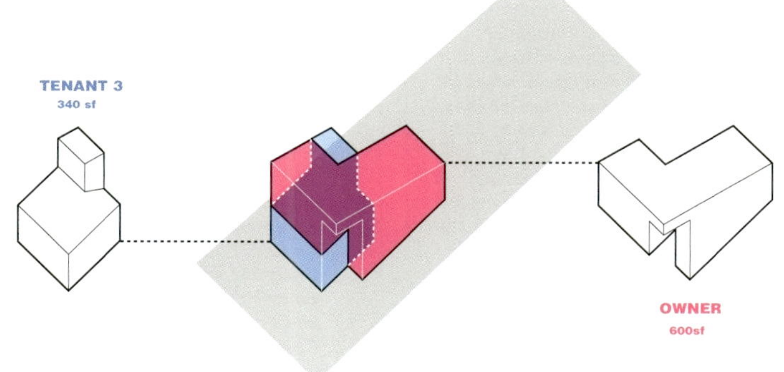

PROTOTYPE REVIEW

I think there's a consistent sensibility to it, but what I'm looking for in terms of adaptability to another site is for that that sensibility to be systematized somehow so we understand what the rules are. I'm looking for more clarity on If that's a game about additive or subtractive volumes or if that's a game about the relationship between building and landscape. It has integrity as a bespoke object. —Ben Pell

TEAM REVIEW

Simon The other comment that I have is that your core—I like it and it's a neat idea—but I wish it was better expressed. I don't think you really get it if you go into the house. It's been eroded so much, especially the stair part, you don't sense a core there. To continue with my earlier thought, we architects are trained to create emotions in other people, and what we really need to learn is to sense emotions in other people, so that we can work with those, rather than trying to do some big thing.

Organschi Those central strong elements—you would never call them the core whatever that is—often have a centripetal, effect and they do grow things out into rooms and out into the landscape.

Göritz I think you need a presence to the street as well as the garden. going back again to the comment about object making, for the same amount of money, instead of carving out the corner, have a future space or a layer that engages with the street and same on the back side. It would allow for expanding horizontally like I said earlier. It's just a simple strategy to do that but all your thinking is revolving around the core.

Bernheimer That's a good point about the grammar in architecture. When you say the core, coming from New York, I think of fire stairs and elevators. It's a building core, it's the structural core so the building can stand up, and it's also the way you get up and down. So when you say core, it means something in vocabulary to me. Maybe it means something different to someone working in a different context say a different city, but this whole issue of the grammar of architecture shows up. So it looks like from where I'm sitting that the core is kind of pseudo-structural, conceptually structural but also spatial, but then it unfolds into the elevation, and as soon as it becomes a part of the elevation it's not a core to me anymore. It may be conceptually a core to you but it's no longer technically a core to an architect, I think that's really important.

Organschi There are two kind of linguistic issues here One is the architectural linguistic, what are the tectonics and how those material transitions happen. I think the real problem in the way that you've presented it is using the term core at all. It's not a core, it's something that sponsors a lot of other things, and by not using the term core you're forced to define exactly what it is and what it does. You guys have come so far with this project, really great job. I appreciate these guys saying what you did because these are really subtle things we can address. That's why design-build is great because we get to address these subtle readings which I think make or break a house.

Team G
Jean Chen, Michelle Chen, Dov Feinmesser, Kiana Hosseini, Anne Householder, Eugene Tan, Winny Tan, John Wan

A house shelters one from the harshness of environment and the turbulence of the exterior—but to be deemed a home, it must transcend the mere desire for protection to take on qualities of comfort and psychological ease. Given the challenge to design a micro-house in an urban neighborhood, the demand for spatial compactness might imbue a house with the characteristics of a confined fortress rather than those of a comfortable home. Without mediation, an abrupt transition from exterior to interior can carry with it unresolved anxieties of the outside. Our design mediates these concerns by considering the house not as an object upon a lot but instead as a landscape. Through a layering of gardens, semi-enclosed courts, and differing elevations, the site becomes the house, and the house, the site. The scheme meanders through a shifting exterior landscape to arrive within an interior that in turn carefully borrows exterior views in the creation of perceived spaciousness. Walls perform all the functions of enclosure, all the while unexpectedly expanding space rather than defining boundaries.

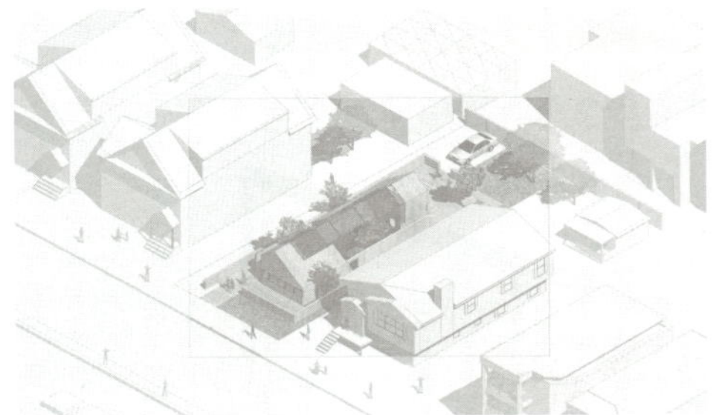

Initial prototype developed by Xinyi Wang

PROTOTYPE REVIEW

There are various alternatives here. One of them is perhaps to expand the house so that this, instead of being just a side courtyard, becomes part of the core of the house itself, which would conspire with the compact nature of the house that you're designing. —Herbert Newman

TEAM REVIEW

Stern Of course it has a gable so I'm very pleased. [laughter] It has the problem of being a one story in a neighborhood of taller buildings. It exacerbates the question of scale that all the other houses also have. It's very beautifully put together. It is very prototypical in my view. The way that it opens up on the side, the proportions and the windows; you seem to be the only team that has really taken care into the proportions of the windows. I'm really impressed. The models are great by the way.

Bernheimer I think it's terrific. I thought making the outdoor spaces that work with the inside is really nice. I think there's a missed opportunity towards the street. I love how you've taken the single gable and opened it up one side one way and the other the opposite way, I think the spaces are very successful.

Betts I would like to see it pushing these two systems to be a little bit dissimilar and not have the outside envelope accommodate the interior. What that would do is create more varied spaces. In the end, I like this project very much, but these interior garden spaces are almost all the same dimension. You have opportunities to have boxes that are not following that exterior envelope, that actually start to fiddle and create other courtyards or more varied spaces. I think the overall strategy is amazing but I'd rather see a more radical difference between that skin and the interior volume.

Shim The purity of the circulation is really important. I just want to rip out all this furniture in the hallway because it's really cluttering the conceptual idea of your project, which has been driven by the core itself. You need to make sure you know what is the key element of your project so the program of residence doesn't undermine the clarity. There are actually ways of incorporating these things in the core. It calls into question whether you really understand how important this relationship is between the inner building and the outer building. I would probably rename your project as a house within a house. I actually think of the core as the inner house and this is the outer house and then an outer layer on top of the outer house. Conceptually it's not a different project; it's a bit more precise about what you're really trying to do.

Göritz I think what concerns me is that the form almost disintegrates. Wouldn't it better if you would have the roof cover the whole thing? Spatially I think that would make this very simple gesture so much more compelling.

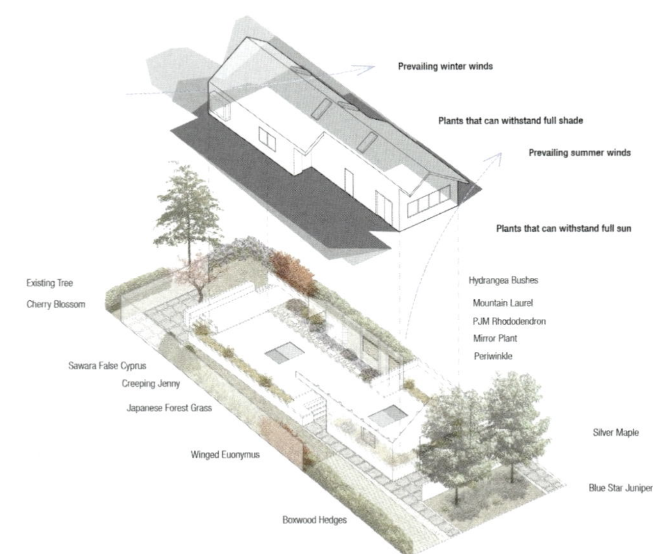

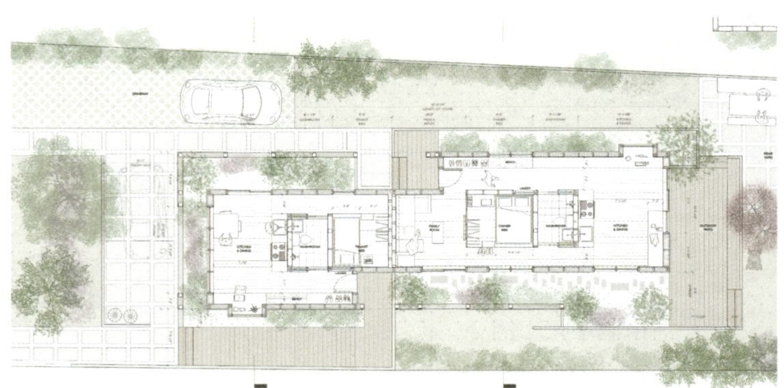

20

BUILDING TECHNOLOGY

Alan Organschi

Cynthia Hsu
Nicolas Kemper
Justin Oh

TILES HILL
WANG SHU

Michelle Chen
Jenny Kim
Richard Mandimika

JEAN-MARIE TJIBAOU CULTURAL CENTER
RENZO PIANO

Michelle Gonzalez
Michael Harrison
Katherine Stege

VENNESLA LIBRARY
HELEN & HARD

INTRODUCTION TO URBAN DESIGN

Alan Plattus

ADDITIONAL INSTRUCTOR: ANDREI HARWELL

This course is an introduction to the history, analysis, and design of the urban landscape presented with weekly lectures and discussion sections. Emphasis is placed on understanding the principles, processes, and contemporary theories of urban design, and the relations between individual buildings, groups of buildings, and the larger physical and cultural contexts in which they are created and with which they interact. Case studies are drawn from New Haven and other cities.

Luke Anderson
Pearl Ho

ROCINHA STUDY—FAVELA IN RIO DE JANEIRO

One of the greatest challenges present in Rio is the rapid transformation and urbanization of the favelas in the city. The favelas, and specifically Rocinha, have only become considered part of the economic urban infrastructure in the last two decades. A "pacification" effort by special police force units was begun in January 2011, and since then there have been numerous steps taken both by the city and the favela residents themselves to make changes in this iconic favela. The city's goal is to ensure favelas are safer places before the World Cup in 2014 and the Olympic Games of 2016. Leonardo Picciani, the State Secretary of Housing in Rio, states that "Rocinha is an emblematic community. It is a community that, since pacification, has been transforming positively and changing the lives of people for the better and property titles are here to crown that work." This project examines this new reality with a critical eye and suggests further improvements to the favela in light of these examinations.

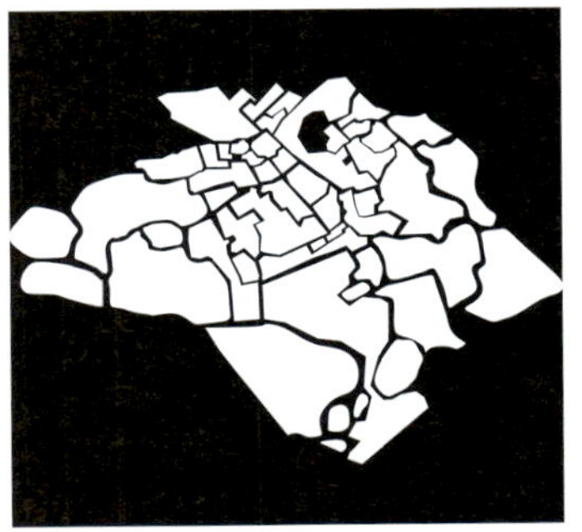

Michelle Chen
Justin Oh

FINLANDIA PARK

On examining a map of Helsinki from 1897, one could see that the infrastructural logic of the city has remained virtually unchanged. Two orthogonal grids at angled juxtaposition were the dominant focus of a map a century ago, and today, it still remains the primary figure for much of Helsinki's urban center. Focusing in on the Töölönlahti Bay, in 1897 there was seemingly little development—aside from the major street Mannerheimintie and the rail roads that cross the bay. The Mannerheimintie still exists today as do the railroads; however, what has changed is the intensity and category of developments along these two major infrastructures in the bay region. Both the road and the railroad perfectly sandwich between them an area of land that has become home to several of Helsinki's largest cultural institutions. However, the way through which this area of civic developments has been unified is still an ongoing transformation.

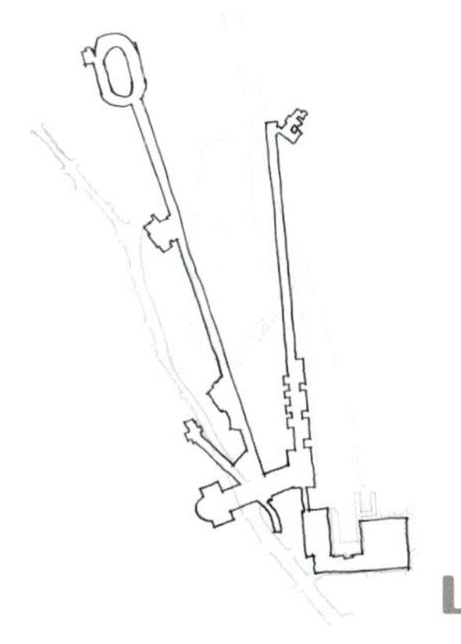

VISUALIZATION III

Ben Pell & John Eberhart

This course provides an introduction to the key relationships that exist among methods of drawing, physical materials, technologies of construction, and three-dimensional form making. The material and formal sensibilities developed in 1015a, Visualization II, are mined to explore drawing as a tool leading to full-scale fabrication. The generation of form through both manual and digital methods is tested through materials and technologies of fabrication. Additive and subtractive processes, repetition and mass production, and building information modeling (BIM) are introduced as tools for assembly. "Assembly" is framed as both full-scale object and "three-dimensional" analog. Exercises and workshops provide students the opportunity to work physically with a wide variety of tools and materials as well as digitally with emerging computer-driven technologies. In this course conceived as a supplement to 1013b, Building Project, students integrate drawing and model-making to develop and propose a construction that can be experienced at the human scale and be understood as an integrated architectural element.

Luke Anderson
Michelle Gonzalez
Michael Harrison
Samantha Jaff
Shayari De Silva
Katie Stege

HOLE TO THE SKY

The site for the installation was the void between the outdoor stair and penthouse on the uppermost terrace of Rudolph Hall. Using the striations of the corduroy concrete as a datum for porosity we suggested enclosure of the space using surfaces comprised of plywood ribs, articulated with a subtle undulation that was reinforced by the mirror placed on the ground. The result, whether perceived from within the space or above, was the illusion of an infinite void, where the distinction between the sky and the ground was blurred.

Lisa Albaugh
Jessica Elliott
Anne Householder
Sarah Kasper
Elizabeth LeBlanc
Caitlin Thissen

WHITE DRAGON

Our final project called for a site specific installation that complimented the formal language of the predominantly vertical front entry stair of Rudolph Hall. The installation mediated two scales—human experience and the building's larger context. Parametric design was used to generate the curved underside of the paper canopy into a straight line across the top. The form was then placed on a colonnade of ascending posts up the stair, inviting interaction and allowing mobility.

Michelle Chen
Jenny Kim
Anna Meloyan
Madelynn Ringo
Dima Srouji

WIGGLE WALL

We were interested in testing paper as a material by transforming the way it behaves and generating three dimensional forms out of the two dimensional, conventional material. For the site, we chose the drawing studio courtyard which had a concrete wall bisecting the space. By repeating these panels we created a wall which enclosed an existing space within the courtyard. By varying the degree of the porosity in the panels, we able to manipulate the light conditions and transform what was once a neglected space into a sacred and private space.

VISUALIZATION IV

John Blood & John Eberhart

This seven-week, intensive course introduces Building Information Modeling (BIM) alongside manual drawing to expand each student's analytical and expressive repertoire. Fundamental techniques are introduced through short exercises and workshops leading toward a sustained study of an exemplary precedent building. Quantitative analysis is pursued through both assembly modeling and visual dissection of both the programmatic spaces and functional elements. Observational and imaginative manual drawings allow for a reconstruction of the design process and reestablish the thought patterns that formed the building's design priorities. These discoveries then are re-presented through interactive, multimedia presentations to describe the building assembly and its design ambitions.

Benjamin Bourgoin

BRITISH ART CENTER
Louis Kahn's Yale Center for British Art stands as a sacred monument to geometry, the arts, and society. In its current state it is impossible to separate the building from its cultural significance. Only in ruin can we imagine its future beyond a museum. Here the Yale Center for British Arts is free of contextual bondage, literally disengaged from the ground and reborn to host a city in the sky.

Hugo Fenaux

ESHERICK HOUSE
The idea of architectural ruin goes beyond the effect that time and the environment has on building materials. In many ways architecture can also be ruined simply through proximity; here the billboard dwarfs the monumentality of Kahn's Esherick House, essentially ruining the intent of the architecture.

Anne Householder

E-1027 HOUSE
After the earth heaved, the morning light revealed that Gray's vision of streamline glass had cracked, its interior open to the salty air. The deck was bestrewn with falling beams and the mast broken, no longer proud. Below, waves clapped a dirge for The House by the Sea.

Vittorio Lovato, Anne Ma, Eugene Tan

TOWER HOUSE
Hastily, this artifact is constructed. Bridging between the sad realities of a broken family and the fantastical desire to escape it, in the eyes of Roberto, this drawing comes to life. His family home, designed by Mario Botta, was not constructed on the hill above Riva; instead, it is deep under the sea. As the family drowns in their own obsessions, the world around him submerges; drenched in imagination.

SECOND YEAR

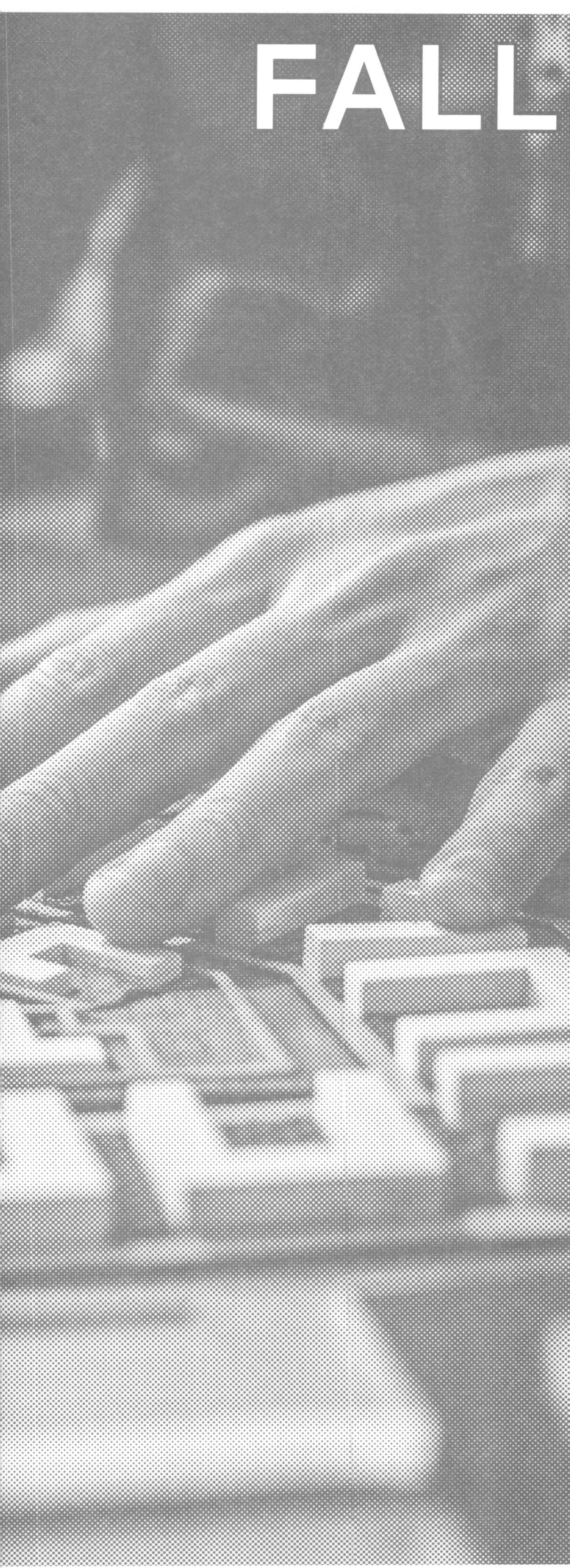

DESIGN STUDIO

This third core studio concentrates on a medium-scale institutional building, focusing on the integration of composition, site, program, mass, and form in relation to structure, and methods of construction. Interior spaces are studied in detail. Large-scale models and drawings are developed to explore design issues.

COORDINATING FACULTY

Mark Foster Gage

FACULTY

Sunil Bald
Martin Finio
Joel Sanders
Michael Young

SOFTWARE INSTRUCTION: MICHAEL LEACH

CASIS HEADQUARTERS

Our design studio is situated at a moment of transition—where history meets technological revolution and where we stake exploratory claims about how we should fuse the history of what Reyner Banham called our 'operational lore' with an empowering future that brings surprising and unexpected possibilities to the practice of architecture. Through the design of a single building, you are being asked to stake such a claim by addressing architectural concerns both ancient and new—including form, massing, program, materiality, lighting, identity, sustainability, context, theory, imagery, politics, affect, tectonics, aesthetics, urbanism, landscape and cultural relevance—among many, many, others. No building can address all of these topics in equal measure, and yet all buildings inherently involve every topic listed. A building is not a free-form collection of decisions—it is a composed construct, operating on multiple ontological levels in precisely calibrated degrees. Your role in this studio is to weave these numerous modes of thinking into a building that crystallizes your point of view regarding what architecture is at this precise and charged moment in time—and therefore anticipate what it can be for a future ripe with multiple forms of emerging possibility.

Students will design a new headquarters facility for CASIS, a non-profit, non-government, unique space organization that seeks out promising research projects and facilitates revolutionary discoveries in the sciences. The building will house several functions, which include an exhibition gallery for display and research associated with the International Space Station (ISS) and Destiny space module, a conference center primarily used for meetings of scientists, researchers and academics, an education center primarily used by students and associated educators, an administrative area, and a payload operations center that enables 24/7 access to research on ISS as well as remote manipulation of experiments and access to the crew. These functions will be supported by required lobby, back of house and mechanical programs. Students are invited to consider how various programs operate in isolation or open and visible proximity to one another, as their architectural ambitions require.

JURORS

Michelle Addington
Stella Betts
Peggy Deamer
Kathryn Dean
Mimi Hoang
Mariana Ibanez
Andrea Kahn
Karen van Lengen
Jill Lerner
Jennifer Leung
Bill Menking
Patrick O'Neil (CASIS)
Lindy Roy
Ken Shields (CASIS)
Kyoung Sun Moon
Tod Williams

CORE CLASSES

4021a Intro to Planning & Development

3021a Architectural Theory I: 1750–1968

Jack Wolfe
Mark Foster Gage

CASIS HEADQUARTERS
Conceived as an aggregation of discrete masses, the CASIS Headquarters is simultaneously massive and scale-less. A rigid, yet voluminous outer-shell is punctured by figural arrays of windows which serve the dual purpose of disrupting the purity and autonomy of the amalgamated masses, while providing visual dissonance that distorts the tangible or comprehensible scale of the building. On the inside, these deep windows create a mysterious light that is employed to create a sense of mystery and is organized to provide direction and points of focus within the voluminous interior. The interior consists of two types of space—the figural void and the residual cavern. The disconnection of the outer shell and inner volume creates opportunities to sculpt rooms and niches—the figural void—while the accretion of massive forms results in organic and complex in-between space—residual cavern.

MID REVIEW

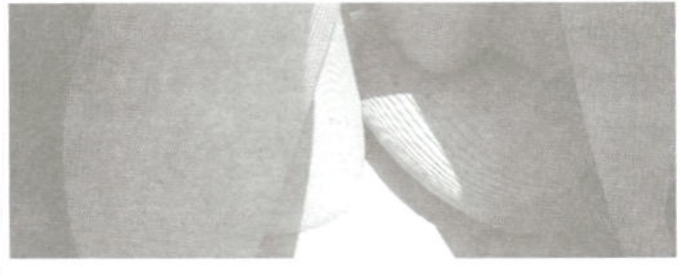

These discreet boulders all use the same language, but they could be radically different environments or experiences on the interior. —Hayley Eber

FINAL REVIEW

Williams You have done a very good job with the language. I think it is important to wonder when you deploy these tools. I just came back from Ronchamp, and thank god that Le Corbusier only did that at that level once. He left it for something super important and this may be that important; this may be the penultimate project. It is too bad when it becomes a de rigueur. So, it is going to be very important to understand where you want to deploy your enormous talents and where at other times you want to be quiet.

Gage Frederick Kiesler did the endless house, which was intended to produce a different form of living for a new age. This is endless, infinite, there are no reference points, it is warped and spatial and quantum, scale-less and has this mystery. There are a lot of things it is doing. I think it is a mistake that you are not explicit about them.

Kahn I am trying to understand a certain disturbing distance that I find between this artifact, which is simultaneously speaking of being on the earth, solid, and very knowable with rocks that are piled up, and then being inside a 1930s sci-fi film with ideas of spaceships that are really unknowable.

Williams Do you see this as poured-in-place concrete?

Finio It would acknowledge that it cannot be the same thing on the outside as it is on the inside. Not to say that it is not the same material, but it is not a single pour. I think the materiality is the most important question at this stage.

Williams I hate your basement. I hate your elevator. You have incredible skill, but you keep going back and dropping my toilet into a straight wall. So, I would not feel good about that if I were you [laughter].

Lauren Raab
Mark Foster Gage

CASIS HEADQUARTERS
This project proposes a headquarters for CASIS that explores the notion of scale, scalelessness, and the relationship of solid to void. The solid object within the project houses mainly private program such as auditorium space, conference rooms, and offices; exhibition space occurs in the area of void around the solid. Experientially, the object becomes an infinite surface against which space objects are displayed, and visitors circle up and around the object to experience this from multiple vantage points.

MID REVIEW

Do you want the instability of the floating boxes or the stability of a central core, or do you play them against one another? —Mariana Ibanez

FINAL REVIEW

Williams The exterior seems to be a little neo-gothic, perhaps something out of the Yamasaki World Trade Center history, and that is not scaleless in my opinion. That is really talking about adding scale to it. The question is, is that a valuable scale or not?

Gage As Martin so brilliantly showed in his installation of a little painting at the Guggenheim [laughter]. At a conceptual level, the ambition to place space objects against a background of vastness I think is an interesting architectural ambition. To do so in a way that is capitalizing on daylighting effects is equally interesting. I do tend to agree that if everything is infinitely seamless, what happens when someone drops a piece of gum or scuffs their shoe? That is a kind of practical problem.

Betts Yes, for me the missed opportunity is in the relationship between the exterior volume and the interior shifting volumes. In every case, they are right up against each other. What I am intrigued by are these floating boxes inside the volume. Whether or not a solid is behind this gauzy structure, maybe it is fritted glass, but if it is right up against it, it is going to do one thing, and if it is three feet away or ten feet away it will give a very different reading of the building and depth.

O'Neil A question on my end, everything looks like it is white on the inside, why did you choose that color? I look at white and if you look at just about any movie about space, there are a lot of corridors and there is a lot of white as it relates to the spaceships they are walking through. Part of me says, because you have the contours and you don't have any hard breaks, the white gives it that futuristic look.

Nicholas Muraglia
Mark Foster Gage

CASIS HEADQUARTERS

CASIS allows scientists to conduct experiments in outer space, testing earthly materials and phenomena in zero-gravity conditions to discover new properties of the world we live in. I was interested in this idea of taking familiar and "earthly" elements from the site context — the ubiquitous corporate slab tower and the constructed ground plane of the plinth — and defamiliarizing them through a series of involutions to generate unexpected and otherworldly tectonic relationships, provoking a rediscovery of the site itself. The familiar of the city is reoffered as something strange, only graspable in its interior by moving through the spatially interdependent bodies of program and structure.

MID REVIEW

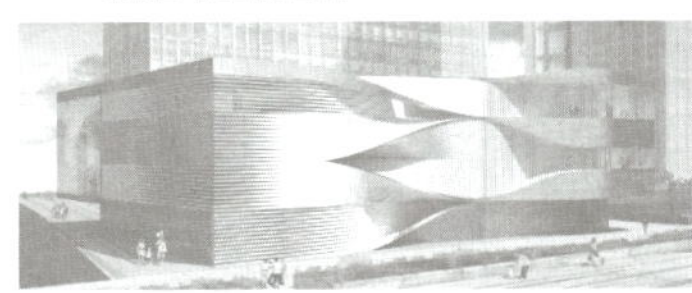

You started by talking about these twisted surfaces, but I don't believe that you're in love with them because your model is just a Xerox drawing. It's just a mid-review, no one expects you to have it all worked out... —Elizabeth Whittaker

Well, I do. —Robert AM Stern

FINAL REVIEW

Gage He's a very twisted soul. [laughter]

Ibanez You're not really taking advantage spatially of the twist and view. The repetition is in the model of floor to wall, wall to ceilings, but the section is still a very conventional section.

Finio The first thing I would want to do, if I made that image, is cut a section through that. Understand what that means. It could be about understanding what it means urbanistically, and the relationship to the city when I'm behind that wall. What is it presenting to the city? Maybe there's a board that's just missing from your work here, the board that shows us how the language was developed, why it matters for this particular project and what it offers, urbanistically, programmatically, tectonically, visually, etc...

Gage There's some unusual dilation and compression of space that's happening but it's not tied into anything else. It's happening accidentally but I think as that gets tuned relative to the program or circulation, this is where it starts to fuse together. If this is a language of vertical surfaces that turn into arches, there's a structural idea to that. You need to tie in this formalist ambition with a structural idea or tie in that formalist ambition with a spatial idea or tie in that formalist ambition with some idea of the city.

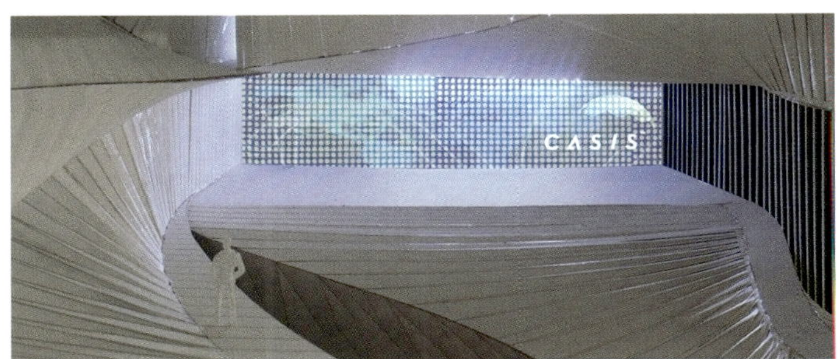

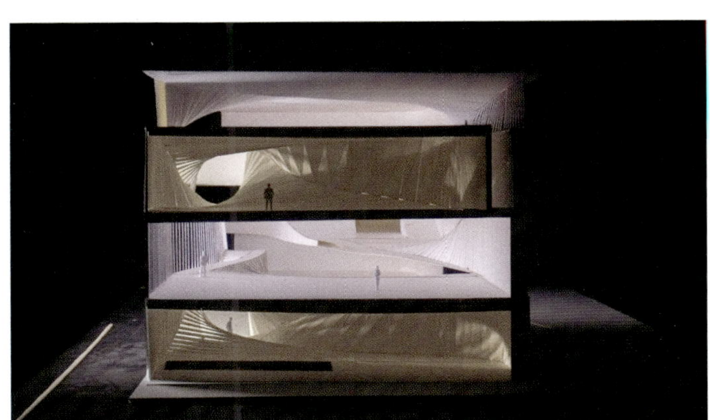

Hui Zhen Ng
Sunil Bald

CASIS HEADQUARTERS

Proposed as an inhabitable sculpture, the CASIS headquarters deviates from the New York City grid typology while still respecting its immediate context. Its foreign form is a negotiation between the need for physical presence among proposed towers on site and its contrastingly small-scale programs. In order to engage the public at street level, the building expands its territory horizontally and claims the adjacent park for its public leisure space. Two solid entities keep distinct users apart, only allowing for cohabitation when similar programs merge and overlap. The exhibition is a journey that starts from the street and ends at the top, where the cores dissolve to form a porous shared zone.

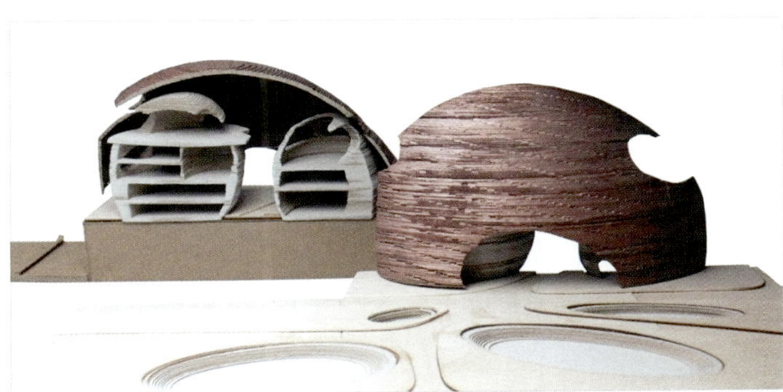

MID REVIEW

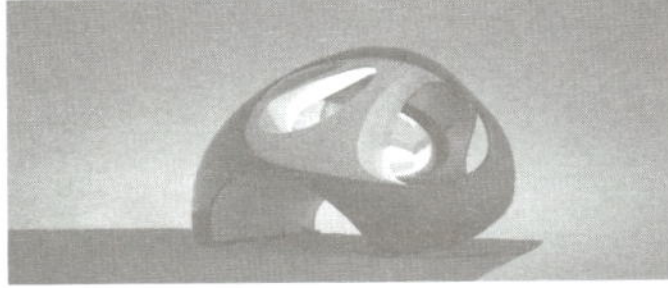

What is the most compelling are the two shells, an outer and an inner. Why can't the space that you need to make be between the outer and inner shell? That would allow you in a more graceful way to get an interior with the characteristics you are trying to achieve here. —Joel Sanders

FINAL REVIEW

Deamer The depressions that you are making begin to indicate that you understand that this egg thing isn't just an object cut off at this plane, but that it is about a container that holds or sculpts it in some way. I think that is all really great. So what I am going to complain about is the moment here, which is if we do not understand the continuity of the egg from the other side, at this level it should come down so you are engaging the FDR people and not just the plaza people.

Van Lengen I like the scale of your project in the site plan, but I have a problem with taking this iconic shape and cutting it up into smithereens. It reminds me of Gordon Matta-Clark in an overlay of one space onto another seeing through. I feel like if I were going to work on this I would think the future is in those oculi that overlap and make themselves finish.

Sanders When I go into an enclosed building and then I find two eggs, the first question in my mind is what are their identities and what is the relation between them. For me right now they remain very independent from one another. I think the whole potential of the project is to infect and allow more dissolving, blurring, and tension between them. To me the richest moment is the dialogue between the two eggs.

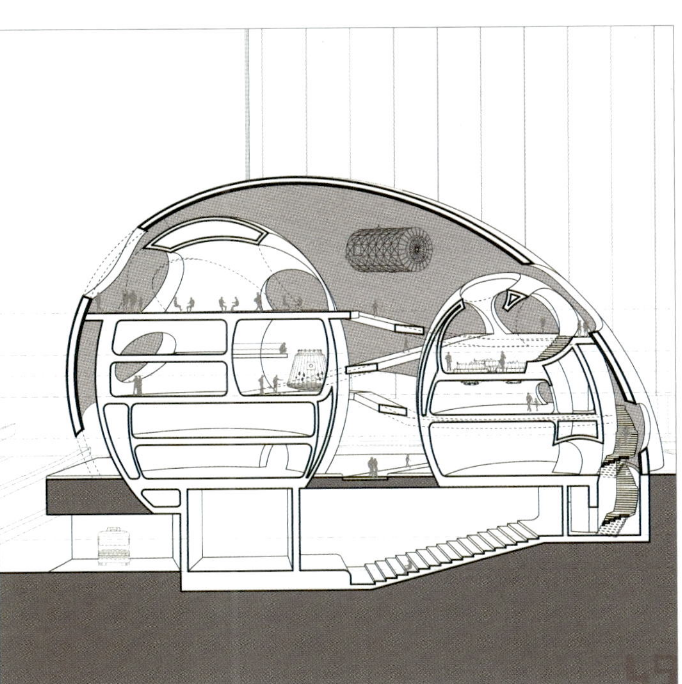

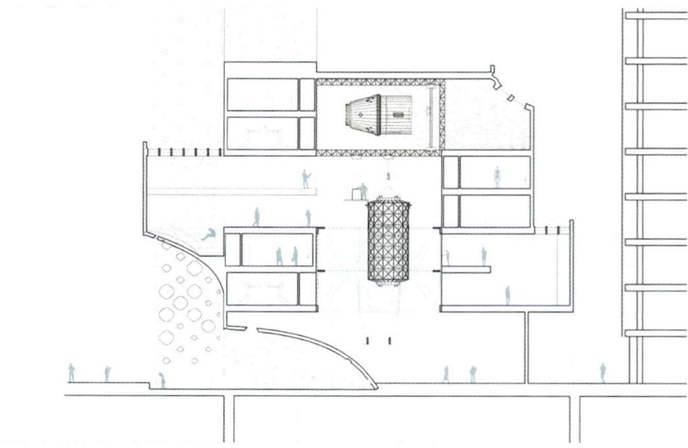

Sungwoo Choi
Sunil Bald

CASIS HEADQUARTERS
Speculating beyond the potential termination of the International Space Station, my proposal for a new headquarters for CASIS is a hybrid typology of office, laboratory, and gallery dedicated to research on space. CASIS headquarters becomes an infrastructure which various private sectors can occupy as tenants, taking advantage of a facility once inaccessible to private sectors. The form is composed of vertical blocks that form the office and gallery, and horizontal blocks that hold the laboratory spaces. While the block retains its programmatic autonomy, compound surfaces mediate the vertical and horizontal blocks in an unexpected way, forming open shared spaces that encourage collaboration among different entities in the space.

MID REVIEW

For midterm, the organization of the project is amazingly clear and extremely succinct. You are exhibiting the work environment and putting it on display. I am bothered by the difference between the middle part and the towers. Internally, the way it works is quite seamless; yet, the seamlessness is at odds with the exterior difference—this is shrink-wrapped and these are the towers. —Mimi Hoang

FINAL REVIEW

Deamer I'm spending my time thinking about the bizarreness of the forms and that in some way it breaks every kind of formal rule that I know. That might have to do with how a curve works against a grid or how a tower works against a something or other, or how certain things that are meaningful in the horizontal dimension maybe don't repeat in the same way in the vertical direction, except for that tower in the corner, which is partly why I think we like it—for many reasons we like it. I think the static nature of that tower in the corner is not yet incorporated into everything else. So except for the two legible aspects of that tower, I like it for its bizarreness. Despite myself! Formally bizarre, programmatically not bizarre, and I have affinities to both.

Van Lengen A curve does have a certain power to it. It has an emotional aspect to it and it directs you in a certain direction. So when you say, well I'll swoop this around and then I'll stop it here because I have another swoop here, I don't think you can do that easily. The body doesn't want to do that. It doesn't want to crash into a wall there, it wants to resolve itself, it wants to go somewhere.

Deamer The curves are imposed after you have added the bars and the towers together. I think part of what you are hearing is that the curves aren't a part of that discourse. We don't see it as an additive or subtractive way; we just see it as a curtain draped over.

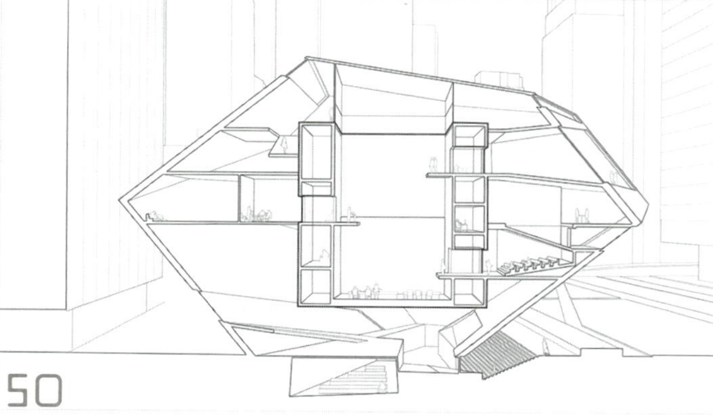

Tyler Pertman
Sunil Bald

CASIS HEADQUARTERS
CASIS serves as the equilibrator between public interest and the private sector. The new headquarters for CASIS serves to explore and develop the complex relationship between these two entities and allows for CASIS to better calibrate that exchange. By rotating and re-orienting the static and platonic form of the cube, new dynamic spaces emerge that facilitate both communication and curiosity. The building allows for both private circulation consisting of meeting rooms and collaborative spaces as well as public circulation through exhibition space, lecture spaces, classrooms and observation areas. CASIS program inhabits an inner, static cube and through its offices allows for exchange and education between CASIS the public and private entities.

MID REVIEW

There is so much productive tension and difference in how you operate between the two surfaces that seems so rich. I can understand you moving away from the cube because you wanted a more complex form, but I would be more convinced with these facets if they had been calibrated to the surrounding buildings or the adjacent plaza. —Joel Sanders

FINAL REVIEW

Kahn How does one translate a motivating intention about the experience of being in the space between into a form? Does it need to be so direct? If that is a diagram of a possible set of experiences, then maybe it needs to be a cube inside a cube. Or if it's really about how you establish the experience of being between two ordering systems, even being between one that might be stable and one that might be moving, perhaps that could happen in a much simpler form.

Williams We should discuss that. I think actual architecture is about use, and use does not allow things to be static. You are constantly changing things, adding layers, rubbing against things and that is precisely what is happening when one is exploring space.

Roy Whether it is a vertical surface or horizontal surface, you are setting up alignments and configurations that can be reconfigured. There is something in here about a Rubik's cube logic that starts to erode the volumes.

Gage I have always liked the interior since I saw your daylighting model. It is really a fascinating object. The box on the outside, to me and I would say to a lot of architects, looks kooky, campy, and kitsch and playful in a Post-Modern way. Does it make you happy that I say that? But if you had the outside one regularized and the inside one kooky, the whole thing would not read as kooky.

Michael Cohen
Martin Finio

CASIS HEADQUARTERS

CASIS is a non-profit company that manages research on the international space station. The company both educates the public about space research and represents corporations developing products in space. This duality manifests itself architecturally in the CASIS headquarters. On the lower half of the building the public circulates around the CASIS program and learns about space. Above, the public occupies the core of the building, where they are the focus of market research. The formal wobble of the building challenges this duality and forces the public and CASIS employees to interact.

MID REVIEW

You can take it much further in terms of the two circles and the distinction between the different revolutions they may have, that's where it can get really smart. There's something about the spatial calibration of two different speeds of revolutions that makes it very machine like. —Elizabeth Whittaker

FINAL REVIEW

Addington The part that really needs to be designed is the part that switches. The moment when you cross that threshold into the inner sanctum is such a key moment, making the people be a part of the thing that's orbiting and being the entity that's being orbited around.

Young You want to somehow tune the entry so that it allows you to go into that solid part and be the most intense conflict between inner and outer shell. It would force someone to go around that wobble, and that would drive the circulation into the tightest points so that the threshold becomes a part of the movement.

Betts I'm wondering if there could have been and iteration where it's more about a carving of the solid on the inside, so that in fact those plates are not sitting in between those other two but in fact impacting a carving out of a space underneath so that that experience becomes more ambiguous.

Young It's a smart move to go from elliptical orbitals to wobbles to get us somehow from using space as a shape reference to a body sensation. One more comment, when I first sat down and looked at this I thought it looked really stubby.

Finio That's the best part about it.

Young I thought it needed to either get taller or get fatter, like bubble out, and then I thought, maybe I'm wrong; maybe we should just go with the awkwardness.

Finio I love this project, I love you, I love the way you set this up. I do feel like the one thing where you really sold yourself short on is figuring out the quality of that interior, what it would be like to occupy either the outward ring or the inner core. I would encourage you to do that, but everything else well said.

Mark Peterson
Martin Finio

CASIS HEADQUARTERS

CASIS is an organization charged with revealing the value of NASA and space research to scientists, private enterprises, and the general public. Conceptually, CASIS acts as a force on NASA—breaking it open—and in that fracturing allows for new connections and ways of understanding.The idea of fracturing manifests in the building as a way of separating the different program elements. In the project, CASIS and the public visitor education component have distinct forms.These fractured masses are then reconstituted into a unified building by introducing a connective skin that not only joins the forms, creating enclosure, but also organizes the building's circulation. That skin serves to mediate the varying levels of privacy, from the open lower levels to the more divided upper-levels.

MID REVIEW

There is a balance in this model between the components, pieces that hold the remnants of program, and the adjoining space that goes out into the plinth and public platform. It is a balance of surface to volume and the amount of circulation. —Leslie Gill

FINAL REVIEW

Kahn The story of the hidden, or the fracture, or the not seen; once you make the symbolic gesture of cracking open, how is that followed through in a material or experiential way as one sequences through the building?

Betts I am curious how this membrane is functioning or performing. I am trying to understand what the interface is between the membrane and the building because that is the connective point. Whether or not it is denying or connecting and engaging; you need to decide which one of those is driving it. It is unclear if you are trying to bring this back together.

Kahn There is a question between conception and construction. Is the concept one thing and the construction another? Or is construction the medium through which architects conceive? Do you engage that problem of the joint?

Williams That is the way science is made. I have got a problem, I have to solve it with the single most direct answer. We have so distorted our world that we see this conceptual stuff as something that we apply some sort of constructional logic to.

O'Neil I remember the story you comprised at midterm on how you fractured things. It was something that was captivating to me because I am looking to be able to tell the story myself, say for instance this ends up being the CASIS headquarters. Personally, I like the story because it is something I can pitch, something that I can ultimately sell, and something that people would buy.

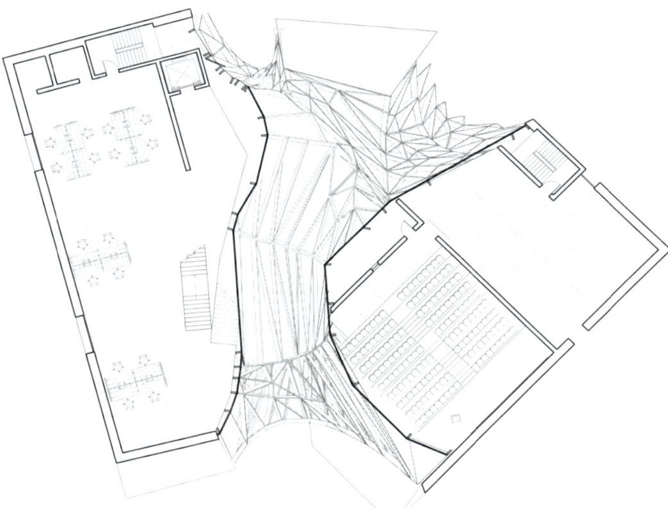

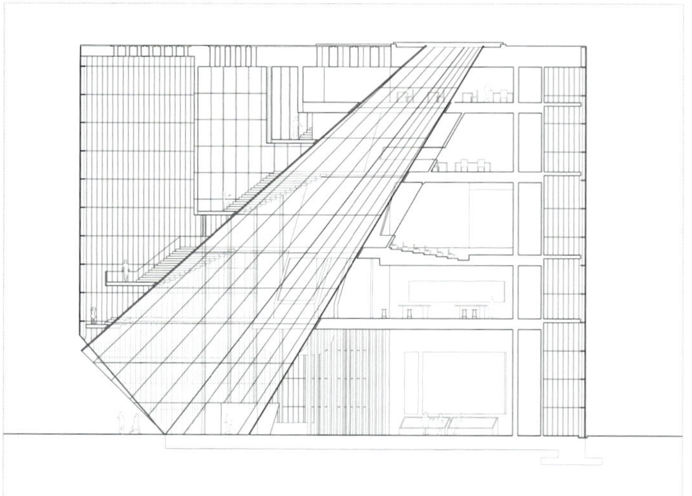

Amy Su
Martin Finio

CASIS HEADQUARTERS
This building serves two primary functions. First, it serves as advertisement for CASIS—it is designed to draw interest and create excitement about space, the ISS and CASIS. Second, it serves to connect people with limited knowledge about space research (tourists and students) with people fully involved in research. Formally and programmatically, the building is organized into a series of three nested boxes, all punctured by a continuous diagonal void that connects the plane of city to the sky. The outer box houses the most public program such as lobby and exhibition spaces. The innermost box is most private, containing offices and research labs. The intermediate box contains shared program—education space, lecture hall, and open labs. As one progresses further into the nested boxes, light becomes more diffuse while attention is focused on moments of clarity—views into more private programs.

MID REVIEW

You are trying to create these layers of transparency. However, maybe there is a way that you can tectonically reach different layers of transparency. That way, you would read the layered space even more so because the structure is changing its dimension as it migrates inside and up. —Elizabeth Whittaker

FINAL REVIEW

Gage When Sejima entered the McCormick Center competition on IIT's campus, Phyllis Lambert was on the jury and saw this scheme with an inch-thick roof that went several blocks long, and Phyllis apparently said, what is going on, this person is an idiot, she clearly does not understand architectural conventions. But it turned out that Sejima along with Arup had actually engineered an inch-thick roof out of exotic material and it was figured out. What I see here is that you are just not showing the structure, I think it would have been a lot more interesting if you had actually engineered the building in a way that allowed you to have these special effects that make it rehearse the qualities that you have in your model.

Williams I think it is better to engineer these things by understanding how much opaque material you need to support the glass layering that you desire here. This layering is absolutely terrific, but at the same time what does it mean when this is filled with stuff that is uncontrollable? That is why the opaque material is my friend. I think you are using it here, but it could be a stronger tool. Once again structure could be used better to achieve what you want to achieve. This is an abstraction, it needs to be somewhere in between.

Sarah Smith
Joel Sanders

CASIS HEADQUARTERS
For a building that was to house both administrative offices and public museum space, I began with a simple bifurcated form. One leg being for 'private' functions and the other for 'public' functions, the two unite at the top of the building to create the auditorium. From the very outset I played with the idea of 'this and that' or seeming opposites, from a programmatic, formal, and conceptual perspective. Formally, the use of the ruled surface—by nature both linear and curved—built upon this idea, as well as served the function for marrying the two programmatic legs of the building. As the semester progressed, the circulation and form of the building became more complex, and rather than two separate means of travel at the different extremities, as with the rest of the building, the systems became enmeshed in a diagonal crisscrossing of circulation from one floor to the next. In turn, the interior floors evolved from flat plates to a network of undulating ruled surfaces, carefully calibrated to respond to the exterior form and the circulation system of escalators and stairs.

MID REVIEW

There is randomness to the way the floors delaminate from the skin. That could be worked more. —Anna Bokov

FINAL REVIEW

Van Lengen What I admire about the move here is that it is a minimal set of strategies. But the curved piece is a hybrid system that isn't hybridized enough, or it is halfway between one thing and another.

Dean I was instantly drawn to the scale shift between the curtain wall and the underbelly of the ruled surface, and the way they scale between the component and the building. I was wondering if there was a way to understand the graining of this model as a way to reinforce or calibrate the interiors. I also wish this incredibly subtle move was a way to start to play with the floor plates and how they touch the skin. The building seems a little bit chopped against the floor plates. Maybe there's a way that the pulling away of the facet can help you navigate so the perimeter also became spatial.

Sanders The biggest challenge I find about this studio, and the purpose of third semester, is sustaining one project for the whole term. I really admired how tenaciously you pursued this idea, and you came up with a subtle way to position the moment of entry in that sequence. Moving forward though, there are other forms of drawings and diagrams that you could use to communicate the qualities of that space. You owe it to yourself.

Benjamin Smith
Joel Sanders

CASIS HEADQUARTERS

This design for the CASIS headquarters building proposes a single system composed of a nested series of shells which grow ever denser towards the center and ever more porous towards the periphery. The shells filter both light and views and create space by acting as floor, wall, display case, and ceiling. Light is filtered through the outer shell, then illuminates vitrines installed in the second shell, and finally penetrates the innermost shell. This geometric vocabulary calls into question gravity and the body's normative relationship to the ground. The innermost shell hovers over a sunken theater and appears to resist gravity. Walls press in as one occupies the convex and concave liminal zone of the public promenade. This tension is ultimately broken as one enters into a central domed exhibition space which also provides a connection back to the exterior through oculi.

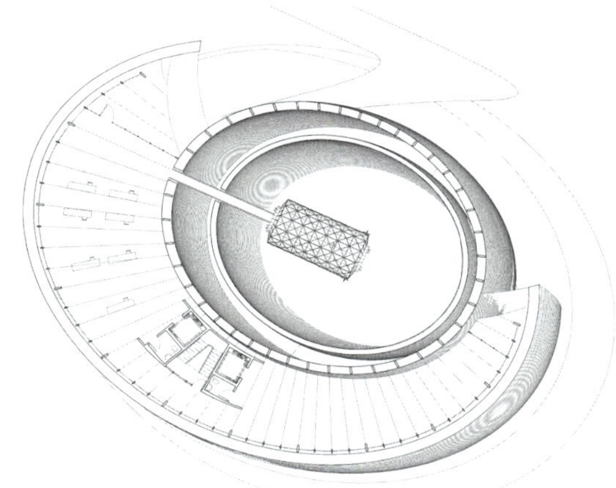

MID REVIEW

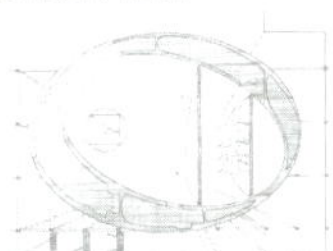

There are three types of space the brief suggests: big space, which only exists metaphorically or virtually; the confined, miniature space of the capsule; and then there is the space that the object sits in, which is the space we occupy and can control. Conceptually, both big space and miniature space might be solved within this building by the layering of the ellipsoid. —Richard Gluckman

FINAL REVIEW

Deamer The possibility of the resonance is between these different skins. I still think that you can break down the skins and the spaces between them. There's rigidity between what happens between skin A and skin B and between skin B and skin C, and that those are such that when there are exceptions they feel slightly awkward. Skin A emerges sometimes but not completely; you might take advantage of the complexity of a multi-skinned thing a bit more.

Dean Even here I'm wishing these things would start to rotate. So that you get a rotation and you would also get compression and expansion in both the plan and the section.

Bald For me, the reason that I feel uneasy about the openness of the outer element is because of the solidity of the inner egg. If there isn't necessarily such a dichotomy between the thing that you render in a solid poché and the thing that you render in louvers, the other thing is that, not just the egg but the tilted egg. I think it gives you opportunities for different orientations from interior floor slab to the outside. It's sort of beautiful, this eyelid pealing up from the louver.

Haelee Jung
Joel Sanders

CASIS HEADQUARTERS

CASIS has three different programs that require different levels of privacy. I separated them into three separate buildings: administration, research laboratories, and exhibition space for the public. The ultimate goal of CASIS is to bring these three programs together and promote interaction and to that end I created three social connectors to link them. The conference and lobby space connects exhibition and research space; the payload operation center plus main exhibition space connects all three; and the lounge space connects office workers and researchers.

On the site, I followed the strong grain of Manhattan that runs from the city to the river. I was interested in the constructed ground plane coming to the river, but instead of a single drop down, I developed a cascade down to the water to experience different levels of the city edge: the highway, the bridge, the constructed ground, and the actual ground.

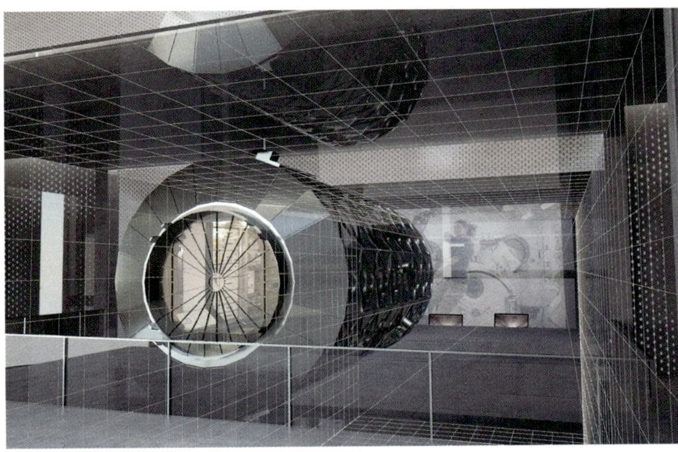

MID REVIEW

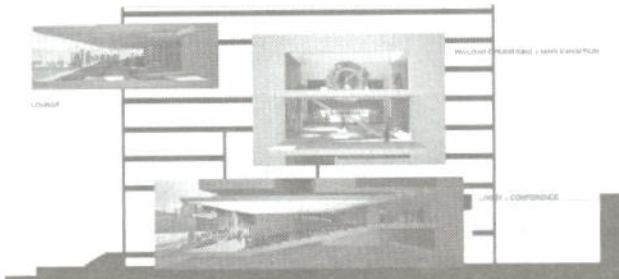

There is this idea of superimposition—of all things happening at once and overlaid on top of each other—but you have separated them in a very convincing way. —Elizabeth Whittaker

FINAL REVIEW

Bald There is something about the clarity of the diagram and then the complexity of the spaces which I think is really commendable. You keep building on spatial complexity by small moves like how the building meets the rest of the site. The one thing I am struggling with is its presence on the site. It reads nicely relative to the slope of the site or the way you manipulate the slope, but it is almost as if you are manipulating a slope to create found conditions. It is not being tested at a more urban scale.

Deamer It makes a more complex project if you think of this not just as three slabs but as six walls that have different conditions. Once we think about those walls then it becomes more infrastructural. I want to understand that ground plane as supporting these walls as it gets less delicate and more infrastructural. Part of what Sunil is describing about not understanding its urbanistic quality is because it is so delicate. That delicacy speaks of another type or location.

Dean The difference between this building and the one we see on the wall is the way those very heavy things hold their own against this location. When you render it so delicately with this column structure, it is a very different project. The bricks seem imported to me, they are beautiful, but space and brick should not be with each other, earth material and space.

Dionysus Cho
Michael Young

GLYTCH

This project sprouted from ideas of space and science fiction. A speculative study of apparent symmetries of mechanical systems, the development of geometries from glitch generation, and the interlacing of reflected human forms, guided the conceptual development of GLYTCH.

The plan is symmetrical, reflected about and highlighting the two central space artifacts—the Destiny module and the smaller SpaceX capsule. Wrapping the Destiny module, continuous circulation takes one from the lobby up into the gallery, through the educational spaces, and up into the lecture hall. The exterior skin consists of an aggregation of shards, a highly articulated structural shell with moments of slippage revealing views within. With the aesthetics of space-mech, CASIS brings back the Space Age with a design that doesn't ground itself with earthly precedent, but truly aspires to bring Space to Earth.

MID REVIEW

It should only be symmetrical to the extent that your face is symmetrical either that or maybe you don't do any of the things that we're saying, maybe you don't make any differences at all you just keep it absolutely, monstrously symmetrical. —Keller Easterling

FINAL REVIEW

Stern I'm going to ruin my reputation by saying that I actually think this is quite an interesting building.

Gage Next [laughter].

Stern That model looks like it's worked out; it looks like it could be made into a building. I think you've made a very interesting urban shape that somehow addresses the entire site.

Hoang What are your thought on its symmetry?

Stern I'm all for symmetry. As far as I can see it's there and it's great [Laughter].

Gage I had a professor back in my classical days who said, always design symmetrical buildings because you only have to design half the building but the truth is that most symmetrical buildings are not symmetrical in the interior. I actually think that you're making much too big of a deal about the interior being slightly asymmetrical when in fact most symmetrical buildings are asymmetrical to some degree small or large. How do you then push the ambition of what you want it to be? Okay it works, symmetry works, Bob likes it, and now what's your ambition toward the appearance or an object that pushes it beyond what's expected. I think that figuring out some of the things it needs, will push you in that direction. The more things that you get to design and fuse together, it's going to make your building more of a building. It's going to make it weirder, which is what you want.

Hoang I was wondering where you were going with this whole theme of taking something symmetrical and making it asymmetrical. I thought that it was leading up to something bigger and perhaps it could. Can you take that theme and really play up the difference on the two sides?

Kara Biczykowski
Michael Young

CASIS HEADQUARTERS

The design intends to act as a transition between Earth and an alien world, which simultaneously refers to leaving behind the present and moving into the future. The building's appearance and relationship to the site separate it from many of the surrounding buildings. The building stands on two feet which arch over a slight depression in the earth that allows visitors to pass through the building during the day and exposes hidden views into the atrium from below. The estrangement of the exterior becomes clarified upon passing through into the foreign interior. The interior ornament which hangs from the ceiling to form a large central atrium is of a higher resolution than the exterior building form. Movement between these two surfaces stirs memories of Earth—the exterior shell—and visions of the future and outer space—the interior ornament. Internal symmetry reinforces these effects of estrangement and unearthliness.

MID REVIEW

I would exploit the idea of resolution, which has everything to do with the distance from which something is viewed. There is a whole range between the hi and lo res that you can experience through distance or material articulation. —Hayley Eber

FINAL REVIEW

Young The heart of your project is these cupolas. They're simulations for astronauts, but she actually took them and they're the interface to look into the atrium, as if looking back at Earth.

Van Lengen It's hard to critique your project because the normal vocabulary we use is difficult to apply. As much as I want to accept the symmetry as a possibility, when it gets repeated those mysterious spaces become predictable. It makes it so predictable that it's not uneasy anymore.

Moon What is the material for those things, the cupola and the outside, and what does that suggest about construction?

Sanders For our generation, when we grew up, the future represented in mass media was space. Most contemporary representations like Gravity are of a dystopian future, or these technologies don't survive. What is strongest about your project is the drive toward a 21st century vocabulary that encapsulates the utopic/dystopic status of space. I also think you're the only person who has taken on the simultaneity of the virtual/actual view, and I want to see perspectives that represent that.

Daniel Nguyen
Michael Young

CASIS HEADQUARTERS
The project proposes a headquarters for CASIS that explores crystalline growth patterns whose aggregations promote a diffuse rather than segregated programmatic organization. The crystal pods themselves collude and collide, allowing for a dispersal of program elements typically thought of as "private" around two cores within the "public" exhibition gallery. Examining the messy relationship between public and private program, this proposal suggests a misreading of programmatic distribution that is reflected in a misreading of form.

MID REVIEW

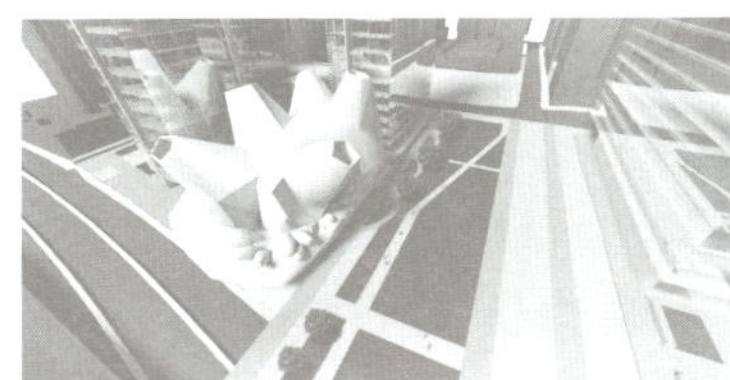

You need to find constraints so that not every wall is moving at a different angle, so there is a datum within the system. Maybe you can do that with floor plates, and maybe vertical surfaces can structure that too. —Maia Small

FINAL REVIEW

Van Lengen There are so many of the crystals—sometimes they face the sky, sometimes they don't, sometimes they're skylights—they lose the force or the direction of what you're trying to do.

Sanders They're more successful from the exterior. I almost read it as a large rock formation. I want to hire you to design the public space and see this as a series of pavilions that are all crumbling, I want to subordinate this thing to the landscape. But the other thing I worry about, you come to inhabit complex geometries, you fill it up with floor plates, that's when you fail.

Dean I agree; it's the floor plates that bother me too. Because of the density and compaction of it, it reminds me of New York City, I can't really touch on why that is. What's interesting, even though these things are decorative, when you push on them they're all structural. Because of the triangulation of it, it has a structural logic.

Young You need to build this model with an inner logic in the manner with which you're building the shell. It reads as just a thin shell on the floor.

Menking It looks like coral. That's how coral grows, in those big clumps. I love these renderings you have of the east side of Manhattan.

Young Is it floral? Is it rough, is it hard? All these questions of different readings of materiality would come to bear on how you find a rendering style to bring that to life.

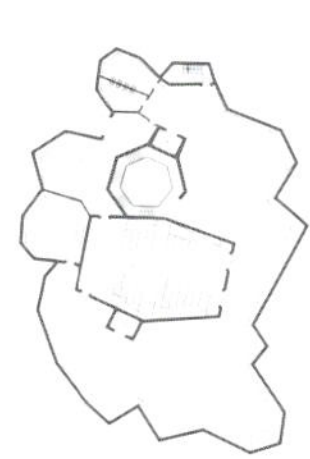

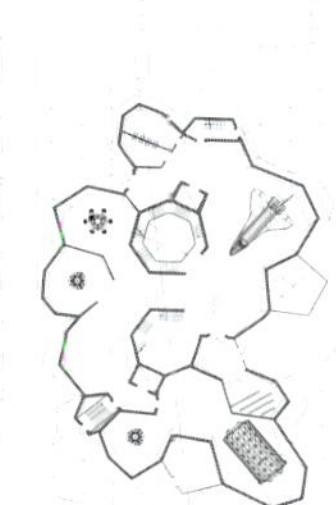

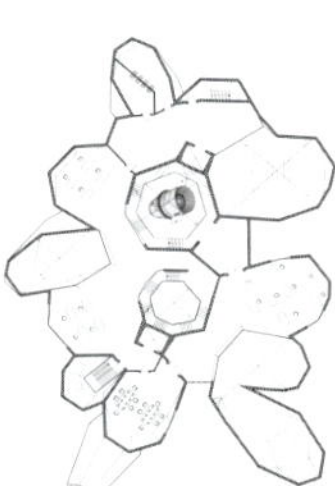

INTRODUCTION TO PLANNING AND DEVELOPMENT

Alexander Garvin

This course demonstrates the ways in which financial and political feasibility determine the design of buildings and the character of the built environment. Students propose projects and then adjust them to the conflicting interests of financial institutions, real estate developers, civic organizations, community groups, public officials, and the widest variety of participants in the planning process. Subjects covered include housing, commercial development, zoning, historic preservation, parks and public open space, suburban subdivisions, and comprehensive plans.

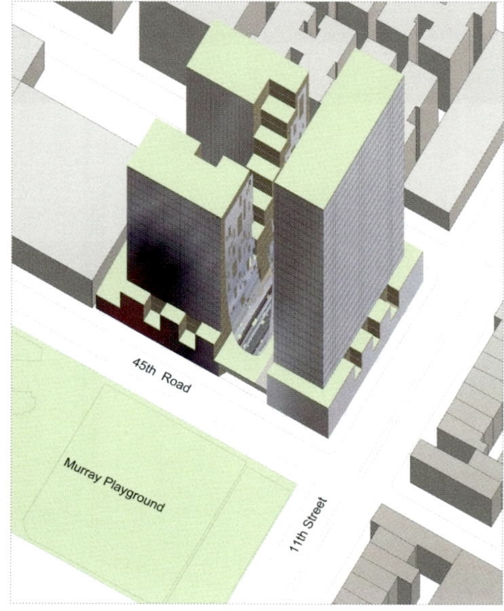

Michelle Gonzalez, Bruce Hancock, Anna Sakellariadis

LUXURY HIGH RISE IN LONG ISLAND CITY, QUEENS
GAME ONE WINNERS

The overall building scheme consists of a platform with retail and community facility space as well condos with three towers with apartment units. The towers "step" towards one another creating a unique form and additional natural lighting. Additionally, unique to this building, is the arcade that runs through it, that will be open and available to the public. The placement of the arcade is in keeping with the overall design of the high-rise complex as the arcade runs parallel to the division between the towers above. The arcade will provide amenities to the building residents, but also create new private market opportunities for investors on the end of the arcade opposite the playground to take advantage of the pedestrian traffic.

Xiao Wu, Benjamin Smith, Sungwoo Choi, Minu Lee, Sonali Bhasin

ENVISIONING A NEW TRANSIT-ORIENTED LONG ISLAND CITY
GAME TWO WINNERS

The Regional Plan Association is committed to improving the sustainability, accessibility and quality of life of the metropolitan region. For our proposal for South Hunter's Point, we draw on our experience with mixed-use development with the Alliance for a New Penn Station, sustainability and public green space with Brooklyn's Waterfront, and transportation with the Second Avenue subway project. Our proposal revolves around transit-oriented development that will foster commercial and mixed-use development in the area, improving the quality of life and the sustainability of our greens.

ARCHITECTURAL THEORY I: 1750–1968

Marta Justo Caldeira

ADDITIONAL FACULTY JOSEPH CLARKE

History of Western architectural theory, 1750–1968, through the close reading of primary texts. Lectures place the readings in the context of architectural history; the texts are discussed in required discussion sections. Topics include discussions of theories of origin and character, the picturesque, debates regarding style, historicism, and eclecticism, Gothic Revival, questions of ornament, architectural modernism, functionalism, and critiques of modernism.

Jeannette Penniman

THE AESTHETICS OF TENSION: PLACING A CONCEPT OF STYLE WITHIN THE STRUCTURAL RATIONALISM OF VIOLLET-LE-DUC

This essay explores three critiques of Viollet-le-Duc's theory of structural rationalism, as well as a close-reading of his Entretiens (Discourses) and Dictionnaire Raisonné, in order to understand how the notion of style or taste might be integrated into his theory. One common element among these attempts to understand style in Viollet-le-Duc's vision is that of time. Viollet's own definition of style depends entirely on the age in which construction and design is practiced (and the corresponding material, technical, and societal circumstances), with style constantly evolving. For Bressani, time is what separates Viollet's conception of an idealized world of the future and the real world of (traditions of) the past; indeed, time is integral to his understanding of Viollet's historical dialectic of man and nature. One reading of Viollet's front-page assertion about the relationship between construction and architecture, in which Damisch perceives a gap for style, would be to see construction as a process, and architecture as a product meant for consumption, in which case they are separated not so much by qualities as by time.

Many of the conceptions of style are further imbued with a sense of tension. Bressani seems to suggest that style is an inevitable part of Viollet's modern architecture, embodied as the tension between old and new; man and nature; real and idealized. This style is both an honest expression of the forces and struggles at play in Viollet's architecture (physical and social), as well as a particular aesthetic with the power to elicit emotion in (i.e., move) its viewer. Similarly, the gap that Damisch identifies as home to potential "style" or aesthetics in structural rationalism is the suspended space between two linked but distinct concepts. The tension between construction and architecture, in both the literal words and theoretical implications of Viollet's proposition ("Construction is the means; Architecture is the results"), is evident.

In seeking an answer to the question of how "style" (aesthetics; taste; beauty) might fit into Viollet-le-Duc's highly rational theory for modern architecture, therefore, perhaps it is best to consider an aesthetic of tension or struggle. Although the critiques explored here understand Viollet's theory in different contexts, they all seem to agree that contradiction, or some sort of dialectic, is a major theme.

Leah Abrams

PRICE AND PAYNE KNIGHT: THE HIDDEN POLITICS OF THE PICTURESQUE

In Distinction: A Social Critique of the Judgment of Taste, Pierre Bourdieu claims that "the 'eye' is a product of history reproduced by education."[1] Debates over the question of taste and preference, particularly aesthetic taste, have circulated for centuries, and not the least were postulated over the aesthetic of the picturesque landscape in the late 18th century. Uvedale Price and Richard Payne Knight acted as two key figures in the elaboration of the picturesque and an analysis of their writings, in combination with an examination of the social and political realities of the period, reveals how theories of taste are closely tied to ideologies of exclusion. As a theory, the picturesque allows for a landscape to be identified, but then as landscape, serves as a platform for the construction and reproduction of social difference, all hidden in a guise of naturalism.

Price's primary concern revolved around defining a specific aesthetic guideline for what constitutes the picturesque. For him, the earlier poetic gardens, though ostensibly naturalistic, lacked traits he saw essential to the genre: ruggedness, variation, age and decay. On one level, it seems as if Price's aesthetic has an even more democratic or egalitarian ideology than earlier forms of the picturesque. He elevates the commonplace, dirty world of peasants and laborers, a world where elements are messy, aged, and crumbling. However, the democratic appearance is mitigated when the aesthetic appreciation is viewed instead as an aesthetic appropriation.

Payne Knight moves away from the characteristics of the physical landscape and towards an understanding of how the landscape is experienced. The mental processes become more important than the physical details. By his definition, the picturesque, intimately tied to vision and imagination, contains the possibility of universal appeal and application. However, Payne Knight also makes it clear that prior education and knowledge are requirements for proper ways of seeing and imagining. Thus the aesthetic of the picturesque garden becomes one that a non-initiated spectator can never fully grasp. Despite its origins in the pastoral, common landscape of the laborer or peasant, Payne Knight's picturesque landscape always remains outside of their understanding.

1 Pierre Bourdieu, Distinction: A Social Critique of the Judgment of Taste (Cambridge: Harvard University Press, 1984)

DESIGN STUDIO

This fourth core studio, an introduction to the planning and architecture of cities, concerns two distinct scales of operation: that of neighborhood and that of the dwellings and the institutional and commercial building types that typically contribute to neighborhood. Issues of community, group form, and the public realm, as well as the formation of public space, blocks, streets, and squares are emphasized. The studio is organized to follow a distinct design methodology, which begins with the study of context and precedents. It postulates that new architecture can be made as a continuation and extension of normative urban structure and building typologies.

COORDINATING FACULTY

Edward Mitchell

FACULTY

Keller Easterling
Jennifer Leung
Bimal Mendis
Alan Plattus

ADDITIONAL INSTRUCTOR: ALEXANDER FELSON

BOSTON SHIPPING CHANNEL AND CONVENTION CENTER EAST

We will be designing housing and commercial facilities to be used during the 2024 Olympic Games and later turned over as market rate housing. The history of a successful bid has had mixed urban success. As the result of a single large development that must, in the short term, be secured from the general public it can result in an urban enclave divorced from the life of the city.

The site is on roughly 101 acres south and west of the Convention Center. The area to the west of the Reserve Channel is manmade land fill and was historically part of the industrial area of Boston and made up a vast infrastructure of rail lines and docks. To the southeast of the site is South Boston proper which up until recently was a working class Irish neighborhood.

This area is a part of a larger urban puzzle of distinct plans being made to develop the South Boston waterfront. Each of these areas has distinct problems of scale, character and urban use. Our site surrounds the Reserve Channel and meets the Convention Center on its western boundaries and the neighborhood of South Boston to its east and south. The main development parcel is controlled mainly by two stake holders—the Boston Convention Center Authority and the Boston Port Authority. A third area is a power plant which is destined to be decommissioned in the near future.

JURORS

Lorena Bello
Denise Hoffman-Brandt
Peter de Bretteville
Howard Davis
Mark Deshong
Alexander Felson
Kurt Forster
Alexander Garvin
Douglas Gauthier
Lisa Gray
Amy Lelyveld
Arianne Lourie Harrison
Andrei Harwell
Brian Healy
John Jacobson
Tim Love
Joeb Moore
David Pieprz
Karla Rothstein
Brent Ryan
Susan Schindler
Georgeen Theodore
Kishore Varanasi
Lynnette Widder
Dongwoo Yim

CORE CLASSES

3022b Architectural Theory II: 1968–Present

2022b Systems Integration

1291c Rome Summer Abroad Travel Awards

Bruce Hancock & Thomas Friddle
Keller Easterling

2024 BOSTON OLYMPIC VILLAGE
Our project fuses the spectacle of the Olympic Stadium with the frequently neglected Olympic Village. We propose a new experience of interactive media in the public sphere. The building is wrapped with a media facade that conveys the excitement of the games as informational updates during the day and as glowing spectacle at night. After the games the building is designed to remain as housing, while using the screen to generate revenue for residential amenities. The on screen images are meant to be brief but immersive, rapidly conveying information in the public domain.

MID REVIEW

I like the premise in which you started talking about media, but it becomes disappointing when it's the same on the outside as the inside, that to me is problematic of what it wants to be and it gives you a condensed region in which you're operating. —Joyce Hsiang

FINAL REVIEW

Garvin I look at that and my initial reaction is you have the best net to gross that I have ever seen because for every third floor you have a corridor.

Love Putting all the spectacle into one part of the project is pretty smart.

Ryan The scheme gains interest to the extent that you maximize the packing of activities within the circle. The rationale for residential to be in a circular form works quite well beyond the Soviet condition, which I am not sure we are seeking to emulate.

Moore It may work, but it is uncanny and shockingly eerie with some of the reverberations out. We are not talking about the elephant in the room, which is the effect, like Boullée's Cenotaph, of this motive machine that operates at the scale of the city. I think that is absolutely fascinating and I am really impressed with how you are tracking it.

Hoffman-Brandt If we take the project for what it is then it works very well. If we were to take this and try to see how we could maximize the future value, is it in the right spot? This could do more and we should challenge it to do more.

Love This is the end game of the Bird's Nest. This would be the last Olympics done.

Moore What I think is fascinating about your project is on one level it is a brilliant proposition that almost everyone here would despise for a number of reasons, but because of that you have accomplished something that is quite hard to do—you have positioned the work in a territory politically, socially, economically, urbanistically, and technologically at all of these border lines. It is precisely in those borders that architecture has its greatest opportunities. I commend you for finding that space.

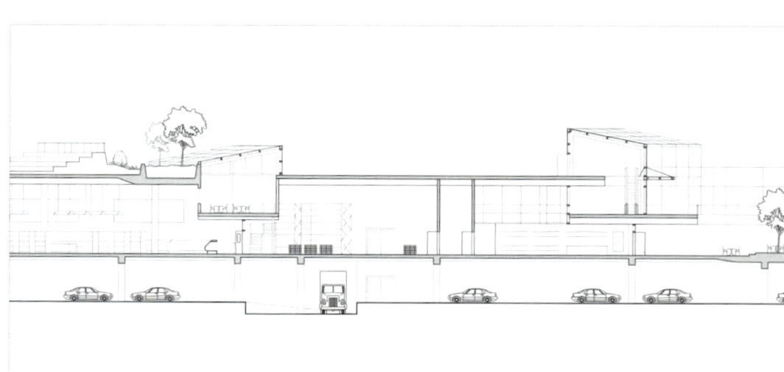

Amy Su & Kirk Henderson
Keller Easterling

2024 BOSTON OLYMPIC VILLAGE
Our Olympic Village proposes a framework for future development, rather than a fully finished environment. We draw on the concept of the 'concourse' that links set pieces of development together, and also grows into a living urban space itself. We place 15,000 units of housing in densely arranged towers along the western edge of the site and their lobbies expand into the primary public and circulation spaces for the urban concourse below. Parking occupies the ground level, due to flooding concerns. We then dedicate the second, third, and forth levels to an open, connected zone of retail, services, and public realm. Internally, these levels link the towers together, while allowing for the urban surprise, encounter, and delight necessary for long-term social value. Externally, the concourse levels modulate their edges to provide access points specific to the surrounding areas.

MID REVIEW

What you're aspiring to develop is a spatial system that can give you the logic of a megastructure at the ground—a consistent, repetitive structure—with different identities occupying the upper levels. —Felipe Correa

FINAL REVIEW

Widder If we laid your project out without any of the wiggles and kinks and funny shaped holes, we'd probably get something that would terrify everyone. I can see a project that is patchier, more selective about occupying the ground, without the whole blanket. For me it's not about rationality, but the redundancy of the experience.

Mitchell The spaces you studied—the shopping mall and the casino—are spaces with a high level of control. So despite the interesting spatial matrix this produces, it has another level of politics.

Easterling If there is a mixture of convention, hotel, and residential, that becomes a very different population than just shoppers. It's a weird lovechild of different kinds of enclosed spaces. Do they have to use the word mall?

Plattus In examples like this that are already built, the towers are carefully positioned so as not to compromise the logic of the shopping mall. What is problematic and exciting about here is that the logics compromise each other.

Easterling What you're hearing is that one expects you guys as parents of this bastard to know everything about its pedigree.

Suhni Chung & Junpei Okai
Keller Easterling

2024 BOSTON OLYMPIC VILLAGE

This urban scheme bases its formal gestures on Boston's existing conditions. Privatized wharfs cover much of Boston Inner Harbor's waterfront, maximizing its shoreline for commercial development. These wharfs are often occupied by mid-rise towers, which consequently make the harbor virtually invisible to the street and devoid of communal spaces. By replacing such buildings with sports facilities, open-air amphitheaters, and food markets, the water's edge can be maximized for public recreation, while maintaining the language of the piers. Initially, these piers built along 1st Street are to be occupied by athletes during the speculative Boston Olympics. A mixed use building lifted two floors above grade traces the north side of the road, creating a threshold from the esplanade into the site. From this large structure, a series of elevated residential buildings branch off towards and into the waterfront, further subdividing the piers into more intimate regions for recreation.

MID REVIEW

I thought the weave of the public space network would have been one of your early diagrams, which is the relationship of ground to water relative to streets. You are blind to the existing city structure. —Amanda Reeser Lawrence

FINAL REVIEW

Widder You need to tell us what you get back from connecting all the buildings. Can you get all the way from one end to the other?

Widder I would have expected you to say, when we went to 1st Street, we wanted to hold on to the tension of the residential neighborhood against the industrial leftovers. One way to do that was to make an incredibly long wall.

Yim You have one strategy for sculpting the water's edge, and another for the architectural typology. They are both trying to maximize waterfront. Flipping the building across the street clarifies both strategies.

Love There is a question of process and methodology. The closer you are to an urban fabric that has other cues, the more moth eaten the diagram has to be. Even if you do not move it, the building form needs to be attacked by the pressures across the street.

Widder Asking what you get back was an attempt to say why did you hold onto the wall? You have to show where your investment is and justify it.

Nicholas Muraglia & Sarah Smith
Edward Mitchell

2024 BOSTON OLYMPIC VILLAGE

Our proposal treated the site as an opportunity to knit together the surrounding neighborhoods of South Boston using a fabric of courtyard typologies; we were interested in the potential of the courtyard fabric to break down the scale of the site and offer private experiences in the city while still creating an overall public weave, providing a unified character for the neighborhood. We were interested equally in planning the "figure" of the city, with a range of typologies which transform according to changing urban needs, as much as the "ground" — the interstitial spaces of the city are treated as an articulated ground plane which unifies the private courtyards, the network of urban courtyards, semi-private greenways, and a densely programmed, activated waterfront as an interwoven, layered system of urban activities.

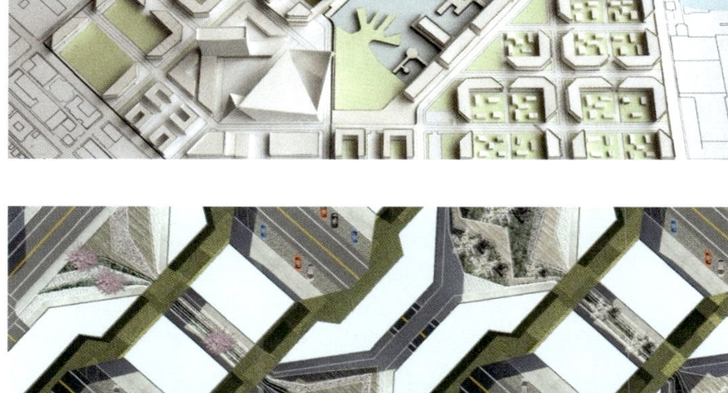

MID REVIEW

I would discourage you from allowing the system to design the buildings. At a certain point you detach from the planning framework and look at the individual building opportunities. We've allowed big projects to coarsen our cities. Stick to your guns about the fine grain you've created. —Alan Plattus

FINAL REVIEW

Gray I would raise the question about how this system touches its edges. If it is your goal to create a pattern that can be inhabited by other designers and planners, I think you should consider how to create more opportunities with a less specific geometry. But it speaks to a real sensitivity to scale, dimension, and height.

Hoffman-Brandt I see an interesting possibility in this corner here, where you've chopped away half the octagon so that you can have a big one, and now you've got one half-size, and you've cut off the leg at the bottom—I know not why, but I'm glad! That kind of variability creates multiple scales.

Bello The idea was that this was all designed for cars, and this was all designed for silence, so it is a binary between circulation and private space. I see it as a little problematic that this is the park and this is the street. You have a lot of roads in your scheme.

Plattus There is no room for contingency in this project because of the excessive preoccupation with pattern. For me the project lacks anything that seems generic where life could occur! Colgate Palmolive used to make a soap called Octagon Soap—probably mercifully outlawed since it was 95 percent lye—but I feel like this is Octagon City.

Rothstein The term "deformation" resonates, to me, with "recalibration"—an intentional adjustment to a set of circumstances. Had the logic been stronger, it would have adjusted a little bit in each context in which it found itself. Where you come into immediate contact with the existing context would have been an opportunity to demonstrate the responsiveness of the system at the edge.

Leah Abrams & Mark Peterson
Edward Mitchell

2024 BOSTON OLYMPIC VILLAGE
In approaching the site as an Olympic Village, we saw the opportunity to transform a part of South Boston that currently has little cohesion into a place with a clear urban center and a unifying identity that would last well beyond the Olympics. In order to achieve this, we focused on the ideas of edge and center.
For the edge, an active waterfront wraps around the entire site, knitting together new and old fabric with shared places of recreation and commerce, creating value and public amenities for both. A series of locks control the water flow and level, allowing the waterfront to serve different uses. In conjunction with a constructed wetland, the locks also help protect the area from storm surge flooding and future sea level rise. For the center, a public park creates a core around which smaller housing districts are grouped, each with its own private courtyard. The smaller courtyards serve as yard and garden spaces for the residents.

MID REVIEW

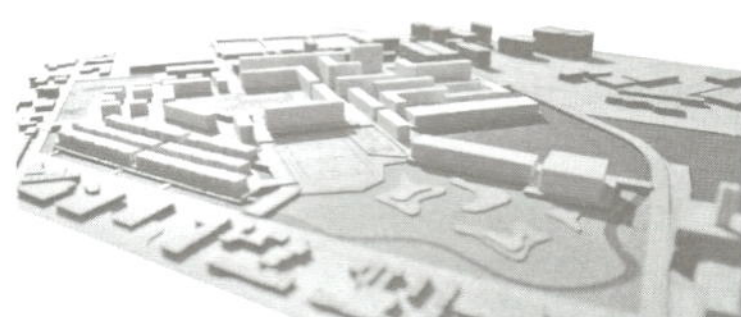

This is very expensive, so out of it you have to draw incredible real estate, communities, social, economic and spatial value. Because if you look at the site, what's left of it now, there's nothing really going on there so you need to do something to create the next new place in Boston. —David Pieprz

FINAL REVIEW

Widder I think one of the most interesting things about urban resilience is the possibility of all these resiliency measures, as kind of Trojan horses for a level of architecture that we haven't seen since, probably, the New Deal. Once you make a gesture like that and commit to that kind of investment, you have to really make it count.

Easterling I think it's a sort of Rittenhouse Square, that's one of the most irritating things people say at this stage but I just end up wondering why it's here, not there. That square might be the way that housing unit is not in its own enclave and your life is not circumscribed by that. Instead, you've given so much to the city that you get to be part of it and you're in the game somehow.

Love In that regard it's interesting to see that this is about as large as Beacon Hill. If you look at Beacon Hill, it's much denser, of course, but Boston is made up of these singular urban districts that are cheek to jowl one to the other, and I think that the success of that as a neighborhood would be precisely its difference from South Boston, but with characteristics that made it equally as memorable and equally as strong. For it to be convincing, it would need to be a desirable place to live, simple as that. What I like about your scheme is that it does get very far with the standard kit of parts of urban design and yet it's the most urban design of the schemes that we've seen so far today.

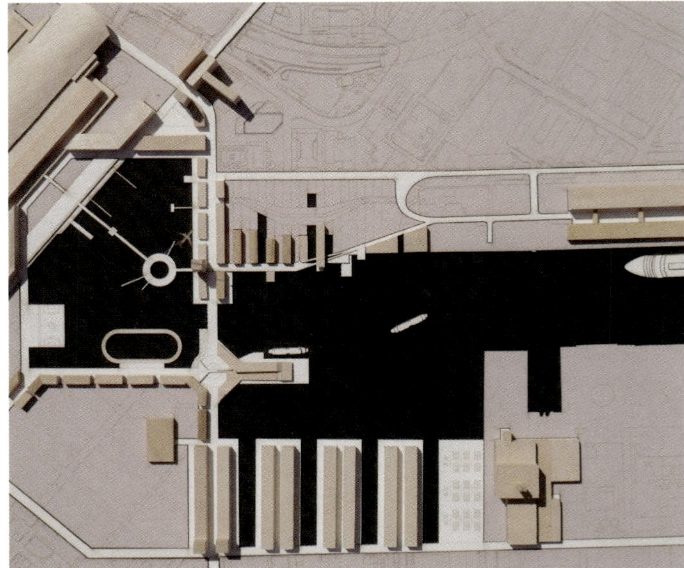

Haelee Jung & Hank Mezza
Edward Mitchell

2024 BOSTON OLYMPIC VILLAGE
The greatest issue we saw in this part of Boston is that a series of very large and important buildings float aimlessly in fields of parking and low scale industrial context. Our primary objective became to negotiate between serving these key points of interest and tying them into the greater fabric of the city of Boston. Our first major move was to absorb the scale of the convention center with a "gasket" of open space. Next, after realizing the importance of Summer Street as a link to the rest of the city, we moved it from its current peripheral location to a location where it can be utilized to better link our site to the downtown, airport, and South Boston, putting our proposal at the center of what could be a major connective hub for the city during and after the Olympics.This created a natural spine along which we placed the majority of our program. At intersection points, we formed nodes which offer access to the future expansion of the Silver Line as well as ferry terminal which we hope will connect our site to the points throughout the northeast coast line.

MID REVIEW

With more density, the perimeter of the water body will be more defined and more urbanized. —David Pieprz

FINAL REVIEW

Varanasi For the first time I can see how the convention center would be nice in Boston, but the intensity of the development you are proposing around this big move is very weak. I would expect to see more intensity around the green or water.

Lelyveld You have been very clear about the roads and the access, which takes the heat off the buildings. After you've attracted people to this place, I would think about where they would land. They are going to fall off the edge, so you need more of a promenade.

Stern It's not the promenade which is the problem. This rather important street crashes into the waterfront. You could solve it if this were a civic building which had a big arch or loggia. It has to be a building you could walk through.

Mitchell At midterm these spines were extremely emphatic, almost a megastructure. When you look at it now, if the Olympics don't come, you can envision where the different kinds of developers would come in. You can break it apart in ways that seem feasible. ite gives it that futuristic look.

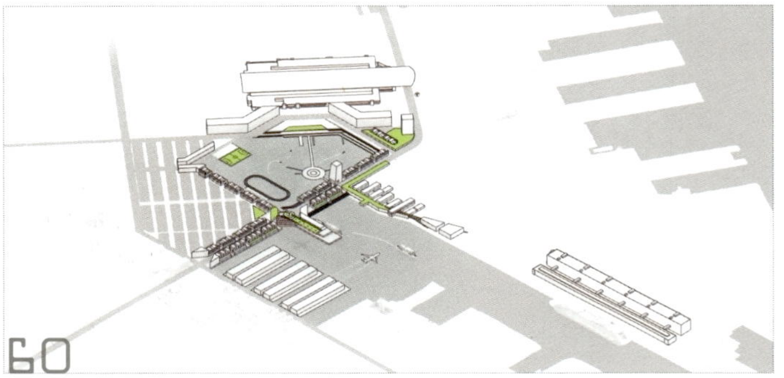

Michael Miller & Emau Vega
Jennifer Leung

HUB CITY
Hub City proposes a weaving of urban fabric and networks across several scales of local and inter-neighborhood connectivity with subway, light rail, bike, pedestrian, car, and water taxi. The architectural form proposes a combination of bar, plinth, courtyard, tower, and landscape typologies which merge and diverge at corners to create multiple datums to establish new ground conditions. Each datum becomes a layer of infrastructure that builds up to create an 'architectural hill' of many networks. These layers culminate with a roof park which provides a continuous surface for public leisure and becomes a piece of the larger Boston park network. The courtyard rhythm oscillates and inverts, becoming interior atrium spaces for events and cultural programs as density increases towards Hub City's cultural corridor, which connects the Boston Convention Center and several large entertainment and recreation programs along its central axis. This creates a new neighborhood which becomes a symbolic architectural hill among the cluster of Boston psychogeographic hill-neighborhoods, playing within and re-imagining the micro and macro identity conceptions of urban and geographic Boston.

MID REVIEW

When does intermodality create connectivity, and when does it create segregation? —Keller Easterling

FINAL REVIEW

Varanasi You're getting caught up in the levels and losing the big idea. You have the convention center that wants to reach the water, you have a neighborhood that wants to get to the water, and while you're bringing in the water, it seems like you're denying the visual access to it.

Deshong The reason for using a network or matrix in making cities is because it creates amenities, civic space, and interaction of activities, serendipitous meetings of people. It's not about this picnic plate.

Lelyveld I don't understand how you put a building over the waterway where you expect to have an amenity and you have people in water taxis. The civic space is completely obscured.

Mitchell This perspective illustrates my point about the separation of infrastructural systems. You've got one guy coming from below. There's a guy on a bicycle, then a subway station, then an elevated public realm, and what looks like another one above that. That's five levels of activity that you're trying to produce, and it's pretty low density. You need more program for this to work.

Mun Hee Lee & Kara Biczykowski
Jennifer Leung

2024 BOSTON OLYMPIC VILLAGE
Our project developed into two large, thin, linear boundaries which took the form of a crescent, both architecturally and in the site's landscape. Large crescent earthworks, resultant of cut and fill to celebrate the water's edge further into the site, provide water collection and protection for South Boston against rising sea levels. Additionally, they double as outdoor training fields and outdoor recreation after the Olympics which include amenities such as Harbor Baths. A binocular effect is produced at the top of each earthwork, or the lobby levels of each crescent housing band, to provide views simultaneously overlooking South Boston in one direction and parkland and the water's edge in the other. Each crescent is formed by two parallel housing bands where an elevated pedestrian street between them becomes populated by both private residents and the public who pass through the lobby partaking in outdoor amenities or enjoying the food and shop vendors. The crescent housing acts as a connective tissue through the site. Its sawtooth form serves to transform from small, private residences into large, public amenities between each crescent where there is a direct public axis to the water for South Boston residents.

MID REVIEW

I'm suspicious of your formal dexterity or ability to zipper black and white and raise and elevate floor planes. I think there's something embedded in your initial investigation. I could see a kind of environmental or ecological model or civil work model where you're talking about what you excavate gets used to create the mounds. —Joeb Moore

FINAL REVIEW

Forster By using black and white, you gave up on any kind of illustrative possibility, and instead, opted for imaginary representation of a character. Did you want the fluidity of the water, which is shapeless and deep, as opposed to the "addity" of the land, which is white and to a surface? Your buildings have the sense of the fluid while belonging clearly to the static earth.

Garvin You actually created a place in common for the use of everybody in the Olympic village, which is part of the program. How you resolve the shape problem, I don't know.

Ryan I read, on one level, an industrial system of denser loft buildings that references a more conventional urban fabric adjacent to the hotel. And then overlaid is this wild, graphic excitement of the sawtooth junction that almost seems like a device that sits at the edge of the different systems. You're quite careful about that, and you transition the sawtooth into different languages of architectural form

Schindler Urban design is not an intuitive practice and I think that with an exercise like this, you really have a responsibility to do more systemic drawings at the beginning that explain the really beautiful moves that you're making. In urban design, intuition is not enough.

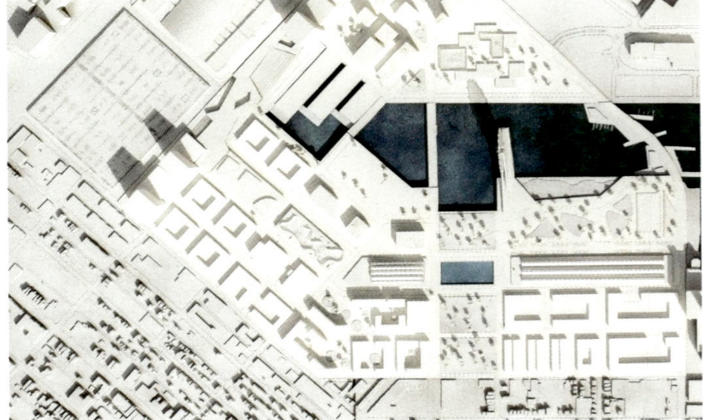

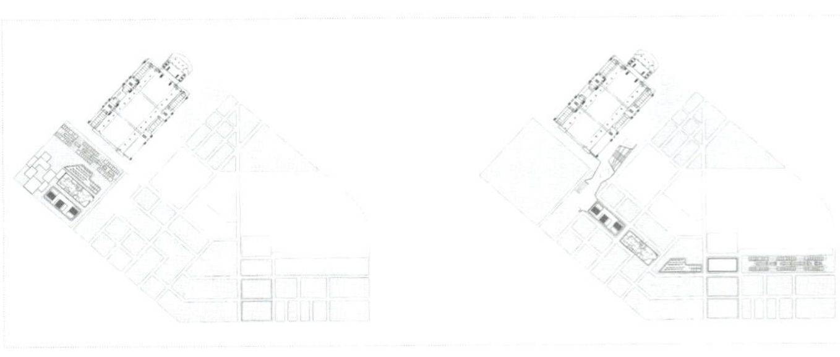

Tamrat Gebremichael & Sungwoo Choi
Jennifer Leung

AN UNCONVENTIONAL CONVENTION

This project reimagines the expansion of the existing convention center as an opportunity to create a new type of urban center in post-Olympics Boston. Instead of expanding the convention center by merely enlarging its current footprint as the existing proposal intends to do, we propose to strategically extend the convention center in a linear fashion across the entire site. As such the new linear expansion serves as a spine for future localized activities and programs to form around it. Hence, the existing convention center is simultaneously expanded in footprint but also reconceived in scale and scope of programs to sustain an intensity of activities in post-Olympics Boston.

MID REVIEW

I think that this project became very interested in being very clear. I think that's helpful, so we reduced things, we get the kind of binary vision. I feel like you got to a good place and I'm really interested to hear these questions; what is it like across the layers? How radical do you conceive the use of some of these spaces? —Jennifer Leung

FINAL REVIEW

Lelyveld So you've broken down the scale but I think that you can keep going down because I like the general concept of the seed here, planting the seed and having it affect different spaces, why can't you use the water, why can't you be more adventurous?

Deshong I wonder why it doesn't invade the water; you don't actually touch the water. You shape it but you don't give it program. I could easily see one of these components becoming aquatic. I think you could set program to that through the agent of water, which would be incredibly rich.

Lelyveld It would make a wonderful swimming pool.

Varanasi There are two layers that you have set up which can be combined given the density you are getting at. One is the waterfront layer and then there is a secondary layer which is happening one block behind. I think they're very much connected.

Deshong What is this building? [A library] Oh, that looks like a market too, but I guess it has walls. These are very beautiful conceptual ideas, but it's the development of those ideas, making them powerful and so provocative graphically so you can see how the scheme would really take off and energize the whole neighborhood.

Mendis I like it because it kind of plays on what the market economy can be and I wonder then why the markets are always segregated. It's about production. I would bring the artistic production into that fold and not some segregated thing that's different from this.

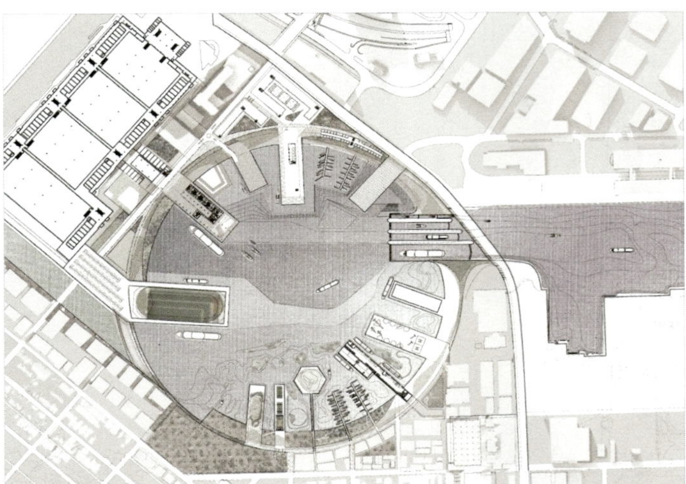

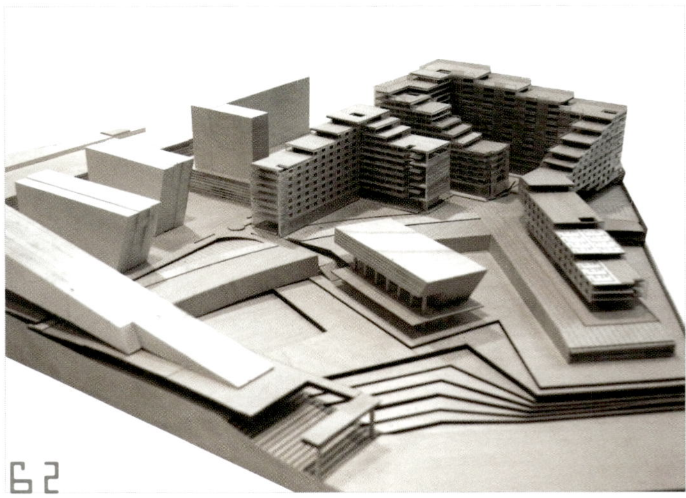

Melody Song & Minu Lee
Bimal Mendis

LOCK CITY

Seizing the Olympics and flood projection as an opportunity, Boston is understood as a continuous manipulation of topography and bathymetry. By managing the gradient between land and water through the system of locks, the project welcomes water as a positive force that makes dynamic public recreation zones, leverages real estate and brings to the fore the legacy of Boston's relationship to water. Like most of Boston, the site itself is engineered from a mudscape to a serrated hard edge. The project continues the historical trajectory of engineering the water's edge and maximizing water-frontage. The project consists of two gestures. A canal along 1st Street bounded by a lock system orchestrates water levels to activate different recreational activities. Secondly, green corridors extending from the new canal to the piers of Seaport District break down the scale of the district into discrete islands to increase the waterfront and concentrate development.

MID REVIEW

You've just excavated a big canal on First Street, wouldn't it be nice if it became a part of an ongoing network. —Ed Mitchell

FINAL REVIEW

Leung It looks like maybe there is a smaller device of encircling, so I'm really curious about the smaller public spaces that you produce.

de Bretteville I'm suddenly realizing that you do this enormous circle and stop. Why isn't there a circular forty story building around the whole thing to make you say, oh my god, that must change when it arrives at the smaller scale side. You lack the notion of continuity here; the only continuous thing is the circle. You need to let it be more relentless. Let it finish out and then look critically at something that's overly continuous and overly drawn and figure out how that becomes particularized. In fact, the circle is not contextual, it's just a circle. It becomes contextual by how it receives, absorbs and responds to its surroundings.

Lelyveld But they've been very clear to mark the boundaries between these rather than blurring it or looking for that other scale.

de Bretteville You've got to see it complete before you can learn. It's got to be there in a way that is aggravating so you know you have to change it. You create a confrontation in order to heighten your awareness of what is necessary. So to create conflict, in your design. I don't see any drawings of circles and the study of how this circle gets occupied.

Tyler Pertman, Mahdi Sabbagh & Jonathan Sun

Bimal Mendis

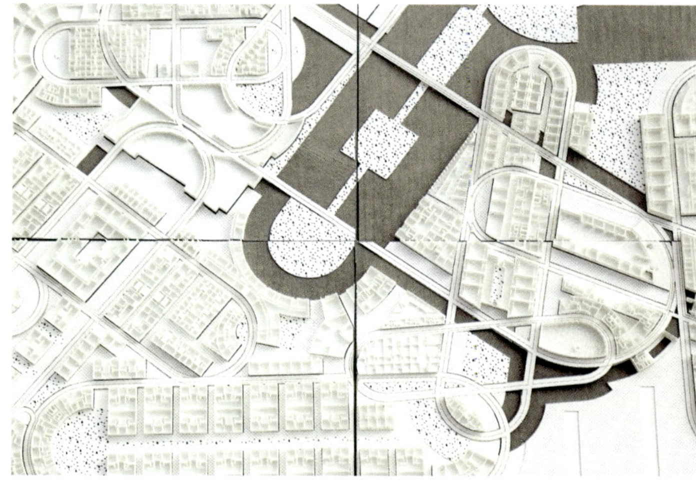

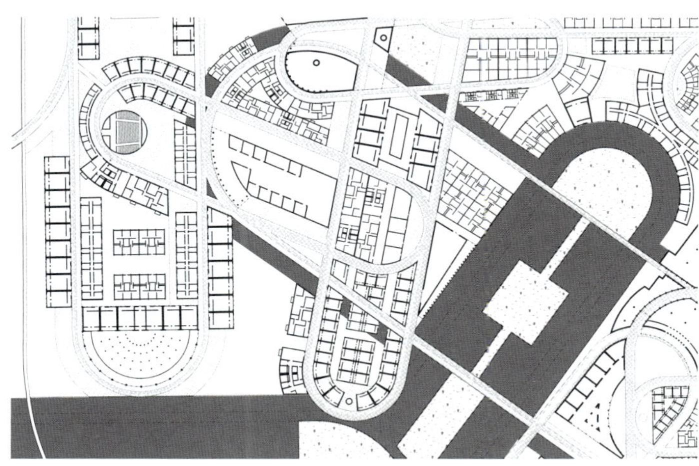

THE OLYMPIC GAME

"The Olympic Game" is an athletic hyper-world, designed as a diverse urban environment, specialized for use by Olympic and recreational athletes. The athletic loop, a symbol of the athletic program, is used as the circulation unit on the site, creating an organizational framework for city-making based on the human scale. Defining each loop with a different program and architectural identity, this framework allows for the opportunity to create a diverse urban fabric by taking advantage of the variety of intersections created by the loops across the site. The loop is inherently specific to the human scale articulate the athletic program by doubling as a site for athletic training. The loop-based framework is replicable and expandable, allowing for the village to be fully integrated into the city after the Olympics.

MID REVIEW

Your generating point is good but when your networks came together, you're not as an architect or urban designer resolving them as places. I don't mind the track form being used as a generator of the plan, it's an interesting diagram, but you haven't been able to give hierarchy to that. —Kishore Varanasi

FINAL REVIEW

Stern The way you've started with these games is so deterministic this is going to be a city for runners. Even runners need other runners and then they develop little runners [laughter]. Then they get older and they want to be in the center, that's what makes a community and so you need places for sitters and standers and all the other kind of people.

Deshong It's a separation between how people build and how people occupy space. it's just a merging of different forms.

Leung There is a big leap between this and something that promises to be so prototypical and iterative. I think what you would want to argue is that this set of software could occur in other parts. I would like to see how you tested these different variations and then what you learned from them. When did you decided too big was too big? That's the promise in here and I like your project, I think there's a real difference between that and what's produced and how you make a decision.

Maya Alexander, Lauren Raab & Benjamin Smith

Bimal Mendis

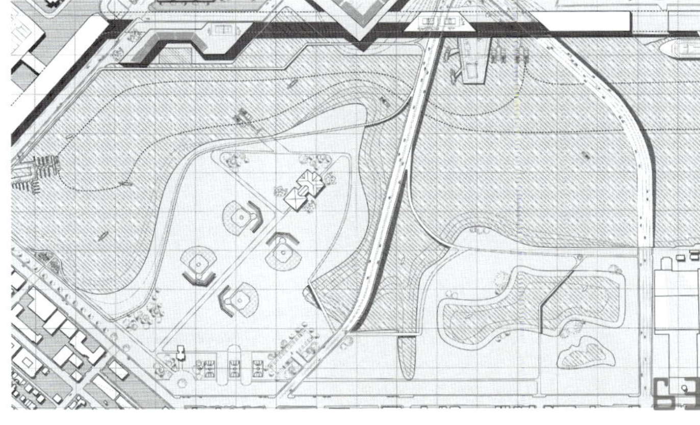

LONGER WHARF

The Longer Wharf proposes a linear residential, commercial, and recreational development along the Boston harbor front. The narrative of a 'linear village' harkens back to Boston's Historical Long Wharf, which was an active commercial and residential hub in the city for over two centuries, but was shortened almost to the point of nonexistence by land infill. In turn, our proposal for a new Longer Wharf links the existing cruise ship terminal to the Boston Convention Center, while extending the conceptual logic of the historical long wharf into the contemporary city. The Longer Wharf, therefore, becomes a new armature for development in Boston by extending the harbor into the city, and ultimately reconnects the city to one of its greatest amenities: the water.

MID REVIEW

The one drawing that is missing is a ground plane drawing. That would explain clearly your aspirations for porosity. Graphic difference between the aerial site plan and a Nolli plan would have erased the presence of the bar except for a dash line in a way that would have strengthened your case. —Tim Love

FINAL REVIEW

Ryan I'm a little puzzled by your presentation of a very polemical form in a very almost domestic, docile fashion. It is a highly differentiated site that you've chosen an identical form for. I don't know why you made that decision but I find that paradox compelling.

Moore It is a lovely presentation but I would argue it's a bit of a caricature right now. You may want to oppose two different mapping methods, Piranesi's along with Nolli's method. You can use the peripheries, the adjacencies to create much more powerful connections socially and economically and historically, that even tie back to the original image.

Forster Doesn't that introduce a very interesting split character? The singularity of such a structure becomes more immune to its surroundings the more it engages its surroundings. Any gesture made intelligently is implying other gestures, which could also be made inadvertently by the changing weather or other tenants or whatever. So the fascination is that what looks so single minded and completely autonomous is a snake with many colors on its skin.

Schindler Nobody's talked what you're doing on the other side. That to me is a completely different approach to the project.

Moore This image here has a panoptic kind of vision and your insistence on the value and the amenity of the promenade, but there's a way in which you're reinforcing ideas about spectatorship that are quite conventional that you may want to break down.

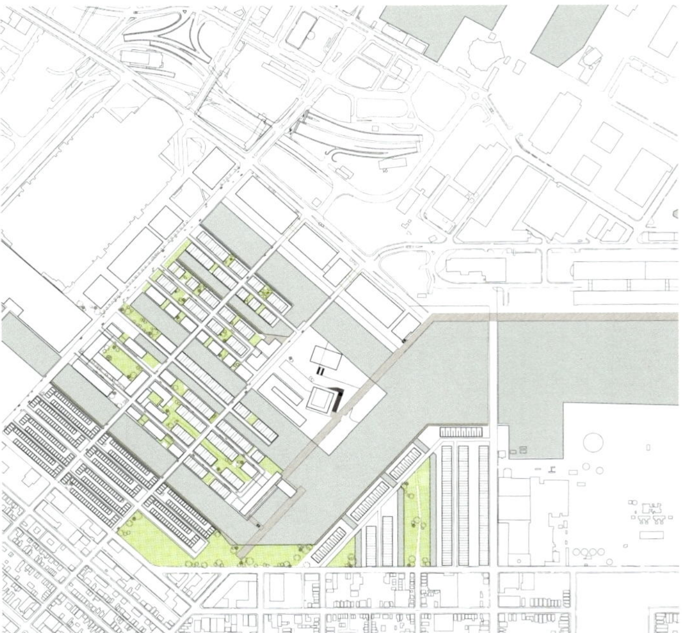

Elena Baranes & Alissa Chastain
Alan Plattus

2024 BOSTON OLYMPIC VILLAGE
Our project approaches Boston as built land with a pier system that mediates the connection between land and water. Our goal was to carry this relationship onto our site, examining the exchange of land and water by pulling the water up to meet the convention center, and in turn building back out into the water using a hybrid landfill and pier system that addresses water circulation and management issues.

MID REVIEW

Even though Borneo Sporenberg is primarily mono-functional—it is mostly housing—there is a huge typological diversity. This is what you are lacking. —Felipe Correa

FINAL REVIEW

Dolman Precedents that have been shown, like Borneo Sporenberg, are preexisting shipping channels. The economics of that huge infrastructure to support this density of housing is very difficult to rationalize.

Love By economics we don't mean actual economics. We mean the kind of setup that the famous Dutch architects are so good at, where you make a proposition that is made plausible somehow by the rhetoric of value added. There probably is a more polemical storyline you need to get people to say yes.

Gray It feels as though the argument could be adjusted slightly. The mixed density might increase so that your argument about relationships to water could be sustained in certain locations, but not across the entire site. That layering of another scale into the project would make it stronger.

Davis As a long term strategy for a single land owner that can justify a decades-long view, like the Port Authority, this isn't crazy. Unlike a developer where you've got to justify the investment of all this infrastructure, they could easily set the stage.

Felson This is a project that manages to bridge between long term infrastructure planning, transportation issues, and multiple land use scenarios with a housing development strategy in the near term. In my mind this is also an adaptive strategy that creates housing framed as a series of piers that could function in the future as a port system.

Plattus But the real challenge is something that Thompson describes in the biography of William Morris as the education of desire. You don't know what you need until someone who is not totally constrained by knowing too much begins that process of speculation. You see what is possible, then go back to the science.

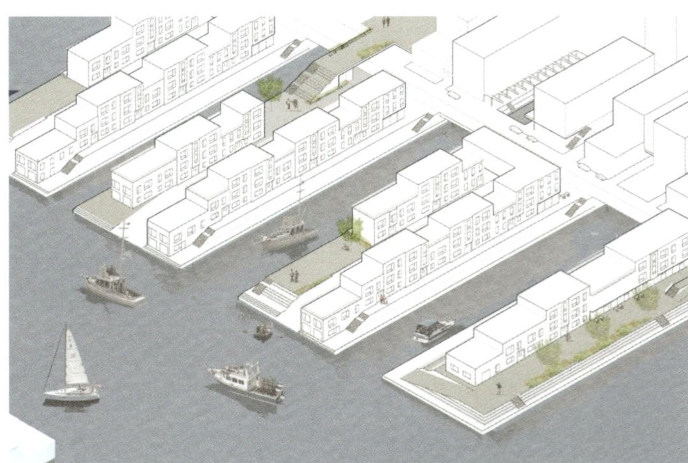

Meghan McAllister & Phillip Nakamura
Alan Plattus

OLYMPIC HARBOR
The New Olympic Harbor neighborhood creates a smaller scale working waterfront for South Boston, providing sorely-needed amenities for Boston's historic fishing industry that has struggled due to market-driven high rise waterfront development. Three different typologies arranged in strips enable the scale change from the convention center to the water front: closer to the convention center, a mid-rise courtyard slab typology sits atop the podium; between D and E street, row homes and small sunken courtyards arise from a mat building; finally, closest to the new working water front, smaller scaled row homes line the fish pier street.

MID REVIEW

You have the green spine, you have the waterfront, but they're existing too independently. —Amy DeDonato

FINAL REVIEW

Gauthier Typologies are a strong way to move through a project this complex as a way to give value without designing every little thing, but what I would like to see is just a few forays into how your concept is polluting those typologies. To me, that's the architecture—the local conditions of the water and the Olympics and the program.

Hoffman-Brandt It's kind of bipolar because you wanted this to be a working waterfront, so that means that your dock levels really do have to engage the water not at the level that the surge does. So, in the sampling, it's a matter of recognizing the whole tectonic shift of the ground level that has to happen to perform at the waterfront in two different ways.

Dolman It's one of the first schemes that has acknowledged the grain of South Boston, and the buildup of density toward the convention center, which I think is a very strong move. I'm wondering if there is a way to use this green space as the surge buffer?

Hoffman-Brandt As the landscape architect on the jury, I have to say, lose the park! Green is not good in this case—it's not performing the way you want it to.

Plattus At midterm there was skepticism from the jury about sustaining very low density waterfront on such valuable real estate. Given what's happening to every American city that's reclaiming its waterfront, where zoning creates a wall of overdevelopment, this is one way to hide the density two or three layers deep in the fabric to make the waterfront look as if it is humanly scaled.

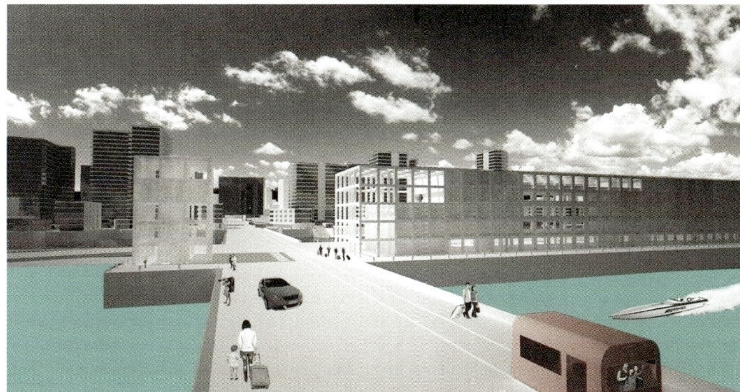

Zachary Huelsing & Zachary Veach

Alan Plattus

2024 BOSTON OLYMPIC VILLAGE

Sample City is a proposed 2024 Olympic village that is composed of artificial waterfronts arranged parallel to one another. The scheme creates an island for future development centered on the convention center and building off of connections to downtown Boston and Logan Airport. Each waterfront condition exhibits a different spatial characteristic, with each edge inspired by pre-existing waterfronts found throughout Boston. The building types and their arrangements are unique to each waterfront, creating a compression of the episodic neighborhood experience of the city.

The disparate, parallel edge strips are connected by a light rail people mover that runs perpendicular to all of the waterfronts. This transportation system begins in South Boston, skewers each waterfront condition, and then connects to Boston's established network of buses, trains, and proposed water taxi system. After the Olympics, Boston will have a new highly connected waterfront system with different building types and urban spatial languages that can accommodate international growth into the 21st century.

MID REVIEW

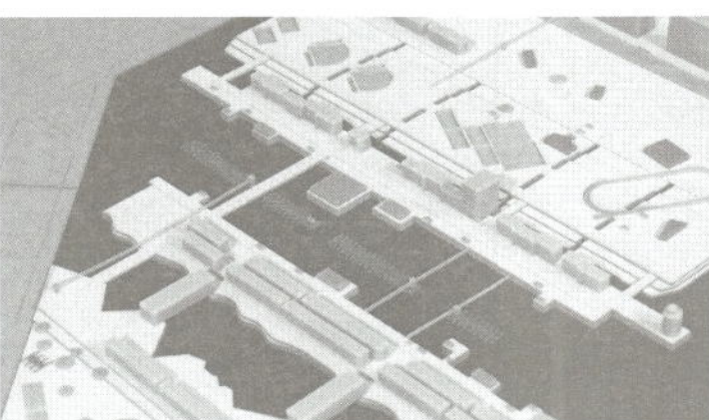

It seems that series of perspectives is a more critical drawing for you in terms of understanding how the parallel bands with the very different spatial characters, programmatic assignments, and intensities work as a series of parallel different experiences. I would say that drawing, in the future, for the final review is the most important drawing. —Tim Love

FINAL REVIEW

Widder It is hybridized with a weird kind of Miami Beach urbanism.

Love The big move is the canal that connects Four Point Channel with the Reserve channel. Your move produces all kinds of frontage south of that new canal which isn't going to have a complimentary identity to a waterfront unit. Development is intensified along the edge, because it's all waterfront property now.

Yim You keep using the word island, but I don't know whether the actual main spine conflicts with that concept. You're building too many connections to the area that you want to preserve from redevelopment.

Mitchell Your big urban gestures produce interesting edges. Thinking the skewer is most important because it's in the middle of your project, rather than what you do to every edge of the site, undermines the larger gesture of the city.

Love Your project has a figure/ground crisis. The edge of your island is actually quite ambiguous. Maybe the mistake was to drive the canal all the way around where it isn't really central to your project. The big island created by the canal is making things have a one sidedness that actually doesn't make any sense.

Widder When I look at your section and I think about the mandate of this studio to include considerations of rising water levels, then I get even more concerned about the way the finger islands are articulated. If you think about the way a storm surge might come through, maybe there's another way to think about the creation of islands that is about leaving strategic pathways for water across the land. It would be less about typologies and much more about a strategic flooding of the land.

Felson One of the steps that I might go through is thinking about how wide a pier do you create and what the distance between one pier and the next is, and how do you play with the scale of the buildings in order to make that distance seem wider. The beach is huge, and that's one of the things that is unconvincing. So I think there's this sort of misbelief over the scale of the beach versus the intricate scale of the building types.

Plattus The move that they made after mid-term to connect the channel was a game changer in a way that was not fully assimilated. The suggestion that you just be more consistent about the edges is the first direction I would explore if you were taking it forward.

ARCHITECTURAL THEORY II: 1968 TO PRESENT

Ariane Lourie Harrison

FACULTY

Marta Justo Caldeira
Chris Cowell

This course is a survey of theoretical and critical literature on contemporary architecture. It explores the texts of postmodernism, post-structuralism, and critical and post-critical discourses, as well as current debates in globalization, post-humanism, and environmentalism in the architectural discipline from 1968 to the present.

Brent Sturlaugson

DISPOSITIF, OR HOW SPACE REGISTERS POWER

Foucault presents evidence of apparatuses of security in describing how a population is controlled through the orchestration of its milieu, or its "medium of an action and the element in which it circulates."[1] Turning to the specific qualities of this milieu, Canguilhem offers insight. For Canguilhem, "In a human milieu, man is obviously subject to a determinism, but it is the determinism of artificial constructions. The spirit of invention that brought them into existence has been alienated from him."[2]

This articulates the securitizing role of artificial constructions—or architecture—in the composition of milieu. Moreover, Canguilhem writes: "The milieu that is proper to man is the world of his perception, that is to say the field of his practical experience in which his actions, oriented and regulated by values that are immanent to his tendencies, carve out certain objects, situate them relative to each other and all of them in relation to himself. This occurs in such a way that the environment he is supposed to be reacting to finds itself originally centered in and by him."[3] For Canguilhem, the milieu describes a space which compels activity. Foucault characterizes this mode of power as governmentality. Governmentality describes an ensemble of tactics that targets a population through apparatuses of security. For Foucault, this operates in a "manner of disposing things so as to lead not to the form of the common good, as the jurists' texts would have said, but to an end which is 'convenient' for each of the things that are to be governed."[4] Much like Canguilhem's milieu, governmentality stimulates certain behavior through its spatial organization.

In a similar fashion, Deleuze and Guattari expound on what they observe as modern power, which "implies processes of normalization, modulation, modeling and information that bear on language, perception, desire movement, etc., and which proceed by way of migroassemblages."[5] Remembering Easterling's description of disposition, governmentality incentivizes the potential activity immanent in the organization of space. In this way, architecture acts as an extension of power, registering a form of governmental rationality. Often deployed as an explanation for complex systems, an apparatus takes on multivalent characteristics. Foucault offers a threefold disambiguation of the concept of apparatus, or dispositif, to explain social assemblages: first, dispositif is "a thoroughly heterogeneous ensemble consisting of discourses, institutions, architectural forms, regulatory decisions, laws, administrative measures, scientific statements, philosophical, moral and philanthropic propositions;" second, dispositif is "the nature of the connection that can exist between these heterogeneous elements;" and third, dispositif is a "formation which has as its major function at a given historical moment that of responding to an urgent need. The apparatus thus has a dominant strategic function."[6] In the first definition, Foucault imbricates architecture among a range of other devices. In the second instance, connections gain agency, and in the third, its strategy becomes apparent. These processes mimic those that occur in architectural production, effecting a notable connection between Foucault's dispositif and the built environment.

1 Michel Foucault, "11 January 1978" in Security, Territory, Population: Lectures at the Collège de France, 1977–1978, ed. Michel Senellart, François Ewald, and Alessandro Fontana (New York: Picador/Palgrave Macmillan, 2009), 21.
2 Georges Canguilhem, "The Living Being and Its Environment[1952]" Grey Room 3 (Spring 2001): 18.
3 Ibid., 26.
4 Michel Foucault, "Governmentality [1978]" in The Foucault Effect: Studies in Governmentality, ed. Graham Burchell, Colin Gordon, and Peter Miller (Chicago: University of Chicago Press, 1991), 101–103.
5 Ibid., 95.
6 Michel Foucault, "The Confession of the Flesh [1977]" in Power/Knowledge: Selected Interviews and Other Writings, 1972–1977, ed. Colin Gordon (New York: Pantheon Books, 1980), 194–5.

Bruce Hancock

OBJECTIVE REALISM AND THE EVENT

The event in philosophy has never maintained a stable relationship with space. As opposed to time in general, the event is most articulate in realism as a specific quantity. For Kant and those after him, there are no concepts outside of the mind, making the specifics of the event less important to idealism. Hence modern architects, who arguably begin with the Enlightenment, pay most of their attention to abstraction and functionalism. To those who subscribe to idealism, the event loses specificity, becomes a generalized idea, and is equated with form. As a new mediated paradigm emerges, a return to a materialist idea of the event reveals new relationships that were previously collapsed into a reductivist dogma. This shift has challenged the meaning of form in relation to the re-emerging event. What is at stake is the degree to which a discourse becomes codified into ideas rather than a recognition of an ever present reality. In the framework of idealism, the idea is tautological; that it may be a representation of a reality is not important, only that the idea has meaning for itself. The realist rejection of framework, leaving ideas in the objects themselves, constantly recognizes the real, especially in relation to the event as a specific point in time.

A model that equates the event phenomenon with a physical thing leads to a conception that opens the gate to a host of meanings, similar to Aldo Rossi's idea of the locus. The architecture of the city easily becomes a complex artifact in this scenario. The city is an object of interpretation. A more contemporary understanding uses the model of realism to allow a mediated scene of events to be unaffected by structure. A mediated world leaves out the possibility of the intent that events emerge from agents acting out of volition. The difference between absorbing a mediated reality and interpreting it for potential action allows the two paradigms to coexist as choices. The architect must understand the creative event both through the agency of interpretation (idealism) and as a flash of the new denying any present structure (realism). This paradox is our imperative.

Laurence Lumley

THE DETAIL; OR, WHY KOOLHAAS IS WRONG ABOUT THE KUNSTHAL

This essay starts with the question of the threat to the detail, an oft repeated concern of certain architectural theorists and practitioners. It attempts to answer this question by laying out what this threat really entails and by analyzing the implications of the positions of those architects who have explicitly attacked the detail. A preliminary general definition of the architectural detail is then suggested, one that can be used to assess these potential 'dangers' and evaluate the continuing significance of the detail today. In so doing this essay seeks to salvage a conceptual paradigm of detailing from within the practice of those very architects who claim to care least about it.

In the first section of the essay three main schools of anti-detail thought, and practice, namely the 'Dutch school', digital design, and 'Junkspace design', are identified and considered. The Dutch concern about detail is that it detracts from the whole, seen as a concept or diagram. The detail is either detailed out or simply un-designed, by using a pre-fab system or component unit. In digital practice also the detail is often designed away, but additionally, through complex strategies of patterning, ornamentation, or fractal repetition, it is erased by its very multiplication—dissolved into itself. In the case of 'Junkspace design' the issue is less one of eradicating details, as one of bad detailing. Here detail is seen as unimportant because it is a crappy, temporary condition that is the inevitable resultant of the tacky, ubiquitous construction materials of the age.

In the second section, a general definition of the detail is offered, reached partly through the comparison of examples. The detail resists abstraction and animates a building in three ways: empathetically—we able to 'feel into' the building, sympathetically—by setting up resonances or dissonances in space that impart a mood; directly—eliciting subtle and specific bodily sensations through those bits of buildings we physically touch and manipulate. As such, details create unevenness in the texture of experience. So a general definition of the detail might be, 'a concrete moment of intensity or inflection that interrupts the even flow of space'.

In the final section of the essay this definition is used to assess the threats to the detail previously laid out. Because they expressly aim at increased abstraction or smoothness, the first two modes of thought are real threats. The threat of Junkspace, however, is questionable. If the detail is essentially a moment of interruption or inflection, the invasion of an 'other' order, then this is precisely the function that the 'junk detail' plays in a architecture whose 'higher order' is one of abstraction and concept. OMA's Kunsthal demonstrates this, for it is a building all about joints and encounters. This is a rushed and fragmented collage of parts, shot through with restless energy. In this early work, Koolhaas managed to subvert the logic of Junkspace, finding a mode of resistance from within.

SYSTEMS INTEGRATION

Martin Finio

FACULTY

Anibal Bellomio
Lisa Davey
Erleen Hatfield
Robert Haughney
Kristin Hawkins
Kenneth Gibble
Laura Pirie
Craig Razza
Edward M. Stanley
Philip Steiner

This course is an integrated workshop and lecture series in which students develop the technical systems of preliminary design proposals from earlier studio work. The careful advancement of structural form and detail, environmental systems, and envelope design, as well as an understanding of the constructive processes from which a building emerges, are all approached systematically, as elements of design used not only to achieve technical and performance goals but also to reinforce and re-inform the conceptual origins of the work. The workshop is complemented by a series of lectures from leading structural, environmental, and envelope consultants.

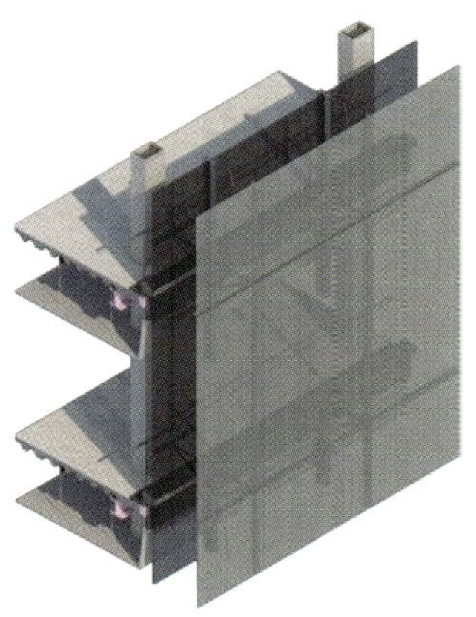

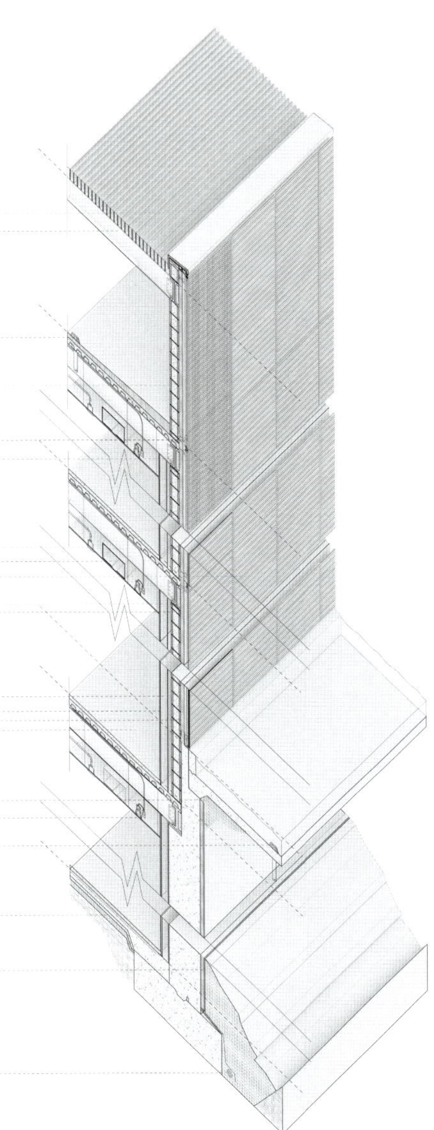

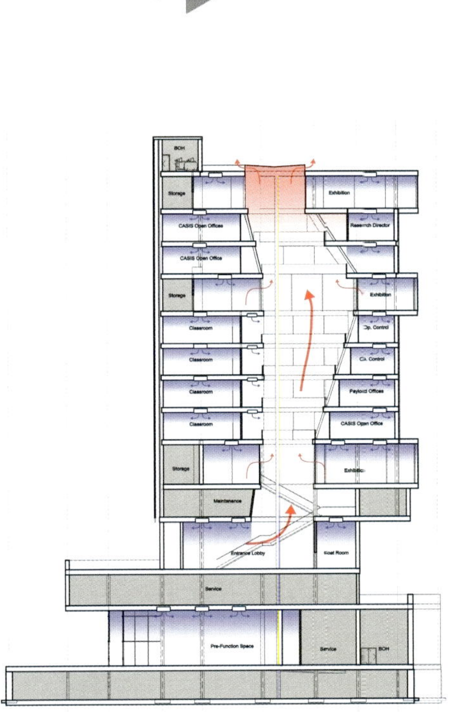

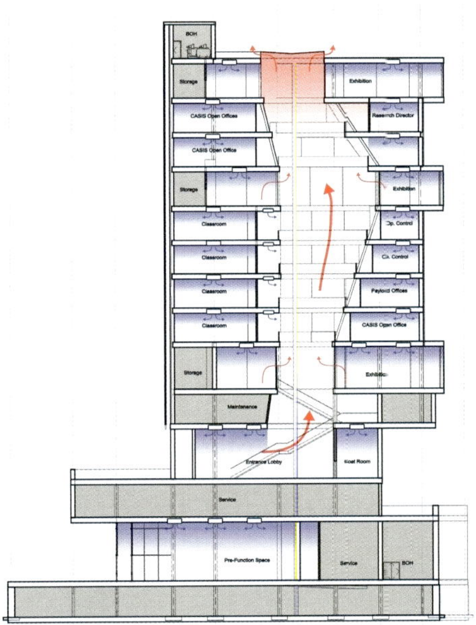

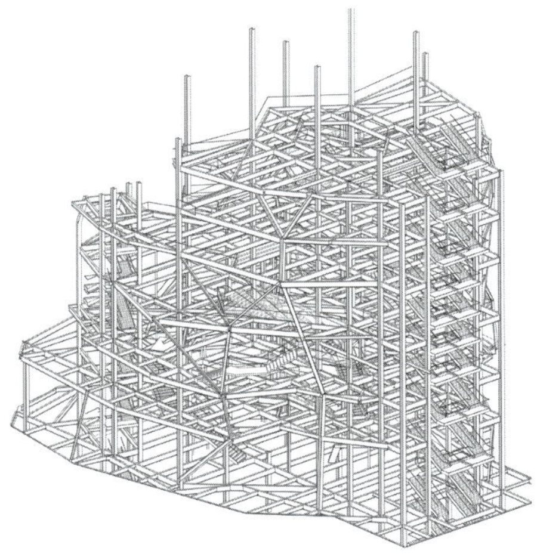

Ross McClellan Elena Baranes J.T. Keeley Meghan Lewis

An early reorganization of the original project's core and internal circulation allowed efficient incorporation of considerations for egress, structure, mechanical systems, and assembly while maintaining the building's original concept of a programmed tower organized around a large vertical atrium. In the second half of the semester, façade materiality was explored in greater depth and original ideas about varying degrees of transparency and solidity toward the surrounding context were able to be developed and fully realized. Collective collaboration throughout the semester furthered the original project and incorporated the required systems without sacrificing the original architectural intentions.

Belinda Lee, Benjamin Smith, Jason Lee

The project is built up in layers. The opaque outer shell houses the mechanical, circulation, storage and other service spaces in small rooms that line the exterior of the building. The facade is built up with a textured cast glass panels backed by a reflective and opaque surface, insulation and non-structural CMU. The textured opaque glass transitions to the faceted, smooth, transparent glass of the interior courtyard that carves away at the solid exterior from the ground up. The structure is steel frame with two large trusses across the top to support a hanging glass conference room.

Dionysus Cho Kara Biczykowski Jack Wolfe

GLYTCH02 is the development of the anomalous GLYTCH as a feasible and complete design from structural to HVAC to building skin systems. The exterior, imagined as folding shards, is broken down into a modularized panel system which divides large triangles into manageable and self-contained curtain wall units. To tackle the heavily articulated façade, an underlying tessellated structural frame wraps the interior space and ties back to a regularized column system. With floor plates which vary drastically from floor to floor and numerous voids and atriums throughout, an intricate web of steel had to be crafted to distribute and support the shifting volumes. At the edge, a circulatory spine doubles as a service one, allowing for both air handling and electrical systems to branch off to each floor. Remaining true to the deconstructed fracturing of its predecessor, GLYTCH02 proves a resultant constructible and cohesive design solution.

ROME SUMMER STUDY ABROAD

TRAVEL AWARDS

David M. Schwarz Architects Internship & Traveling Fellowship

Established by David Schwarz (M.Arch. 1974). Provides a non-graduating student with a summer internship and a traveling fellowship.

Meghan Lewis

THE AFTERMATH OF RUIN PORN: AMERICAN RUINS IN GLOBAL CONTEXT

The historical, cultural, and aesthetic value of architectural remnants that is celebrated in many European cities has been avoided heretofore in American cities. The American relationship with ruins is partially a result of its relatively short architectural history in comparison with its European counterparts, but also to its tendency to erase or export the devastation of war, natural disaster, and economic crisis. Previous to the phenomena of American post-industrial ruins, nature played the role ruins play in other countries, inciting nostalgia and offering a conduit into our cultural origin story: Manifest Destiny. As these ruins evidence, the tangible remnants of America's recent past tell a different origin story. The ruins of capitalism have begun to accrue so quickly that an attitude must be taken towards their destruction, restoration, reconstruction, or re-use. The recent influx of literature in the past several decades in response to the public demise of Detroit and other cities exposes the struggle architects and planners are currently undergoing to find an American narrative for the role of these spaces in the urban built environment. The eager consumption of the imagery of these ruins leaves little direction for the local populations suffering adjacency to what may be an emotionally turbulent or physically dangerous architecturalization of memory and nostalgia. The lack of precedent in American cities has led some to turn to iconic ruin environments of ancient civilizations in Europe for comparison, in search of a cultural response to obsolescence or preservation. Through the David M. Schwarz Travel Fellowship, I studied the potential (or lack thereof) of the ancient ruins of Turkey, Greece, and Italy as a lens for understanding the future of our own American landscape.

George Nelson Scholarship

Established in honor of George Nelson (B.A. 1928, B.F.A. in architecture 1931), architect, product designer, and writer, by Herman Miller, Inc., and Mrs. George Nelson. Awarded each year through a competitive application process to a second-year student in the first professional degree program for support for an independent course of study.

Jack Wolfe

BRAZIL MAYBE

In his 1928 Cannibal Manefesto, Oswald de Andrade polemically argues that Brazil's history is typified by cannibalisms of other cultures. He advocates for the Brazilian people to continue this metaphorical tradition in order to detach themselves from oppressive impositions of European cultural and religious ideals, such that Brazil might re-establish their own imagination, sentiments, and expression. To Andrade, cannibalism offers the possibility of improvement, it is a positive destruction. According to legend, and undoubtedly propaganda, the indigenous Tupi warrior ate captured warriors of other tribes in order to obtain their positive attributes. Thus, when Andrade provokes the nation to act cannibalistically towards the European influences on Brazilian society, he is not rejecting the West, but advocating for the absorption of their commendable qualities into a transfigured body that is distinctly and undeniably Brazilian.

Absorption and transformation became the unspoken mantra of Brazil's modern architectural movement. The cannibalistic approach to Corbusian Modernism exhibited first by the Carioca School architects Oscar Niemeyer and Lucio Cost, and later by the Paulista School architects Paulo Mendes da Rocha, Joao Batista Vilanova Artigas, and Lina Bo Bardi exemplifies the Brazilian capacity to absorb foreign influences and translate them into unique, local pieces. My aim is to analyze, capture, and re-present the iconic buildings of the second half of the 20th century, not as emblems of their utopian conception, but as cannibalized entities that have experienced the jaws of contemporary Brazilian culture. In order to better understand the Carioca and Paulista schools of architecture, it is important to understand the artistic, cultural, and architectural lineage. Therefore, the study includes the documentation of colonial, slave, tribal, baroque, and modernist architecture, art, and urbanism as they exist in Brazil today.

Takenaka Corporation Summer Internship

The Takenaka Corporation, one of Japan's leading full-service architecture and construction companies offers a three month summer internship in the Architectural Design section of its Osaka office. A monthly stipend is provided for the duration as well as round-trip airfare.

Phillip Nakamura

JAPANESE URBANISM

My interest is in the observance of density and scale in Japanese urban form; in particular, the ways in which Japanese architecture responds to and is impacted by density and scale. Despite the need for more space, sprawling, even tedious projects continue to be built alongside the ultra-efficient. For example, the ground is made and remade in the large infrastructural architecture of train stations while at the same time taller and taller skyscrapers continue to be built. As a result, I propose to examine examples of historical, informal, and urban forms in Japan in their approach to density and scale. Ultimately, density and scale are issues dealt with by all architects, and the Japanese approach can be broadly informative.

POST PROFESSIONAL

POST PROFESSIONAL DESIGN STUDIO

This studio is specially designed for incoming post-professional students to introduce them to the School's educational program and faculty. Each student is given the opportunity to examine in depth a sequence of design problems.

COORDINATING FACULTY

Edward Mitchell

FACULTY

Aniket Shahane

CENTRAL SQUARE CAMBRIDGE

This studio examines how one represents, analyzes, constructs and projects the future design of an urban site. There are two competing but at times complementary ways for architects to approach city making. One approach examines the city as a series of distinct physical spaces and generally operates by establishing typological standards and identifies and constructs significant and iconic public spaces—streets, squares, and parks. This establishes the grammar of city making to construct a comprehensible fabric. The second approach is concerned with the city as a technical object that organizes time—the operational aspects of the city—as well as space. This method envisions the city as the performance of both large and small scale infrastructures that support the operative vitality of the city. These infrastructures may include operations as extensive as an urban aquifer or as intensive and focused as the establishments of devices like fire stairs. Both are critical in giving form to the urban realm. We could say that the first conceptual method is linguistic while the second is functional, but clearly the two methodologies inform one another.

Urban design is by nature a complex endeavor with immediate as well as long-term effects. Proposals at the city scale involve negotiations between public and private interests; global, regional and local forces and needs; collective and individual expression. The process confronts urban designers and architects with many potentially conflicting demands involving, among other things, rights (individual vs. collective), design language (personal versus common), design focus (landscape, building form, infrastructure systems), and design attitude (traditional versus progressive).

Any design proposal does more than simply solve a given set of immediate problems. An urban design proposal embodies a position about, and has consequences for, urban life and urban form. In urban design the term "program" has a more open-ended meaning than when applied to a single building. Urban design programming involves a process of ascribing value to different needs, demands and desires. Your projected urban vision for the Central Square district will be the result of negotiating between, and determining the relative value of, various possible urbanisms. At the city scale, the term "site" also has broad implications. Urban design site boundaries are both political and ideological points of contestation. In this studio, we ask you to consider how intervening in a specific and limited location in downtown Boston can initiate a larger plan and longer-term vision through urban and an architectural scale propositions.

The Post pro studio has been engaged in exploring the recent broad urban initiatives in New England to extend the commuter rail systems and to re-inhabit its historic town centers on the Massachusetts south coast and in Boston. This year with representatives of Twining Properties and CBT Architects in Boston who are working on this project while we are developing our own work.

JURORS

Brian Healy
Lydia Kallipoliti
Susie Kim
Alfred K. Koetter
Keith Krumwiede
Michael Kubo
John McMorrough
Kim Poliquin
Robert A.M. Stern
Alex Twining
Kishore Varanasi
Sarah Whiting

Karolina Czeczek
Kate Lisi
Central Square Cambridge

Feldman Nominees

Central Square in Cambridge characterizes a mix of programs and activities. It is said to "be messy but in a good way, where a 99-cent McDonalds and a $6.99 carrot-beet juice with wheatgrass boosters can co-exist." Central is inherently not one thing, but rather an intricate network of many, diverse parts. There is a collection of many small elements—parking lots, murals, and benches—that create their own networks. Currently they are overpowered by the large street-block-building structure. The large and the intricate are out of balance, which has created dull public spaces, limited to the linear edge of Mass. Avenue.
With our scheme we attempt to preserve Central's unique atmosphere with all its messiness and unpredictability by introducing a new urban order. A building matters but not more than the space between the buildings. The organizational porosity encourages a meandering cross-movement through the site, dissolving the linear barrier of Mass. Ave. and creating a more rich urban experience. We took elements existing on site; downplaying the role of big components (buildings, roads) and amplifying the intricate ones (trees, lamps, benches). By creating a new relation between big and intricate we achieved a place with little hierarchy; a spatial matrix capable of unifying on an urban scale while respecting the identity of its components; fields of intensity overlap, amplifying the intricate, making a tree or bench no less significant than a building.

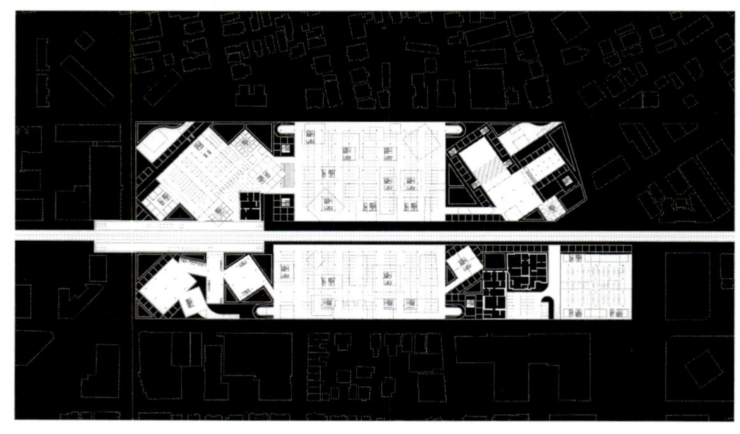

MID REVIEW

If you're densifying our cities, I don't have to get in a car and go to the mall to do my shopping. Some of the typologies that exist out there, in the burbs, have to make their way into Central Square. —Kishore Varanasi

FINAL REVIEW

Varanasi What this challenges and what Mass. Ave. already does is that it's not about the automobile; it's about the pedestrians. And for years we have sort of built this idea of the street wall that reinforces this movement of automobiles. Is that still relevant as we are moving away from the automobiles, or do you blur the edge, and you don't do it everywhere but in special places. This is where there is a giant souk and what's tremendously interesting about this is, the size of the buildings doesn't matter anymore. Nobody focuses on the size of the buildings. It's the network and the underground that makes it as an interesting strategy. So I can plunk a big loud building there and nobody gives a shit, right? So, it's not about the typology but your figure is really overpowering the form itself, which I think is a very interesting strategy.

McMorrough I appreciate the ambition and I understand that the change is in thinking about traffic but given the character... Not even the character, this isn't about ambiance. Given the throughput of Mass. Ave., is this a good candidate for this kind of approach and if it is, than how is it achieved, not just generally, but specifically?

Twining The pedestrians feel like they own it.

Mitchell You have a kind of oscillation, it's in a different degree with a kind of complex figure ground work that you and Susie do, you know, that's one technique and this is another one. That's kind of interesting and I think that lineage is worthy of some discussion. Traffic being traffic and that's important, but I think these other things in this project raises some stakes here that are interesting.

Healy I think, there's an organization of the buildings, which are random, if not arbitrary. And way finding, or how you find your way through these is interesting. You talk about the blue... I don't know how I get to the front door and know where I'm going at all. So you still rely on Mass. Ave. as an organizing device and I'm wondering whether Mass. Ave. is consistent with the random organization of figural buildings. I mean, it seems residual, that's my question. So, does Mass. Ave. really need to be there at all? Because, related to the rest of the site, how do I know where to go? I mean, I'm fascinated by being in there, and I guess at some point you'd figure it out, but it is not the traditional organization of a city along the street.

Kim But what I'm saying is that urban design is all about making value. It's really like a game of chess. If I do this, what's the result?

Mitchell What's interesting is that they actually buy out a lot of FAR by making a ground floor. They actually have a parking garage and shopping mall underneath this stuff. So they actually get close to the new FAR. You've cut through this project in certain ways the intensity reads and then it dissipates from another approach and I think that's kind of what's interesting about it. I think the more you would study the kind of perspectival looks of this, it would be ever richer; you'd keep developing that technique throughout the project.

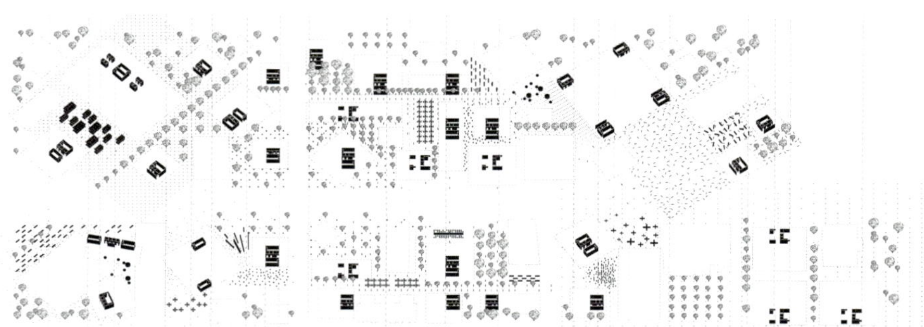

Raphael de la Fontaine
Katarzyna Pozniak
PIT

The public infrastructure terminal (PIT) acts as a public foundation, supporting and negotiating two thousand new residential units in Central Square. The PIT borrows principles from the success of Boston's great streets and vast landfill projects of the 19th Century. Utilizing the underdeveloped superblock located North of Massachusetts Avenue the project proposes a 60' deep excavation, allowing for 8 full stories of residential housing, while maintaining the relatively low elevation of the existing streets. The underground terminal is connected to the existing infrastructure of the T-stop and streets. Moreover, the terminal redefines the public realm by interlacing all degrees of public program including transportation, parking, shopping, recreational park and residential lobbies. The hybridized program creates a new active park-scape that mediates between public and private areas. An integrated cultural performance venue activates the site at night. Situated at the end of Main Street, it creates a more definitive square that is visually connected with the urban fabric across the Charles River.

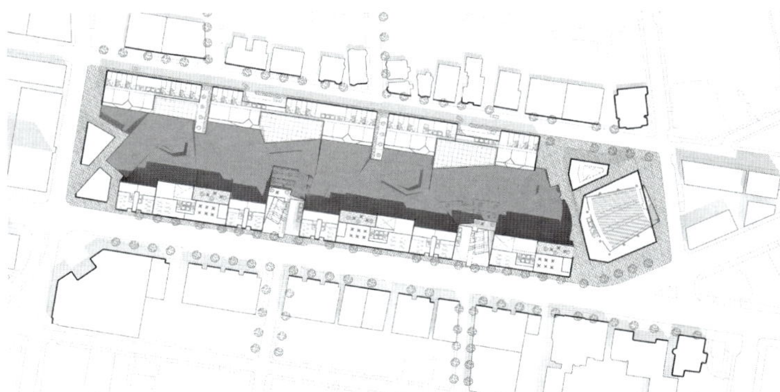

MID REVIEW

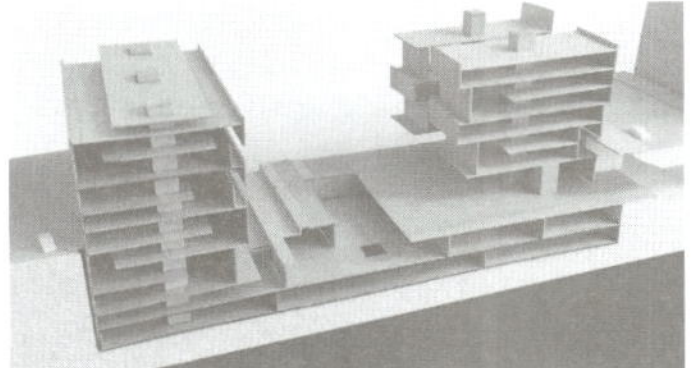

But unfortunately, you look at that and it is potentially really deadly, to overlook this massive depressed mall and really feel like it's no place you want to go. —Elihu Rubin

FINAL REVIEW

Twining You know, I think from last time when we met at the midterm, that you really pushed this a long way At the midterm, it was a bit stark and scary. It was below ground, but it looked a little daunting. But now you've made it a lot friendlier. But with all your levels and your added civic program, à la, the market, now you can start to warm up to it and understand it a lot better. What's interesting is people who live in Central Square, they complain that there's none of those bigger box uses. That they have to go to the mall, Cambridge-Side Galleria, you could actually hide them down here and fit them next to all the funky small stuff, so it really could work.

Varanasi If it's a mall, you have to get your diagram right.

Whiting Is it a mall? Is it a mall or is it not a mall?

Twining A terminal [laughs].

Kubo Actually, I think what it feels like closest to me, is actually one of those transfer terminals at the end line of an "L-Way". It's where everybody parks their car in the morning on the way to work and that's precisely where you have a supermarket and all these things because when they come back at the end of the day, they go to the supermarket before they get in their car and that's interesting.

Mitchell I think there's a reason; I don't think they're presenting this the way they should because the thing about quietness makes no sense. There's a certain pressure on the urban infrastructure of Boston to produce this new kind of space and investigate that fully, I think you've actually done that but you start talking about a quiet residential district, it isn't the same project.

Kubo But that argument makes it sound like a polemical project camouflaged by a total none polemical project?

Mitchell This is the Yale polemic project.

Kallipoliti That's exactly what I thought.

Kubo And the argument you just laid out was, its taking a suburban condition and in a radical way. Taking the suburban condition of this quasi-mall, the quiet condition of being isolated from the city and basically dumping it into the city in a very aggressive way and that induces a series of very nicely done moves to open it up, to lighten it, to stitch it in, to make the blocks kind of low, to make the blocks contextual... All the stuff that happens above it to stitch it into the urban fabric is like the non-polemical, kind of nice contextualist repertoire. But just the basic project of saying I want to put a suburban condition into Central Square, Cambridge is a polemical project.

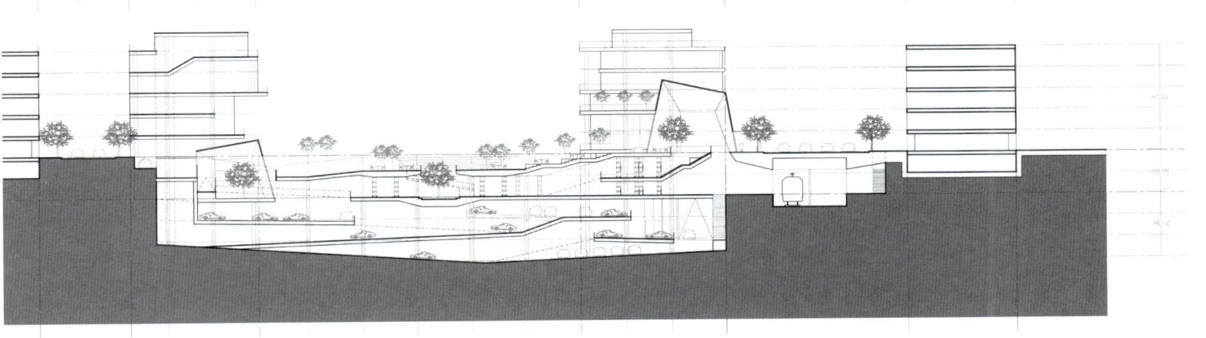

Daniel Luster
Olen Milholland
Cambridge Common

The Colonial Common was a space of everyday interaction, a place where the layers of the city could overlap—it was a place of montage. From an urban standpoint, Boston is made up of figural green spaces that are connected into networks of public spaces. Cambridge, however, lacks such a central space as the old common has been subsumed by Harvard University. Central Square—the new center of Cambridge and the intersection of three major arterial roads—is the ideal place for a new kind of public space, a new common. The overlap of people, nature, cars, shopping, and social gathering creates a synthetic environment. It is a place of the everyday. We propose a new park that splits Mass. Ave. into two one way streets, pulling it apart to make space for the park and pull it into the community. New development, in the form of linear towers hovering over the plinths of the park-scape, reinforce the edge of the park and give the new common a clear edge and definitive reading as a new central space for Cambridge.

MID REVIEW

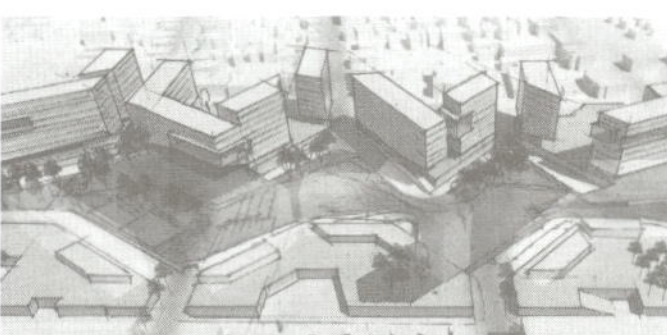

The problem with the up and down at the level you have it is that you never see. Unless you get up on top of one of the hills, which is a little more privileged and private, you don't have a sense of the overall figure as an open space. —Tim Love

FINAL REVIEW

Krumwiede Rather than just, could you have a 200 by 800 or 1,000 foot long park on the south and a 300 feet by 800 feet deep, or whatever, on the north, Mass. Ave. runs right down the middle, you have your buildings float across the top of the park and it's so easy. Your answer to Brian is we raised it so we can connect to the plinth we put on the second level. We raised this and then we had to do this to respond to the thing the thing that we already did. And I remember at the midterm, this has been the weirdest review, coming to the midterm and final, which I had never done, to realize, you might as well not have a mid-term review because no on listens to what's said at the midterm review [laughter]. So you come back and you say the same things.

Mitchell At least the diagram changed.

Krumwiede Well, I know, but I remember flipping through diagrams and going stop at this moment. So I'll shut up except for saying, everything I said at the midterm, I believe is correct.

Mitchell You're just like Bob [laughter].

Twining It seems like one of the dilemmas we had at the midterm is a couple things we talked about, some of which I think you've evolved. The difficulty in having all those edges where cars are going under, some of your renderings show some pretty interesting approaches to that. The bigger issue we had though, was you're building this amazing huge green space but you can never, unless you're at the top of one of those hills, you can never quite grasp it even as big as it is. Now, maybe that's on purpose, but it also seems it's a little bit of a lost opportunity.

Twining I think, in a way, that this is a new prototype. That's why we're all having trouble with it. I don't know if it'll work or not, but I think that that could be the applicable statement.

Kallipoliti Maybe it doesn't matter anymore what I want to say. I forgot. You're clearly very competent. Your drawings are really fascinating and your renderings. I really like the kind of flexibility of the surface that you're creating your park in a way that it both reaches the fringes of the community but it creates its own commons, as has been said. What I find a little bit less convincing is the kind of elevation of the housing which is completely detached from that commons and that kind of strange connection with what you said before, the Radiant City. This is basically a kind of hygienic project, which creates a kind of new fabric, like a cleaner version of a city. So that, to me, is a little conspicuous and what I'm lacking in the renderings is a confrontation with the real, a counterpoint where what you're suggesting comes in contact with the existing condition of the grain of Cambridge, because they all look very James Bond like.

Julcsi Futo
Read Langworthy
Urban Flotilla

Central Square is ethnically, culturally and architecturally diverse, but it lacks density and public space, and therefore lacks identity. This project harnesses the diverse forces of the site and orchestrates them to create a strong urban and architectural identity, while maintaining its multiplicity. The dialectic of diversity and identity is explored through the fine line between mega-structure and urban aggregation. Starting with identifying, framing and connecting leftover spaces on the site, the project weaves together the existing with the new structure. Through capping the building height at 86 feet the project tests how the dynamics of compression produce new kinds of shared spaces. The resultant relationship between old and new activates the previously neglected spaces—rooftops and back alleys—and creates new opportunities for urban community. What emerges is a recharged area with a great increase in FAR, allowing new residential, commercial, and collective gathering spaces, without building towers or a tabula rasa approach. Ultimately this creates a strong identity for the neighborhood and allows the existing diversity to remain, while strengthening the vitality and variety of activities that occur in the area.

MID REVIEW

Is it about a platform. At the top as a new city level or is it about this kind of organic growth that happens? Maybe it can be both, but as you move forward, that needs to be cleared. —Amanda Lawrence

FINAL REVIEW

Varanasi There's a contradiction going on. I love the scheme and we talked about it the last time too. All of your drawings there are quite fascinating until you got to the last one where you're building off of this smaller module. We're not talking about an urban renewal project of wiping it down. You can basically take the voids and start to build, but then I question your need to homogenize and connect everything into a sort of big block. Because the beauty of taking it each block by itself is that it reproduced the granularity of Central Square in three dimensions and plan but the moment you sort of connect everything as one project, that's where I have a problem. I think it's a beautiful project but then the third diagram and the forth diagram then say, OK, I'm going to just now do this...

Kubo What do you feel like you are gaining from emphasizing the parceled approach as opposed to just saying, it's going to be a much bigger block, bigger parcels or a huge mega-structure. Because it seems to me like you keep oscillating in your moves between one and the other. You talk about certain things like the whiteness of all of it, as a thing that binds it together, and that somehow masks over the fact that they are completely different facades, presumably with a lot of different materials. It seems to me every time you do a move that emphasizes the one you almost hedge your bets by the other, so I just wonder if you're pushing the parcel, what do you think is the big payoff for that decision?

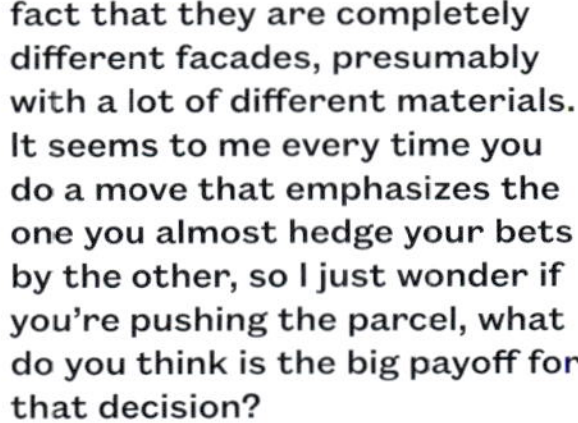

Koetter Isn't this just infill? I can understand the black and white thing, but it looks just like infill to me.

Kallipoliti Vertical infill.

Healy What's the benefit of maintaining the existing buildings, what do you get from that? Forget the reality of structure or how you build it.

Whiting They keep people like you happy [laughter].

Healy I'm not happy, I'm not happy.

Kubo Keeps the community board happy.

Twining I think the strength of the project is the tension that we're all feeling between being a mega-structure but being made out of all these fractured crazy pieces with the volume and the open spaces, to me that's the power of this. You're asking a macro question which is, is this the right place to put density in the city of Boston, right?

Healy Yes, and I was following up on Susie's, assume it happens, it's a good idea and you guys are brilliant and it works and people want to be there, what's the impact on Central Square and on the infrastructure and other things?

Mitchell Actually, this building would be interesting, not as a residential thing but something like a high school or something. Because the courtyard you've got, I never thought of that, it looks like the public high school where everybody sits out on the steps and then you could integrate those.

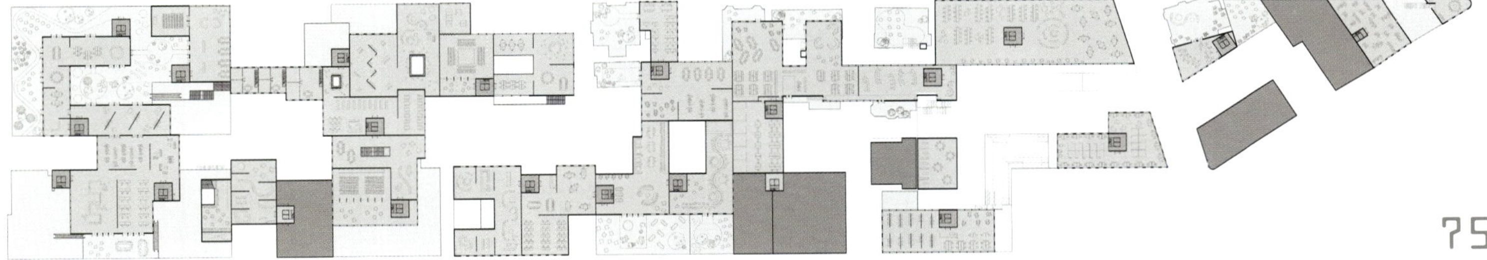

ADVANCED STUDIOS

ATHENS, GREECE

Elia Zenghelis

ZURICH, SWITZERLAND

Demetri Porphyrios

RIOJA, SPAIN

John Spence, Patrick Bellew and Andy Bow

MUMBAI, INDIA

Bijoy Jain

LOS ANGELES, CALIFORNIA

Georgina Huljich and Marcelo Spina

BEIJING, CHINA

Alan Plattus

ROME, ITALY

Peter Eisenman

HELLENIKON METROPOLITAN PARK AND URBAN DEVELOPMENT

Elia Zenghelis

The William B. and Charlotte Shepherd Davenport Visiting Professorship of Architectural Design

ATHENS, GREECE FACULTY: ANDREW BENNER

The Hellenic Ministry of the Environment, Planning and Public Works launched an open international ideas competition in 2004, for the design and urban development of the Hellenikon Park in Athens. A number of sport facilities had already been built on the site for the 2004 Athens Summer Olympics and these had to be integrated within the proposed design for the park. These are still there but to this day they remain unused and their condition is rapidly deteriorating. In 2005 the winner was announced: an international team led by architects David Sereno, Elena Fernandez and landscape architect Philippe Coignet. During the economic crisis of 2008, the Serero plan was shelved. However, in 2010, the new Greek Government commissioned the Barcelona Strategic Urban System office (BcnSus), under the aegis of Josep Acebillo, the eminent Catalan Architect-Planner and teacher, to make a new proposal.

Acebillo presented his masterplan for the Hellenikon park, as a Strategic Urban Model, in Athens, in the summer of 2011. The project, consisting of an acupuncture program of public spaces, was aimed as a socio-economic catalyst for the city-region of Athens; it proposed a reduced park of 260 hectares (642 acres, or 20647sq.ft.), conceived as a public space, connecting the sea to the neighboring districts. But, importantly, it consisted of a mosaic of urban clusters. These included primarily a high diversity of housing typologies, but also offices, retail and services to foster a Mediterranean way of life; roads and parking facilities. As neo-tertiary provision, the project encompassed proposals for a financial and governmental district near the old Saarinen terminal, an international Center for education and business, and a research and development center, related to new media technologies. Finally, it proposed an underpass connection to the sea, with public waterfront facilities, around a renewed marina.

These will be typologies that the studio will re-examine.The economic crisis, and the ensuing demise of the government sponsoring it, saw the demise of Acebillo's strategic plan and finally that of the idea of the Park, as a public resource.The current administration is now considering other uses for the space, and, neglectful of its appeal as a public resource and its potential as a fitting site for valuable social amenities, it is planning to surrender it to the exploitative prospective of the private sector and to the realm of financial speculation. This plan runs counter to the original idealism of the park and to the aspirations of both the local communities and the general public. There is a public outcry, demanding the creation of a profitable but public resource, with housing, social, educational, commercial, business and other communal facilities, set within a Public Park. The studio will intend to pick up the gauntlet and develop a project that returns to the original idea and offers new, inspired and sustainable proposals for this prime, but luckless and mishandled site.

OBJECTIVES

As already stated, the transfer of Athens airport from Hellenikon to its new site in Mesogeia in 2001, made available a large piece of prime land close to Athens, ten kilometers from the Acropolis and lying on the Saronic Gulf. The planning and management of this extensive area, 530 hectares (1309 acres, 28685sq.ft.) remains as unique an opportunity as it was before the economic crisis, for Athens to reclaim an inhabited and public green area badly needed to improve the quality of the city's environmental problems. The original aim of the competition, which was the realization of a XXI century urban park of exceptional scale and remarkable design is still valid today.

In this context, the site of the former airport in Hellenikon has the potential to operate as an urban project of international scope and at the same time be an influential measure for upgrading Athens as a renewed economic, environmental, and innovative developmental center.

JURORS

Ioanna Angelidou
Cynthia Davidson
Peggy Deamer
Monia De Marchi
Keller Easterling
Peter Eisenman
Maria Giudici
Christopher Marcinkoski
Emmanuel Petit
Marcelo Spina
Georgeen Theodore
Theodossios Issaias

Feldman Winner

Bryan Maddock
Long Center

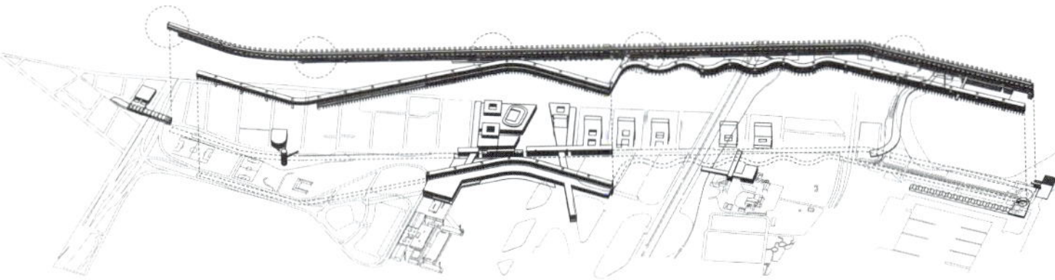

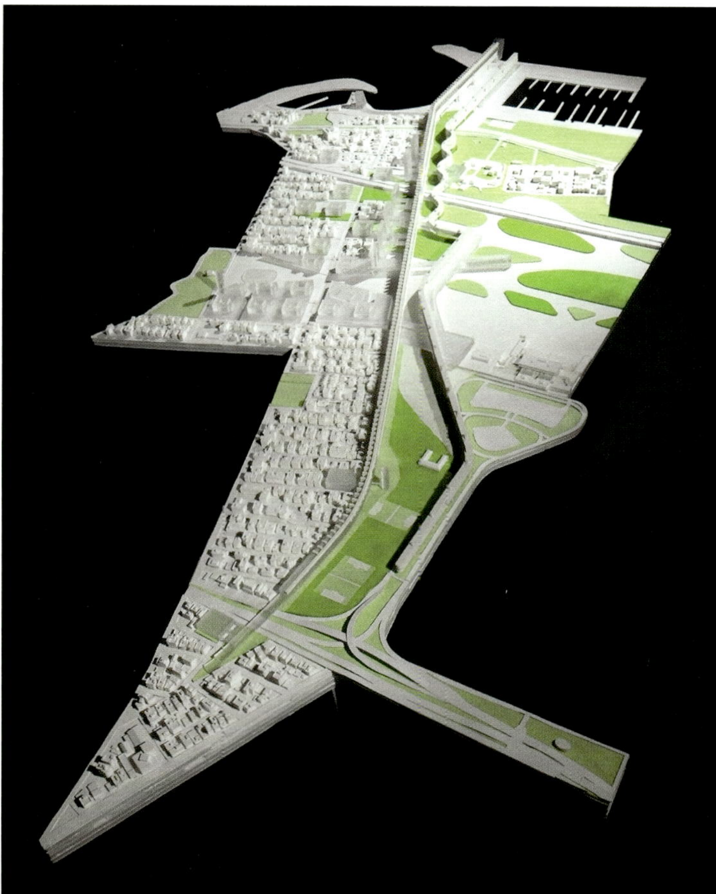

Utilizing built form as a strategic carrier of culture in opposition of the status quo, the project links the disconnected suburban mountain communities in the east with the sea to the west while simultaneously cutting the massive Hellinikon airport into distinct zones. This new linear centrality is a moment of productive tension and transition between the expansive landscape of the airstrip and the dense energetic randomness of the sprawling polykatoikia. Clear intentions and means of operation make the monumentality of the architecture an accepted and pro-active participant in the city. The long and wall-like nature of the architecture evokes imagery of the 'Long Walls' of Ancient Greece that connected Athens to the port city of Piraeus, while simultaneously presenting itself as a modern day stoa and processional urban experience not unlike the Acropolis or the ancient city of Delphi. As a pair of long buildings, the two housing lines converse across a newly established and hybridized linear park while opportunistically enhancing and introducing shared programs along their lengths. The parts and the overall strategic form collectively constitute a city that fearlessly and optimistically reintroduces an architecture that can generally be a more important and vital force in our lives while countering any preconceptions we may hold of what a city may be.

MID REVIEW

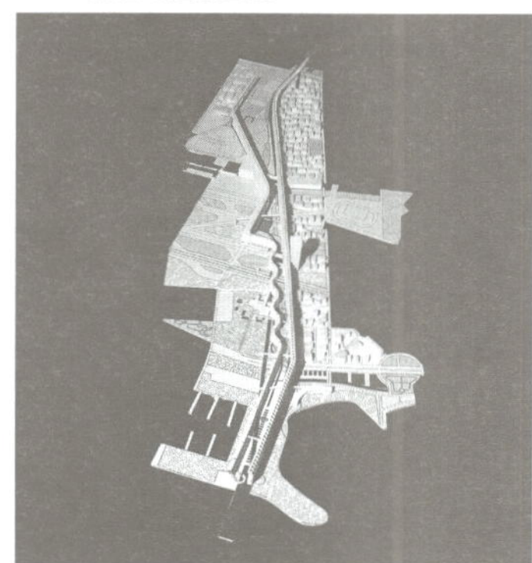

I think it's a superb scheme but I expected the project to have something to do with the shore line. Either you find a relevant urban point to connect to the water front or this is the right scheme in the wrong place. It seems to me the wiggly line, formally is very well done, but it's a little bit like Brazilian modernism. In Brazil, it looks like this because it's related to the topography or to the mountains, here it's not. It seems like a formal device and one that's not multivalent. —Emmanuel Petit

FINAL REVIEW

Eisenman You know you really don't have to say anything. It's a very clear project and the more you talk the less excited I am about it. I can imagine a lot of exciting things going on. One of them is, you haven't used the runway so bravo for going against the conventional wisdom. It's the first project that connected inboard neighborhoods to the sea in a reasonable way. Connection to the south of the site is significant.

Giudici It's also very strong by doing very little. There's a lot that you're just letting be.

Marcinkoski If they got chopped and it wasn't two buildings but it was 20 buildings, 50 buildings, but they were all aligned in the same way, is it the same project?

Maddock No, I think that especially with the prompt of the studio, the idea of proposing a big building that can act as a city is a strong idea to go forward. I think that you do have to propose a mega gesture in a project like this to provoke interest in questioning the city.

Marcinkoski The reason I ask is when you really look at it you have a lot of different segments. I think you can have the same project that is equally provocative and robust that clears out this part of the city and reinsert something into it that doesn't have to be a singular building, it could be an accumulation of things and from my point of view works exactly the same way.

Deamer What I like about it is the twoness of this. The twoness is essential and that is part of the playfulness. It seems to me that once you have two of them you're giving yourself a new formal type. Also, how you begin and end the thing is an issue. This is not how I would end it nor is this where I would end it. I would give more thought about that particular destination.

Spina Your presentation is great but I would like to know what the drawings are a little bit more.

Eisenman No one knows what your students drawings are for sure, so why do you need to know?

Spina Just my nature. I do agree with the comment that maybe in the seed of the project there's intelligence and an attitude towards the linear but it doesn't mean that it has to be one building. It could be a number of things. In fact intuitively you've made the differences and that could naturally happen if there was more lateral engagement similar to the other side. To me what's interesting is the attitude towards the rest of the site, that this thing could not only be the project but could also be an attitude towards other parts, it could be shorter but function in a similar way. You said this is not a 21st century project. It takes on multiple typologies; it's not just a bar.

Zenghelis It's not so much a question of whether its presented for any particular century, I think its whether it's socially relevant.

Eisenman The real question I have is at what point would this building become too long? I think he's very lucky that the ocean is here.

Petit I am bogged by this discussion about this thing of "now". There's a sense that there's no pure form but it is composed of multiples. I find it very different from some of the generic forms we've seen, which I would locate in historical time at a certain moment. I find it very of now, because of the multiple typologies. If you just take this form, we've seen it, we've seen this elbow shape we've seen the line, we've seen the double line. It's never been seen composed this way.

Swarnabh Ghosh
Tactical Stitching

The project stitches together the three distinct landscapes of the site to create connections between them while preserving and making apparent their distinctness. An infrastructural plane undergoes a series of transformations to function variously as pier, ramp and volume, absorbing existing infrastructure and negotiating topographical variation. The plane 'thickens' to accommodate energy infrastructure and communal workspaces, and is anchored by large housing slabs which accommodate public program at their lower levels. The base of the slabs as well as the surrounding structures perform the role of programmatic knots that accommodate convention and exposition spaces, institutional facilities, cultural facilities and park infrastructure such as greenhouses and nurseries. A series of slabs are introduced to the eastern edge of the site, one of which plugs in to the Saarinen building.
The combination of the horizontal plane and vertical slabs define physically, as well as visually, the boundaries of the site, orchestrate public activity and intensify the experience of the vast open space occupied by the runways. A third typology, the mat, is introduced on the waterfront, which is reshaped and houses an artificial beach, series of conditioned pools, a new marina as well as desalination and purification infrastructure. As the largest and one of the last remaining publicly owned sites in Athens, Hellenikon is representative of a potentially powerful public center for the city and this project attempts to recast it as a decidedly public park for the citizens of Athens—a large scale assemblage of public infrastructures nourished by intense habitation and activity.

MID REVIEW

You're relying heavily on axonometric and plan. You could actually contrast the notational medium of the flat second dimension that gets the cross section to expose this kind of social depth, so you're forced to collage in a hybrid of new and existing landscape and program. —Joeb Moore

FINAL REVIEW

Giudici You're justifying your choices with functional or pragmatic reasons which is fine but in a way it needs to be more aggressive and less polite. My big doubt is about these slabs. Are they always the same element? Because when you explain how you placed them it makes sense functionally, but when I look at the model spatially I wonder what kinds of experience you imagine creating.

Ghosh I think the idea behind the slab was to use a fairly ubiquitous housing type to orchestrate certain things that would happen in the band. I think it was a way to create series of edges for things to happen in them without really dealing with the inside.

Marcinkoski Is it intended to be something that structures future occupancy or is it a fixed idea? If it is fixed, it's problematic, but if it's understood as an armature and infrastructure for transformation there's potential there. I don't think you've grasped that potential.

Deamer I'm wondering how you did these renderings and believe that you weren't doing a scheme that is anti-urban because these are so unbelievably empty it seems you completely enjoy the untouched condition and the emptiness.

Spina I think it's a super challenging and complex problem. The scale is just really hard to grapple for any architect so I have to give you credit just for the fact that you did something here. [laughter] I sense that having gone there, being on site, being on the runway, it was probably quite shocking because you seemed to have fallen in love with the possibility of the site to actually remain empty. There's something quite dystopian about it. My view is that when you're working at a scale like this, you can't pick and choose reality; you have to take it as a whole or you have to dismiss it. The reality is that the concrete is there and it's too complicated to try to turn it into a park, another reality is that I don't want to live in that slab and feel like I'm in Russia before the wall came down.

Zenghelis It's true, when one is there, you're struck by the kind of other worldliness of the place, and this other worldliness is what one wants to keep because it's really quite striking.

Petit I think this project at some point stops being able to be discussed as an architectural project and it becomes a political social project. I've seen these projects in many places. They are very charming but they are ruins of a social system that has collapsed. You seem to enjoy that ruin. Maybe that is your political take on this, to revive this kind of socialism. I wouldn't want to live in one of those but I can see how for an architect its super sexy to design a slab like that.

Easterling Could you look at that and imagine that this is not really a fixed composition but it's just a cross section, a string which other things crystalize? That's not what this is but with half closed eyes, you look at it in a slightly different way out of the land of architectural myth and imagine it in Athens.

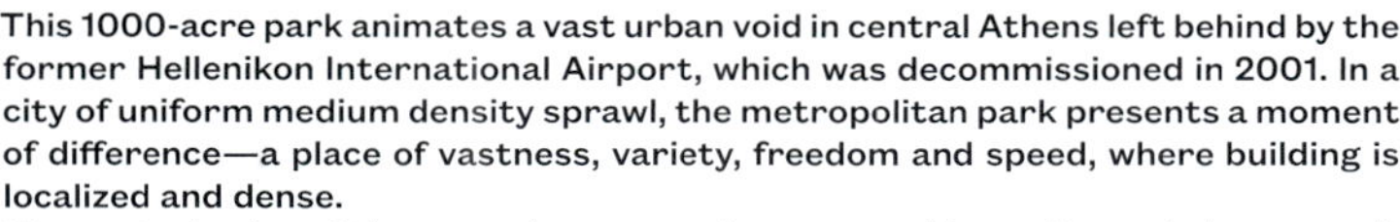

Alice Tai
Violette de la Selle
Hellenikon Metro Park

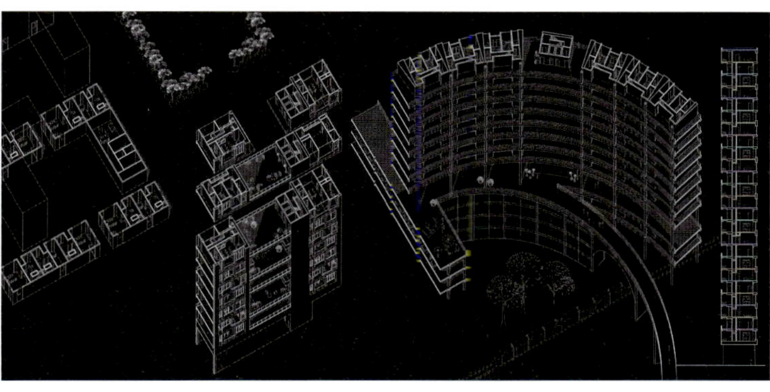

This 1000-acre park animates a vast urban void in central Athens left behind by the former Hellenikon International Airport, which was decommissioned in 2001. In a city of uniform medium density sprawl, the metropolitan park presents a moment of difference—a place of vastness, variety, freedom and speed, where building is localized and dense.

The central spine of the area, the runway, is converted into a Formula 1 racetrack, attracting the general public into the heart of the site for a spectacular event of speed and exhilaration. At the pinnacle of excitement, on the day of the race, the course occupies the full length of the runway, connecting four distinct conditions of the site: the conventional green forested park, populated by pine trees, with serpentine roads winding through them; the new residential neighborhood of the geometric sublime, where groves of trees, parking structures, courtyard houses, and high-rise apartment blocks are organized into a dynamic grid composition; the original apron of the Hellenikon airport, fronted by the Saarinen terminal, left completely empty, which becomes an attraction in its own right as a site that invites myriad kinds of occupation, from international trade shows to farmers' markets to local sporting events; and finally, the coastal road that has been relocated directly onto the runway and widened into a twenty-two lane stretch of mega-highway, which affords Athenian drivers the thrill of the race as a part of their daily driving.

MID REVIEW

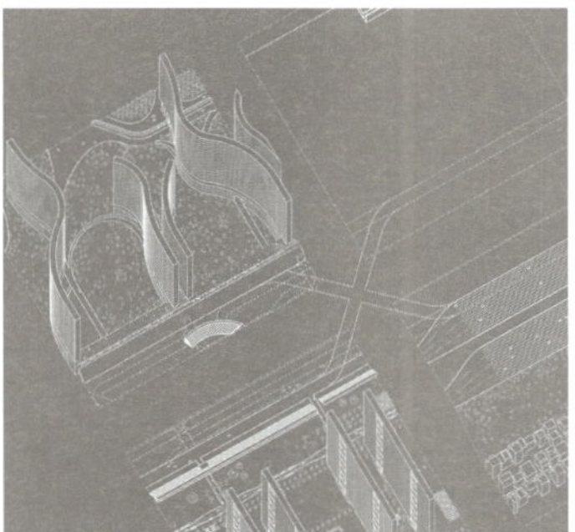

Trying to keep that runway you actually lose that monumental feature, whats impressive about it is the shear length of it and the hard definition of the edge which now has this kind of confetti of program around it. —Joyce Hsiang

FINAL REVIEW

Stern What does a project based on movement mean?

Tai Here we are with this enormous site. And we can't possibly program all of it and occupy all of it so what we're doing is providing a system which changes and that is the racecourse. That's a dynamic event but it can't be used every day so it's reconfigurable.

Stern How can you say that racecourse is reconfigurable? The one in Berlin was there before Hitler, it survived the whole Second World War without being reconfigured

de la Selle Actually it has been because a part of it has become the Autobahn. It's a part of the way you access the city. So we have moments where the ghost of the race track that's used as a Formula 1 racetrack for one week of the year becomes a part of the scenography of the road that everyone in Athens will use.

Eisenman Let me ask you a question. I used to live next to a racecourse and it was hell, a real hell. So let's assumes there's no course there. It looks to me like the same project.

Marcinkoski All of the other projects have struggled with the vastness of the site. You've actually concentrated the program and activity into a scale that is almost close to believable. When you're saying all of these little incremental pop up things are happening on the apron of a runway or a formal airport, it's hard to imagine those registered because they're so small. whereas in that space you've defined that is quite concentrated, you can totally buy that these things would happen there. If you have 50,000 people living on that, you can imagine a public sphere that would occur in that area. It has nothing to do with the race track.

Stern What you don't have is a simple diagram of how you thought the site could be organized and maybe that's the problem. For me, this is very picturesque; it's filled with tropes from LeCorbusier's projects. Filled with certain romantic notions he had about driving on roofs of buildings and things like that and that's okay, I love revival. I love revival architecture. [laughter] But you're not saying that this is LeCorbusier's idea, this is how we did it, and this is the diagram. It's just a bunch of stuff.

Petit What I find crazy is that you get the same criticism that you got at the midterm. I would not sell it with Formula 1. The idea that's most interesting is the diagram where you take that longitudinal space and then dock on a series of different structures. You should say it could be Formula1, but it doesn't need to be. That axon could be the beginning of a very metropolitan building. The idea that you have a plinth filled with probably commercial stuff, then you can walk or drive on top of that, and then you have residential above, that's very metropolitan as a typology. These buildings here could become less slab-in-a-park and more slabs in a complex relationship with plinths and topography, reorienting them to that central space.

Stern I don't think buildings are boats that get docked. I don't think people want to live in that condition of urbanism if they had a choice, and I think urbanism is more complicated. It's perhaps less neatly diagrammed but it can be diagrammed.

Theodore One of the things that we haven't really seen in any other project is the way that you've used time and thought about occupation. You've created a series of public spaces that can be used by other people in the city which we haven't seen yet.

EMBASSY OF THE CONFEDERATION OF EUROPEAN STATES Demetri Porphyrios

Louis I. Kahn Visiting Professor

ZURICH, SWITZERLAND **FACULTY:GEORGE KNIGHT**

Over the years, I have spoken extensively about architecture as the representation of construction and use. This semester, my design studio will focus on architecture as the representation of venustas. An ancient preoccupation of architecture and a term imbued with various meanings—proportion, beauty, propriety, social meaning, symbolism—venustas invariably reveals the priorities, values, sense of judgment, and aspirations of a given culture and period. In all cases venustas demonstrates the power of ideas and their ability to change and regenerate society.

The background of the studio's narrative is that the European Union, as we know it, will in time dissolve and reconfigure itself as the Confederation of European States. The embassy of this confederation in Europe will be located in 'neutral' Switzerland and will comprise a research and development, financial and cultural centre. The embassy buildings will be located in Zurich.

JURORS

Thomas Beeby
Kent Bloomer
Kyle Dugdale
Bryan Fuermann
Bijoy Jain
Marianne Khoury-Vogt
Barbara Littenberg
Alexander Purves
Jaque Robertson
Robert A.M. Stern

Feldman Nominee

Ann Morrow Johnson

Embassy of the Confederation of European States

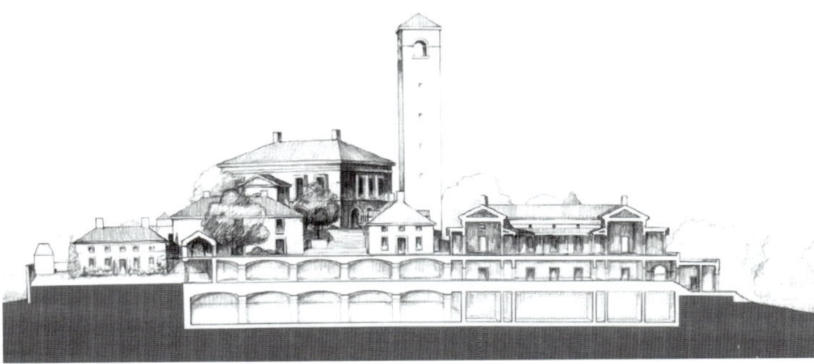

The project called for an embassy of an imagined Confederated States of Europe to be located on a lakeside site immediately south of Zurich's center. In an effort to straddle the conflicting priorities of maintaining public access to the park and establishing an appropriate level of security for the embassy grounds, the project proposes a sectional organization. The ground level is public; it allows pedestrians to continue along a waterfront path that hugs the lake-shore all around Zurich. The majority of the park remains public and is supplemented with formal gardens, food, beverage, and retail venues, and street access. Lastly, from the waterfront path the public can access a belvedere, which provides sweeping views of the lake and Alps beyond but which also announces the presence of the embassy as one approaches from downtown Zurich.
The embassy itself is raised several stories up from ground level, which allows the considerable service and security requirements to be tucked below grade while the buildings themselves are provided views of the surrounding landscape on multiple levels. The buildings making up the embassy surround a central urban square which opens towards an upper plaza and the embassy's Events Hall. This placement allows the embassy's most public spaces to maximize waterfront views and overlook the public spaces below.

MID REVIEW

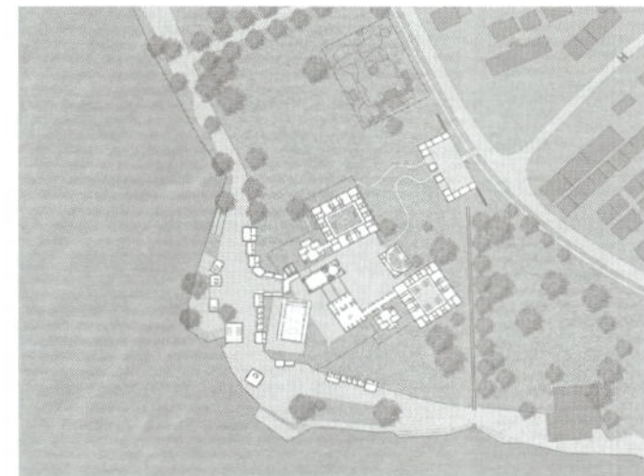

Since the whole thing is built up, a citadel, why not do that with elements of the composition rather than moving earth? —Elia Zenghelis

FINAL REVIEW

Bloomer It is so refreshing to see manual graphite drawings and watercolors. You have to grant that it is a domestic typology, which in fact is precisely what makes it work. If you were to go back into the history of large, important government buildings they traditionally followed the domestic type.

Robertson What is nice about this little model, is that you can almost guess the country that it might be coming from. It looks like it could've been something that you pulled out from down in the village, which is what you want. You don't want this parking flown in on the express. It looks like this could be Switzerland.

Porphyrios And it can be Europe. If there is an essence, a kernel of what Europe is really about, it is really that moment of feudal Europe actually becoming nineteenth century mercantile Europe. That moment will never get lost. You managed to do that without referring to specific styles. From a distance it looks and smells like Europe, but it could be any style. I've been telling people, do the massing, forget the detailing. The massing is how a person from a distance affects you. You remember a person for another reason—the gait. But buildings don't have gaits, they're static.

Khoury-Vogt A lot of students have talked about the importance of the promenade, but not a lot of people have spoken about how this ties to the existing fabric. I can't imagine a building that would turn its back to that, and you deal with that very nicely by having these three streets that meet in a pretty simple building, and that then disperse you into the rest of the site.

Porphyrios I also appreciate that it's a-stylor. It is basically a box with windows and a couple chimneys and a front door.

Bloomer But not a-typological. Children will draw that house.

Beeby I wonder about the base. The base structure is out of scale. The windows are too small.

Stern What you should've drawn is an elevation, which is not a section. A real elevation.

Porphyrios What is fantastic is the plan has this slight turn, so nothing is square, nothing is oblong. That actually gives life to the spaces. That brings me to classical antiquity, which is not a strategy of establishing ceremonial spaces, but of using the buildings themselves to make the spaces. One may actually think this is a court. But it is made by the location of the buildings.

Jain What's interesting here is in the dimension there is an ambiguity. The building that sits on top, when you look at that plan, has a different structure from the other footprints. There is that continuous scale shift between plan and section and elevation.

Purves I'm wondering about the enlargement of scale, suddenly going up to the scale of the larger buildings, using exactly the same fenestration patterns of the smaller ones. Is that intentional? It's very abrupt. Look at the final model, which is very crude in comparison to the drawing. It makes you wonder whether the model is being built at two different scales.

Robertson In the end, you will begin to think about, don't spend money on this, spend it on that, because that's much more important. You say, how can I do that parking garage dumber. I'm serious. Push it in the landscape? But this is nice to finish on because the style is still unidentified. There are actually Palladian elevations in it. The virtue of Palladio is that he never dies. All the best New York buildings were built before the Second World War. Most of the stuff we've built since is junk. This is a heart lifting conclusion with Demetri, who is really good at what he does.

Jon Swendris
Embassy of the Confederation of European States

The newly formed United States of Europe has decided to build its first embassy in neutral territory on a prominent parcel of land in Zurich, Switzerland. Located along the large lake that surrounds the city known as the Zürisee, the Embassy is to serve primarily as a private complex in a very public area. The main components of the program include a lecture hall, library, event space, housing for ambassadors and administrative space.
Following extensive research into the deep structure of the courtyard building type—tracing variables such as size, proportion, porosity and development—as well as the organization and history of Swiss urbanity, the embassy is formed around a series of interior courtyards that expand and contract along a central axis. These courtyards range from private and intimate to grand and ceremonial. The entire complex is situated on its own 'island' a 215 meter by 60 meter landmass that makes a historical nod to prominent, albeit smaller barges that once lined the banks of the Limmat River. Locating the complex on its own piece of land also prevents the embassy from disrupting the kilometers long linear park that wraps the periphery of the Zürisee. This precarious position alleviates the burden of immediate, physical security such that expansive colonnades and porous facades can remain open to views both within and unto the campus and the mountains beyond.

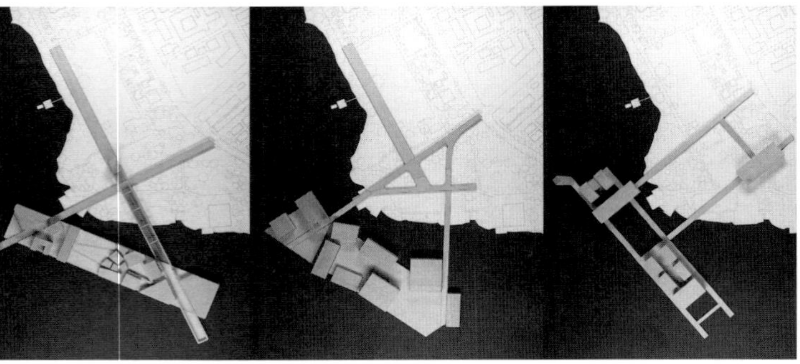

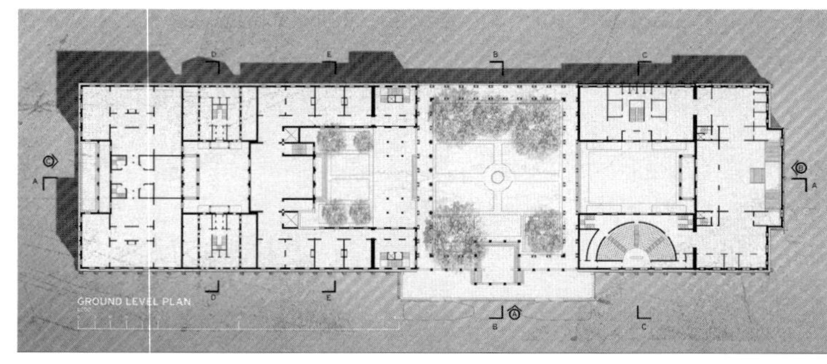

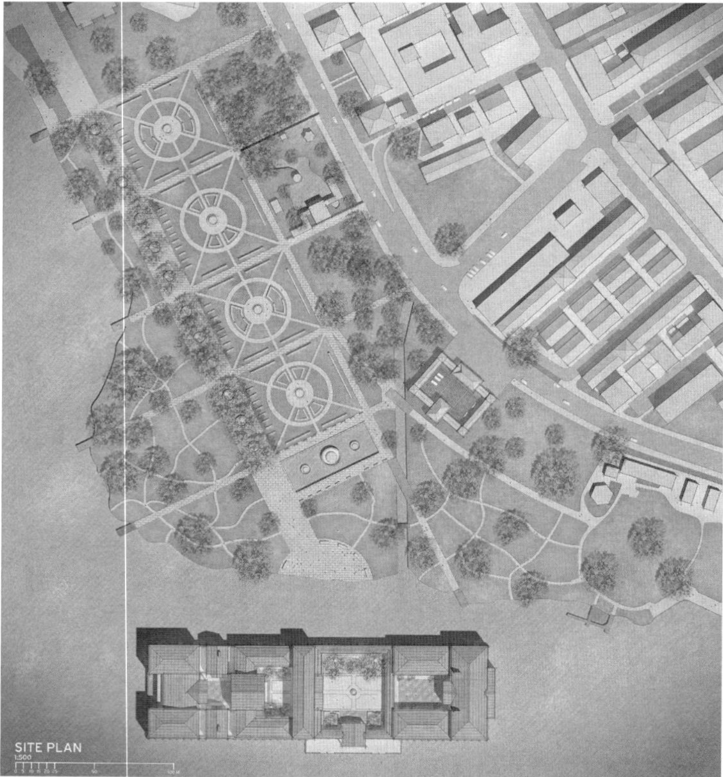

MID REVIEW

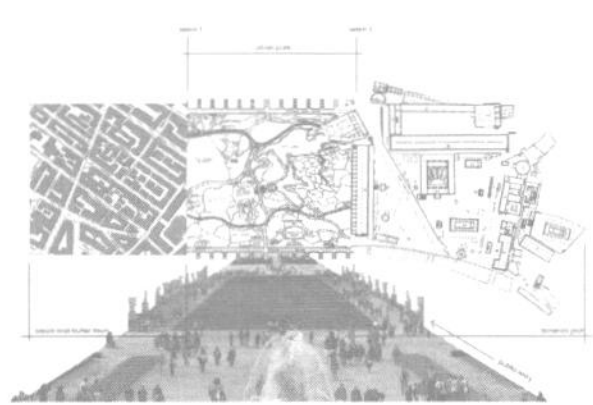

The forms on the barge or island should have resulted from the choice to locate them there in the first place. —Alexander Purves

FINAL REVIEW

Purves Where would you arrive by taxi, in the underground?

Porphyrios You can't go by taxi. Invitations are arranged ahead of time. It's like going to the queen, you know that Bob. [laughter]

Stern I have never been to the queen, but if you can arrange it I'll clear my schedule. [laughter] If you go to the White House, where I have been, you can go by taxi. You just get out of the car outside the gate.

Bloomer I'm concerned with the water. You're going to lose a tremendous amount of pageantry of going onto a boat. In that respect I don't understand why you just don't build a bridge. I think the majesty of entering this important building would be so much better. It's a funny way to approach it, from the bottom up.

Jain If you think about the Lake Palace at Jaipur, there is a very clear procession of getting to the palace through the water. There is a whole promenade, a series of pavilions and steps that you have to descend, so in a sense that's the foyer between which you have the water and the palace. Without that the building would just float away.

Khoury-Vogt I agree, and also there is something compelling in your scheme about how succinct everything is. I like the fact that it's not disparate buildings. To me the missing connection is how the land connects to the building.

Beeby I have a question about the roofs. Why did you decide to articulate the roofs as separate buildings? You could have done one building.

Swendris We studied what made up the core qualities of Euro-pean-ness in towns all over Switzerland. We all gravitated to the accumulation of different buildings that have accrued over time and that create residual spaces, not all based on the same plan.

Littenberg But this is built all at once.

Purves And why is that considered better?

Stern I wouldn't have looked at any architecture in Switzerland. This happens to be in Switzerland, but it is the united nations of Europe. I would look at the great civic buildings of the cities that would be part of this new association.

Dugdale The project as a whole would be stronger if you could make the connections between the three elements more explicit, so that each one gave some sort of clue as to the meaning of the other, and we were able to read this as one entire design rather than as assemblage of parts.

Littenberg I wanted that square to have something to do with the semicircle here. There is a whole promenade ending up at this circle. I would turn the axis around so that the pavilion, which is a park-like feature, is on the park, and instead of having this blank arcade you use it as a destination.

Bloomer From a nautical perspective, this looks much more industrial than governmental. This is a very typical situation in a harbor where you align your warehouses and factory moorings exactly this way. It's an easy thing to have happen when you're building on the water's edge, because that's where the industry was until very recently. That's a typical, almost garden variety Gloucester, Massachusetts elevation.

Stern You know, the Beaux Arts system was really good, because you would have to come up with a scheme in 12 hours, and you could not depart from that for 6 or 12 weeks. You'd stick with one idea and develop it. That's a remark for the end. Here there is too much time churning around and not enough time developing the building, which is what architecture is about.

David Burt

Embassy of the Confederation of European States

As an embassy located along a 4.5 km lakeside park in the heart of Zurich, this project has a responsibility to be completely private and secure, as well as public and free. This concept is at the heart of the project, which explores the creation of the first embassy of the theoretical United States of Europe. By organizing the buildings on a series of plinths, both security and access became possible. A formal square marks the center of the project, with the Chancellery and Consulate defining its edges. Each of these buildings is connected to their corresponding ambassadorial residences through a formal garden. On a lower plinth, and adjacent to the central square, is a less formal urban space that contains the more public programs of the embassy: library, art gallery, and event hall. This space opens up toward the lake and city park, and provides the possibility of interaction between the private and public aspects of the site.

MID REVIEW

It doesn't seem like there is a hierarchy from the secure areas, how people filter across the site. —George de Brigard

FINAL REVIEW

Robertson I'm kind of at a loss. Embassies are very specific building types. This is almost like the embassy is but a device to have other interesting buildings, like your library and museum. I just don't get any real feeling of the purpose of your embassy, although they're nice drawings.

Stern The embassy building, while it's centered on the garden, seems rather casually located to the entrance square, and indeed the entrance to the building doesn't exactly sing in your plan. In other words I suppose the criticism you're being hit with is it's a lovely scheme for a park with little pavilions in it, but it's not convincing as an embassy building.

Khoury-Vogt When I first got Demetri's program, I struggled with the fact that an embassy almost needs to be like an enclave and a fortress, and on the other hand it has a clear public function. How are you responsive in any way to the existing fabric of the town, which is quite beautiful, and secondly, to the public functions of your project, which are in many ways the more interesting spaces where people will gather.

Littenberg You've chosen to take one of the four constituent elements of the program, which was spaces for social events, and atomized that program into a series of activities and pavilions which have an overlapping purpose, or shared use, with the embassy itself. If you're saying it's a garden scheme, are the basic functional units organized as a kind of checkerboard plan, where you pass from one pavilion through a public space to another? How would the ambassador get to his office? He would drive. He would go around and be dropped off.

Porphyrios But that has been very common until the beginning of this century. People had umbrellas and coats. All of that is nonsense with all due respect. That it has to be packaged into some sort of conveyor belt is an Americanization of his scheme.

Stern Demetri I hate to disagree with you but Palladio used arcades.

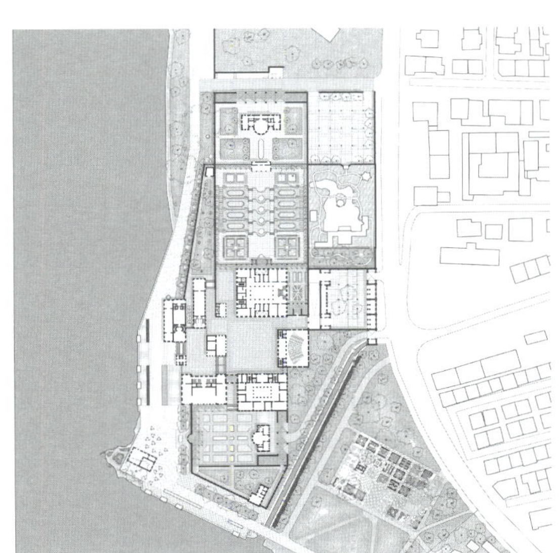

Eleanor Measham

Embassy of the Confederation of European States

The project deals with the rich and diverse cultural influences from the composite member states by framing spaces for exhibition and performance of each nation's cultural heritage. There is a degree of implied neutrality in the construction and design that denies the adoption of any architectural 'style' or specific national traits whilst offering a framework to house requisite political, social and cultural events. The building complex is situated in a park on the lake front of the Zürisee where the program is distributed between carefully composed buildings. These buildings are arranged dependent on internal programmatic relations and connection to the park and city beyond.

This complex opens up the clandestine activities associated with government deals and closed-door politics. The courtyard layout surrounding a public gathering space allows the visitor to see all buildings at once, whether publicly accessible or not. Each building is directly tied to the neighboring parkland and the greater landscape of the lake and extended views. The visitor access is necessarily limited, but there is an openness and transparency to the design and organization of program that challenges preconceptions of the traditional impenetrability of a typical embassy building.

MID REVIEW

The security issue is what you're really trying to solve in this extreme case of public/private interaction. —Anne Fairfax

FINAL REVIEW

Porphyrios There are no shows there. Theater in the classical manner is the place to be seen. All of those things you call entertainment are what the embassy does to introduce and agree upon contracts. All of those people are invited specifically by the government, they show up, and by the end of the visit, which might take a year or an hour or two, a contract can be made. And then there are meetings in which they sort out the details. When you go to the Queen, you just have to make an appointment like three months ahead, and if you manage to make the appointment, they know everything about you, more than you know yourself. [laughter]

Robertson There are a lot of things about your proposal that are very nice, but one of the last things one would do is go out on the water, because one of the great things about the end of that vista is you see it's a park. If you saw a big blob of a building out there it wouldn't be anywhere near as appealing.

Littenberg You talk about the buildings integrating into the landscape. And there are a lot of walls that are extensions of the building. Is that what you're talking about? Retaining garden walls that attach the buildings to the landscape? I would argue that one of the dilemmas is these things are all autonomous whole objects. It tends to look like somebody came along and did a bad addition, it's just sort of glued on. I'm asking if it's not a conceptual issue, and if there's something about the bases of these buildings that maybe has a horizontal continuity that works with the garden walls but also allows them to pull into the architecture.

Porphyrios This is a fantastic scheme. I learned something in school, the more people praise you, they don't understand. When you critique someone, you have to be very clear why you're critiquing. Praise—this is beautiful, and this and that—is not specific. Beware of those bringing praise.

A SUSTAINABLE BODEGA (WINERY) AND HOTEL COMPLEX John Spence Patrick Bellew and Andy Bow

Edward P. Bass Distinguished Visiting Architecture Fellow

Eero Saarinen Visiting Professors

RIOJA, SPAIN FACULTY: TIMOTHY NEWTON

The students will be tasked with the design of a medium sized Bodega that will produce wines to the Biodynamic standard in the Rioja region of northern Spain, capable of producing up to 500,000 bottles of red and white wine per annum. Attached to the bodega (or related to it) will be a 4/5 star hotel comprising 30–40 rooms, together with a restaurant of approx. 100 covers, a bar, spa, business and medium sized conference facilities and potentially some sports activities.

Independent from the hotel the bodega will have visitor facilities in the form of a presentation space, tasting room and retail outlet to facilitate wine tours around the property so that visitors get a clear understanding of the processes involved, the seasonal nature of the activities and the time needed to make great wine. Additionally the Bodega could include an attraction designed to encourage visitation and tourism, and be in keeping with the concept of wine, or the region. (e.g. a museum, an amphitheater for concerts, local produce production facilities such as cheese or chocolate etc.) As part of the project the students will also be asked to develop branding and marketing materials for their Bodega.

FOCUS AREAS

To expand on the three points above, the studio critics will particularly focus on the following in the delivery of the project:

1. Innovative and beautiful design which should be inspiring to visitors but relevant to the local area and climate, and to Rioja and wine in particular.
2. Environmental respect and sustainability. The design must be centered around the development of a design proposal that addresses issues of social, economic and environmental sustainability design in a holistic and integrated way.
3. Commercial viability, both in a PURE operational sense, but also from a point of view of being able to attract visitors and have an element of uniqueness about it.

WHY RIOJA?

Wine has been produced and consumed in the Rioja region since pre-Roman times, and has always had a strong focus in society, not only as a drink but also through religion, celebration and community. The region is stunning and provides a magnificent backdrop for any architectural project.

RIOJA TODAY

Spain is an extremely fragile economy at the moment and has an unemployment rate of over 25%. This is particularly bad and visible in rural areas, and Rioja is no exception. Many once thriving traditional villages are now virtually deserted and the proud Riojans struggle with a lack of employment and a need to move to the cities.

The region needs to rely more than ever on its 2 strong USPs: the famous wine trade and its attractions as a tourist destination. Students will be encouraged to consider the need to create a facility that supports both of these activities, thus producing employment and helping maintain community and local activity and opportunity.

THE SITE

John has identified a beautiful site on one of the greatest Estates in the region, the Dinastia Vivanco near to Haro, and has identified a parcel of land in a stunningly beautiful location with a backdrop of a church, a hill, rows of vineyards, and the river Ebro which will be as the location for the design project.

JURORS

Michelle Addington
Deborah Berke
Anthony Fieldman
Dana Getman
Georgina Huljich
Mark Loeffler
Joeb Moore
Alan Organschi
John Patkau
Demetri Porphyrios
Amir Shahrokhi
Hugo Urquiza
Mark Simon

Feldman Nominee

Katie Stranix
Bodega Aldea

Tourism is one of the major energy-consuming sectors, placing a heavy burden on local economies, cultures and environments. I was interested in alleviating this problem by creating a self-sustaining bodega/hotel complex whose architecture is strongly rooted in the physical and cultural context of Rioja. The winery acts as a central organizing element, much like a cathedral or a public plaza, upon which the rest of the complex aggregates.
The building acts as a marker within the landscape to simultaneously attract visitors and relate to the architecture and social spaces of neighboring medieval towns. The complex additionally contains a conference center, restaurant, spa and hotel ensuring commercial viability during the offseason. Tourism becomes tied to production through programmatic adjacencies, exposing visitors to the inner workings of the bodega.

MID REVIEW

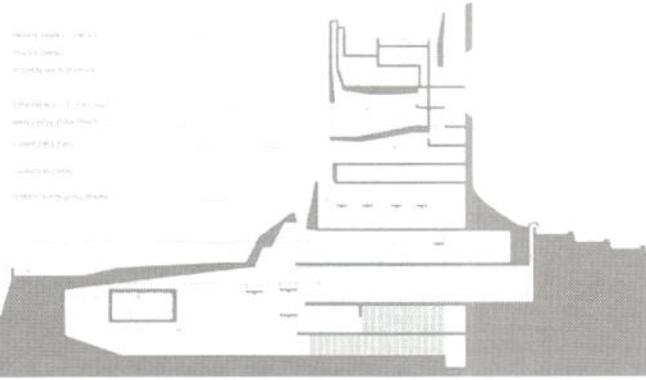

The tower is very churchy. It reminds me of Firminy by Le Corbusier. You have to do something to the tower to give it some sort of dimensional reading. —Robert A.M. Stern

It talks about the larger process of why you would want to make an icon. You recognize the icon would refer to the winery. The fact that it is mute, I really appreciate. I like its stumpiness and that it comes from the Earth. —Peggy Deamer

FINAL REVIEW

Loeffler I made a note when you finished up your midterm that it needed vernacularization. I think that you are downplaying it a bit, but you are realizing the ecology of a Spanish or Mediterranean village.

Simon This is terrific. I really appreciate the clarity. I appreciate the effort to fit into the landscape even though you are trying to be iconic. It looks Spanish to me. It wouldn't fit in in Denmark or Sweden.

Fieldman It looks a little like Morse and Stiles to me [laughter]

Organschi So, I don't mean to be mean, but I'm really confused by what motivates the architecture. You originally had this idea of the landscape swooping up, the vines disappearing into this stone, and that diagram of the climb in the landscape. Yet, I don't really understand if it is not an icon, why you have a tower. I really appreciate the thoughtfulness of the different moments, they are really good, but how do they accrue? What do they produce?

Huljich To me what you tried to do from the midterm until now is remove the tower from its idea of monumentality by cutting windows. What I really appreciated at midterm—yes it could have been a church, but who cares—was that it was so robust, so monolithic. Now everything has started to be broken up. A monolith or this very robust form that was so important to me in the midterm has now started to suffer this surgery. That is the type of negotiation where you do not concede and say, no, I cannot cut a window. A monolith does not allow me to cut a window. How do I solve this? You can start to rearrange the program.

Patkau Is the notion of a monolith essential to the concept of this project?

Huljich No, no, no I don't think so.

Fieldman John I was going to ask if the monolith or the icon is a concept.

Patkau The point I am trying to make is the stone that is so evident in your drawings is wallpaper, something you simply applied to the surface. It seems to me that you could have had a very legible, powerful, and beautifully experiential scheme had you stuck to principles.

Addington I feel the opposite. What I like to see is how the architecture begins to take advantage of or even create opportunities for interacting with the environment. I actually get the connection between the building and the opportunities for environmental behaviors—the gravity that comes from within the system, the breakdown of the tower into components, the terraces that create the perfect environment for clerestory lighting as well as those shaded areas.

Fieldman This is like a professional project. I am not burdened by the midterm, nor am I bothered by images of churches. It is a tower and you clearly want a marker in the landscape. In a sense, what I wish happened is you exploited the verticality to then influence some of the things I think you were interested in. You could have really taken the uniqueness of that vertical form and influenced another clear part of the studio brief and agenda.

Shahrokhi I just want to comment on the village. You went from the focus on the tower to a notion of the village. Of the villages you visited in the region and the central square, those configurations are all dependent on shading from the surrounding buildings. The central square in your village is the one place in your project you do not want to be because you are bombarded with sun and heat.

Moore I imagine it could be interesting if you understood them as two different systems; the village as an aggregation, and then tower. The problem with the tower, for me, is when you decided to put the conference spaces on the top, it went against the idea that this tower is a machine for fermentation. The whole tower is in fact about gravity and wine.

Fieldman Amen.

Ian Svilokos
Bodegas Terraplén

Terraplén translates to mean embankment, possibly earthwork, or terrace. The winery and hotel act as a natural continuation of the landscape built up and held by these walls of rammed earth, which course through the site. By using the physical substance that is not only close to the site, but is the site, the building visually expresses the project's deep connection to the beauty that is the Riojan terroir whilst being a zero-carbon, sustainable gesture.
The winery is condensed, compacted, efficient, and hidden away, while the hotel spills out into the landscape, puncturing the rammed earth walls reaching toward the light. As a guest enters into each programmatic element belonging to the hotel, he/she moves from a space within the walls, through the walls, and then into the light. Lastly, the site gives us wind. With the given topography, the wind is strongest at the ridge, rising up along the landscape from the east creating a specific microclimate. The building orients itself south to north with a thin plan, allowing the possibility for cross ventilation when appropriate and needed, while protecting the exterior public space surrounding the pool on the west from strong winds.

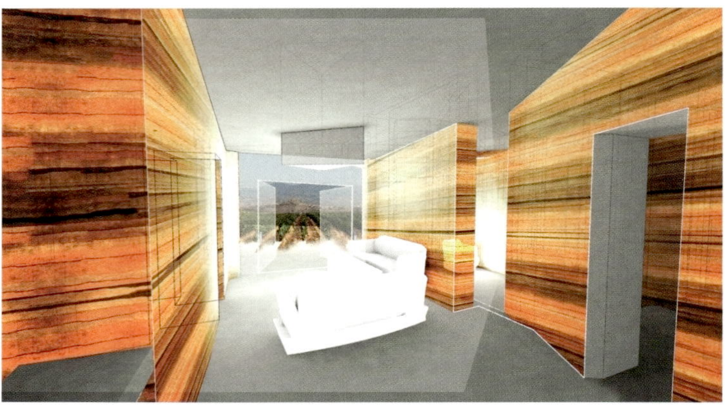

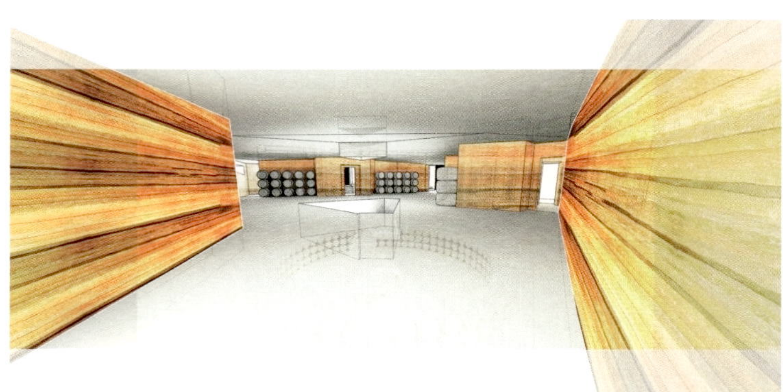

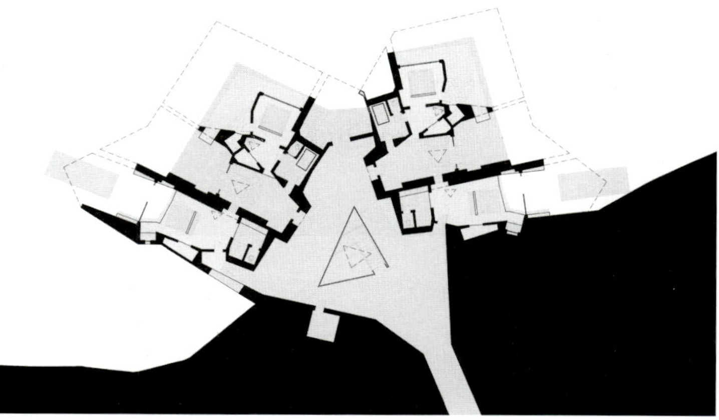

MID REVIEW

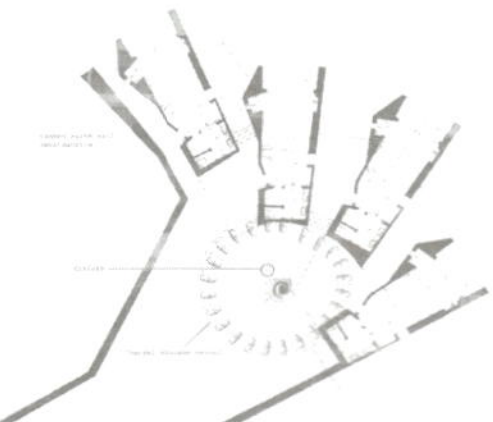

Studying the poché in plan might help. Is the line paved, a cut, or part of the earth? Then how are the hotel rooms and other spaces relating to that? Are they excavations from the line, something organically growing from it, or a little bit of both? —Dana Getman

FINAL REVIEW

Berke I feel as though you have set up a parallel relationship between the guest and the grape. This could be good, as it was I'm sure when you were in Spain. [laughter] So, the grapes come in at one end and leave as wine at the other; it is a very linear thing. But to be a hotel guest is not linear; it is circular. You leave your room for breakfast, you play with your family, you have sex with your lover, you go out for another meal, and so you go round. The line that reflects wine makes the issue of actually being here very difficult for a guest because every time I do this I am traipsing the same line. So you either say let's make the section richer so every time I take that trip I can discover something else; or, in fact, does this need to crank further so by the time I get to the end I can make my way back to the front?

Organschi We all have these internal disciplinary concerns of how to make form, what it means, and its reference to landscape and topography and I think you have really captured that well. So the idea of using thickness materially is evocative here, both as an environmental function and service, but also as an aesthetic concern.

Huljich I think, as I cannot say I like or I dislike the actual form, the clusters are working and I like the sensibility in how it is rendered in the physical model. You worked with the sensibility of adding thickness to the line at various levels, which I think is really interesting. That was a great opportunity to create a new order of rooms whose organization does not have to differ much from the other ones. They should be a little more incorporated.

Shahrokhi I would like to pick up on that point and talk about drawing a little bit. The architecture is very well described in plan. What we do not see described is the landscape in drawing form. The landscape is integral to the architecture; where lines intersect, where lines go from topography to architecture. Adopting that and working through that would have been very helpful.

Berke In missing the landscape, the lines that we are missing are the lines of the vineyard. If you had drawn those and actually explained how close those rows of grapes come to the force field of this building you created, or how they get distorted if they are running parallel to it, it would inform the creation of your exterior spaces, swimming pool, nice clusters of guest rooms, and different pathways.

Simon I think what you have tried to do is blur the edges and make your line the vine, which to a certain degree the vine is a line. I find this very beautiful, the imagery and the design is very compelling. You lose something that could be even more powerful when you take that image of the vine and the line and confuse the two.

Patkau What strikes me with this project and what is very common with student projects is the relationship between the spaces that are programmed and the spaces that are serviced and it leads to the question of the disposition of those spaces. What I see here is a very small hotel, forty rooms, which has, relatively speaking, a very large area. I'd rather see a hybrid SUV.

Organschi It's a gas-guzzling compact car.

Porphyrios I would like to congratulate you, which is actually quite rare.

Newton Hold on we'll stop there [laughter].

Porphyrios Almost when you look at it, it is as if you made up the site yourself to allow for these sorts of roots. I don't think it is a line as such, although you started with a metaphor of the line, it is really a root. You have managed to deal with this project absolutely fantastically. I really congratulate you and I wish I had been here at midterm.

Charles Hickox
Bodega and Hotel

I came to Rioja to design a structure that would architecturally integrate the production of the highest quality wines with a luxury resort. The structure can be reduced to three components: steel trusses which cradle hotel rooms, hotel restaurants, bars, offices, gym, and spa; a ground level, terraced along the terroir, that hosts entry lobbies for both the hotel reception and wine tour departures; and public exterior plazas, restaurant, and wine tasting room. Carved into the earth below, the winery drops in level, sequentially, according to the stages of the winemaking process.

MID REVIEW

It is a little bit of a catalog. The way you are materializing the scheme of the project, in that every single part is responsive to a specific problem, it needs to be orchestrated into a larger idea. —Georgina Huljich

FINAL REVIEW

Simon Well this is a dramatic gesture. If we are going to be sustainable, we have to figure out how to get this much drama without this much steel and a lot less stuff. That is my primary complaint, but it is beautiful and a very interesting concept.

Organschi This is like a Yale 1985 project, which is it combines a literary reference which is uprooted in the project with structural heroism which has no purpose other than to celebrate the form. Why do you need to have a rock concert on a flood plain?

Moore I think there are some basic moves that are smart and sensitive to where it is situated. There are moments in your project where you are setting up a very simple tension between the grata and wine production. The winery is actually in these cavernous underground spaces and the hotel, which you lofted up, in this incredible infrastructure of steel.

Huljich It is hostile. To me that brings up the issue that came up in a few projects, which is the appropriateness toward the site, towards program, and towards its peers. Now the good news, beyond that, I think it is a really competent project and well developed. If you want to get rid of the discussion about hostility, you can shift it to one of taste. There, I think it is absolutely great. I love the section on the physical model. The way that nothing is necessarily adjacent to anything else is quite smart because you are eliminating the fact that you have to deal with material adjacencies which would bring a whole new set of conflicts.

Patkau I wonder about your ambition for the epic. I wonder if you could have abandoned the steel structure and used all of the techniques of sustainability that you have referenced in your drawings to create an epic statement, which would have been appropriate to the mission of this studio.

Porphyrios Correct me if I am wrong, I think he uses epic in a totally different meaning. I asked my daughter the other day, what is epic? She said, dad you don't know? Epic is beyond cool.

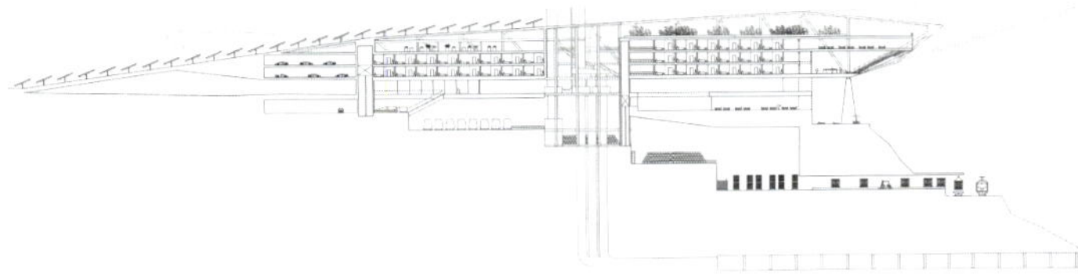

Nicholas McAdoo
Viña Luna

The cycles that occur at a winery and vineyard—those of grape-growth, biodynamics and vinification—are to a large degree governed by the movements of the sun and the moon. This project attempts to tie into these cosmological forces and the cycles they influence by adopting a circular form, which, derived from historical examples of solar and lunar tracking devices, allows for an omnidirectional orientation toward the Rioja countryside. Buried underground to take advantage of the cooler temperature is the gravity-driven winery. Suspended off the ground is a ring composed of hotel rooms interspersed with a restaurant, bar, library and tasting room. The plinth contains the spa and full moon theater and is otherwise flexibly programmed based on the time of year and the solar and lunar positions.

MID REVIEW

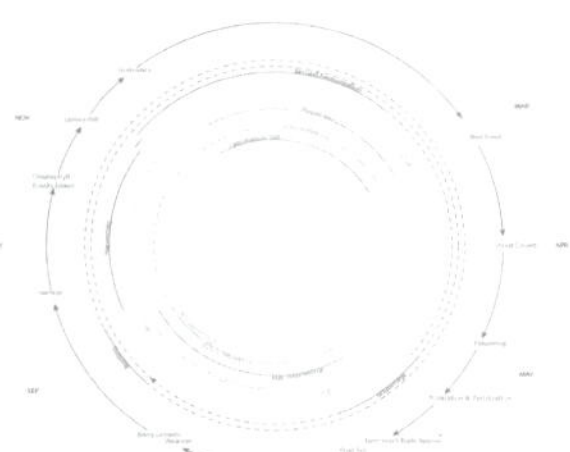

The strictness of the plinth needs to be diminished. There is a play of the offsetting trays in plan that could also occur in section. In that case, you will start to integrate the program in different ways without losing the diagram. —Georgina Huljich

FINAL REVIEW

Fieldman There is a huge amount of work and there is a clear parti. There is a lot of great strength in the clarity of it.

Getman One thing that is interesting about it that could be an opportunity is there are a lot of communal aspects to wine making in that region, but in a hotel you really want to be isolated. What could be nice about this is you have complete isolation when you are in your room, but as soon as you pass that threshold you have the opportunity for this really central space.

Simon In that same regard, I am always very dubious about raised buildings, because they are great in theory, they are great at that scale, but the experience of walking under a building like that is not very pleasant. That got me to thinking, why isn't this simply on the ground? There is this wonderful relationship between the ground and the sky. Instead of floating one above the other, you have the chance of actually embedding this circle in the ground.

Porphyrios But then he has no project.

Simon No, he has a great project!

Porphyrios He has no project because that image is really a pre-judgment in his process of design. We all have pre-judgments in our designs. We all have initial sketches.

Moore No you can still do that, just plant it on the ground.

Porphyrios No, I get that, but then it has no strength. It's not an idea.

Moore Another way to register your project is through time and less through its placeness, its form, or its shape. There would be this syncopation and connection between different cycles of time.

Organschi We could just say it is not a circle. Having said that, a circle is fine; go for it. Then make something of the temporal aspect. Then I think the project starts to get rich. There is something about this project that lacks materiality and that is powerful. I do appreciate the austerity, it is very beautiful.

STUDIO MUMBAI AT YALE Bijoy Jain

Norman R. Foster Professorship of Architectural Design

MUMBAI, INDIA FACULTY: TOM ZOOK

The architecture of water throughout India defines a spatial realm that is simultaneously sacred and mundane, private and shared, spectacular and subtle. In a history that extends back thousands of years, spaces for storing water are connected with religious structures in a tradition that seamlessly unites a spiritual consciousness with basic human activity of drinking, bathing, and washing.

Water is the essence of humanity that binds us to one another. Like animals drawn to a watering hole, human civilization is based on an ability to share water.

Studio Mumbai at Yale will travel to India to study the architecture of water. Through guided research, each student will study the atmosphere of specific sites in India and seek to represent the essence of that condition through construction of physical models made in sand, wax, aluminum, plaster, and bronze. Students will define their own method of making in various mediums as an apparatus that gives form to an experience of reality. A second model in bronze will be made later in the semester that transposes the quality of the site in India to another local site of each student's choosing where the student can conduct further research as the semester progresses. All aspects of the studio process will be documented and presented as hand crafted books. Though the work will take place in New Haven, Studio Mumbai's members and craftspeople, techniques, and resources will be made entirely available throughout the semester.

JURORS

Sunil Bald
Nancy Clark
Rod Henmi
Thomas Hsiang
Alan Plattus
Surry Schlabs
Robert A.M. Stern
Stanley Tigerman
Billie Tsien
Tod Williams

Feldman Nominee

Daniel Jacobs
Metronome

The post-industrial prairie-scape between the Farmington Canal and the New Haven reservoir provides a fertile landscape of oppositions for proposing a new live/work paradigm. The programming of the site evolved from a small-scale community foundry to an agricultural landscape of amaranth, producing the pink-red dyes for use in an associated fabric dyeing facility. Inhabitants of this world operate along the lines of the crop rows bracketed by monolithic walls—hung with drying fabrics and replete with deep red soaking pools—concealing concrete, cubic, perforated shells which contain private dwellings and public spaces within. This series of thresholds involves the spectator (the cyclist on the path, the driver on the bridge, or the passing pedestrian) in these layers of public and private life/space and allow for a glimpse into the metronome of the working residents. The primary public gathering space is located far from the urban paths, comprised of a threshing floor where the heaps of amaranth are gathered and a covered space where the plant is processed with water from the reservoir. Adjacent to the covered space, and within the raised pine forest, a path leads to an isolated descent down a staircase culminating in a landing with two large rooms, providing the working residents with access to the reservoir.

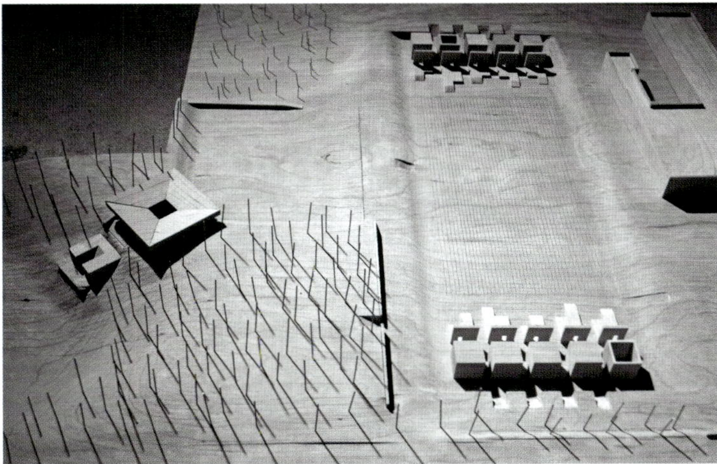

MID REVIEW

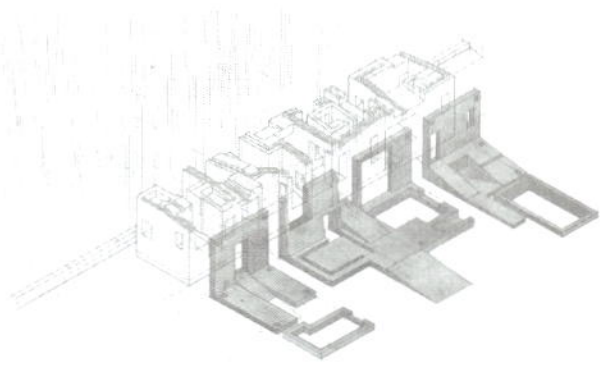

One thing I feel is the absence of the human subjects—the path on the ground in relation to these things. The missing element is the marking of the ground in a more general sense. —Kenneth Frampton

FINAL REVIEW

Tigerman Once again somebody benefitted from the trip to India, and actually came back and drew.

Stern He used to wear a coat and tie before the trip. [laughter]

Plattus I had the feeling when you were presenting that there was an element of free association masquerading as narrative. A little bit like Phillip Johnson and his site, it becomes a sort of autobiographical narrative in a way, ex post facto, so we accept its coherence at a certain level it is a life. Or is there a kind of pleasure in the fact that these things have been detached from their original purpose, so that they stand more like follies in the landscape, that have a poetic but not really a narrative dimension. The process seems to me to be incomplete in a curious way, in that what allowed you to discover the site—the canal/greenway path—has now been cast as an afterthought. On a bicycle this is a five second experience, even if you're pedaling casually, and that's not what you want.

Jain So the idea, the way he frames it, is that there are two points of entry into that space between these two concrete blocks. That's where he's allowing the possibility that it could be a five second experience, or you could spend an hour or a day. What I find curious about it is what's adjacent to that pathway. The pink wall and the pink garden are what might suggest the slowing down.

Bald I was wondering if this wall had been painted black when you got on the site, would you have made a coal mine? [laughter] It speaks to a process you've undergone of how to you riff from what you find. You saw the wall as a solid thing, so the work became a foundry. Then you stepped back and the color became the next thing to riff on. So okay, it is an amaranth field and there's communal farming. Those are really interesting ways of working, but then it's a question of what do you arrive at, when do you stop.

Tsien For me it is very important to understand how this is not a folly. As a folly, I find it very upsetting. If it turned so that these pieces were not simply a false front with a stage, but made a place for each essential cube to either expand or contract, then it becomes a little bit tougher because it becomes a place to live rather than a stage set.

Schlabs I actually think the fact that this false front accommodates private work space but puts the inhabitants on stage is what makes it interesting. The one communal aspect of the program is isolated in the woods in the most private spot on the site, whereas the most private areas are right up on the trail. The power of the project is in those contradictions.

Henmi I will bring up one comment, probably the only reference to Bijoy's studenthood. I used to teach Bijoy. From your beginnings, which were rather frenetic but interesting, in a kind of Loos interlocked manner to the final project which is kind of stripped down and quite minimal in many respects, I can see that Bijoy has influenced you in a good manner. Even as a student he was very minimal in his approach and obviously he makes strong, simple buildings.

Stern There's always some review where people say at the beginning they love the project, but then by the end you wonder if they still like it anymore. [laughter] I still like the project, and I think it's poetic, and it's a kind of poetry that doesn't come down the road all that often. Maybe there's a place for some soft places in America in our wasted industrial landscape. There are many compositional subtleties which I think are what you take with you as you go on to other projects over and over again in your career. So, I would compliment you, and if this is what Bijoy did for you, great.

Tigerman You better cherish that moment because not many compliments come out of Bob's mouth. [laughter]

Scott Parks
Desert Citrus

Based on studies of the 1870s cattle drives from South Texas to Abilene, Kansas, my project's focus is the precious relationship to scarce water concealed in aquifers beneath the arid plains of West Texas. The site I chose is nestled into the continental divide near Marfa, Texas and contains a dry creek bed, or arroyo, that floods with rainwater intermittently. An expansive circular earthen wall, the main architectural move acts as both a dam to collect flood waters and a wind-blocking device that protects the vast, paradise-like citrus orchard. The buildings are simply constructed of adobe and contain both infrastructure for farming and shelter for ten families and twenty visitors. The second storey of the main residences has sweeping views of the top of the orchard canopy out to the desert. Large "sky courts" within the building complexes create needed voids in the forest for gatherings or individual pursuits of any type.

MID REVIEW

How does optimizing one condition for the crop create another condition for human habitation? I'm looking for the connection between those two optimized environments that is played out through a means of marking the land. —Sunil Bald

FINAL REVIEW

Tigerman It reeks of utopian precedent. It really is an oasis. This could be the desert, whether it is West Texas or West Arabia. It's a desert, and water is precious. The subject matter of the studio is a precious matter. I will think about this project quite a bit later when I'm back in Chicago, and where we stand as a civilization with respect to water and aquifers and so forth. It brings up a lot of stuff that is not all happy ending stuff. If we don't use water judiciously we're in big trouble. Again it goes back to your trip to India, and coming back and knowing your own culture, having been in an utterly other place.

Parks A big obsession of mine at the beginning of the semester was the Becher photographs. They did this incredible catalog of water towers. They are all static forms; they don't communicate what's going on inside of them.

Williams This looks like a watering arc—like a crop circle. Within the circle you've got some inconsistencies that I'd like to point out. You've said that you actually created a dam here, but the water won't flow through this way, it will actually create a big puddle. So, then I wonder about how one crosses the arroyo. They may be shallow, but they're always a little bit of a dip in the land. That makes me wonder how are the buildings disposed on the land? Do they want to address the arroyo? The natural growth around the dam will create a very different vegetative state here along the arroyo. You could almost track the system that you water this by, and create an architecture regulated to that. This is what you've not done. As an architect, formally, that's too many mistakes within your own brilliantly described idea.

Bald If you think of some of the 19th century utopian models where you might have a contained community, there would be metrics that governed the relationships between parts, whether it was internal like Broadacre City, or external. The drawing instrument for the circle was a beautiful analog between your conception of the project and something mechanic that might inscribe a boundary or fertilize an area.

Tsien If you used this as the generator, then your decisions could fall from that, and they're not so subjective. It's interesting that the last project and this one both talk about crops, although you're being interrogated much more seriously about the legitimacy of your crop. I think it's this drawing of the circle.

Plattus There's a very interesting figure-field reversal from the Islamic and Arabic tradition of the orange courtyard, of orange trees, that you get in a mosque like Cordoba, where the image of paradise is the enclosed courtyard with a very limited number of gridded orange trees. You've apparently explicitly reversed that figure-field relationship and taken the limited paradise, at least within a larger field, and created the qualified illusion of this continuous field, within which the courtyard occurs.

Clark I also think that the crop here is a generative device. Whereas previous projects change very easily and probably could have changed again, they seemed more incidental.

Henmi This is not just a question about the diameter of the circle in terms of the logic, principles, and what drives you as a maker. It's about interrogating the principles that drive the original thing, the lifestyle in the place.

Tigerman What is really interesting is that you managed to get Tod really worked up.

Williams It happens every once in a while. You too, Stanley.

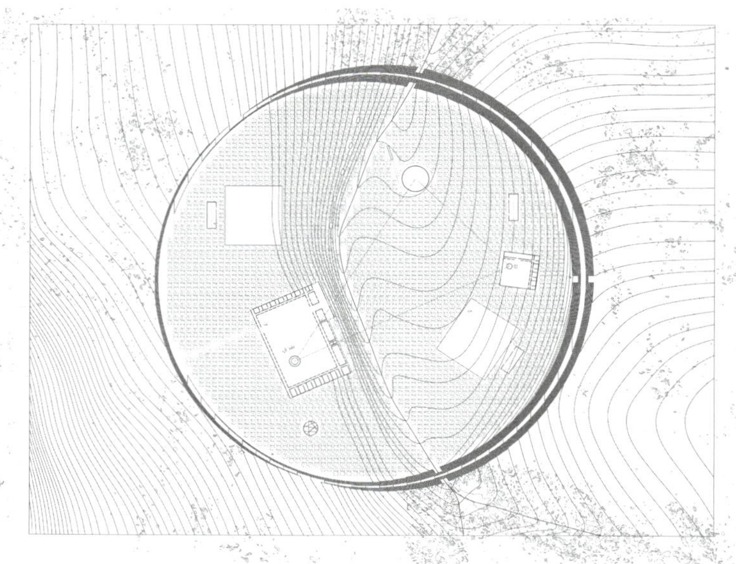

Mark Tumiski
Seaweed Harvesting Facilities

My project for a live/work infrastructure on the East Providence waterfront establishes a reciprocal relationship of 'give and take,' whereby bioextraction—the removal of macroalgae blooms from an ecosystem—turns a byproduct of local urban runoff and wastewater treatment into a beneficial resource (seaweed for compost, fertilizer, agars, alginates and eventually food). This cleanses the bay of excess nitrogen, creates demand for low and high-skilled labor, and reactivates a local awareness of place. The site plan embraces the idea of coming and going, with primary facilities anchoring both ends, while workers traverse the expanded tidal zone and drying platforms over the course of the day. The occupation of this abandoned brownfield reunites residential East Providence with the city's working waterfront across the bay.

MID REVIEW

What are your methods in terms of manipulating the earth? There is a light touch in terms of topography, and you should reconsider your tools. —Margie Ruddick

FINAL REVIEW

Henmi My question is about the village. That is, about the language of that grouping of buildings. I wonder why would the language depart from the linear, and the length, and the parallelism to the river to such a degree?

Tsien For me the most powerful thing was this idea of extending into the water and then making these various kinds of textures that would keep a residue behind. That would say the opposite direction, which is that you do more with less. In the end it's a pretty peripheral activity. So if you had less could it be somehow more powerful?

Tigerman The one thing he does convey to me, and it is very clear, is not only the final condition of life marked by death, but also the modesty of his understanding of his place in the larger scheme of things; how architecture at some level matters so little and is so fragile, and ultimately, like the metaphor of life and death, is only there for a time. I'm glad you brought up the photos, but I'm much more interested in the stuff and this final project. It is about architecture and the very small impact it has on much larger issues.

Plattus You have to pay Stanley's fee not as a critic, but as a shrink.

Tigerman There are a number of ways we all respond to the authority of natural forces. One of them is to cluster. I think the village thing is a natural impulse in the face of the authority of water, which will overrun. Not that it will ultimately protect us. He's taken a number of different attitudes and postures about where this site is.

Clark But then I also wonder why he doesn't continue with the idea of extension into the landscape. I see these early models, and suddenly you become tentative about extending those lateral moves against the shoreline.

Hsiang What if you turn the model 180 degrees, because we never approach the site this way. This is a relationship issue in your approach toward the horizon line. Once you look back, you realize there's a wall behind you. Maybe some walls are a façade because they're articulated inside and outside, or they're walls to retain the earth. Your approach is about the length, about the horizon line where the water meets the sky. It is also about the cross section, and if that is introduced, that means you have a series of lines to articulate the separation of earth.

Allen Plasencia
Black Everything

Black Everything is a monastery for the Trappist order. It is designed to house twenty permanent monks and accommodate up to twenty guests. The program includes designated spaces for prayer, work/production, gathering, cultivation of local fruits, kitchens, and dormitories.

The concept for Black Everything stems from a swim I used to do as a child in the Florida Keys. The swim takes place through a dredged channel toward a natural estuary. I focused my design process on the experience of this swim, in which the depth of the dredged channel creates a brief moment of blackness within a bright and colorful context. This momentary appearance of black water resonated with me, and through the use of different mediums (making, painting, poetry, sculpture), I created an architecture—a building that embraces the blackness. The building is porous; it becomes a diaphragm inhaling and exhaling the blackness into the surrounding mangroves.

MID REVIEW

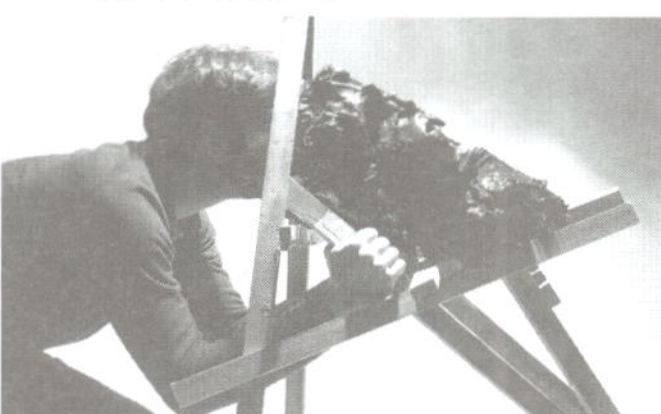

You need to focus on your relationship to the blackness, and how you were able to overcome it. —Bijoy Jain

FINAL REVIEW

Clark At what point did you program it? How committed are you to that program?

Plasencia Not super committed. It could be a nail salon. [laughter]

Tigerman I realize you're saying it tongue in cheek, but does program have an impact? Is it by accident that it's oriented correctly east-west for monastic life?

Plattus I think the process is sort of Aldo Rossi-like. Aldo would latch onto these very powerful memories of pure types, that may have had a functional connotation at one time like a lighthouse or a theater, but then they would be emptied of mere function and be reincarnated as pure monument. In other words, new rituals are invented to fit the abstracted emptiness of the monumental form. I think your process is more akin to that, given your mix of personal, typological and environmental memory, than it is to a program-driven process. I'd pitch it that way.

Tsien In a certain way I think it's the gift that's been given to everyone in the studio, in that it appears to be free of a certain level of program. I imagine what everybody will come back to at a certain point is the actual inhabitation of these amazing places, because that is the next step. I think it can happen without destroying the power.

Clark It is a powerful project and it speaks a lot about Florida, the karst topography and the caves. You're in the darkness searching for the light, the fear of cave diving in the limestone.

Jain It's interesting considering what he did to get here. At some point he took all the water out and dammed the space to overcome the black water...

Multiple No!

Jain Then he filled it half way, and eventually at some point I remember him saying, I'm going to keep the water the way it is. This whole journey of dealing with the presence of the black water; the project is set up to assert that resistance.

Tigerman The fact that somehow he was able to recover his early younger experiences swimming—that's actually a long swim...

Plasencia My parents didn't know I did it. [laughter]

Clark You weren't afraid of alligators?

Plasencia There are no alligators, it's the Atlantic. There are sharks though.

BRUTAL BEAUTY

Marcelo Spina
Louis I. Kahn Visiting Assistant Professor

Georgina Huljich
Louis I. Kahn Visiting Assistant Professor

LOS ANGELES, CALIFORNIA **FACULTY: NATHAN HUME**

PILES, MONOLITHS AND THE INCONGRUOUS WHOLE

"Reyner Banham insisted that a brutalist building should produce an affecting image, "something which is visually valuable"; and while classical aesthetics would presume this value to accrue in pleasure of something beautiful, for New Brutalism "image may be defined as quod visum perturbat -that which seen, affects the emotions," with pleasure, displeasure, or, pointedly, an admixture of the two."

Mark Cousins, "The Ugly," AA Files 28 (1994): 61, quoted by Timothy Hyde in, "Piles, Puddles, and Other Architectural Irritants", Log 27 (2013): 73

Moving a step beyond from what we now perceive as a process of cohesive formal homogenization in the last two decades, the studio aims to explore the formal and aesthetics possibilities of incongruity in architecture. Rather than a naive return to collage, which suggested a collision of multiple opposites to produce disjunction and fragmentation, the studio will examine degrees of formal indeterminacy and visual inconsistency as productive means to generate a more genuine and unexpected whole.

With the overt intention of exploring mute forms of iconicity in architecture, the studio will reconsider the formal economy and ruthless aesthetics of brutalism, especially its reliance on robust massing, volumetric piling, and a sensibility towards monolithicity. Using specific digital techniques and mathematical definitions to simultaneously deploy multiple packing primitives while also articulating monolithic compositions, the studio will explore formal contrasts between cohesive wholes and random piles.

Formal ambiguity and ambivalence of reading will be mobilizing mechanisms to subvert notions of typological and aesthetic fixity. At the center of this is the idea of dichotomy, which implies that by combining opposites, contrasts will either dissolve or become fuzzier, the whole entering into a more complex state of dualism.

With the expectation that mute iconicity will come to define not fluidity or singularity, but incongruity and ambivalence, the studio will move well beyond brutalist's assumptions of regularity, uniformity and its much critiqued atmosphere of totalitarianism. In that regard, the studio will engage the polemic ambition for physical movement and social connectivity, which as part of brutalist philosophy has become a vital component of today's mobile urban society.

ACADEMY MUSEUM OF MOTION PICTURES

The project will be a new building for the Academy Museum of Motion Pictures at Los Angeles County Museum of Art [LACMA] Campus. The studio will use as its basis the recently announced proposal by Renzo Piano: a 290,000 sq.ft. new building addition to the existing May Company Building on Fairfax and Wilshire. The new project will include a 1,000-seat theater, more than 10,000 square feet devoted to the history of the movies, a public piazza, the museum lobby, a cafe and a gift store. The new building will also include a two story 12,000 square foot "making of..." demonstration room for 150 people to recreate the experience of real-life theatrical moviemaking

Consistent with the "tabula rasa" trend initiated by Rem Koolhaas's proposal for LACMA in 2001 and continued by Peter Zumthor's latest plan, the studio will contemplate alternatives to the assumption that the May Co. building is to be kept. Rather than simply reconverting the existing building, adding to its back as proposed by Renzo Piano's current scheme, the studio will pursue bold new visions. These visions will reconsider the museum's urban presence towards its immediate context as well as within the Wilshire corridor, the cultural implications of a new access and, the making of a different kind of icon in a city of icons.

JURORS

Anna Bokov
Lise Anne Couture
Winka Dubbeldam
Hernan Diaz Alonso
Mark Foster Gage
Timothy Hide
Ferda Kolatan
Keith Krumwiede
Thom Mayne
John McMorrough
Edward Mitchell
John Patkau
Steven Phillips
David Ruy
Joel Sanders
Michael Speaks
Robert A.M. Stern
Michael Young

Feldman Nominee

Constance Vale
Incongruous Monolith

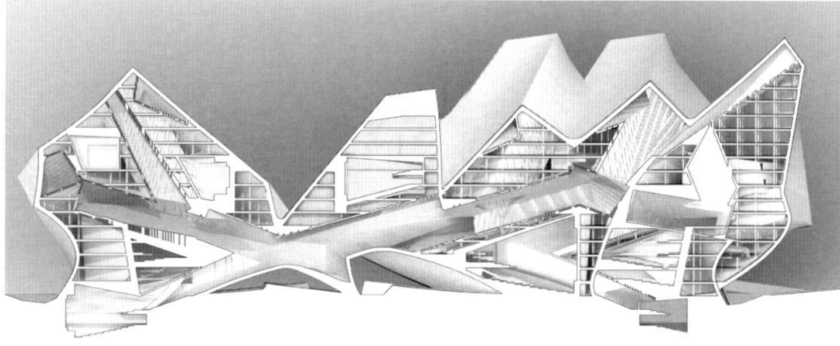

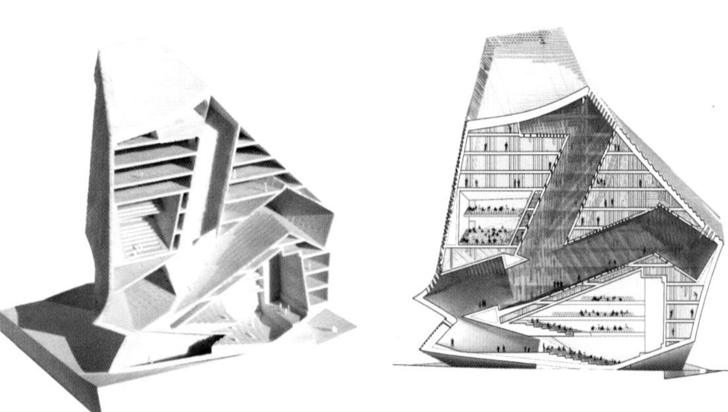

In order to achieve monolithic qualities three primary formal strategies are employed, referencing those same qualities found in the bunkers of Paul Virilio located along the Atlantic Wall. First, mass is made to appear "upturned" and "tilted," as if "weight displaces volume over time,"[1] reinforced in shadow distribution across the façade's texture. Next, earth is seen as "no longer being good lodging" due to an apparent "dematerialization of the ground"[2] through a formal insistence on verticality and in the shift of the predominant mass above the ground plane. Finally, the primitives are made to "interpenetrate" leading to a "confusion of the animate and inanimate."[3] Their forms are coincident and rotate around a hinge point, creating an internal sense of motion.

The resultant monolith is in effect a slightly lifted pyramid, with its internal primitives acting as narrow tunnels. A figure-void relationship is created in which solid program acts as a thick poché, wrapping around the central void of the primitives. The convergence of these primitives results in an atrium that carries light to the interior, provides circulation space on the lower horizontal levels, and allows in views from the adjacent floor plates through the pores of a micro-texture in the more vertical forms above. The monolith retains its status as such not only for its formal qualities, but in its "inward looking"[4] attitude. It is in effect "a single object folding back on itself."[5]

1 Virilio, Paul, and George Collins. Bunker archaeology. (New York: Princeton Architectural Press, 1994), 38.
2 Ibid., 41.
3 Ibid., 44.
4 Johnston, Pamela, ed. The Function of the Oblique: the Architecture of Claude Parent and Paul Virilio, 1963–1969. (London: AA Publications, 1996)
5 Ibid, 9.

MID REVIEW

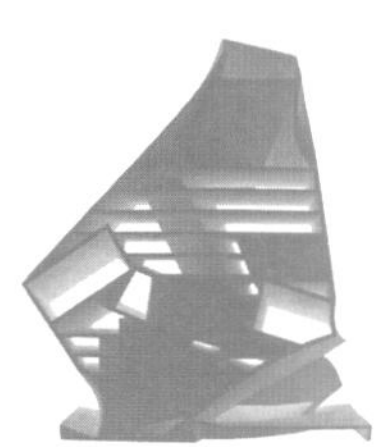

I think you can expect more from your research in bunker archaeology. If this formal paradigm could be made into an organizational paradigm, whereas there used to be a band window in a bunker to see the whole horizon and shoot people, now it sits vertically or obliquely in space. In the bunker archaeology paradigm, there is more to be taken than just the formal vocabulary, but a whole lexicon of how to organize space. —Emmanuel Petit

FINAL REVIEW

Phillips I don't know if you know the artist Joel Shapiro—look him up you'll love it.

Mayne To me this is the fourth morphology. The inside-out, this being two forms that have space between, and the outside-in, that wasn't quite there. It's really interesting because your strategy for attacking the initial object, which is just the provocation, seems to be imbalanced somehow with the power of the form, and you're getting a lot out of it.

Ruy Why is the indifference to the ground necessary—essentially a desire to make a generic tabletop? Why is it important to the architectural project, your project, to make the ground disappear as a product?

Vale I wanted it to act monolithically, so the context is less important to that.

Hide I don't understand why you're not answering David's question in terms of what you talked about. With the destabilized ground, the ground is no longer of substance. It is the turning of the oblique inside.

Diaz Alonso The question that David is posing is, I would say, super important because I think it would tilt. We do an automatic link between the monolithic and the object, which I would say is not always the case. It depends on how you treat the ground and how you treat, in this case raising it, that would push the project in one direction or another. I would argue that it has been a problem in the last twenty years—the over manipulation of the ground. We've tried to conquer the ground as part of the figure problem.

Gage This is like a little building inside of the building. I think that's the thing about the monolithic. It is almost like you are producing an exterior condition inside your building.

Mayne In plan you get these very odd conditions. It reminds you that you're not developing this thing planimetrically or sectionally. It's a three dimensional idea, which you are looking at as CAT scan, which is useful in another way, but not as the original generate. It's a complete shift of how architecture is made in the end of the 20th century from the 90s. It starts all over again. The plan is gone as an idea.

Sanders I think what is brilliant about this project is that it achieves that radical disassociation between exterior and interior, but through the vehicle of this exquisitely delicate louvered façade.

Young I'm going to give two comments. There is something in the posture of this project where we are always turning away from it. As if you're trying to talk to somebody and they keep turning their head away from you so you can't actually address them yet. The other one is, I would love to see that full-bleed color rendering of this thing.

Mayne It seems like you're struggling with some of your own conventions. There are so many opportunities. I mean you've cut through it, and that's major. After that the opportunities are the various chance behaviors between the demands of the interior and the skin. That's the spontaneous combustion between two things which creates invention.

Craig Rosman
Porous Monolith

My project looks at the idea of muteness, and the challenge of creating an object with its own agency. With no information to reference, the object needs to generate its own internal set of data. The project focuses on techniques to produce internal information and to transform that data into several aesthetic outcomes of envelope, texture, and volume. The overlap of aesthetic regimes negates the possibility of a singular sensual object and instead proposes a multilayered, eidetic object.
To do this, I started in an object-oriented programming environment and wrote a program that creates a set of vectors. The vectors define the discrete primitives and monolithic boundary in aggregate, are de-featured to complicate a reading of figures, and then scaled to fit the site. In order to test this process, I treated the results as found objects, looking at eidetic properties: sphericity, top-heaviness, chunkiness, and precarity. The texture of the envelope destabilizes the building's relationship to time and scale, as the voxel detail reveals itself upon closer inspection. A further confusion of spatial identity occurs on the interior. In contrast to the blank exterior, a highly articulate volume created by the overlap of several boxes forms the interior.

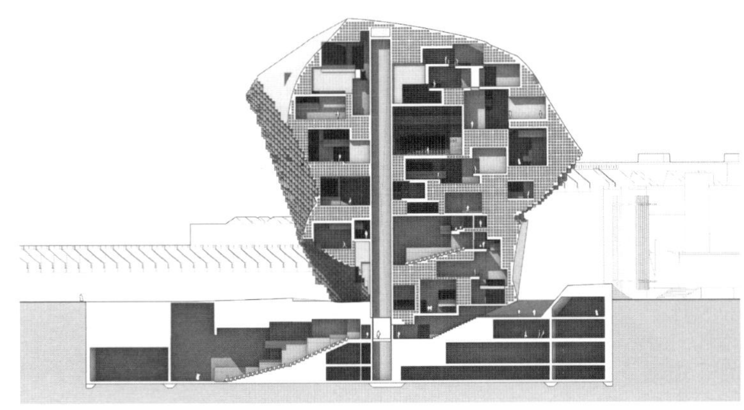

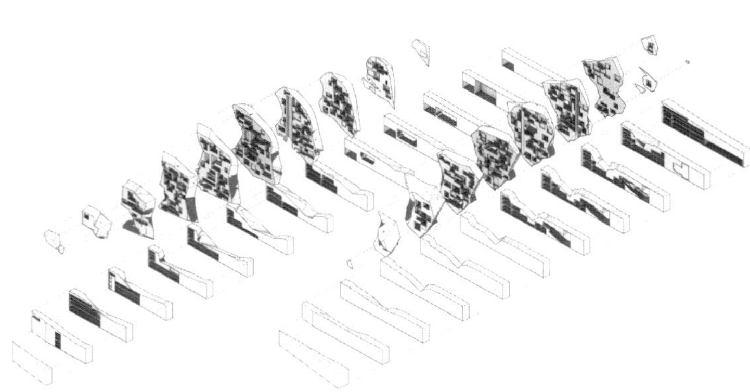

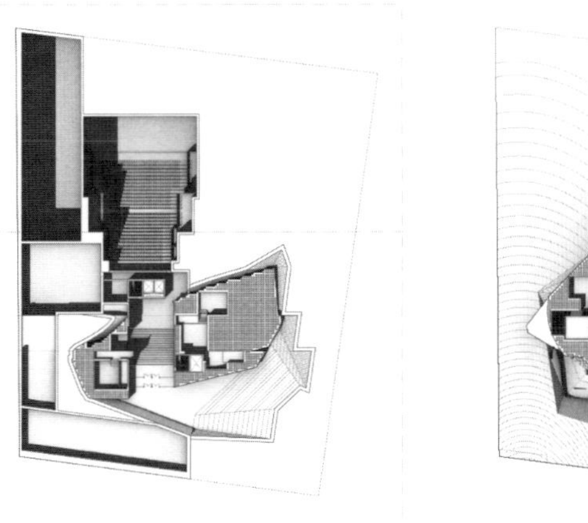

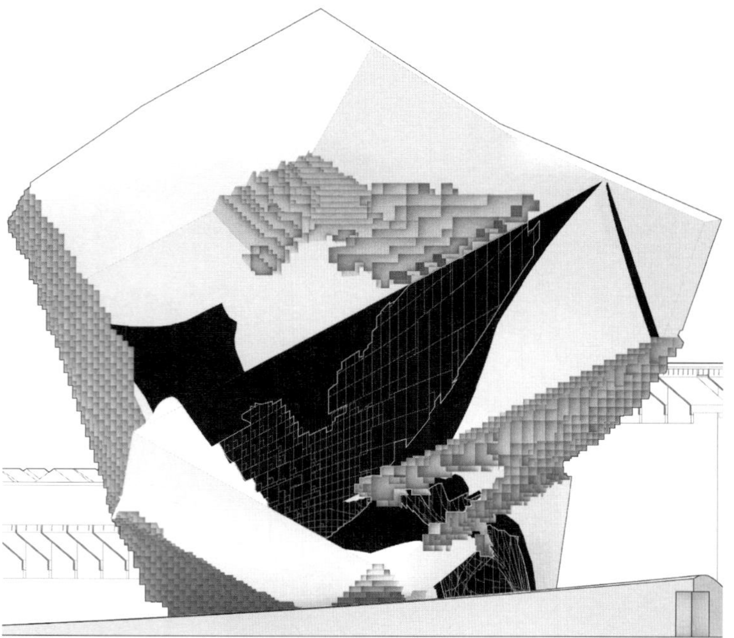

MID REVIEW

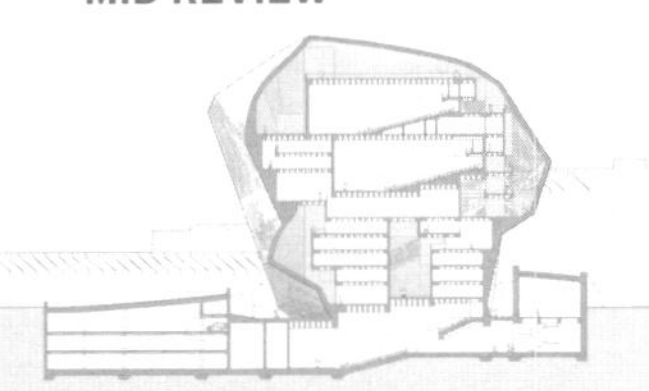

This seems to have a clear relationship to the outside. Even though it might not be an elegant or functionalist one at all, it is an expressionist one. Going back to the discourse, if you think about monolithicity as something that expresses mass and weight—certainly this one tries to do that. —Anna Bokov

FINAL REVIEW

Dubbeldam Do you understand how weird it would look to stick a door in there?

Gage We keep insisting that we read these as where's the structure, where's the front door, how does it fit into the context. I feel like these projects are asking larger questions than we're answering by talking about them so pragmatically.

Hide Do you think the project is against reading though? It's not against reading.

Mayne It's not; I think it's a burden. This is Yale. And he still uses the word poché. What I would assume though, is that seeing is forgetting. The word poché should be eliminated indefinitely in your project unless you reinvented it through your process. I'm an old guy and I'll tell you planimetric was already gone twenty years ago as an organizational idea. You're completely embedded in a planimetric idea that has nothing to do with the project. It's an absolute three-dimensional, spatial project. It's about an organization of an inside and an outside, the wall and the skin, on and off.

McMorrough I would say it's a diagram of how to occupy something monolithically. Conceptually, 100%. Spatially, I'm not sure yet. There is a kind of programmatic alibi that sets up the condition of muteness. This weird building has just three auditoria, nothing else. There is a sufficiently idiosyncratic programmatic need that forces this condition of the monolithic because, typologically, you don't need the windows. In this sense, the typology needs the monolith rather than the monolith being inserted on it.

Gage Poché is just a tool that allows you to not have to put aspects of architecture in relationship to one another. So, with poché your interior doesn't have to line up with your exterior. It's just a gasket that allows you to maintain an independent object-quality of things. That seems like a perfectly monolithic idea for producing interior and exterior figures and shapes.

Diaz Alonso Think of this paradox of a building being solid or monolithic, which we know is not true. Yet, if you allowed yourself for a second to think that could be possible, the building would deliver something like this. It is not just poché, but it's all the consequences of being in a complete solid.

Huljich I don't completely agree with you Thom. I think it begins to read thick enough to, first of all, be removed from an idea of an object inside an object that I think many of the other projects tried to do. This one shocked us.

Mayne You can't be a pluralist. If you participate in pluralism, it's called being bipolar. You're either one or the other, but you have to discuss the meaning of the poché drawing and what it represents in terms of your conceptual strategy.

Spina We're interested in dichotomy as a word of pushing this kind of indeterminacy. The project introduces different iconographies. One is a massive thing you're going to read from far away. Then, I don't think this is poché, these are just thickened walls. The issue of texture is quite present, especially in this little model. If you think of brutalism, that sort of béton brut started as a mistake, and it became an aesthetic. This would be the other way around, in which you would actually make an aesthetic look like a mistake. In that model, it doesn't look so articulate, it doesn't look so refined. I find that an interesting provocation.

Phillips Architectural representation becomes extremely important in this project. You've created a building where you understand it from the outside, which has nothing to do with how you experience it from the inside. However, you're never going to know or understand that poché on the inside of the building. The only way you can even understand this project is through section and sectional model. It's a provocation; it's actually inter-disciplinary.

Justin Nguyen
Medusa

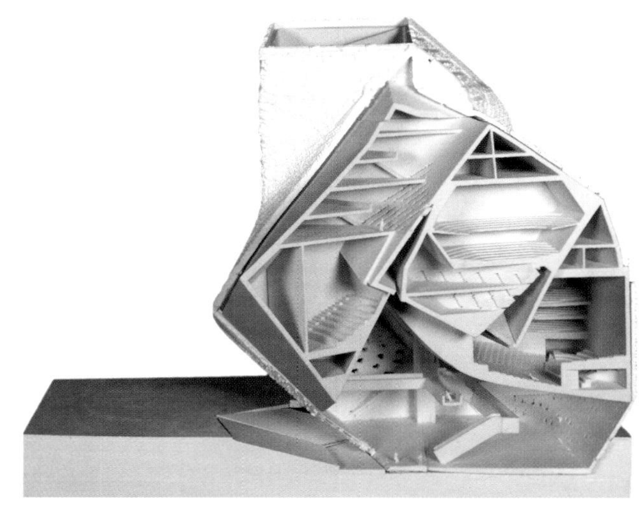

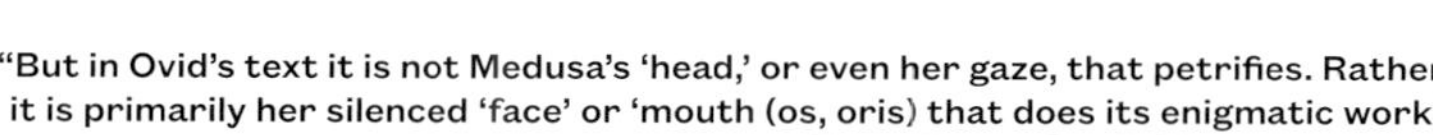

"But in Ovid's text it is not Medusa's 'head,' or even her gaze, that petrifies. Rather, it is primarily her silenced 'face' or 'mouth (os, oris) that does its enigmatic work."
—Enterline on Ovid's Metamorphoses

Considering the incongruous formal relationship between cohesive wholes and random piles, this project is interested in the possibility of multiple and paradoxical readings within the monolith. Rather than assuming the mute iconicity of the architectural monolith as a lack of articulation, blankness is defined in terms of multiple and contradictory part to whole relationships as described by Kipnis' concept of Intensive Coherence—further recalling his account of Frank Gehry's Vitra Design museum.

The monolithic arrangement is additive rather than subtractive, such that a heterogeneous yet cohesive whole suggests no single dominant in either the organization of the initial massing, the internal volumes, the wrapping of the envelope or the dematerialization from the texture. Multiplicity through layering produces an unstable and ambiguous dialogue between inside and outside, background and foreground, vertical and horizontal. The Medusa-like form distorts and dislocates elements which "seek to engender shifting affiliations that nevertheless resist entering into stable alignments." (Kipnis, Towards a New Architecture). The misalignment and miscoupling of the original organization of primitives attempt to create a reading that is both and neither part (pile) or whole (monolith).

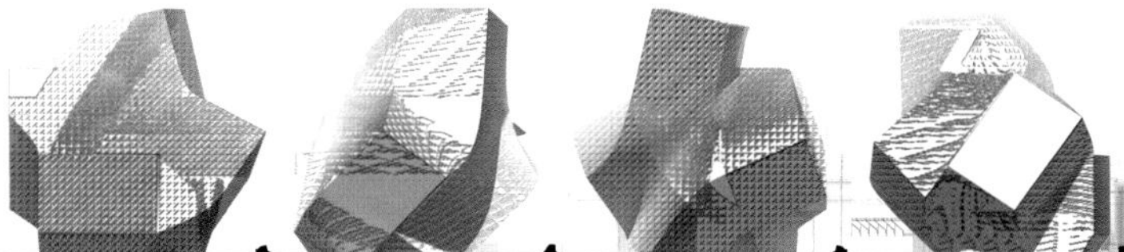

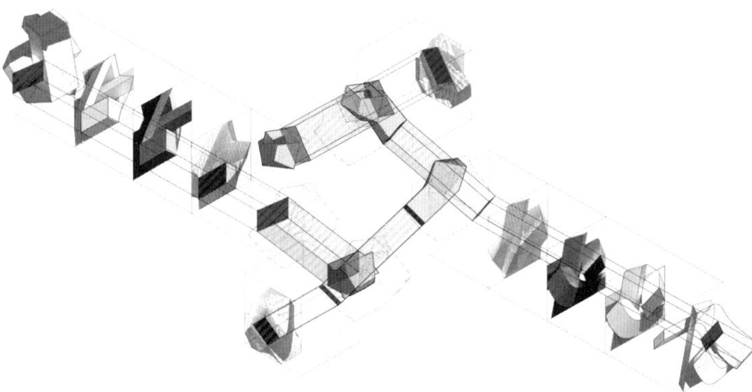

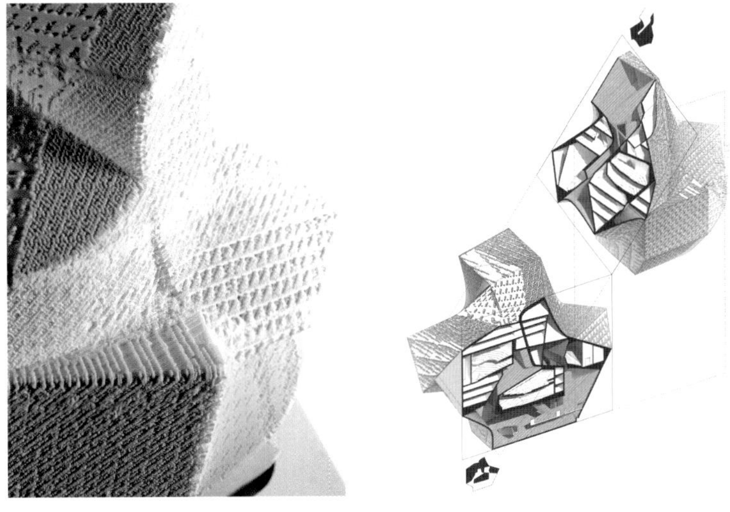

MID REVIEW

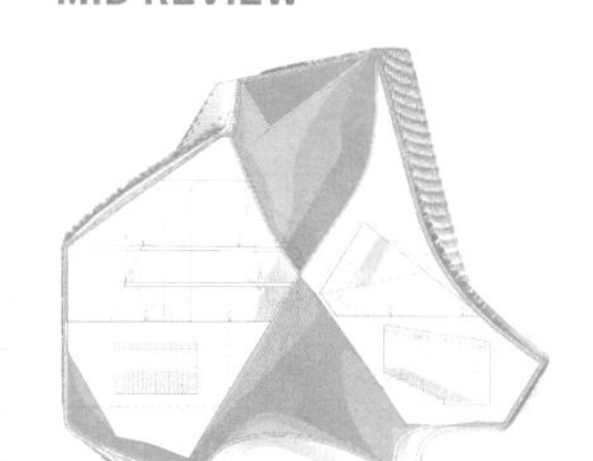

I think this studio needs to theorize what the interior of a monolith is. If we think of buildings that could quickly be classified as monoliths, I immediately think of Casa de Musica, which runs into the same problem when reading the interior. If the idea of the monolith for this studio is going to be successful it has to go beyond the idea of the monolith and the wrapper. What is the interior of a monolith? —Emmanuel Petit

FINAL REVIEW

Diaz Alonso To me your project is like a friendly monster, it is not aggressive enough. I think it makes too many concessions to the standards of architecture. You need to truly make the context surrender to the object. Also, the texture the corduroy concrete is one thing, but what is it trying to do for you project? To me the edge requires another layer of sophistication which is not clear yet.

Gage It's best when the skin hides those moves. The skin becomes the mediator between the action and the form.

Mayne You have totally destroyed the notion of edge which is the project. Can I draw on these?

Diaz Alonso You have to sign it so they can sell it immediately [laughter].

Mayne Everything is about the edge. This is the void that comes through and you don't want to fill it with horizontal stuff.

Spina Thom, you go from jury to jury, school to school, and comment that this is a great project if you didn't put in all the slabs. For me this is what architecture is made of. If you actually think of a monolith, if a building is full, it is full of slabs. You are going to have to choose selectively where you do it.

Diaz Alonso To me, I have an issue with a wall to wall slab, not with a slab per se. So for me it's always more successful when you have anomalies in relation with the slab.

Gage I think the floor line isn't the problem. I think you're accepting the ceiling as an offset of the floor. If you thought about the spaces as monolithic, you would have much more ceiling articulation. If you accept that everything is uniformly a slab then you are essentially adopting the politics of the envelope argument by Alejandro—that the only efficacy, the only power left in architecture, is in the two inches of the façade. However, if you cut the slabs two feet from this object, the floors, all of the sudden, look like an object and not a wall.

Mayne This is using edge, periphery, and boundary as the organizational idea. It is the utilization of that surface as an organizational technique, which is a completely new idea. It is expanding notions of how we organize complex space. That is why the figure ground completely destroys that. It completely obfuscates the major part of the project, which is the edge. Then, it seems to me that the interior condition is important, if not more important, than the surface as it finds itself in relation to its interior and exterior. In fact, it seems to make the project extremely interesting. You're given clues that you see the object, which now reappear in a very different form as you experience the building.

Phillips I think, Thom, the enigma is not meant to be satisfied. When you go inside you may not see what you expect to see and when you leave you may not understand the building any better. It breaks certain obvious rules of architecture.

Mayne I think that's asking a lot. You can't be Miles Davis before doing your 10,000 hours. I'd be happier with the 4,500 mile mark now. This is a really beautiful project. There are a load of possibilities. I'm critical precisely because I buy into the potential of the project. I'm looking at it and I'm ready to go. Let's figure this out.

CHINA STUDIO Alan Plattus

Professor of Architecture

BEIJING, CHINA **FACULTY: ANDREI HARWELL**

This studio will be the fourteenth year of the Yale School of Architecture China Studio, and the third year of a new collaboration between Yale and Tsinghua University School of Architecture in Beijing. With this studio, we are also continuing a projected three-year investigation of urban development and redevelopment in the historic and contemporary Chinese capital city, with a particular emphasis on models of sustainable mixed-use and neighborhood development, in part funded by a grant from the Yale School of Architecture's Hines Fund. Over these three years the China Studio will study the impact of preservation, infill and new development on three sites along the historic north-south axis of Beijing, moving from the center outward to the urban periphery.

The first year's studio focused on a sensitive site immediately adjacent to the Forbidden City, where existing fabric and preservations-based design restrictions severely constrained new development, and the second year's site was a mainly open superblock between the Third and Fourth Ring Roads, originally cleared for the 1990 Asian Games and later used by the 2008 Beijing Olympics, lying as it does at the southern end of the Olympic Axis. This year's site is along the southern extension of the axis, just to the south of the reconstructed Yongding Gate, and so just outside of the historic Ming Dynasty city, and includes an interesting mix of institutional, commercial and residential development from different eras. The site lies on both sides of the axis and encompasses 146 hectares between the Second and Third Ring Roads. It will be served by a stop on the projected extension of Line 14 of the Beijing Metro system with immediate access to the new Beijing South Railway Station. The area is already characterized by its association with the garment trade and the local authorities are interested in encouraging the development of a world class fashion district. Given its size and mixed character, the site presents the challenges and opportunities of thinking critically about the urbanistic significance of the unit of development in contemporary Chinese cities, as well as the sensate relationship of new and existing development. In addition, students will be asked to consider the changing meanings of Beijing's historic axis and the relationship of the site to the axis, as well as the potential of the site as a model for sustainable urban development at the levels of the district, the neighborhood and the individual project simultaneously. Projects will therefore encompass both large scale issues of urban infrastructure and ecology, as well as finer grain issues of urban fabric, building typology, local use and image.

As in past studios, Yale students will travel to China, tour the site and other relevant sites and projects in and around Beijing, meet with local planning officials, and, most importantly, collaborate with their counterparts, graduate students at Tsinghua University, to develop preliminary site analysis and design concepts. This interaction will continue throughout the term via video conferencing, and Tsinghua students and faculty have been invited to participate in final reviews at Yale. All students considering participating in the studio should make sure that they have a current passport in their possession, with sufficient space for a Chinese visa.

JURORS
Patrick Bellew
Joseph Clarke
Songzhou Dai
Piper Gaubatz
David Kooris
Karen Van Lengen
Gary McDonogh
Dennis Pieprz
Joel Sanders
Zhengxu Shou
Robert A.M. Stern
Hui Wang
Wenyi Zhu

Feldman Nominees

Tyler Collins
Ivan Farr
Super! Expo Urbanism

This proposal for Beijing urbanizes the expo through a highway-infill strategy that connects the existing fabric with a distributed architecture of variously scaled displays, small shops, workshops and walkable streets. A flexible city, Super! takes advantage of the existing Beijing South Railway Station as a link for regional and national travel suggesting its surroundings as an ideal location for expo facilities that enable both large and small scale gatherings and display. The proposal juxtaposes a variety of scales that have often been separated into discrete entities maintaining little relationship with their context. Through a dense network of tree-lined streets, granular block structure and the blending of seemingly disparate scales of use, Super! argues for the viability of the expo as a diverse and lively urban fabric. The combination of exhibition facilities, shops, residential towers, conference workshops and loft spaces throughout the district reframes commercial activity in Beijing by connecting production, marketing and consumption in a synthetic entangling of uses typically kept separated. By breaking them into workable pieces of urbanism through a variety of scales, the expo's typical footprint is fractured to produce a series of lively urban spaces in-between that invigorate the district during off-times and takes advantage of temporary visitors.

MID REVIEW

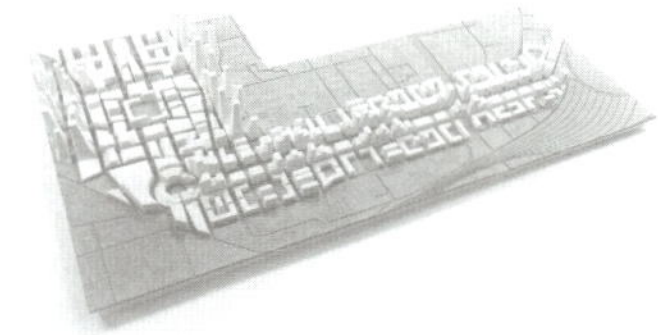

It's important for us to challenge you. I kind of long to mess it up a bit. At the moment, it's just too ordered. The way we do these things in the office is we build big models and we move bits and try other things out because that's actually how decent cities evolve. —Andy Bow

FINAL REVIEW

McDonogh I think it raises a question that actually goes back to some ideas about moving in and out. I'm trying to think about the rhythm of the space within the city, because there's also dead time when the exhibit closes and I have this sense that for eight hours or twelve hours, it's going to be this kind of cemetery in the middle of city. I think it's interesting to try and rethink the expo center and also to try and think how it fits into the needs of Beijing. This would seem to be something that fits the whole city in a way different from the other projects. Moving the vitrines down actually might make it more interesting, to walk through at night for example, but it's too monolithic in its use.

Kooris On the land use-transportation connection, the fine scale nature of your urbanism is a direct result of how you've treated the road. You've calmed the road, which implies a much greater reliance on transit; but then you have this very high density stuff set back from the main corridor. So I think taking a step back, looking at the high speed rail access and the metro station and making sure that your densities respond more to proximity to those two amenities, will allow you to have the more fine grained approach that you've taken to the street network.

Pieprz What intrigued me, and the way I thought you were headed, is an exhibition area, but it's not a monolithically managed exhibition. It is thousands of incubator industries, so it is small scale people that never have access to these mega exhibitions. There might be exhibitions going on in like four blocks and the others are carrying on with other things. There are exhibit boxes or pavilions scattered throughout; it's taking the monolithic idea and really smashing that to pieces.

Sanders The idea of interjecting a program that doesn't seem obvious is fantastic, but it also requires a lot of research and analysis of the way in which existing film studios work like existing expos, not to confuse them but as a way of reinventing them. I think what your ambition is has reverberations of potential. It's not only for the city of Beijing but as you say, it is for typologies that kill the urban fabric, like a cemetery. So how do you break down the scale and make these into 24-hour places that allow a city to thrive? How could you take that, which normally is about these giant, vast open spaces that can be easily serviced, and allow those specific activities to take place while still allowing what you planned?

Plattus I like the reflective zeppelin. That's how you know what's happening on the roof.

McDonogh What is that exactly? And what is the exposition that actually has you hanging a whale there, just out of curiosity? I think it should be a sperm whale rather than a killer whale, a celebration of 12 Monkeys or something [laughter].

John Farrace
Michael McGrattan
Infilling Infrastructure

Beijing is a city characterized, especially in recent years, by mega-scale development. The city is organized by enormous blocks and streets, and has continued to move forward with developing mega scale urban projects.
Coinciding with this super development has been a renewed interest in a smaller, tight knit fabric, perhaps as a relief from the large scale development prominent throughout the city. Qienmen St, the redevelopment of traditional hutong fabric into shopping streets, MAD's hutong bubble, and the back lakes area among others have all shown a renewed interest in this type of world.
This proposal is a tightly knit network of regularized streets, canals, pedestrian pathways, and pocket parks beginning by generating a unit of development that was flexible enough to create small scale urban spaces, but could also be altered to frame larger public spaces. The unit consists of 12 meter wide bars that can be varied in lengths that are ideal to accommodate flexible uses. The proposal also redistributes the primary central road across the site and creates a more regularized street system to break block sizes down, disperse automobile traffic, and create a more pedestrian oriented world. The buildings were designed to frame particular public spaces, at a scale that was able to mediate between the large and small fabric across the site. The three overlaid networks consisted of a dedicated pedestrian street, green spaces and waterways that play up existing historical elements on the site and separate the pedestrian from primary arterial roads. The edges of this system act as appendages that allow for existing neighborhood fabric to tie into new development. The system is anchored by three different types of major public spaces.

MID REVIEW

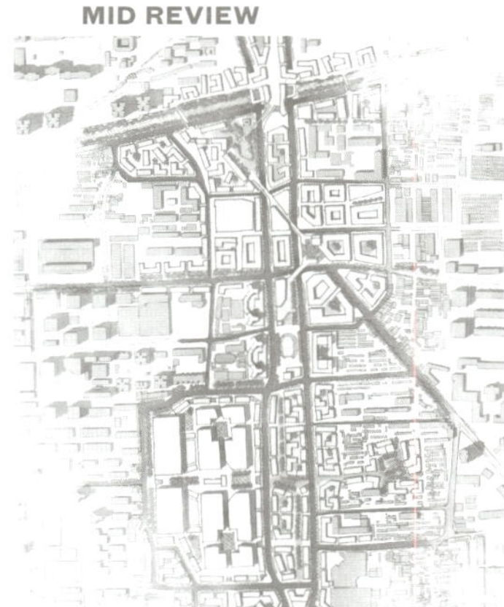

What I'm hearing are two very interesting but completely different alternatives. One would divert the axis and make a new neighborhood. The second one is the scheme that says work with that axis. Which project do you guys want to make? —Joel Sanders

FINAL REVIEW

Pieprz My instant reaction is that it's a very sophisticated development of components and you can imagine actually being in this thing, walking through the district. But it has a very small town-like attitude. It doesn't sound like it's in a 15 million person city on the main axis, which is totally, totally suppressed in a sort of brilliant disguise. Look at this drawing, it's an amazing piece of the city, but just four blocks away is one of the busiest train stations in the world, five times as much as Grand Central. Yet, there is no clue in your project that that is hovering so near. So it's a fascinating project, very well presented, but it raises a lot of issues.

Gaubatz This is a place that would be really nice to live in, you know, it feels like a real living space. It may be problematic in this location to the extent that the axis is really important; it's got a huge significance. I could see this being a brilliant way to deal with a gate to the east, but I think you'd find some resistance locally, people feeling like erasing the central axis is not what they want to do. It's part of this whole conceptualization of how the city has been and is growing. That being said, this really has the feel that when you walk in it, it's not like somebody planned one big huge monolithic thing, it's going to feel like real space.

Wenyi For this very specific site, south used to be the strong axis, and a certain element that should be taken into account is the Tiantan, the Heavenly Platform. That used to be a very important site in Chinese history. This was the place the emperor made dialogue with heaven. In Chinese history, we don't have so called religion, but even above the emperor there is a heaven. Twice a year, for spring and autumn, the emperor prayed to heaven and then went to another pavilion at the end of the axis and prayed for the harvest. There also has to be a height limitation here. When you stand on the platform you should just see a breathtaking view of the sky.

Bellew To me this view provokes the question of what does the city of the future, with less emphasis on the car, start to look like? Can we bring it back down to a different grain? It is a bit of a cop out to assume you can take these traffic lanes and divide them into four. If you were to improve on this, definitely work on the whole cycle network idea, build that up. I think more interesting, perhaps, is a slightly larger transport infrastructure. Perhaps you look at a trolley bus system to link back to the railway system. You're building big infrastructure here, so you could provide a lot of people with trolley buses to link back to the central station. How does all that stitch together? I like the way it comes out.

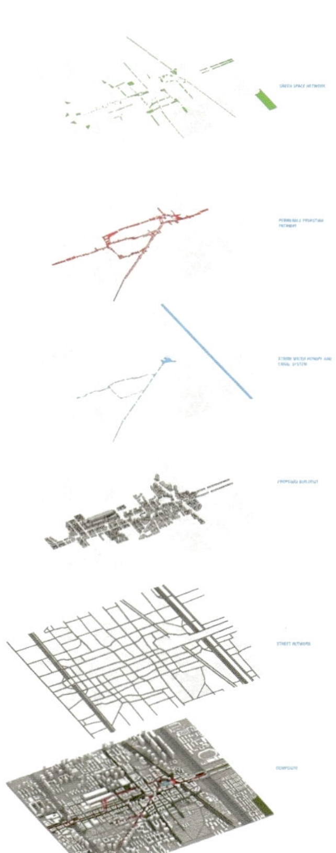

Russell LeStourgeon
Caroline VanAcker
From Metropolitan Axis to Localizing Grid

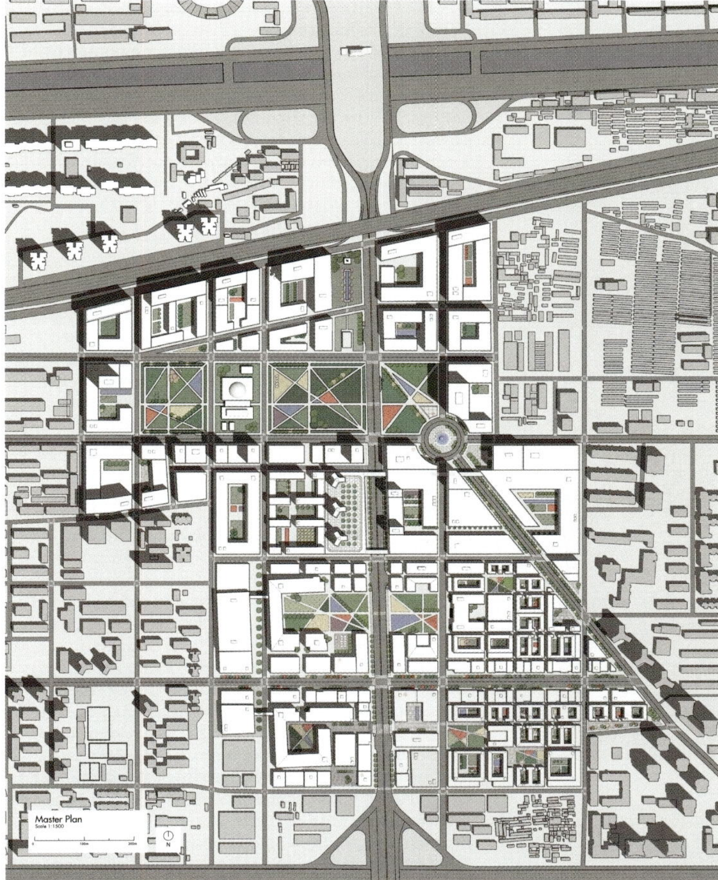

In central Beijing, the historic axis serves as a potent, symbolic connector of the city's history and culture. In southern Beijing, however, it is instead an obstacle. Sixteen lanes of traffic make what should be a celebrated zone into little more than a highway—its overwhelming scale must be dealt with in order for any kind of future development to be successful. This project proposes to first reduce the size of the axis road on our site, redistributing its traffic onto several new north-south avenues between the Second and Third Ring Roads. These are crossed by a number of east-west roads that restructure the urban form. Together, this grid system extends the influence of the axis across the site, connecting it to landmarks such as the new rail station.

Based on an analysis of existing programs in the area, this proposal focuses on three main zones of use, each organized around an open space arranged perpendicularly to the axis: a business district to the north, a hospital/wellness campus, and a live/work/retail village on the old site of the Bairong Mall. Although the three respond to different functional requirements, they each contain a mixture of commercial, residential, and institutional space. The grid provides a framework for new typologies of development units, ranging from traditional Chinese courtyard residences to podiums and high rise towers. In this way, the introduction of a grid system allows streets to be connective rather than divisive, localizing the urban energy of the axis.

MID REVIEW

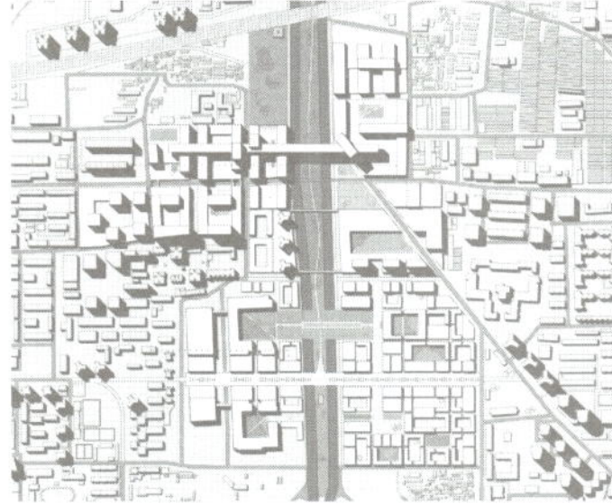

In 25 years time, the love affair of the car will have gone. In this area, there will be master sectioning, there will be mixed uses, it will no longer be 1960s planning. It will be much, much richer. If I were you, I'd switch the computers off and I'd build one big model —Andy Bow

FINAL REVIEW

Pieprz They're narrowing the axis and saying, OK, it is still very wide, in the hierarchy it is the most important, and they're knitting together this network of streets which is providing choice, so that you don't have to only go in that main axis. You can now circulate through the district on the secondary avenues and filter through the whole district. It breaks down the blocks; it starts to make more of a series of interconnected districts that are two halves of an interconnected superblock.

Stern I have a little experience with Chinese planning at this point and there are rules that exist that make traditional, conventional urbanism almost impossible. Like virtually every apartment has to face south, for example. You have this monster road, and it's not going away. Why not say it is a river, like the Hudson or the Seine, and it divides two parts. You put a couple of bridges across but don't pretend that you can unite it.

Plattus Bob, that road is very wide in this section, it narrows down, it widens out, it narrows down. It has been made ten lanes, sixteen lanes, but in fact, the normal north-south circulation in the area has been completely blocked between the ring roads other than that one road. It's an artificial creation. It is not a natural feature like a river.

Van Lengen They also did something interesting that I don't think is complete yet. This area is the most interesting because...

Pieprz It leads right to the station.

Van Lengen Yes, it leads to the station. It opens up and it just wants to end here. So I think you just...

Pieprz You should have carried it on.

Van Lengen Yes, and then you don't have to jump over the street, because you've made the connection from the city to the big train station through the space, through the axis. Then, this bothers me a lot because it downplays how important this transition really is; you just want it to open up and see the historic gate. Nobody else did the east to west axis here which I think is a really interesting move on your part. Also, instead of this large scale model, I would have taken a section view. Because this shows southern facing buildings sloping down and going this way and I think it could have given a great, rich idea in a sectional cut.

Hui I really like your design proposal and your humble and logical way to integrate real dimensions in such a special site. I see from your drawings and your models that you have a very solid, fundamental skill for traditional design and I really appreciate that. There's just one small thing I want to argue with you, and that is the different scales. I think the nearer to the gate, the smaller the scale; the bigger scale, far from the gate.

Plattus Having a significant public space perpendicular to the axis rather than smack on it may actually end up doing better for both.

Stern That was your achievement. But that circle with that fountain... Wow [laughter]. They might actually build that.

A PROJECT OF AGGREGATION Peter Eisenman

Charles Gwathmey Professor in Practice

ROME, ITALY FACULTY: AMY DEDONATO

Departing from previous studios, the challenge of this exercise is to re-define the term—aggregation—as a critique of the digital, which has become synonymous with homogeneous, continuous space. The idea of aggregation aspires to challenge the self-similar repetition and spatial continuities that have become the hallmark of algorithm-driven design, today the most prevalent strain of digital practice. In a recent interview, Patrik Schumacher writes: "Give me any collage of unrelated elements and I can generate connections and resonances, invent correlations. So I reject the pure interruption, the pure discontinuity, collage."[1] If the algorithm provides the possibility of smoothing over differences by absorbing them into a cohesive system of controlled relationships, its outcome arguably falls back into the Modernist vein of consistent, homogeneous space. It is a critique of this tendency today that animates the possibility of an aggregated project.

The capacity of the digital to produce a multiple is arguably a reaction to Albertian principles that underpin the metaphysical project in architecture. In this proto-humanist context, Alberti first defined space or spatium and more specifically posited that all space is homogenous, meaning that all objects exist within a consistent and calculable medium. Alberti's theory of homogenous space first raised questions regarding the nature of space and the difference between surface and spatial objects. Spatial homogeneity projected the idea of the organism, that all parts relate to a whole and that all objects in space are bound to one another through universal, mathematic relationships.

Jump to today. The digital, in a subconscious attempt to overcome these Albertian principles, has an advantage in its ability to produce an inconsistent multiple, or non self-same repetition. While Alberti's notational systems transcribed a single design by a single author, computation has the capacity to produce multiple iterations that the designer must choose from. In Alberti's case, "the author of the drawing becomes the author of the building."[2] Today the computer is the mediator and the generator of the multiple. The idea of the inconsistent multiple is one possible critique of Alberti, in that it questions the idea of authorship and challenges former ideas of space that were predicated on homogeneity.

If parametric or algorithmic-based design paradoxically lapses back into homogeneous space, how might an idea of aggregation produce the possibility of heterogeneous space, or more specifically "heterogeneity within an intensive cohesion rather than out of extensive incoherence and contradiction?"[3] The studio will attempt to define the possibility of an aggregated project as a means to critique parametric methods of homogeneous space formation.

In relation to the digital in architecture: what is the contemporary status of the ground in relation to literal and metaphysical presence? How does the digital platform—essentially a groundless interface—change the way space is bound, controlled, differentiated, or conceptualized in the first place? If the digital platform is a replacement for the literal ground, in what ways can one manipulate the platform in order to destabilize preconceived notions of ground?

1 Patrik Schumacher, "I am trying to imagine a radical free-market urbanism," Log 28, Anyone Corporation, 2013, pp 39–52

2 Mario Carpo, The Alphabet and the Algorithm, (2011)

3 Jeffrey Kipnis, "Towards A New Architecture," AD Folding in Architecture, Profile No. 102, John Wiley & Sons Ltd (London, 1993), pp 102

JURORS

Lucia Allais
Andy Bow
Mario Carpo
Henry Cobb
Preston Scott Cohen
Cynthia Davidson
Peggy Deamer
Emmanuel Petit
Ingeborg Rocker
Stanley Tigerman
Anthony Vidler
Sarah Whiting
Mark Wigley
Elia Zenghelis
Guido Zuliani

Feldman Nominees

Brandon Hall
Evan Wiskup
Biblioteca di Roma

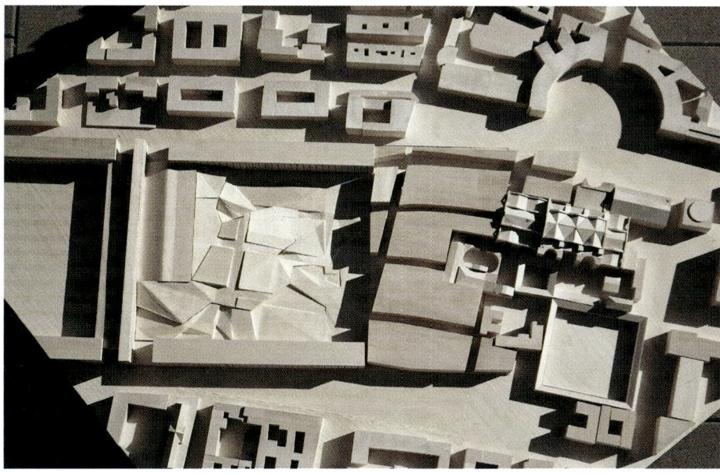

This project interrogates the idea of aggregation through the analysis of homogeneous and heterogeneous space as a construct of the existing condition of Rome. At the scale of the city, realized and unrealized axes that resulted from the Sixtus V plan create a heterogeneous organization with pockets of gridded streets producing zones of homogeneity. The project is located between the Baths of Diocletian and Termini Station. By extending the linear organization of the station, the project partially contains the Baths with a new homogeneous infill while framing the architectural intervention of the library. The intervention is both figure and ground, referencing the homogeneous infill adjacent to it while using the internal structure to further explore the relationships between the programmatic elements such as library, lecture hall, and museum which orient themselves to the realized and unrealized axis outside of the frame. In this way the project creates a new entrance to Rome which reveals past, present, and unrealized conditions of the city.

MID REVIEW

FINAL REVIEW

Rocker What I find really interesting is that the roof of the station becomes now a piece of ground and whoever arrives more or less has to slip into the ground condition. I think that is a very bold move in a good way. The figure remains being figure and yet it is submersed in the ground, and then there is this other axis coming across which becomes a figure and a ground at the same time.

Zenghelis One of the deductions is that the Sixtus the Fifth axis in this particular part of the city is irrelevant. It does not impinge on it. So why would you then begin to reproduce it in your project?

Rocker The whole point is that there is an ambiguity of these two things.

Allais Arguably urban spaces are ambiguous, so it is fitting that one arrives into the station into a condition of spatial ambiguity.

Zuliani Well you enter an interior space, there's no ambiguity there. Only the space outside plays that game.

Petit What I don't understand is why we have a grid inside rather than a striation. Those blocks talk about striation and the station is based on lines that all come in, and you are exactly nested in between those two. Why wouldn't you play on the striation rather than the block grid structure, which is for me completely foreign in this place?

Wigley On one level there's great intelligence of the work, except for these long sections, which unfortunately may give us the truth of the project. Why would you introduce a pseudo-grid when the actual grid is in operation? I don't have great suggestions for you for what to do with those stupid blocks. One is to make your landscape keep coming, just getting lower and lower. Even consider the possibility of reversing the landscape so actually it starts to climb up. I think you could forget about the figure and figure and say, would I like to go downhill or go uphill? You can throw your logic in at the end.

Zuliani It has an extraordinary clarity in relationship to the terminus. I mean those two blocks I find absolutely stunning. But you can simulate non-texture or non-ground very easily without having big lumps of wood. This is where the model kills the analysis.

Wigley It's like people hacking away at a parmesan wheel and half way through there's this faceted quality which doesn't really mean anything, though if you were in a Peter Eisenman studio you could say it's an aggregation of removals.

Carpo The smooth transition of continuity and homogeneity of space is what you were asked not to do. You're trying to find a way to look digital, and not smoothly digital. This digital looking monster in the middle works precisely because it is in the middle, because it has a frame.

Allais In new media this is called compositing, which means that difference is not smoothed over. I think although there are clearly formal problems to your project, the sort of exaggeration that you arrive at speaks to the urban condition. Compositing may very well be the best way to come up with a formal aggregation strategy.

Wigley When your analysis produces lousy stuff, get rid of the analysis.

Deamer I see this project as being completely didactic. You're bracketing off the whole city so you can show your experiment, this versus that. The arbitrariness of the decisions of how you laid out the library is exactly the problem.

Whiting For me the aggressive landscape is not designed enough above and below. The library actually seems too small underneath it to pull off that gesture at an urban scale. It is a residual of the pieces that you're bringing onto the site. The fact that it is so loyal to your analysis should be shed. I think what you see in this project is the confidence that it will get better in the next iteration.

Elisa Iturbe
Brittany Utting
Contested Rome

In the unstructured space of the Piazza de Termini, the library operates as a territorial stitch between the two potent objects of the site: the Baths of Diocletian and Termini Station. This new urban void enclosed by the incomplete frame of the library negotiates this restructuring of the site, producing a network of figured voids now oriented around the object of the Baths and aligned to its original axes. The spatial logic of the library belongs to both objects and thus flaunts its duplicity, oscillating between a state of belonging to and subversion of its urban context. What results is a schizophrenic landscape twisted between two constructs of space: the bath's aggregated logic of spatial modules and the homogenous linear expanse of the train station. The northern bar of the library resurrects the former frame of Diocletian, occupying the space of the bath's original outer wall. The eastern and western bars of the library repeat the framing logic of Termini, however reoriented to the baths and obscured by the homogenous infill of context. The bars of the library thus carve and are carved by the context, contaminated by their own terms of spatial negotiation.

MID REVIEW

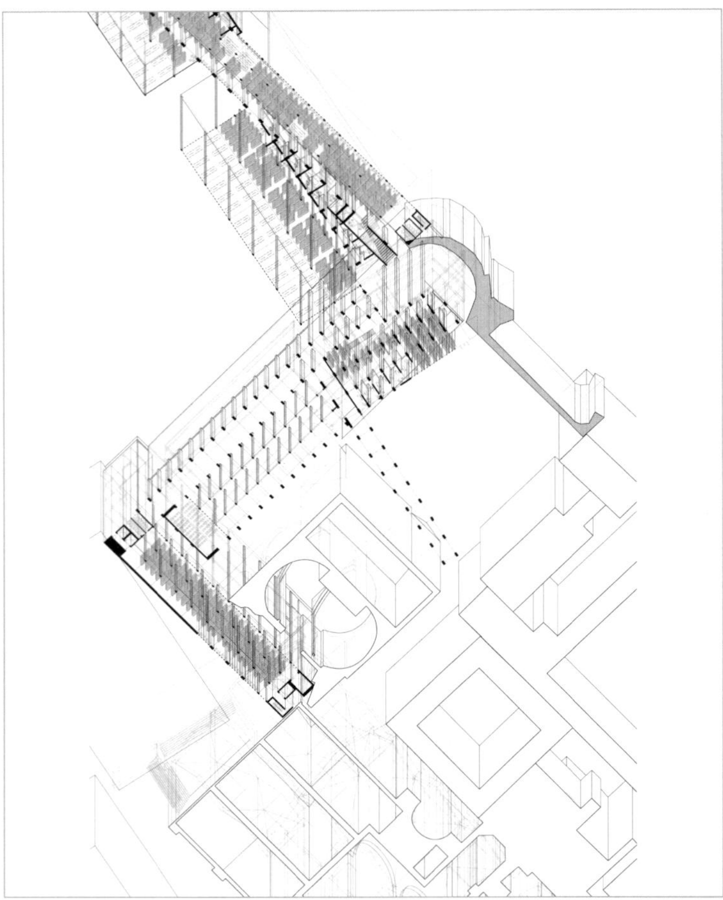

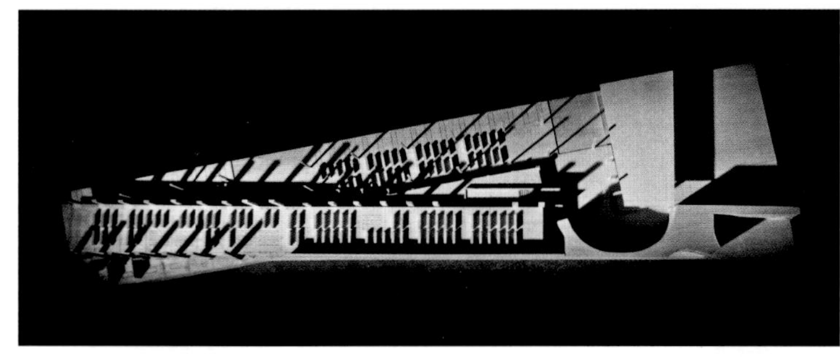

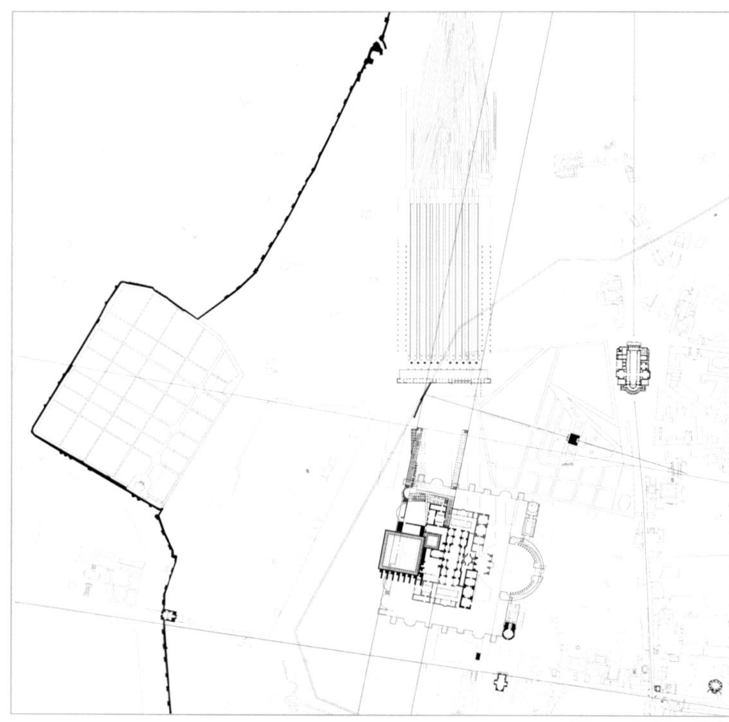

FINAL REVIEW

Petit It is a funny idea to put a facade in front of all these aggregated spaces becauseisn't that a way to smoothen out the difference? Isn't that the San Marco kind of way of absorbing difference in a common form of structure?

Davidson Or was it just that you moved the objects together and they've become so blended that if I didn't know Rome I would think this was some poche space from relatively self-similar architectural fabric? It really seems like the objects have created little minions. It's more of a camouflage than it is an aggregation of dis-aggregating

Eisenman They are dealing with the major railroad station of Rome. You can't arrive into a back alley. So the question is, is that scale inappropriate to the scale of Termini?

Tigerman No, it actually is appropriate because you understand that the trains come and they stop and they filter through. I don't see the relationship to the modular cellular condition of the baths. What you've done, appropriately, is favor the train by creating a great space for arrival because currently they arrive at nothing. What you haven't done it seems to me is pick up on the cellular activity, which could have been happening on the perimeter.

Zuliani The outer perimeter of the bath seems to be completely lost as a trace. You've kept the physical remains but you haven't used the perimeter to make a space within a space within a space in order to develop that cellular aggregation.

Petit There is a disconnect inscribed in the way Peter describes this studio, because how do you want to do aggregation and at the same time make people pick one of three typologies? For me that doesn't work and this is one of those projects where that problem is visible. We're dealing with a very conventional core typology, and once we go into the typology there isn't much that can move without destroying the whole project.

Wigley I think the description of the project is very good and the analysis is very interesting but the model is not as satisfying. You said you wanted to structure the void and if that's the case, only voids can be structured? The reverse side to this is that you can only get something out of nothing. At one scale your frames are dissolving and at another they're being undissolved. It all boils down to feeling like you need to do more interlocking. Also, all wood models are a waste of time. They are what architecture use to mean. Especially here.

Deamer The way that I was thinking about it wasn't the wood but solidity. You really want to read all the complexity of what you're doing with halls versus walls. We can't see columns versus walls. I think a lot of the stitching happens not necessarily where we have slippage of spaces but where there is porosity and where there is no porosity. When I look at this model, the most intriguing part for me is exactly where I can see a colonnade that doesn't actually make a courtyard. We want to see continuity but where we would expect to see it we're not seeing it. It's not wood, it's solidity that's not helping.

Bow When you travel around Europe and you go to all these great cities sometimes in great buildings you arrive in spaces that are dark, threatening. I love the idea of a cultural building here, I love the idea of making the space smaller, and we can talk endlessly about where's the front door and how the three fragments of the buildings actually work as a library. But for me it is all about the ground plane.

Allais In response to the idea that the scheme of the courtyard is the proper way to experience urban space or the proper way to give a sense of arrival to Termini Station, I think that this is what dictated the heavily processional, axial or beaux-arts nature of your urban plan, which bothered me. If you look at your drawing you have two notions of urban experience. One is this idea of terminus or arrival that requires mass space. If you look at the baths plan it has a different idea about urban space, which is arguably much more appropriate for the typology.

TENNESSEE VALLEY
Greg Lynn

HOUSTON, TEXAS
Pier Vittorio Aureli

REYKJAVIK, ICELAND
Deborah Berke

LONDON, ENGLAND
Frank O. Gehry

VIENNA, AUSTRIA
Brigitte Shim

DHAKA, BANGLADESH
David Adjaye

LIBREVILLE, GABON
Dan Wood

REYKJAVIK, ICELAND
Peggy Deamer

BRIDGE DAM DIKE

Greg Lynn

William B. and Charlotte Shepherd Davenport Visiting Professor

TENNESSEE VALLEY FACULTY: BRENNAN BUCK

This studio will indirectly address the issues germane to the New York Metropolitan Area raised by Hurricane Sandy as a method of engaging an ongoing local discussion that has larger consequences beyond the region. Instead of beginning by forming a problem from outside the discipline, our studio will begin by stating worthy intra-architectural problems that would change one's design response to the emerging challenges to design civic infrastructure in densely populated urban areas.

EXPANDED FIELD

Attention to the architecture of infrastructure comes and goes but presently infrastructure is a distinctly American and global question. Often, infrastructure is an opportunity to marry monumental form with structural expression and/or landscape design. Participation in the studio will involve a clear position on the status of monumental form and civic expression. Given the present journalistic and perhaps professional climate of aversion to civic expression this should be a hot button issue for everyone.

INFRA-INTERIOR

Infrastructure is often without volume and civic interior experience. This semester we will imbue infrastructure with internal experience, character, and identity to avoid the design of empty facades cladding large urban machines; even if it forces functions and experiences in unprecedented ways. This might also raise ideas about the boundary between public and private development.

FORMAL ENGAGEMENT WITH NEW MATERIALS AND MECHANICS

Everyone will be asked to look at: new materials and their structural and formal implications, such as the composite Neal Bridge in Maine; new mechanisms for extracting energy and directing natural forces, such as the Bath County Pumped Storage Station in Virginia; and a new paradigm for relating to a global ecology which is in transition with rising sea levels and changes in weather patterns.

DESIGN DEXTERITY

The studio will select three sites and three infrastructure building types that suggest different design problems in their site, typology, urbanism, and structure. Every student will quickly conceptualize a bridge, a damn, and a dike as a method of defining an architectural problem for themselves; such as the relationship of architecture to landscape, machine, roadway, water, topography, structure or other problems germane to the design of infrastructure.

JURORS

Michelle Addington
David Adjaye
Mark Foster Gage
Frank O. Gehry
Chuck Hoberman
Walter Hood
Jeffrey Kipnis
Nicolai Ouroussoff
Robert A.M. Stern
Stanley Tigerman

Feldman Nominee

Constance Vale
Cyclic Metamorphosis

Dams built in the 20th century utilized grand neoclassical façades to monumentalize the ingenuity of man. This proposal for a dam shifts the emphasis from the wall to the dam's moving parts and the spaces they envelope. Two key moving elements, the lock and gantry, are reinterpreted in their means of motion and form, as a set of rotating conic volumes. One complete revolution of the lock causes the water level within it to gradually fill and conversely drain, allowing boats to reach both river levels through the course of a 360 degree turn. The effect of both large moving objects on the exterior is a temporally transforming facade. On the interior, an oculus in the turbine hall, and linear aperture on the lock, allow both spaces to perform as inconstant observatories, charting their own engineered cyclic motion and the natural cyclic motion of the earth in relation to the sun. Both forms embedded in the dam wall are the result of subtractive operations made on two perfect conic volumes, causing these forms to be read as their primitive geometric source and as a more complex set of derivative surfaces that avoid a simple scalar reading. Sited along the Housatonic River, this dam is proposed as a replacement for two existing non-navigable dams. Consolidating these dams into a new dam with a lock will make the lower portion of the river navigable to the Atlantic. The new dam will also connect two currently isolated state parks that meet the river on either bank, and will merge their existing system of trails. One could equate its sublime qualities to those of a cathedral, presenting the question, how can architects engage infrastructure's potential as a new kind of monumental public space?

MID REVIEW

They are twins or a couple. Right now, they are autonomous to each other; one is for boats and one is for people. I want to find more spatial and programmatic tension between the two of them. It is a composition and right now they are not far enough apart to argue their isolation from each other. —Joel Sanders

FINAL REVIEW

Tigerman I've never seen something like this. A damn turbine is one thing, but to see it in another light, historically somewhere between Piranesi and Boullee, you really got it. The experience, spatially, is another look at monumentality. From that side it is brilliant.

Gage The fact that your project actually moves is incredible; coordinated with the actual geometry, I think it is stellar. There is something so epically ancient and monumental about this that it approaches the quality of the sublime, which is almost religious in its effects.

Ouroussoff What is interesting when you are talking about Boullée and Piranesi; there is something very nostalgic about this idea of being able to produce pyramids again. There is not any effort to minimize it. It is partly so beautiful because it is unashamed and celebrating that kind of scale. You could argue that every resistance to scale through Post-Modernism turned out to be a farce because scale just became bigger and bigger in terms of economics. Scale has always been there, but we are always trying to mitigate or hide it. People are afraid to celebrate it.

Lynn It is not a very big size; it is a very big scale.

Gage There is a tendency, which is a kind of a Rem-ing or Diller and Scofidio-ing of architecture schools, where you show the back stage or someone changing their clothes to make the project interesting. I appreciate your scheme because architecture makes the architecture interesting. In that sense, I think it is the Gehry of architecture student work; it is not the stuff or people you necessarily fill it with.

Hoberman Jumping back to the technical, just thinking about this massive turning element, could we just float it? If it is water at the lower level, could it just be like a boat? Build this boat with some gaps and some bumpers.

Gehry The imagery says everything.

Addington I am really interested in why you sited it the way you did. You seemed to choose a spot where you are not looking to make a reservoir, but it is a very discrete slice and not changing the flow of the stream that much. It is very intentional, and actually, completely out of scale for the type of work it is doing.

Ouroussoff It is about the two extremes of scale. It is meant to be two or three people walking through the space.

Hood In a way, this is geologic time. As you are hiking out, you can see things one way and by the time you get there they are another. That notion of finding something in the landscape, I find pretty powerful, especially thinking about the temporal quality of it.

Ouroussoff The slowness suits it. The funny thing is, at the beginning we were asking how often does this happen, as though we needed the experience to speed up. However, here slowing down makes complete sense, since the locks are used so infrequently.

Addington That is what I find intriguing. It is that one time per year when the gantry is up, which is when the valley is working.

Lynn We found there are a lot of people in the Tennessee River Valley that track this; on their computer, it is their home screen. You see when the flow is, you see when they are going to spill. There is a culture of river watching.

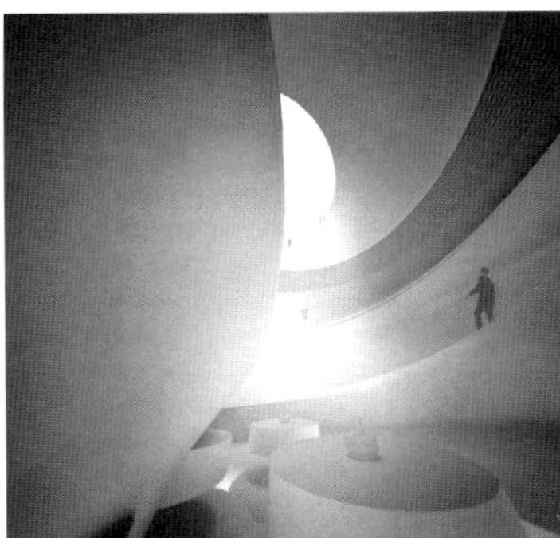

Justin Nguyen
Carapace

The civic character of typical dams is defined by two problems: their elements are either underground or highly internalized and their elements are experienced as disparate parts. This project uses the lock to reveal what would otherwise be underground or internalized functions—the penstocks, the spillways, the powerhouse and the turbine hall—by exposing them throughout the internal façade of the lock, similar to the Pompidou Center. Translating underground into underwater, the dam dramatizes this experience by submerging and revealing its elements within the space between the upstream and downstream of the river. This dam then unifies all these parts with a formal language of interiority and transparency that folds them into the wall of the dam; while this interiority is expressive, the rest of the dam's wall is muted. These elements become figure and relief along the wall of the lock, creating a new space that is both exterior and interior.

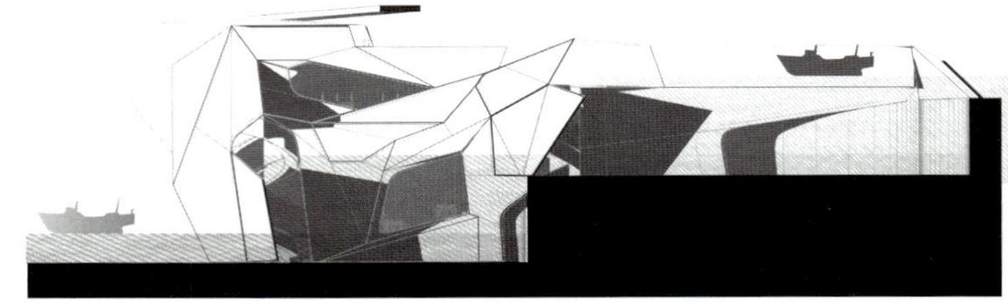

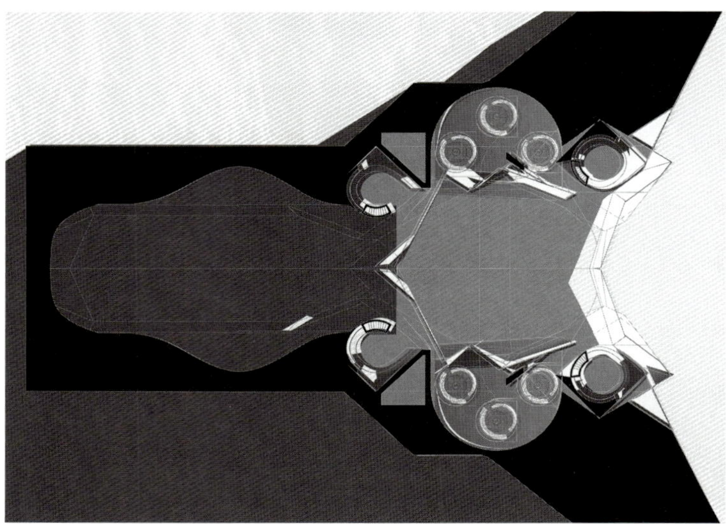

MID REVIEW

This is a fabulous interior elevation. What I appreciate is the development of a language. This is a strange constructed cliff face which is between sculpture, architecture, nature, and topography. You see this especially in the dynamics of how the section would work with constant change in relationship to the water. —Joel Sanders

FINAL REVIEW

Kipnis It is a threatening experience and a very particular architectural language. It is not an accidentally threatening experience. So, why is that? Everything is about increasing its intensity and its anxiety. This makes me like it, but why?

Tigerman It is about architecture. Dams have that threatening quality. The threat is always there, however, it is implicit. What he does is make it explicit. This is a threatening experience and he is finally revealing it for what it is, at some level.

Lynn It is calm on the outside and threatening on the inside because it's very blank.

Kipnis If you have a phobia you do not find out how bad it is until you are inside [laughter].

Lynn It is very blank and it is involuted. Everything is happening in this chamber.

Kipnis And you play "Death and Transfiguration" by Strauss when you are inside [laughter]. This is an architectural language you are interested in and you took the studio as an opportunity to explore it further. That is good. That is enough for me. So it is not that in the project you saw an opportunity to rethink the status of the dam. Instead, you have this goal of finding out your relationship to this body of formal work so you continued it in the studio.

Ouroussoff You are rewriting the narrative for him basically, right? You started by talking about exposing a machine, in which case everyone would have expected something very different.

Kipnis He is trying to find a way to apologize for the work. He did this work. What he did not want to get up and say is that, I understand this project, I worked it out, but I am interested in a certain kind of architecture, a certain formal language—and I wanted to continue that interest in this studio—because he thought he would get in trouble or something. There is no language I like better.

Tigerman When Greg stood up and showed the two doors that open and close, and when you are inside them, and those things are compressed; that is a threatening experience. It is very interesting that you decided to reveal and elaborate on that. It is very different from entering the Panama Canal, Chicago River Change, or the Brenta Canal. I admire that you decided it consciously.

Kipnis When a captive audience is put through that without any will, then you have different ethical options and responsibilities.

Lynn Why wouldn't everyone want to go see this?

Kipnis I'd be there in a minute.

Tigerman Absolutely. In a vessel.

Gage The production of terror is not foreign to the languages of architecture.

Hood It is interesting how it is so concentrated on one experience. You have eliminated every other part of the program.

Adjaye This is the genius of the project. I actually find it theatrical.

Ouroussoff Do you see the humor in your own project?

Tigerman Not humor—maybe irony.

Gage This is one of the most intense architectural places on Earth, if it is built. It has something to do with the mechanical idea of the sublime.

Ouroussoff It goes back to surrealist images of the machine and sex. It is Duchamp.

Tigerman I think it's a wonderful project. And it is—which I can't say for all of the projects—it is architecture, straight up.

Charles Hickox
HV-ERS

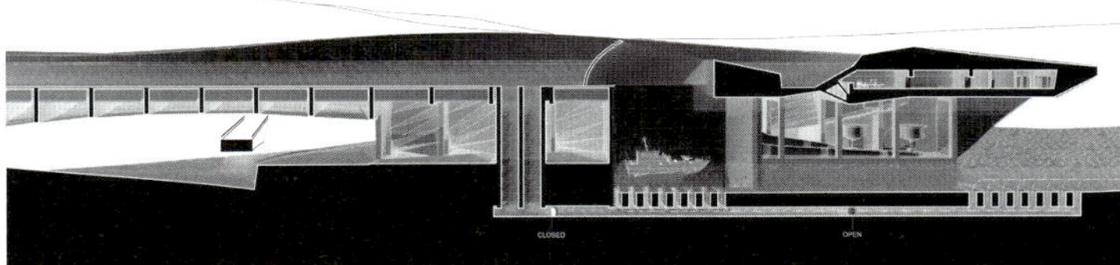

The Housatonic Valley Electric River Station proposes to resolve the primary adverse environmental impact associated with the introduction of a hydroelectric dam facility into a river system. HV-ERS extends from the generation station upstream to a point on the river which is naturally higher. The river is split into its natural flow and a new flow in which the water level is maintained at its current level until it reaches the HV-ERS basin. At this point, the water is fed into penstocks and forced through turbines, which creates electrical power without disrupting the continuity of the Housatonic River.

HV-ERS depends on a more dramatic topographical change than other dam types. For this reason it is especially suited to a rapids condition, such as Great Falls in Canaan CT, a half mile chain of rapids over which the Housatonic drops one hundred feet. Through HV-ERS, boats which would be wrecked by rapids on the existing rocks can bypass treacherous conditions on an even water level which terminates in a lock at its basin.

HV-ERS is situated mid-river and wrapped by continuous bands of broad pedestrian boardwalk, winding up from the river level, basin, and along the channel. Its support structure is skinned in reflective panels which take on the light and color from the river's surface. Strategic gaps between buttresses allow visitors to peer into the power station without posing a risk or nuisance. On the top of the basin the visitors are floating above the river, on the bottom, they are enveloped by it.

MID REVIEW

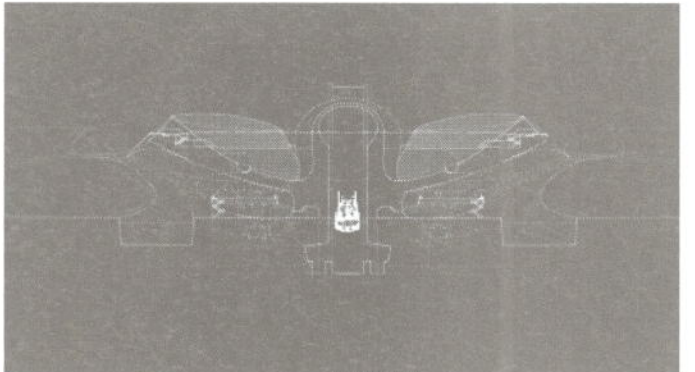

The great early dams of New England, like Kensico, were built out of stone. That automatically connects the man-made object into its natural setting; whereas, the use of concrete automatically divorces the building from the site. Don't be embarrassed to use natural materials. —Robert A.M. Stern

I think this wants to be plastic. Many of the other projects are looking to nineteenth century nostalgia; I would try to go more towards Starship Enterprise. —Greg Lynn

FINAL REVIEW

Gage Everything we have seen today is a connection between two points—a span. You have turned the dam into an object. It switches back and forth between human circulation and boats, and that is ingenious. The question should be, for Michelle, if this is a hydro-dam, is the architecture dramatically in excess of what it is doing?

Kipnis It looks like the Starship Enterprise landed and got beached, and now the Dilithium crystals cannot be found anymore, so they have to generate energy with water.

Gage Everyone is asking about the architecture and what they really want to know is why it looks so Calatrava-like.

Kipnis Nah, Calatrava would never make a great beak like that. This is Donald Duck. This is great because it has a sense of humor. Have you ever seen any sense of humor, on purpose, from Calatrava?

Hood When the water comes in, why is there a bulge right before it gets to the end? Are you bringing in the same amount of water the entire way or do you need to hold a different capacity at different points? Is there something hydrological about this form or is it much more of a gesture?

Lynn Consistently, you have kept the language and let's say the tectonics uneasy. It has been Starship Enterprise, it has been post-industrial...

Ouroussoff The language is different in the images too. I keep seeing lampshades in those turbines. It is very different in terms of the way it is shown in the drawings and the model. You are still struggling to get to a language.

Gage I think this spaceship direction is wrong. The highly polished character is wrong. I think the massive ruin that is somehow foreign and ancient is a more interesting direction that you already have going with the materiality. The highly overdesigned, aerodynamic—unless it is ironically a duck, and pop and funny—just does not feel quite right.

Kipnis I am on the pop and funny side.

Hoberman I would like to recognize this project as one that says, let's rethink how a dam works. In my experience as an engineer working with architects, one of the dilemmas with the architectural process is invention and innovation are not really a part of the program, yet they should be. This is a project that does not belie the details at the very end, so I think it is great.

Ouroussoff You know this is like a Kazuo Shinohara house with extremely muscular structure for a very small space—it is really hard to believe the structure makes any sense, but it does in the end. It has to be that muscular. On an infrastructure scale if you have all of that water held up in the air, it actually makes structural sense. It could also give it a visual language that makes sense.

Kipnis We have been talking about alternatives to machoism, and to find a durational sense of humor—not wit, not irony—is one of the possibilities. That is why, for example, I picked the duck-billed platypus to be biologically more accurate. It is great that you can come out of a studio with five or six ideas when, coming in, I did not think there were going to be any.

Hoberman That is the great idea of giving a problem that nobody has thought about for one hundred years.

PRODUCTION/REPRODUCTION: HOW TO LIVE TOGETHER Pier Vittorio Aureli

William B. and Charlotte Shepherd Davenport Visiting Professorship of Architectural Design

HOUSTON, TEXAS **FACULTY: AIDAN DOYLE**

THE PROJECT OF THE DOMESTIC

Departing from the rich legacy of emancipatory movements in the United States, our Spring studio asks that we rethink the architecture of domestic space as way to imagine alternative forms of life. The studio will begin with a rigorous study of the house as both an economic/political apparatus and an architectural space, encouraging students to propose different modes of housing within our contemporary condition. A great emphasis will be given to the role of the house and housing within the context of American cities. While the history of European cities has largely been shaped by the invention and development of Public Space, the evolution of the American city has been largely driven by the politics of home-ownership. The studio will focus on the city of Houston which is one of the most "archetypical" American cities, embodying the most relevant forces and conflicts that have shaped urbanity in the United States. Houston embodies a city with no zoning, no urban rules at large, but where economic, political and racial factors have strictly determined the form of the city.

We might say that Houston represents—in its most concise and extreme form—the 20th century capitalist city. It is a city in which concepts of individualism, home ownership and suburbanization are the sine qua non of development. The challenge of the studio is to rethink this condition not by large-scale reform or planning, but by the careful reform of domestic space itself. The hypothesis put forward by the studio is that by changing the nature of the domestic, more general issues about political economy and governance will be questioned. What forms of life can be imagined as alternatives to the one enacted by the single family house? Is it possible to live together with social relationships that do not rely on the family as the only form of human association? Finally, can we imagine a new "Grand Domestic Revolution" within the current of today's insurgent political forces?

RESEARCH STRUCTURE: HOUSTON AS A PARADIGM / A PROJECT FOR HOUSTON

The studio will be conducted as a Thesis studio, which means that the students are responsible for their own brief. The brief is an integral component of the project and it cannot be assumed as a ready-made starting point for design. The first month of the studio will be dedicated to the study of Houston as a paradigmatic urban condition. Research will be organized into three trajectories—urban politics, urban form and specific projects of housing in the US. The goal of this first enquiry is to define Houston as a paradigmatic model of 20th century urbanization. The studio assumes that only by conceptualizing the existing city it will be possible to define a possible project for its future.

By focusing on one of five given themes of living conditions, each group of students will develop a domestic prototype whose goal is a wider application within the city urban form. Each prototype should clearly articulate a specific living condition that challenges current housing habits. Although the prototype will be developed as an architectural example, the premises for the latter are to be defined through careful analysis of the subject(s) at stake. We expect this exercise to test the utmost basic conditions of architecture: enclosure, separation, and inhabitation. A fundamental aspect that must be taken in consideration is comfort in a domestic interior. Comfort can be understood as having a space that is generous in size, but also as owning an individual room of one's own no matter how small; it can be conceived as quantity or quality of lighting, as the possibility of silence, or as the presence of a significant view from one's window. Therefore, the elaboration of an idea of interior—both from the architectural and the environmental point of view—will be at the core of this year's advanced studio. The relationship between immaterial needs, ambitions, and desires, and the movement of the body in space, its physical presence in a specific place, is at the root of such a research. The goal of the studio is to develop a strategic plan for Houston that uses the prototypes as complementary parts.

JURORS

Ioanna Angelidou
Andrew Benner
Cynthia Davidson
Peter Eisenman
Keith Krumwiede
Lars Lerup
Mary McLeod
Stanislaus von Moos
Emmanuel Petit
Alan Plattus
Albert Pope
Matt Roman
Surry Schlabs
Robert A.M. Stern

Feldman Nominees

Daniel Jacobs
Brittany Utting
Alcova

Because of Houston's tactics of territorial annexation and leap frogging developments, the outer loop is a patchwork of linear gaps and interstices, empty spaces between places, and excluded as other and outer. These spaces function as buffer zones between suburban enclaves belonging to neither, and therefore maintained by no one; ownership is both contested and blurred. We are proposing the archetype of the wall as a typological solution for these linear domains and a space in which to restructure the project of domestic inhabitation. Opposed to the autonomous unit of the home, the linear archetype is instead a homogenous bar with an open and negotiable interior, countering the paradigm of partition and subdivision within domestic space.

The inhabited wall becomes a cabinet for the body, containing in its poché the spaces for reproduction and thus freeing the space of the dwelling for living and working. The necessary infrastructure for living—bedrooms, bathrooms, kitchens, laundry, storage—are embedded within wall niches and alcoves in measured intervals. By compressing all of the functions of living into the wall, the resultant spaces are allowed to be empty. They are freed from domestic infrastructural requirements, clearing space for the self-employed, the freelancer, and the entrepreneur. We are reclaiming the generic character of the home and reorganizing it into a highly specific cabinet of living and labor, which introduces the body as a centerpiece for a restructuring of domestic space.

MID REVIEW

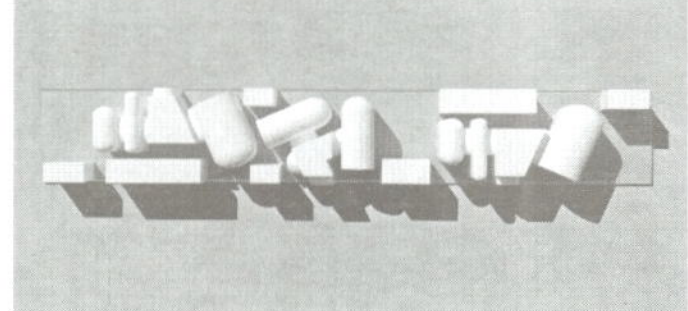

Are there rules that keep it so pure? The homeowner's association next door says no gnomes in the garden, but this also looks very strict. —Keller Easterling

FINAL REVIEW

Aureli This is a community, not a house. It's not a traditional domestic space. It's a community that works by people trusting each other, living together, sharing the space.

Stern But for how many? You can't afford to have such an amount of shared space for so few people. It doesn't make sense, communal or not. From the drawings I calculate about 50,000 square feet of space for 250 people.

Plattus The inhabited wall, whether you buy it or not, makes a certain amount of sense given the geometry of the site. At the end of the day there are less than 200 square feet per person in this scheme. Bob, I doubt you have recently done a residential project, including dormitories, where you've been that economical. We were talking as if this is the most profligate project in the world.

Lerup This is a proposition, however absurd it might be, on how we exist. Whether it is exactly right in terms of numbers, who cares? This proposition suggests another way of dividing night and day.

McLeod Can I suggest exploring Kahn further, and looking at his beautiful monastery project? Instead of poché, it's objects in a courtyard. I would love to reverse this scheme. I have no trouble thinking of it as a commune—as zones.

Petit I would like to question the symmetry of this. The sun still comes from one side and not the other, and orientation matters.

Pope The intimate spaces in the poché are always fixed. You can maximize the flexibility in everything else, and I agree, the symmetry is not helping you do that.

Krumwiede You would never read the symmetry from an urban standpoint. It's so long you would never see both sides at once. The massive north face and massive south face are fundamentally different, with different lighting conditions. If the project were to move forward still on its own terms as a commune, I think you would look to incorporate other parameters that wouldn't undermine the basic social argument. The adjacent spaces would be a lot more flexible if you didn't have that singular solid wall.

Lerup It's a clever move to insert something very large, because this space needs framing. So then it is not autonomous, it is about its context and the more regimented, larger and impressive this is, the more clarity you will get. It's a very important aspect of Houston's fragmentation. Your site is an area that nobody knows how to occupy. We've had very few projects attempt to sew it together in some way, or make it more clear where the borders lie.

Krumwiede There is a sense in many of these projects of something deeply Houston, with an absence of any sense of Houston's climate.

Schlabs On that note, Mary brought up Kahn earlier. The Kahn projects that this compels me to think of are the ones he did for India and Bangladesh, where he wrapped the buildings in ruins to mitigate the climactic effects of living in a tropical environment. There's plenty of room for Kahn here, but it's the tropical Kahn.

Aureli For me what is most important here is the idea of the alcove—to rethink it. The alcova is the way, before conventional apartments with bedrooms and bathrooms, housing used to be. The way it is presented here it is an archetype rather than a specific solution.

Lerup What I like about all the schemes is they go back to this question, how to live together. This is a question that is poorly answered in Houston, there are very few alternative ways of living that are really interesting. We who are Houstonians appreciate a view from the east on this. Thank you very much. I hope this is soon over and we can have martinis.

Elisa Iturbe
Laurence Lumley
Asylum

Immigrants—both documented and undocumented—operate from a cultural, economic or legal periphery from which they cannot take access to urban and natural resources for granted. As it stands, documented immigrants lucky enough to be offered housing are usually placed in unsuitable converted apartment buildings that hide them from the city. Meanwhile, undocumented workers are an unrecognized but hugely significant part of our labor force. Our project, then, is to design a new housing typology that, through land access and opportunities for self-sufficiency, addresses issues of integration and visibility. We seek to make the immigrant community and their productive labor visible within the city, and to create a third condition between exception and assimilation (the usual choices offered to new arrivals); one in which the migrant is granted both a right to be a stranger and the right to place and home.

The scheme consists of a sequence of bands, comprising residential bars (formed from a repeated module of 30 private cells sharing generous communal kitchens and two courtyards for outdoor living and working), labor bars (equipped for agricultural production and storage), kitchen gardens, farmland, and un-programmed open spaces that allow for the activities of the informal economy. All these spaces are connected by a central spine, planted with live oaks, creating a space of non-vehicular circulation shaded from the Texas sun. The spine is lined with market stalls where the produce of the land and the products of the informal economy can be sold to the city. In this way our project opens up access to the city, subverting the prevalent spatial structure of Houston, the isolated subdivision, and making visible the labor of an otherwise invisible population.

MID REVIEW

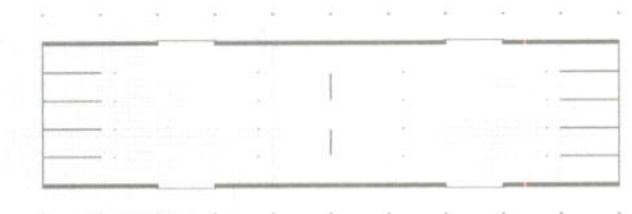

It is autonomous, but only in a bargain. Ironically you have freedom because you are interdependent. If your neighbors know you are stable, you create a market of protection that keeps you from being ghettoized. —Keller Easterling

FINAL REVIEW

Petit I understand the idea of alienation, I understand the history, but I would like to hear you say more about the kind of alienation that you suggest and if it would be effective in this context. Despite its absolute beauty, I would question if alienation can be effective when it has absolutely nothing to do with the context you've implanted.

Iturbe We are less interested in alienation, and more interested in autonomy, and the idea of a subject who by nature has to operate outside of the system.

Petit I get that. But just take the redness. We know what these bright colors would mean for Barragán, but here, what is the redness of this doing? How does it relate to this cultural context?

Lerup What I like about this project is exactly this largesse. It asserts itself in these little housey-houses. This is a large piece that's put in, taking the social model of the Russian concourse or the kibbutz.

Plattus At the same time, what I've liked about this since I saw it at midterm is that kind of industrial scale. You could do this in a compact area, but the space is there so fill it up. These are really big barchesse, working barns that are themselves architectural arms. It reminds me of the Palladian villa that has no villa, it's all barchesse. Farmyards actually work like this on working farms. In good weather people will bring the table into them and have a meal outside.

Davidson The question is who made the meal. The same person who's doing the laundry?

Stern Fine, I have another question. You are institutionalizing the decentralization of a city that is one of the most decentralized cities in the United States. Does that bother you? You're also institutionalizing—you're locking into a moment—the immigrant population, as though many of them don't want to integrate with the larger, let's call it Anglo, model. Which is not true. Many do, some don't.

Krumwiede What would it mean to you if we said, what if it was not migrant workers, or undocumented workers? Would this be good housing? I want to see how we might dislodge this from your subject and start to see it on other terms. The undocumented worker, they're not all farmers. What you're looking at in Houston, the policies that produced the decentralization you're talking about, they adapt and typologies are inhabited in different ways. I would like to speculate how this might be inhabited by a different class of worker, a family perhaps.

Pope It doesn't work, but it could. I don't think this is a city of the dispossessed; it's an alternative urban model. There is something abstract about the renderings that makes me think it's not a do-it-yourself project. It's something more institutionalized. It's not an alternate city but the next city, built in the interstices of what exists, but ultimately built to replace what exists.

Aureli For me, every project starts with a specific subject. The Palladian villa is a response to a specific subject, but at a certain point it can become a general paradigm for the city. They are not addressing the subject of the dispossessed. It's a particular subject that is very ubiquitous but invisible. They are addressing a subject that now lives in many different kinds of situations, giving them some kind of recognition through housing, but I think the structure is resilient enough to allow a transformation.

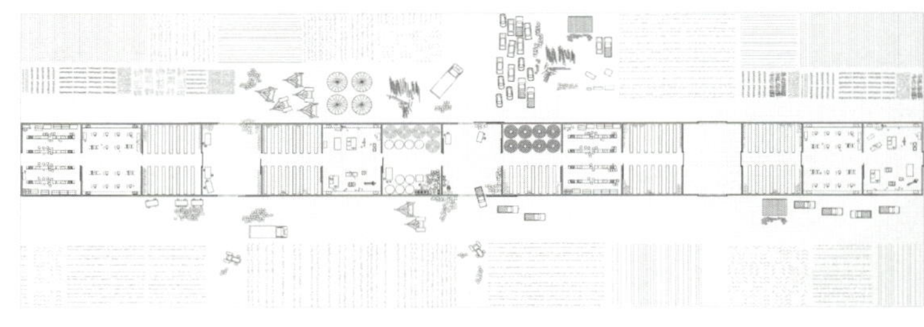

Brandon Hall
Lodge

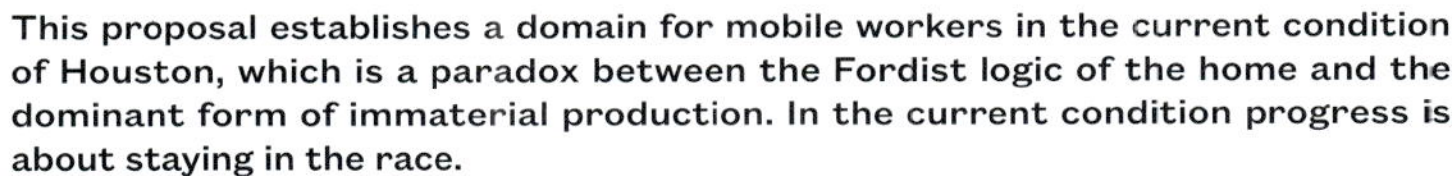

This proposal establishes a domain for mobile workers in the current condition of Houston, which is a paradox between the Fordist logic of the home and the dominant form of immaterial production. In the current condition progress is about staying in the race.

The project questions not only the home but also the individual, understanding that the development of technology has created a new condition of living, starting from scratch. The subject longs to free themselves from experience and the exhaustion that comes from devouring everything, both culture and people. Just in time production processes have undermined the typical economic condition, devaluing work. Rather than innovating, contemporary labor is forced to respond to current economic desires. Simultaneously, the conflict between the speed of information technology and the slowness of life creates a struggle. How can an individual exist in this dual condition?

Despite a commitment to the place and the work, the mobile desires only to lodge; to have habitation or quarters; to come to rest; to stick. The contemporary American condition is driven by the ideal of home and land ownership, framed by the narrative of the American dream. While the single family home supports a certain way of living, it also promotes a static form of life, tied to the investment of the home. New forms of work have promoted new forms of living, where the individual must be highly mobile in order to capitalize on opportunity.

As a critique of the generic hotel which is placed in the speed-zones of major cities, this project integrates simultaneously with the context and the employer, tailoring space to the kind of work needed and establishing proximity to the place of work. The project utilizes interstitial space to deploy three distinct typologies as strategic interventions in the contemporary suburban landscape, addressing conditions found in the zone between the ring roads of I-610 and I-8. The conditions are the parking lot, the suburban lot, and the lacuna (vast open space). By matching these conditions to the typology of the mat, the tower, and the cabin, the project seeks a legible domain for the subject who is often confined to a replicated spatial product.

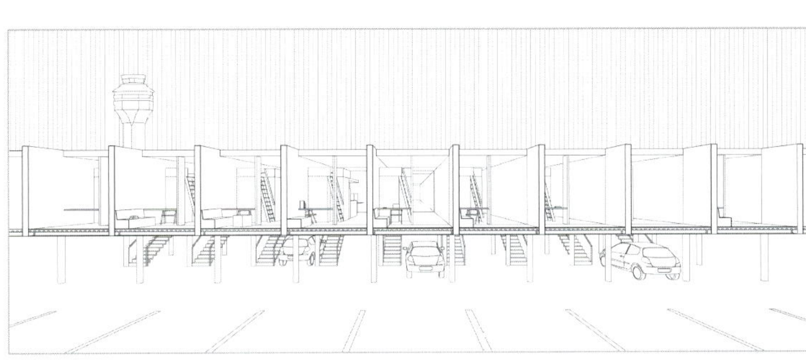

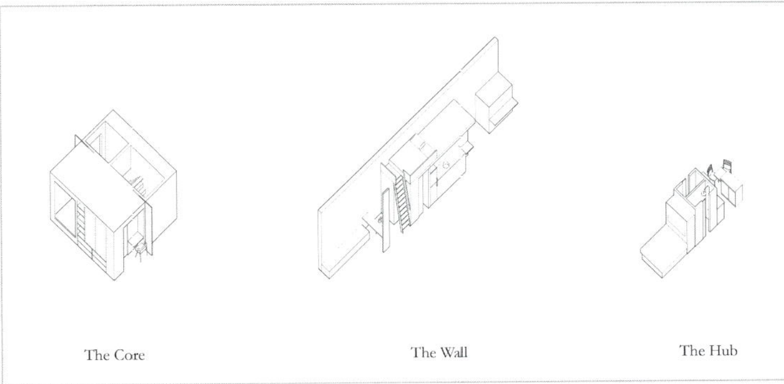

MID REVIEW

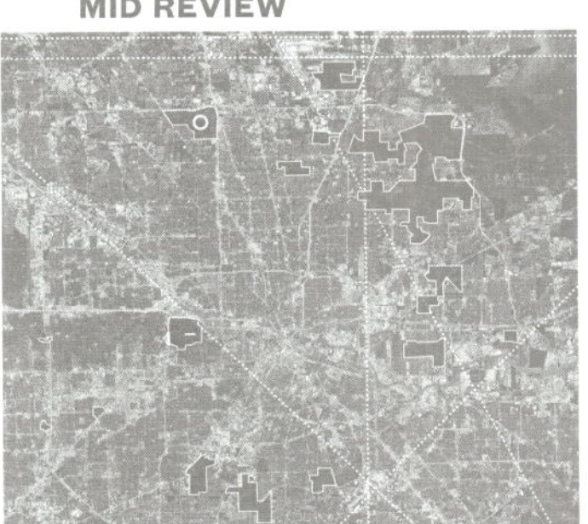

I see these as potentially symbiotic conditions but at very different ends of the spectrum. I wonder if you'd like to position it that way, or if you see it as studies of the same problem. —Alan Plattus

FINAL REVIEW

Lerup This project appeals a lot to me because there is that suggestion that the collective is virtual. Ultimately, that is a much more viable model than the physically expressed collective.

Pope You use a single subject to describe all of what you've done, but I can't imagine more different scenarios. They seem to be the opposite of what you described as the single subject position, which interestingly enough you call a worker. I'm not quite sure that generic term applies anymore, and it may be the thrust of the argument or the proof of the project that you can't forge a single identity out of this group of people.

Davidson What unites these three different things is a community of isolation. I don't know where the community comes from except the repetition of units—there is no exchange.

Petit But you can't just accept the isolation. That would be stepping into nihilism. You're an architect and you must have some sense of optimism about the future, but it seems that you helped the apocalypse come a little faster. The ambition to visualize something, especially in this studio, is to pay attention to a problem that exists. That's not nihilist. It's constructive.

Schlabs Charles Bukowski said he wasn't a misanthrope, he just liked sitting alone in a room drinking and smoking himself into a stupor. I don't think this is necessarily as cynical as you make it out to be.

Krumwiede I don't think he's trying to produce an environment for the digitally connected yet socially isolated worker. We all want those moments of isolation sometimes, but don't demonstrate a uniform behavior or emotional state continuously, we vacillate.

Plattus So whoever lives in this is probably going to have a storage locker somewhere. They may have a locker in a gym or health club. So scattered around the urban no place will be these equally single purpose minimal facilities which are part of the hidden infrastructure that supports what you're doing. I think you got caught up and fetishized just the architecture of the individual unit rather than the range of spaces that are actually like it and connected to it.

Eisenman Here we are debating a sociological and anthropological issue, of which we know little, rather than accepting the sociological premises and saying, is this a good example of wanting to be alone, architecturally?

Aureli It's accepting the extreme banality of the housing landscape, hoping that by making it explicit you can relieve it.

Stern Other people have argued that the typical American suburban house is not banal. The coding and the interesting things in the façade that are derived by many moves from historical prototypes mean a great deal in instinctive ways to the people who live there.

Angelidou You have models of individual types, but you didn't smash them together.

OPNA Deborah Berke

William Henry Bishop Visiting Professorship of Architectural Design

REYKJAVIK, ICELAND FACULTY: NOAH BIKLEN

"All human beings have three lives—public, private, and secret." —Gabriel Garcia Marquez

"The fantastic advances in the field of electronic communication constitute a greater danger to the privacy of the individual." —Earl Warren, 1963

"Secrecy is for losers. ... "
—Senator Patrick Moynihan, 1998

In this studio we will design an institute and advocacy center located in Reykjavik, Iceland dedicated to issues of digital transparency, internet privacy, and free speech.

REYKJAVIK, ICELAND

Iceland is emerging as a potential global free speech safe haven apace with the needs of our contemporary digital age. Iceland's 2008 banking crisis provoked widespread concern about issues of corporate and governmental transparency and raised questions regarding the role of the internet in public life. In the aftermath of the crisis, Iceland's parliament's passed the Icelandic Modern Media Initiative (IMMI), which attempts to rethink the necessary protection of free speech in the internet era, the Icelandic court ordered credit card companies to process donations to Wikileaks, and social media platforms provided an arena to advance a crowd sourced alternative constitution. Iceland boasts the highest percentage of households with connection to the internet in Europe and a nascent industry in geothermal powered data centers.

INSTITUTE AND ADVOCACY CENTER

This studio project—the design of an institute dedicated to issues of internet freedom—takes place within the context of an ongoing and contested international debate about the relationship between internet privacy, access, free speech, and security. We will begin the semester by researching the "architecture" of the internet, data-mining and surveillance, changing understandings of privacy, the politics of access, encryption protocols, and open-source networks. Through sketch problems and the analysis of architectural precedents we will explore the spatial implications of digital surveillance and privacy. Finally, we will trace the architecture and visual style of "cypherpunk" culture, surveillance, and internet activism through film—the glow of the computer screen, fluorescent lighting and reflective glass, the sleek whites, grays and blacks, the alluring repetition of the powder-coated servers, the distinct hum of data storage facilities, the hoodie.

After the studio trip to Iceland the students will begin the design of the 50,000 square foot institute and its site in Reykjavik. The studio program will include public spaces for receptions, events, lectures, and installations, studio spaces for audio-visual production and transmissions, lab spaces for workshops, office and back of house spaces, a guest house for visiting scholars and researchers, and an approach to digital security and storage.

This studio takes as its premise that architecture has a role to play in the debate about digital protections, access, and security. What is the architecture of digital freedom and radical transparency? This studio will examine the spatial implications of the tension between user friendly accessibility and the cumbersome requirements of encryption. Students will be asked to confront the performative requirements for the architectural envelope in regards to the Icelandic climate and energy use, daylight control, institutional brand identity, and transparency. We will explore the ideas of threshold between open and secure spaces, the demands for adaptability required of spaces that incorporate technology, and the relationship between virtual surveillance and physical space. Through the lens of architecture we will challenge the well-worn binaries of open/closed, transparent/opaque, public/private, and seamless/discontinuous. The studio will work primarily in perspective and model, with emphasis on the relationship between digital processes and materiality.

JURORS

Peggy Deamer
Kyle Dugdale
Martin Finio
Cathleen McGuigan
Mary McLeod
Dan Michaelson
Emmanuel Petit
Damon Rich
Robert A.M. Stern
Mason White

Feldman Nominee

Kate Warren
1V2364DcfvQvud9s9

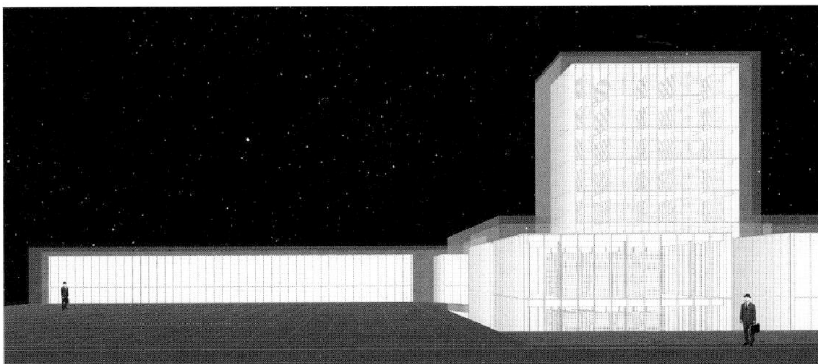

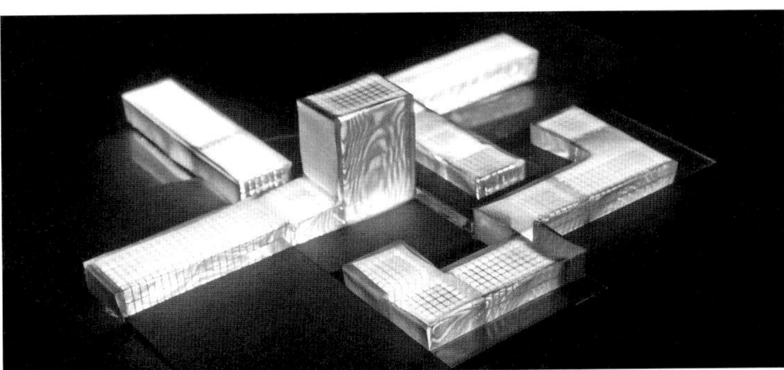

This proposal uses the World Wide Web as a metaphor for the formal generation of the building—in the contemporary sense of how we use the internet, we are in a constant balancing act of protecting our personal information while taking advantage of conveniences the internet offers. We may believe our personal information is protected by "secure" sites, but time and time again the insecurity of the internet is revealed. The program of this building contains a similar contradiction—on one hand, it is intended to be a building of public outreach through education programs on computer literacy and the current state of surveillance. On the other, it contains asylum apartments for people taking advantage of the initiatives' freedoms, as well as containing a data center that would cater to clients and organizations wishing to store sensitive information.

The building separates these major functions into four separate wings—a secure wing, with the data center and apartments; an administrative wing, with offices for the day to day running of the institute; an event wing; and a public outreach wing, with workshops, fabrication labs, and a library. These four wings are connected by a two level networking system—on the lower level, it is a lobby, while the upper level is a public pathway that connects to a 30km waterfront walk circumnavigating Reykjavik. The entire building is covered by two layers of metal screen. This screen acts as a sort of layer of encryption over the building by giving the building a monolithic appearance during the day and providing a reading of the interior by night.

MID REVIEW

The screen is our life. There is a one to one relation between the black screens and the volumes they enclose. It is interesting to think about that in all its meanings—architecturally, socially, projection, etc. How can the outer layer become something more than just referencing the inner layer? What does it become as a larger component of the project? —Martin Finio

Your project, at this point, is too nice. —Pier Vittorio Aureli

FINAL REVIEW

Finio I think it's incredibly beautiful and deft and sophisticated. Having said that, I still want more! I still feel like there's so much more that we can't see that you know about the project that I'd love to be able to make manifest.

Michaelson On the most basic level it is a really good strategy to solve this brief through a campus or a system of separate moving pieces. It helps you avoid the problem many previous projects ran into of attempting to totalize the solution into a single cosmology. Now, you have this set of parts that can be combined in different, more unpredictable programmatic relationships. Plus, it not only echoes network architecture as we see on the internet, but it also echoes the architecture of the computer—subsystems separately engineered to make a whole.

Deamer I see it as a Magritte, a kind of strange surreal, one that has a not-worked out quality and isn't a real place. This is a ghostly place and it doesn't want to articulate its difference. I look in here and I don't think, oh wow, those are cool spaces. I think they are creepy! Maybe you wanted to be creepy.

Warren That was an intention, something that is a little bit unknown.

Rich This is why I found it ironic that Emmanuel was speculating about the urbanistic qualities here. I think at midterm someone, it might have been me, named this project 'The Black Mass.' I read it as a strong criticism or skepticism about the program you were given.

Stern I am with Peggy. It's sort of a creepy scheme. It's also very suburban in my view. If you're going to do a very minimalist architecture, like was done in California—which is odd to see in Reykjavik by the way—it is usually done in a very temperate climate friendly to architecture, as was done in the 1950s and 1960s by Raphael Soriano or Craig Ellwood.

McGuigan I think it is so interesting that Bob evokes California when I can think of few places that are less indoor-outdoor than Reykjavik. Wouldn't these buildings have screens everywhere and be creating an internal climate and world against this really inhospitable environment? I'm wondering why you might not actually create a place that had more screens and virtual views.

Petit I'd agree with that because, at first, when you started presenting I thought this was taken from a Godard movie. However, with Godard, you have Paris represented through reflections of Paris in glass. You barely have glass. In fact, you have screens so that you do not have the reflections. I kept thinking, what can we do with that? Now that you mention the virtual views, that might be exactly it! Meaning, your building could cause the kind of disorientation that Godard was interested in, but instead of having reflections of real Paris in real glass, yours would be a virtual world of screens meeting real screens and that would cause disorientation. And if that was the idea...

Stern I'm lost...

Petit Well that's the point! [laughter] And why do you need the tower, which gives you an orientation as if this was a little village, which you do not want it to be. Why is the foundation so centralized and based on the square? It is like a humanist plan; what has that got to do with any of this?

Katie Stranix
The OPNA Institute

This studio project is for an institute and advocacy center dedicated to issues of digital transparency, internet privacy and free speech. The Institute and a fully functional data center coexist in an effort to reveal the physical space of data to the public. By uncovering these ordinarily inaccessible spaces, humans have the opportunity to physically interact with the essential infrastructures they virtually engage on a daily basis.
The OPNA Institute brings the infrastructure of data to the forefront as a didactic effort to increase public awareness of the physical ramifications of digital activity. The user of the building is exploiting the nature of the data center architecture rather than be exploited by it.

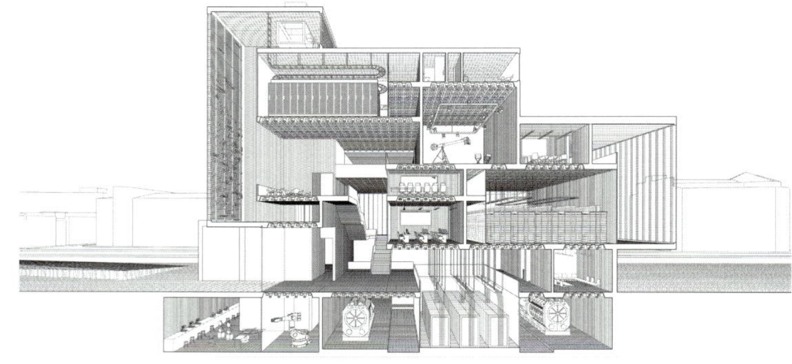

MID REVIEW

There is a sort of sublime and terrifying beauty to your project. For the first time we are confronted with architecture that is not made for humans. For a didactic purpose, you allow people to understand what experience we are confronted with, but you have to be consistent. In a way, this could be a sort of data center museum of information. —Pier Vittorio Aureli

FINAL REVIEW

Stern This is a beautiful presentation and it is not an uninteresting building. It does not quite look like what it might want to be—it does not look urban in a funny way. It looks almost—you're going to kill me—like a beach house.

Berke I'm going to kill you.

Stern Well Peggy and I agree about this; there is something about the scale of it. Also, you do not have one drawing that bangs the arrival sequence home. How do you get there; what are the most important things about arriving at the building?

McLeod What I'm struggling with is the overall organization feels a bit arbitrary. It is in and out on all four sides almost, except the one tape wall, which has some constancy. I can't help it, but I also thought of Paul Rudolph and this building—I mean I felt there was this constant sectional shift.

Rich Sometimes as a guest critic you misremember midterm, but if I remember at all accurately, you professed a lot of interest at midterm for disassembling this inherently non-human space of the data center and choreographing this visit to it. This kind of representation undermines what I've loved so much about what you professed at midterm, which was an interweaving of public and private space.

Michaelson I agree. I thought there was a lot more clarity; it was this very involuted little knot with a very clear path. What you have is wonderful to look at, but it is very complex and flat.

Stranix What I took away from the mid review was that it was too didactic, that it was very choreographed.

McLeod Well, maybe it is at the point where some of that didactic quality would help clarify the situation. And, if I were you, I might have answered Bob that you wanted a museum of this data material and made that very clear. It was about showing all the guts.

Deamer I agree because when I hear that story about docents it is like, Oh! Yes! This is as much about educating the viewer as in a museum. Here, it is not as straight as possible, and so the things that you love—this is going to be cruel—are reduced to features, and that's not helping you. So then the complexity of this looks like you're completely fearful of that repetition.

Petit I totally agree with Peggy. I thought the way you started your presentation was great. I mean to finally see servers—I mean we haven't seen servers all day—so you showed them. Then all the qualities that you described are evident in your building, and the server spaces are just reduced to fish in an aquarium, which you put into a house that has nothing to do with the aquarium. So I too expected to see very repetitive, linear spaces where the long chain would be the trick. Then suddenly cubes come in, and the cubes, they get nested within one another, something that servers will never do; they cannot do. The seriality is killed by giving each cube a different expression and orientation. I think the server spaces are so linear because every server looks the same, is oriented the same way, and functions the same way; and you negate all that in your architecture. The whole technology stuff—the fish in the aquarium—they are really just a gimmick to become a decoration on a wall, or window. So you did not activate those very things that in fact you wanted to point to which are so different for this type of building.

Berke Propose it as an aquarium.

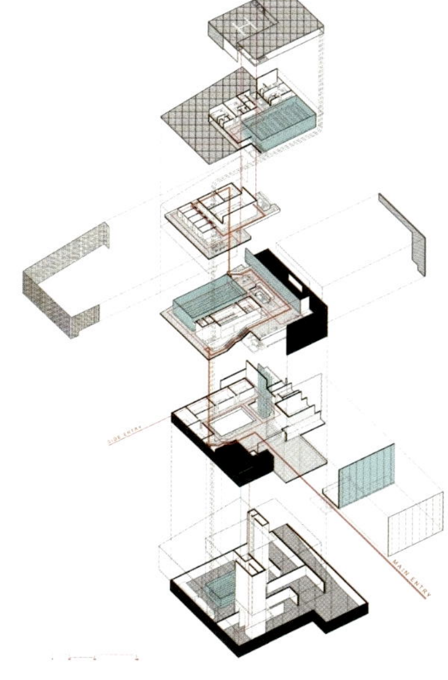

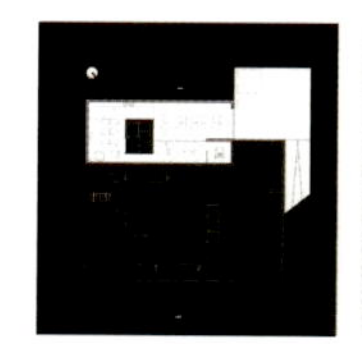

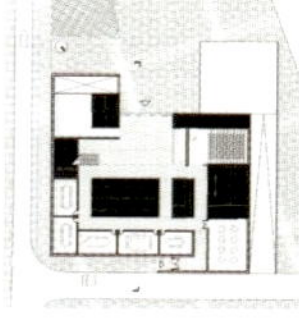

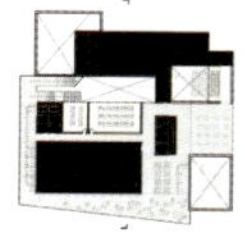

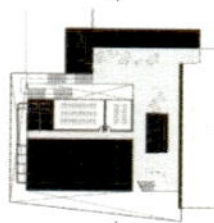

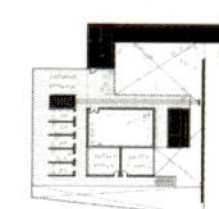

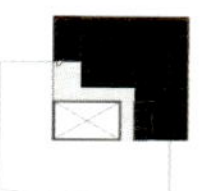

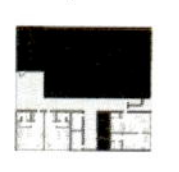

Alex Sassaroli
Yfirborð

In the popular local culture of Iceland, the thermal bath is the space of social interaction. The bath, in contrast to the digital space of private anonymity found in social networks, is a corporeal space of public intimacy. Local politics are discussed vigorously and consensus found in the space of the pool, whereas digital space fosters polarization and alienation.
This project, a headquarters for a new institute focused on internet security and digital freedom, leverages the infrastructure of the digital to build productive realms of intimate social interaction. Located on the harbor of Reykjavík, this project interweaves surfaces capable of producing unforeseen or novel forms of interaction, allowing it to oscillate between a landmass and a landscape. The interior contains large open surfaces and floors to produce social interactions a stereotypical project of this typology would not engender.

MID REVIEW

The incredible stress of the digital age—basically our cognitive abilities are stretched to the limits—is even more stressful than physical labor. In that sense, you are reclaiming the body and acknowledging that we are not just brain. This would be a very polemical statement. Your project is a contemporary version of the Roman bath, which was a way for people in an incredibly dense city to reconstruct their own reciprocity. —Pier Vittorio Aureli

FINAL REVIEW

Finio I love looking at your building—it feels very convincing. I have much more trouble looking at it once I see how you have sited it.

Petit Well I tried to find a way to talk about the form and I must say I am a little bit at a loss. If you say it's geological, then I look at the mountains and I try to understand what the relationship is to your building and I miss it. Aren't there steps missing that help us understand this has to be the form? It is clearly not determined by program. You just stuffed a turkey, meaning here is a form and you stuffed in the program. It is not the monolith you are talking about when you slice these guys to let in light—that negates the monolithic appearance of it. It becomes an insect more than a geological thing, in that case, and you have a series of shells.

McLeod I would like you to talk a little about the tension between the two strategies in two sections—one looks like the strange rock floating above ground and the other looks like you are trying to mold the landscape. They seem a bit at odds, how something that is so much about distorting the ground plane suddenly becomes an object floating above.

Rich This, along with a few previous projects, has a tempered brutality. On one hand there is a desire to do something that is aggressive—the geological building—but then you also want it to be polite—lifting up its skirt so you can see the mountain beyond. One idea that stuck with me from your midterm is the pool and its relation to the notion of public intimacy. Is there a way to resolve that oxymoron, which is a beautiful and romantic image in some ways—and slightly awkward.

Jonathon Meier
Mute Icon

This project creates a dual reading of form that floats between iconicity and contextual muteness. Adopting the scale and rectilinear footprint of the nearby buildings, pedestrians and drivers approach the building on the oblique. Requiring movement and exploration to be understood and gradually revealed, the building becomes increasingly transparent and fluid toward its center.
While the form is completely contained within the boundary's four corners, the form subtly absorbs circulation flows from outside the boundary. Upon approach, the loose, horizontal formwork of the concrete comes into focus, which gives the forms a subtle and imperfect texture that moves with the form's directional flow. Toward the center of the facades, the concrete strips away to become a louvered veil over the apertures reinforcing a transparency gradient from the building's boundary to its center. At the heart of the building, the surfaces become completely transparent.

MID REVIEW

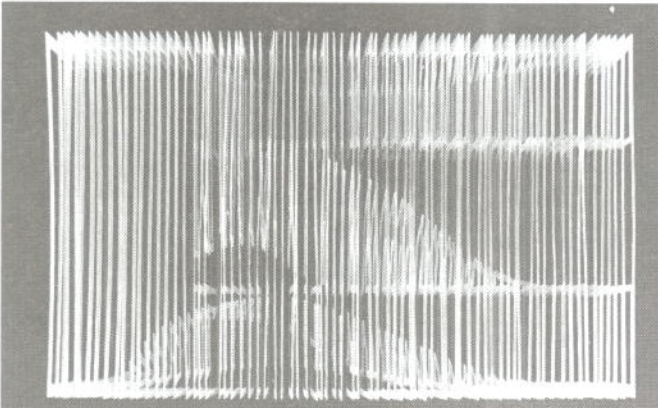

What is very interesting about this model is you are almost putting together Peter Zumthor and Patrik Schumacher, which is a very unlikely marriage of styles. The strength of your project is this model. Take pictures of it and try to understand what you have done. —Pier Vittorio Aureli

FINAL REVIEW

Deamer These spaces are fabulous. I really admire what you have done here. It seems to work really well with your idea that it is a simple rectangular building that finds fluid spaces. The one thing that I question is the poured nature of it.

Finio To me, that's the only issue with this project. I agree that the confidence within which you have solved complex fluidity is really commendable. That said, the fact that the striated openings are constricted to bays seems very much against the idea of the building itself.

Petit There is this dialectic between the orthogonal box and the rich interior that swirls around an atrium that is very contemporary and a convincing technique. What I question is how you stuff the functions into this plan. The plan is kind of out of control. There are rooms, toilets and stairs everywhere.

Rich Since midterm you have really focused on the formal resolution of this building; programmatically, maybe not quite as much.

Petit How about putting potatoes inside that plan—instead of having these conventional enclosures, what about potatoes? This geometry has been tried by SANAA, for instance, and they do not define frames because it just does not work with this kind of free floating interior form.

McLeod Certainly at the entry I would love to see something more engaging with the stair and the auditorium being distorted. The entry could be absolutely magnificent. I think you could use potatoes. I think you could look at things like Strasbourg.

Finio There is certain program that needs to be at the edge—that needs a window. You could be much more strident about that defining edge and then your bathrooms could be your potatoes. They could be the objects that float as infrastructural kiosks within the space.

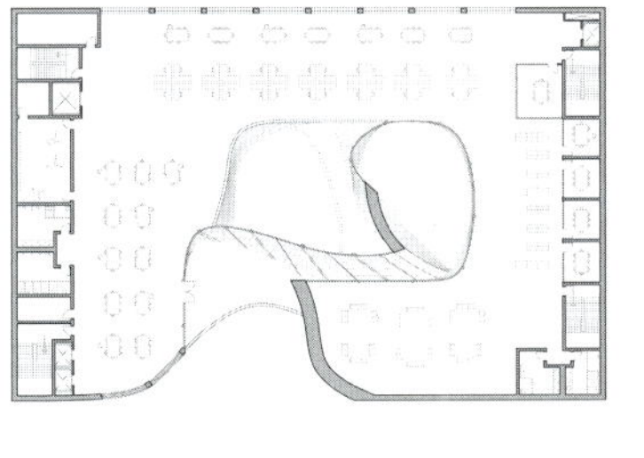

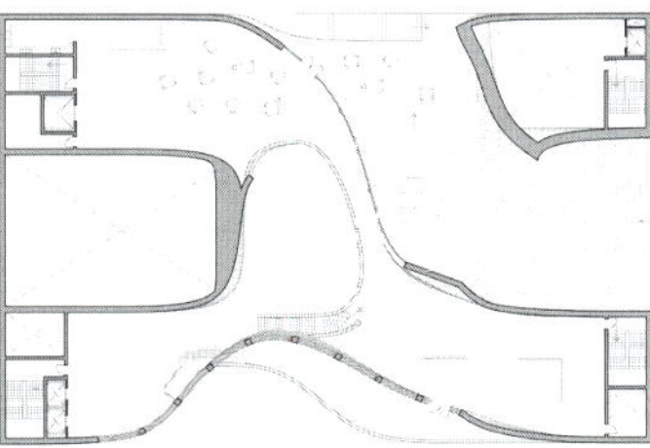

BARBICAN CENTRE CONCERT HALL Frank O. Gehry

Louis I. Kahn Visiting Professor

LONDON, ENGLAND **FACULTY: KATHERINE (TRATTIE) DAVIES**

Completed in 1982, the Barbican Center is a brutalist complex of performing arts venues, the largest of its kind in Europe, centered within the Barbican Housing Development by Chamberlin, Powell and Bon. Despite prior attempts at renovation to address ongoing issues of design and organization, the Barbican continues to seek alternatives and solutions to the problems present at the existing complex, now a Grade II Listed Building.

This Studio will take on the challenge of designing a new concert hall for Barbican Centre to replace Barbican Hall, currently a subterranean 1,949 seat theater, hosting classical and contemporary performances, home to the London Symphony Orchestra and the BBC Symphony Orchestra.

The new site for the hall will provide an opportunity to radically re-imagine the role of the Concert Hall within the Barbican Centre, responding to changing audience expectations for the arts and visibly addressing the ambition for the Barbican to serve as a cultural quarter, engaged and equally welcoming to residents and audience.

With a new external expression, students are asked to design a space for the experience of music from the inside out. Students will consider the dynamic relationship between audience, stage and performer. They will consider how live-performance and artistic expression effect change through shared experience and how architecture can engage with and transform site and context.

The studio will be run in close collaboration with Ara Guzelimian, Dean of the Julliard School. The semester will begin by meeting with Mr. Guzelimian in New York followed by a tour of Lincoln Center for the Performing Arts and Signature Theater. Following initial discussions, students will undertake collective research on the site as well as precedent studies of concert hall typologies and music performance history. Throughout the course of the semester students will meet with a variety of specialists, such as musicians, conductors and acousticians, in order to better understand the specific nature of the project and to assist in the development of each individual's design proposal.

For travel week, students will visit London to review the site and current facilities of the Barbican Centre, then travel to Paris to tour IRCAM, La Cite de la Musique and the Paris Opera and then to Berlin to see the Berliner Philharmoniker.

During Spring Break, the students will additionally travel to Los Angeles to visit the office of Gehry Partners and tour the Disney Concert Hall.

Throughout the semester the studio will attend live concerts and performances in the Northeast, including a performance at the Richard B. Fisher Center for the Performing Arts at Bard College.

For their individual projects, students will design independently and will be encouraged to investigate their personal approach to the given design problem. There will be a strong emphasis on large scale physical models throughout the semester as a primary design tool.

JURORS

Joseph Clarke
Kurt W. Forster
Sam Gehry
Paul Goldberger
Ara Guzelimian
Sir Nicholas Kenyon
Greg Lynn
Robert A.M. Stern
Stanley Tigerman

Feldman Nominee

Ivan Farr
The New Barbican Centre

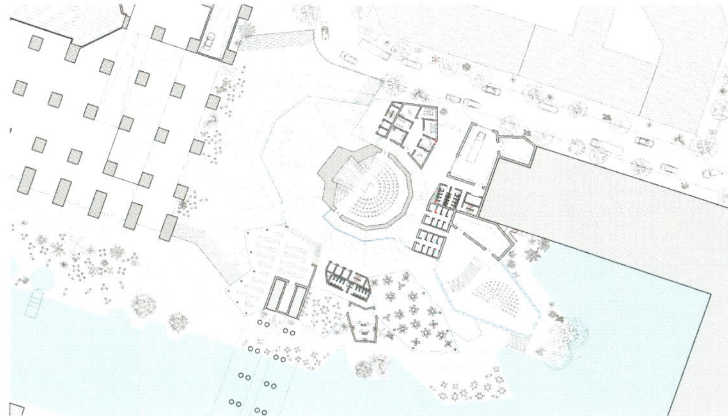

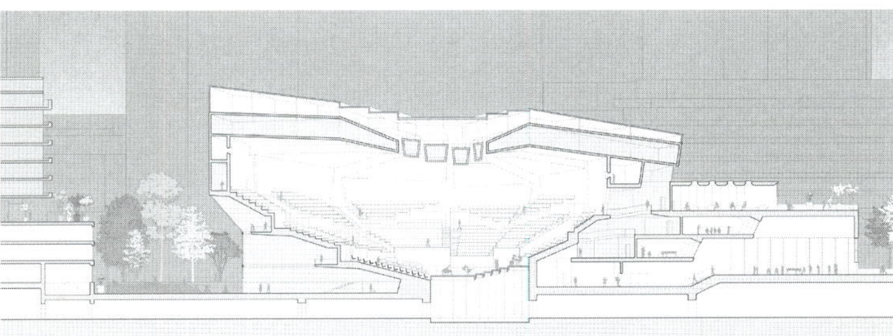

The Barbican Centre is an iconic masterpiece of British brutalist architecture which has acquired a notorious reputation for its innate qualities as a fortification: it is a thick, impenetrable poché in the midst of a porous medieval street structure. To tackle the issues of physical, visual and aesthetic access, my proposal excises an existing part of the Barbican Centre to make room for a plaza that grants direct passage into the infamous compound.
The New Barbican Concert Hall building sits adjoining the plaza, partially hovering over it to amplify the urban gesture. The performance space is housed within this exterior form as a nested object that is pulled away from the staggered interior spaces to create a network of dynamic canyon-like foyers. The concert hall is designed as a series of tiered seating sections which vertically shear past one another to construct dynamic viewing experiences as well as to create an acoustically heightened performance space.

MID REVIEW

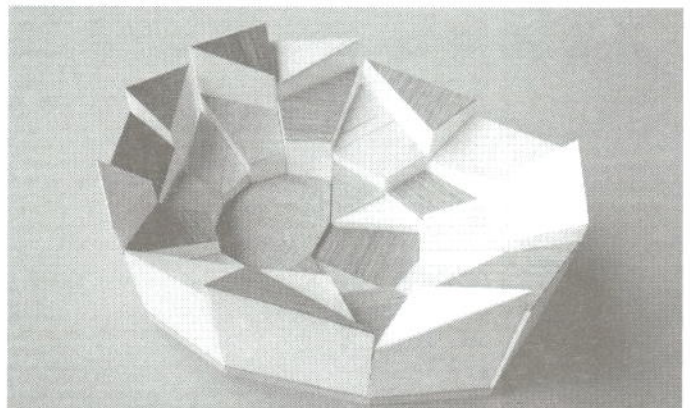

When we design performance spaces, we usually start by thinking about the relationship between audience and performers, which is what really shapes the room. In Berlin, the way the vineyard is broken up creates intimacy. By breaking the spaces down it's a way to create more intimacy rather than alienation. —Craig Webb

FINAL REVIEW

Goldberger It seems to me that the divisions between the different levels, which in plan create a contorted star, allude a little bit to what you are talking about, so that is one place in which they do come together. A lot of biomorphics.

Forster In theory one could imagine taking a similar segmentation turned outside, and then the exterior would retain some of the impressive calming effect and equilibrium. Your hall seems serenely resolved, what would be the problem with such a hall? But from the outside it does retain allusions to something which is rather tensely caught between spiky and...

Tigerman Kurt, it's really interesting when the model is here, it's as if the hall is embraced by the musicians. The practice halls, the recreational aspects, and the hall are presented therefore as almost an isolated purity, which is really interesting.

Goldberger Given your mention of the Berlin Philharmonic, I wonder, one could argue that the hall is too soft. That it's too pure and symmetrical, given where your interests actually lie and the larger things you are actually trying to do.

Lynn With those entries into the hall, if they have some presence in the foyer or the lobby, then it really works and should be transparent at those places. You said I know I need some bathrooms, and it is just a plan, but they are in the really wrong place. I think it should be much more open like it is in your sections so that you see this thing surrounded by the porcupine, and there is space in between the two with catwalks or something and it really becomes a ceremony to go between your hall and the prickly stuff.

Tigerman Actually Greg, the hall is embraced by the back of the house stuff, which is in turn embraced by the Barbican, I mean in the spirit in which Eero Saarinen talked about when something is part of the next largest thing. You would have to have gone to the Barbican, which of course you all did, to understand that the Barbican could embrace something which in turn could embrace something else, which in turn could finally be pure and unencumbered by bathrooms. They may be in the wrong place, but if you've got to go you'll find it.

Stern Everybody has jumped in and picked at you in one way or another, but I'm not sure anyone has said what I think is a very beautiful scheme, very beautifully presented, and very interestingly evolved as you've organized your process. That is very important to be noted at the end of the term's work. I wouldn't want to make Frank mad, but it actually manages to be Gehrian in spirit but not look like a Gehry concert hall, which is pretty tough to do around here.

Guzelimian Also it just acknowledges the reality that lots of people live here and that they have spaces enhancing where they live, that by creating those public spaces it becomes a destination other than for its concert hall usage.

Lynn Do you really need all the water? Are you related to Bruce Farr? He's a famous naval architect and I wondered because of all the water... But anyway would you have to have all the water? Or if you drained that and made it into more of a plaza would it work? Because it's a great waterfront concert hall but that isn't much of a waterfront.

Stern The Barbican is a very strange place. I mean there are so many people said to be living there, but every time I go there, I've never seen a soul. Not a soul. And I've never told anyone when I'm coming.

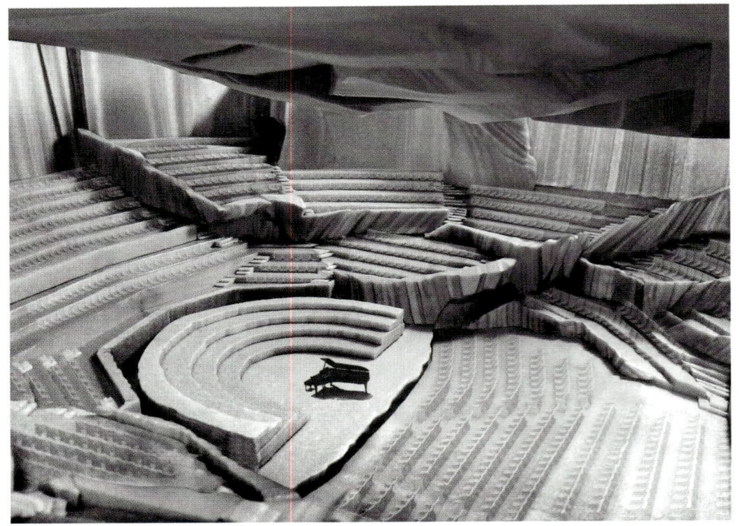

Danielle Davis

Ivan Farr

John Farrace

Jing Han

Alisa Hintz

Kyeong Jae Lee

Michael McGrattan

Eleanor Measham

Christian Oncescu

Kataryzna Pozniak

Raphael de la Fontaine

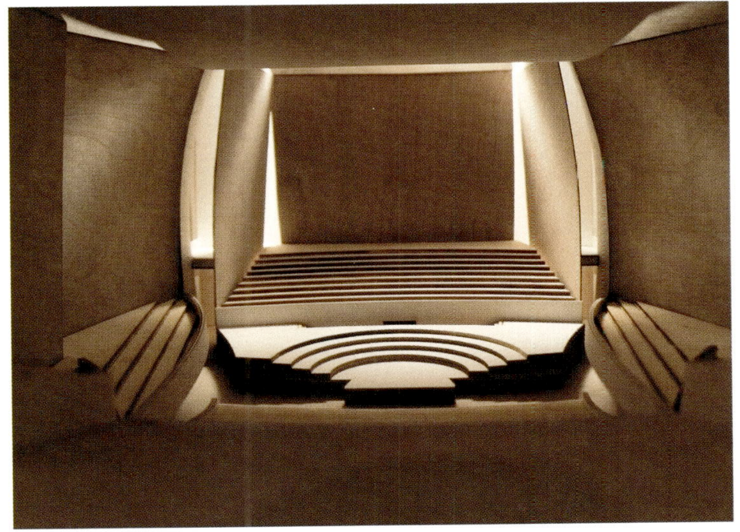

Ian Spencer

BE MY GUEST: THE INTERCONTINEN-TAL HOTEL Brigitte Shim

The Eero Saarinen Visiting Professorship of Architectural Design

VIENNA, AUSTRIA **FACULTY: ANDREI HARWELL**

This studio will explore architecture and the threshold / calculated balance between public and private space and its impact on modern life. The vehicle for this exploration will be the hotel which is a building type that uniquely combines, intertwines, embraces, and engages both the public and the private realms. The hotel by its nature is a zone of transition between many extremes. The studio assumes that the urban hotel is a compelling tool for the transformation of our urban fabric. The hotel has been and remains a testing ground for social change where the conventions of gender, race, class and spatial norms can be wilfully tested, reconfigured or abandoned.

The studio group will travel to Vienna, Austria where the building project site is located. Students will have the opportunity to visit the site many times, observing the subtle shifts in its surrounding urban context at different times of the day and night. Tours of iconic Viennese hotels as well as significant contemporary and historic buildings in Vienna have been organized. Curators from the Architekturzentrum in Wien will share knowledge on evolving local urbanism and the pressing contemporary cultural issues in Vienna. As well, a New York field trip to several iconic hotel buildings has also been organized.

In the contemporary hotel, the local resident and the global traveler collide, intersect with and overlap within the traditional hotel program. Students are asked to consider both the local and the international as active players in the evolution of the new hotel typology. This advanced option studio invites speculation, rethinking and reinvention of role of the urban hotel in shaping the future of our cities.

JURORS

Sunil Bald
Deborah Berke
Karla Britton
Kashef Chowdhury
Joseph Clarke
Kenneth Frampton
Elke Krasny
Alan Organschi
Billie Tsien
Mason White

Feldman Nominee

Olen Milholland

Intercontinental Ice Plaza Hotel

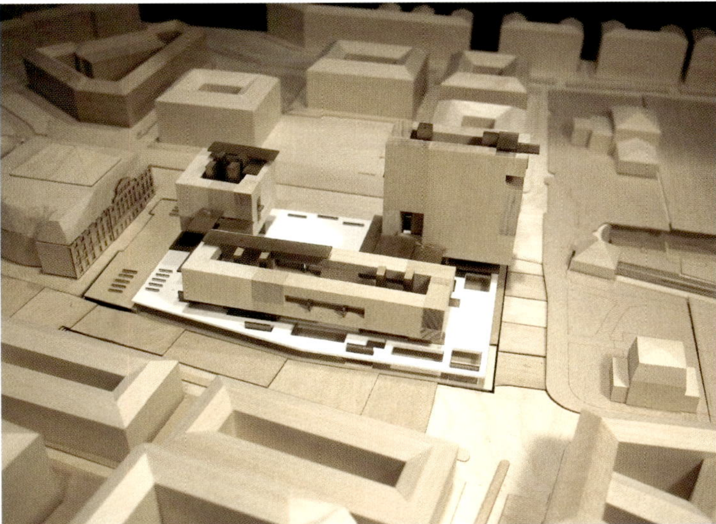

The Vienna Skating Club has long been part of Viennese society, and what was once held up as a spectacle and heralded for its ability to bring people together in communal activity has become suppressed and hidden behind closed walls. The current ice rinks found in Vienna are in a social black-hole abutting the Intercontinental Hotel and the Vienna Konzerthaus, but engage neither and remain hidden from the street. This project sets out to reimagine the ice-skating rink as seamlessly integrated into the public realm. It refigures the site as one large sheet of ice that is both visibly and physically accessible to everyone. Much like the Dutch Painter Hendrick Avercamp's paintings depict, society would occur on the ice, blurring the distinction between plaza and ice rink. This new free space allows for a programmatic mixing that brings a multitude of different groups together inhabiting a frozen tabula rasa.

MID REVIEW

Ice is such a strong conceptual idea. In the summer you also need the conceptual clarity or the metamorphosis of ice into water. For me it's the inverse of the ice as water. There needs to be different ways of using water that offers back these amenities while fitting within this conceptual underpinning. —Brigitte Shim

FINAL REVIEW

Organschi If you take this too far, you have to deal with mechanical systems for freezing ice. Those things are worth maybe not literalizing, but I do appreciate how this plays out, how the shuffle board becomes the curling, which is actually a legitimate tradeoff. I think it's an exceptional space.

Tsien You are very inventive, so when you say that there are three different lobbies, then as a part of your story invent a different way of checking in. It's like a kiosk at an airport. Many people are lucky that Bob is not here, [laughter] but Deborah is here, and she knows. Once again I would push you to be even more inventive and rethink the system if you are rethinking the conventions.

Britton Your project raised a question I've been struggling with all day, which is the issue of the character, the appropriateness of the formal language in a particularly charged setting. I can't get over the symbolic importance of this site in relationship to the historic city, but somehow I feel like people are perhaps not grappling enough with the problem of cultural heritage and tourism. The symbolic significance of this space and its connection to the future of Vienna in this project hasn't been proved enough. Do Miesian-like towers belong here?

Bald It is a problem with a project like this how you deal with the elevation, how you play with it in terms of a reading of character, scale, patterning, and structure, which is something that often gets negated when you construct an elevation of this size. Today, we think more and more in terms of skin, and skin is more talked about in terms of patterning in some way. We saw in a couple of projects where you see the structure on the first level but once you reach the façade, it is pure patterning. The negation of pattern in some respects is what you're doing for the sake of effect. At the same time, it begins to avoid certain questions or issues of efficiency. Hotels are generally marketed less in terms of the exterior experience but more about the interior experience. It's not necessarily a worthwhile investment to put layer upon layer on a façade; they will invest more on the interior. It challenges you to think about this conundrum.

Berke If you were to actually build the necessary service area, not just for the hotel, which is really significant, but also for the programs that you are suggesting here, it would give more meat to the ground level and would make this a better plan. The little walls that are shooting around and the elevator shafts don't anchor the plan for the kind of building you're trying to make, but in fact all the stuff that would be required to make this work would give some strength to the ground.

White It is still existing as little bit of a "ba-dum ching". You skate everywhere, put on your skates and arrive at your apartment, be careful if you didn't bring your skates, walk carefully if you're going to get a drink. It's a bit tongue and cheek. Many are talking about the technological requirement but I am interested in the urban risk of treading across this plane. How many people would just no longer short-cut across this site?

Frampton I think there is more to it than that. Very clever scheme, an ice sheet, but as soon as you say that, the question of the ground and the concept of ground is gone. The other thing I do not agree with has to do with the ground again. You can't do this number where the side walk becomes a forest. There's a distinction between a public domain and a civic domain, and you can't then turn it into an orchard for god sakes. It is still very abstract. You have to be careful about that because unfortunately people buy this stuff, and then it gets built. [laughter]

Daniel Luster
The Intercontinental Hotel

This project is located at the eastern edge of the important Stadt Park and a block to the south of the Ringstrasse in Vienna, Austria. The new hotel—which takes the form of the typical Viennese block, or Hof—establishes new public space, mediates a new social and natural landscape which connects the concert house to the park, and creates a new architectural promenade for the hotel itself. This is accomplished by allowing the solid, stone clad ring of hotel rooms to float above a dynamic landscape plane which folds up into the court of the hotel activating the interior single-loaded corridor. Space for ice skating is created—on multiple levels—for the Vienna Skating Club in the adjacent plaza that fronts the concert house. This is accomplished by the manipulation of the plane of the landscape. The hotel lobby is situated below the floating ring and the plane of landscape and acts as a point of connection for the various programs of the project.

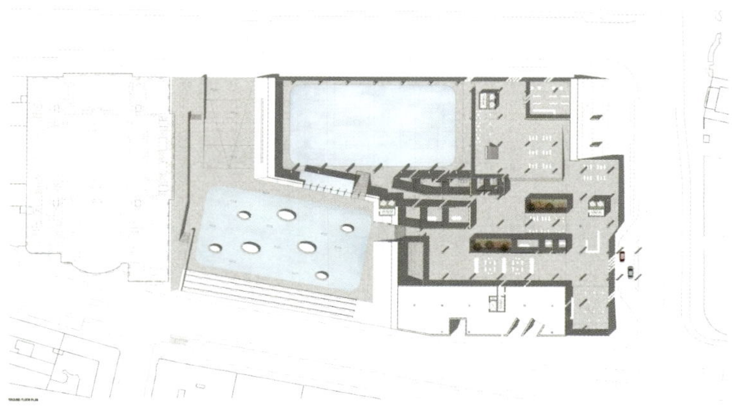

MID REVIEW

He has to redo it
—Robert A.M. Stern

FINAL REVIEW

Chowdhury I think this project makes a very confident case for the site. Not over-doing this ice skating thing. The use of the block to follow the urban fabric with the courtyard in the middle, and how the courtyard opens itself to the changing landscape during the seasons, is very interesting. My only issue would be the ground floor. Where your spaces are sprawling, it lacks definition, which is in contradiction to what you are doing here because your project is more architectonic and your spaces are not.

Frampton It is a very interesting platform you're adopting, this rather large scale version of this perimeter block, and putting all the accommodation in it is a very productive idea. I think gestures like this, a monumental staircase and another one going up, they are so powerful you have to arrive at something because it must occupy an important space. So when you arrive, when you finish climbing the stairs, what do I have before I get to the top of the staircase? I was talking to Eeva-Liisa about this today and she said one of the great things about Aalto is the great space you find you arrive at. It is latent in this project; it is a very clever project. But when you go a bit further you can't really figure out the place you arrive at, the plan is even missing. One other thing, if you get to do the Baumschlager Eberle, you can't cut it up like it is a piece of cheese.

Tsien You've been asked to deal with some rooms, at least some hotel rooms. I can imagine that it is because Brigitte wants you to focus on human scale, and because you are grappling with a project as a whole the spaces tend to become huge. I see vertical spaces that are really really tall. Everybody is inflating everything to get the effect but the idea is smaller and more human scale. In the future everyone needs to go back to that. Tables that are ten feet apart, have you ever been in a restaurant like that? It's smaller and more intense.

Krasny I really like this form, I think it is very elegant, but when I looked at what you referred to as the public space, it is rather difficult because you have one space for winter use that is described here, and it is not quite clear what it can be in the summer. It is very unresolved in the proposed use and implementation. It can be this lived experience you are arguing for running from a public park all the way to the concert hall, but I think what they would actually want is a very distinct division between them. They would want to keep the public apart from the audiences, unless they are invited as their so called target group.

Frampton Another thought that has been on my mind all day. This is a comment that has to do with architectural education in general, and to which extent students are encouraged to consider typological presence. The typological proposition drives everything. Start to look at this thing and think about the fact that this is a square with a courtyard, a corridor all the way around, floors designed with rooms sitting on top of a podium, and with an axis and asymmetrical movement. The asymmetry itself in section and plan can negotiate public access and hotel-only access. I was looking at this plan and thinking, it looks like you had to do a plan underneath a square so certain things came down, certain columns, they're there but what sort of place is that? It's a place you're stuck with in a way even though you designed it. And the other thing that occurs to me is, what does it feel like to be inside the hockey rink? What is that space really like? In a way it is an honorific space, it is a place where really serious skating goes on. If you had the asymmetry that would activate the square or the courtyard, then you could play with the thing at other levels, perhaps you yield to spaces that are more honorific, and you would not need to cut into the cheese. [laughter]

Christian Mueller
Intercontinental Vienna Hotel

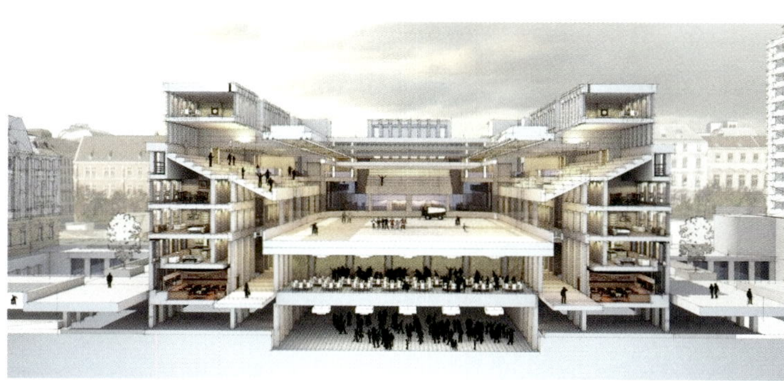

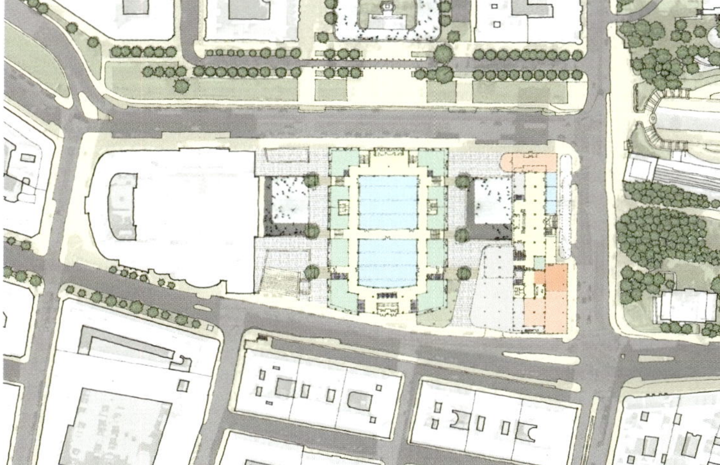

This proposal retains the existing Intercontinental Vienna Hotel (Holabird & Root, 1962) and resolves the brief's programmatic additions with a new, mid-block building that creates two new gassen, or alleys, enhancing connectivity between the Ringstrasse to the north and the residential neighborhood to the south. Rather than treating the entire block as a unified development, this proposal sees value in the heterogeneity of multiple buildings from different periods, and the liveliness of the public realm created at their interstices. As such, the proposal hopes to restore a human scale to a site currently defined by infrastructural and automotive-scaled boundaries, extending the medieval-derived Viennese urban fabric.

The multiple programmatic zones of the building—retail, residences, ice skating, conference—are deliberately scrambled in section, forcing new social adjacencies and interactions. The resulting complex—in contrast to the hermetic, self-contained bubble of the current Intercontinental—is a public promenade of seeing and being seen, that builds on the long tradition of other Viennese civic institutions like the Staatsoper. Likewise, the presently-consolidated activities of the Eislaufverein will be dispersed across the site to further activate the interior and exterior public spaces.

MID REVIEW

You are doing smart studies about massing and urban fabric, but I think you're going too quickly to the building that you imagine should go there. I am not saying don't do classical buildings or Otto Wagner buildings, but they should remain less politicized visually or aesthetically for a while so that you can really find out what the solutions are. Take this chance in this studio to get an idea of the big urban moves and then we can talk about Otto Wagner. —Alan Organschi

FINAL REVIEW

Frampton The cubic, the metrics is very interesting idea. But once you set it up, I don't see why you part from it. The nine square operation, where the central square is larger. Why would you part from it? Having put this rather formal idea between the existing concert buildings, it suggests a strong gesture.

Organschi This project has taken a very different turn since midterm. It seemed to me that you were very interested on the exterior of trying to find a formal language that would integrate it, particularly with your interest in Otto Wagner. You were interested in celebrating the hotel through this idea of the atrium and drawing attention to its symbolic importance in a historic site. Here it seems as though you have gone in the direction of pseudo—1960s superblock. It completely overwhelms those previous intentions. I guess I'm curious what happened to those renderings. You were so interested in tracing your experience of Vienna.

Shim The two pedestrian walk-ways are key elements to the project. It is actually quite a different response than the projects we have seen today. The core or the inner part of the block becomes the public zone that carries the weight. It would have been really lovely to see a section through those spaces, because in a way they are quite different, one with the concert hall and one with the existing hotel. It would be more interesting to understand more specifically what their characters are and how your new building contributes to these two different spaces. They are also asymmetrical in their dimensions and proportions. We see it sort of in plan, but it is hard to really get a handle on the specificity of how that would work. I like it as an urban gesture; I think it is a really strong part of the project.

White There is a question of is it a big building, or is it a shrink wrapped collection of ten individual buildings? The balance you are playing tilts more towards the building that has been put through the cheese grater. I wonder if there might have been more play, and I do not know to what degree you might call it tweaking Wagner. It is always a dilemma when you are working with a significant historical architectural figure within their own city, how to play that right. I am more interested in the game of is it a big building, a single building that has been sliced, or many individual buildings that have been bundled or gathered. That second version could enhance a bit more the individuality along the street with an inversion of facade types. You always have your base and your top tier; maybe there is a chance to invert that sometimes or even thicken the armature at some points.

Benner The negotiation between the resident and skater, which in every other project has been completely segregated, is mixed in sequence into the building. That goes again back to the plan how do you control bringing people into the project, how do you allow people up to that level? You can begin to see in the striation of the section how that might happen. I see the promise of this amazing light condition that could happen on the site and at the same time create this social milieu in the project.

Clarke I would also question how you interweave the public and private programs. The residential apartment part of the building would normally be the most private area, but you are cross-programming it with the most public facility, and we are wondering where the two kinds of public and private realms should intersect.

HYBRID TYPOLOGIES: GARMENT FACTORY COMMUNITIES David Adjaye

Norman R. Foster Professorship of Architectural Design

DHAKA, BANGLADESH FACULTY: BRIAN BUTTERFIELD

WITH KASHEF CHOWDHURY OF STUDIO URBANA, DHAKA

More than 78% of Bangladesh's export earnings come from the garment industry which is the single greatest source of foreign currency in Bangladesh. The sector employs around 3.5 million workers, of which around 80 percent are women. The garment sector has a greater potential than any other sector in terms of employment and foreign exchange earnings to reduce poverty and make a contribution to the national economy. However working conditions are poor as Bangladesh's factories do not comply with international labor practices that ensure the social welfare of their employees. As a result, there is a rising fear in Bangladesh that the garments sector may face a decline in demand from global brands if it does not reform its labor practices and start to provide living wages, social services, and educational opportunities such as trade schools and women's centers.

Lutyens' Delhi, Le Corbusier's Chandigarh (with social housing by Maxwell Fry, Jane Drew, and Pierre Jeanneret), and Louis Kahn's National Assembly building in Dhaka will be used as lenses through which we will examine the regions architectural legacy—from late colonialism to modernist examples of post-independence nation building. Students will examine the local urban ecologies of the garment industry districts in Dhaka and propose hybrid building (or campus) typologies that address the needs of an emerging middle class—or at least examine the notion that coupling new factory buildings with housing and social or education programs could perhaps foster more upward mobility for factory workers, especially women. Students will engage in the analysis of a garment district quarter and choose a site within to propose an industrial program paired with a social, educational, and/or housing component. With Corbusier's Chandigarh, and Kahn's Bangladesh as Utopian precedents, this studio will be analogously Utopian but focused on an architecture that is scalable to that of local urban ecologies and the hyper topologies of global capital networks. As opposed to the notion of nation building that drove the post-independence architecture of the 60s and 70s—it is now the demands of the global economy, combined with the rapid urbanization of Bangladesh as workers stream in from the countryside, which calls for a responsive architecture for new worker communities.

Bangladesh has a 50 year legacy of modernist architecture from the forming of the nation in 1971 to present. Kahn's National Assembly was completed in 1974. This and Corbusier's Chandigarh are examples of architects working in another world—projects situated in a geography and context outside of their culture, though both projects are operationally very different. If Corb's Secretariat can be seen as a variation on the Modulor, a Unite dropped into a foreign context as a symbolic catalyst, the architecture of Kahn's National Assembly building is perhaps more mutable and culturally aware of the aesthetic heritage of the region. As opposed to the mimicry of modernist utopian tropes, this studio will engage in the back and forth of research and design, drawing from the layered, complex tectonic palette and spatial typologies of the region, until a responsive architecture to fit the contemporary global culture and economy emerges at both architectural and urban scales.

It is important to note the impact of contemporary technology and computer aided design and fabrication on the future of garment industries in places like Bangladesh. Non-mechanized garment factories are beginning to feel pressure to modernize their operations as technological advances in garment manufacturing are allowing a significant number of manufacturing operations to come back to first world nations—this will have a direct impact on labor conditions and the economic factors driving new factory architecture.

JURORS

Tim Altenhof
Pier Vittorio Aureli
Kashef Chowdhury
Nikolaus Hirsch
Robert A.M. Stern
Chris Van Bergen
Stanley Tigerman

Feldman Nominee

Allen Plasencia
Shelter Factory

The garment industry is struggling with identity and cultural relevance. The economic position of Bangladesh is drastically being influenced by the global forces, and fundamental aspects of Bangladeshi culture like live and work are being reinvented. This reinvention and new production of goods has separated the contemporary Bangladeshi culture from the traditional processes of cultivation and production. Shelter Factory is located in the river delta of Bangladesh; it proposes a jute manufacturing facility that doubles as a cyclone shelter.

The building acts like a bridge. Its embankments are designed to extend the dry season by 45 days and protect a select portion of jute crops from the monsoon floods. Shelter Factory consists of permanent concrete piers that are anchored by the embankment system. The permanence of the walls is contrasted by the temporary timber structures that infill the infrastructure. A series of courtyards provide light and access while mitigating the water-to-jute relationship. During the dry season the building is utilized as a factory for the production of jute products, while in the wet season it serves as a bridge and flexible public space.

MID REVIEW

You need to be careful that you're not perpetuating what they already know how to do. You're on a very slippery slope in my opinion. And to not recognize urbanism as it exists in Dhaka, you may not like what it looks like, you may wish that cities looked the way they did 50 years ago, but that's just a part of life. I am wondering if you are not just evading modern life. I can't but believe that Bangladesh is going to change, so where are you in that change cycle? —Robert A.M. Stern

FINAL REVIEW

Tigerman I have one criticism. The housing in the embankment is orientated willy nilly, it needs to be orientated.

Stern Will people live in your building?

Hirsch And they would process the jute as well? It would become a production facility?

Plasencia It is left open as a very flexible floor plate in a sense that this varies in dimension. These walls also vary so that if there is a specific program that requires a different dimension, that can be accommodated. It's left as a flexible system and the instruments are just set in place to cultivate jute.

Stern What is the material of these walls?

Plasencia Rammed earth with concrete mix, no reinforcement. It's timber structure.

Aureli I like the simplicity of the project. You have a very clear reference to the energy and the deviance that happens across the country. A plan would have been nice to see, it's a very simple open building and you have been very precise about elements and even the structures.

Plasencia All of the structure that's happening in this direction is according to the 45 degree in case there is a flood. The silhouette of the building in this direction is almost like a ghost figure and in this direction it's very heavy.

Aureli In a sense this project reminds me of this idea that it can be very romantic in a sense, a building that can respond to unexpected situations. You can't just make a building; it always becomes a ruin by default. It's interesting that only certain kinds of buildings can have the resilience to accommodate difference problems and different uses. It's interesting because these kinds of structures are more infrastructural, like bridges, buildings with more generic use, buildings that have a level of simplicity in the structure. I love the model; the model is the best way to convey your presentation. I think a project needs to have an impact. I wish you had been more confident with your architectural statement. I think it's architecturally very powerful.

Chowdhury I think this is very good project, you're working with the flood. To be frank I wasn't sure at mid review, I wasn't sure which way you were going. This shows that you're really working on it and this really works in a situation that is away from anywhere, your place is in the river's end. One thing I'm not too sure about is this rammed earth, I said this before, even if it has concrete mixed into it. I would be very surprised if these hold, but that's a small issue. Maybe you can have a very thick brick wall as well. You're structure is like a bridge that you can walk across. You need to very precisely measure the levels so that you're really working with the flood.

Tigerman It's a terrific project.

Adjaye That's all you need to hear. [laughter]

Tigerman I've seen this guy before, he's a good guy.

Adjaye The reason that you probably didn't get as many comments is that you're very much in control of the elements and the program.

Tigerman Well you clearly understand the conditions. It's a very needed kind of structure throughout the area south of Dhaka. Rammed earth, it's only a function of a 50 year flood, the velocity of the water to find out the added mixture of concrete. You can go from rammed earth to straight out concrete and you can find that out, it's not a big deal.

Adjaye This project is exemplar, and your tenacity is exemplar.

Matthew Rauch
Rana Plaza Memorial City

The city of Dhaka, Bangladesh, is not a traditional city with a defined core and periphery, but rather a collection of centers consisting of large-scale institutional and manufacturing districts. The typical factory complex in Dhaka is poorly planned, colliding with the informal settlements that grow around it and leaving no room for public life. Because of the large number of factories that make up the fabric of the city, the factory is an ideal type to introduce a new sense of monumentality and civic identity. This proposal is located in the garment-producing suburb of Savar, at the site of the tragic Rana Plaza factory collapse that occurred in April 2013 and claimed over 1,200 lives. The excavated foundations of the collapsed building are repurposed as a sunken memorial space, and a grand civic axis connects this memorial site to an existing temple complex to the east.

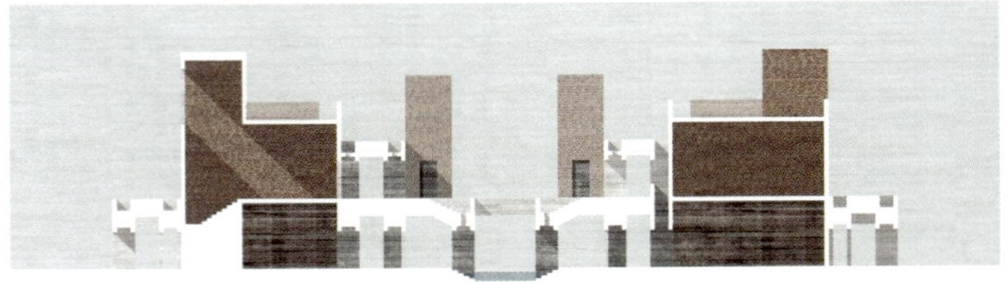

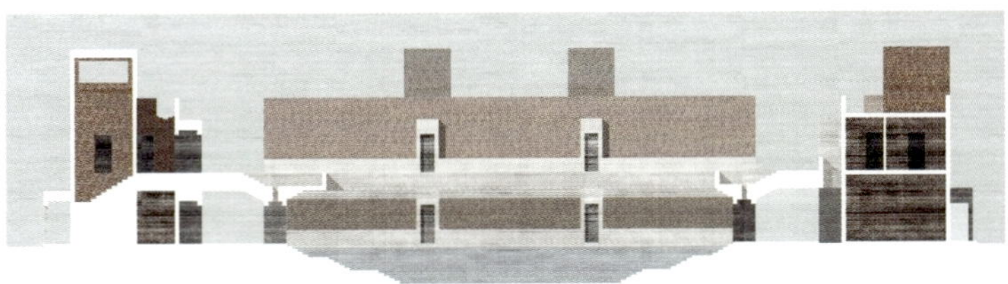

MID REVIEW

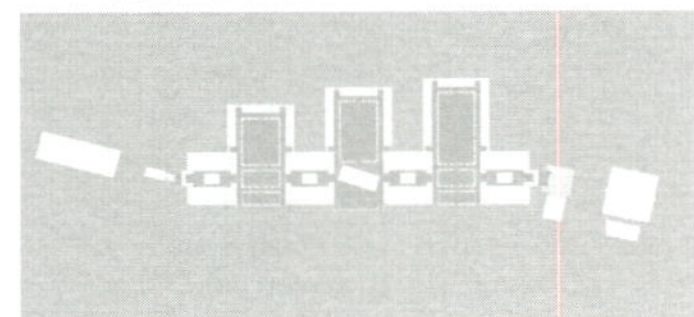

I think the idea of turning labor and housing into a memorial and a connection to the past is very powerful and you need to keep remembering that as you carry through. I think going around the Rana Plaza and the ruin is where your project is at, nobody else has picked that up. It also talks about emerging dignity; it's actually very difficult to do. —David Adjaye

FINAL REVIEW

Aureli It's a very beautiful project and it's very much under control. I like the images, there is something very specific about your graphic presentation it makes me wonder where you referenced. I was a student in the 90s, when this kind of school was still alive and actually we were forced to draw like this but by hand. We had to basically color this with pantone markers. It's an old school approach to presentation which I'm very fond of. Placing the mosque in the middle of the octagon must be a very strong gesture culturally, but what does it have to do with production? Using religion to make people work more productively, which you know has been the case. Your ambition to transform a productive space into a civic space by enforcing a strong mentality, it's very precise. Here is your position, here is your approach, there is no question about that, but the question is why. It's very controversial. It's a very strong position combining religion and production. There is no question that the mosque in the context plays an important role and I'm sure people would use it, but more than anything else the question is for you. There is something very strong that cannot be argued by just saying this is something that is used. One of the most interesting projects for a factory is in Berlin. It was designed to have a clear statement that production and factory had to have the same role in the city as the church, and of course there was a clear agenda behind it. The president of the factory saw the industrial revolution as a new ethos, as a new cultural direction. Factory can't just look like a factory; it has to look like a monument. I think you have a position and there's a history of that but I think you have to be a little bit sharper. It's a project, and the gestures are so strong that it requires a certain position.

Adjaye Your project is the only one that takes on another idea of another state form. It's a utopia. It's a way to place an entire life and history into this moment of the disaster which creates this negative. You're making this absolute pure thing. The cartography of the whole thing is the Greek temple. It's the Bangladeshi Greek temple of living, work, public life, religion, and ruins, past and present, and I was really shocked that you even dared to go this path. What is very clear is that this public space was so important that this statement or this image is never really seen, but it's actually experienced. It became clear that there was another agenda that articulated the architecture.

Altenhof It is risky to also approach it from a western viewpoint I guess.

Adjaye Totally risky.

Altenhof I haven't been to Bangladesh but the way that the temples are integrated into city fabric, into everyday life, one puzzling aspect that struck me every time is how polluted these divine sites are many times. You expect these places to be sacred spaces, but in yours they're completely entangled into the everyday.

Adjaye This is not expected to be a shrine, it's a living place, it's an idea of an idealized system, to use architecture to make an image of an idealized moment in a place which is just about things that are produced out of need fundamentally. When you have a culture where you haven't produced the reflection of the image, I think it's critical to produce the image and this project tackles that problem head on and uses the device of the tragedy. Using the idea that death is a really powerful thing and that the carnage of death is a powerful image and you need to create another image, in our culture the tombstone, to replace the decay of death. To create an idealized place on top of the carnage is very powerful discourse.

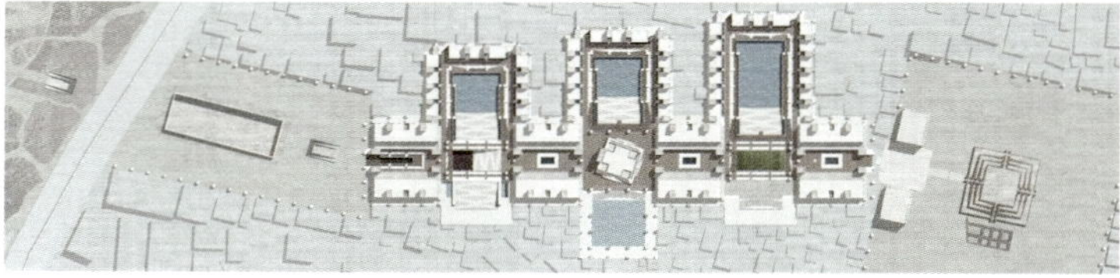

Tyler Collins
Filter

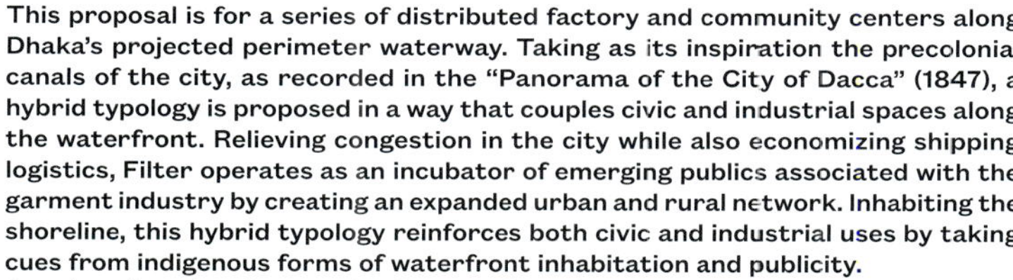

This proposal is for a series of distributed factory and community centers along Dhaka's projected perimeter waterway. Taking as its inspiration the precolonial canals of the city, as recorded in the "Panorama of the City of Dacca" (1847), a hybrid typology is proposed in a way that couples civic and industrial spaces along the waterfront. Relieving congestion in the city while also economizing shipping logistics, Filter operates as an incubator of emerging publics associated with the garment industry by creating an expanded urban and rural network. Inhabiting the shoreline, this hybrid typology reinforces both civic and industrial uses by taking cues from indigenous forms of waterfront inhabitation and publicity.

A series of sectional strategies form the interface between city and water, carving out of the shoreline marketplaces, promenades, loft spaces, docks, a central ghat and a charbagh. Imbricating the garment industry with a variety of urban publics, Filter acts as an architecture of threshold, scripting movement between city and water to produce a series of spatial conditions for public and industrial use. Solidifying its presence as an urban infrastructure of Dhaka, the proposal's austere brick massing acknowledges Bengali brickyards while incorporating metal jali screens for thermal comfort. A hybrid typology that creates an inhabitable porous edge, Filter embeds Dhaka's emerging industry and publics in an architecture of the city.

MID REVIEW

Your project is really sophisticated and really accomplished. I'm curious when you start to show this architecture, I think the conversation becomes about what architecture means in Bangladesh. You have a very definite image, creating these extraordinary moments. The justification is there, you have factories that just use the waterway and avoid the traffic, and then you make these gateways; but then you make this architecture. It's the only part where you don't describe why it is what it is. —David Adjaye

FINAL REVIEW

Hirsch Interesting proposal in a context of many cities in the western world trying to get rid of all the industrial infrastructure that blocks the view from the sea. You're doing the opposite. You're trying to invent the new hybrid model that combines industry and culture.

Aureli There's this fetish of the waterfront having to be public space. I think what you're doing is providing a public space but maintaining its industrial preoccupation. Apart from that, the most interesting part of the project for me is the sequence of sections. It seems that you have designed it through the site. The waterfront fetish is always about the view, and your project seems to point out the problem of this, and introduce something that is not yet the expected. I think it's a very resolved project but it needs a stronger statement about what is at stake here.

Tigerman If the community center was in between the two factories, all of a sudden you have this mix right within the project itself of allowing people to participate in factory, cultural life of the city, and the archival. With a very slight modification, this thing could become much more democratized. Right now the community center is shunned off to the side and I would say it's not necessary. One could imagine interspersing them with these other guys and it would become sort of a paradigm, and it becomes a model for zoning so that you can't just build isolated factory stuff on one side and cultural stuff on the other side, it's mixed together. If you're doing a factory, you have to have a cultural center, and you could do that very simply just by changing the colors. Purple green purple orange purple. [laughter]

Adjaye You started studying factories, different kinds of factories, the kinds of spaces that are in factories and what they mean. It has been slightly lost. What I like about the project is the opportunity of creating infrastructure but not disconnecting infrastructure from architecture, making the infrastructure and architecture work with the public realm.

Tigerman If it had been this other way, then the access to the river edge between the buildings could be very clearly articulated and all of a sudden become democratized. Capital produces, as capital often does, cultural and archival stuff like museums. I think you're well on the way, you shouldn't be bashful in saying this is potential zoning, all of a sudden, business doesn't suffer, culture isn't shunned aside but they're sort of integral and they feed back into the city fabric.

Chowdhury I think it's one of the very few projects that uses the river for transport which is important because Bangladesh is a network of rivers. More importantly, you're opening up a front to the river as well as a destination. You have those steps which become a new gateway to that part of old town where the people can come and gather. You're not only using the river, you're working on the water, you're taking water in, and you're providing facilities for the public. All of it is working and this is probably the only space they will have, in that very congested, very dense area at the back. So this really creates a new civic space, and as Stanley said, if you blend it more with the production facilities, then you're encouraging more of this interaction and real life into the facilities. There are a lot of things happening at different levels and that is what the complexity of this project is about. That is what the beauty of this project is about.

BOULEVARD TRIUMPHANT Dan Wood

Louis I. Kahn Visiting Assistant Professorship of Architectural Design

LIBREVILLE, GABON **FACULTY: BRANTLEY HIGHFILL**

Gabon is a small country in West Africa with big ambitions. The nation is currently embarking on its second modern wave of urbanization and development. Its first, following liberation from France in the 1950s and the discovery of oil off its coast in the 1960s, resulted in a master plan for the capitol Libreville by early eco-urbanist Marcello D'Olivo and a number of optimistic, modernist buildings and infrastructure. This new wave, initiated by President Ali Bongo Ondimba, has the goal of moving the country into the ranks of emerging economies, as oil supplies taper, through a transition towards industrialization, services and green jobs and development.

This studio will focus on one of the two major axes created by D'Olivo's plan—the Boulevard Triomphal—as the locus of a new, forward-looking image for the city. This boulevard leads inland from the seacoast and is the location of major public buildings including the Gabonese Parliament and many embassies and government ministries. We will look at how the introduction of new sustainable infrastructures, including transportation, waste and energy can both transform the boulevard and create the opportunity for new representative public architecture. By extension this will provide a physical manifestation of the country's goals and offer a model for a progressive 21st Century Africa.

The class will research precedents of other transformative infrastructures, from Haussmann's Paris to Foster's Masdar, as well as general research into contemporary Africa. We will develop together a new master plan for the Boulevard Triomphal in advance from our trip to Libreville in February. In Libreville, we will be hosted by the Agence Nationale des Grands Travaux, currently carrying out more than 70 large-scale infrastructural and architectural projects throughout the country. The remainder of the semester will be spent developing individual projects for new public buildings and complexes along the boulevard.

JURORS

Amale Andraos
Ben Aranda
Nathan Browning
Glen Cummings
Mark Dolman
Keller Easterling
Jorge Otero-Pailos
Nicolai Ouroussoff
Brigitte Shim
Marc Simmons
Robert A.M. Stern
Neyran Turan

Feldman Nominee

William Sheridan
Getting Around

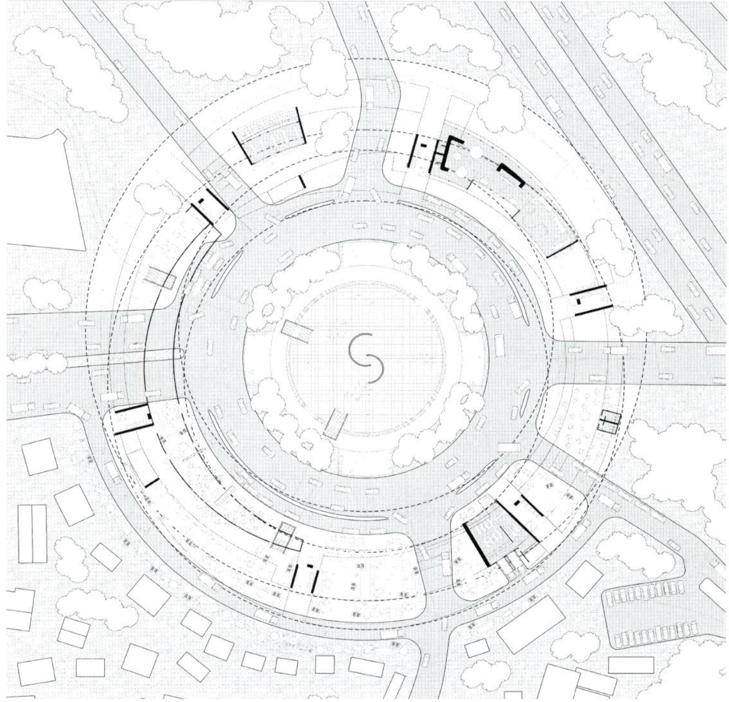

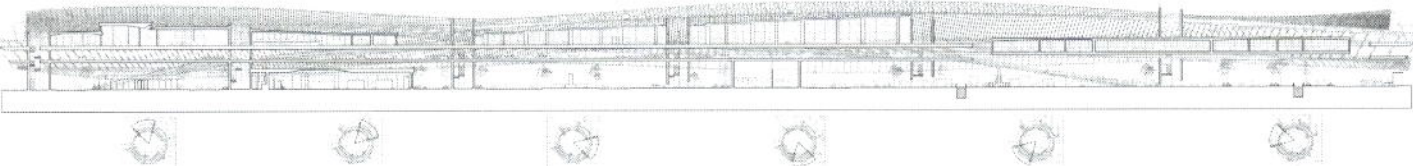

This project is sited on the Boulevard Triomphal: the Place de la Paix, a roundabout where the boulevard meets the city's ring road before continuing on to the Cité de la Démocratie. This location can operate as a central hub for the entire city with easy access to most destinations. The site would be transformed into a hub for the taxis/taxi-buses of the city and it would function as the main point of transfer for most trips. Curbside loading and unloading would occur at the periphery of the rotary, where simple signage that clearly labels destinations throughout the city would allow for much more efficient commuting. The building itself would help facilitate pedestrian movement around the rotary by providing a continuous circulation path above street level. It would also establish a stronger connection between the Boulevard Triomphal and the developing civic and cultural campus in the Cité de la Démocratie.

Wrapping this new taxi hub with a market that can leverage the influx of commuters to the site marks a first step in recoding the urbanism along the Boulevard, transforming it into a bustling pedestrian thoroughfare. On ground level, an open market interfaces with the existing informal settlement to the south of rotary. Facilities for the new, expanded taxi-system wrap the rotary at the ground level. A new welcome center for the Cité is located on the ground level as well. Two long ramps capable of accommodating small vehicles allow for easy access to the two levels above, which provide further open-air market space. Conditioned spaces selectively wrap the perimeters of the market rings, housing a control center and offices for the new taxi system headquarters, a new Department of Motor Vehicles, and public bathing facilities.

The integration of infrastructure and public space promised by this confluence of programs around a new, busy transportation hub proposes a new urban idea for the city. The Place de la Paix has long been an important site for civic protest. Now, despite relatively little program explicitly dedicated to civic functions, the site is transformed into a newly visible and therefore powerful civic space.

MID REVIEW

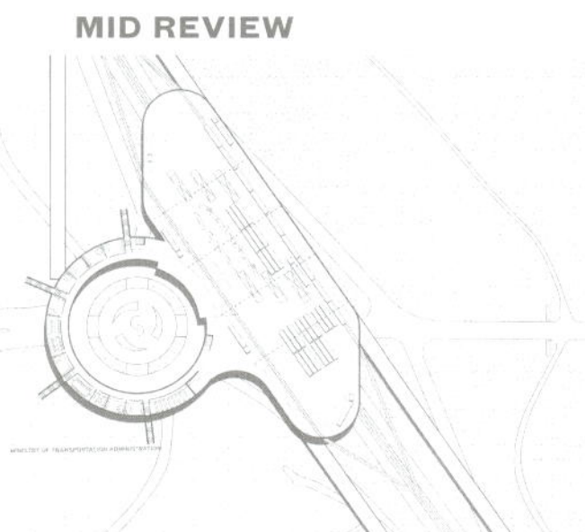

It's a bridge infrastructure, sort of 1960s in a way, monumental. A pure geometric form would reinforce that monumentality. —Greg Lynn

FINAL REVIEW

Aranda The premise of this studio is about how tropical modernism is able to create local identity, somehow tapping into infrastructure and large scale moves, such as transportation, circulation, and light. It also needs to offer an identity and monumentality. I think you've really done it.

Stern That poor monument in the center would be gone. If you had extended your idea under the road, with a sunken court in the middle and more shopping down below, and allowed people to go under, up, and crisscross, I think you would enrich the density and probably the centrality of this scheme. Give it more energy. Right now everyone is kind of chasing a tail around the edge.

Simmons It should still have all the same dynamism, people should still be able to pick up their taxis, but they shouldn't have free form access to these upper levels and the middle layer. I think if you start really looking at flows on the site, it would start to inform a different way to weave it all together into a three dimensional project. Right now, it seems like circle, section, canopy, each in isolation. It looks dynamic, but it's too static.

Andraos Just to Mark's point, I actually appreciate the complexity as a result of simple moves—this layering and slight twisting. My concern would be more a question of scale. It seems very single-minded in terms of scale. Is there more of a gradient, are there more zones, do you negotiate the circle by differentiating these core moments? How do I know where I am in the circle?

Shim I also think there's a deliberateness to where the cores are that is the next level of development. Right now, they are evenly distributed. Their locations need to register the key functions of the market, especially if we imagine it being food goods.

Stern With respect to the main axes in classical architecture, you would have a big arch here. It would help people see into it. Right now it has the quality of being under a freeway. Look how Frank Lloyd Wright took his building over the road in Marin County; one architecture people size and one architecture car size.

Turan When we use the word infrastructure it's usually an extension of the land. I like the ring language, and the way you represented these conditions, almost classically, that makes the chaos even more.

Easterling I think you're inflecting the idea of crowd in a very interesting way, because this is also kind of a stadium. One imagines that there would be another kind of urbanity, another kind of urban pleasure, another kind of urban practice in looking at people that is different than anywhere else.

Dolman These are all over Japanese cities going to and from train stations, because they had that issue where people walk out on the streets. They do functionally work as an infrastructure, with this three dimensional space below and above grade, but the those spaces are so large, they aren't programmed at all. There are kids playing music, people selling things, etc. In this particular site the center becomes important, but if this were a typical cross intersection the same strategy could work.

Adam Wagoner
Gabon Bleu

Gabon, a coastal African country located on the equator and 80% covered in rainforests, is highly informed by water. However, the country suffers from a general disregard of water as an important resource. With no real country-wide sewer system, 67% of Gabonese lack modern sanitation facilities and 12% lack access to clean drinking water. Gabon needs a new direction for how it manages water infrastructure. This system should not merely be a continuation of the standard western model of isolated infrastructure; it has the opportunity to become visibly integrated into people's daily urban and ecological lives.

The proposed site for the first of these interventions in the capital city of Libreville would be located at the bottom of a large water shed area in a location that allows for easy access to the economic and governmental buildings along the Boulevard Triomphal, the surrounding housing neighborhoods, and the country's main university. This plant can then become an asset for the adjacent neighborhood in other ways, combining the utilitarian functions of water purification with social programs that can feed off the byproducts of the plant's processes, such as laundromats, pools, restrooms, car washes, cafeterias, bars, meeting rooms, media labs, auditoriums and galleries.

Arranged into a vertically stacked system, this new water treatment plant and community center would become the tallest structure in Gabon establishing itself as an unavoidably visible statement about the importance and potential of water and water management for the future of Gabon as a developed country.

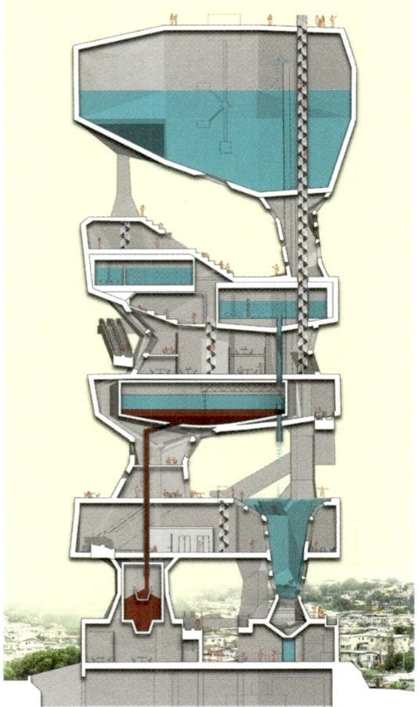

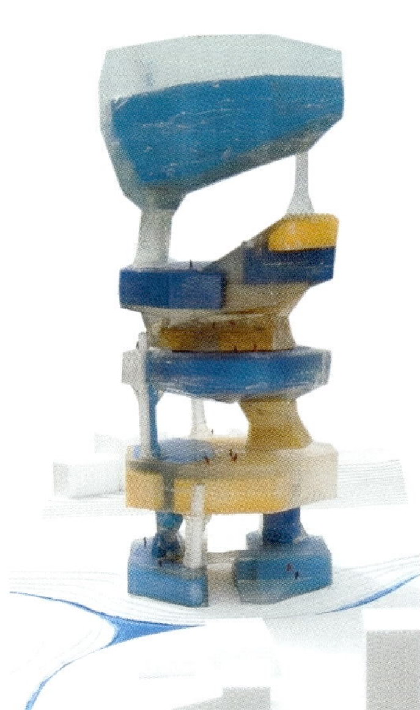

MID REVIEW

The water could play a greater role in your form making.
—Ariane Lourie Harrison

FINAL REVIEW

Andraos You know every single inch of the project and how it works. Beyond function, there is a history of the water tower as icon. In countries like Gabon, which are emerging, they are looking for what can be iconic and still have meaning for the public. In this case the system and the icon start to work together in really interesting ways.

Simmons You started from the idea that these things are usually flat, and there's probably a good reason for that. It's probably cheaper and more efficient. Obviously there is a sense that cities need towers. That looks like it could be housing or an interesting hotel. How many stories would it be, twenty? It would be the tallest building in Gabon. That's quite a gesture.

Wood You can see in the rendering that the second tallest is also a water tower.

Ouroussoff There is this idea of the tower as a sort of monumental figure of modernization that relates to a type of urban experience that might not necessarily be this one. The idea of adding land to the bay is today a typology you see across the developing world as a symbol of modernity. I don't know if this figure of the skyscraper is anachronistic now, and whether there was an opportunity to think about a horizontal figure of modernization.

Turan I don't see it as a water tower. It's an infrastructural monument. The system is visualized and verticalized, like a church. I think you should grasp that in the project. If it turns into a machine that just happens to be vertical...

Cummings I am no expert in sewage treatment, but there are two principles massive amounts of surface area, and long durations of exposure to the sun. I'm thinking about how that gets incorporated into the tower form, which opens up a really interesting possibility of how you multiply the surface area and dramatically decrease the speed of water moving through. Right now your base level process seems to be in conflict with the form.

Stern I would like to come to the idea of more of these across the city. It starts to address this bigger question about identity, which has woven through the entire day. This new architecture is about giving a presence or identity to this emerging country that wants to reinvent itself. The idea that you can treat this as a prototype for different neighborhoods becomes more interesting as opposed to a one-off. Even the form you're working with can be adaptable in relation to orientation, wind, and view, which creates specificity with each neighborhood condition.

Dolman Back to this question of the tower and the symbol; if you were to build a conventional tower, the first thing you do would be the core and shell. You've pushed the idea of what it is to make a tall building by asking us to think about a different program, water and how it circulates, as opposed to people. These could be different around the city. Infrastructure becomes sculptural form. You've made certain choices that are not bound to the pure working of the pipes. Most of it, in fact, is about expressive form.

Ouroussoff When you talk about the different activities in terms of program, you should be much more selective about what you include. There is a sense that you need to pack things with program, otherwise they won't be alive. It's a default position that is often very counterproductive. In this case, I think you want to get rid of the café. What if the spaces are more specifically public, like the public swimming pool? It is infrastructure, so it is about a collective relationship to the city, not an individual experience. This is symbolic of what everyone needs water.

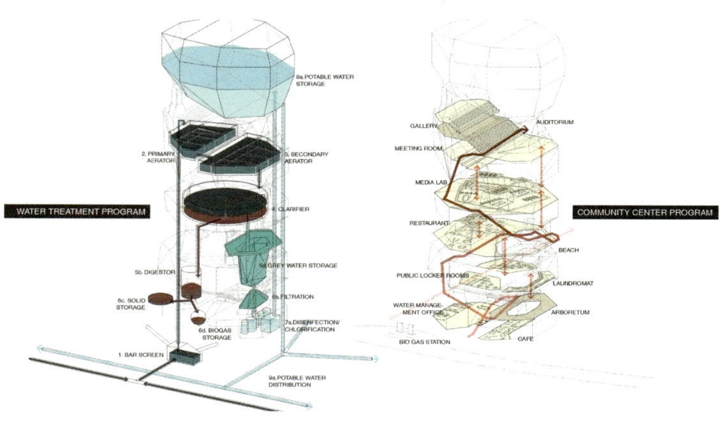

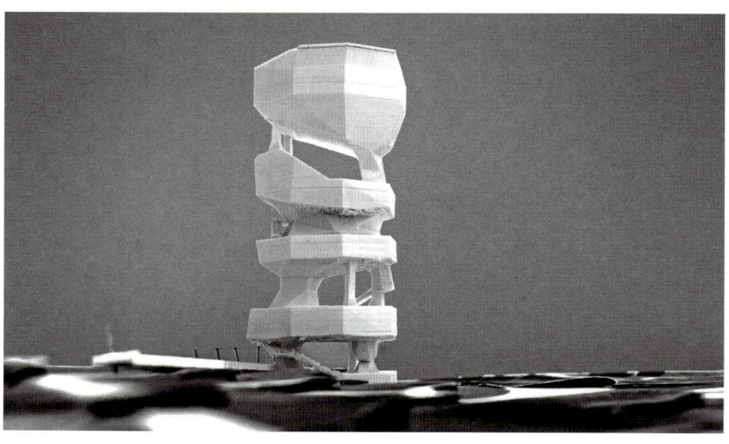

Jacqueline Kow
Interfaith Gabon

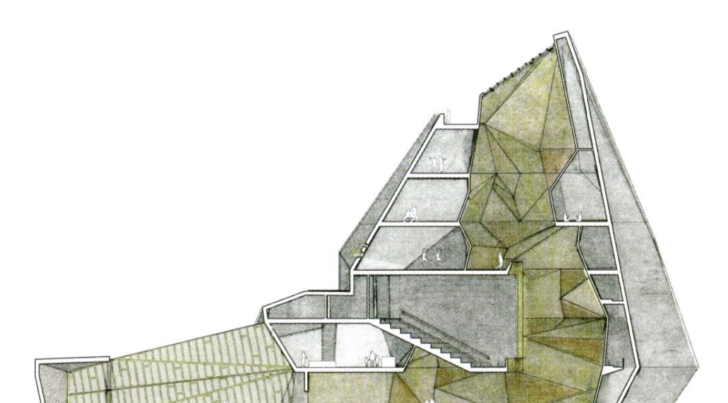

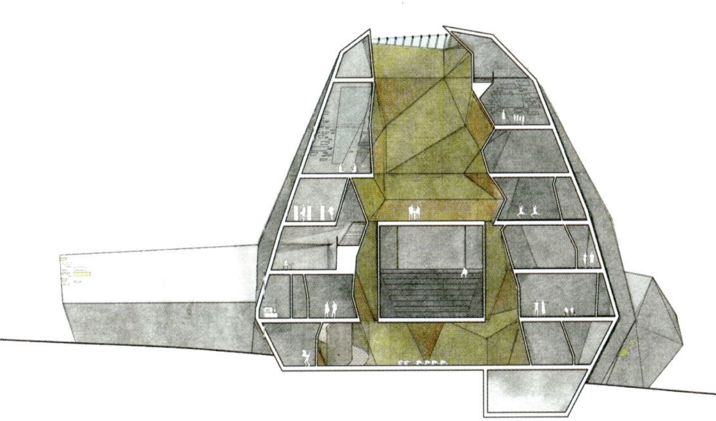

This project proposes an interfaith chapel right off of the Boulevard Triomphal in Libreville, Gabon. Religion has always played an integral role in the community and culture of the country, and with increasing religious diversity in the country, the city is primed for an iconic building that celebrates and preserves the religious culture of the country. In studying several religious typologies and recognizing the opportunity for taking advantage of exterior space, the building is centered around two types of ritual space: the courtyard and the chapel. While these spaces allow for all liturgical practices to occur, there is no demand for specific forms that are generally associated with specific religions.

The form of both the chapel and courtyard are instead shaped by the spatial demands of the program that the interfaith chapel can spur in a city like Libreville. The interfaith chapel goes beyond just a religious space, by offering a piece of social infrastructure that is currently lacking on the Boulevard Triomphal. The building has a youth club, auditorium, exhibition space, and library that allow for different means of engagement to religious artifacts. At the very top of the building, there is also a public platform that allows for one to look back onto the rest of the city and back down on to the central chapel.

MID REVIEW

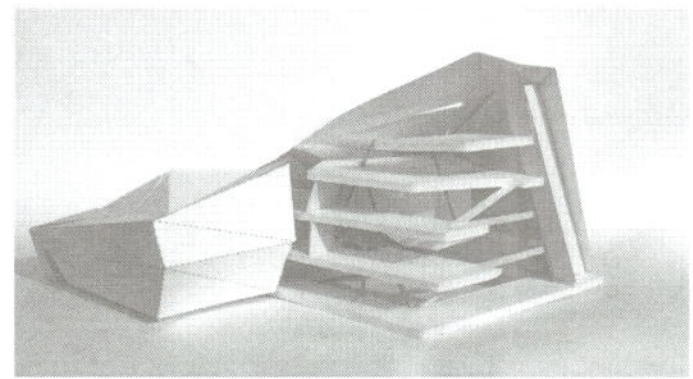

The material quality of the interior needs to reinforce the reading of the void. —Joyce Hsiang

FINAL REVIEW

Shim The fact that it's wood or gold—it's some other special material—depending on the time of day, this light would reflect and refract and actually illuminate the space from within. It's a challenge designing an interfaith space because you have to be generalized to work. Your abstraction of light as the generator that ties them together is a good call. I have lots of questions about the massing and location, because it feels so context-less.

Otero-Pailos This interfaith idea as an emblem of the aspiration of the country is brilliant, especially given that the President converted, which is also a political act. Then, to turn it into some sort of major monument is almost more important than actually whether people do or do not practice anything inside. Every time I go to an airport I document interfaith chapels. That's where you always find them—terminal C, lower concourse. If I don't have access to the VIP lounge, I go straight to the interfaith chapel to work. No one is there! [laughter]

Ouroussoff I assume it's intentional, but this is ambiguous on so many levels. It is not on the main axis of the city, it's slightly removed, like you're trying to find a place in between. It's monumental but it's not, because the space is so small that it can't be used in a monumental way. Even that viewing deck on the roof—St. Peter's has a walkway inside the dome—you do not normally think of a church having a viewing deck, which is oriented toward the axis but not quite. What are you viewing? It's those details that would charge it more.

Turan I like the unfamiliar object. Not only that it's not a circle or a square, but that you can't pin it down as an object. I agree with the comments that the unfamiliar object works really well for an interfaith chapel. You can't pin it down, and that's the point. However, there needs to be some other element that is controlling it. You're a little conservative about that.

Andraos There are two ways you can do this. You can bring us into your iterative process, where there is a beginning and 100 iterations based on orientation and quality of light on a completely formal level. Or, another way would be with reference to relative histories and types.

Easterling What seems very deliberate to me, and perhaps politically charged, is the fact that not many people are allowed to collect. The other thing, which is not the field condition of the mosque and not the hierarchy of the church, is the concentricity of the move. We face the central space as an individual, not a large group. That is very pointed, maybe even dangerous.

Aranda Something I would like to applaud is the techniques of ruination. You have deliberate moves against yourself and against a single reading. Nothing is perfect or whole. The models of interfaith are about this kind of incompleteness. I also like that you don't really know what you did to produce that. In this age when we have so many bombastic positions about what architecture is, what it isn't, and what it should be; I applaud the intuitive approach.

Otero-Pailos If you look at these types of religious buildings in let's say Chandigarh or Brasilia, you have the cathedral as a monument because there is nothing around it—it all has been cleared. There is another tradition of the church building or temple as the site of accretions, markets, etc. You have a corporate lawn around your building. This is standing in a long European tradition of the monument on the lawn, a 19th century tradition. You could have moved it to an even deeper prehistory that is more attuned to what this city is like today.

THE URBANIZATION OF THE REYKJAVIK DOMESTIC AIRPORT

Peggy Deamer  Professor of Architecture

REYKJAVIK, ICELAND

This studio will emphasize the external conditions within which architecture operates. The actual buildings we produce are the tip of an iceberg resting on a set of procedures, institutions, manufacturers, and regulations that architects organize. The smarter we are about these conditions, the more power we have. The more we gather intelligence about these conditions, the richer our architectural acumen.

This studio will situate itself in a number of these conditions—that is, in specific constraints emphasizing the fact that architecture doesn't spring from our heads alone. We will, first, be working in Iceland, a country—remote and small—that has special resources and special scarcities. Its main resource is renewable, geo-thermal energy; another is its aluminum industry. Its scarcity of other industries essential to construction, however, makes it dependent on external sourcing.

We will therefore be working with a specific industry, Seele glass facades—a German company that will supply the material and industry lacking in Iceland. They are chosen as well to take advantage of the expertise that they offer, a material and production intelligence that will limit our material palette on the one hand but enhance our expertise on producing a smart facade/building on the other. It also adds to the complexity because these highly technical facades are not inexpensive and are shipped from global locations; procurement and scheduling become part of the design logic.

Finally, Iceland has the advantage of being small, nimble, and responsive to individual initiative at the same time that it has the disadvantage of being capital-challenged and in a financial crisis. Thus, they, as a population and a government, can be highly responsive to design vision at the same time that they are strapped for cash to support it. Our program, a badly needed and highly controversial new domestic/international airport, operates in the center of that tension.

JURORS

Peter Arbour
Daniel Barber
Annie Barrett
Anna Bokov
Alexander Felson
Rainer Hirth
Timothy Hyde
Theodossios Issaias
Steinthor Karason
Eeva-Liisa Pelkonen
Dan Wood
Frano Violich

Feldman Nominee

Thom Medek
Flugspitali

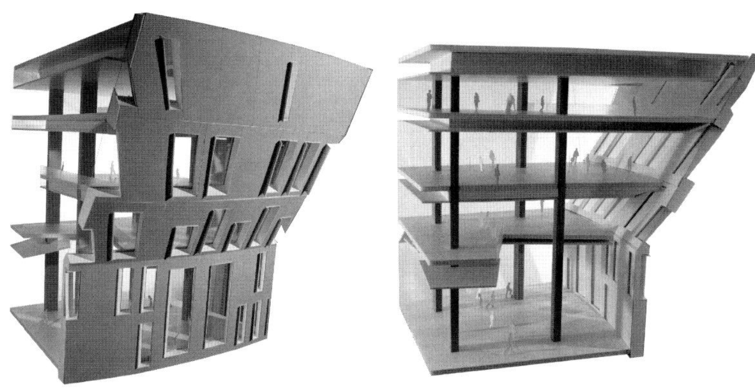

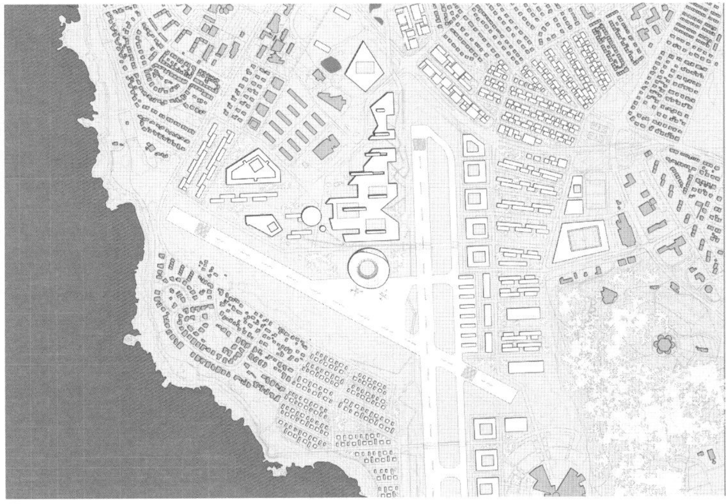

The regional airport situated near Reykjavik's city center is the source of one of Iceland's most heated political debates. Evenly divided, nearly half of the country's population depends upon the airport for commuter use, while the rest regard its location as a noise pollutant taking up valuable land preventing growth of the city's center. More important, however, is the dependence by those residing outside of the city on the airport for transport to the country's only hospital suitable for emergency care.
This proposal advocates for repositioning these conflicting views as potential opportunities which allow for moderate development of the site to meet the city's need to grow while also constructing a hybrid hospital, airport, and resort building used not only to serve the needs of the people, but also to spur medical tourism as a model for benign and sustainable economic growth in a country struggling to recover from recent economic collapse.

MID REVIEW

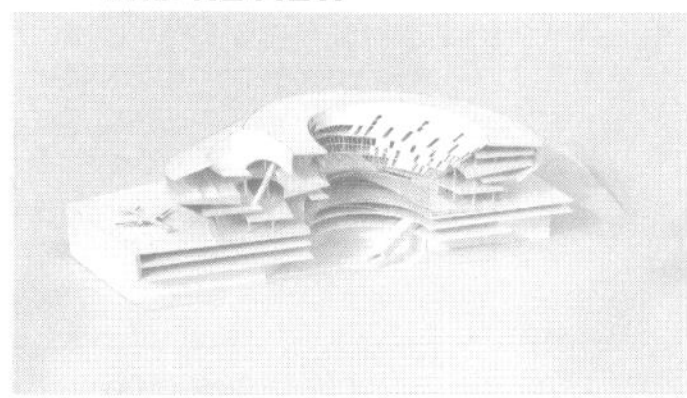

The fact that you're drawing this as a circle also indicates something and that's the fact that if you transcend the local conditions and you go to more abstract conditions of serenity or democracy, the power of the circular form takes a new level of affability. But it doesn't translate so easily down to the local setting. —Hilda Guner

FINAL REVIEW

Pelkonen I have some problems with the narrative, but I have to say, this is one of the most accomplished buildings, I love the way it looks and whatever program would go there, I would still love it. It is so elegant and such a pleasure to look at the spaces inside the incredible form making, it's just perfection. So it's just the narrative and this whole question about two hospitals and the tourism aspect of it. But I think it's an incredibly accomplished building.

Karason There are two projects here. In Iceland we tend to argue over everything. There is this necessity for the airport, for the people who live on the island, but they normally fly in with much smaller planes. Ten passenger planes with room for one stretcher. And you know that would work. The tourism, they would all arrive in the international airport. I think the project would gain a lot if you would go either way.

Violich I would expect that the deformation, getting back to Anna's point, would have had much more impact in the distortion and I think it would have been an exciting moment architecturally, because you obviously have the skillset to take that on. Somehow I would expect that geometry to shift so that the north is actually open to what they call the light sky. It's not about the sun, it's how much light is in the sky. So, I think it is a sectional thing and a bit of a detail remark but I would have been interested to see how far you would have risked destroying the circle before you got to the edge where, crap, I'm starting to lose it.

Hyde You don't really need the circle; you just need hermeticism to deal with this idea of the closed loop of the airport hospital connections outside of Iceland. So there are other ways to produce hermeticism without the geometry of the circle. That would have been if you identified or affiliated some of the form with the light as Frano was saying but thought of organizational modes of hermeticism, because you deal with hermeticism basically with elevators.

Pelkonen I love the plan, in a way, talking about hermeticism, I think it's kind of a building that you can tell is bursting out of its seams. It starts very proper; you have the buses and the logic, closure and then in the top floor it wants to burst out of its seams. I think it's great, so maybe it should become a clinic for schizophrenics [laughter] who want to fly out of the window because it does get more and more open.

Deamer Part of me is saying break open the circle and then we could figure out how to connect it to the hospital, but on the other hand the hermeticism is absolutely essential to its nature. There's this on-going tension about what it does as a kind of power source, whether it's an internalized energy or whether it's a hub that connects other things.

Karason Dealing with light in Iceland is extremely difficult. The light there is, relative to winter and summer, really even. In the spring and fall it is extremely contrasted, it is ever changing. It is really unbelievable. This comes again to the scale of the project. The trees there won't get ever one ray of light, sorry. When you are describing your façade and you are dealing with the light and at the same time, the scale of the building, I mean, this is the north side and it is incredibly cold and that's the main entrance? This north side of the building with overhangs, they're really, really hard. Just the scale of things, the scale of the city, the scale of the buildings there, the scale of places there, it's not by accident that they are like that. I say this in general, this is something that you have to look at and have to take seriously.

Mark Tumiski

Icelandic Connector: Domestic Transit Hub and Urban Bridge

This upgrade to Reykjavik's controversial domestic airport enables arrival in the heart of the city while reuniting its north and south districts across the main arterial road—establishing a civic gateway linking urban and rural Iceland. The building design is a product of the urban and detail scales; my curtain wall proposal aims to capture and reflect the constantly changing colors of the arctic sky while utilizing the hovering roadway to reflect light into the sunken concourse. Vehicles, pedestrians and programs are braided together in plan and section, maximizing adjacencies and disrupting the linearity of the bar.

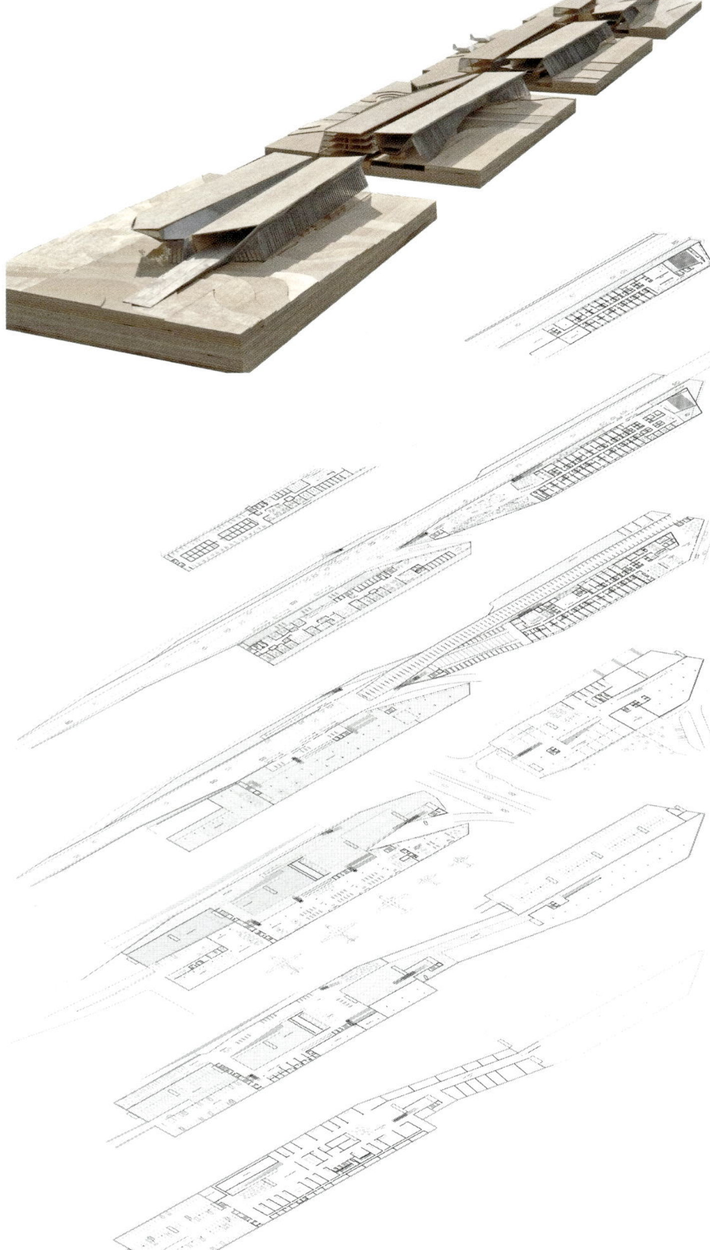

MID REVIEW

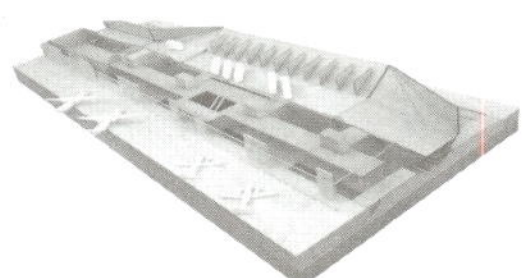

I've been struck all along by the amount of effort you're taking to put the buses on the raised story. I would think about that very carefully. I haven't heard from you or in the discussion a logic that should suggest why it shouldn't be lower than higher. —Daniel Barber

FINAL REVIEW

Barber It has a real robustness to its functionality, even if it's only symbolic, but it feels a little untested. Why are you bringing down light into the second concourse and putting a road up top when you could just put everybody up top and put the road down? I'm sympathetic to the notion of this being a bridge across the space that the highway contains, you know, in the sense of the scale of the roads in Iceland that Frano referred to, and I like the way that you're really exercising some of the capacities of the curtain wall system to transfer light. But I'm not totally on board with how that gesture becomes possibly superfluous if you just shift some of the programing around.

Hyde The reason I support the inversion is that I buy this braiding of the city and the airport, certainly in contrast to the previous project. So this is really trying to think of how you integrate the city into the terminal. As you say, it's big, but it's not an exaggeration of scale. Even if the inversion is a contrivance and the curtain wall then solves that contrivance, it's a worthwhile because it braids a city scale and a city experience into the terminal and you can imagine here that there is an elasticity in the parti. The hotel could be bigger or smaller, you could have more offices and less hotel, so the ratio of different programs doesn't really matter, that's variable. But you've actually figured out a system for braiding those kinds of elements together.

Barrett You started by talking about your project as a gateway, and I wonder about your attitude to the roof which in a way is a fifth façade of the building, especially because it's an airport. There is a little bit of biomimicry going on, I don't know if it's twisting roots or braiding, but I wonder why you didn't take a landscape approach to the roof other than the deck. It seems like it wants to be a mineral in the landscape.

Pelkonen Bringing the street in brings up another issue that is particular to the airport typology, especially of a certain scale that you never experience the building from outside, or hardly ever. The only time is if you land and you see it from the window. Who would know what Frankfurt airport looks like? You experience it from the interior, it's a building that's pure interiority, it's quite fascinating actually. I think all that action that you show in those sectional models, that's the project. There's a wonderful project, well not so wonderful, kind of a creepy project, by Kevin Roche, the Union Carbide building that brings the highway inside. He made the point that you never experience a building outside, you are always inside and therefore the building should provide inside what it lacks outside; you have different types of environments, different types of light conditions that it delivers on the interior.

Deamer At a review between the mid-term and this one, the critics suggested that all of this really amazing work about the facade and how it manages light should be brought into the interior, so it shouldn't just be a spectacle on the outside. The solution to the light and the curtain wall that begins to work at the cross grain would be an entrance into the reprograming issue. Because the less this has become just a bar building, the more it is on the verge of actually telling us how we can break the typology, how we can get another reading besides that linearity. The light penetration as a counterforce going in would then break it even further.

Hirth Getting off the plane, arriving is the one moment when you confront your wall head on, otherwise you're always moving alongside it. So there is this one part of the building where you are on the transverse grain, going through the wall, and you have pockets signifying a door of some kind, but that is deeply unfortunate. That seems antagonistic to everything else you're doing. Until you figure out how to put a door to go that direction, it's a big gray area.

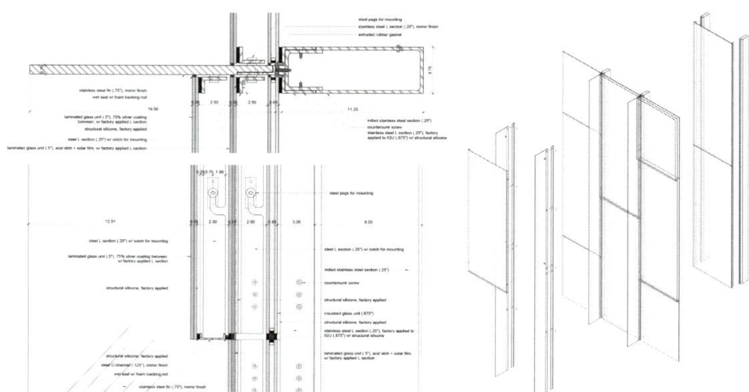

Jason Roberts
Reykjavík Domestic Airport

The odd pairing of a domestic airport within downtown Reykjavík is amplified through a single gesture. A linear building combines city functions with airport functions, at once connecting the city and staging new public experiences close to but separate from aircrafts.

MID REVIEW

How would you feel if it got a lot messier? Because right now it's this clean line with big, empty hallways, but when you park planes in it, you're going to have taxiways, you're going to have baggage tug paths where all the baggage comes through. If this gets inserted into reality, it's going to be a long line with lots of bits and pieces breaking it up and splitting out. Would that hurt the diagram? —Daniel Barber

FINAL REVIEW

Wood The why is so important, and you can't say it is dogmatic. Dogmatic and dogged are two different things. It's like a dogged expression because relentless is dogged. Dogmatic means there is some incontrovertible truth behind it. What is the truth that you are presenting? Because it's like we're looking at the interior design of New Babylon or Superstudio, which didn't have interior design because it was about this dogmatic concept about contemporaneity and future and life and political situation, whatever, there was a dogma.

Pelkonen This is not high tech. This is low tech, skylights and concrete. That's an interesting paradox. You want the airport not to be high tech, not fluid but archaic. Do you see it? Was it intentional? Because that's interesting; slowing it down. Not the fast airport, the slow airport.

Felson Take a stance on what you are doing and be able to say yes it would undermine the project or, or no it would make the project better. With such an intense project you're putting forth, you really want to know and I think you should think about this for the next day or month. I'm not saying you haven't considered that but if someone says cut off half your building, I would expect a strong response: you can't take that away from me. The project is so strong and that's what's so interesting about it.

Violich That raises the question, what came first, landscape or the bar. In your mind, you could say both but let's say you can't. It very interesting that the bar is driving the landscape and there is more landscape than bar. So it's an interesting thing to consider the idea of enfilade rooms, you itemize the bar and it is responsive to a greater landscape infrastructural approach, meaning you have to get from one room to another through that soft infrastructure as opposed to through a harder one. It's a choice to make and that's why I ask what came first. An architect will always have the bark on first. It's in our DNA but I think I just raised the opportunity that the other might come first.

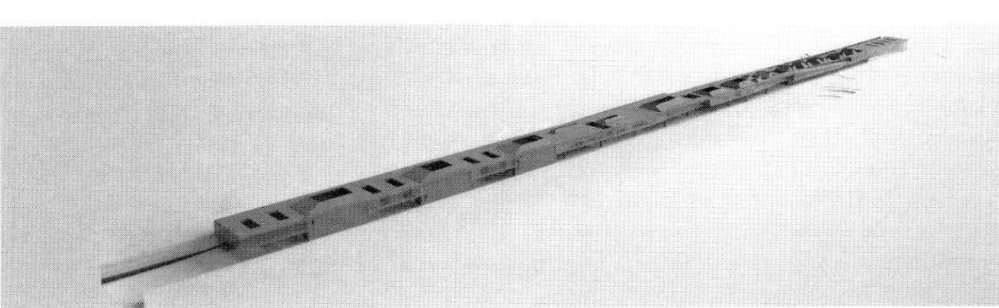

Kailun Sun
Reykjavík Terminal

The project tries to find a new meaning for the airport terminal inside the city. In the proposed master plan of Reykjavik, an under-utilized runway is eliminated to give space for the extension of the city grid in the southeast direction. On the other hand, a cardinal city grid is laid out as the extension of Kópavogur, the neighboring city, to meet the extended city grid from Reykjavik.
The new terminal is chosen to be located at the intersection of two grid systems as the new transportation hub of Reykjavík that combines the airport terminal with the local bus terminal. This terminal organizes and directs different scale circulation flows using folding surfaces, to integrate the exterior landscape and the interior programs. To better separate traffic flows both programmatically and conceptually, a double skin façade system is introduced. While the outer skin emphasizes transparency and the boundaries of the terminal, the inner skin serves the function of acoustic and thermal separation.

MID REVIEW

I really like the way that you've done this folding and pleating in ways that are programmatically driven. Providing a different sort of logic to that formal gesture. It seems like it needs to be worked out in much finer detail. —Daniel Barber

FINAL REVIEW

Barrett One way that might help would be to think about the way that you're programing it. The exhibition seems a little bit vague, and a different way to think about it would be instead of programs in a building, think about programing as a city. So park, parking lot, you know, whatever those ingredients of the city are and think about those scales other than the building program scales. Similarly, you have this beautiful form making but maybe one that is not really aligned to multimodal transportation. You don't see the turning radiuses of the planes and the buses that you would probably see, so thinking in that programming language from a planning perspective as well as from the architectural scale might help the project. It is really beautiful to think about the inside/outside as a way of engaging the curtain wall.

Barber A lot of this is playing around the potential of the dual curtain wall. You separated them in the two pretty different systems, and yet, you're producing these huge volumes that need to be conditioned. The urban porosity, and even more so the square where the different curtain walls have different planer systems, don't have to coordinate themselves to different planes.

Arbour The project reminds me a little bit of the dome proposal over Manhattan by Buckminster Fuller. In that case he's got one tool, you've given yourself two. You have the red stuff and then you have these transparent vertical walls and so it's almost a satellite city. You could see this housing taking place inside, you could see streets in here. The complexity and the urban idea of what goes on in a structure that large can include a bus and an airplane and a street and a house and you know, retail and whatever else, an exposition space.

MASTER OF ENVIRONMENTAL DESIGN

COORDINATOR: EEVA-LIISA PELKONEN

MED COMMITTEE
Michelle Addington
Peggy Deamer
Keller Easterling
Karsten Harries
Alan Plattus

VISITING CRITICS
Daniel Barber (UPenn)
Timothy Hyde (Harvard)
Jonathan Massey (Syracuse)
Mari Lending (Oslo Architecture School)

2ND YEAR STUDENTS
Anuj Daga (advisor: Eeva-Liisa Pelkonen)
Ayeza Qureshi (advisor: Keller Easterling)
Britton Rogers (advisor: Elihu Rubin)
Jessica Varner (advisor: Peggy Deamer)

1ST YEAR STUDENTS
Benyameen Ghareeb (advisor: Todd Reisz)
Eric Peterson (advisor: Peggy Deamer)
Eric Rogers (advisor: Peggy Deamer)
Andrew Ruff (advisor: Eeva-Liisa Pelkonen)
Brent Sturlaugson (advisor: Keller Easterling)

True to the legacy of the MED program, while this year's graduating class represents a wide range of backgrounds they share the passion for looking at the built environment through a variety of intellectual lenses. Anuj Daga was fascinated by the circulation of images and how they shaped not only his own architectural education but the rapidly changing built environment in his native Mumbai; Ayeza Qureshi pursued the enigma of the absence of a valid map for his native Karachi; Britton Rogers, a practicing architect active in preservation movement, wrote about Longwarf, a strange relic from New Haven's industrial past that survives till today; and Jessica Varner, who came to the program via California, wrote about Co-Evolution Quarterly, a quintessential San Fransisco-based magazine from the early days of the environmental movement. The synergies between these disparate topics was apparent in the colloquium they helped organized in spring 2014 under the rubric "Powers of Ten" bringing together speakers within and without Yale to talk about the built environment from the scale of the satellite image to the particle of dust.

The topics of the first year students make their shared interest in the political dimension of architecture and urbanism manifest while the sites of their explorations vary greatly from Blackhills of North Dakota, to New York, Edinburg, and Kuwait. Many of them used the summer to conduct primary research; Andrew Ruff will travel to Scotland on a Paul Mellon travel grant and Brent Sturlaugson to Blackhill on a state AIA grant.

Anuj Daga
In the Place of Images

The thesis explores how circulation of different formats of visual media ties into the built environment of cities in India. Analysis of different artefacts like publications, people, films and buildings articulate different themes through which global architectural expression in India can be possibly read. The title, In the Place of Images presents thus, a subtle contradiction. While the notion of 'place' is understood as a primal location through which a being operates and locates oneself in a particular physical setting, technology and media have brought this relationship into dialectic with image production. By challenging the fixed idea of 'place' with the flow of 'images,' one recalls the categories of the 'scapes' given by anthropologist Arjun Appadurai, which restructure the conception of the world through flows of technology, media and capital instead of the established cartographic boundaries. In the process of architectural design, different formats of media from this fluid space get tied together, and morphed into physical reality—a "place" of sorts—in unexpected ways. The thesis lends the concepts of 'misreadings', 'misprisions', 'confluences' and 'leakages' to understand the hybrid visual architectural landscape of Indian cities.

"Cambridge Circus is in which UK City?" asks Prem, the anchor of the show "Who wants to be a Millionaire?" in the movie Slumdog Millionaire, to the contestant Jamal who is a mere chai-wallah (tea-maker) in a call centre in Mumbai. Jamal's filmic navigation in order to guess an answer to this five-million-rupee-question frames an interesting picture of the how spaces that actively participate in import and export of data, products and people (along with images, ideas and lifestyles) take physical form in a city like Mumbai.

The Oscar-winning film offers thus a window to new types of environments that shun our pre-existing notions of architectural or urban space located in real time and place. Rather, these new building types—call centers, hotel chains, malls, are all sites that have seemingly no qualities that we normally associate with architecture; their main function is simply to facilitate the circulation of images, identities, capital, people and products through them. The film—at times comic, depicts how these new types of spaces, which become more and more common after India liberalized its economy over the 1990s, are active sites of various flows that transcend national and local boundaries sometimes in strange and uncanny ways. In doing so, they have not only become the means, but also the products of circulation of ideas and images.

Ayeza Qureshi
Mapping Power: the political instrumentality of the map in Karachi

Karachi, one of the world's largest urban agglomerations, is spread over 3527 square kilometers and has a population estimated to be greater than 20 million, yet it is arguably a city without a map. Since partition, in 1947, the colonial City's inherited forms of organization and representation have steadily declined. Under the relatively new State of Pakistan, this decline has resulted in the absence of a comprehensive master plan and a legible map of the contemporary city in the public domain. The thesis explores the political instrumentality of the map in the increasingly polarized and conflicted megacity of Karachi. A comparative, chronological analysis focuses on the association between maps, power and politics—how the map affects the city's capacity for communication and decision-making. The study explores the interdependencies between individual gains and the success of the rising megacity, that have thus far, supported its development in the absence of a legible image of the city. If the map is to be useful for governance in fragmented and conflicted environments, what does the history suggest about its future as a technology for mediating complexity, conflict and human wellbeing?

The production and distribution of spatial knowledge in Karachi has had a significant impact on the access to and the management of resources across socio-economic and political classes of society. The map assisted the modernist state to articulate authority by cultivating legibility in the territories and people it ruled. Authority was established not only by making the subject coherent to the state, but also the state visible in the everyday life of its subjects. The absence of the map thus signaled the absence of demonstrated centralized control or authority.[1] If Karachi is a profitable endeavor, why is the State not more interested in coordinating and communicating control to its citizens?

The traditional model of control that reinforces legibility blurs in the context of Karachi. As political parties fragmented and multiplied, consensus generated by above-the-table negotiations was fraught and often stalled, as in the case of city master plans. If power was subject to consensus, and consensus could not be manufactured, its alternative, dissent, became an equally effective way of control. Through forms of resistance, dissent survives in its ambition to compromise control or conversely reinforce control in spaces of conflict.

If Karachi is a success, it is not in the measure of its space standards, a preserved or marketable aesthetic, and the standards of sanitation or the quality of their building materials. If maps are the fundamental elements of communication and decision making for the built environment, then the case of settlements, which have been communicated and negotiated in their absence, is an important one to consider. In such environments, what is the value of conventional orders of representation as tools for establishing control? What does the history of the map's association with power, politics, and culture in Karachi suggest will be its future as a technology for mediating fragmentation and conflict, in order to improve access to essential services required for human wellbeing?

1 Sahoutara, Naeem. "These unmarked maps of Karachi are no better than wallpaper, say judges." Newspaper. The Express Tribune, International Herald Tribune, October 26, 2012.

Britton Rogers
Long Wharf: Twentieth Century Industrial Renewal in New Haven

The Long Wharf Industrial Park was an attempt by urban planners to address the changing form of industry. Along with politicians, they diagnosed the growing economic necessity for the City of New Haven to remain relevant for manufacturers. One of several redevelopment projects in the city's urban redevelopment program that began in the 1950s, the Long Wharf project was unique to New Haven in that it was the only project created on new land, for the purpose of the renewal of industry. Its genesis is in the physical and functional relationship to the Connecticut Turnpike, which enclosed a marshland that was filled to create the district known as Long Wharf. The form and use of the newly created land followed a specific spatial paradigm: the industrial park, which had its origins in nineteenth century industrial cities and became a dominant form of land use across the country. Composed largely of unremarkable one-story factories and warehouses the district contained one monument by Marcel Breuer for the Armstrong Rubber Company; the one building in the district that has been vacant almost as long as it was occupied.

Long Wharf was able to lure industry to remain in New Haven because it was designed to meet changed needs of manufacturing for corporations. It could host companies that needed flexibility to respond to technological change. The wide open, flat spaces made companies who located there able to capitalize on truck transportation, a modern technology presenting new options for shipping in the 1950s.1 New types of public-private relationships were forged in order to adapt to these rapidly shifting industrial practices, as evidenced by the story of New Haven's relationship with Sargent and Company, a large, local hardware manufacturer.

Now on board, Sargent was an anchor tenant, along with the Wholesale Food Terminal Corporation, who could be accommodated at the site as well. The new industrial park's design was printed in a publicity brochure by the Redevelopment authority. Reading the plan, we see that it imagined buildings lined up with consistent setbacks along the highway, a modern language of large floor plates connected by driveways and parking. Unlike many industrial parks that developed at the time, the design did not turn away from the highway. Parking was not in front, but in the back of the buildings as a buffer between the rail yards. The plan reveals a gesture of campus planning with a mall of sorts shown down the center, with paths crossing. This mall was oriented perpendicularly to the turnpike, symmetrically between exit and entrance ramps. At the time, campus plans were being applied to industrial, research and development office parks, as well as corporate estates. It seems like an awkward application to us today because of the orientation to the turnpike, but this shows the emphasis that was placed on the new means of travel to be faced, not ignored or hidden from. The plan shows three important elements that never materialized: a port with rail connection which was a needed increase for the city's port capacity, a heliport as an attempt to modernize the city's transportation links that was important for corporate leaders, and a public marina in the harbor. Marc Levinson describes a significant shift in transportation technology in Box: How the Shipping Container Made the World Smaller and the World Economy Bigger. Princeton, NJ: Princeton University Press, 2006.

Jessica Varner
Ecology, Expertise, and Exchange: CoEvolution Quarterly (1974–1984)

This thesis will examine the link between the little-known, science-focused journal CoEvolution Quarterly (1974–84) and the changing agency of environmentally focused architecture within a larger debate of ecology. Founded under the editorial hand of Stewart Brand, CoEvolution Quarterly began by foregrounding a network of architects and designers as primary participants in the wider ecological exchange amongst scientists, businessmen, politicians, artists, and intellectuals alike. The community of contributors—the circle of friends—created the diverse conversation. While the editors talked to the readers, the contributors communicated amongst each other, and the journal spoke to the environmental issues at hand; in short, the journal's form took on its theoretical premise—the conversational, connected environment centered around ecology, exchange, and expertise.

CoEvolution Quarterly began as a critique of the large-scale cybernetic systems of the 1950s and 1960s, instead promoting small-scale, connected theories exemplified by the journal's scientific leaders—James Lovelock, Lynn Margulis, Paul Ehrlich, and Gregory Bateson. Presented in 1975 by James Lovelock and Lynn Margulis in the sixth issue of CoEvolution Quarterly, the Gaia Hypothesis proposed that earth is a living series of interconnected relationships, a conversation amongst parts, thereby rendering it impossible to consider the environment or nature separate from humanity. Similarly, Ehrlich's theory of coevolution and Gregory Bateson's ideas of connected-systems were presented in CoEvolution Quarterly the same year.

This conceptual systems shift signaled a marked difference in perceptions of environmental hierarchy and the notion of exchange; no longer were nature and culture in conflict, nor was nature a pure, pious thing and culture a messy "other;" everything was in conversation. Every scale and particle, human and nonhuman, now had a voice. Thus, the role of architecture and of the architect transformed within the environmental conversation; architectural practice and product were no longer isolated within the field but instead a necessary component of the larger biosphere and an even larger dialogue.

Also, the journal's criticism of expertise led to both a crisis and opportunity of the expert. As scientists turned to architecture, architects to politics, and designers to science, the position of expert was up for grabs. In turn, language and representation shifted within CoEvolution Quarterly. Architects and designers took the opportunity to define environmental design as a political, technological, social, scientific, and aesthetic dimension. As architecture absorbed all it could, its potency dispersed, and in the end the only expert left standing was the panacea of technology and the gauges of performance.

This thesis highlights the aspects of ecology, exchange, and expertise in relation to key players and the representation presented in CoEvolution Quarterly. Messy and emboldened, the artifacts, personalities, and the conversation presented reveal the shifting debate in design and science from form to performance. Architecture and its changing definition is highlighted as a primary actor in the environmental project. The introduction reviews the history and context of CoEvolution Quarterly, looking primarily at how the conceptual framework and transformation of ecology, exchange, and expertise manifested new agency to designers. The first chapter addresses the specific transformation of ecology and architecture in CoEvolution Quarterly through the work of the New Alchemy Institute and Dr. John Todd. The second chapter addresses the changing nature of expertise through the work of Day Chahroudi, the founder of Suntek, inventor of Low-E technology, and other solar material technologies. The third chapter reviews the changing face of exchange within CoEvolution Quarterly through the dialogue between Sim Van Der Ryn, the State Architect of California, Stewart Brand, and California Governor Jerry Brown, Jr. Finally, the coda addresses the moment of reprieve in ecological emphasis and CoEvolution Quarterly's end alongside technology's rise in the mid-1980s. As technology and performance became the barometers for success within both the scientific and architectural context, exchange diminished and the conversation quieted.

As the contemporary conversation shifts back to issues of the environment and the connection in architecture to ecology, exchange, and expertise reemerges, these questions remain: how can we establish a value system in such a dynamic, nonhierarchical ecological system? How do technology and science inform the conversation? How can the architect within this system define their role in ecology-based design in a world of experts? How can architecture be extra-disciplinary without losing its identity?

Benyameen Ghareeb
The Urbanization of the Kuwaiti Population

The housing scene in Kuwait today shows several 'districts' or areas that differ based on socio-economic and racial factors. Some of these divisions result from sequential expansion over time i.e. center to periphery, while others are argued to be created intentionally by the State. Locals that mostly lived within the old center prior to modernization inhabit the several 'rings' of neighborhoods surrounding the historic center. These areas have the greatest real estate value due to perceived prestige as well close proximity to downtown where most jobs exist. It is also a testimony to being one of the 'originals' that were in Kuwait before wealth arrived.1 The next set of areas beyond these neighborhoods generally house the second generation of the first suburbs' inhabitants. The third area with the least real estate values includes Al-Jahra (an old village about fifteen miles west of the old center) and its adjacent neighborhoods, as well as the urban settlements in the far south.

It is argued that the government intentionally housed Bedouins in these neighborhoods that were naturalized in the past few decades. The reason behind this strategy was in order to control this population both politically (in parliament to ensure seats with government support) and physically against protests.2 Bedouins began to settle in urban areas seeking improved living conditions due to tough desert life and dwindling grazing fields in the 1950s and 1960s. Due to a lack of accommodations within the city, they squatted in shanty villages (barastis) near Al-Jahra or Fahaheel in the south (where they had relatives). It is speculated that when the government naturalized these populations, it did not include them in the regular housing application system, but rather gave them land in neighborhoods that were farther away from the center and near the distant villages.

Another significant change brought about by the State was regarding the traditional family structure. Bedouins were moved from extended family households into single-family detached houses. This move was potentially to weaken bonds between families and their tribal leaders and on the other hand strengthen the relationship with the State (or Al-Sabah).3 Finally, Bedouins were further divided according to 'noble' and 'non-noble' tribes in different suburbs.4 In general, these neighborhoods are denser than 'model neighborhoods' by using attached housing and smaller lots.

This complex dynamic coupled with a growing housing backlog and an unaffordable real estate market has engendered interesting migration patterns and an unofficial market of bartering and trade-offs between citizens.

---

1 Farah Al-Nakib, "The Bidoon and the City: An Historical Account of the Politics of Exclusion in Kuwait," in Al Manakh 2; also Ali Al-Zubi, "Urbanization, Tribalism, and Tribal Marriage in Contemporary Kuwait." Order No. DA9932953, Wayne State U, 0101

2 Shafiq Al-Ghabra, Lecture at the Yale Law School Middle East Legal Studies Seminar. New Haven, January 17, 2014; Al-Zubi; Crystal; and al-Haddad

3 Crystal, 89; and Mohammad al-Haddad, "The Effect of Detribalization and Sedentarization on the Socio-Economic Structure of the Tribes of the Arabian Peninsula: Ajman Tribe as a Case Study." (Phd diss., University of Kansas, 1981)

4 For more information on the segregation of tribes see Al-Zubi

Eric Peterson
Planning for Crisis: Redevelopment, Governmentality, and "Urban Crisis" in New York

Amid scarce public resources and a lack of political will, how do cities undertake large-scale infrastructure building? Whose interests get prioritized and who should pay for development? These were some of the questions facing public officials in New York in the late 1960s and which led to the creation of the Urban Development Corporation, or UDC, an organization given radical powers to attack some of the city's most pressing problems. This project examines the trajectory of the UDC, arguing it was pivotal in the transformation in the means through which large-scale infrastructure building happens in New York. As the post-war project of urban renewal unraveled amid debates over the role of government planning in urban reconstruction, the UDC created an innovative if contradictory model, using private money, financed through municipal bonds, for the purposes of social good. Between 1968 and 1972 it was the largest builder of subsidized low-income housing in the country. When federal funding for low-income housing was abandoned in the 1970s, the UDC became implicated in New York City's larger debt crisis, nearly defaulting on $2 billion in debt. After the crisis, the organization became a key tool for public officials to expedite the building of privately funded development projects such as the erection of large corporate office complexes.

The UDC's financing model created a process of financialization that ultimately limited how public officials could undertake large-scale urban development projects as they became increasingly tied to private financial markets. Born out of contestation over the proper means and outcomes of public planning for development, the experience of the UDC offers key insights into the ways decision-making over public urban development shifted from the community block to the boardrooms of the city's most powerful banks, and from the public realm to private development markets. The UDC's evolution complicates normative narratives about the end of urban renewal, and sheds light onto the enduring yet transformed means through which public officials outsource and subsidize the redevelopment of urban space.

Eric Wycoff Rogers

Architecture and Reproduction

I argue that architecture plays an essential role in the reproduction of capitalism as an economic system. I use the term "reproduction" because it implies the contingency of the process of capitalist accumulation on its prerequisite inputs—those inputs that are required for overcoming capital's inherent contradictions: labor, the means of production, and the political system that organizes labor into specifically capitalist relations of production.1 I engage in a general consideration of the processes involved in the reproduction of the capitalist system, focusing on the roles that non-market entities play in reproduction, specifically the state, civil society and the family. I show how the state has been steered politically by civil society organizations which have served as a kind of federation of professionalized think tanks, using expert knowledge to form upper-class consensus. Focusing on the programs of specific civil society organizations throughout history, particularly surrounding the City Beautiful Movement in the United States, I trace the ways that the state was increasingly induced to adopt policies about urban land use that would secure optimal results for capital's survival and growth, by replenishing the basic inputs required for capitalism's reproduction.

The state accomplishes such an ensuring, I show, by ordering spatial configurations that maximize consumption as part of a larger absorption strategy in an economy that constantly struggles to find investment opportunities for surplus capital seeking valorization. Also, and quite crucially, I demonstrate that these urban policies, functionally consistent with the Enclosures Acts, and commented on by Marx and Adam Smith, and called by these thinkers "primitive accumulation," accomplished an integration of non-capitalist-produced value, which, through its integration, makes up for the deficit of value that accumulates from the gap between total wages and total value of commodities (as Marx's labor theory of value demonstrates). Specifically, and increasingly in the post-colonial world, this has largely been achieved through the reconstitution of the worker by the family—shielded from the volatility of the market by this incentivized social unit. The state has materially and culturally encouraged the proliferation of the family as the primary social unit through the zoning of single-family dwelling-specific areas, selective guaranteeing of loans for family-sized, suburban houses, the construction of roads, park systems for easing the strain of urban families, and various other subsidies. The creation and preservation of these non-market pockets is not an aim in and of itself—at least not for capital. What makes the family so economically productive is that it is simultaneously given a haven and separated from other families to prevent them from becoming a dominant, socialized mode of non-capitalist production. This separation is mediated through commerce, and generally involves third parties, generating capital. The point is not to create a stable basis for the family for itself, but to establish the family as a protected pocket out of which labor may reproduce itself for use in the market, as well as to create pockets for the production of consumption. What is thus inscribed into the urban fabric by state intervention, in addition to private pockets for family activity is a system of mechanisms for harvesting non-waged labor power.

This thesis project attempts to demonstrate the architectural history behind this aspect of the modern capitalist economy's development, considering the development of urban planning, zoning, the development of civil society groups before, during and after the Progressive Era, and implementation of the policies pioneered by these groups, as well as their alteration and further development in the hands of the state in the form of the New Deal. I then consider the changes that have occurred in the world of urban planning in the neoliberal era, in which credit and mortgage debt came to play a more significant role in the reproduction of the economy, shifting the emphasis away from the architectural origins of the planned economy.

In a final essay, I explore the possibility, within the economic-historical context that I describe in earlier chapters, for an exploitation of the aggregated pockets of non-capitalist space by both capital and non-capitalist modes of production.

There must be constant, and ongoing intervention in order to preserve the preconditions of production in an economy that, "while it produces, and in order to be able to produce in the future, [must] reproduce the conditions of its production. It must therefore reproduce: 1) the productive forces [labor and the means of production]; [and,] 2) the existing relations of production [capitalist relations of production]." Althusser, Louis, Etienne Balibar, Jacques Bidet, and G. M Goshgarian. On the Reproduction of Capitalism: Ideology and Ideological State Apparatuses, 2014. pg. 48.

Andrew Ruff

Terra Incognita: Projective Symbols and Speculative Cities

In medieval and Renaissance cartography, the representation of new territories often grafted symbols and mythical creatures into the illustrated landscape. This practice created a discrepancy between the objective geographic survey and the interpretation of space through symbolic imagery, a paradox which was most articulated within terrae incognitae, the dynamic, uninhabited lands dwelling on the tenuous horizon of the known universe. Here, the symbol served as a projection of man's desire to occupy the unknown, operating as a metaphorical threshold between the impossibility of the infinite and the tactility of the immediate.

The emergence of new states within the global political arena offers a contemporary corollary to these mythical illustrations. While monsters and the dragons operated as a means to symbolically occupy the untraversed and unstable spaces of early cartography, emergent countries and cities utilize similar symbolic armatures as they engage international politics. In order to delineate themselves from the homogeneity of transnational, globalized culture, these new political states project their identity through the creation, manipulation, or destruction of symbolic urban space. This thesis speculates that the threshold and the boundary are unique typologies of urban space through which political entities attempt to project the myths of the state, myths which manifest as a mutable, and potentially ambiguous, assemblage of symbolic forms ingrained in the fabric of the city.

Just as sea monsters symbolized the complexity of emergent space, these symbolic urban spaces are the dragons of the city: offering the ideal medium to embody discrete spatial symbols which occupy and define the otherwise homogeneous horizontality of urban development. Ultimately, this project posits that the city is a construct at the intersection of material, spatial, and political symbols; necessary symbols which offer a means to critically engage existing formal systems and to speculate new urban spaces through the apparatus of symbolic projection.

Brent Sturlaugson

Land and House, or How Space Registers Power and Economy on Pine Ridge Indian Reservation in South Dakota

This thesis uses space as the registration of dissonance between competing modes of power and economy on Pine Ridge Indian Reservation in South Dakota. Historical documents depicting changes in reservation land articulate a shifting balance of power relations, while different housing types reflect diverse economic activity. Through these devices, space inscribes the machinations of conflicting powers and economies.

Archival evidence provides spatial artifact of power. In the late eighteenth century, representations of indigenous nations remained unencumbered by territorial attribution, thus retaining liberty as points in space. In the mid nineteenth century, lines enacted boundaries between tribal groups and established sovereignty among nations. In the late nineteenth century, land within these borders gained attributes, and became tangible planes. In the early twentieth century, organization of volumetric space compelled the behavior of boarding school students to perform according to a script. Analysis of these artifacts reveals different modes of power through their representations of space. In turn, these spatial deposits influence the complexity derived from contemporary land issues on Pine Ridge.

Archival collections depicting different housing types register historic changes in economic activity. In the late eighteenth and early nineteenth century, tipis facilitated subsistence practices and precluded accumulation. In the late nineteenth to early twentieth centuries, log cabins accommodated the provisions of an aid economy, and in the mid to late twentieth century, both prefabricated units and trailers ushered in an era of renewed reservation aid combined with an increasing circulation of different forms of capital. While each period drew from additional economic means and featured houses apart from its categorical imperative, the main economic activity of each period proceeded by way of a unique housing type.

UNDERGRADUATE ARCHITECTURE MAJOR

DIRECTOR: BIMAL MENDIS

The purpose of the undergraduate standard major in architecture at Yale is to include the study of architecture within the broader context of a liberal arts education. While the core requirements focus on architectural design, the overall curriculum includes theory and history of architecture, leading to a bachelor of arts degree. In this manner, students are prepared for advanced study in architecture, art, history of art, city planning and development, the social sciences or public affairs.

Senior Research Colloquium for Urban Studies
Karla Britton

This course is intended for students who seek to carry out independent research projects in their senior year in architecture, urbanism, design, or related fields. Under the guidance of the instructor and members of the Architecture faculty and visitors, students present and define their proposals, complete and discuss readings, and seek criticism for individual research agendas.

Students write on subjects of their own choice related to the design, history, theory, and criticism of architecture and urbanism. Some recent research projects, for example, have focused on issues of the economic, developmental, and cultural forces of the global city. Students have also used the colloquium to deepen their independent research carried out during prior summer travel in urban centers in such diverse locations as the Middle East and Africa; Western Europe and the UK; North and South America; and Central and Southeast Asia.

CYNTHIA DENG
The Legacy of New Gourna: What can we learn from Hassan Fathy?
In our current world of fast-paced urbanization and global links there is an increasing concern that new construction uses up shrinking natural resources, impacts local ecology in destructive ways, disregards the specifics of local context, and remains imposed by or only accessible to relatively affluent classes. In light of the concerns about sustainability and building, the work of Hassan Fathy has recently resurfaced in the literature of environmental architecture as an alternative sustainable development model. Fathy advocates for mud-brick architecture, community engagement in construction, local knowledge systems, and revival of vernacular building methods among other things. Yet, examination of sources reveals that Fathy's work has not yet been comprehensively situated in a critical framework of architectural discourse. In order to advance Fathy's ideas as a potential model of sustainable urban development, especially in developing countries, it is essential that we address the problems that arose and critically examine the issues surrounding his approach. Using the example of New Gourna village, Hassan Fathy's ideas are investigated through their relationship with western modernism and tradition. His ideas are directly influenced by underlying political currents of nationalism, colonialism, and westernization. Understanding the village through multiple lenses is crucial to a wider consideration of the relevance of Fathy's ideas today.

MAX POMMIER
University Typology: Architectural Mutations in Higher Education
From Joseph Ramée's Beaux-Arts proposal for Union College (1813) to Frederick Olmsted's arcadian master plan for Berkeley (1865), the campus found, in America, a fertile plain of opportunities for spatial experimentation. Despite the multiplicity of aesthetic styles and visions present in these early explorations, the essential philosophy of the campus remained one of humanism. This narrative stressed the complete and balanced life of the student, with ample time for leisure, reflection, sporting activities, cultural outlets, and a connection to nature reminiscent of the bucolic groves of Plato's Akademe and Aristotle's Lykeion. This script drew some inspiration from the residential college life of Oxford and from the Greek word schole (which stood for "leisure" as well as "school"), but took on a life of its own through the campus.
The propagation of this script across a built landscape led both to the programmatic diversification of spatial objects and increasing complexity of the relationships between these objects. Gradually the campus became an abstraction, a term that divorced itself entirely from its original object form (that of the college yard) and assumed the role of the active form, handily taking charge of the various scripts needed to successfully code the American campus university.

ANNA RENKEN
Urban Laboratories: The Interventions of Marco Casagrande and Mary Mattingly
I will compare Marco Casagrande's Organic Layer with Mary Mattingly's The Waterpod Project; Casagrande's Ruin Academy with Mattingly's Flock House Project; and Casagrande's Nomad City / Aurora Observatory with Mattingly's Wearable Portable Architecture.
The Casagrande projects generally take the form of modifications to existing, static, relatively permanent urban forms. In contrast, Mary Mattingly projects are often more ephemeral and mobile. The Casagrande projects tend to involve more direct interaction with existing communities, which raises questions about the position of the outsider or visitor. Mattingly projects tend to involve situating new smaller communities or organizations relative to urban communities, which raises questions about the degree to which the intervening gestures are integrated into or separable from the existing communities.
Through these studies, I will focus on the scale of the body, whether in the process of the design gesture or in the form that casts the body as an isolatable environment—almost as a site of its own, or something in between. Looking closely at how Casagrande and Mattingly have framed their own projects will be crucial to my analysis. What do these projects suggest about current conditions and what conjectures might they be making about future conditions?

Senior Design Studio
Turner Brooks & Adam Hopfner

In the context of the intentions of this studio, the non-human bat makes a major contribution to the discussion by his non-visual assessment of space. Always measuring its changing configuration by the beeps he sends out and the echoes he receives back, he is like the ultimately engaged space lunatic aficionado—always locating himself with exactitude within the space, always swerving and never blundering, the space prompting him like a dancer in an elegant ballet. To be a bat trapped in Francesco Borromini's St. Ivo might be as close to ecstasy as it gets. The project is a temporary structure on the face of a quarry wall in Guilford, Connecticut that creates intimacy and immensity.

SAMANTHA MONGE KASER
The details of the quarry face shape the structure, creating a balance between tension and compression, cradling and release. The net guides a fragile intimacy and is minimally intrusive to the ecology of the quarry and the uncut granite. It is morphed into a series of distinctive tectonic roles and molded to accommodate the different postures of the human body.

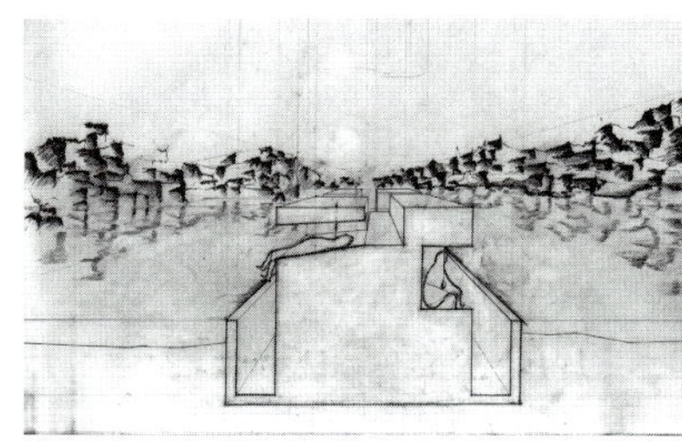

KUANG HE
The objective is to participate in the conversation between the intimate and the immense, the natural and the man made, and to find an interior that holds the body in a cozy position in relationship to the rock surface and the vast void inside the quarry. The intent of my project is to occupy the bellybutton of the quarry, and to create a procession that celebrates the journey to and from the habitat.

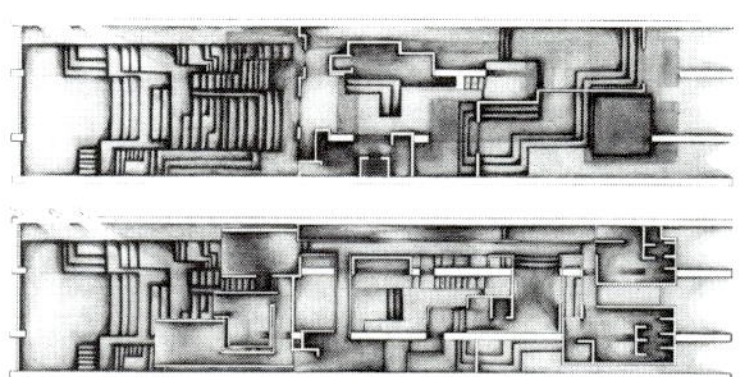

ELIZABETH GODAR
Music Haven: a new home for a string quartet. This proposed permanent home for Music Haven, a local nonprofit, creates a liminal space fitting for both the position the group in the city of New Haven and it musical experience. Four thick concrete walls define the space, giving the building an imposing, or even absent appearance from the street where it aligns with the adjacent house fronts. On the interior, it explodes into chaotic, endless spaces that weave against the grain of the larger defining walls.

Methods and Form in Architecture II
Joyce Hsiang & Sunil Bald

The culture of food and eating is a universal activity of collective social interaction. This studio will examine, question, and re-invent the activities surrounding dining and food preparation as a locus for social activity and architectural investigation.
1. Projective Drawing of a Recipe; This exercise begins with a recipe and projects the processes, procedures, sites, and contexts that underlie the construction, presentation, and consumption of the dish that the recipe describes.
2. Bento Box; Students will use clues from the first exercise to make their own version of a bento box that makes this universe physical and implies the relationship of parts and sequence of the meal.
3. Productive Landscape; This project will translate the site of a meal for two, as organized by the bento, into a landscape for the communal cultivation, preparation, and consumption of food on a given site.
4. Eating Hall; The students' final project is to design a public eating hall that celebrates the production and culture of food.

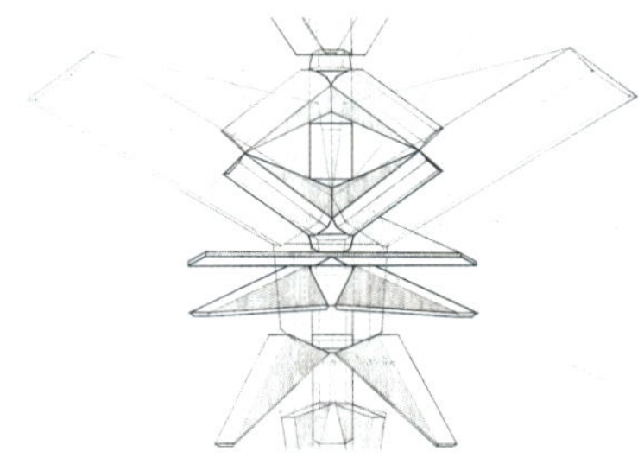

ARIEL FLOTTE
Food Container
The bento box was re-imagined as a complex multipurpose food container, whose unfolding structure expressed a sequence of dining spaces rising from the Farmington Canal and interweaving with a walkable roof structure connecting Yale's courtyard system.

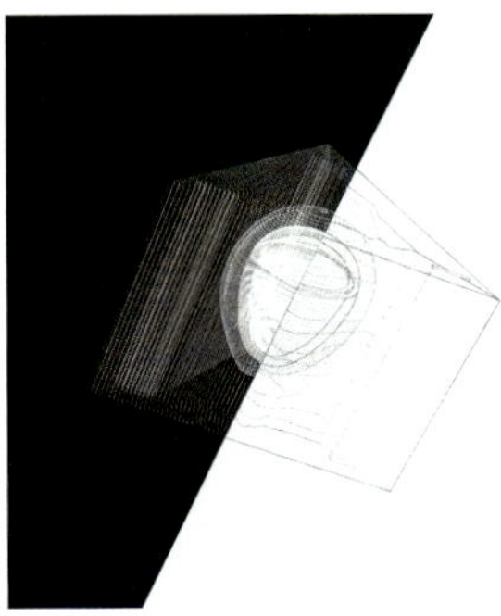

ELIF EREZ
Yogurt
Designed to accommodate the incubation and production, as well as the consumption of yogurt and an accompanying meal for two, the Bento Box addresses the discrepancy between the traditional culture of yogurt making and its modern, industrialized context of consumption.

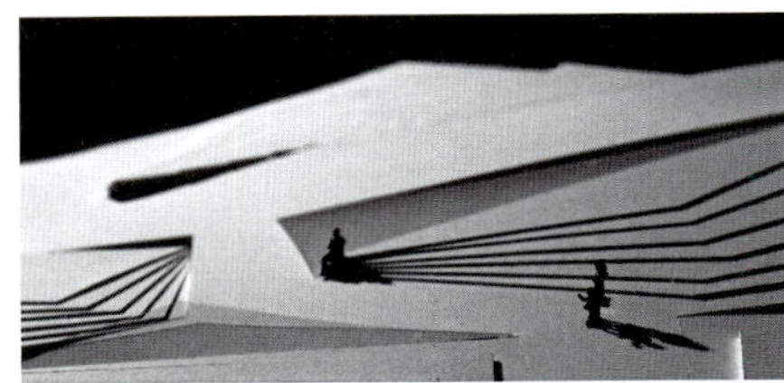

KATRINA YIN
Tea Leaves
The site exercise is a geometric interpretation of the movement of tea leaves, furling and unfurling with the extraction and introduction of water, into a fully occupiable terraced landscape.

The Analytic Model
Emmanuel Petit

Introduction to the history and practice of architectural analysis. Students produce drawings, models, and diagrams of significant architectural works in order to facilitate a comprehensive understanding of specific architects, buildings, and contexts. Description of a variety of approaches and the reciprocal relationship between analysis and design.

EDWARD WANG
Nichinan Cultural Center by Kenzo Tange
The Nichinan Cultural Center, with its sloping concrete masses and irregular perforations, deviates from traditional vertical building hierarchies and instead presents meandering sequences of tectonic elements that support each other democratically. In this study, details are treated as important generative moments, pointing to larger themes of fragmentation, disjointing, and delamination.

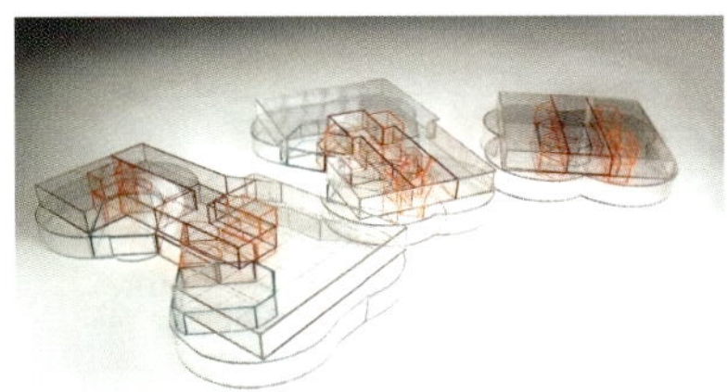

JUAN PABLO PONCE DE LEON
Nijmegen Museum Project by Aldo van Eyck
The building's program is like a coded set of rules which determine how spaces gradually become subject to forces of expansion, contraction, translation, and rotation. For example the main interstitial spaces between the galleries in both floors, shown in red, are subject to forces of compression that break their original form.

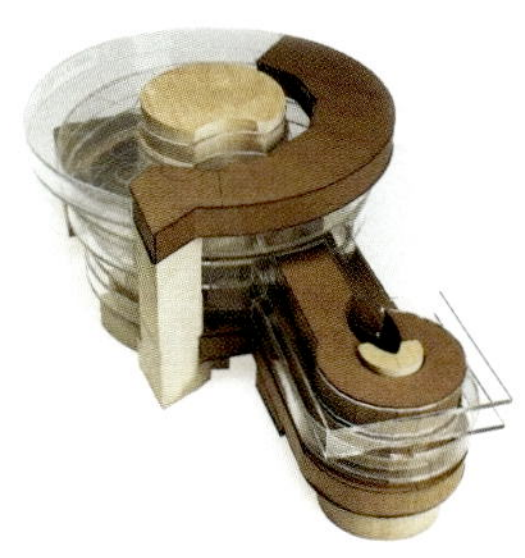

ISABELLA KLITZ
Guggenheim Museum by Frank Lloyd Wright
The Solomon R. Guggenheim Museum's open spaces define the building and hold its real mass. The building's structure has two cores that attract its other elements. These two cores are the open center of the main spiraling gallery and the miniature version to its left. Out of the open center of the main spiraling gallery grow the triangular staircase and L-shaped gallery space. These four multi-story vertical masses support the five horizontal layers.

Senior Design Studio
Steven Harris & Marta Justo Caldeira

In this undergraduate design studio, students lead individual design investigations, focusing on independence and precision in the deployment of design ideas. Emphasis is given to visual and nonverbal presentations. Students develop a three dimensional component, such as large scale mock details or other visual means of presentation, which might include photography, film, video, or interactive media.

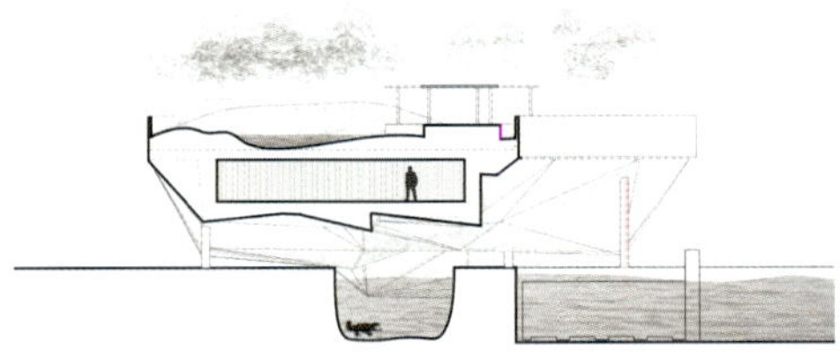

OLIVER BRADLEY
This project, located in Loxahatchee National Park in the Florida Everglades, is an industrial piece of infrastructure designed to remove phosphate pollutants between the water source, Lake Okeechobee, and the Everglades. My project plays with the complex relationship between natural and artificial that exists where a large-scale intervention is required to maintain the "natural" landscape. My project elevates an undulating picturesque parkscape on top of the industrial phosphate removal plant, a representation of our natural ideal, which is in fact the most artificial strip of landscape in the area.

ELIZABETH GODAR
For the Hydrology Center, my analysis of the site and water treatment strategy led me to create an edge condition that would both treat and visually indicate water quality as it reaches the Everglades. A wall composed of the research and water treatment facilities extends along the edge of the Everglades, adjusting as changes in treatment are necessary, and visitor program weaves around it as a long linear park.

SYDNEY SHEA
The Hydrology Center is based on a series of slats, a flexible form which allows for control of water and light; these slats create a structure which also shapes human circulation, confronting its visitors at every turn with the water its mechanical systems are filtering. The building itself is a massive aeration system: wind turbines first draw the water within the canal into a holding tank, then drop it down through a series of waterfalls and louvered slats into a shallow pool, where the newly-aerated water is filtered through a field of aquatic plants to remove problematic pollutants.

ELECTIVES

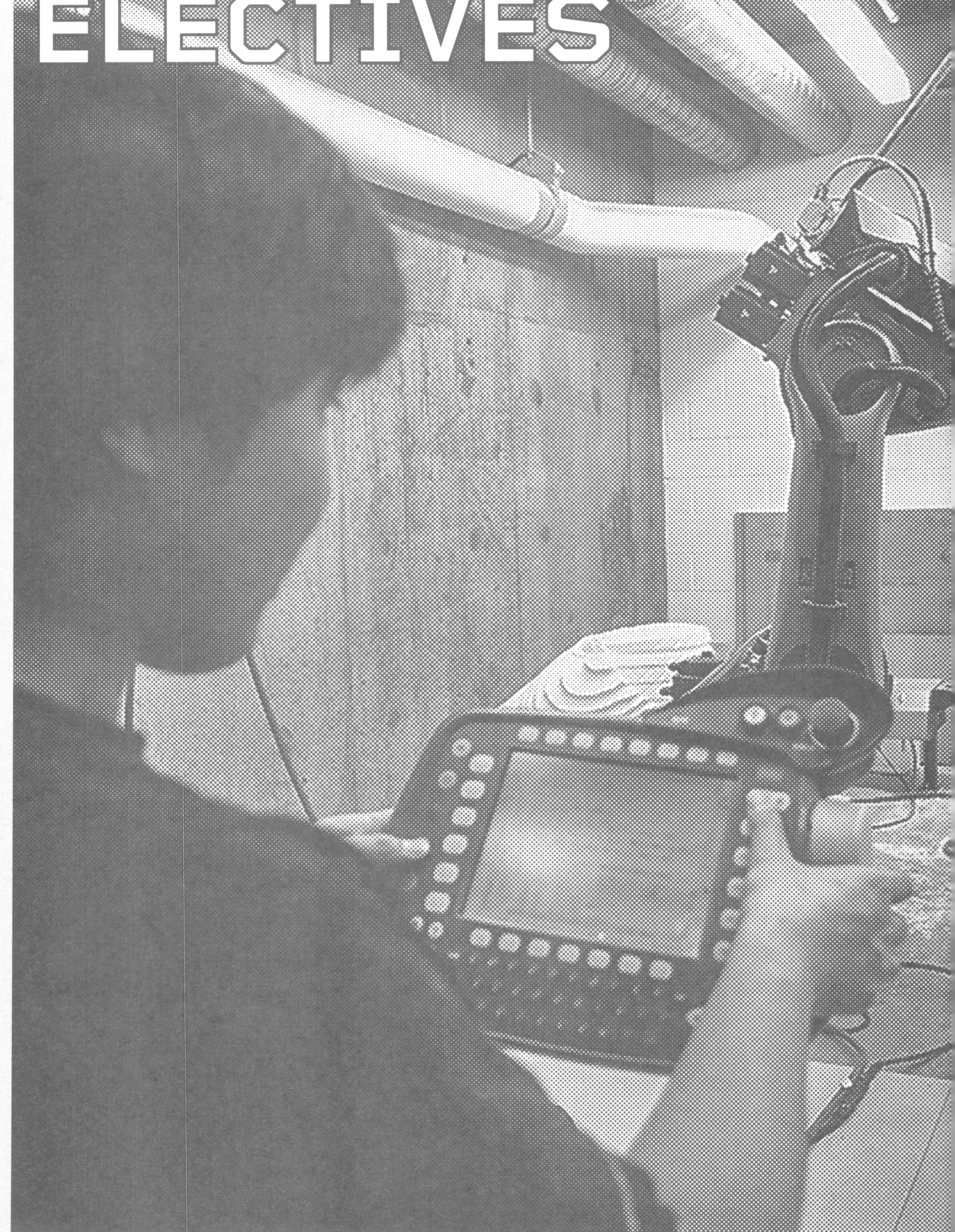

FALL

COMPUTATION ANALYSIS & FABRICATION

John Eberhart

This course investigates and applies emerging computational theories and technologies through the design and fabrication of a full-scale building component and/or assembly. This investigation includes various static, parametric, and scripted modeling paradigms, computational-based structural and sustainability analysis, and digital fabrication technologies. Students work in pairs to design, analyze, and fabricate a full-scale constructed piece.

Julcsi Futo
Daniel Luster
Olen Milholland

THE GOLDEN FLEECE

This site specific installation in the sixth floor studio entrance of Paul Rudolf Hall is an exercise in perception, tactility and displacement. This division of space and circulation sets up a dialogue between the two sides of the plane. One side is tactile, covered in sheep skin, while the other side displaces the viewer to the outside through the glass as it is covered in reflective, mirrored golden film. Thus the viewer, after inadvertently choosing a side—by opening one of the two doors—is confronted with two different forms of perception.

Elvira Hoxha
Katarzyna Pozniak

LENS

This 2'x2' window screen prototype is designed to filter light through its organic porous structure. The panel thanks to its sculptural qualities casts shadows that activate the interior space, while the red filters embedded within it refract the light. The lens is composed of 13 3D printed pieces. The final structure is a singular piece of a bigger system that could be mass produced and applied to larger surfaces.

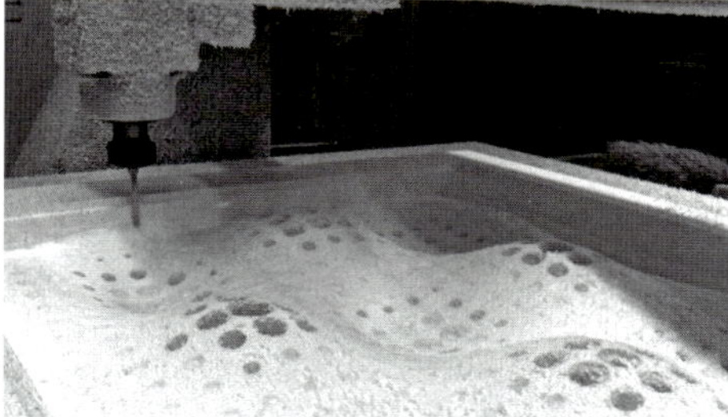

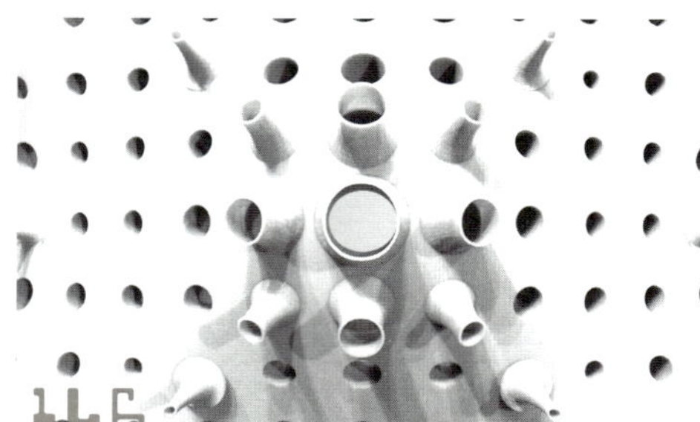

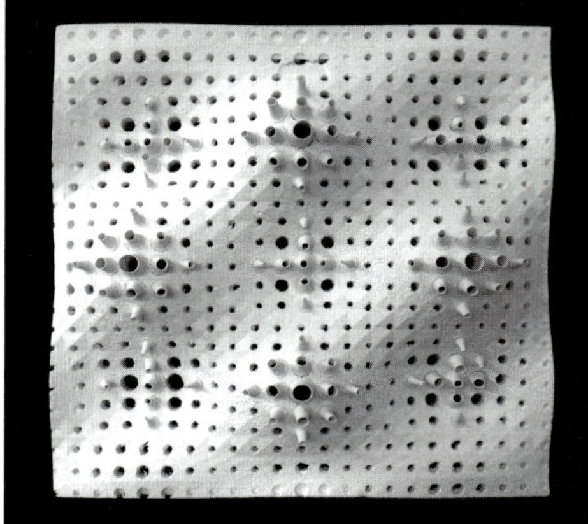

Karolina Czeczek
Raphael de la Fontaine

PARABOLIC SUNSHADE

The parabolic sunshade creates focused multidirectional lighting. The consistently distributed holes along the surface have various sizes. The size of the holes is determined by their sectional location. Additionally, the directions of the holes remain always perpendicular to the surface at their location. To accentuate the directionality, perpendicular hollow "plugs" with different sized openings are extruded from the holes. For the fabrication process, a 3-axis CNC mill was programmed with various sized drill bits, utilizing the "flip milling" technique to accomplish the consistent thickness. The plugs were then 3D printed in the plaster printer and attached to the surface of the foam.

DRAWING & ARCHITECTURAL FORM

Victor Agran

This course examines the historical and theoretical development of descriptive geometry and perspective through the practice of rigorous constructed architectural drawings. The methods and concepts studied serve as a foundation for the development of drawings that interrogate the relationship between a drawing's production and its conceptual objectives. Ultimately, the goal is to engage in a larger dialogue about the practice of drawing and spatial inquiry. Weekly readings, discussions, lectures, and drawing exercises investigate the work of key figures, such as Brunelleschi, Girard Desargues, Piero della Francesca, and Brook Taylor, in the development of orthographic and three-dimensional projection. After midterm, the course takes a more experimental approach, and students interrogate the relationship between manual and digital practice.

Elena Baranes

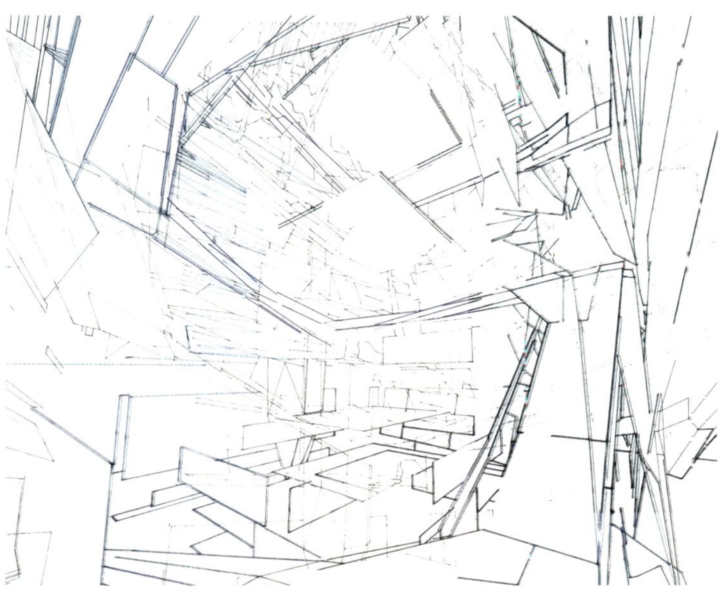

Michael Miller

The most productive moments in the act of physically drawing space, objects, and projections are the opportunities to invent between these poles through the slow process of creating. In the space of the mind one is able to represent the ambiguous, play with incomplete form, and layer perceptions of time and depth one could never perceive, all executed in merely straight line.

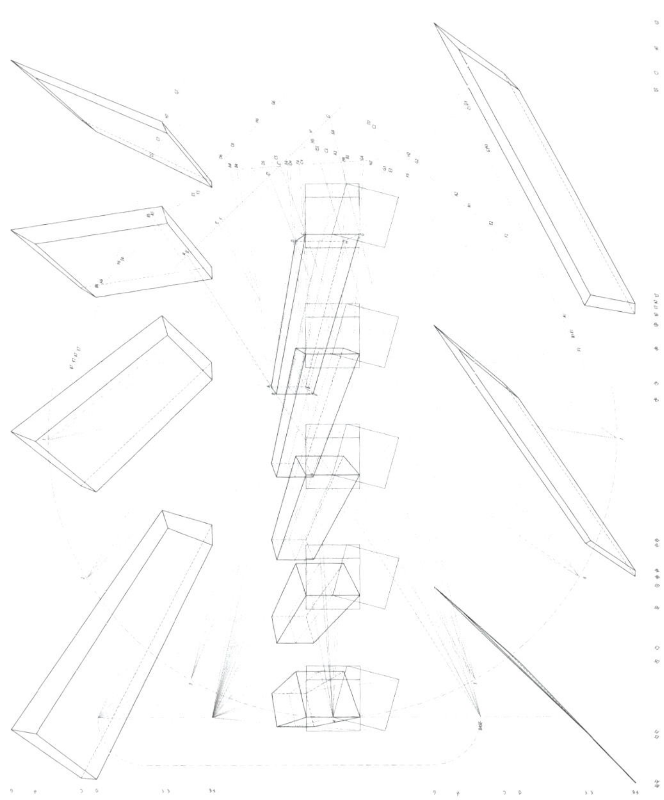

Grant Scott

The first series of projections are along the central horizontal axis, where Taylor's method was employed, with the projection point moving in relation to the projected object at each instance. The final instance of the projection was then treated as a 3D object from which to project 7 more images, which are shown above and below the horizontal central axis. Each of these was projected from a new position around the object (indicated by the stations around the circular construction line) onto the planes with the notational markings. The newly projected objects were reconstructed using these projected points.

Jonathan Sun

The generation of a hypothetical, exponential massing strategy is documented as a ribbon wrapping around a core. The axonometric progression is overlaid onto a two-dimensional graph of the unwrapped ribbon. The drawing is an exploration of the ability that graphic representation has in representing generative and geometric concepts.

COMPOSITION & FORM

Peggy Deamer

This seminar, consisting of weekly exercises, addresses issues of architectural composition and form. Leaving aside demands of program and site in order to concentrate on formal relationships at multiple scales, these exercises are intended to establish proficiency with "the language of architecture" as well as encourage confidence in personal, formal proclivities. Students are responsible for their weekly designs as well as for critiquing the projects of their fellow students; the goal is not only formal and compositional dexterity but also eyes that can see the organizational paradigms at work in any piece of architecture.

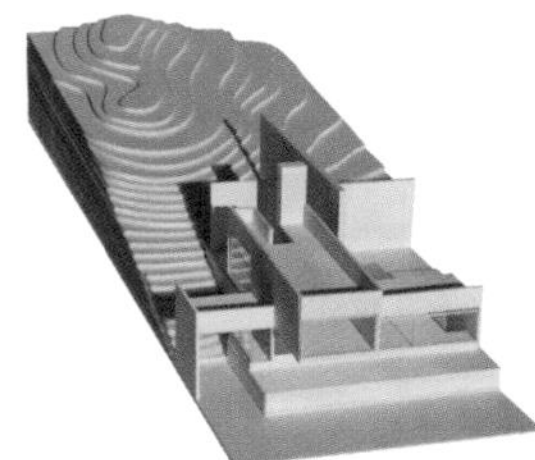

Mary Burr

This design for a house consists of two bars stacked perpendicular to one another. The assignment prompt was to reinterpret a section drawing that was given to us (of an unknown building). The provided section showed a ground floor with a cantilever above it, projecting out of a steep hillside. This reinterpretation finds an inherent proportional logic in the given section by basing the design off a 15'x15' modular system, in the form of an asymmetrical cross. Two retaining walls amplify the cross form of the building, as well as the formal thrust into the hillside.

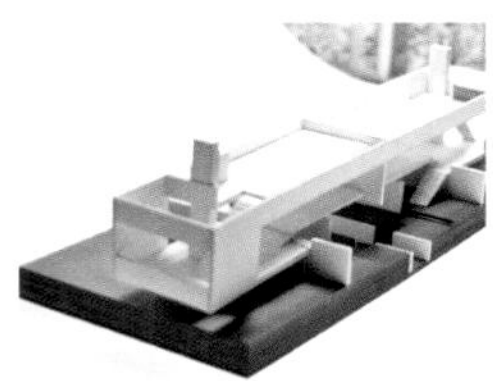

Phillip Nakamura

This project imagines the section as a cantilevered house placed upon a continuous infrastructural track. At the ground level the tracks sectionally filter between pedestrian and car traffic up into the house. Due to this extreme cantilever, the form is mirrored to rely upon each neighboring unit. Replicating this mirrored bar multiple times results in an additional cross-grain to form courtyards at the interstices between each track and housing unit.

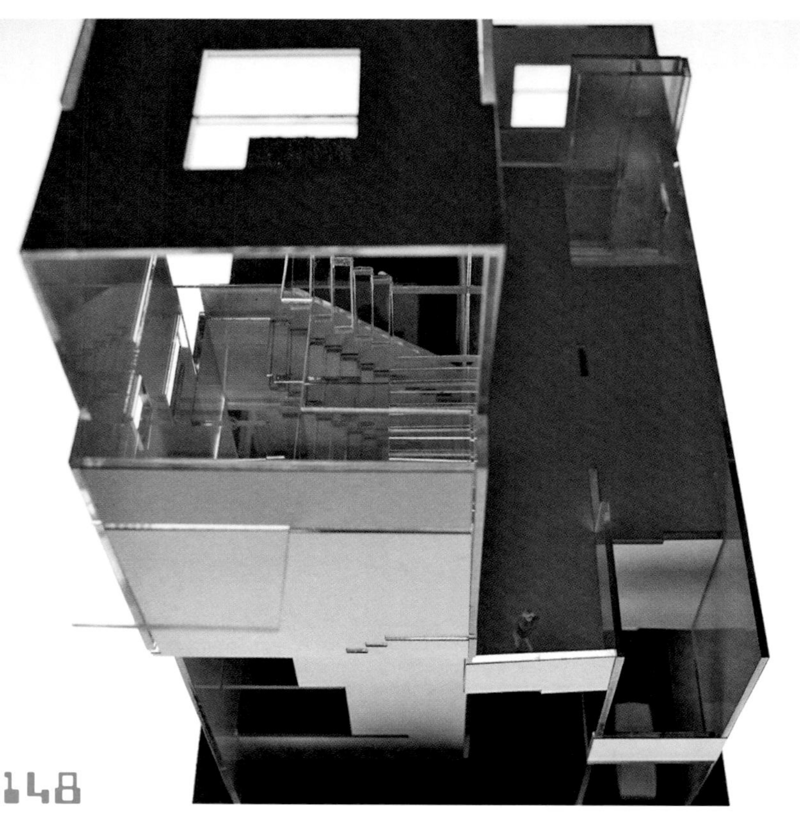

Tyson Jang

What are the consequences of rotating a sectional drawing along its dominant axis and overlapping this rotated drawing onto itself? This project investigates the spatial consequences of working within such a prescribed set of compositional operations. The relative nature of terms such as "top" and "bottom" is revealed in exciting ways with consequences to both the conception and (projected) experience of the project.

INNER WORLDS: THE POLITICS OF AFFECT

Brennan Buck

Affect is commonly understood as a personal emotion—precognitive and thus unspeakable, beyond the limits of discourse. Within our discipline, this dilemma is amplified by the residue of architectural phenomenology that linked emotion and bodily experience to reductive essentialism. These two critiques—that affect is nondiscursive and inherently conservative—are undermined by an "affective turn" in other fields. Over the past two decades, developments in philosophy, sociology, and neuroscience have redefined affect as a state or capacity beyond the individual and capable of influencing not only our moods, but also our ideas and our collective culture. This seminar examines contemporary ideas of what Nigel Thrift calls the "spatialities of feeling," the nonrepresentational yet potentially political impact of the built environment. The first half of the course focuses on readings and discussion before shifting in the second half to individual investigations of existing public spaces conducted through analysis and drawing.

Andrew Ruff

Ralph Bunche Park, a one acre public park opposite from the United Nations Headquarters in New York City, provides the only space for political action within close proximity to the UN complex's demarcated international zone. The highly politicized extraterritoriality of the United Nations contrasts vividly against the isolated, deterritorialized public sphere of the park, a civic zone which is clearly subordinate to the political entities who meet in the General Assembly. Despite the fragility of this small space to host political activities, the park offers a unique opportunity for protestors to occupy a highly visible, though easily policed, space located directly along the arrival route for UN ambassadors and politicians.

Laurence Lumley

This project explores the potential of affective design to disrupt and alter the feeling of an existing space. Walter Benjamin said of architecture that "it has always represented the prototype of a work of art, the reception of which is consummated by a collectivity in a state of distraction". He did not mean this to detract from architecture, far from it: "A man who concentrates before a work of art is absorbed by it. In contrast, the distracted mass absorbs the work of art." Architecture has this distinct power, precisely because it can insinuate itself into, and hence shape, the being of those who use it without requiring their conscious attention. Through this project I sought to establish specific affective devices and a theoretical framework to understand their operation on the subject.

Leeland McPhail

Yale University's institutional power and authority are conveyed on Chapel Street as one has already entered the quasi-campus. Louis Khan and his Yale Center for British Art stand opposed, formally, linguistically and materially to the Yale Art Gallery designed in part by H.I. Feldman. As a pair, they sit heavily, weighing on the passerby. By saturating every single atom with light using the banality of hang lights, this project assumes the role of arbitrator, both dissolving the power of the Institution, and rebooting the pedestrian out of a mostly pedestrian experience.

DESIGN RECONNAISSANCE

Mark Foster Gage

Significant advances in technology and material intelligences have ushered in an era of explosive innovation in virtually every discipline of design. In an effort to capitalize on these developments for architecture, this seminar proposes a new model of design research—that of the military reconnaissance mission—not into physical territories but rather into other industries. The sole purpose of such research is to discover innovative methods for creating, manipulating, and fabricating new genres of form and function for potential use in architecture. The course researches the tools and related expertise found in industries such as fashion, automotive and industrial design, robotics, jewelry design, and, increasingly, biology and the manipulation of cellular structures. Students research design methods, tools, and materials specific to these disciplines and convert this newfound expertise into a series of self-determined research projects. Experts from these disciplines participate in the seminar throughout the term. A series of field trips is required to visit key figures and facilities from the aforementioned industries.

Andrew Dadds

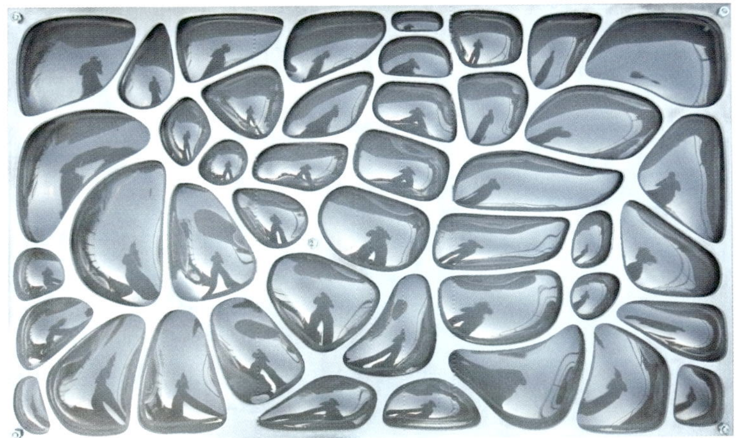

Madelynn Ringo

ONE TO ONE: FURNITURE DESIGN FOR THE ARCHITECT

Brian Butterfield & Evan Sabatelli

Architects produce the idea of a building—to be built at full scale—through scaled drawings. In this seminar, students are asked to immediately work at full scale to design a functional prototype for sitting (chair, stool, or bench). Designs are refined iteratively through the considerations of aesthetics, function, cost, and the market, elements that inherently influence design resolution. All assignments include drawings at 1:1 scale, the only scale at which the structural and material limitations of a given design are encountered. Short case-study presentations examine architects influential to the history of furniture design, examining their iterative processes of creating furniture prototypes that reinforce their own architectural principles or aesthetics. The primary materials and material quantities used for the final project are finite, not to dictate formal consistency across projects, but rather to allow for group critiques of inventive joinery methods and material expression.

Thom Medek

Miron Nawratil

Mark Tumiski

STRUCTURES & FACADES FOR TALL BUILDINGS

Kyoung Sun Moon

This seminar investigates the dynamic interrelationships between technology and architecture in tall buildings. Among the various technologies involved, emphasis is placed on structural and façade systems, the separation of which in terms of their function led to modern architecture and allowed the emergence of tall buildings. This seminar reviews contemporary design practice of tall buildings through a series of lectures and case study analyses. While most representative structural and façade systems for tall buildings are studies, particular emphasis is placed on more recent trends such as diagrid structures and double skin facades. Furthermore, this seminar investigates emerging technologies for tall buildings and explores their architectural potentials. Finally, this course culminates in a tall building design project and presentation.

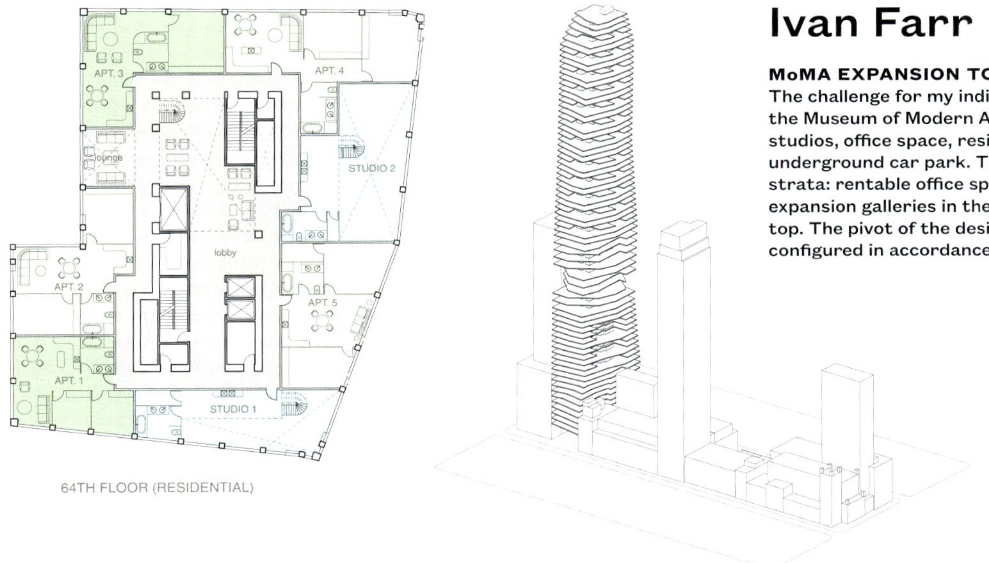

64TH FLOOR (RESIDENTIAL)

Ivan Farr

MoMA EXPANSION TOWER

The challenge for my individual project was to create a skyscraper that houses the Museum of Modern Art expansion galleries, corporate art galleries, artist studios, office space, residential space and various amenities along with an underground car park. The skyscraper is divided into three programmatic strata: rentable office space with corporate art galleries at the base, MoMA expansion galleries in the middle and residential space with artist lofts at the top. The pivot of the design comes in the core layout, which has been sized and configured in accordance to the programmatic adjacencies of the floors.

STUDIES IN LIGHT & MATERIALS

Michelle Addington

This seminar provides an overview of the basic characteristics and families of "phenomenological" materials, with a special focus on materials and technologies that have a relationship to light and vision. Materials and technologies, such as LEDs, smart glazing, displays, and interactive surfaces, are examined in depth, and some of the contemporary experiments taking place in the architecture profession are explored. Throughout the term, students catalog relevant properties and begin to develop a mapping between behaviors and phenomena. Students have the opportunity to interact with some of the well-known architects who are at the heart of the current experimentation. Each student learns how to coherently discuss material fundamentals and comprehensively analyze current applications. The seminar culminates with each student focusing on a material characteristic with which to explore different means of technology transfer in order to begin to invent unprecedented approaches and applications.

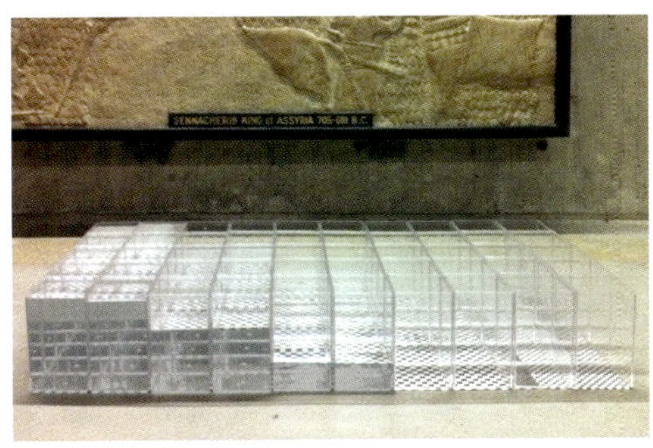

Mansi Maheshwari

The final project dealt with the understanding of reflection and refraction of light through a particular media in order to create a displaced surface. A grid of thin acrylic material formed the structure of the installation. This was then filled with water in varying depths. As the angle of refraction depends on the thickness of the media it passes through, the varying depth created a series of displaced surfaces that appeared at different planes. The installation created an illusion of a staircase from a plane surface.

Ross McClellan

Developed around Plexiglas's optical qualities of simultaneous reflectivity and transparency, this window installation improves the space in which it sits by transforming a quotidian beam of sunlight into a brilliant and dynamic radial display. A series of calibrated Plexiglas fins are oriented to redirect rays of sunlight while simultaneously preserving the original view through the window. The patterns of reflected light constantly change with the moving sunlight, washing a variety of radial patterns and ruled surfaces onto the adjacent wall.

Jonathan Swendris

LIGHT MODULATING PANEL

This panel's primary concern was to modulate light in two distinct ways with minimal user participation. To do this, the panel is comprised of a bundle of cylindrical tubes. Fiber optic rods are positioned within the interstitial space between the tubes. When standing in front of the panel, one can look directly through the tubes and beyond. From an oblique angle, the depth of the tubes prevents light as well as the view from passing through. At this angle the fiber optics sandwiched between the tubes become highly visible, and in contrast to the open tubes, much brighter.

MATERIAL FORMATION IN DESIGN

Kevin Rotheroe

This course presents historical, contemporary, and emerging methods of material formation from a designer's perspective. Emphasis is placed on processes useful for custom architectural fabrication, especially those that enable students to capitalize on opportunities generated by computer-aided design and manufacturing (CAD/CAM). Distinctions between direct and indirect making are emphasized in terms of the formal freedom various techniques afford designers. Students are encouraged to cultivate specific aesthetic interests and experiment with the translation of variations into a series of material prototypes in order to benchmark results and better inform their own design process going forward.

Ross McClellan

This experiment explores multiple layers of information held within a single surface, generating an artifact with the history of its own formation process evident in the final object. The process preserves the original while allowing the creation of multiple custom cast pieces through a single thermoformed mold.

Kyeong Jae Lee

The essence of natural beauty lies in its generative purity—the process of formation is untouched, uninterrupted by humans, who can only engage in artful, sectional revelation after the fact. I see great beauty in the section of geographical stratification—in layers and layers of time built upon one another sheared and penetrated by subliminal force at an enormous scale. Instead of replicating the phenomenon itself, I elected to adopt the process in order to control the purity of its formation, and at the same time, establish an agenda to generate iterations that can be endlessly reproduced and further transformed. The final production is a juxtaposition of layered porosity that can either perform as an architectural surface or an architectural volume.

Emau Vega

A series of panel prototypes are produced from manipulations of image scans of an initial basswood hand carved panel. Beginning with a hand-carved panel allowed for a freedom in design that is achieved through simple intuitive moves that are applied directly on the material. By scanning to "digitize" the initial model, the new genre of formed panels registers new data from traces of the material properties of the basswood which begin to add a new layer of complexity and texture to the digital forms.

PARALLELS OF THE MODERN

Robert A.M. Stern

This seminar puts forward the argument that what many have accepted as the mutually exclusive discourses of tradition and innovation in the modern architecture of the first half of the twentieth century–respectively identified as the "New Tradition" and the "New Pioneers" by Henry-Russell Hitchcock in his Modern Architecture: Romanticism and Reintegration (1929)—in fact share common genealogy and are integral to its history. The seminar explores in depth key architects working in the "New Tradition" and goes on to explore its impact for postmodernism in the 1970s and 1980s. The possible emergence of a new synthesis of seeming opposites in the present is also considered.

Mary Burr

DUDOK: STYLE & SPIRIT

Just as Dudok adeptly gave a new answer to the town hall problem, he also responds to a new building type of the time: the department store. The De Bijenkorf department store in Rotterdam dates to 1930. Compared to the urban fabric surrounding it, the hulking mass was an imposing new scale, "a stranded ship in the centre of Rotterdam."[1] It maintains the signature play of vertical and horizontal elements that mark his work before World War II. Given its commercial function, where increased square footage equates to increased profit, and street presence is the primary gesture, Dudok's architectural response aptly varies from that of the Hilversum Town Hall. Rather than a sculptural monolith, De Bijenkorf sits on the corner, presenting two large glass walls to both streets. Two strong verticals mark the corners of the entry façade and offset the transparency of the glass walls with unbroken solidity. The façade is glazed yellow brick atop reinforced concrete and he accents the spandrels with black white and gold stones. At night the glass box was meant to emit a glow of light, drawing customers in like moths. The style duly responded to the building's commercial spirit.
De Bijenkorf was destroyed during the bombing of Rotterdam and Dudok proposed a new design, which was never built (while a scheme by Marcel Breuer was). His new proposal at first seems completely at odds with the usual 'Dudokey'[2] play of solid and void, deep horizontals offset by vertical punctuation. The new scheme was a solid box with a uniform masonry pattern applied to the facade and small round windows in each panel. Gone are the unbroken masonry walls, the dramatic Wrightian horizontals. While this may seem like a non sequitur in his oeuvre, it is completely in keeping with Dudok to surprise, responding with a fresh style to a new programmatic prompt. In this case, the programmatic flaw with the first building was that the company displayed cases in front of the windows, blocking natural light from entering. Dudok's response was to use artificial light, and celebrate this uniquely modern opportunity to seal off a building from sunlight.
Dudok welcomed the innovation and stylistic influences of Modernism, without letting it become the theoretical or formal driver of his work. Despite the criticism Dudok received, he remained stalwart in his attitude that each project deserved a specific typological, contextual, and spiritual response to form rather than the canned rulebook of orthodox Modernism. His longtime assistant and later partner, Robert M.H. Magnee wrote in 1954 that "Dudok never joined an architectural movement, in fact "movements" hardly touched him."[3] It is his resistance to polemic, and his resistance to the style in fashion, that contribute to the longevity of his work. Dudok recognized that different programs called for different modes of expression, and that various forms can satisfy the same program—social housing is not a style, a town hall is not a style. Construction is not a style.

1 Van. Bergeijk, Herman. W.M. Dudok. Rotterdam: Uitgeverij 010, 2001. Print. p15.
2 Jordan, R. Furneaux. "Dudok and the Repercussions of his European Influence." The Architectural Review (Jan 1954): 237-241. Print.
3 Magnée, R. M. H.. Willem M. Dudok. Amsterdam: Saane, 1957. Print. p20.

UNIVERSALS

Keller Easterling

The seminar explores the pleasures, perils, and potential productivity of architecture's love affair with, or faith in, systems of standards. From the belief that the proper combinations of geometry would actually generate transcendence in ecclesiastical architecture, to the various adoptions of a neoclassical language for the redemption of buildings or cities, to the modular systems that would allow modernism to rewrite the world, to the hidden mysteries of ISO's (International Organization for Standardization) supposedly rationalizing decisions, episodes in the alchemy of standards feature many architectural disciples. This seminar studies the ways in which the desire for standards has created isomorphic aesthetic regimes as well as productive renovations of construction and assembly. The seminar also explores the more expansive organs of decision-making that overwhelm and dictate to the architectural discipline, trumping the internal theories of design society with universal standards of much more consequence. While the seminar revisits familiar architectural theory, it also visits some less-familiar episodes such as Eiffel's prefabricated cathedrals designed for distant French colonies, the origin of Sweets Catalog, the context of Konrad Wachsmann's modular systems, or ISO's control over everything from credit card thickness to construction industry protocols.

Daniel Jacobs

BUILDING BLOCKS: INTEGRANT MOLECULES FROM TOYS TO AUTOMATA

The idea that architecture could exist solely as a megastructure into which humans could input generic prefabricated blocks was already a major component of the architectural/urban design discourse, especially in the work of Eckhard Schule-Fielitz or Yona Friedman. These megastructures allowed for "rigid systematization" simultaneous to infinite individual freedom.1The human, not the structure-as-machine, is again the center of the interaction. The addition of armature and superstructure, both in Price's InterAction Centre as well as the Study for an Urban Agglomeration by Schulze-Fielitz from 1964, allows for the constant game of addition and subtraction of solids and voids in the urban spatial configuration. The armature allows for Fröbel's blocks to exist in reality, and the pervasive universalizing Bravais lattice and its extents govern the urban form.
Throughout the 1980s John Frazer continued exploring the Human/Machine interaction through computation and what he termed Machine-Readable Models, culminating in the Universal Constructor of 1990. This inquiry sought to achieve "intelligent physical modeling" in which human-controlled physical models were used as input devices for computer software and algorithmic analysis. These models ultimately settled on the form of cubic blocks embedded with sensors and signaling devices which would allow the computer to track their location, communicate to a person where they should be moved, or respond to the placement of a block by a human.

Charles Hickox

Georges Bataille and Le Corbusier in the nineteen-twenties and thirties represent "dialectical opposites of modernity: the modernity of discipline versus the modernity of desire."[1] Bataille urged for an artistic movement of horizontal transgression, towards the base, ugly and absurd. Only by rejecting the canonical laws inherent to artistic, architectural, and governmental power structures, in which played out an eternal endgame of idealism—the human could sidestep the oppressive forces which muffle desire, that alienate internal experience. Le Corbusier, on the other hand, impelled society towards scientific rules which he believed would produce a happier and healthier status quo for the human inhabitants of the built environment. Architecture, rather than the oppressor, was humanity's great liberator. Le Corbusier's vertical conception is expressed in the absolute ethical dimension of uprightness, the upright human body, the right angle, according to which architecture became possible. If Le Corbusier talks about the horizontal axis, it is always to subordinate it to the vertical axis"[2] Bataille saw the vertical as the alienator of horizontal urges, that the horizontal would dislodge transcendental dogma in favor of a profane immanence.[3] Indeed the humanoid icons of these two men provide visual evidence to support their directional tendencies: the Acéphalic Man with arms horizontally outstretched and the Modular reaching for the sky.

1 Lahiji, Nadir. "The Gift of the Open Hand: Le Corbusier Reading Georges Bataille's La Part Maudite." Journal of Architectural Education, Vol. 50, No. 1 (sept. 1996), P. 51. (1996). Digital. The author of this characterization, claims to owe the dialectic to which these two players are appropriated to Hal Foster in Compulsive Beauty(MIT)
2 Lahiji, P. 61
3 Lahiji, P. 61 Lahiji states that he is paraphrasing Lecht in "Surrealism and the Project of Writing," I could not, however, locate the original text.

Skender Luarasi

THE NON-STANDARD UNIVERSAL IN THE ARCHITECTURE OF BERNARD CACHE: AN ONTOLOGY OF THE POINT OF VIEW

The aim of this paper is to investigate the concept of objectile, or the non-standard object, as a universal in Bernard Cache's work. The concept of objectile in Cache's project is closely connected with geometry as a means of constructing the universal aspect of objectile. This connection, however, is part of a larger historical and philosophical context, in which geometry is used as a means to demonstrate and construct the concept of the universal. Therefore, in this paper I rely on Cache's own texts and other texts that deal explicitly with the concept of Objectile, as well as other texts that deal with the philosophical significance of geometry as the language of the legitimation of the universal.

HUMAN/NATURE: ARCHITECTURE, LANDSCAPE, TECHNOLOGY

Joel Sanders

Our global environmental crisis poses the challenge of devising a new model of ecologically responsible interdisciplinary practice that brings together two disciplines—architecture and landscape architecture—that have been professionally segregated at least since the nineteenth century. The first half of the term looks at this issue from a cultural and historical perspective, tracing the ideological origins of the architecture/landscape divide to another Western polarity—the false opposition between nature and culture, human and non-human—dualisms that are deeply rooted in Western literature, philosophy, popular culture, and even notions of gender and sexuality. The seminar explores how this way of thinking has impacted design practices in America from Frederick Law Olmsted in the mid-nineteenth century to Ian McHarg and Robert Smithson in the 1960s and 1970s. During the second half of the term the focus shifts to consider contemporary trends, examining the work of a diverse group of architects, landscape architects, and artists who have been undertaking groundbreaking projects that dissolve traditional distinctions between building and environment. Three converging design directions that unite this otherwise heterogeneous group—topography, bio-computation, and ecology—are identified, and the affinities and differences between them are discussed.

Leah Abrams & Phillip Nakamura

HOW THE WILDERNESS NARRATIVE INFORMS AMERICAN MASCULINITY

Film illustrates the cultural manifestations of the wilderness: natural landscape is portrayed as alien to civilization. Through the conquest of this wilderness, the main character's masculinity is reinforced. In Stagecoach (1939), Ringo journeys from the wilderness back to civilization. His return functions as a realization of manhood by becoming defender of justice and domestic ideals, reinforcing the narrative of a hero's journey requires returning from nature back to civilization.

In Into the Wild (2007), Chris' self-imposed exile shows a shift in the narrative structure in the wilderness. The new narrative posits that the realization of masculinity comes from leaving society behind and pursuing a personally transformative journey into the wilderness. Ringo's journey plays upon foils where we understand masculine characters through their relationships and service to female characters in the rugged wilderness. It ends with him settling in society. Chris' journey, on the other hand, becomes one of self-discovery through his self-denial; it is an existential pursuit of an idealized wilderness.

Kara Biczykowski, Nicholas Muraglia & Constanza Alcaron

HOW THE WILDERNESS NARRATIVE INFORMS AMERICAN MASCULINITY

The polemics of Post-Minimalism challenged the devices of control latent in the art institution which have been internalized as "natural" and thus inform our perception of the world in concealed ways. Artists such as Robert Smithson critiqued the Greenbergian Modernist attempt to render invisible these mechanisms which reveal the "everydayness" of art and remove it from a transcendental realm. In particular, the critique of the Modernist thinness of the frame is crucially important to our discussion of how the frame operates as an active agent in the work of art; we are asked to question those latent social and cultural assumptions which filter our perception of the frame's content.

Robert Smithson's "Non-Sites" operate as an allegorical sectioning out of the world; a bounded section of the Site put into a frame. This act of framing Nature becomes integral to the work, rather than peripheral and concealed.

Theodossios Issaias

REPRESENTATIONS OF NATURE AND 19TH CENTURY URBANIZATION

The dipole of Man and Nature, culture and natural environment, closed and open system, is a highly simplified interpretation that prevents us from reaching this historical conjuncture in its essence. The intention of this research is to shift the attention from the binary relation to the amalgamation of the two concepts in modern architectural thought and its socio-political implications in the context of the 19th century western civilizations. The research question lays on the multiple definitions assigned to Nature and seeks to identify how they were integrated in the architectural discourse and vice versa.

SPATIAL CONCEPTS OF JAPAN

Yoko Kawai

The seminar explores the origins and developments of Japanese spatial concepts and surveys how they help form the contemporary architecture, ways of life, and cities of the country. Many Japanese spatial concepts, such as MA, are about creating time-space distances and relationship between objects, people, space, and experiences. These concepts go beyond the fabric of a built structure, and encompass architecture, landscape, and city. Each class is designed around one or two Japanese words that signify particular design concepts. Each week, a lecture on the word(s) with its design features, backgrounds, historical examples, and contemporary application is followed by student discussion. Contemporary works studied include those by Maki, Isozaki, Ando, Ito, Kuma, and SANAA. The urbanism and landscape of Tokyo and Kyoto are discussed.

Laurence Lumley

THE KAZE-NO-OKA CREMATORIUM

The Kaze-no-Oka Crematorium is the culmination of years of research by its architect, Fumihiko Maki, on traditional Japanese spatial concepts.

Maki carefully choreographs the nature of the light from outside that enters the building. Diffuse, indirect light is used in the ceremonial rooms to create a floating sense of stillness and eternity. The vibrating, rippling light of water introduces animation and life into the building, a contrast to the shadowy atmosphere of death within, and perhaps an intimation of the world to which the mourners are soon to return.

Spatially the binaries of compression/expansion, directional/centered, hiding/revealing, and the careful attunement of spacing and interval, modulate one's sense of time, as understood in the concept of 'ma'. Through the idea of 'shintai' as being bound up with the world, we can see how the spatial manipulations of the architect enmesh the inhabitant of the building into the deep, inner space of oku. So in the Kaze-no-Oka crematorium, the layout of spaces is intentionally not rational and linear, but rather takes the user on a circuitous journey or circlings, repetitions, and returns, that never reaches a definite goal but elongates and ceremonializes the movement of approach.

J.T. Keeley

ANIMATING JAPAN-NESS: HAYAO MIYAZAKI AND THE ART OF JAPANESE CULTURAL SPACE

In Spirited Away Hayao Miyazaki creates a story which resonates with the philosophy of Tetsuro Watsuji, one of Japan's most important cultural philosophers. The heroine, a young girl named Chihiro, journeys from a bland suburban world, the new Japan, to an amusement park which comes alive with symbols of Japan's layered cultural historyThe subdivision represents a nonspecific, globalization space—a place that denies the possibility of personal and cultural development. Miyazaki has spoken at length about the problems he has with such spaces and he has said that Chihiro's initial irritable behavior is meant to show how these spaces create immature people.

Her adventures in the spirit world change her personality and even her physical appearance. Taking on the uniform of a Taisho-era schoolgirl or maid, she becomes an independent and heroic figure. And although the viewer sees the suburb only once during the film it stands in stark contrast to representations of the spirit world.

Before she can return to the suburban world, which might be categorized as "real," she will find a new, stronger version of herself in this complex and complicated vision of Japanese culture.

Jeannette Penniman

URBAN SHAKKEI: THE CHANGING NATURE OF BORROWED LANDSCAPE IN TOKYO

The contemporary Tokyo skyline is at once one of the world's most recognizable, and one of its most anonymous. Relentless, compounded by poor air quality, and—outside of a few distinct landmarks—homogenous, the Tokyo megalopolis has in many ways become a city defined by mid-ground landscape. This is significant for a city originally planned around distant vistas, in a culture that values the layering of spaces and objects to create depth through the concept of oku. One of the most standard practices in Japanese gardening technique is the borrowing of distant landscape, or shakkei. Traditionally found in the sprawling rural estate gardens of Japanese nobility, shakkei cannot remain relegated to the country if it is to remain relevant to an increasingly urban-centric Japanese culture. Ironically, it appears that in modern Tokyo, the best opportunities for employing shakkei to reintroduce oku are in the massive private developments that characterize more and more of Tokyo's growth.

By consolidating built square meters in tall, distinctive buildings at the center of open space, these developments both create new objects to be captured that are more visually unique than the relentless built fabric of undistinguished midrise building, as well as layers of open and built space to add complexity.

THE DIGITAL TURN

Mario Carpo

This seminar discusses the present state of computer-based design and fabrication by situating today's digital turn within the long duration of the history of cultural technologies. It assesses the technical logics of hand-making, mechanical reproductions, and digital making, focusing on the invention of architectural notations and of architectural authorship in the Renaissance. The seminar then outlines a tentative history of the digital turn from the early 1990s—from the Deleuzian fold to free-form, topology, and formalism; from mass customization and nonstandard seriality to recent developments in digital interactivity, building information modeling, self-organizing systems, and digital form-finding—questioning in particular the digital reversal of the early-modern and modernist principles of agency in architectural design and probing the import and consequences of these trends for contemporary practice. Students test these interpretive patterns by developing a case study of their choice (of a media object, object, building, software, or technology).

Ian Spencer

Continuing exponential development in scripting and computational prowess has allowed algorithms to expand their applicability beyond deterministically linear problem solving and into the hermeneutic iterative processes of design problems. As such there are two parallel narratives that can be traced through this new applicability—design to criteria, whereby given geometry is manipulated algorithmically to optimize certain parameters; and design to procedure, whereby the algorithm is expected to self-organize into a previously unknown geometry. The key difference between the narratives is the stop-point or completion of the algorithm. While optimization algorithms have defined stop points, so-called morphogenetic algorithms do not. This crucial distinction limits the topological variation of the former and the wholesale applicability of the latter. A genetic algorithm generates solutions to optimization problems by using a search heuristic to imitate the "survival of the fittest" evolutionary processes of inheritance, mutation, selection, and crossover. A population of potential solutions (phenotypes), each with a corresponding set of properties (genotypes) is evolved toward better solutions. The algorithm terminates when either a maximum number of generations has been produced, or a satisfactory fitness level has been reached. The design to criteria narrative uses, as its fitness function, quantifiable (and scriptable) entities such as material properties, applied forces, prescribed displacements, and volume constraints.

Laurence Lumley

What is particular about the digital art of our time? In this study I sought to trace the roots of current digital art practice through the history of conceptual art. By discovering its lineage it is possible to see what the current turn in digital art is. I argue that what unites conceptual art through the 20th Century is a turn away from matter towards the algorithm (such as Sol LeWitt's instructions) and ultimately the pure abstract idea (as in Lawrence Weiner's sentences). Now, in the 21st century, it would seem that technology has realized the dreams of conceptual art. As Mary Ann Doane has pointed out "the cultural dream of the digital is a dream of immateriality" in which information or representation appear to exist nowhere and media are 'virtual'. And yet it is at this very moment, perhaps not coincidentally, that art practice seems to be turning back again towards the material, a move that is manifesting even in the work of those artist explicitly engaged in the digital.

Swarnabh Ghosh

The architectural rendering is undoubtedly the most ubiquitous form of architectural representation today. Apart from revolutionizing the profession of architectural illustration, this phenomenon has led to the emergence of a very important stakeholder in the profession of architecture—the individuals and organizations responsible for the production of these images—organizations like MIR, DBox and Luxigon. Luxigon, perhaps more than any other rendering company has gained immense popularity and received a lot of attention in the last several years. The founders of Luxigon, unsurprisingly, are vocal advocates of Photoshop and attribute much of their success to their sophisticated use of it in an artistic, almost painterly manner (as described by one of its founders in the issue of CLOG dedicated to the subject). Photoshop is perhaps the single-most indispensable tool for the production of architectural illustrations today, giving retouchers and illustrators unprecedented control over visual effects. On the other hand, the specificity and variability afforded by Photoshop has turned its use into a proprietary platform.

WHOLE DICHOTOMY

Marcelo Spina & Georgina Huljich

Used by Rodolfo Machado and Rodolphe el-Khoury in 1995 to describe a series of projects that deliberately did not articulate a part-to-whole relationship as dictated by classical doctrine, "monolithic architecture" became the predominant architectural form of the "avant-garde" in the past two decades. The monolithic project is identified by its iconography, latent muteness, scalar ambiguity, and indifference to both program and context. This seminar aims to elucidate the critical lineage and contemporary relevance of monolithicity in architecture by revisiting some of its most relevant contemporary and historical examples. Considering that as a productive allegory, the use of the term monolithic in architecture relates more to problems of representation than to those of construction or material assembly, students are asked to analyze, theorize, and generate alternative instantiations for "monolithic" projects.

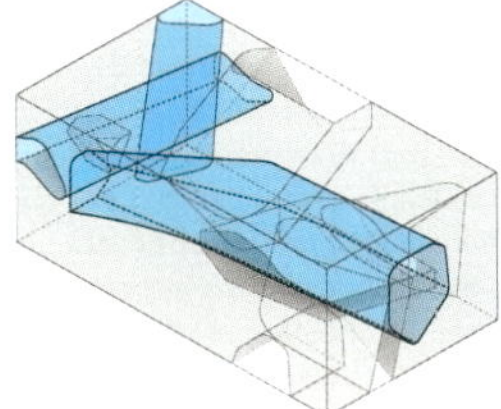

Jacqueline Kow

STEVEN HOLL'S TRAJECTORY TOWARDS MONOLITHIC ARCHITECTURE

The Tianjian Ecocity Ecology and Planning Museums both represent additive and subtractive form-making in their purest monolithic form. While the two museums come from their own respective lineages, their formal similarities produce tensions that a monolithic building normally would not have. If there is any relationship between the two, it is that the subtractive monolith acts more like a fabric building because it expresses a box primitive as its form and therefore is more introverted than the additive monolith.

Evan Wiskup

FROM SUBJECTIVITY TO OBJECTIVITY: PARAMETRICIZING MONOLITHICITY

The crisis in the discourse surrounding monolithic architecture is within the subjective nature of its very own defining characteristics. Since its first inception by Rudolfo Machado and Rodolphe el-Khoury in 1995, monolithic architecture was established as a set of contradictory forces and paradoxical relationships. This essay posits the possibility that the defining variables of monolithicity can be clarified through an objective set of relationships rather than subjective opinion. In doing so, a case for the parametricization of monolithicity will be made through a close reading of Wang Shu's Ningbo History Museum.

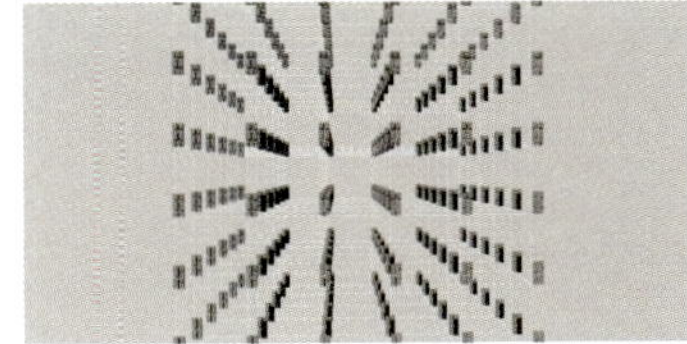

John Farrace

BRUGGE CONCERT: COMPOSITE MONOLITH

The Brugge Concert hall justifies a new category of monolith and an amended definition of the composite monolith. This new type of monolith is characterized by multiple, but limited figural readings of a project and is produced by a continuous skin that blurs the boundary between separate elements. These additional readings are not just allowed to occur, but are in fact encouraged by the implied continuities between different geometries set up by the designer. Finally, the composite monolith should be amended and re-understood as merely virtual.

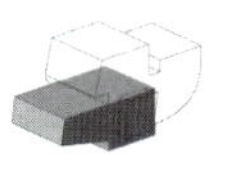
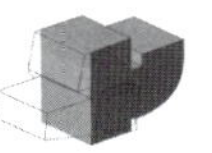
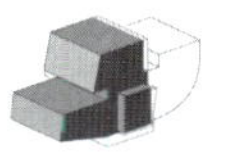

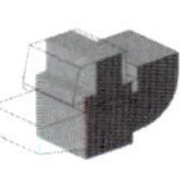
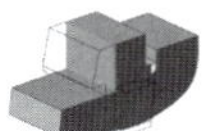

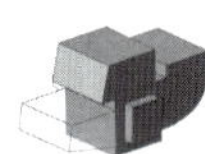
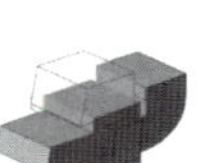

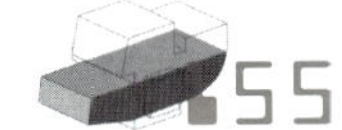

AMERICAN CULTURAL LANDSCAPES

Dolores Hayden

After a brief review of Native American and colonial settlements, this lecture course surveys the growth of towns and cities between 1800 and 1920, then examines the shift between 1920 and the present, when residential and commercial activities move away from city centers into diffuse, automobile-dependent metropolitan regions.

Brent Sturlaugson

THE ARCHITECTURE OF ASSIMILATION: SETTLEMENT PATTERNS ON PINE RIDGE INDIAN RESERVATION, 1804–2013

Housing on Pine Ridge Indian Reservation in South Dakota has received international attention for its spectacular disrepair.[1] Severe overcrowding, structural deterioration, and extraordinary energy consumption pervade the residential landscape, and in this environment the effects of the longstanding dispute between the United States government and the Lakota manifest themselves in the architecture of everyday life. Over the years, both public and private initiatives have attempted amelioration by providing additional housing units of various construction techniques and site design; however, these programs fail to consider infrastructural implications of housing that have been overlooked in the urgency of providing basic shelter. Moreover, references to Lakota culture in recent developments misappropriate earlier spatial practices, resulting in the creation of inhospitable environments. Missing from existing research of housing on Pine Ridge is a detailed account of settlement patterns and structures during the period of transition from nomadic to sedentary practices, a period in which architectural and infrastructural interventions by the United States government transformed traditional ways of life. Three periods of analysis constitute the basis for investigating the imposed transitions in Lakota settlements on Pine Ridge. The first period, 1804–1851, corresponds to a mode of existence observed in the years between contact with the Lewis and Clark Expedition in 1804 and treaty negotiations that began at Fort Laramie in 1851.[2] The second period of analysis, 1851–1961, marks a transition between nomadic and agrarian spatial practices of the Lakota. The third period of analysis, 1961–2013, concerns contemporary residential development on Pine Ridge. At its core, the inability to understand cultural differences of inhabitation plagues the residential landscape of Pine Ridge.

1 Raquel Rolnik, "Report of the Special Rapporteur on Adequate Housing as a Component of the Right to an Adequate Standard of Living, and on the Right to Non-Discrimination in This Context," United Nations, Human Rights Council, Thirteenth Session, issued February 12, 2010.

2 Jeffrey Ostler, The Plains Sioux and U.S. Colonialism from Lewis and Clark to Wounded Knee (Cambridge: Cambridge University Press, 2004).

Daniel Luster

THE FIRST TRANSCONTINENTAL RAILROADS: TWO APPROACHES

In the second half of the 19th century the impact of the railroad on the American landscape, the economy, and society at large was indelible. Perhaps the most important moment in the history of the railway system was the crossing West by the great transcontinental lines which linked the two coasts of the United States for the first time, an event which forever changed the United States. The ceremonial connecting of the Union Pacific Railroad (UP) with the Central Pacific Railroad (CP) in Promontory, Utah in 1869 was a moment of national pride. However, this railroad was enshrouded with controversy as both companies making up one line across the country were government-established and government-subsidized companies, yet they remained for-profit, private corporations. This created a situation where the public bore the risk and the private companies took the profits. Moving from one scandal to another, the executives of these railroads, along with many of the well-connected political class, successfully transferred massive amounts of public wealth and land into their own pockets. This is compounded by the fact that the US military used the railroads as a guise under which to wage a brutal war on the Plains Indians.

By comparing the subsidized UP and CP with the privately funded Great Northern Railroad (GNR), it becomes clear that the commonly accepted understanding of the necessity for government intervention in the first transcontinental railroads should be reconsidered. The waste, fraud, abuse, and destruction of the UP and CP line were not the only ways to accomplish large scale railroad infrastructure projects in the 19th century.

James Hill's GNR was as an economic and cultural experiment unique not only for its own time but the contemporary period as well. The GNR offers the possibility that through voluntary actions in the market, society can operate in a more peaceful, more "civilized" way—while still accomplishing grand and wonderful things.

GLOBALIZATION SPACE

Keller Easterling

This lecture course researches global infrastructures as a medium of transnational polity. Lectures visit the networks of trade, communication, tourism, labor, air, rail, highway, oil, hydrology, finance, and activism. Case studies travel around the world to, for instance, free trade zones in Dubai, IT campuses in South Asia, high-speed rail in Saudi Arabia, cable/satellite networks in Africa, highways in India, a resort in the DPRK, golf courses in China, oil-financed development in Sudan, and automated ports. These investigations begin in transnational territory where new infrastructure consortia operate in parallel to or in partnership with nations. Not only an atlas or survey of physical networks and shared protocols, the course also considers their pervasive and long-term effects on polity and culture. Infrastructures may constitute a de facto parliament of global decision making or an intensely spatial extra statecraft.

AJ Artemel

THE THIRD BOSPHORUS BRIDGE

One of the major catalysts for the Gezi Park protests was the removal of trees from the center of Taksim Square, an act that mirrored a larger scale removal occurring in the same moment: the clearing of millions of mature trees in a hundred-meter-wide swath through the forests adjacent to the approach roads of the third bridge across the Bosphorus, to be completed around 2016. Photographs of the felling emerged during the summer of 2013, renewing the anger of environmental activists, who fear the loss and division of wildlife habitats and the destruction of the broad-leafed knapweed and small meadow saffron.

When Prime Minister Erdoğan was mayor of Istanbul in the mid-1990s, he stated that construction of a third bridge would amount to the "murder" of the city, its forests, and its water system. And yet, the Turkish Parliament has exempted this and other major projects from filing an environmental impact assessment, a move that the Turkish Chamber of Architects and Engineers would contest if its power to contest urban planning decisions had not been unilaterally revoked by the Turkish Parliament due to the Chamber's rebellious response to the Gezi Park protests.

The purpose of these fires and bulldozing activities is fairly clear to most Turkish urban planners, who have learned from the experience of the past two Bosphorus Bridges that construction is soon followed by a relaxation of zoning regulations on land surrounding approach roads and the expansion of the city northward.

Istanbul was left relatively unscathed by the global financial crisis of 2008, so rampant land and real estate speculation continued unabated. Recent years have seen a mushrooming of skyscrapers, shopping malls, and gated communities across Istanbul, supported by rich investors from the Middle East, Europe, and Russia. The third bridge will serve as yet another infrastructural anchor for this sort of financially, environmentally, and socially precarious urbanism.

Benyameen Ghareeb

KUWAIT: THE TRANSFORMATION OF AN OIL STATE

"Financial Danger Begins in 2021,"[1] read the front-page headline on Al-Qabas, a prominent daily Kuwaiti newspaper, on June 8 2013. The threat, based on a government-issued report, was referring to Kuwait's annual spending budget outgrowing its annual returns (mainly from oil exports) in a mere eight years. How is one of the most affluent countries in the world, so minute in size (area comparable to the state of Connecticut), with only 1.23 million citizens, able to spend more than it can make in one year?

A significant sum of the spending budget is directly attributable to the country's transformation in the fifties from a primitive mercantile trading port town into a modern socialist welfare state by providing benefits to its citizens, both directly and indirectly, through spatial and non-spatial incentives. The spatial incentives, supported by oil wealth and served free of charge to all citizens, consisted of state-of-the-art infrastructure, health and education services (schools, universities, clinics and hospitals), a housing welfare program in the form of suburbs (free land grants and long-term low-interest loans or ready-built houses), and a modern central business district. The non-spatial, on the other hand, was a combination of providing limited citizenship as well as benefits accessible only to the lucky few.

In this paper, I am interested in exploring how this oil wealth was used as a tool by Kuwait's ruling family, Al-Sabah, to maintain a stable hegemony over alternate powers in the country, as well as tracing the various methods that were used to leverage foreign investment to benefit the domestic market and population.

1 Saba George Shiber, The Kuwait Urbanization: Documentation Analysis Critique = Al Madianah al-Kuwaytiyah. Kuwait: Kuwait Govt. Printing Press, 1964, LIX.

SUBURBS

Keller Easterling

American downtowns have declined in size and influence since 1920 as suburbs have come to dominate urban regions. After considering the history of diverse suburban landscapes, this seminar explores definitions of sprawl linking impoverished inner-city areas to growth on metropolitan fringes. Representations of suburban built environments in photography, films, and literature are examined.

Theodossios Issaias

ENCRYPTING ARCADIAS: NATURE, CITY AND ORDER IN THE AMERICAN SUBURBS OF PARKSIDE AND BROOKLINE

The origins of the first American organized suburban communities have been the subject of extensive research and debate. Their genealogical investigation consists of a wide variety of urban practices from villas, parks and speculative developments in England, to the design of romantic cemeteries and communitarian settlements. Despite their multiple and often contradictory objectives, the common denominator is the expression of conflict between city and nature, agrarian gentility and emerging urban capitalism.

The first romantic suburbs designed by Frederick Law Olmsted evolved after a series of endeavors to reconcile this dichotomy between city and nature. In this regard, they were expressions and progeny of the urban theories and practices of the nineteenth century that aimed to reform the city and society comprehensively. In contrast to the common approaches that examine the first romantic suburbs as remote and isolated communities (as the name 'picturesque enclaves' implies), the research paper aims to analyze them in conjunction to the cities they were adjoining and attempts to reveal the political and cultural implications of their reciprocal and often contentious relation.

Craig Rosman

FROM OPEN LINKS TO PRIVATE PARKLANDS: GOLF IN AMERICAN SUBURBS, 1895–1930

The period of American golf course construction between 1895 and 1930 is considered a 'Golden Age' because of the exponential expansion of the game and formalization of strategy in golf course design. Although golf was identified as a perfect leisure activity for burgeoning suburbs, architects needed to transform golf's customs, culture, and places from their modest roots in Scotland to a more sophisticated and exclusive product in order to integrate them with picturesque enclaves.

The purist infatuation with the links as the only true landscape for golf led C.B. Macdonald to design the first true championship level links course in the states, National Golf Links of America in Southampton, NY. At the National, in search of variety, Macdonald had translated a vernacular form, the Scottish links, and formalized it into a new typological language. Inadvertently, his design separated proper links derived course design and stroke play from less legitimate forms of the game.

Meghan Lewis

THE LAWN EPIDEMIC: A CRITIQUE OF CONTEMPORARY RESPONSES TO THE NATURE-SUBURB CRISIS

The desire to abandon cities to live closer to natural environments has drawn Americans to urban edges since the 1820s, yet rarely has nature in suburbs been codified and understood. Designers of newly imagined suburbs claim to have a different, ecologically-friendly relationship with their environment, while in reality they respond only to the most recent shape of suburban neighborhoods—edge nodes and rural fringes. To study the shifting definition of nature in suburbs, I began by identifying the landscape typologies found within each of the seven historic patterns of suburban neighborhoods established in Dolores Hayden's "Building Suburbia" in an attempt to avoid regional or typological bias. I then examined Lewis Tsurumaki Lewis's proposal "New Suburbanism: Prototypical American Suburb" and WORKac's "Nature-City" as two radically different examples of idealized future suburbs that share rhetoric and strategies with many contemporary proposals.

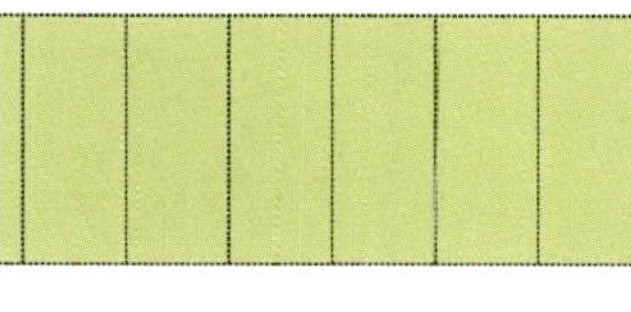

GHOST TOWNS

Elihu Rubin

This is an advanced, interdisciplinary seminar in architectural history, urban planning, vernacular building, the politics of preservation, collective memory, tourism, and, ultimately, urban sustainability. Looking at a broad spectrum of failed or almost-failed cities in the United States and across the globe, this seminar uses the ghost town and its rhythms of development and disinvestment to establish a conceptual framework for contemporary urban patterns and processes. Students develop skills in urban and architectural research methods, visual and formal analysis, effective writing, and critical reasoning.

Zachary Huelsing

HAIR IT IS: SOCIAL AND FORMAL TROPES AND THE DESTRUCTION OF PLACE IN RURAL AMERICA

Salons at first appear to abandon modesty in an attempt to assert themselves as expressive places with unique characters. Perhaps this is an effort to suggest the importance of personal style, but the competing desire to create a salon with unique flair while also hewing to cultural expectations collide to create methods of representation that are shockingly consistent once compared over a large geographical area.

An appeal to beauty, design, style, or fashion sets salons apart from barbers. Implied by this gesture is a sense of currentness. No business would hope to survive by peddling in outmoded fashion sensibilities, but the signage used by many salons has the unfortunate effect of expressing what was in vogue at the time the sign was made.

The effort to convey the product offered by the salon has led many salons to utilize artwork that is emblematic of then-current dictates. The fact that these trends, by definition, extend past locality is a possible reason for why the associated imagery shown on some signs is not only similar, but sometimes exactly the same.

The shortest route by car linking Columbia City, Indiana; Grand Ridge, Illinois; and Carthage, Illinois is 376 miles. But all three cities feature salons that utilize the same dramatic, messy-haired couple to express what sort of style a potential client might expect.

In Learning From Las Vegas; Venturi, Scott-Brown, and Izenour write, "The big sign and the little building is the rule of Route 66." In Las Vegas, they see that, "Symbol dominates space. Architecture is not enough." The phenomenon of de-emphasizing architecture and replacing it with another symbol is not unique to Las Vegas, nor is it specific to highways that are defined by fast moving cars. The analysis of the ways that hair salons attempt to play a part in defining a character for a place shows that much of what is signaled is divorced from the structure within which businesses reside, and is instead telegraphed through adherence to social norms that manifest themselves through signage.

Melody Song

Designed by Marcel Breuer, the Armstrong-Pirelli building (1968–1969) lies vacant. The tower faces the interstate highway, its central void scaled to allow a view of New Haven beyond. Once meant to advertise to automotive clients the prestige and promise of the Armstrong Tire Company in the newly developing Long Wharf area and as monumental "gateway" to New Haven, it now carries an IKEA billboard.

Purchased in 2002 by IKEA, the building is viewed as a liability to the business; only after much local protest and the mayor's insistence against its demolishment, IKEA conceded to keep the tower but amputate the long two-story "base" of the building for parking. Currently the building is under lock and key due to safety reasons of being filled with asbestos. The project is a campaign manual for the long term goal of adaptive re-use, and the short term goals of: 1. Conducting New Haven Preservation Trust sponsored tours of the asbestos-free 1st and 2nd floors; 2. Creating site-installation and re-use as gallery, studio space or extension of IKEA; 3. Creating a social media platform that documents the Pirelli building over time and garners funding for its asbestos cleaning and reuse. The manual identifies the protagonists involved and their objectives (e.g. the interests of the NH Preservation trust, NH Urban Design League) as well as lists IKEA points of contact. A promotional video storyboard illustrates the history of the building and juxtaposes the Bauhaus inspired IKEA furniture and brand identity with Breuer's work.

HISTORY OF WESTERN EUROPEAN LANDSCAPE ARCHITECTURE

Bryan Fuermann

This course presents an introductory survey of the history of gardens and the interrelationship of architecture and landscape architecture in Western Europe from antiquity to 1700, focusing primarily on Italy. The course examines chronologically the evolution of several key elements in landscape design: architectural and garden typologies; the boundaries between inside and outside; issues of topography and geography; various uses of water; organization of plant materials; and matters of garden decoration. Specific gardens or representations of landscape in each of the four periods under discussion—Ancient Roman; medieval; early and late Renaissance; and Baroque—are examined and situated within their own cultural context. Throughout the seminar, comparisons of historical material with contemporary landscape design are made.

Ann Morrow Johnson

PLINY THE YOUNGER'S TUSCAN VILLA

Expanding on an earlier assignment to draw the plan of Pliny's Tuscan Villa, using only his text for reference, this project allowed the villa to be examined in three dimensions. There is a great tradition of architects and scholars performing the exercise of drawing Pliny's plan, and rather than beginning from scratch, this model is based on Schinkel's interpretation of the Tuscan Villa. Schinkel produced ground and second level plans, a single section, and a single elevation. This information is translated onto the remaining facades in order to create a complete model that shows how Schinkel might have intended the resolved design to appear in the round.

Jason Roberts

BRION CEMETERY

Carlo Scarpa's masterwork the Brion Cemetery in San Vito d'Altivole is remarkably singular. However, the elements used draw upon a rich history of Western European landscape architecture. This project, creating a high-resolution model of the cemetery, is based on a rigorous study of the scarce existing documentation of the project and, most heavily, photographs. Through its formation, one is able to observe the sloped concrete enclosing wall, the two distinct entrances, the chapel, two covered burial areas, the euripus, the prato, a private meditation pavilion, and the reflecting pools.

Constance Vale

WATER & WILL: VILLA D'ESTE

The garden of Cardinal Ippolito II d'Este built in the hills of Tivoli marks a moment of exceptional brilliance in the use of water within landscape architecture. The work of architect Pirro Ligorio's significance is owed largely to a series of fountains he employs in shaping the viewer's temporal and sensorial experience. This is accomplished both by means of the layout of the garden and through the strategic control of water, through pipes and spouts, clarified by Charles W. Moore. Simultaneously, it displays iconographical themes, identified by David Coffin in his Villa in the Life of Renaissance Rome. The garden demonstrates Cardinal d'Este and Ligorio's attempts to display Herculean strength, controlling natural forces in one of the greatest combined feats of engineering, architecture and landscape.

Eleanor Measham

VILLA LANTE GARDEN

This drawing of the Villa Lante is one piece of a project that touches on the role of water in the history of selected landscape gardens across Europe. The project as a whole deals with the notion of three natures as revealed through the treatment of water. Throughout history and cross-culturally, water in the garden has held particular symbolic, spiritual, and metaphorical values. It has been treated in various ways that reflect philosophical and cultural ideas of the age within a historical garden context.

Villa Lante, a refined and elegant garden from the Mannerist phase of the Italian Renaissance, adopts the richness of allegory and metaphor in its water sequence to enhance the choreographed relationship of grottoes, fountains, parterres and pools. A watercourse punctuated by fountains and manipulations provides the dominant central axis to which all other elements fall secondary. It is clear that Villa Lante embodies the three natures as part of man's fall from a perceived Golden Age however there are parallel readings, such as the popular belief that the fountain sequence in fact bears some allegorical reference to the four elements of Nature.

SPRING

BOOKS & ARCHITECTURE

Luke Bulman

For architects, the book has been a necessary (if not essential) tool for clarifying, extending, and promoting their ideas and projects. This seminar examines the phenomenon of the book in architecture as both an array of organizational techniques (what it is) and as a mediator (what it does).The book has been the preferred mode of discourse, outside of building itself, architects have chosen to express their intellectual project. Lasting impression relies partially upon durability of message, and symbolically at least, the book remains the objet par excellence among media. In addition to this usefulness, the book finds itself in a privileged position as an instrument of discourse. Despite claims that it is an antiquated tool among an expanding world of media alternatives, it is exactly the book's resistance, weight, displacement, its old-fashionedness, which seems to safeguard its value as an instrument of thought. Simultaneously, there is a natural affinity between the objects of the book and architecture; they can be seen as analogs. Each is a medium that organizes material using spatiality and temporality; a progression through a group of pages proceeds just as a sequence of spaces are navigated.

Nicholas Muraglia

256 IMAGES THAT MATTER TO ARCHITECTURE

I was first interested in the task of establishing what "matters"; to do this requires as a personal definition of what is at the core of architecture, as much as speculating what is at its boundaries and outside of them. After all, the act of architecture is an act of definition in its etymological sense, "to set bounds". What are the established centers of architecture, and what are its corresponding fringes and boundaries? And how could I test the limits of the center/periphery relationship through the inescapably dialectic format of the book spread? I started with pairs of images which looked closer at the centers and boundaries of architecture, against the architecture of centers and boundaries—the cultural, epistemological boundaries or the literal, physical boundaries, both which equally structure our experience of the world. The image pairs start as distinct and antithetical, reinforcing a center/periphery binary, while still possessing some visual rhyme which allows a conversation to emerge between the two images. Reaching the end, the full-bleed images read less as distinct pairs; the center and the fringes bleed into each other across the spread, complicating what exactly is center and what is fringe.

John Farrace

2:3/1:3

This book consists of a selection from Finnegan's Wake, upside-down and in pink, by James Joyce and various lyrics, right-side up and in black, by Riff Raff. Accompanied with each section is a series of images. Images in pink apply to Joyce's passages and images in-color apply to Riff's. The images were organized in a way that would underline overlaps. The book is 100 pages and oscillates between lyrics from Riff Raff songs and sections from Finnegan's Wake. All content is continuous and page numbers are irrelevant. It can be read right side up or upside down or not.

Stephanie Lee

256 IMAGES THAT MATTER TO ARCHITECTURE

The postwar culture of consumerism, tied heavily to the American Dream, had its rise and eventual decline in the 20th century. Promoted as the ideal way of living, every citizen dreamed of owning a single-family home, which led to the booming growth of the suburbs in the mid-century. The 256 page book illustrates its seemingly endless construction, and the numbing homogeneity of suburban housing developments. Using aerial images of tract housing, advertisements from the Sears-Roebuck catalog, and art images from photographers such as Robert Adams, it presents an array of images related to the environmental and human effects of this dream.

ORNAMENT THEORY & DESIGN

Kent Bloomer

This seminar reviews the major writings governing the identities of and distinctions between ornament and decoration in architecture (e.g., Owen Jones, Riegl, Sullivan, Goodhue, etc). Modernist actions against ornament are also examined. After individual student analysis of Victorian and art nouveau production, the focus is on the designing of ornament in twenty-first-century culture.

Zachary Veach

The taxonomy of phosphene groups indicates that some of the earliest forms of visual language had a sense for symmetry theory as well as an understanding of the 'form constants' as described by Heinrich Klüver. This indicates a relationship between the geometric patterns and forms of a variety of formal traditions in ornament and the predispositions to certain pattern-forms created by the visual cortex, or as some have speculated, by the organization of retinal cells. By tapping into these seemingly universal forms, I am attempting to create an ornamental system which references both the contextual specifics of that which is being ornamented and to universals that are rooted in the visual language of pattern recognition and the history of traditional ornament.

In this particular project I am linking the taxonomy of ornamental systems to the taxonomies of organization within the building. The organization of the contents of this seed library are linked to this diagram and then expressed through an ornamental system. It occurs at moments of public/private thresholds, providing a link between the exterior world, the interior organization of the building and its contents, and through to a long tradition of communicative ornament rooted in these form constants and phosphene groups.

Michelle Gonzalez

The phenomenal generator of a system of ornament should be recognizably derived from the geometrical components of a building at large. In order for the system of ornament to pay homage to that which it is auxiliary to, it must take precedence from the building itself; this yields a direct relationship between the components of a building and allows for the metamorphosis of form and construction. For this study, I am taking the Saarinen Chapel at MIT and applying ornament to its exterior by using the building's formal qualities as the initial generator. Given the Chapel's clear formal strategy, I am analyzing its geometric components and relationships in order to design and embed ornament in the building and awaken the subdued structural components. This project dissects a building's geometries both two-dimensionally in plan and elevation and three-dimensionally as a massing in order to use fragments of the building's formal qualities as the initial and phenomenal generator of the ornament. The geometries from the overall building overlap, link and reconfigure and the new ornament awakens in response to a building's construction. This allows for the new collaboration of form as an initial generator to come into dialogue with the structure of the building.

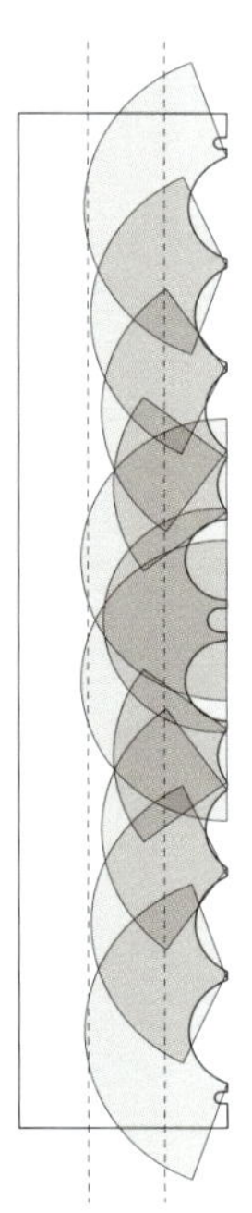

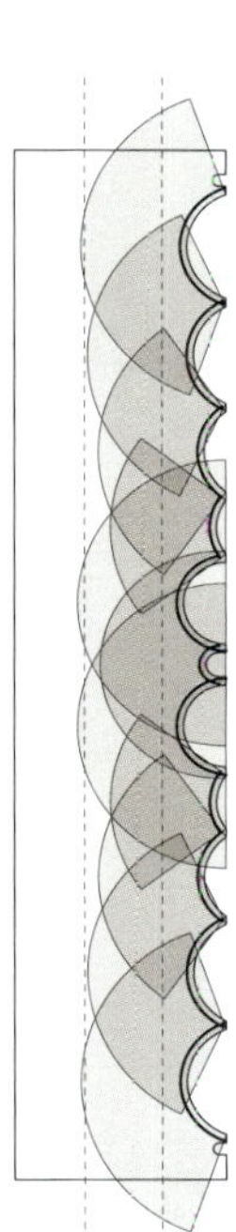

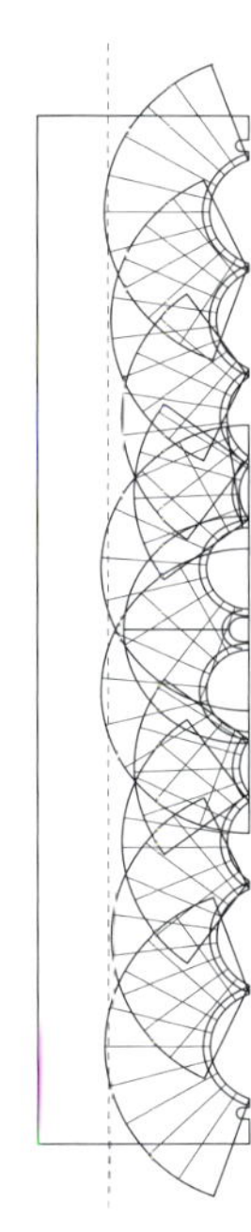

Jessica Flore Angel

This project of ornament for the Yale Center for the British Arts reacts to the pervasive use of ornamental wrappers in the contemporary practice of architecture. These articulate surfaces, which most of the time cover the entire building, are utilized to provoke an immediate visceral effect through the juxtaposition of repetitive panels. As a result, the structural and material identity of the building disappears behind this extra "decorative" layer. This ubiquitous modus operandi is frequently perceived as a reinterpretation of Gottfried Semper's theory of ornament due to its literal or metaphorical use of fabric. However, in his drawing of the primitive hut for the World Exhibition of 1851, Semper shows explicitly the wooden structure that holds the woven mat. This duality and exchange is fundamental in order to acknowledge the tectonic and geometrical qualities of the building. As a result I chose to implement an ornament on the north facade of the Yale Center for the British Arts. The abstraction of the geometry of the Bradford pear trees dialogues with the existing concrete structure while holding the ornamental fabric veils, which have replaced the steel panels. In reference to Louis Kahn's fascination for ruins, the building is projected in a phase of entropic decay, in a far future where foliage and nature have taken over architecture.

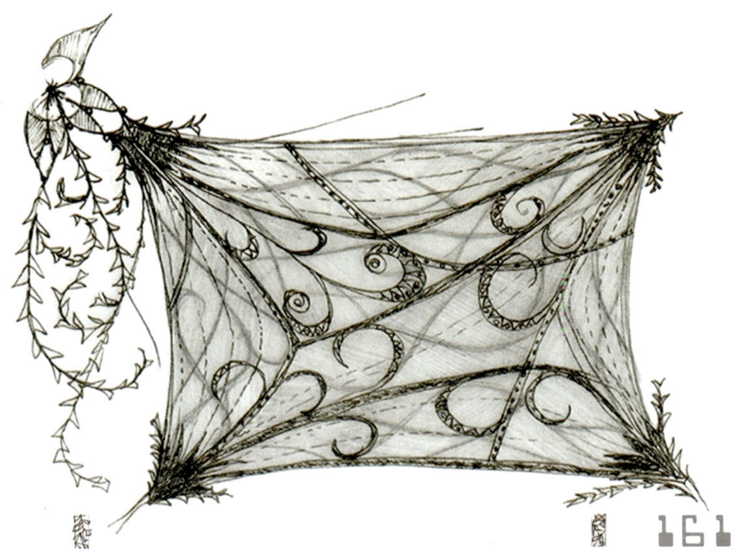

DIAGRAMMATIC ANALYSIS

Peter Eisenman & Amy DeDonato

The recent exhibition of the work of Le Corbusier at MoMA exposed the general public, students, and teachers alike to a display of human artistic passion and production rarely seen in an exhibition of architecture. While there might be much to quibble with in the current sobriquet of landscape as a generator of the work, there can be no doubt of the impact of the exhibition on a generation of young students for whom Le Corbusier and the idea of architecture and a discipline as something more than a sustainable environment is sometimes often forgotten. Clearly with such a figure there can be no single interpretation that would be adequate to explain what has been witnessed, but nevertheless, explanations and deeply held points of view are not necessarily in agreement. All such history can be seen as a matter of value judgments. It is these such value judgments that a course in diagrammatic analysis attempts to question.The proposed seminar will open a very specific discussion on the work of Le Corbusier based on two of his canonical writings: The Five Points of Architecture and the Four Compositions. These texts will be read through a series of buildings and specific writings as they evolved from 1914 to 1965 and will be augmented by more general readings as well as other points of view from visiting theorists like Stanislaus von Moos, Anthony Vidler, Kurt Forster and Pier Vittorio Aureli. The class work itself will in no way present an unbiased point of view, but it will act as a complement to the aforementioned commentators.

Anthony Gagliardi

PAVILLON SUISSE

This analysis of the Pavillon Suisse tracks the destabilized center of a four square grid as it causes the deformation in a series of vertical planes and an ambiguous reading of the columnar organization. Introducing the dormitory as a "table" building, and datum against which to read the conceptual transformations, the implied center shifts off the axis of the four square producing multiple centers.

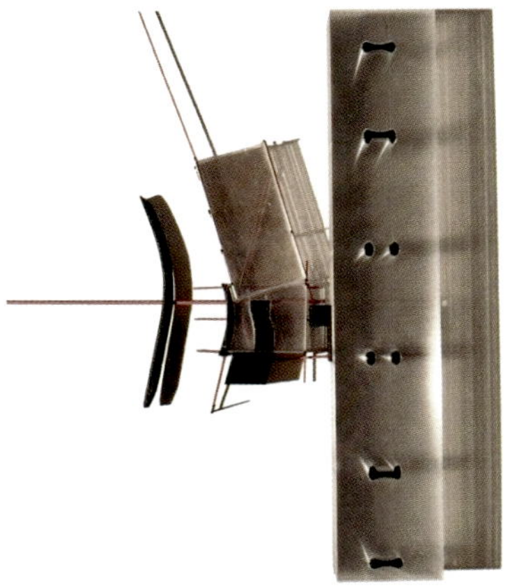

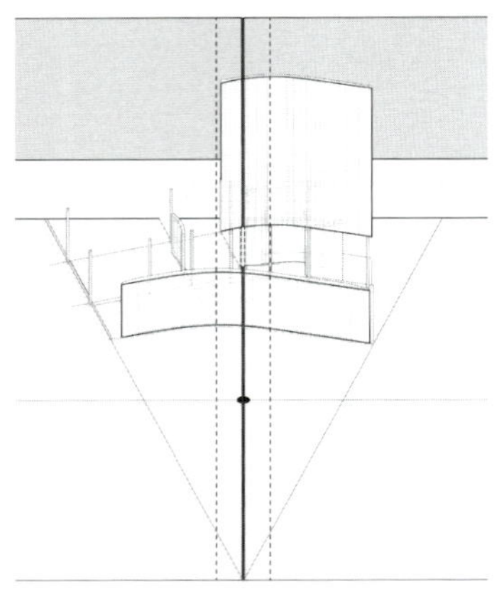

Sarah Kasper

MAISON LA ROCHE JEANNERRET

Analyzing La Roche Jeanneret reveals a virtual framework of two intersecting planar axis from which the façade surfaces push and pull. Façade deviations from the original axis planes establish a balanced composition of shifting surfaces and initiate entry into the off center atrium space. By manipulating the façade surface and hinging the building at the intersection of the axis planes, the atrium emerges as a shifted central void from which surface manipulations guide an inwardly focused promenade into and out of the voids bracketed by carved out solid spaces.

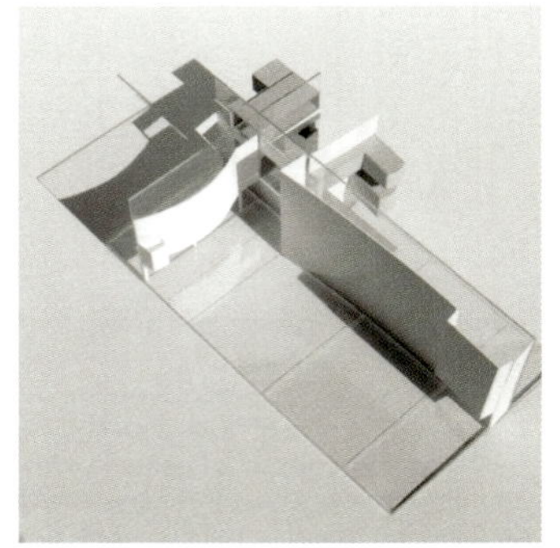

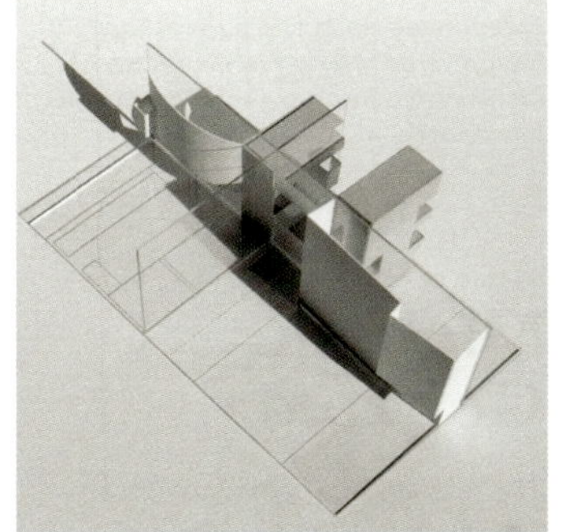

Andrew Sternad

VILLA STEIN

For the Villa Stein at Garches, alternatives to Colin Rowe's well known reading of the building as a series of layered vertical planes were investigated. First, an investigation of erosion from a solid—finding the David within the stone—attempted to locate critical figures within the mass of the building. Later, internal figural elements were measured as deviations from the structural grid, suggesting that entropic spaces press outward to fill their container and reinforcing Le Corbusier's Second Composition.

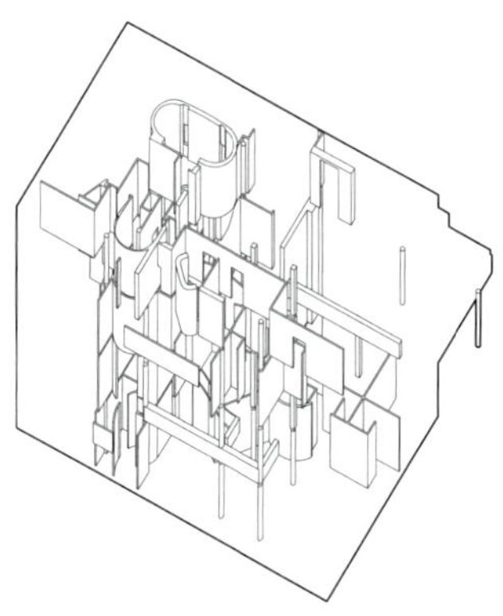

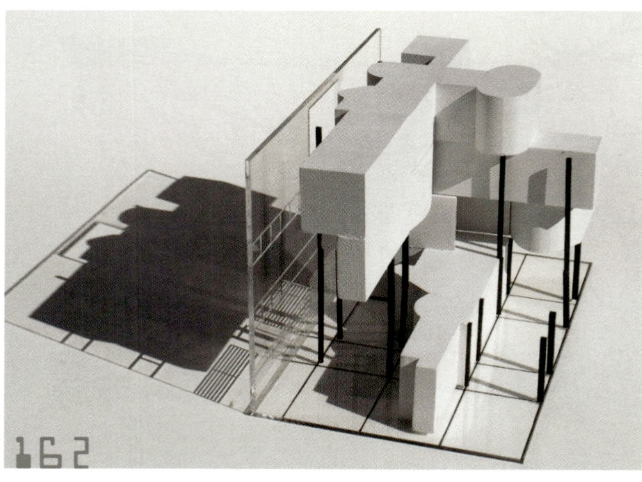

Phillip Nakamura

MILLOWNER'S ASSOCIATION BUILDING

The Millowner's Association Building shows the idiosyncrasies of Le Corbusier's post-war buildings. Corbusier establishes the familiar elements of the Five Points and Four Compositions particularly through free plan and the Garches prototype. The architectural promenade is manifested through the ramp that establishes the central axis of a conceptual nine square grid in the actual building's structural grid, which is marked by the full-height column. The nine square is then denied through a conceptual carving of the extended threshold of the brise soleil and exterior staircase. Figures set within the grid remove and absorb continuities of the structural grid; the result of which maintains balance in the composition.

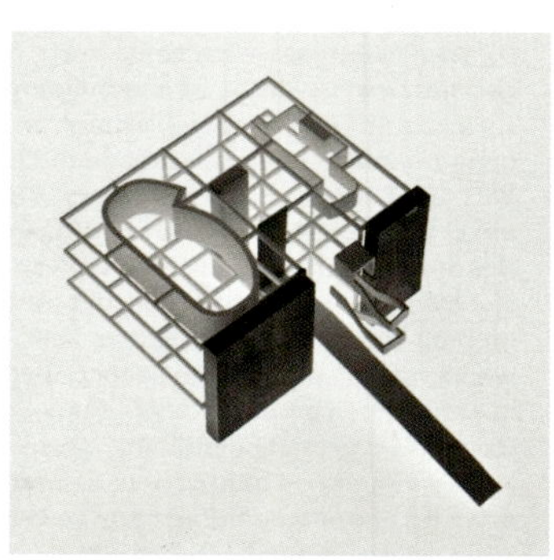

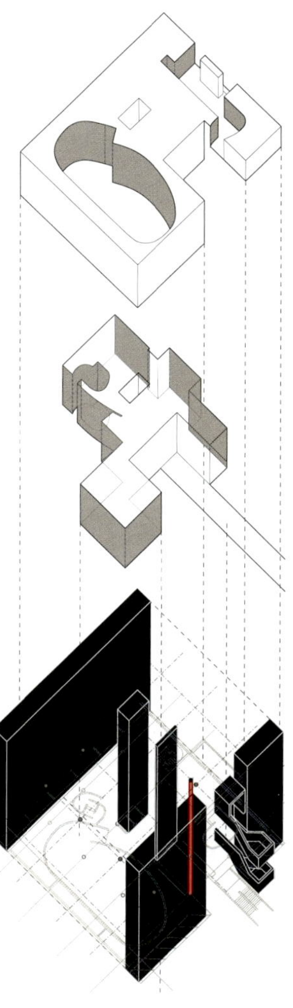

DRAWING PROJECTS

Turner Brooks

In this course each student comes up with a subject matter to pursue in drawing throughout the semester. There are weekly group meetings to discuss the work as it evolves over the course of the semester. Much of the discussion focuses on the act of 'seeing' and finding the 'mark' on the paper which conveys the varied meanings of the subject matter. At the end, each student has a 'body' of work.

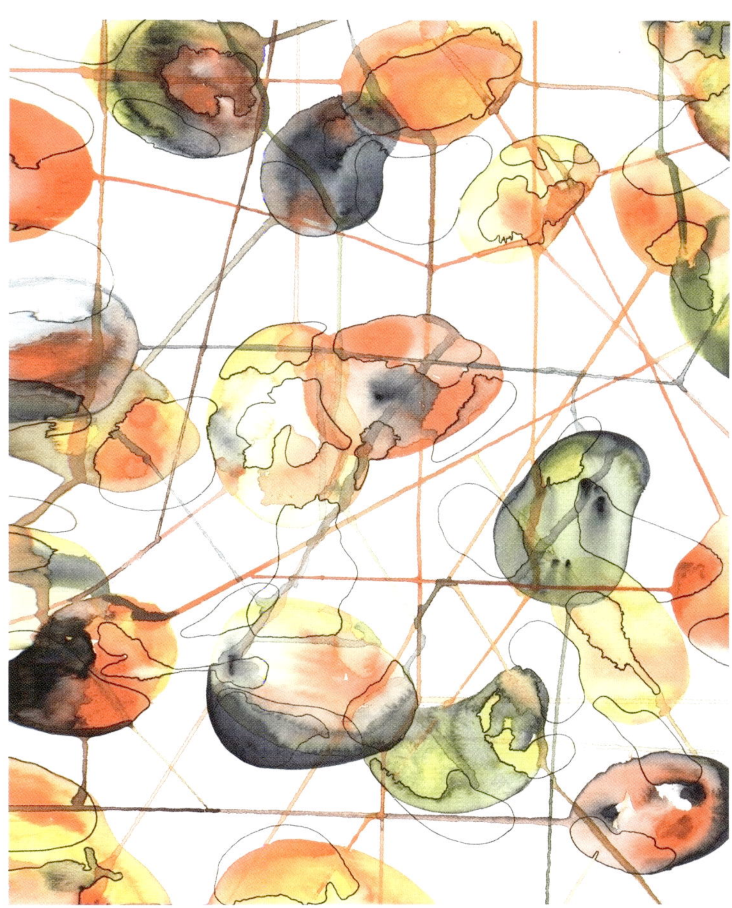

Julcsi Futo

Eleanor Measham

Andrew Dadds

DISHEVELED GEOMETRIES

Mark Foster Gage

For the Spring of 2014, the focus of this course will be one on digitally re-inventing the analogue technique of "kitbashing" to, as a class, produce a single large-format 3d-printed volume or room. The seminar is funded at a significant level by Autodesk towards this end. As the final design allows, we may also CNC mill portions of the volume or room in solid Carerra marble through an ongoing affiliation with the Digital Stone Project. As part of the latter there will be the opportunity for one student to study digital stone carving in Tuscany to further develop a portion of the project for one month over the summer, as was the case with last year's seminar. Kitbashing originally emerged from the hobby of plastic model building, and involves using pieces from multiple model kits, glued together in unexpected arrangements in order to produce objects that seem strange and otherworldly. This technique was adopted heavily by designers of 1970s science fiction films such as Alien, Star Wars, Blade Runner and numerous other films that predate the emergence of digital special effects. We will be digitally "kitbashing" in much the same way as these early special effects pioneers—by relying on existing forms that are radically recombined, but also mutated, fused and mistreated in novel and creative ways. For us this involves not plastic model kits and glue, but the 3d scanning of found objects using our smartphones, and the downloading of existing objects from large online object sharing clearinghouses. We will kitbash these objects by organizing them in vast numbers and forcibly manipulating and mutating them into massive figural arrays which read texturally.

Dionysus Cho
Anne Ma
Daniel Nguyen

KITBASHING
Through collaboration with Autodesk, this project aims to develop an aesthetic direction and effective workflow to create a high resolution 3D printed physical space out of the conglomeration of disparate digital entities. With the advance of technology, the sci-fi world of kitbashing and unlimited ornamentation/articulation is entering the real world. Form is no longer reliant on arranging and manipulating primitives, but is manifested as an aggregate of objects composed to enclose volumes. This particular composition includes a juxtaposition of notable cute objects adjacent to hard edged, streamlined volumes which induces multiple layers of estrangement and ambiguity that is augmented by a material disregard for any original "intentions" these objects might have had.

PARTS IS PARTS

Ben Pell

This seminar examines the component nature of architectural production, specifically at the interface between the customarily distinct practices of fabrication and construction. Looking at a range of historical and contemporary examples, the seminar explores ways in which constructional techniques and typologies have been both restricted and propelled by limitations of scale—often provoking new directions in design technique and production technology. Readings and case studies in the first half of the term are used to outline the history and theories of modern production practices, from 1851 to the present, and serve as the basis for a series of material studies to be produced at full scale. The course culminates in a final design project and presentation.

Jason Lee
Emau Vega

DOLOS
Like the Greek god of trickery and guile Dolos, our project addresses the part to whole relationship with a cunning deception which blurs the reading of the part to the overall monolithic body it composes. Our project is composed of singular modules which are sculpted to give a reading of a component made of multiple parts when in reality the module is the only part. As the modules aggregate to compose a larger body, the reading of the part is further blurred. Additionally, the application of a dazzle paint camouflage pattern was intended to further conceal the part to whole relationship. The final prototype is made of carbon fiber as a response to the desired qualities defining a monolith, qualities of seamlessness and continuity.

PATTERNISM

Brennan Buck

Over the last two decades, digital form has energized Modernism's neutral field to produce undulating surfaces tense with potential energy. Topological surfaces, deployed at an architectural scale, define spaces of constantly shifting size, proportion, and orientation. These surfaces are enabled by calculus rather than geometry and are characterized by vectors and flows more than stable points and planes. This seminar proposes that a formalism combining the continuity of topological surfaces and the articulation of tectonics, enabled by the precise modulation of computation, might catalyze a more diverse mode of formal continuity: pattern.

After briefly establishing a theoretical foundation, the seminar focuses on exploiting the full potential of Grasshopper software. First through the lens of material flow (structural loads) and then through spatial experience, poles of repetition/redundancy/continuity on one hand and stocasticity/variation on the other hand are explored. By modulating the relationships between objects and spaces, the seminar investigates multilevel structural and spatial hierarchies—hierarchies of position, scale, and connection—while maintaining what Gregory Bateson called the great aesthetic unity that patterns produce.

Belinda Lee & Constance Vale

This three-dimensional structure emerges in the overlay of two distinct grid systems: a grid of nested planes that hierarchically increase in density, and of a series of scaled spheres occurring on the same grid. These spheres manifest in the system as Boolean difference operations performed on the planes, thus generating the reading of a third system. Volumes within the interior are delineated in two distinct ways, by planar surfaces with cut circular openings and in the confluence of many edges creating a porous poché. The resultant system of discrete chambers is disrupted by a larger spherical Boolean that compositionally unifies multiple cells. Views through the interior occur on any 45 degree oblique axis, the axes along which the Boolean spheres deteriorate the planar grid. The flatness of elevation, with its circular openings, causes the spherical Booleans executed on the angled planes beyond to be read as a series of elliptical edges. A secondary two-dimensional pattern is applied to the planes, decreasing in density as these planes angle away from the oblique axes and approach the orthogonal axes. This both reinforces the reading of these planes along the oblique and allows the two-dimensional circles to operate autonomously on the planar surfaces.

Nicholas McAdoo & Justin Nguyen

This project looks at the relationship between exterior and interior by reconciling the diverging part to whole relationships among computational and compositional themes in digital form. If computation generates a field of self-similar parts that lacks an overall external figure and if composition produces a monolithic figure that is spatially uniform, this project creates internal organization from external figure. By subdividing the figure into recursive scales of figures and voids, the external figure—a bunny in this case—challenges homogeneity by organizing both internally and externally a series of linked, non-intersecting, irregular tetrahedra. These linked volumes create a continuous poche that generates cellular voids within the bunny - each autonomous yet connected to its neighbors. The result is a porous network of cells that allows light and shadow to define the quality of the interior space.

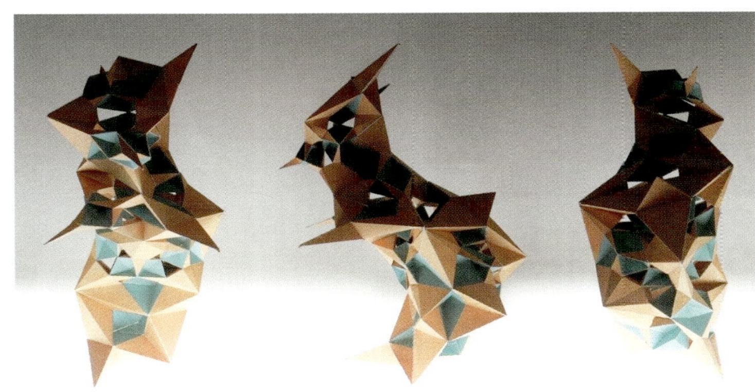

Charles Hickox

Our project superpositions two divergent organizations of self-generation: one could be characterized as an internal system which grows outwardly, the second system demarcates the space of enclosure. The internal system is initiated at a single point and grows radially through diagonal iterative branches. The enclosure system is built by the regular repetition of cubic cells, which are arrayed equally in the X,Y,Z dimensions, forming an aggregate cube. The branches of the internal system are translated into cells which grow outwardly, transitioning in scale from units which equal the cells of the the enclosure system to much larger. The interface of these two systems remains, at the origin, the membrane between enclosure and interior cells have a one to one relationship; the balance shifts outwardly with many enclosure cells interfacing with one interior cell. The membrane between cells defines two simultaneous interior/exteriors as each "interior" acts as the "exterior" for the other system.

FROM BOGARDUS TO 3-D PRINTING

Peter de Bretteville

Architectural practice has been profoundly affected by new tools of representation that are now leading ever more directly to both fabrication and actual erection of buildings, at the center of which are robotics and 3-D printers. Software has replaced the physical "kit-of-parts" as the instrument of standardization, resulting in systems in which the parts are infinitely customizable. This has increased the necessity for architects to seriously consider the techniques and strategies of prefabrication. What are the architectural implications of this, and will a new language emerge?

This seminar begins with five lectures: New Materials at the Turn at the Century; Cast Iron and Other Systems; Postwar Explorations 1940–55; Systems and Techno Fantasies of the 1960s and '70s; and Emerging Methods, Robotics, and 3-D Printing. These lectures set the stage for the students' research into materials and a system or systems that are presented to the class and that culminate in an illustrated paper as well as a 3-D printed model describing the system, including all of its components.

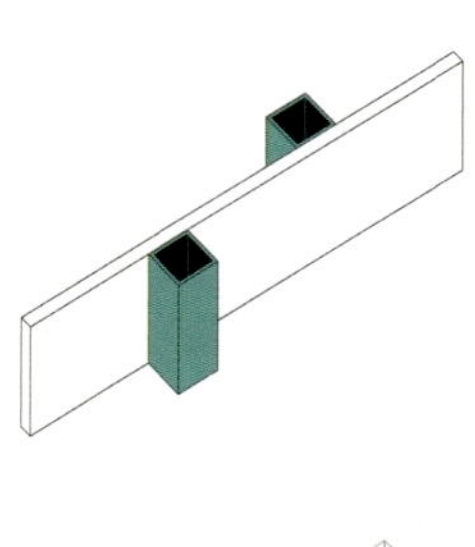

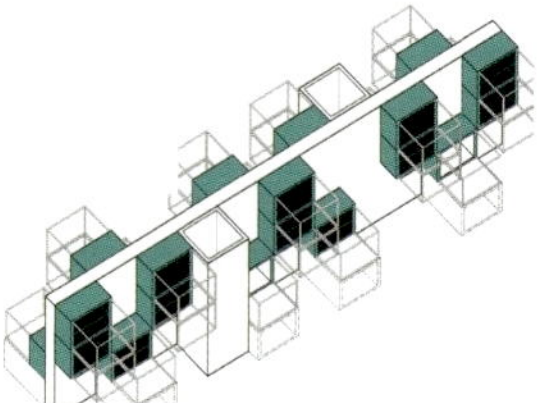

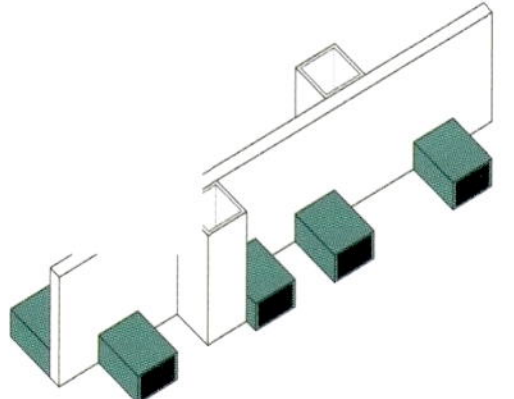

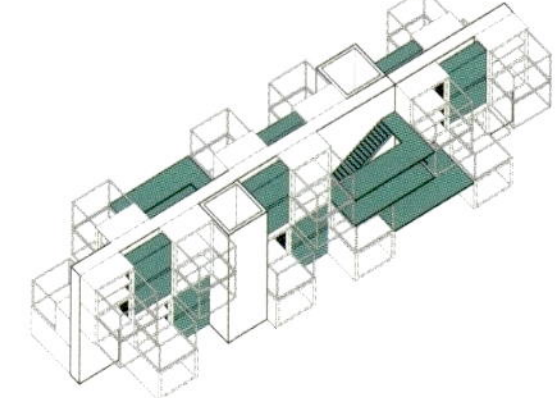

Suhni Chung & Katarzyna Pozniak

ZVI TO COMPLEX FRAME
The residential tower reinvents the morphology of the modular system of Ramot Polin apartment complex in Jerusalem. The "Zvi to Complex Frame" project, inspired by Zvi Hecker's organic structure composed of repetitive prefabricated modular dodecahedrons, proposes a vertical system with customizable parts. Hecker's design has proved to be unsuccessful. Unusable walls, narrow balconies, limited lighting conditions, and bad ventilation forced residents to extensively alter their living units. Our project adapts the geometrical language of Hecker's residential neighborhood, while improving its dysfunctional components. The vertical structural frame with customizable 2-story apartments offers more space, more daylight exposure, efficient circulation core that facilitates communication, variety of public and private spaces such as unit-shared courtyards, private balconies, and occupiable green roofs. The design of the tower was informed by the software and 3D printing techniques as the instruments of standardization, resulting in a system in which parts could be infinitely customizable, while the whole structure could grow and evolve in response to different climates and geographical locations.

Kiana Hosseini & Elizabeth LeBlanc

This class focused on distilling the principle aspects within a building and utilizing these aspects as a point of departure from which to formulate our own critical creation. We extracted from the Loblolly House by Kieran Timberlake the idea of designed prefabrication. Although, the project was highly efficient in its execution of a prefabricated method we critiqued its application to only accommodate one family and its fixed configuration. As a result our critique seeks to diagram how the general form of the project could be aggregated and still function.

John Farrace & HoChung Kim

As the global population flocks to urban centers around the world, it is critical to consider alternative ways of living, building and designing that can accommodate this profound shift towards high density living. The complexity of this is increased by new building technologies, namely 3D printing, CNC milling, robotic assembly processes and other ways of computer aided manufacturing. Additionally, as global economies become more interconnected to, and codependent on each other, the need for systems that can integrate into existing production workflows are critical to the success of new concepts.
We looked at one attempt to tackle the pressing issues of mass urbanization, the Kurokawa Capsule Tower in Tokyo. Tokyo is the second most expensive city in the world per square foot at $7,600. The tower has 140 capsules, all to be occupied individually. It is required that all of the capsules be removed and replaced at the same time, every 25 years. Over 40 years have passed and the capsules have not been replaced, leaving only 30 capsules that are actually being used today.
In response, we propose CAPS-L, a capsule tower with multiple scales of interchangeability and more complex organizational possibilities. CAPS-L is composed of capsules that are about 10 feet wide by 20 feet long. The dimensions allow for the blocks to rotate and flip and still nest into each other, in the same way bricks in a game of Tetris stack. Each L shaped capsule is equipped with a robust structural frame that carries all utilities and hangs directly, individually off of the core.
The fundamental idea about CAPS-L is that it can accommodate for a huge range of configurations that produce a variety of spatial organizations—from open outdoor space to semi outdoor space to interior, private space. As each unit wraps around the core and other capsules, voids are left, and new interiorities are strung together to create dynamic spaces and multi-unit residences.

ROME

Stephen Harby, Bimal Mendis & Alexander Purves

This intensive five-week summer workshop takes place in Rome and is designed to provide a broad overview of that city's major architectural sites, topography, and systems of urban organization. Examples from antiquity to the present day are studied as part of the context of an ever-changing city with its sequence of layered accretions. The seminar examines historical continuity and change as well as the ways in which and the reasons why some elements and approaches were maintained over time and others abandoned. Hand drawing is used as a primary tool of discovery during explorations of buildings, landscapes, and gardens, both within and outside the city.

Amy Su

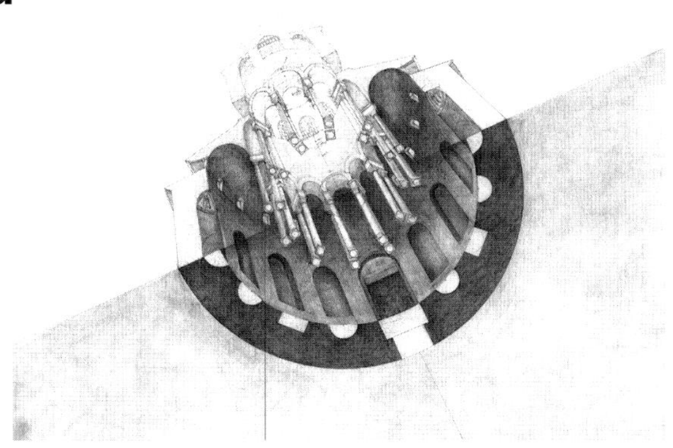

Jack Wolfe

Kirk Henderson

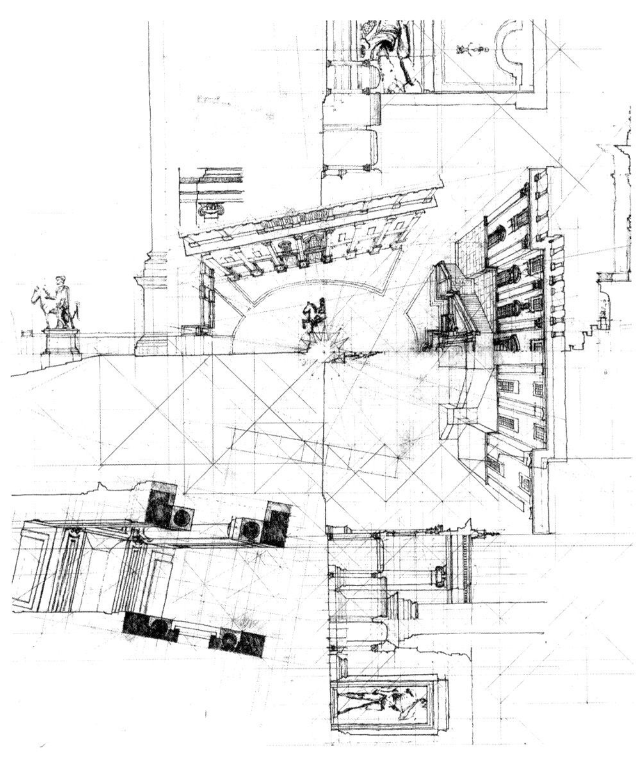

Belinda Lee

MATERIALS & MEANING

Deborah Berke

This seminar urges students to probe material usage, in terms of detailing, context, embedded meaning, and historical precedent. The course examines how variations in joinery affect a built work, what opportunities materials afford architects in design and construction, how architects make material selections and decisions, and what meanings material selections bring to a work of architecture.

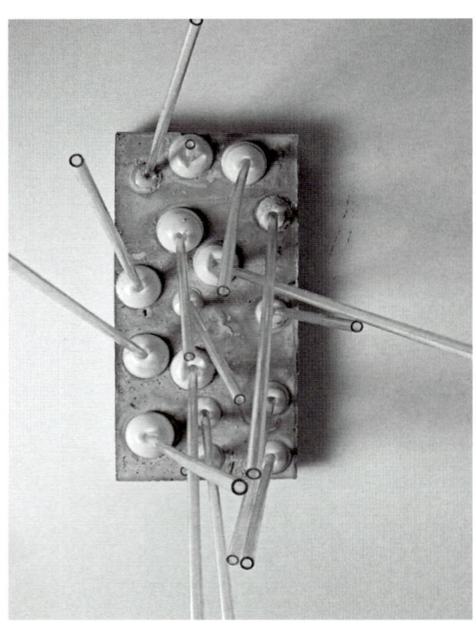

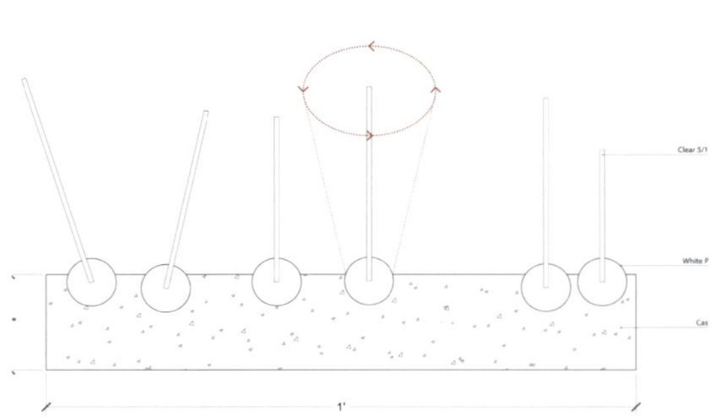

Jie Tian

This imaginative and unexpected way of material assembly pushes the joint to evoke subtle sensations visually and physically. Ingenious and yet deceptively simple, this project presented a desire to experiment with the material property of concrete and plastic. Being cast more than halfway inside the concrete, the ping pong balls are locked, while their smooth surface allows their free movement inside. The plastic tubes held by the ping pong balls therefore, control their rotation. This is an interactive design full of fun and engagement.

Eleanor Measham

The joint is a study of a wall section where red oak planks both act as the formwork for casting and as a hung panel, flush to the lower, exposed concrete. Through continuous vertical panels and the expressed grain throughout, the joint explores the relationship of the two materials in both design and construction.

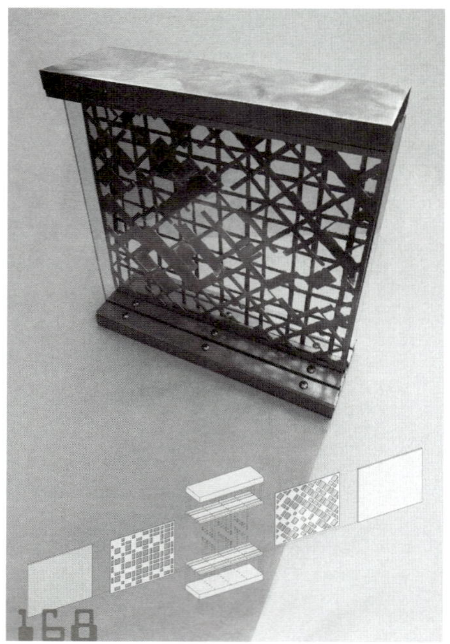

Talia Pinto-Handler

The cut metal joint is shown composed strictly of aluminum and glass, and explores the structural and ornamental potential of both materials. Aluminum sheets are cut into two grid patterns on the plasma jet cutter. These panels, as well as two made of glass which are installed outboard of the cut aluminum, are inserted between aluminum bars above and below, via channels built into the bar structure. The entire system, which comprises one single unit, is to be arranged as one of many, with increasing and decreasing levels of transparency to suit the programmatic needs of the interior space beyond.

CRAFT, MATERIALS & COMPUTER-AIDED ARTISTRY

Kevin Rotheroe

This course reviews materials and computer-aided manufacturing processes especially suited for digitally crafting aesthetically unique architectural components and surfaces. Cross-fertilization of digital and conventional modes of making is emphasized, as this approach often generates economically viable opportunities for creative expression. This is a hands-on, project-based seminar addressing fundamental theoretical issues in the transformation of ideas into material reality via representations, hand-operated tools, and CNC-automated forming devices.

Amir Karimpour

In exploring Islamic geometries and patterning, two main aspects were put into direct friction: the free form arabesque and rigid, strict geometrical derivations. The geometrically constructed Islamic pattern served as an underlying framework for subsequent, more intricate patterns to grow from. These subsequent arabesque patterns created a grain of fluidity across the piece, both in directionality and gradients. These constructed drawings were then digitized and fabricated to explore different material properties and effects.

Ivan Farr

The topic of my semester's exploration in materials concerns translation between analog and digital media. For the first stage of my project, I created original hand-made concrete casts (eventually painted silver) which were then 3D scanned into a workable Rhino mesh. In the second stage, I proceeded to 3D print the scans and capture an inverse mold of them with a casting rubber compound. For the third and final stage, I cast wax over the rubber mold and experimented with embedding organic objects. These three discrete steps allowed me to create an analog object, digitize it and fabricate a hybrid of the two states. My process commenced with an opaque concrete cast which morphed into a nuanced translucent surface.

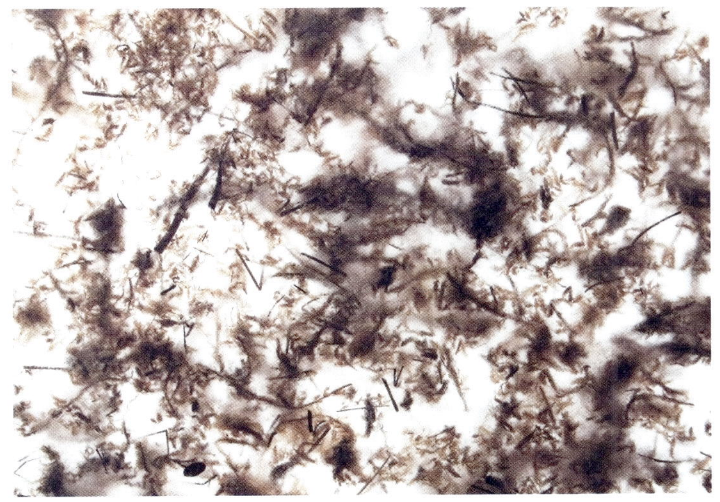

Jack Bian

The final exercise is an exploration of the architectural frieze. Through history, three unifying elements of the frieze have been observed: symmetry, narrative, and linkage. The creative process was informed by sampling disjunctive objects, collaging them to create an ornamental surface and mirroring them to create classical symmetry.

DESIGN COMPUTATION

Jason Bond

The capabilities and limitations of architects' tools influence directly the spaces architects design. Computational machines, tools once considered only more efficient versions of paper-based media, have a demonstrated potential beyond mere imitation. This potential is revealed through design computation, the creative application of the processes and reasoning underlying all digital technology, from e-mail to artificial intelligence. Just as geometry is fundamental to drawing, computation affords a fundamental understanding of how data works, which is essential to advance the development of BIM, performative design, and other emerging methodologies. This seminar introduces design computation as a means to enable architects to operate exempt from limitations of generalized commercial software; to devise problem-specific tools, techniques, and workflows; to control the growing complexities of contemporary architectural design; and to explore forms generated only by computation itself. Topics include data manipulation and translation, algorithms, information visualization, computational geometry, human-computer interaction, custom tooling, generative form-finding, emergent behavior, simulation, and system modeling. Using Processing, students develop computational toolsets and models through short, directed assignments ultimately comprising a unified, term-long project.

Ryan Connolly

APPOSITIONS

This software was developed to explore an architecture of Appositions, or the act of placing together or bringing into proximity or juxtaposition. Rather than enable the creation of a finite architectural object, this software instead offers the possibility to quickly test variations in order to gain a broader understanding and appreciation of the system's compositional logic and architectural potential. Utilizing a physics engine, varying boxes are created and brought into contact via user control, by connecting their corners or midpoints to the corresponding positions on other boxes. With the ability to move between plan and a full 3 dimensional environment, it is possible to simulate the spaces between the boxes, the relationships between the modulated spires, or how the system interacts with the static circles, demonstrating the ability of the system to interact with a site condition. With precedents ranging from Iranian bazaars to Louis Kahn's Fisher House, Appositions is a system that is both fluid and precise.

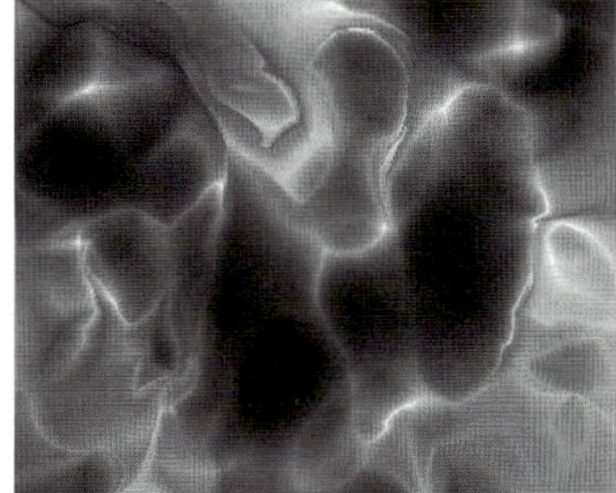

Kate Warren

FAÇADE VISUALIZATION

In my proposal, the building is covered by two layers of metal screen that visually play off one another in the wind that is common in the harbor on which the building is sited. In developing the application, I became interested in creating a tool that could be applicable to more than just my studio project through a wide range of user customization options as well as the possibility of output in a number of different media, including images, videos, and GIFs. The interface for the application is designed to maximize user-customization. The basic framework is two grids overlaid on top of one another, one fixed and one in motion. The user interface allows flexibility in the grid spacing, line weights, opacity, shadows, and color, as well as customization of the physics controlling the motion of the flexible grid and its relation to the fixed grid. Additionally, the user can choose to auto-animate the application or control it with a mouse.

Dionysus Cho

SPRAY

SPRAY is an interactive piece that untethers painting from the human hand with the aid of a crafted mech-anism and a Processing based digital interface. A spray can, suspended with a finely tuned mechanism, is actuated through a Processing script—a control interface allowing for orchestrating a sequence of motions—and an Arduino microcon-troller. Propelling the device with the release of air, SPRAY produces a hectic and random piece tracing strokes of its travels as a result of controlled activation—both timing and pressure—of a spray can.

EXPLORING NEW VALUE IN DESIGN PRACTICE

Phillip G. Bernstein & Brian Kenet

How do we make design a more profitable practice? Design practice has traditionally positioned building as a commodity in the delivery supply chain, valued by clients like other products and services purchased at lowest first cost. Despite the fact that the building sector in its entirety operates in large capital pools where significant value is created, intense market competition, sole focus on differentiation by design quality, and lack of innovation in project delivery and business models have resulted in a profession that is grossly underpaid and marginally profitable. The profession must explore new techniques for correlating the real value of an architect's services to clients and thereby break the downward pressure on design compensation. This seminar redesigns the value proposition of architecture practice, explores strategies used by better-compensated adjacent professions and markets, and investigates methods by which architects can deliver—and be paid for—the value they bring to the building industry.

Brandon Hall & Caroline VanAcker

HALCYON BUSINESS PLAN

Currently, architecture firms operate on what we call a "ribbon-cutting model." They sign one contract with one client group for one building. Once the building is delivered and the contract fulfilled, the firm's responsibilities end and the business relationship is—for the most part—dissolved. However, buildings last much longer than the time it takes the architect to construct them. In fact, this initial building cost is only five to ten percent the total lifetime cost of the building. Why are architects abandoning their ideas, their buildings, their clients, and their relationships when that other ninety percent is still on the table?

Our practice concentrates on three main areas of practice: Habits, Creations, and Networks. We expand the box of services of traditional architecture (the "ribbon-cutting" model) in both directions. In the beginning, we study the habits of users, modeling pre-occupancy. Then we create an intelligent building system optimized to meet our established targets. At post-occupancy and beyond, we mine the data continually generated as our buildings are in use. This information goes back to re-inform our network of initial metrics, as we continually recalibrate our standards to best model and complete outstanding projects. The linchpin of this effort is Halcyon's proprietary automation/integration software that models a building's health and performance. We have fundamentally reconsidered what it means to make architecture, as our building is therefore the hardware partner to our software. Our value - and our payment structure—is tied into the results from these two components working in tandem over the course of a building's full lifecycle. Not only are we providing a uniquely well-designed building from the outset, we can prove how much better it is, whether that be through saving money or improving results. As the clients' needs change, we can readjust the built environment to align it with any new benchmarks.

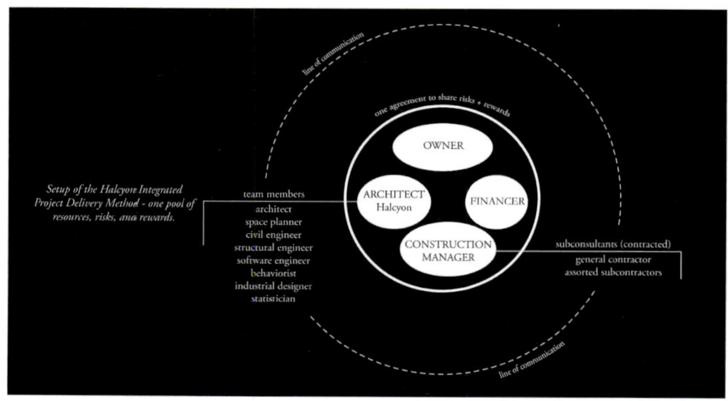

THE CONSTRUCTION OF EXACTITUDE

Karla Britton

This seminar critically considers modern classicism not only as a compositional design method and as an evocation of precedents, but also as a language of clarity, reduction, and economy resistant to an unquestioned avant-gardist predilection for the "new." Beginning with the fixed principles that were the legacy of nineteenth-century French and German Neoclassicism (unity, symmetry, proportion), the seminar continues up through the Rationalism and Formalism that followed the Second World War. Issues explored include the concepts of the ruin and monumentality; the Modern Movement's analogies to the classical; and the representation of interwar national and political ideologies. Works studied include those by architects, literary/artistic figures, and theorists such as Richardson, Garnier, Perret, Le Corbusier, Rossi, Asplund, Lutyens, Terragni, Speer, Mies, SOM, Kahn, Valéry, Gide, de Chirico, Calvino, Rowe, Krier, Eisenman, Stern, Porphyrios, and Colquhoun.

Jacqueline Kow

ACCEPTERA AND THE GÖTENBURG LAW COURTS: A QUESTION ABOUT STYLE

The introduction of acceptera uses the role of marriage in human society as a metaphor for explaining their thoughts on the role of architecture in society. They argued that the three major theories came out of the prevalent attitude of the society. "Not truth but social adaptability makes a theory powerful."[1] While the manifesto isn't explicit in connecting individual theories to architectural thought, there are some clear correlations that can be set up if one buys into their argument that architecture like marriage is also a product of the time. The first theory proposed by Lewis Henry Morgan was that marriage followed the laws of evolution.[2] The implication of this was that society has been evolving from a primitive state towards a higher form. However, this theory began to be problematic for maintaining the status quo, as it was then interpreted that we were always in a state relative to the past and future and that the present was never the culminating point. This became the basis of many social radicals and therefore the theory became objectionable to the bourgeoisie. The theory by Edvard Westermarck that followed fell in line with the broader social theory at the time: current social values have always existed in humanity.[3] Westermarck proposed that monogamy and marriage have always existed and that all other forms of social relationships, such as polygamy, were deviations.

The equivalent architecturally of these two theories could really be read in the architectural debate of the time. The first would have suggested that Modernism should be the style used because it was the most advanced form of architectural expression having evolved from all previous styles. The second would more directly suggest Laugier's theory of the primitive hut as the origin of architecture and in turn promote classicism over all other styles that deviated from it. What Asplund and the other authors of acceptera present is the architectural version of the third theory of marriage. The third theory proposed by Robert Briffault's The Mothers states that monogamy was not inherent in humanity, but became the standard due to poverty and economic demands on families. The implications of this are that the state of marriage is the product of the demands of the time, not tied to morals or history, but out of necessity.

1 Asplund et al., acceptera, 148.
2 Ibid., 145.
3 Ibid., 146.

Xiaodi Sun

PARALLEL PROJECTION AND THE REPRESENTATION OF ARCHITECTURAL MODERNISM

The Enlightenment pursuit of empirical reasoning put Renaissance rhetoric in relationship with intellectual clarity. Especially in the nineteenth century, architectural representation as addressed by Auguste Choisy, viewed the oblique parallel drawing as a tool which could convey the possibility of direct measurement and the logic of construction. In this manner, since the nineteenth century parallel projection was used in the West as a means of conveying a concern for "truth" and rationality in architecture.

In the East, however, perspectival drawing since the medieval period was dominated by certain painting genres which emphasized place-making rather than rational understanding. Evidence for this place-making may be seen in the yamato-e style painting which underscores a concern with the tension between stable and transient elements. These paintings demonstrate a concern with space that does not underscore the Western privileging of a rationalist approach towards architecture.

Written by the famous female writer Murasaki Shikibu in medieval Japan, Tale of Genji is a novel that renders the love story between Prince Genji and a number of court ladies. In scrolls like Genji Monogatari Emaki, the oblique appearance of architecture was planned out and positioned purposefully to establish "stages" for the stories. The oblique angle even lends the viewer an extra dimension of emotion when figures in the painting were positioned at direct confrontation with the angled space.

WRITING ON ARCHITECTURE

Carter Wiseman

The goal of this course is to train students in the principles and techniques of nonfiction writing as it applies to architecture. The course includes readings from the work of prominent architects, critics, and literary figures, as well as reviews of books and exhibitions, opinion pieces, and formal presentations of buildings and projects. Class writing includes the development of an architectural firm's mission statement, drafting proposals for design commissions, on-line texts, and other forms of professional communication. The main focus of the course is an extended paper on a building selected from a variety of types and historical periods, such as skyscrapers, private houses, industrial plants, gated communities, malls, institutional buildings, and athletic facilities.

Zachary Huelsing

LAMBERT'S CAFÉ

To describe the experience of walking into Lambert's Café, situated along the highway that many snowbirds take on their annual trip to the sunny shores of the Gulf Coast of Alabama, is to do away with the conventions often utilized when describing a restaurant. Smells do not readily spring to mind, and the only color worth mentioning is brown. Bric-a-brac lines the walls in an effort to create a "homey" environment that harkens back to some vague notion of the early twentieth century, but the reality is that the assemblage only achieves banality. POW flags, state flags, and rocking chairs all tug at any real American's heartstrings as he or she shuffles past the neon sign, "Outhouses." All of the red state kitsch one could dream up is contained under one roof. It is a home for these simple artifacts. However, to be more precise, it is "the home of throwed rolls."

The experience of Lambert's naturally ends with dessert, and the menu only offers banana pudding. By nature, pudding is fairly straightforward affair, but leave it to the folks at Lambert's to exploit it in order to add to the chaos. Every hour or so one of the servers utilizes the loudspeaker, cutting off another play of "Cotton Eyed Joe" to announce to all diners that all who wish to get a free desert only need join the rapidly forming conga line. YMCA blasts through the restaurant as half of the patrons gesticulate to the song, led around the dining room by a dutiful employee. The ruckus subsides, and everybody sits back down only to be greeted with another announcement. The kitchen has plumb run out of pudding, y'all! The restaurant does away with any potential profit to be had off of people who might have actually wanted to eat dessert. But then again, this place was never about the food.

Ian Spencer

VOID AND GRAVITAS: INSIDE THE NEUE WACHE

Architecture cannot guarantee a specific feeling. It can make one feel, certainly, but to say each visitor is made to feel the same is a tenuous position. The difficulty is one of representation. In a language as abstract as architecture, the depth of feeling is translated into a spatial idea, an atmospheric sensation. It does not show sadness, it shows void. It does not show excitement, it shows detail. Architecture does not ask us what we feel; it asks us to reconsider what makes us feel. And the Neue Wache asks this quite directly. Interred in the Neue Wache are the remains of an unknown German soldier and an unnamed concentration camp victim. The shrine does not redeem. It does not recall, it does not recite, it does not remind. It reveals. It asks that we consider the nature of human frailty, the depths of grief, and the poignancy of the object. The statuary in the tympanum depicts the goddess Nike deciding a battle, intended as a tribute to Prussia's role in the Napoleonic Wars and a symbol of liberation from invading forces. Now, I think, it symbolizes victory over the dangers within, and liberation from the recent past.

Adam Wagoner

THE ROUNDHOUSE

The door of the dark, damp locker room opens to the THUD THUD THUD of hands and feet. The sound hits you immediately, reverberating through your bones. Then the band strikes up, da DA dum da da DAA, brightly, loudly. You run forward into the light. Hundreds of people, standing, cheering, waving, line the interior of a bright, white, domed space, all centered on a glowing, wooden, basketball court. In the age of ESPN and 24/7 sports coverage why are so many people attending a high school basketball game? The answer to this question is in the physical space itself and what that space represents to one small Midwest town.

The Roundhouse is a powerful space because it represents something larger. It holds the combined memory and pride of a population's history, accomplishments and culture. Young children throughout the town are still shooting hundreds of baskets in their driveways, dreaming of a future in the spotlight, and as long as this desire is still there, the power of the Roundhouse as a community conductor is still alive.

RELIGION & MODERN ARCHITECTURE

Karla Britton

The design of religious architecture challenges the creative capacities of prominent architects, yet this domain has largely gone unnoticed within the field. In an inter-religious and inter-disciplinary context, this seminar offers a fresh examination of the history of modern architecture through a close analysis of a single building type—the religious building (mosques, churches, synagogues, and temples). Drawing on guest speakers, this course opens a discourse between the disciplinary perspectives of philosophy, theology, liturgical studies, and architectural history and theory on the influence religion has come to exert in contemporary civic life, and the concretization of that role in the construction of prominent religious buildings. Questions addressed include: How can the concept of the "sacred" be understood in the twenty-first century, if at all? In what contexts is it intelligible? In a pluralist society, in which the spiritual is often experienced individually, how can architecture express communal identity or tradition? How are concepts of the ineffable realized in material form?

Raphael de la Fontaine

THE REPRESENTATION OF A LOST HISTORY: THE GREAT BURIED MENDEL SYNAGOGUE OF BUDA

This paper retraces in detail the steps taken by archeologists to restore the narrative of a once-flourishing Jewish Hungarian community. This community's remarkable integration into the medieval Hungarian elite was manifested by their prominent location within the Castle District of Buda. Following the 1970's accidental, yet extraordinary, discoveries of two distinct Jewish medieval quarters, including numerous Jewish dwellings and several sacred spaces, archeologists faced the challenge of representing these findings. The Great Mendel Synagogue was the ultimate discovery. However, the ruling communist government at the time actively hindered the excavation of the synagogue. As a result, the amazing story of what is arguably the largest medieval synagogue in Europe remains buried under the modern streets and houses of Buda. The current paper engages in, and furthers, the complex reconstruction process in light of recent renewed interest to excavate the buried synagogue. The extensive excavation efforts in the old town of Buda raise challenges inherent in the process of restoration, which demand the determination of an accurate historical narrative. In this paper, I condense comprehensive findings based upon established as well as independent research carried out over the course of the last year. Data includes interviews with local authorities, stepwise analyses of two proposed restoration strategies, as well as drawings and photographs produced while visiting the site.

Eugene Tan

RELIGIOUS PARKS: SACRED SPACE

These raisons d'être of religious parks are too similar to be coincidence. The respective founders were individuals who knew little about craft but personally invested time, money and effort into making gardens and sculptures. These parks were never intended to be private monuments or pleasure gardens, but spaces for everyman. Perhaps it is this devotional and benevolent craft that produces sacred space; in the same way liturgy and religious practice in places of worship make them sacred. To appreciate these parks for what their founders intended, we need to doff the muddying lens of contemporary society, or look past the weeds and rust of abandonment. These parks call us to look beyond what the modern world looks for in 'amusement' and see them as what they were intended to be: sacred space which exists, almost ineffably, somewhere between religious monument, folk art, public garden, and pilgrimage site.

Vittorio Lovato

HIGH-TECH LITURGY: SACRED PIXELS, DIVINE REPLAYS, SPIRITUAL BROWSERS

In an age of digital browsing and personally directed experiences, architecture has been continually pushed aside in favor of the digital screen itself. These applications define not only our imaginary digital identities but also religion itself. Making it easier for people to determine what is the best way to practice, apps integrate themselves into the religious experience by offering substitutes for books, prayer beads, and church buildings; they essentially redefine the typical codified rules that define a given religion. The customization of religion challenges not only the legitimacy of the experience and the practice but also challenges what is being worshipped. The domination of the user and the ability to control the way religion is performed invalidates previous notions of religion and religious architecture, suggesting new ways to design space in this new religious landscape.

THE AUTOBIOGRAPHICAL HOUSE

Kurt W. Forster

Architects and artists have long built dwellings for themselves (and for surrogate clients) as showcases of their art, sites of collecting and teaching, and as retreats from professional life. From Thomas Jefferson to Philip Johnson, from John Soane to Eileen Gray and Frank Gehry, building a house of one's own often harks back to Renaissance models while experimenting with new manifestations of the architect's evolving role. This seminar examines key examples of buildings as well as wide-ranging readings in autobiography.

Leah Abrams

THE ROOM, THE HOUSE AND THE LANDSCAPE: THE AUTOBIOGRAPHICAL TERRITORY OF VIRGINIA WOOLF

The built environment features prominently in Virginia Woolf's work, never as a neutral backdrop but as an active character that has been heavily informed by her personal history and participation in the modernist project to restructure the spaces of private life. Woolf's spatial explorations are evident on three scales, the room, the house and the landscape, and manifest most vividly in her two most autobiographical tracts, A Room of One's Own and To the Lighthouse.

Woolf explores the space of the room in A Room of One's Own, which cleverly combines autobiographical content, fiction and a cultural critique. Woolf does not name the protagonist, either as herself or otherwise, which allows her story to also speak for the collective. The book becomes both an autobiography of the self, and of the everywoman. Though this is can be viewed as an autobiography of an interior life of both a personal and collective nature, it is not merely a psychological exploration—the interior life always has a spatial counterpart. In the end, Woolf is calling for material changes in the organization of domestic and architectural interiors. The act of writing, of authorship is not dependent on gender, knowledge is not dependent on masculinity, but on having a physical, discrete, private space.

The house and landscape both become active forces in To the Lighthouse. The novel's two central women, Mrs. Ramsay, the mother, and Lily, the artist, serve as the most autobiographical characters, standing in for Woolf and her mother. In the novel, as also in life, the two women represent a traditional vs. modern binary.

Ross McClellan

An investigation of the domestic territories occupied by the Bloomsbury Group led to an understanding of Monk's House, Charleston House, and Berwick Church as found objects transformed over the course of their inhabitation. The culminating physical models appear initially as basic typological forms of farmhouses and churches, but opening each reveals the introduction of "significant form" aesthetics to the interior surfaces in a manner similar to that deployed by the Bloomsbury Group. The standard, anonymous shapes that initially existed as nothing more extraordinary than a hollow shell become filled with life, character, and color. The house becomes a canvas, and each brushstroke captures a small bit of personality and writes a small phrase of one's autobiography. The vivid and authored interior is not a work of art, but a trace or memory of life, belief, and character. The models are meant to represent the ideologies and aesthetic philosophies of the Bloomsbury Group: that a thin coat of paint can turn the most standard typological house into a singular and unique autobiographical home.

Peter McInish

OVER THE VOLCANO: LUIS BARRAGAN'S ITINERARIES IN THE LANDSCAPE

In 1945, with the help of a few investors, Barragan acquired 1,200 acres on the southern fringe of Mexico City—roughly adhering to the site of an ancient lava flow, El Pedregal. The land was considered undesirable, despite the inevitable outward growth of the city. Like the paintings of de Chirico, Pedregal was a setting almost devoid of life, but one that had clearly witnessed catastrophe. A windswept and sunbaked terrain of igneous rock and cacti, it was the perfectly hellish landscape in which to intervene. Surveying the land with the painter Gerardo Murillo and the photographer Armando Salas Portugal, Barragan was determined to frame the vast site as an inhospitable wasteland. By orchestrating their drawings and photographs, he would playfully expose the irony of situating a paradise in utter desolation. The development's early marketing materials would run on the disparity between these starkly brutal images and the tagline "el lugar ideal para vivir"—"the ideal place to live."

ART IN ARCHITECTURE

Stanislaus von Moos

Architecture's changing coalitions with the sister arts have been an important factor of its evolution since the Renaissance. Ignoring or actively severing that connection has been one way for functionalism to break away from historicism and to engage in new forms of interactions with the sciences and with social dynamics. As a result, the call for a "Synthesis of the Arts" as promoted by CIAM after World War II is but one theme within a wide spectrum of promiscuity that characterizes the condition of architecture in its relation to painting, sculpture, and other forms of artistic and visual practice ever since. Introductory classes on Le Corbusier, the Smithsons, Venturi and Scott Brown, Koolhaas, Herzog & de Meuron, and other architects examine the role of surrealism, art brut, conceptual art, pop art, or minimalism, and their related philosophies in shaping the ways architects organize, discuss, and promote their work.

Tamrat Gebremichael

TRANSCENDENCE IN THE WORK OF GORDON MATTA-CLARK

In 1976 Gordon Matta-Clark broke into the Institute of Architecture and Urban Studies in New York and shot out the windows of the gallery with an air rifle. This aggressive act would come to define the perception of this young artist's work as reckless and ultimately as anti-architectural. Peter Eisenman likened the stunt to Kristallnacht. Matta-Clark's full body of work and the manner in which he practiced and documented his work, however would suggest that he has a much more sophisticated and paradoxical relationship with architecture. In 1975, a year after Louis Kahn's death, Matta-Clark completed Day's End, where he cut away part of the floor and roof of an abandoned industrial warehouse on a pier in Manhattan. A year before that, Kahn had completed the design for the National Assembly Building in Dhaka, Bangladesh. These two projects offer a striking contrast in motives yet employ a comparable formal operation of placing large holes on walls. In Dhaka, Kahn's design was intended to celebrate national identity and hope towards the future. On the opposite side of the world, Matta-Clark was marking the bygone prowess of New York's industrial era by cutting away the walls of an abandoned warehouse. Where Kahn hopes for the permanence of his edifice in Dhaka, Matta-Clark critically challenges architecture's perceived permanence. In a sense, Kahn and Matta-Clark are starting their project from opposite ends of the timeline. While Kahn is constructing towards an eternal presence, Matta-Clark starts out his project from the building's expiration date.

Nicholas Muraglia

DISTURBING SELF REFLECTIONS

In the age of the "selfie", of social media and NSA surveillance, the notion of the self as a function of being watched is an extremely relevant issue. How do we define our most private, intimate notions of the self in relation to the watchful gaze of the exterior, public Other? How do we see ourselves in private, and how do we see ourselves when we are being watched? How do we construct the self as we watch others? "Self-reflection" is an important term to consider in discussing these questions. Self-reflection carries both the meaning of the literal, optical reflection of the self in the mirror, but also the figurative meaning of reflecting on the nature of the "self". Le Corbusier's Beistegui penthouse and Dan Graham's Alteration to a Suburban House might, at first, appear to be very different projects with different theoretical agendas; the former being a built work from 1930 typically situated within the rubric of Modern Architecture, and the latter operating as a conceptual art piece from the late seventies. One is an architecture for the elite, seemingly closed off and hidden to the city, but open to the sky, while the other is generic, suburban, standard, exhibitionistic and open to the street. Comparing the two projects will hopefully open up more discussion about how the projects situate themselves in the context of the art-architecture complex.

Skender Laurasi

THE CONSTELLATION OF SUBJECTIVITIES IN SIGFRIED GIEDION'S HISTORIOGRAPHY: FROM YOU=ME TO YOU+ME

This paper investigates the relationship between architecture and subjectivity in Sigfried Giedion's historiography, and how this relationship changes from his early (pre-war) to his later (post-war) work. This investigation is bounded by two extrema: Building in France, Building in Iron, Building in Ferroconcrete published in 1928, and Architecture You and Me: The Diary of a Development published [in English] in 1958. This investigation is provoked by the dialogical theme of Architecture You and Me, and the general observation that there is a shift between the latter and his earlier book, Building in France. Starting from this general observation, the paper puts forward the hypothesis that if Giedion's Architecture You and Me suggests a subjectivity constellation of YOU+ME, then his early work in general and Building in France in particular suggests a subjectivity constellation of YOU=ME. In order to investigate this hypothetical shift from YOU=ME to YOU+ME, I define and frame these terms in relation to the principle of construction, and how this principle is in turn played out on several levels in Giedion's historiography: the construction of the book, the construction of architectural object and the construction of subjectivity.

LAUNCH

Keller Easterling

This seminar studies the designer as entrepreneur. Contemporary entrepreneurs usually understand not only how to capitalize a business but also how to play market networks with the viral dissemination of both objects and aesthetic regimes. While the architecture profession has absorbed many of the technologies that markets use in their population thinking, practice is nevertheless structured to support architecture conceived as singular creations. This seminar considers both historical and contemporary moments in architectural and urban design when architects conceived of buildings, building components, or formats as repeatable products—products that, in the aggregate, may have the power to create an alteration to a local or global environment. Each week, the seminar considers the work of two or three architects together with texts that provide critical and theoretical inflection. The final project is a business/design-plan wherein students serve as each other's publicists.

Robert Cannavino & William Sheridan

GMUNI

GMUNI (a term co-opted from Google Bus protesters) is a proposal for a system that better integrates city and regional transportation networks in the San Francisco Bay Area by supplementing MUNI services in the city and re-imagining the commuter train experience to the exurban corporate territories of Silicon Valley. The deal would be structured as a public-private partnership.

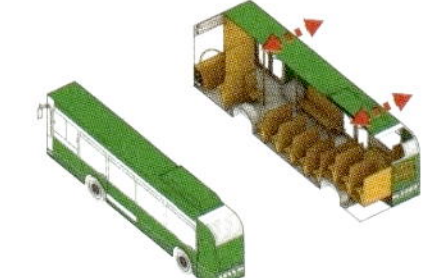

Jonathon Meier, Craig Rosman & Dennis Tseng*

SUPERLET

Here in the United States city centers are losing their character and their affordability by erecting soulless towers housing myriad ultra-expensive apartments and condominiums within shells of mediocrity and awkward floor plans. In response, we propose Superlet, a new type of commodities exchange that will have a significant effect on the way we envision our neighborhoods, our cities, and our skylines. We envision Superlet as a system to facilitate the efficient trading of affordable housing credits amongst developers and small landlords, helping to foster customizable buildings with character, while simultaneously giving landlords incentives to create and upgrade affordable housing units. All the while economic diversity is maintained, and wealth is created for both parties and for the community. Superlet is the invisible tool for shaping the topography of cities and neighborhoods, allowing them to evolve organically, becoming more and more dynamic.

* Yale School of Management '14

Maya Alexander & Zachary Veach

HUBSTORE

How do we tap into the spatial network of the online commerce paradigm while also reinvigorating underutilized urban sprawl? With the HubStore, we see an opportunity to hack this unbridled growth while also capitalizing on shifts in e-commerce. This in turn can produce a new urbanism that is mutually beneficial to corporations, consumers, and property owners.

The new HubStore piggybacks on Amazon's warehouse network but creates a physical storefront that is responsive to a far more dynamic relationship between consumer and supplier. By reintroducing the physical market into these massive existing online markets, we see the opportunity to naturalize our distribution systems by participating in a city-making which crystallizes urban space along preexisting flows, resulting in a thickened web of cities and distribution infrastructure.

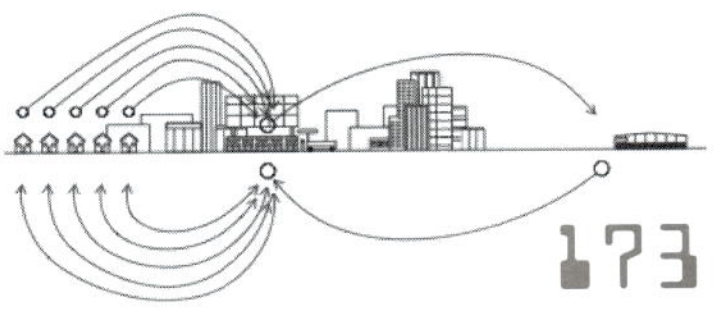

SCHINKEL & THE EUROPEAN CITY

Kurt W. Forster

The Berlin architect Karl Friedrich Schinkel, widely traveled in Europe and in close touch with architects from France to Russia, England, and Italy, helped reshape the city of Berlin by means of numerous inserts and partial expansions, creating new types of public buildings, spaces, and parks. Schinkel's pictorial invention—his panoramas, theaters, and residences—reconfigured the scenario of the city. This seminar attempts to grasp his ideas of topography, landscape, and culture at a time of swift transformation of the European city.

AJ Artemel

SCHINKEL'S SUBURBAN CHURCHES AND BERLIN'S INDUSTRIALIZATION

On February 29th, 1828, Karl Friedrich Schinkel received the contract to design two new, enormous churches—accommodating a congregation size of 2,000 to 3,000 people, far larger than almost all of Berlin's existing churches—for the suburbs growing to the north of the city. In 1830, all work on the project was halted for a period of two years, during which the budget available for the churches shrank even further. When work resumed, in 1832, Friedrich Wilhelm III asked Schinkel to prepare new designs for the churches, and increased the number to be built from two to four. Schinkel faced a difficult design problem in realizing twice the number of buildings with far less money. Construction on St. Elisabethskirche had already begun, so Schinkel had to shrink the plan in mid-construction. He then used this plan for the other three churches: St. Johannis, Nazareth, and St. Paul. Indeed, the differences between the designs of the two phases are so striking that the cause of this difference bears investigation. Why was the design process stopped, and was there more behind the design changes than simple budgetary concerns could account for? These questions are closely linked with events occurring in the city of Berlin during the Vormärz Era, spurred by a transition from a society framed by the ideas of the Enlightenment to a society facing the new pressures of industrialization. The design of the Vorstadtkirchen marks a turning point for Schinkel as well, as he begins to assert a legacy and look forward into the coming age of iron.

Evan Wiskup

Wilhelm was designed in 1829 by Freidrich Schinkel. The Palace is located on the corner where the Unter den Linden and the Pariser Platz meet and is directly across from the Brandenburg Gate. The site for the project has historically been situated in an 'in-between' zone in Berlin. Looking at the 1688 map of Berlin, it is possible to discern what would have been relatively newly formed Unter den Linden and the future location of the Brandenburg gate. The Pariser Platz and the Spree River are still taking shape during 1688 with the Spree not yet modified to where it would be during Schinkel's time. The future site for the Palace for the Prince in the 1688 map is at a transitional point between the Tiergarten and the Unteden Linden. With the Brandenburg Gate not yet built at the time the 1688 map was drawn, the site for the palace plays the significant role as the entrance into the fortified area of Berlin, acting as a critical transition from the wild and uncontrolled natural world outside of the walls of the city into the manicured urban landscape beginning with the Unter den Linden. If it were placed in the 1688 map the corner of the site for the Palace would serve as a monumental device calling attention to and acting as a gate or threshold to Berlin.

William Sheridan

SCHINKEL, THE ARCHITECTURAL IMAGE, & DISJUNCTIVE IMMERSION

One might assume that Schinkel is susceptible to Michael Fried's complaints regarding theatricality in art and image-making. He was, after all, of an inherently theatrical disposition and dramaturgical values and scenographic devices suffuse his oeuvre. However, Schinkel challenges the macho absorption/theatricality dialectic of Fried who criticized the 'theatrical' aspects of painting for diminishing the objecthood of the image by tacitly relying on a beholder. Schinkel's image-making is predicated on a sort of theatrical illusion involving an act of dislocation that opens up a gap between image and viewer. He actually applies this conception of the image as a device for aesthetic displacement and imaginative transport to the theater through his stage designs, drawing up a radically new contract with theatrical audiences regarding their suspension of disbelief.
Schinkel's new notion of theatrical illusion is static and highly composed; its intention is to produce a dislocating atmospheric environment by way of near-panoramic images. Crucially, his conception of theatrical illusion depends on the recognition of image as image, as autonomous object.

ARCHITECTURE & CONTEMPORARY LABOR

Peggy Deamer

This seminar examines both the practical and theoretical parameters that affect architectural labor today. On the theoretical side, texts are examined related to material/immaterial labor, the creative class, the performance of craft in the digital age, and the labor distinction between craft and design in architecture. On the practical side, students are asked to make surveys of architectural firms with regard to the following issues: Who does what work in the hierarchy of the office? What in this work is considered to have craft and/or design input? Who are considered to be designers? What work is given to consultants? What is outsourced and why? How is compensation determined for staff and consultants, and is it in relation to design and/or technical skills? Who manages the workflow? Is there a BIM manager, and what is that person's background?

Jean Chen

WAGE VALUE OF ARCHITECTURE

With society constantly reciting the adage "Do what you love and love what you do," the idea of "labor" is often an unpleasant one to associate with one's career. Yet it is precisely because people nowadays are free to pursue their love and passion instead of following a familial career path that wage becomes especially important in a career like architecture that has previously been considered a gentleman's profession and not a breadwinning career. Indeed, if architecture is to be an available career choice to all those with talent and commitment, and not just the lucky few with means to support this "passion," one must learn to regard architecture as "labor" and "work," and consider its values and wage situations. This paper begins with writings by John Mill and Adam Smith to understand "labor" and its relationship to wage. Through these, we come to the realization that wage isn't just a number we assign for people to make money, but is inextricably tied to population ratio, demand, and valuation of work and labor. With increasing focus on mental and creative labor, the diminishing presence of physical labor raises difficulties in determining value of labor by physical hours and physical products.

Dov Feinmesser

LABOR TIME – WORK TIME

In industries where the volume of production does matter, time is very carefully managed. Research is continually done alongside improvements in the facilities and machinery to constantly measure how much product a given individual can, and should produce within the agreed upon measure of time. With creative ventures however, this is not typically possible. The subjectivity of the product's value makes the time invested in its production beyond simple objective measure. The value of the product is therefore measured in time by the worker, and not the industry. A painter, outside the influence of market, evaluates his work not on the cost of the paint or canvas, but on the time it took to acquire the skill to master the technique and produce a painting. The same could be said for a sculptor or a graphic designer. The loss of distinction, however, between work-time and non-work-time, coupled with the fact that architects desire to consider themselves within the fold of creative product deliverers, has greatly diminished their ability to valorize architectural work.

Meghan McAllister

RETHINKING ARCHITECTURAL AUTHORSHIP AND ITS DISCONTENTS

In 1989, Denise Scott Brown wrote an essay criticizing the sexism inherent to the star-system of the architectural profession. Twenty-five years later, there are more female architects, but the gender gap is still significant for those registered with the AIA. Scott Brown made it clear how the concept of co-authorship was difficult for critics and clients to understand, and this was often the basis for her role being overlooked. The idea of the "master-creator" is significant to society's perceived value of architecture as well as to architectural pedagogy.
This paper investigates how a new type of authorship might be defined for architecture. I analyze the history of authorship within the profession, as well as philosophical critiques of authorship, focusing on texts by Barthes and Foucault. Additionally, I explore how in the post-war era, new forms of practice have attempted to address issues of authorship. I ultimately argue that the product of the architect should be reconceived as not a singular object, but rather as an artistic service-based process that is at once physical, social and temporal.

MODERNIST HISTORIOGRAPHY

Stanislaus von Moos

This reading seminar proposes a close-up examination of some key texts of modernist historiography. The seminar explores the way in which the method of history writing interacts with the practice of contemporary architecture and the nature of the media used in its promotion. The following questions are addressed: In what way has Henry-Russell Hitchcock's view of modernism been shaped by his understanding of Henry Hobson Richardson and/or Frank Lloyd Wright? In what way does Giedion's view of modernism relate to Le Corbusier? What was Kahn's and Venturi's relevance for the critical positions developed by Vincent Scully? In what way, if at all, have those critic/historians retroactively influenced the course of architecture?

Theodossios Issaias

POLITICS OF THE PRIMORDIAL

The warm afternoon of February 1st, 1954, Jawaharlal Nehru (Prime Minister of India) and Jacqueline Tyrwhitt ('U.N. technical assistance expert', CIAM secretary and Giedion's close collaborator) visit a replica of Mahatma Gandhi's hut in New Delhi.[1] The 'primitive building' is part of a demonstration village for low-cost housing constructed by the Indian government at the idyllic location adjacent to Purana Qila, Delhi's fifteenth-century fortress. The village of eighty homes is the main feature of the International Exhibition which was scheduled to coincide with the United Nations Regional Seminar on Housing and Community Improvement. The four week seminar, organized by Tyrwhitt, is attended by international modern architects, CIAM delegates, government officials and technical experts from South East Asia (Burma, Ceylon, the Fiji Islands, Hong Kong, India, Iran, Iraq, Japan, Laos, Pakistan, Puerto Rico, Singapore, Thailand, and Vietnam).[2] Additionally, the UN sends participants and representatives from Afghanistan, Australia, France, Greece, India, Israel, the Netherlands, the UK, the USA, and Yugoslavia. The seminar includes lectures, design workshops, educational trips and screenings of film-documentaries that provide general knowledge on local building materials and construction methods. In this context, before their very eyes the frames of the movie How to Build an Igloo start rolling.[3] The movie captures the ingenious building process of temporary dwellings that Eskimos of the Arctic Circle developed over centuries.
What is the affinity between the replica of Gandhi's hut, the Igloo at the Arctic Circle, the international crowd of policy makers, and the CIAM delegates? How could those worlds be reconciled?
During the first decades after World War II the architecture discipline retracted to the beginnings of mankind. Faced with the devastations of WWII and its aftermaths, historians revisited with a new impetus the prehistoric times and were influenced by the work of contemporaneous anthropologists and archeologists. Equally, the cold war geopolitical context and the efforts to negotiate the post-colonial demands of nation-states played an integral role in this paradigm shift.
The search for a universal language of cooperation and global peace as promoted by the international institutions and transnational organization (i.e. UN, UNESCO, World Bank) found it's nesting ground in the primordial existence. Fossils, rock formations, ancient settlements, architecture without architects and the significance given to the so-called 'primitive' creativity aimed to mediate the obvious rupture between the pre-war aspirations and the post-war ruins. Historians, such as Sigfried Giedion, would instrumentalize the primordial to reaffirm the modern project, although through the construction of a different narrative.[4] The paper 'Politics of the Primordial' examines this paradigm shift within its historical causality and political intentions; a shift that challenged the precarious dipoles of modernity and tradition, universality and locality, Western-Eurocentric hegemonic representations and the post-colonial era.

1 United Nations, "United Nations Seminar on Housing and Community Improvement," February 1, 1954, http://www.unmultimedia.org/s/photo/detail/337/0337730.html
2 Jaqueline Tyrwhitt, "Mary Jaqueline Tyrwhitt in Memoriam. Issue," Ekistics 52, no. 314 (January 1978): 396–558.
3 M. Ijlal (Muhammad Ijlal) Muzaffar, "The Periphery within : Modern Architecture and the Making of the Third World" (Thesis, Massachusetts Institute of Technology, 2007), 37.
4 Indicative are: The Commission on Aesthetics—Attitude Toward Primitive Civilizations at CIAM 9, Aix-en-Province, 1953 as well as Giedion's 1957 Mellon lectures on Constancy and Change in Early Art and Architecture and the publication of the first volume of The Eternal Present in 1962.

PEDAGOGY & PLACE

Robert A.M. Stern

In preparation for the celebration of the School's centenary in 2015–2016, this research seminar proposes to examine, in detail, key instances where architecture school buildings and architecture pedagogies manifest a close reciprocity. Where appropriate, the implicit reciprocities between pedagogy and practice will also be considered. The seminar will be the basis of the Spring 2016 exhibition, Pedagogy and Place: Celebrating 100 Years of Architectural Education at Yale. Along with lectures by the instructor documenting the story of architectural education at Yale, there will be roundtable discussions with faculty and individual presentations by students devoted to the analysis of other examples of instances where architecture school buildings and pedagogies were conceived as a unity. Building upon class presentations and faculty workshops, students will pursue individual research on specific buildings/pedagogies with the idea of documenting and illustrating their interrelationships. All in all, the intention is to identify and interpret how architecture facilities foster — or discourage— collaboration within the discipline and the influence of the studio model on other disciplines. Questions that will be asked include the following: How does the architecture school reflect the pedagogy of the larger university? How do architecture schools shape studio culture and student life? How have pedagogies responded to social and political changes?

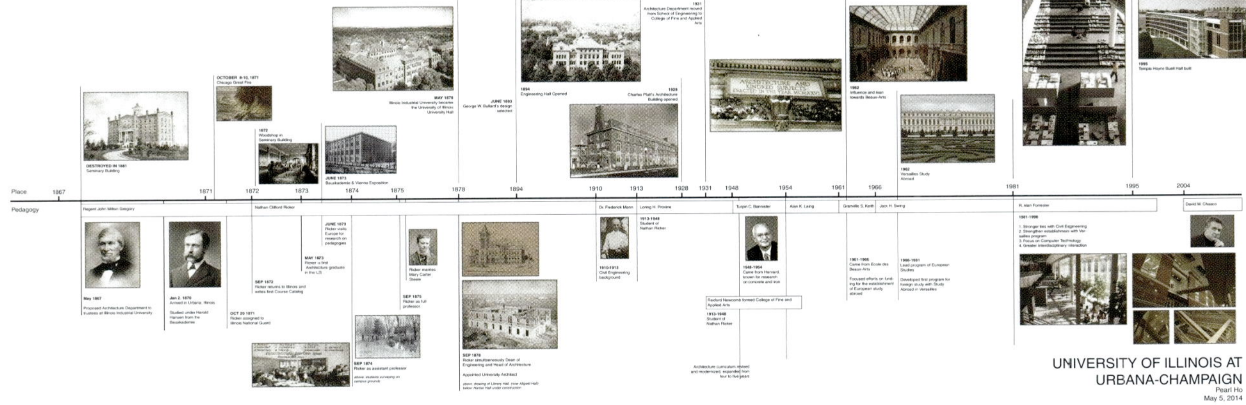

Pearl Ho

UNIVERSITY OF ILLINOIS AT URBANA-CHAMPAIGN

The case study of pedagogy at the University of Illinois at Urbana-Champagne revealed a distinctly parallel relationship between the life of Nathan Clifford Ricker and the school's journey of development. Ricker was the first Architecture school graduate in the United States, and wrote the very foundation courses that Illinois eventually built their program upon. Since Ricker's professorship, three different buildings housed the School of Architecture. The study traces the translation of academic spaces chronologically, and ultimately demonstrates the alignment between pedagogical shifts and each new building.

Matthew Rauch

THE UNIVERSITY OF MINNESOTA SCHOOL OF ARCHITECTURE

The essence of natural beauty lies in its generative purity—the process of formation is untouched, uninterrupted by humans, who can only engage in artful, sectional revelation after the fact. I see great beauty in the section of geographical stratification—in layers and layers of time built upon one another sheared and penetrated by subliminal force at an enormous scale. Instead of replicating the phenomenon itself, I elected to adopt the process in order to control the purity of its formation, and at the same time, establish an agenda to generate iterations that can be endlessly reproduced and further transformed. The final production is a juxtaposition of layered porosity that can either perform as an architectural surface or an architectural volume.

CITYMAKING ON THE ARABIAN PENINSULA

Todd Reisz

From eighth-century Baghdad to twenty-first-century Masdar, the Middle East has been approached, from within and without, as a susceptible terrain for creating cities. This seminar considers the histories and mythologies of city-making on the Arabian Peninsula, focusing on urban planning since the early twentieth century. Modern city-making is discussed as a globally induced building boom, delivered by figures like American oil men in Saudi Arabia and Sir Norman Foster in Abu Dhabi. A regional survey includes an inspection of Gulf cities (Abu Dhabi, Aramco company towns, Doha, Dubai, Jubail, Kuwait, and Riyadh) and their earliest attempts at modern urbanization. Arising themes and particularities are discussed. Historical context, mostly in the first half of the term, provides students the means to analyze forces and ideologies shaping the newest cities and mega-projects in the region and beyond. The course is not so much a geographical study as an investigation of the pervasive contemporary forces in urbanism and globalization. Whenever possible, the week's discussions focus on a particular Gulf city as the exemplification of chosen themes. Beyond just sociology and urbanism, reading and discussion materials include primary historical documents and historical and contemporary journalism.

Swarnabh Ghosh

RAK POST URBANISM

Ras Al Khaimah (RAK) occupies the position of a proud underdog in the United Arab Emirates. With no significant oil reserves, its economy has never been reliant on hydrocarbons, growing instead, by diversifying into infrastructure, logistics and manufacturing. This two-part project investigates the growth of RAK and the financial instruments employed by the emirate to position itself as a rising economic player in the region with affirmation from a number of global investors and credit rating agencies. More importantly, RAK's hesitation to go down the path of high-density oil urbanism has unlocked its potential as a powerful alternative to the model of growth adopted by its neighbors. Another aspect that has historically set RAK apart from its neighbors is its unique geology, landscape and soil quality. With steady runoff from the Hagar Mountains in the North, RAK has the highest percentage of arable soil in the UAE. This is reaffirmed by its rich history of small-scale agricultural production that continues to thrive in the form of a small but significant agricultural sector that is mostly informal and incremental. The second part of this project proposes a vision for Ras Al Khaimah—'RAK 2030', which leverages its nascent 'post-urban' form of growth to propose a horizontal, decentralized model of habitation supported by an economy structured around desalination and agriculture. Instead of trying to 'urbanize' in a conventional sense, RAK 2030 seeks to strengthen the emirate's traditional dispersed settlements—its villages and its farms—with the aim to develop a resource and knowledge economy based on innovation in infrastructure and agricultural practices for arid environments.

AJ Artemel

REBUILDING ABADAN

Abadan, Iran, has been both an extremely prosperous city and an extremely destitute one since the British discovery of petroleum nearby in 1908. From then through the 1970s, Abadan was a company town, site of the headquarters of the Anglo-Iranian Oil Company which later split into BP and the National Iranian Oil Company. During this time, the refinery grew to occupy the entire center of town, surrounded by dense areas of housing for Iranian workers, and sprawling garden suburbs for British managers and other international professionals. And despite being excluded from many of the amenities enjoyed by these international workers, Iranians flocked to Abadan to partake in its prosperity. Soon, though, Abadan became one of Iran's poorer cities. From 1980-1988, the city was shelled to ruin during the Iran-Iraq War; the refinery, and much of the city's housing, was destroyed, and the population fell from a high of almost 400,000 inhabitants to just 64. Today, the city has still not recovered, the profits from its refinery, still operating at only 60% of its capacity, being used to subsidize the rest of the Iranian economy rather than for rebuilding.
In many ways, Abadan was the first 'oil city' of the Persian Gulf, having served as a base for oil extraction for almost 20 years before ARAMCO started drilling in Saudi Arabia. But Abadan has now been far surpassed by former competitors around the Gulf. The proposal for this class thus investigated ways in which to first restore Abadan to its former level of development, and then to begin attracting new prosperity.

Anne Householder

GATEWAY TO THE GULF: THE CRITICAL CONNECTION BETWEEN DJIBOUTI AND YEMEN

Since the Global Food Crisis in 2008, the Gulf States have been heavily investing in farmland overseas. Today, imports in the Gulf account for eighty to ninety percent of food production. Thus, the emirate is investing in 'Breadbasket Africa' for agriculture production and to position itself as a gateway for investment flows and trade in the southern hemisphere.
On the other hand, Africa is faced with an ever increasing population. Africa hopes that relations with the Gulf will bring them the expertise and finances to support the young generation. By one account, Africa requires thirty billion dollars a year to meet investment requirements in the fields of energy and power.
A network of ports on the Red Sea, Arabian Sea, and Persian Gulf linked through a regional railway and strategically located silos would provide both governments with needed supplies and mutual exchange. The proximity between Djibouti and Yemen lends itself to be the ideal connection and center of trade. Should infrastructure bridge the borders as planned, a series of new 'breadbasket cities' would be organized to efficiently export goods while also catering to a large population of workers and tourists.

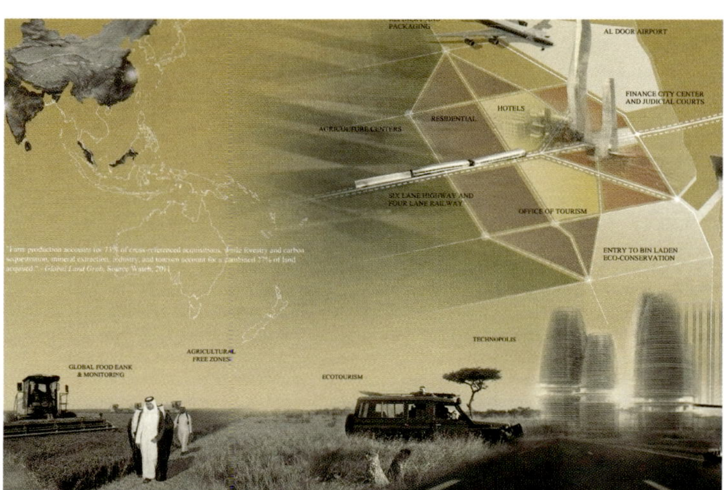

INTERMEDIATE PLANNING & DESIGN

Alexander Garvin

This seminar examines the interaction of property development and planning with local market conditions, financing alternatives, government policy, and the political context at the community level. During the first part of the term, students learn how to analyze a specific neighborhood (in New York City) by using fundamental planning techniques and examining national trends within that neighborhood. Topics include housing, retail, and office development; zoning; historic preservation; transportation; business improvement districts; and building reuse and rehabilitation. In the second part of the term students prepare recommendations for the neighborhood that will meet the conflicting interests of financial institutions, real estate developers, civic organizations, community groups, public officials, and a wide variety of participants in the planning and development process. The end product is a printed book presenting the results of their work.

Brian Hong[1]
Sungwoo Choi
Kirk Henderson
Amir Karimpour
Read Langworthy
Kate Lisi
Christian Mueller
Lauren Raab
Joseph Yu
Starling Childs[2]
James Santana[2]
Michael Harvey[3]

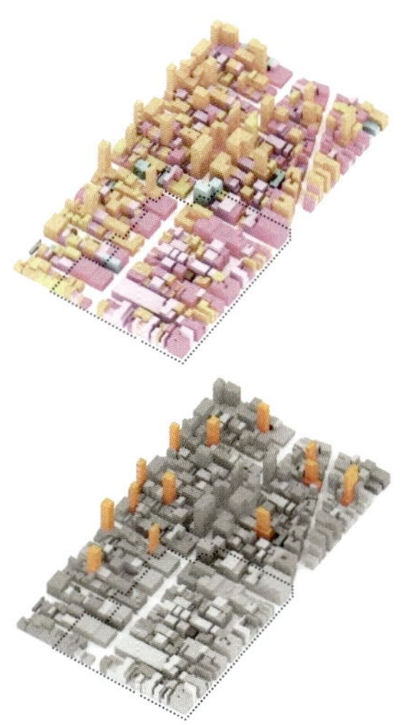

CITYMAKING AT THE EDGE OF EVERYWHERE
The central question of this booklet asks not how to define a "new" Manhattan. Instead, each proposal seeks strategies for re-inhabiting this portion of vital city fabric, and to find a balance between the existing physical city, Manhattan's historic legacy, new growth, and a revitalized public realm. Nestled between well-established regions of the city such as Chelsea and 34th Street, our area of study defies a singular definition or characteristic. Much of the streetscape is governed by its immediate commercial activity, though the recent revamping of Broadway suggests a more pedestrian-oriented approach may be desirable. Diversity has long been the area's strength. New development opportunities, however, herald a period of growth and change. The area's vintage building stock offers many conversion opportunities to new offices and residences. The dense transportation infrastructure, new hotels, and increasingly high-end entertainment outlets suggest the area is primed for a fashionable, upscale class of residents and consumers. As is ever the case, moneyed interests will inherently come into conflict with ideals of historic preservation, neighborhood character, and collective quality of life.

1 Teaching Fellow
2 Yale School of Forestry '14
3 Yale School of Drama '14

BUILT ENVIRONMENTS AND THE POLITICS OF PLACE

Dolores Hayden

Call it the built environment, the vernacular, everyday architecture, or the cultural landscape, the material world of built and natural places is intricately bound up with social and political life. This research seminar explores research methods and sources for writing the history of the built environment, including maps, aerial and ground photographs, planning documents, landscape analysis, and GIS. It includes readings from history, geography, anthropology, and architecture as well as readings on narrative and graphic strategies for representing spaces and places. Students present papers. Sections from longer theses or dissertations in progress are welcome.

Katherine Stege

THE MATERIAL LIFESPAN OF SEATTLE'S LARGEST HOOVERVILLE
One cannot sketch economic calamity, paint social welfare policy, or photograph a man's sense of independence. Mere forms of visual representation fall flat when faced with the tangled push and pull of such factors, lacking the inherent dimensionality needed to illustrate economic, political, or cultural dynamics. Informal settlements, such as Seattle's depression-era Hooverville, however, link the physical to the conceptual through the rise and fall of the built environment. Instigated by the drastic economic downturn following the stock market crash of 1929, propelled by failed political and social systems, and reinforced by cultural necessity, the first individual shacks of Hooverville rose out of the tide flats in 1931. In its ten-year lifespan, the rise and fall of Hooverville's material landscape visualized the tangled interactions between positive and negative economic, political, and cultural forces of the time. As illustrated by the physicality of Hooverville's material existence, the complex interplay of economic, cultural, and political forces constructed the development, maintenance, and eventual destruction of Seattle's largest informal settlement.

Eric Peterson

FROM URBAN RENEWAL TO URBAN ENTREPRENEURIALISM: THE NEW YORK STATE URBAN DEVELOPMENT CORPORATION, THE MUNICIPAL BOND MARKET, AND PLANNING FOR BATTERY PARK CITY
The creation of Battery Park City played a key role in the transformation of Lower Manhattan from the historical center of the city's maritime and industrial economy to a postindustrial hub of finance and corporate headquarters. Beginning in the late 1960s and evolving dramatically until their realization in the early 1990s, plans for the neighborhood suggest how its development helped reconfigure municipal government to deal with the challenges and new realities of this new age of the city's history. Officials originally proposed a massive megastructure, which folded subsidized housing (including low- and middle-income housing), commercial office space, and public community and health centers into a single structure built atop landfill created by the construction of the adjacent World Trade Center. The project was conceived during a high point of postwar liberalism in planning, when public officials continued to emphasize large-scale infrastructure building to address myriad crises, from industrial decline to a shortage of affordable housing.
In 1979 a new plan for Battery Park City, heralded under the direction of the quasi-public authority the Urban Development Corporation, or UDC, was formulated around rescuing investment in the project's bonds, which were in jeopardy of default. This new plan abandoned the megastructural design in favor of a New Urbanist schema that emphasized a piecemeal development of the site.
Divested of its original social aims, Battery Park City's transformed goals realigned public development around the market mechanisms that had enabled its early development through municipal bonds. Born amid contested debates over the shape and means of planning for public development during a transformational period in the city's history, Battery Park City's development through private finance and quasi-public authorities had the effect of foreclosing these debates in ways that have had lasting implications for how development happens in the contemporary city.

Chessin Gertler

FALL RIVER, MA
Fundamental to the challenge of how to incorporate the presence of the river into the urban fabric of the city of Fall River is the complex residual relationship between the two entities created by the existence of the mills. Functionally, the mills operated by means of the river's water power, so the associative connotation of the mill with the river was strong. Symbolically, the presence of the river also manifested itself in the wealth that the mills created.
There exists, however, a striking binary between the urban face of the mills' front with its symbolic gesture to the river's generative capacity and the urban back, where the river's relationship to the mill was exclusively pragmatic. While the backend waste and its hidden disorder of the mill typology in many ways does not differentiate it from any other built typology with a service end, the shared space of the harnessing of the building's power source, its tangible intervention on an environment, and its avenue of waste disposal, creates a dialectic as to the multivalent nature of this environmental intervention. Through the simultaneous centrality to its population's economic sustenance and its relegation to concealment by the architectural forms which subtly masked the reality of its presence, the social relationship with the Quequechan River found itself increasingly marginalized and unhealthy through Fall River's periods of urban expansion.

URBAN RESEARCH & REPRESENTATION

Elihu Rubin

Every day, architects and urban designers make proposals that shape the public and private realms of the city. This seminar sets out to contextualize the social and political ramifications of these interventions; to intensify the designer's tool kit of deep, sociohistorical research of site and place; and to cultivate a reflexive practice that considers seriously the social responsibilities of both the architect and the urban researcher. In the classroom, and in the field, this seminar introduces a diverse set of methods for studying the urban environment, from the archival and visual to the observational and ethnographic.

Mun Hee Lee & Tyler Pertman

A CROWN STREET STATE OF MIND

The research and representation here serves to explore the ideas of mood and urban perception. Urban research, when constrained to the senses, retains a low degree of statistical significance. How do we turn the derived into data? How can we understand words like "romantic", "busy", "heartwarming" and "beautiful" in quantifiable terms? Our research aimed to blur the distinctions between anecdotal evidence and empirical evidence by surveying a random sample of 30 people on Crown Street. These individuals were asked to describe their current state of feeling in one descriptive term followed by their impression of the street in another descriptive term. These two terms were then charted and graphed in a number of different ways to allow for a new way of reading the urban environment to develop.

J.T. Keeley & Amy Su

CROWN STREET NIGHTS

In this video we explored the qualities and personalities of Crown Street by night. As a major restaurant, club and bar hub in New Haven, Crown Street is host to a vibrant set of characters who venture out even in the most bitter winter weather to imbibe, eat and dance. We focused on the experience of the bouncers who man the doors at Crown Streets most popular hot spots. As active filters between the public and private, they have a unique vantage point from which they can observe Crown Street. By asking them about their experiences, we were able to compile a personal analysis of the street as well as a brief history of club life on Crown.

Sarah Smith

CROWN STREET COGNITIVE MAPPING EXERCISE
INTERACTIVE CROWN STREET

With Crown Street's close proximity to the Yale Campus and one of Yale's commercial avenues, Chapel Street, I wanted to examine how the Yale community saw and experienced the street and how we, as a group and as individuals, recall the landmarks, the scale, the geography, and the sequence of places we visit and know in our daily lives. The following prompt was given to a group of people:"Please take five minutes, and draw Crown Street from memory. This is a cognitive map, so please draw in a map view primarily, but if it helps to visualize things in other perspectives, do not hesitate to draw what is in your head. Please attempt to fill the page as best you can do not use any kind of reference." Twelve of the participants' contributions were compiled to create a palimpsest of cognitive map.

HISTORY OF BRITISH LANDSCAPE ARCHITECTURE

Bryan Fuermann

This seminar examines the history of landscape architecture and of the idea of nature in Britain from 1600 to 1900. Topics of discussion include Italian and French influences on the seventeenth-century British garden; the Palladian country house and British agricultural landscape; Capability Brown's landscape parks as national landscape style; garden theories of the picturesque and of the sublime; Romanticism and the psychology of nature; the creation of the public park system; arts and crafts landscape design; and the beginnings of landscape modernism. Comparisons of historical material with contemporary landscape design are emphasized throughout the term. The collection of the Yale Center for British Art is used for primary visual material, and a trip to England over spring break, partially funded by the School, allows students to visit firsthand the landscape parks studied in this seminar.

Alice Tai

A British Landscape Primer is a visual lexicon that uses annotated hand-sketched vignettes to render key elements of British landscape design in the seventeenth and eighteenth centuries accessible to a general audience.

Christian Mueller

This catalogue creates an unconventional narrative by linking two brief epochs in design not usually considered in relation. Bookending the 18th century, the short-lived English Baroque (1699-1726) and French Enlightenment Rationalism (1773–1799) explored remarkably similar themes of geometric primaries, austere expression, and idiosyncratic form. Without seeking to demonstrate influence or awareness of precedent, this catalogue investigates the shared formal concerns of the two movements, primarily through the lens of landscape structures – gatehouses, monuments, bridges, and follies.

Constance Vale

TYPOLOGY OF MOUNDS

Historically, earthen mounds have been created for a range of functions, beginning with burial mounds and military fortifications, and later employed in the spatial organization of gardens, and the shaping of earth art and public space. The four primary formal categories this matrix investigates are object based primitive geometry, object based complex geometry, field based primitive geometry, and field based complex geometry.

Thomas Day

STOWE: A GUIDE BOOK TO THE LANDSCAPE AND GARDENS OF THE HONORABLE VISCOUNT COBHAM

My work uses the proliferation of monuments in the gardens of Stowe as a point of reference within the tradition of guidebook history. Through juxtaposition, re-siting, reframing, and other compositional or conceptual devices the project is a way to re-view Stowe via the lens of contemporary art and sculpture.

INDEPENDENT STUDIES

Brandon Hall

ON BIGNESS: THE AIRPORT AS THE URBAN INTERSTICE

ADVISOR
Keller Easterling

The last decade has been marked by a plethora of infrastructure investments into the airport. While the tragic events of 9/11/2001 marked a critical moment in the history of the United States, it also arguably reinforced the use of the airplane as both an image and weapon of modernity. What we have come to understand as the airport has taken on a far more immersive experience, yet the growing itinerancy of the population has led to the explosion of air travel globally. This has led to a different kind of architecture which prefaces the projection; build as big as you can. What has emerged is an architecture which is massive and powerful, yet demonstrates the hegemony of protocols rather than any real ingenuity.
What is put forth in this research project is not an overarching solution, but rather an agglomeration of research and ideas about what the airport is and what it will become. The attempt is made to both connect to the airport's resiliency and also its currency. At this pivotal point in which the airport has become difficult to describe, and even more difficult to draw, propositions towards its decoding must be made in order to recognize the airport not only as an agglomeration of protocols, but as a productive form of urbanism, in which politics, economics, culture, and infrastructure are all present, and the ability to intervene may once again be realized.

CHECK-IN	SECURITY	IMMIGRATION	LOUNGE	BOARDING	PLANE
PREMIUM STATUS ECONOMY	STATUS PRE-SCREENED STANDARD	CITIZEN VISITOR	LOUNGE ACCESS NO ACCESS	FIRST CLASS BUSINESS CLASS EXECUTIVE PLATINUM PLATINUM PRIORITY ACCESS GROUP 1 GROUP 2 GROUP 3 GROUP 4 GROUP 5 GROUP 6	FIRST BUSINESS ECONOMY

Swarnabh Ghosh

DELHI MUMBAI INDUSTRIAL CORRIDOR

ADVISOR
Keller Easterling

When (and if) it is completed, the Delhi Mumbai Industrial Corridor will be the largest and most expensive infrastructure project ever undertaken on the Indian subcontinent. Stretching more than 1480 kilometers between New Delhi and Mumbai, the DMIC, termed a 'mega-project' in infrastructural parlance, is projected to cost over 100 billion dollars.
The DMIC comes cloaked in possibilities and aspirations, which not only appear manifold, but in doing so, transcend political, financial and economic ideologies with alarming ease. This project attempts to create a visual cartography of the DMIC—its physical characteristics as well as the variegated relationships between the numerous actors involved in its conception and execution. Perhaps the most challenging aspect of trying to unpack the DMIC is its refusal to present itself as a singular entity despite the deceptively straightforward 'pyramid' of players that are responsible for its delivery. In fact, it is this 'looseness' which lends the DMIC a specter-like quality, intermittently present in mainstream media and drawing room conversations, but never concrete and rarely instantiated. It is also a great example of a project where a study of facts, numbers, statistics and projections are increasingly futile as they are constantly shifting. Perhaps, this, if anything is its one recognizable quality – a small but steady reformulation of its scope, extent and objectives, brought about by myriad financial, political and economic considerations.

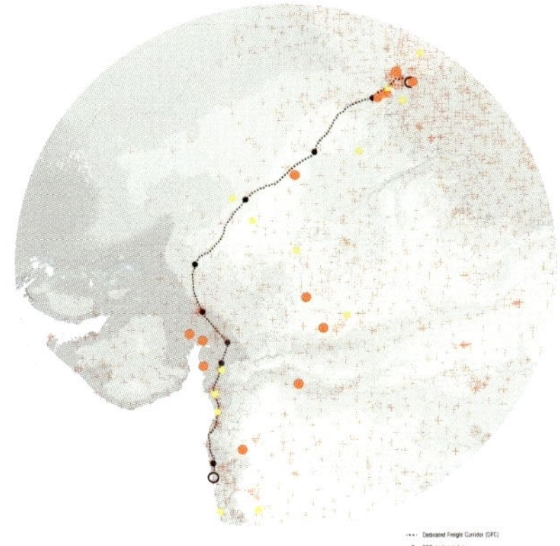

Mahdi Sabbagh

BEDOUIN LANDSCAPES IN COLONIAL EXPLORATION: CHARACTERIZATION OF BEDOUIN SPACES IN LATE 19TH–EARLY 20TH CENTURY BRITISH TRAVEL IN PALESTINE

ADVISOR
Todd Reisz

This paper argues that through exploration, travel and surveying in Palestine, British explorers imagined and invented a Bedouin landscape. This is not to say that there were no Bedouin landscapes, but the British imagination formulated a narrative on Bedouins that delineated a cultural binary and tribal political boundary that did not previously exist.
I use the work of travelers, surveyors and colonists who were interested in the climate, landscape, architecture, societies and customs of Palestine, in order to extract their views and perspectives on the Bedouin population. Between the late 1800s and 1946 British travelers and explorers produced an incredible amount of texts and visual documentation, including maps, textual description, photography and eventually aerial photography. In this research I study the travel texts of Claude Reignier Conder, Ellsworth Huntington, Reverend George Robinson Lees and Gertrude Bell. Here, whether the travelers had drawn accurate illustrations is irrelevant. Their illustrations were presented as a newly re-discovered world. The Bedouin populations were rarely the main focus of such texts, occupying the fringes of the accounts, especially through the Beersheba area and on the peripheries of major cities such as Jerusalem and Hebron. Nevertheless, explorers visited Bedouin communities, studied them and were often hosted by them. Through the close reading of such texts, it became apparent that there was a distortion of space and time through language, a deliberate literary tactic used to describe Bedouin cultural landscapes. The accumulation of this cultural narrative, I argue, is fundamental in understanding the politics and policies of the British Mandate. The eventual establishment of the British Mandate sees with it a rapid sedentarization of Bedouin communities, especially in the Galilee where they were better documented than the Bedouins of the Beersheba district. 11 Sedentarization of Bedouin communities became a systemic policy under the British Mandate and introduced the reality of new sedentary Bedouin communities: a paradox that redefined the very definition of the term "Bedouin" in the early 20th century.

EVENTS & PUBLICATIONS

FALL/
SPRING

AUGUST 29, 2013
E.P Bass Distinguished Visiting Fellow

John Spence
Five Star Hippie

I am a university dropout, the least educated person in the room. I am not a developer and I am not a really a hotelier. I am an entertainer—I always wanted to be an entertainer—and a salesman, and we view our job as entertaining clients. We don't view ourselves as in the lodging business. We think when people come to stay in a resort they need to be entertained from the time they arrive to the time they leave.

One thing I am very proud of is that we have zero debt: I have never borrowed a penny from anyone, either personally or in business. I was at a conference recently and almost got thrown out when an arrogant developer said he had done a billion dollars in sales and raised some two billion dollars in debt, and I asked, "Why is that so good?" So we believe in not having debt.

What do we do? We pretty much have three stages of business. Number one, we are a developer and a property sales company. We acquire land or resorts in prime locations, usually good land to be ahead of the game because you cannot compete with the megacompanies, and we lock it away to master plan or renovate and improve it—but whatever we do we throw our magic fairy dust on it and make it into a product that is better than the one we acquired. We then sell the units to individual clients. So our goal is find a good land or resort, make it sexier, and then sell it.

Stage two is where we work as a hotel and/or resort operator. We lease the properties back in some form, manage the resort like any hotelier, and build relevant on-site amenities such as restaurants, bars, and spas. In stage three we are an ancillary and brand-related service provider. We finance and facilitate sales through our own finance company, operate third-party beach clubs and spas, and own concierge services and holiday clubs. We are vertically integrated and laterally diversified.

What we are doing now is picking up assets in Europe, renovating them, and marketing them back to the Asians, who saw the Sound of Music and spent their youth dreaming about going to the Alps and the Scottish Highlands.

SEPTEMBER 12, 2013
Brendan Gill Lecture

Sylvia Lavin
Architecture That Is Near and Architecture That Is Far

The 1970s were really at the cusp, the breaking point between the past and the present, a moment in which we thought we knew. It is a period that many of the people in this room lived through and know in a certain way, but it is also passing into a historical frame, which means we have to understand it in a different way.

There was a lot of traffic between Yale and Los Angeles back then, lots of characters going back and forth. We have to understand that it was not just people like Peter Cook and Craig Hodgetts that were moving back and forth across the country, but architecture itself was being mobilized and uprooted from a relationship to place through the development of publications.

All of this moving around not only mobilized architects and architecture but also significantly transformed what you might think of as the devices of design. It was no longer pencils and models... but automobiles, helicopters, and cameras. Those tools became part of the standard repertoire of architectural equipment, just as today you would not be able to do your site documentation without an iPhone. When you think about these systems of mobilization, you can understand the relationship between art and architecture, and the different kinds of perspectives: views from above, thinking about the ground plan in a different way, really transforming the discipline from within.

Materials were being activated and transformed. ... There is probably no more famous material in Los Angeles than the stud. We think of Los Angeles as the city of studs: architects go crazy for studs. They build houses with way too many studs; they fantasize about buildings without any clothes on, with the studs open and exposed.

This was also the moment in which the do-it-yourself movement became significant, both in terms of activating new publics for architecture and for rethinking how architects designed, moving them away from a fascination with the final object and toward process. I think the 1970s was exactly that moment of potential when many things are up for grabs and therefore full of possibility for the present. So they seem very near, and they are very far, and in that distance is a kind of a gift that is received well by young architects today.

OCTOBER 3, 2013
Paul Rudolph Lecture

Philippe Rahm
Atmospherical Cube

Why do I have a link with art? It is not with plastic art but more to find a place where it can challenge the language of architecture. As an architect you use a language, sometimes one that already exists and sometimes one you have invented, to ask new questions and maybe to find some new solutions—and I think the art gallery is a place where you can challenge this language. Maybe my interest in architecture—and why I want to challenge its language—from my dissatisfaction with the idea that everything was linked to the solid, the visible, and the façade, and I thought that instead architecture is really related to the void, the emptiness, the space. This is the most important difference between sculpture and architecture: sculpture is a solid object that you are in front of; space is an object you go inside of. If we want to define the space itself, we know that it is not only air; there is a chemical quality to this air, there is an electro-magnetic quality to this air, there is some biological value to this air. The body is not neutral inside this space: you receive something, perhaps some light, and you have some reaction. Focusing on the main target of architecture, the space itself, the exhibition was the place where we started to analyze some new tools to establish a new element of architecture.

In France we tried to take the reality of the interior as a kind of climatic pocket space where you are protected from the rain, cold, and wind. We designed the indoor atmosphere so that during the winter the house is twenty degrees Celsius, which is to jump in one second into a tropical climate, like going to Spain or Morocco, when it is cold outside. The idea is to start to design a climate and then find a program from the function, so architecture is a background—a geographical or atmospherical background—and everybody is free to have their own interpretation of the space. Like when you are in a natural landscape and a tree protects you from the rain, so you are free to choose the atmosphere, and this is what I tried to do.

OCTOBER 10, 2013
Myriam Bellazoug Memorial Lecture

Timur Galen, Nader Tehrani & Preston Scott Cohen
Client Building

Timur Galen: Being the Goldman Sachs Guy, I am going to sketch the business case... I am going to start in the mid-1990s: In anticipation of becoming a public company, Goldman Sachs went about a very purposeful structured program to invest in a corporate infrastructure it thought necessary to compete in the securities business. ... What did we bring to the engagement of 200 West Street? A 75,000-square-foot site, with about 1.8 million square feet of FAR, a very complicated planning history, a very rigorous business plan, over two billion dollars to invest, a management team with a growing sophistication in its understanding of the business and its ability to execute in the marketplace, but most importantly an abiding conviction that design, both physical and operational, was the essential ingredient in taking what otherwise might have been a corporate commodity and turning it into a strategic asset for the firm and its people.

Nader Tehrani: In being asked to do a project for Goldman Sachs on that particular site, we were very conscious of the uniqueness of New York, a place where things are big, monumental, and colossal. At the same time this was occurring at a moment when we were all very conscious of the particular nature of the site, on the oblique corner directly overlooking the tragedies of 9/11.

Scott Cohen: At first, Harry Cobb asked me to apply for one of several interior projects for 200 West, but given that I am naturally attracted to peculiar and tightly constrained sites, I liked this site between the building and a neighboring hotel. In this geometrical narrative, I was not particularly interested in Cobb's original plan for a flat, sloped, rectangular canopy constrained within the straight part of the passageway. I wanted the canopy to be a separate geometric entity lodged between Goldman and the hotel.

There is a tension between two kinds of sponsorship: patronage and clientship, a distinction brilliantly articulated by Robert Gutman, wherein the first confers virtue involving benevolence, such as the production of civic and community space, and the latter sees the building as a commodity measured by its exchange value.

OCTOBER 14, 2013
Louis I. Kahn Visiting Asst. Professor

Marcelo Spina
Current Dichotomies and the Predicament of the Whole

We live in a field prone to dualisms, oppositions, and strong categorizations. So while I think not everything is completely compatible and some things should come to violence, there are many important oppositions to be debunked. The tectonic approach involves engaging some of these dualities, accepting inconsistencies, and working through productive incongruities. Our interest in constructive dichotomy stems from the possibility of challenging fixed notions of part-to-whole relationships, producing new authenticity as well as new audiences for architecture, which can question the role and the status of the icon, and more importantly its architectural image. Our projects tend unequivocally toward a unified whole, in which internal dichotomies create formal, scalar, material, or grammatical labels; for instance, monolithic forms always undergo moments of continuity, transition, and estrangement, either by accepting or by being disturbed by other objects or forms.

Figures and voids, and the idea of interstitial space, are quite important, especially in relation to mass, as is the condition of how these buildings and certain congruities they express as a robustness on the outside, but also imply an interiority that is maybe different, and the figurality of that difference as it reveals the possibilities of tension.

The form of the object is not just the object itself—or the building—but also the field around it, including the cultural and historical habits, behaviors, customs that configure and impinge upon the object. The most important thing about this dichotomy is the single character, so the idea of practice on one side, the personality of the architect trying to think within the world and all of the things that relate to the building and discipline, and the mutual relationship between the things, the idea of actually working, but also to have a certain autonomy and be able to challenge it.

The issue of mass is at the center of what we are interested in, and one of the things that defies easy categorization. The sort of finitude of the building, its shape in the context, and the pressures on its exterior are not just purely problems of volume, but those of volume inflected by internal conditions of the building, and the instrumentalities of such, in terms of building codes.

OCTOBER 31, 2013
Eero Saarinen Lecture

Toni L. Griffith
Detroit Future City

Eero Saarinen's father, Eliel, who practiced urban planning in Europe, wrote the book City: Its Growth, Its Decay, Its Future. I was elated to see a connection to Michigan and Detroit in his prediction of a future: in light of the current increase in civic decay, it is apparent that if things are not conducted in a manner that will lead to proper decentralization, the future will surely bring sad consequences. Unless surgery of decentralization is undertaken in time and conducted in an organic way, coming generations will witness constantly growing slum areas. Saarinen predicted this in 1943.

Saarinen's design studios were suggesting something called "organic decentralization," in which even within the city limits, you would be much more prescriptive about how you would save and harness assets and try to order the city in a much more efficient way.

What we needed was an operational and functional yet aspirational strategy for how to transform Detroit into something different, something that could be more productive now for the 700,000 people who remain there. So, Detroit Future City was a three-year planning process with a comprehensive team of consultants from the United States and abroad in the fields of urban design, planning, architecture, economics, real estate, and finance.

Our plan looked at five framework elements: the equitable city (economic growth), the image of the city (land use), the sustainable city (city systems), the city of distinct neighborhoods, and a strategic approach to land assets. One of the things that was also very important to this work was recognizing that the transformation of Detroit was not going to happen overnight, so we would have to build a framework strategy that imagined different horizons of implementation.

And we only have to remember Rome, one of our most famous shrinking cities, which was nearly double its size, area, and population many hundreds of years ago. It is now a thriving city—and we hope that someday Detroit will be in same space.

NOVEMBER 7, 2013
Norman R. Foster Visiting Professor

Bijoy Jain
Praxis

After studying in the United States and then returning to India, I was looking for some way to find a space... where more than fifty percent of the landscape is actually built outside the scope of formal architecture, outside of what we do. ... I remember the first project I did was a series of formal drawings... and not a single drawing was used. It was all done through gestures, communications, storytelling, and drawings on a wall because most of the people who build in India do not actually know how to read drawings. So you can see here the density of the formal and the informal, and how they overlap.

In the last twenty years there has been rapid economic growth and a kind of juggernaut has taken over. My interest has been the idea of a potential overlap, not of whether it is traditional or contemporary culture, but that the two poles are not actually opposing each other, instead they are meeting and moving away, meeting and moving away.

One of the things I want to bring to the fore is that for a country's population of a two hundred million people our organizing principle is chaos. Everything is based on that idea because there is negotiation in that. If there are systems as a population, or a culture, we would possibly implode.

If you have been to India you know that everything lies between a yes and a no. So if you are asking a question, and there's a nod—is he saying "yes"? And he says "no." Is he really saying "no"? And again it's the nod of the head, this gesture that works between the yes and the no. What is interesting is not one or the other, but the resonance of those two points.

Studio Mumbai is set up with a few architects and a lot of builders; they are professional artisans, some of them with a lineage of ten, fifteen, twenty generations. (Some of them exaggerate and say fifty generations.) More than fifty percent of Indians know how to build in some way, and we should find a way to tap into that resource.

This idea of ebb and flow is in the nature of how things are carried out in the country, where there is a large exodus to the villages before the monsoon. These are primarily the builders of these constructions.

NOVEMBER 21, 2013

Arnold Aronson
Ming Cho Lee and the Transformation of American Stage Design

Ultimately what allowed Lee to develop a unique style was his ability to absorb a wide variety of disparate influences, many from outside the American scenic vocabulary, and synthesize them into a coherent approach.

Of all Lee's contributions to American scenography, perhaps the most important is sculptural. Measure for Measure pushed Lee in a new direction. Director Michael Kahn asked to set it in the meat-packing district of Manhattan—at the time a gritty neighborhood, not the chic enclave it is today. The result was fascinating. Lee used the same vocabulary—an upper stage at the rear, reached by stairs on either side—but the scaffolding and pipes were industrial and functional, stripped of any decorative sensibility... The metal structure above, supported by vertical pipes, provided the vertical thrust necessary to emphasize the volume of the stage. It was a jarring, almost threatening juxtaposition to the romanticism of the park. I think many people do not realize the centrality of Lee's responsibility for introducing an industrial sensibility to the American theater.

Nine Songs is based on a poem cycle by Qu Yuan, from the third century BCE. Lee created a series of panels that flew up and down, and side to side. Together they formed a painting of a lotus blossom, by noted Taiwanese painter Lin Yu-san, that gets deconstructed as the panel sections move. The orchestra pit was turned into a water tank upon which lotus blossoms floated. Once plucked from their roots, lotuses will wilt within two hours, even in water, and the dance was timed to the wilting of the leaves. At the end of the dance Lin added an homage to Chinese martyrs from ancient times to Tiananmen Square. The dancers fell one by one until the stage was covered with bodies and then began to rise slowly and move off, returning over and over with lighted candles until the stage was filled with four hundred candles in an undulating pattern. The back scrim then rose to reveal a curved ramp covered with another four hundred lit candles that seemed to merge into an infinite sky of stars. "The dance doesn't really end," Lee says. "After the applause it just continues. There were people who sat in the audience for ten minutes or more just watching the candles."

SEPTEMBER 5, 2013

Unfinished Spaces

Directors:
Benjamin Murray, Alysa Nahmias

"Cuba will count as having the most beautiful academy of arts in the world." —Fidel Castro, 1961

Cuba's ambitious National Art Schools project, designed by three young artists in the wake of Castro's Revolution, is neglected, nearly forgotten, then ultimately rediscovered as a visionary architectural masterpiece.

In 1961, three young, visionary architects were commissioned by Fidel Castro and Che Guevara to create Cuba's National Art Schools on the grounds of a former golf course in Havana, Cuba. Construction of their radical designs began immediately and the school's first classes soon followed. Dancers, musicians and artists from all over the country reveled in the beauty of the schools, but as the dream of the Revolution quickly became a reality, construction was abruptly halted as the schools were deemed irrelevant in the prevailing political climate. Forty years later the schools are in use, but remain unfinished and decaying. Castro has invited the exiled architects back to finish their unrealized dream.

JANUARY 30, 2014

The Making of an Avant-Garde:

The Institute for Architecture and Urban Studies, 1967–1984

Written, produced and directed:
Diana Agrest

The Institute for Architecture and Urban Studies (IAUS) was a non-profit organization founded by Peter Eisenman and dedicated to critical architectural debate. The Institute operated in New York and became a center for architectural innovation, reinvigorating theoretical discourse worldwide. International figures who collaborated with the Institute included Richard Meier, Rem Koolhaas, Charles Gwathmey (M.Arch '62), Frank Gehry, Robert A.M. Stern (M.Arch '65) and many others. The film presents the legacy of the Institute through a series of interviews with its primary participants, who reflect on the Institute's continuing impact on the structure of architectural theory education and the professional practice of the discipline today.

Diana Agrest is a professor at the Irwin S. Chanin School of Architecture at The Cooper Union.

JANUARY 4, 2014
Norman R. Foster Visiting Professor

David Adjaye
Work

It is nice to be back in this hall, though I have a very faint memory of it, due to its intensity. Metropolitan Architecture was really trying to engage with the idea of the continent not as one of the AFRICA division into fifty-two countries, which have now become fifty-four, but to reimagine the context of the continent through its geography and its cultures and different sorts of habitations, and to understand the habitations that are present in the continent, where they might be, and why they are where they are.

We take on some projects that require an investigation, a topology test, or a reboot, and if they come under the umbrella of houses but talk about the ongoing discussion of the domestic realm, its lowest form, and its working class, right through to the very wealthy people. So it is really the whole range that we test as much as possible and retrieve four types: the working-class house, sort of a middle-class house, two middle-class houses, and a wealthy person's house.

We won the Smithsonian competition four years ago. It was an international competition on the Washington Mall, the twenty-third Smithsonian. ... The museum is dedicated to the history of the African-American and the African-American lens as a way to understand what America is. It has about thirty thousand pieces, but it is really about the narrative of the journey from Africa, the agrarian slavery and landscape, the migration into the urban landscape and cities, the explosion of art and music, and so on.

We won the competition by saying that we would make a building not like what you generally find in Washington, but something with a new kind of profile. The site is very close to the Washington Monument, so I argued that the building had to fall somewhere in between an artwork and a building.

JANUARY 16 , 2014
Louis I Kahn Visiting Assistant Prof.

Dan Wood
Behind the Scenes

When we started the office we were just coming out of OMA and did not really know what kind of architects we were going to be, or what our voice would be. We saw two possible paths toward a possible future. One of them I would call the Archigram or the Ant Farm route, basically you end up at the same place. The Archigram route is the ivory tower, where you are thinking, drawing, developing your voice and ideas in isolation through academia and competitions. The Ant Farm was inspired by Archigram, but the model was just to go out and do it. And they built inflatables and organized a media van and filmed performances. We took the Ant Farm route and called ourselves "Work" because we wanted to define ourselves through work. We set down rules in 2003: Act bigger. Stay global. The inside is different from the outside. Plants and animals are important. Finally, when in doubt, paint it blue. We had a series of five-year plans. The was, "Say yes to everything." We are just going to do everything possible and take everything as it comes, including teaching. We did fifty or sixty real projects in that five-year period, and hundreds of other things on the side. And some of the things we did never went anywhere.

We are always looking at the relationship between architecture and power, so at one point I decided to map all of our projects in relation to the instigating forces that organized the project, and we used John Kenneth Galbraith's definition of where power comes from. Power can come from wealth, property, organizational or institutional power, or the force of knowledge and personality. Most of our projects come from the latter: people who gained power through the force of their personality, the things that they think about, or the knowledge they have gained.

Our attitude is to push the power ball, a kind of Sisyphean relationship. Architecture and power are always related; one does exist without the other. I mean, power can exist without architecture, but architecture certainly does not exist without power. Power builds up to a pressure point where powerful people feel they need to express themselves through architecture, and normally go broke.

JANUARY 23 , 2014
Myriam Bellazoug Memorial Lecture

Sean Keller
Automatism

What is needed now is the maturation of architectural practice and criticism beyond isolated positions, so that computational methods can be considered within rather than simply against historical and aesthetic contexts.

Stanley Louis Cavell, professor of aesthetics at Harvard, chose the term automatism rather than one of the more established possibilities, such as medium, form, or genre, reflecting the importance he attaches to the idea that, at the level of artistic process, there is something automatic in the practices he identifies as automatisms.

One could say that what architects must propose today to greater and lesser degrees are automatisms of automation. That is, an architect must attempt to wrest a substantial way of practicing out of the various, and variable, constellations of automated technologies available.

As Cavell sees it, the Modernist artistic process runs between two unacceptable poles: systemization and chance. On one side is the risk of "total organization," demonstrated by the compositions of Karlheinz Stockhausen, where artistic responsibility is displaced by an empty formal system. On the other side is the "radical ceding" of artistic control, and even the dissolution of art itself, proposed by John Cage's chance operations.

I propose that Cavell's concept of automatism suggests what a "critical" contemporary architecture could be— critical in a Kantian sense of questioning its own ground—one that encompasses but also moves beyond the automations of computation.

... the limitations of applying such a concept to architecture seems to lead to the familiar situation in which "serious architecture"—or simply "architecture"—is only a minor subset of building. I'm not sure that another possibility exists within late Modernism. For his part Cavell recognized the similar condition of art but was careful to characterize it in a manner that may give us some small comfort: "While the community of serious art is small," he said, "it is not exclusive—not the way an elite is exclusive. It is esoteric, but the secret is open to anyone.

FEBRUARY 13 , 2014
D. Roth and R. Symonds Lecture

MARCH 31 , 2014
Gordon H. Smith Lecture

APRIL 3, 2014
W.H. Bishop Visiting Professor

APRIL 10 , 2014
T. E. Lenahan Memorial Lecture

Trevor Paglen
Seeing Machines:
Geographies of Photography, Control, and Our New Algorithmic Overlords

Overall my projects tend to be about seeing, in a way, and trying to push vision and seeing and perception to the point where it breaks down. I am really interested in what the line between the knowable and unknowable, the visible and the invisible, is; for me that is a way to continually see the world with fresh eyes. We can keep pushing the world until it breaks, and then we can see something new and different. That is really what I want out of art— things that help us see who we are now.

Within the overall project of seeing, invisibility, and perceiving limits, I have been very interested in state secrecy and have done a number of projects about the question of how to see secrecy.

People tend to think about secrecy as what you get to know about versus what you do not get to know about... I think that is completely wrong: I do not think about secrecy that way at all... I think of secrecy more as a way of doing things, a kind of organizing logic, a logic of organizing activities, institutions, and infrastructures that has political, economic, or legal dimensions, and of course even cultural dimensions. It is a way of doing things whose goal is invisibility, silence and obscurity. In this way secrecy is something that in geography we might call an abstract space because it does not really exist: instead it is a logic. It is a set of immaterial ideas that are applied to things but that do not exist in any sort of physical way. In the real world secrecy can exist only insofar as its logic is applied to stuff in the world, the material world that everything in the world is made of. So in real life secrecy is made out of infrastructures.

Seeing at an extreme, seeing at a distance, and seeing what happens when vision and perception starts coming undone. We see a classified image of the premier U.S. chemical weapons testing range, but it is also a photograph of what it looks like when you push the physical properties of vision as far as they will go. It is literally a photograph of what it looks like when vision begins to collapse. ... What I want out of art is things that help us see the world that we are living in, things that help us see all the things that are going on that in many ways we do not know how to see, or do not know how to notice.

Jim Eyre
Exploring Boundaries

I have four themes. One of them is manipulation, which is not as sinister as it sounds. It is really just about configuring materials and the various tectonic elements to achieve what we are trying to do in terms of form. The second is collaboration, which is really about our relationship with nature. Thirdly, regeneration takes many forms, but for me it is about working with existing buildings and the aspect of memory and identity; and the fourth is celebration, which I will come to a little bit later. Often we are blurring the boundaries between disciplines, but principally we work at the boundary of architecture and engineering. We really enjoy working with engineers who have a good understanding of architecture, and they can be structural or civil but also environmental engineers, and occasionally we stray into sculpture, which is considered by many to be dangerous territory.

Now you would expect architecture to be fertile territory for technical innovation, but in the construction industry innovation is actually agonizingly slow. The reason is that every building is its own prototype, so there is a limit to what you can do each time. Technology is often transferred from elsewhere. I have always been interested that architecture straddles the line between science and art: science of course being the tangible, finding out how things really work or what really exists, and art being rather more like holding up a mirror to ourselves. But I think that in technology, often seen as a branch of science, creativity is still king, and innovation comes from applied inventiveness. It is very different from pure science, the scientific method of data gathering and proof. So in architecture creativity can be technological or just aesthetic.

The twentieth-century construction industry really got too utilitarian in periods. If you have limited resources, you should do things for the lowest cost to spread benefit across society; but that does not always work in the direction you want it to because ingenuity gets directed to cost instead of well-being in the widest sense or the efficient use of materials. This is a really aggressive approach if it is erosive or applied to the environment, which deserves our respect and is far too valuable to ruin. After all, as architects we actually believe we are enhancing people's lives with what we do.

Deborah Berke
Out of the Ordinary

I have long been interested in the everyday and the ordinary. This is the new ordinary—as of Monday there were more than 430 million of these (iPhones) in the world; that was Monday, who knows what it is by today.

I like the regular and the useful, but I want them to have a more resonant meaning and connection to everyday life. I believe one has to believe in something and have those beliefs manifest in the work, which is what I am going to talk about.

I think architecture should effect change in a world that is changing very rapidly. Much has been said about the dramatic new world created by the Internet and other forms of electronic communication and computation, but finally, with the exception of my nice little boat, buildings do not move: they sit where they are built and a rapidly changing world whizzes around them. Buildings collapse an enormous amount of time, energy, and materials into a single moment; they collapse the efforts of many into a single object. Another idea I am interested in is going back to that seemingly simple object again and again and finding something new. I want to embrace a back-to-basics approach to architecture, maybe with a little twist of social responsibility, not groaning over community participation but relishing in it. I think it is important to take pleasure in designing the working parts of your architecture as much as the image making. I like making the architecture of the back of house, and the key to our philosophy of practice is to acknowledge the collaborative nature of the endeavor.

Being an architect is more like being a playwright and less like being a painter because you are so dependent on the skills and commitments of others for the realization of your work. I do not think architecture is problem solving, although in the process of making architecture there are certainly plenty of problems solved. For me architecture is about making something you believe in, something that expresses your beliefs, about doing many things simultaneously, many of them burdensome, like the building and zoning codes, ADA and LEED standards, irrational expectations of clients, and conflicting expectations of many communities. ... I am interested in the explicit and the implicit, the invisible and the visible, the unpredictable but inevitable space, light, form, material, function, program, environmental and community responsibility and engagement—and the poetry of everyday life.

Anette Freytag
Back to the Roots:
Topology and Phenomenology in Landscape

I have developed a framework and I have developed a framework and tools to recall the potentials of landscape architecture—at ETH we call this approach topology. Although I am convinced that we could create and maintain an environment that is both livable and beautiful, even in the midst of a rapidly changing world, I am more and more disheartened by examples that seem determined to prove the opposite true. This is an example of our overwhelming daily reality.

Today's architecture has very often disconnected itself from the terrain and the soil. Landscape architecture has followed this trend. Our environment is dominated by the logic of finance, and finance is not economy, as sociologists recently stated at the conference that our chair organized. Financial capitalism has nothing to do with economics anymore. It permeates everything.

Art has become the placebo of our time. Remember how Patrick Blank's vertical garden was called an ecological art form? The superficial emphasis on artists in landscape projects threatens to raise the real competences of the discipline. In Europe landscape architecture has been turned into a mere festival. Urban space is increasingly dominated by temporary gardens. A quick smile on the faces of people who walk by and then an admittedly positive kind of activism has become more important than the correctly executed craft of the landscape architect.

The strongest motivating force for achieving the objectives of landscape architecture is undoubtedly the environmental movement as carried out in Europe since the 1960s. It has generally dictated people to be the enemy; this movement propagates without people.

I am also convinced that the landscape architect is the ideal urbanist and that the landscapist attitude should be the promoter of urbanism today. I still struggle with the program of landscape urbanism, at least how it is interpreted in Europe, which only works well as a large-scale strategy, but at the small scale has little concern for the physical well-being or the interaction between humans and nature. In brief, it mainly ignores the topological and phenomenological dimensions of landscape architecture because here you are up but there you are down.

With landscape you find yourself always in the labyrinth of Daedalus, and if you want to feel comfortable you need topology and phenomenology.

OCTOBER 3–5, 2013
J. Irwin Miller Symposium

Exhibiting Architecture: A Paradox?

Organized by Eeva-Liisa Pelkonen, Carson Chan, and David Andrew Tasman

The ambition to exhibit architecture always entails a paradox: how to exhibit something so large and complex as a building or a city or how to represent something as elusive as an architectural experience that unfolds in space and time?

While the story of major museums and their role in shaping the history of modern architecture has been largely told, this symposium will bring together historians, curators and practicing architects to explore how architecture has pushed exhibition as a medium in its own right and how exhibitions have shaped the discipline of architecture by posing questions that are historical, theoretical and critical. Rather than focusing on major historical surveys where the exhibit is treated as a descriptive event, this symposium will focus on exhibitions where architecture is used as the medium, at times becoming architectural reality in its own right. The symposium will also explore the condition wherein architecture itself has come to mimic exhibition and display strategies, making buildings into producers of scenographic sequences and atmospheric affects or, in some cases, into objects on display. Various exhibition techniques and formats that have emerged through experimental architectural exhibitions as well as fertile institutional settings and curatorial practices that have explored alternative modes of public engagement will be explored.

OCTOBER 4, 2013
George Morris Woodruff, Class of 1857 Memorial Lecture

Barry Bergdoll

"Out of Site – In Plain View: The Symbiosis between Exhibiting and Projecting the Modern"
Keynote Lecture

In the past few years the spectacle of architecture has been everywhere, even if the press is filled with discussion of the eclipse of Starchitects. Indeed with Koolhaas's appointment as the director of the 2014 Venice Biennale of Architecture, one might wonder about our current period of Starcurators, where curators are often as famous as contemporary artists and architects, and the word curate has been applied to everything from meals to clothes. But what does it mean to exhibit architecture? Isn't architecture already on display once it is built?

The architectural exhibition is—with few exceptions, as perhaps in the case of the plaques of the New York City Landmarks Commission—a radical deracination of architecture. The architectural display starts then from a lack, some might even say—in the case of fragments of an act of destruction or violence and from something that is a poor reflection of the monumental grandeur and place-making of the art of architecture.

But what, I asked myself, would it mean to craft a history not of the poor substitute that is an exhibition condemned to work with placebos but of the potentialities of the architectural exhibition? To ask why the habit of exhibiting architecture in the gallery first became common practice during the Enlightenment, in London in the 1760s, soon after in Paris, and then by the end of the eighteenth century, in Berlin, St. Petersburg, and nearly every other European city in which there was an academy—with isolated and quite specific cases half a century earlier, notably in Papal Rome. And to ask to what extent did the phenomenon of displaying architecture change the very nature and possibilities of architecture? With "Out of Site: In Plain View," I propose that part of the very essence of a self-consciously Modern architecture is wrapped up in the ability to put it on display—to take it out of its original site and return it to plain view—and that in fact the exhibition has been a vital instrument to some of the greatest features of modern architecture since the Enlightenment: the emergence of a critical discourse on the public character and responsibilities of architecture; the invention of a history of architecture with its consequences for the exploration of architectural meaning and its capacities to build national, regional, and local identities; and the capacity of architecture to project entirely new programs and environments that we associate with the very condition of the avant-garde. At nearly every step of architecture's modern history and of the history of architecture as Modern, exhibitions have been an integral part of the life of architecture, an enabler as much as a reflection. Today I see new potentials for the architectural exhibition since inevitably I speak to you in a hybrid voice, as both historian and curator.

FEBRUARY 20–22, 2014
J. Irwin Miller Symposium

Digital Post-Modernities

From Calculus to Computation

Organized by Mario Carpo

In the course of the last twenty years digital technologies have changed the way architecture is conceived and made. New architectural theories have responded to and interpreted technological change, and since the early 1990s a new, theoretically driven digital style has deeply marked the history of architectural form.

But today's digital style is no longer that of the 1990s. While many intuitions and anticipations of the architectural avant-gardes of the early 1990s have already become a reality, digitally intelligent architecture is now facing new challenges, prompted by rapid techno-social change, disciplinary constraints, and ideological straitjackets.

This symposium will convene protagonists from different realms of today's digitally intelligent architecture, and invite them to assess the way their own digital work has changed over time, or relates to the work of their predecessors or followers. By looking at our digital present in a historical perspective, and emphasizing the continuing rift between our modernist and post-modern allegiances, this symposium reflects the vitality and diversity of today's digital design scene, aiming to highlight some of the oppositions that animate today's digital discourse among the design professions.

FEBRUARY 20, 2014
William B. and Charlotte Shepherd Davenport Visiting Professor

Greg Lynn

"Old School Digital"
Keynote Lecture

In terms of my personal ambitions, and to some degree those of the Canadian Centre for Architecture, this is not a history of digital technology, nor is it scholarship. This is really archaeology. It is not about practices; those projects are like core samples of practices in some way. ... We are generating an oral history where we interview everyone, the teams and collaborators and associates; we are trying to inventory the actual equipment, the hardware and software that was used in the offices, and we are comparing it with both digital and analog material. One of the interesting things in the Yale show is that the computers, manual drafting, and model building were more or less running at the same speed at this time, so it was very easy to test the two mediums against each other and cross back and forth.

It is very hard to theorize tools that have not been well documented or understood in a generalizable way. So part of this show is to clarify what the roles of software and hardware were, and to make the documentation accessible to scholars.

In an interview Peter Yesios, said I am going to have nothing to talk with Peter Eisenman about in terms of working with a computer, and then by the end of the project he realized Peter was a computer. He described him as a speaking computer, and I remember very well Peter's desire for a procedural process, something that was reversible where you could make sequential decisions and then go back and change a decision in the chain and replay the design process, which was what he saw in the digital technology of the time.

Many people think digital technology was cooked up in the attic of Columbia University and paperless studios, by people of my generation, but the fact is that a bunch of older dudes who already knew what they wanted to do were using computers to digitize things they were already looking at—it was not only kids.

These five projects describe five trajectories by people (Greg Lynn, Peter Eisenman, Frank Gehry, Chuck Hoberman, Shoei Yoh) who had a design intelligence that guided the computer and were not born digital—this was not something that came as second nature to them the way it would to most of the students at Yale right now. As a postscript, none of these people really thought that the critical part of computers was important, as we do today.

* YSOA Symposia posters designed by Pentagram, New York

AUGUST 28, 2013 – NOVEMBER 9, 2013

Everything Loose Will Land: 1970s Art and Architecture in Los Angeles

Curated by Sylvia Lavin
Photographed by Richard LaPlante

Reframing Frank Lloyd Wright's famous quip, "Tip the world on its side and everything loose will land in Los Angeles," this exhibition explores the intersection between architecture and art during the 1970's in the City of Los Angeles.

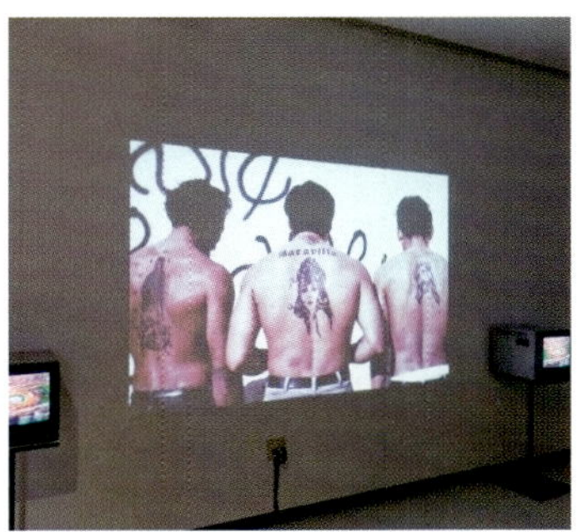

NOVEMBER 20, 2013 – FEBRUARY 1, 2014

Stage Designs by Ming Cho Lee

Curated by Ming Cho Lee, Lee Savage, and Brian Butterfield
Photographed by Marty New

Yale's School of Architecture and School of Drama are teaming up this fall to present "Stage Designs by Ming Cho Lee," a retrospective of the award-winning designer and Yale professor's work in theater, opera, and dance. Since the 1960s, Lee has been one of the world's most celebrated and influential set designers, particularly during his tenure with the New York Shakespeare Festival and at the New York City Opera. He is renowned for his meticulous attention to precision and detail, and his models have been described as works of art in themselves. "Stage Designs by Ming Cho Lee" will showcase some 65 of these models, along with sketches and photographs selected from the nearly 300 productions he has designed.

FEBRUARY 20, 2014 – MAY 3, 2014

Archaeology of the Digital

Curated by Greg Lynn
Photographed by Rich House

Archaeology of the Digital looks at four pivotal projects that established bold directions in architecture's use of digital tools: The Lewis Residence by Frank Gehry (1985–95); Peter Eisenman's Biozentrum (1987); Chuck Hoberman's Expanding Sphere (1992); and Shoei Yoh's roof structures for Odawara (1991) and Galaxy Toyama (1992) Gymnasiums.

MAY 18, 2014 – JULY 26, 2014

OUTLOOK Year-End Exhibition of Student Work

Curated by Brian Butterfield and Alison Walsh
Photographed by Rich House

The school of architecture publications office directed by Nina Rappaport, published new volumes of books in the on-going series that are described here:

Renewing Architectural Typologies: House, Mosque, Library

The fifth title in the Louis I. Kahn Visiting Assistant Professorship book series, Renewing Architectural typologies: House, Mosque, Library features the three advanced studios led by Makram El Kadi and Ziad Jamaleddine (L.E.FT Architects); Hernan Diaz Alonso; and British firm AOC (Tom Coward, Daisy Froud, Vincent Lacovara, and Geoff Shearcroft). Edited by Nina Rappaport and Leticia Almino de Souza ('12), it includes interviews with the architects about the work of their professional offices and essays on the themes of their studios. The book is designed by MGMT Design and distributed by Actar.

Rethinking Chongqing: Mixed-Use and Super-Dense

Edited by Andrei Harwell ('06), Emmett Zeifman ('11), and Nina Rappaport.

The book documents the work of the school's seventh Edward P. Bass Distinguished Visiting Architecture Fellow, Vincent Lo, of Hong Kong-based Shui On Land, and Saarinen Visiting Professors Paul Katz, Jamie von Klemperer, and Forth Bagley (B.A. '99, M.Arch '01), of the firm KPF, assisted by Andrei Harwell. The advanced studio developed ideas for a dense, mixed-used site at the central rail station of Chongqing, in western China. The book features interviews with Jamie von Klemperer and Vincent Lo about working in China and an essay about the growth of development in the region. The book is designed by MGMT Design and distributed by Actar.

ON DEMAND SERIES

The "On Demand" Studio Series grows with new books featuring the advanced studios. These books are designed to guidelines set by MGMT Design and published by the school in small runs and then available through the school's Web site—www.architecture.yale.edu.

Assembly

The book Assembly documents the 2012 design-build project at the Yale School of Architecture: a pavilion on the New Haven Green for the International Festival of Arts and Ideas. The project was initiated by students in the post-professional program and was constructed in the school's fabrication labs. The book includes a description of the design and building process as well as a series of essays and interviews on integral themes, including the teaching of digital fabrication in architecture by Mario Carpo the Vincent Scully Visiting Professor, critic Michael Young, engineer Matthew Clark, Dean Robert A. M. Stern, assistant dean Mark Foster Gage, and critic Brennan Buck. Student David Bench and engineer John Lacy speculate on the visual effects of the pavilion and digital production in general. Assa Abloy supported the project and its publication.

A Train of Cities

In addition to A Train of Cities, which presents the work of the three post-professional studios led by assistant professor (adjunct) Edward Mitchell and professor (adjunct) Fred Koetter was published last summer. The book analyzes and recommends ways to revitalize the Massachusetts south-coast communities along the commuter-rail routes by networking their physical and economic patterns. With the demise of lucrative industries, the power of cities and towns declined throughout the twentieth century, and the construction of the interstate system damaged the infrastructure and identity of many of these communities. In the 1990s, the Southeastern Regional Planning and Economic Development District began plans to open up former commercial rail lines as commuter routes from Boston to the south coast. The book analyzes the historic structure of these areas, with student work done in Taunton, Fall River, and New Bedford projecting the potential for education, new industry, housing, and agriculture as sources of economic growth and development that could lead to future potential for these older industrial cities.

Knowing How in Downtown Las Vegas

Published this winter is a third book in the Studio Series, Knowing How in Downtown Las Vegas, on the work of professor Keller Easterling's Spring 2013 eponymous advanced studio. Her studio focused on understanding and configuring new programs and potentials for downtown Las Vegas sites. The students took on the task of remediating environmental and developmental issues—problems related to infrastructure, water, garbage, suburban expansion, or energy. These issues were addressed with health conscious high-rise buildings resembling giant TVs, a new construction technology for weaving an infrastructural/architectural skin, a pneumatic building for experimental foods and scented atmospheres, a swimming pool long enough to serve as urban transit, and a system of water tanks dramatically exposing the city's infrastructural underbelly. In addition to the tangible built structures, students were also tasked with creating an amplifying and multiplying "active form" that would operate in less obvious ways. The studio strove to be a precedent for the improvisation studio that values not only knowing that but also knowing how.

YALE URBAN DESIGN WORKSHOP 2013–2014

DIRECTOR: ALAN J. PLATTUS **PROJECT MANAGER: ANDREI HARWELL**

Founded in 1992 by Alan Plattus, then Associate Dean and Professor at the Yale School of Architecture, the Yale Urban Design Workshop (YUDW) is a community design center based at the School of Architecture. Since its founding, the YUDW has worked with communities across the state of Connecticut, providing planning and design assistance on projects ranging from comprehensive plans, economic development strategies and community visions to the design of public spaces, streetscapes and individual community facilities. Clients include small towns, city neighborhoods, planning departments, Chambers of Commerce, community development corporations, citizen groups, and private developers. The YUDW is currently located in a storefront space on Chapel Street in New Haven's Dwight neighborhood, two blocks from the School of Architecture.

In all its work, the YUDW is committed to an inclusive, community-based process, grounded in broad citizen participation and a vision of the design process as a tool for community organizing, empowerment, and capacity-building. A typical YUDW project may include design charrettes, focus groups, and town meetings, as well as more conventional means of program and project development. These projects are staffed mainly by current graduate professional students at the Yale School of Architecture supervised by faculty of the School, but often also include Yale College undergraduates, recent graduates of the School as full-time staff, faculty and students from Yale's other professional schools (including the Law School, the School of Forestry and Environmental Science, the School of Management, the School of Public Health and the School of Art), as well as outside consultants and other local professionals.

Recent and current projects include downtown and neighborhood plans for the Connecticut towns of West Haven, Woodbridge, Bridgeport, and Milford, and a redevelopment plan for the former site of the town hall in North Branford, CT. In 2014, the YUDW will complete a comprehensive master plan for Fishers Island, New York, which will address the stabilization of the year-round population of the Island. The YUDW is also working with the Avery Copp House in Groton, Connecticut to develop a concept for a Thames River Heritage Park between Groton and New London, Connecticut.

In May 2014, the YUDW returned to Middle East to continue its work on the planning and design of the region's first trans-boundary Peace Park. In collaboration with NGO Friends of the Earth Middle East and faculty from Bezalel Academy, the YUDW led a charrette focused on the detailed planning of the proposed southern gateway to the Park at the Old Gesher compound in Israel, where three bridges from the Roman, Ottoman, and British periods span the Jordan River. The YUDW began its work on the Jordan River Peace Park in 2008 when it led a major international design charrette in Jordan, bringing together faculty and graduate students from Yale with Jordanian, Palestinian, and Israeli architects, engineers, and students.

FACULTY ASSOCIATES
Alexander Felson
Edward Mitchell
Douglas Rae

FELLOWS 2013–2014
Jasdeep Bhalla
Stephanie Lee
Michael Miller
Matthew Rauch
Jack Wolfe
Daria Zolotareva

Donors

FRIENDS
Nancy Alexander
'79 B.A., '84 M.B.A.
Anonymous (3)
ASSA ABLOY
Charles L. Atwood
Autodesk, Inc.
Michael C. Barry '09 B.A.
Deborah Berke & Partners
Architects LLP
A. Robert Bissell '72 B.S.
Bluebeam Software Inc.
Howard M. Brenner '54 B.A.
Carolyn Brody
Gordon M. Burns '75 B.A.
Centerbrook Architects
and Planners
Xiaoling Chen
Chiang Ching-Kuo
Fdn/Scholarly Exc
James C. Childress
William D. Chilton
Richard D. Cohen
Thomas J. Deegan-Day
'89 B.A.
Elisha-Bolton Foundation
Frank O. Gehry '00 D.F.A.H.
M. Ian G. Gilchrist '72 B.A.
Graham Foundation for
Advanced Studies in the
Fine Arts
Julia & Seymour Gross
Foundation Inc.
Steven Harris
The Hearst Foundations
Andrew Philip Heid '02 B.A.
Judith T. Hunt
Elise Jaffe + Jeffrey Brown
Susie Kim & Fred Koetter
'93 M.A.H.
The Kohler Co.
Ken Kuchin
Elizabeth Lenahan
Lost Tree Club, Inc.
Keith G. Lurie '77 B.A.
MakerBot Industries, LLC
Anne Kriken Mann
Gilbert Maurer
Louis C.S. Ng
Helen W. Nitkin
Hilda Ochoa-Brillembourg
Michael A. Pearce '09 B.A.
Cesar Pelli '76 M.A.H.,
'08 D.F.A.H.
Pickard Chilton Architects
Inc.
William L. Rawn III '65 B.A.
William K. Reilly '62 B.A.,
'94 M.A.H.
Joseph B. Rose '81 B.A.
Robert Rosenkranz '62 B.A.
Carolyn Greenspan &
Marshall S. Ruben
'82 B.A.
Melissa G. Vail '74 B.A.
& Norman C. Selby
'74 B.A.
Brenda Shapiro
Jon Stryker
David M. Schwarz
Architects, Inc
Oscar Tang '60 B.E.
Jeff C. Tarr
Elpidio R. Villarreal '85 J.D.
Betty L. Wagner
Anne C. Weisberg
Mathew D. Wolf
Pei-Tse Wu '89 B.A.
Arthur W. Zeckendorf

1940
Russell P. Morse

1942
H. Dickson McKenna

1944
Leon A. Miller

1949
Frank S. Alschuler
Theodore F. Babbitt
Jack Alan Bialosky, Sr.
Charles H. Brewer, Jr.
Augustine J. Palmieri
George D. Waltz

1951
Stanley B. Brundage*
Phelps H. Bultman
Ross H. De Young
Martha Cantwell Meeker

1952
Frank C. Boyer, Jr.
James A. Evans
Donald C. Mallow
Vincent M. Milone
Lawrence Frederick Nulty
James E. Palmer

1953
Duncan W. Buell
Andrew S. Cohen
R. Edward Harter, Jr.
Milton Klein
Julian E. Kulski
John V. Sheoris

1954
Charles G. Brickbauer
George R. Brunjes, Jr.
James D. Gibans
John F. Lee, Jr.
Boris S. Pushkarev
Roger L. Strassman

1955
John L. Field
James Leslie
Sidney M. Sisk

1956
Gerald E. Henniger
Walter D. Ramberg
Stanley B. Wright, Jr.

1957
Ernest L. Ames
Edwin William de Cossy
Charles A. Ferrari
James H. Handley
Richard A. Nininger
William L. Porter
Richard Elliott Wagner

1958
James S. Dudley
Harold D. Fredenburgh
Mark H. Hardenbergh
J. Arvid Klein
Allen Moore, Jr.
Malcolm Strachan, 2d
Michael W. Stuhldreher
Harold F. VanDine, Jr.

1959
Bernard M. Boyle
Frank C. Chapman
Peter B. Frantz
R Leslie Harriman
Louis P. Inserra
Robert M. Kliment
Earl A. Quenneville
Bruce W. Sielaff
Lewis I. Schwartz
Terry G. Twitchell
Donald W. Velsey
Carolyn H. Westerfield
Andrew C. Wheeler

1960
Lawrence N. Argraves
James B. Baker
Thomas L. Bosworth
Richard S. Chafee
Bryant L. Conant
John K. Copelin
Alexander Grinnell
Michael Gruenbaum
Louis B. Joline
Julia H. Keydel
James D. McNeely
Oscar E. Menzer
Robert A. Mitchell
Konrad J. Perlman
Walter Rosenfeld
Gertrude O. Seibels

1961
Paul B. Brouard
Robert W. Carington
Peter Cooke
Warren Jacob Cox
Francis W. Gencorelli
Charles T. Haddad
Lewis S. Roscoe
W. Eugene Sage
Bradford P. Shaw
Wallace E. Sherriff
Stanley Tigerman

1962
James L. Alcorn
David W. Fix
Richard A. Hansen
Tai Soo Kim
Keith R. Kroeger
James Morganstern
Leonard P. Perfido
Renato Rossi-Loureiro
Meredith M. Seikel
Ming-Hsien Wang
Donald R. Watson
Myles Weintraub

1963
Austin Church III
Howard H. Foster, Jr.
Ward Joseph Miles
F. Kempton Mooney
Robert T. Simpson
Louis H. Skidmore, Jr.
William A. Werner, Jr.
John V. Yanik

1964
Philip Allen
Lucinda L. Cisler
Theoharis L. David
Peter Jeremy Hoppner
Charles D. Hosford
Augustus G. Kellogg
Judith A. Lawler
Charles L W. Leider
Robert A. Nerrie III
Joan F. Stogis

1965
Michael J. Altschuler
Thomas Hall Beeby
H. Calvin Cook
Richard C. Fogelson
Peter L. Gluck
Norman E. Jackson, Jr.
Isidoro Korngold
Thai Ker Liu
Gary L. Michael
John I. Pearce, Jr.
Alexander Purves
Elliot A. Segal
Robert A.M. Stern
Frederick C. Terzo
Leonard M. Todd, Jr.
Jeremy A. Walsh
Arnold N. Wile

1966
Andrew Andersons
Emily Nugent Carrier
Richard C. Carroll, Jr.
James Scott Cook
Loren Ghiglione
Frank S. Grosso
John S. Hagmann
Michael Hollander
William F. Moore
Myron B. Silberman
W. Mason Smith III

1967
William H. Albinson
Edward A. Arens
R. Caswell Cooke
Charles M. Engberg
Alexander D. Garvin
Glenn H. Gregg
Walter A. Hunt, Jr.
Chung Nung Lee
John W. Mullen III
Charles S. Rotenberg
Theodore Paul Streibert
Darius Toraby
William H. Willis, Jr.
Robert M. Winick

1968
Frederick S. Andreae
Robert A. Busser
Gail H. Cooke
Peter de Bretteville
John Fulop, Jr.
Christopher C. Glass
Susanne Feld Hilberry
John Holbrook, Jr.
Gerard Ives
Erno Kolodny-Nagy
Peter C. Mayer
Peter Papademetriou
Franklin Satterthwaite
Donald R. Spivack
Salvatore F. Vasi
John J. Vosmek, Jr.
Thomas R. Welch
James C. Whitney

1969
Stephen Harris Adolphus
John Badman
James E. Caldwell, Jr.
Robert J. Cassidy
David B. Decker
George T. Gardner
Harvey R. Geiger
William H. Grover
Eric R. Hansen, Jr.
Roderick C. Johnson
Raymond J. Kaskey, Jr.
David H. Lessig
William B. Richardson
John H. Shoaff
Kermit D. Thompson

1970
Richard F. Barrett
Roland F. Bedford
Paul F. Bloom
F. Andrus Burr
Michael G. Curtis
Steven B. Edwins
Peter Van W. Hoyt
Marilyn Swartz Lloyd
Kathrin S. Moore
James V. Righter
Steven G. Rockmore
Daniel V. Scully
Jan A. Van Loan
Jeremy Scott Wood
William L. Yuen
F. Anthony Zunino

1971
William A. Brenner
An-Chi H. Burow
Rockwell J. Chin
Edward F. Cox
Mark J. Ellis
Anita Holland-Moritz
John Jayner
Robert L. Miller
Humberto L. Rodriguez-
Camilloni
Peter J. Wood

1972
Marc F. Appleton
Paul B. Bailey
Edward P. Bass
Frederick Bland
Stephen J. Blatt
Philip Mack Caldwell
Roberta Carlson Carnwath
Heather Willson Cass
John H. T. Dow, Jr.
Joseph A. Ford III
Coleman A. Harwell
William H. Maxfield
Keiichi Okamoto
David B. Peck, Jr.
Barton Phelps
Jefferson B. Riley
Paul W. Scovill III
Mark Simon
James L. Strickland
Carl H. Wies
Roger Hung Tuan Yee

1973
Russell E. Bloodworth, Jr.
J.P. Chadwick Floyd
Stephen R. Holt
Everardo A. Jefferson
William M. Mack
Nancy Brooks Monroe
Robert D. Orr
Karen Rheinlander-Gray
Steven C. Robinson
William A. Sterling
J. Lawrence Thomas
Stephen C. Thomson
R. Jerome Wagner
John W. Whipple
Robert J. Yudell

1974
Gordon M. Black
Jonathan G. Boyer
Sara E. Caples
Eric A. Chase
Andres M. Duany
Barbara L. Geddis
William E. Odell
Thomas C. Payne
Patrick L. Pinnell
Elizabeth M. Plater-Zyberk
Barbara W. Ratner
Barbara J. Resnicow
David M. Schwarz
Richard A. Senechal
George E. Turnbull

1975
Tullio A. Bertoli
Douglas J. Gardner
Karyn M. Gilvarg
Susan E. Godshall
Keith B. Gross
Edwin R. Kimsey, Jr.
Francis C. Klein
Larry W. Richards
Hervin A. Romney
Andrew K. Stevenson
J. David Waggonner III

1976
Benjamin M. Baker III
Shalom Baranes
Henry H. Benedict III
Richard K. Charney
Robert S. Charney
Anko Chen
Stefani Danes
Daniel F. Kallenbach
James R. Kessler
Roy T. Lydon, Jr.
Eric Jay Oliner
Adrienne K. Paskind
John K. Spear
Barbara Sundheimer-Extein
Scott Van Genderen

1977
Calvert S. Bowie
Louise M. Braverman
Peter D. Clark
Bradley B. Cruickshank
W.J. Patrick Curley
Eric W. Epstein
Barbara Fabiani
Barbara Flanagan
Carl M. Geupel
Jonathan S. Kammel
James Hirsch Liberman
Kevin P. Lichten
Randall T. Mudge
Andrew K. Robinson
Charles B. Swanson
Stephen M. Tolkin
Alexander C. Twining

1978
Philip H. Babb

Frederic M. Ball, Jr.
Judith M. Capen
Shiao-Ling Chang
Kenneth H. Colburn
Ralph A. Giammatteo
Cynthia N. Hamilton
John W. Kuipers
William H. Paxson
Daniel Arthur Rosenfeld
Julia Ruch
David Spiker
Margaret T. Weidlein
Brigid C. Williams

1979
Steven W. Ansel
Jack Alan Bialosky, Jr.
James Leslie Bodnar
K. Daryl Carrington
Richard H. Clarke
Jeffrey P. Feingold
Bradford W. Fiske
John Charles Hall
Kevin E. Hart
Michele Lewis
Gavin A. Macrae-Gibson
Richard L. McElhiney
George R. Mitchell
Thomas N. Patch
Jon K. Pickard
Miroslav P. Sykora

1980
Jacob D. Albert
Turan Duda
J. Scott Finn
Alexander C. Gorlin
Stephen W. Harby
Mariko Masuoka
Ann K. McCallum
Julia H. Miner
William A. Paquette
Joseph F. Pierz
Laura H. Prozes

1981
Richard L. Brown
Michael B. Cadwell
Douglass W. Cooper
Mark Denton
Michael E. Hassig
Brian E. Healy
Mitchell A. Hirsch
T. Whitcomb Iglehart
Michael G. Kostow
Jonathan Levi
Jane Murphy
Spencer Warncke
Diane L. Wilk

1982
John A. Boecker
Carolyn Brooks
Michael B. Burch
Domenic Carbone, Jr.
David P. Chen
Bruce H. Donnally
Raymond R. Glover
Kay Bea Jones
Thomas A. Kligerman
Charles F. Lowrey, Jr.
Theodore John Mahl
Paul W. Reiss
Janet S. Roseff
Martin K. Shofner
R. Anthony Terry

1983
Maynard M. Ball
Anthony Stephen Barnes
Phillip G. Bernstein
Carol J. Burns
Stuart E. Christenson
Ignacio Dahl-Rocha
Stefan Hastrup
Erica H. Ling
Elisabeth Nan Martin
Elizabeth Ann Murrell
Nicholas J. Rehnberg
Jacques M. Richter
Gary Schilling
Brent Sherwood
Sonya R. Sofield
Robert J. Taylor
Nell W. Twining
David M. Walker
Michael R. Winstanley

1984
Bruce R. Becker
David P. Bolger
Kenneth A. Boroson
Paul F. Carr, Jr.
Michael J. Chren
Marti M. Cowan
Teresa Ann Dwan
Douglas S. Dworsky
Blair D. Kamin
Elizabeth M. Mahon
Michael L. Marshall
David Chase Martin
Kenneth E. McKently
Scott Merrill
Jun Mitsui
Lawrence S. Ng
David L. Pearce
John R. Perkins
Jennifer C. Sage
Kevin M. Smith
Mary E. Stockton
Sarah Taylor Swearer
Sarah E. Willmer

1985
Barbara A. Ball
Rasa Joana Bauza
William Robert Bingham
Robert L. Bostwick
M. Virginia Chapman
Michael Coleman Duddy
Jonathan M. Fishman
Andrew M. Koglin
Lucile S. Irwin
Charles H. Loomis
Chariss McAfee
Richard G. Munday
Roger O. Schickedantz
R. David Thompson

1986
William Bartow Bialosky
Timothy Burnett
Margaret J. Chambers
Carey Feierabend
David J. Levitt
Nicholas L. Petschek
Whitney F. Sander
J. Gilbert Strickler
John B. Tittmann

1987
Mary Buttrick Burnham
Soo K. Chan
William D. Egan
Elizabeth P. Gray
Andrew B. Knox
Douglas S. Marshall
Craig D. Newick
Lilla J. Smith
Duncan Gregory Stroik
Jennifer Tate
William L. Vandeventer

1988
Atowarifagha I. Apiafi
Hans Baldauf
Andrew D. Berman
Cary Suzanne Bernstein
John David Butterworth
Aubrey L. Carter
Allison Ewing
Natalie C. Gray-Miniutti
Charlotte B. Handy
Drew H. Kepley
Ann Lisa Krsul
Thomas F. Marble
Oscar E. Mertz III
David H. Must
Alan W. Organschi
Elaine M. Rene-Weissman
William Taggart Ruhl
Gilbert P. Schafer III
Matthew Viederman

1989
Edward R. Burian
Larry G. Chang
Darin C. Cook
John DaSilva
Steve Dumez
Thomas J. Frechette
Jennifer A. Huestis
Timothy C. Joslin
Kevin S. Killen
Scott A. Kirkham
Frank Koumantaris
Stephen D. Luoni
Cherie H. Santos-Wuest
Caroline A. Schiele
Robert Ingram Tucker
Randy Wilmot
Koichi Yasuda

1990
Charles S. Bergen
Patricia Brett
Stephen Brockman
Stancliff C. Elmore
Roberto J. Espejo
Kristen L. Hodess
David E. Houston
Jeffrey E. Karer
Marc D. L'Italien
David Clayton Miller
Deborah R. Robinson
Marie B. Wilkinson
Scott Wood

1991
David M. Becker
Sophie Harvey
Joseph W. Moore
Dominic L. LaPierre
Linda Stabler-Talty
Alexander M. Stuart
Claire E. Theobald
Michael W. Wetstone
Kevin Wilkes

1992
Andrew James Abraham
Peter Kevin Blackburn
Kelly Jean Carlson-Reddig
Betty Y. Chen
Larry G. Cohen
Frances Douglas Corzine
Perla Jeanne Delson
Alisa R. Dworsky
Frederick Adams Farrar, II
Bruce Marshall Horton
Maitland Jones III
Douglas Neal Kozel
James A. Langley
Daniel P. Towler-Weese
Lynn Waskelis

1993
Gregory M. Barnell
Benyamin Ber
Sari Chang
George Andrew Clemens
Timothy Charles Geisler
Richard G. Grisaru
Louise J. Harpman
Michael A. Harshman
Tara L. McCay
Gitta Robinson
Evan Michael Supcoff

1994
Brendan Russell Coburn
Mark C. Dixon
Pamela J. Fischer
Paul W. Jackson
Mark R. Johnson
William J. Massey
Tania K. Min
Edward B. Samuel
Albert J. Tinson, Jr.
Mimi H. Tsai

1995
Matthew K. Bremer
Carolyn A. Foug
George Craig Knight
Aaron M. Lamport
Michael Henry Levendusky
Jonathan Paul Siegel
Todd Thomas Stodolski
John Christopher Woell

1996
John B. Clancy
Don M. Dimster-Denk
Russell S. Katz
Michael V. Knopoff
Chung Yin J. Lau
Thomas A. Lumikko
Nancy Nienberg
Steven A. Roberts
David A. Thurman
Mai-Tse Wu

1997
Victor E. Agran
Alexander O. Barrett
Richard Kasemsarn
Drew Lang
Peter D. Mullan
Jeffery Ryan Povero
William James Voulgaris
Shawn Michael Watts
Andrew Paul Wolff

1998
Carl F. Bergamini
Lana Berkovich
Paul J. Boulifard
Marjorie K. Dickstein
Edward B. Gulick
Karl A. Krueger
Faith Rose
Elizabeth P. Rutherfurd

1999
Elizabeth Marie Bester
Jonathan David Bolch
Kimberly Ann Brown
Yoonhee Choi
Eric Richard Clough
Martha Jane Foss
Bruce D. Kinlin
Moshik S. Mah
Aaron W. Pine

2000
Benjamin Jon Bischoff
Dominique D. Davison
Joseph Shek Yuen Fong
Oliver E. Freundlich
Timothy R. Hickman
Donald W. Johnson
Thomas Matthew Morbitzer
Soohyoun Nam
Michael J. Tower
Cheng-Hsun Wu

2001
Ghiora Aharoni
Mark Foster Gage
Jeff Allan Goldstein
Alexander M. Hathaway
Christopher M. Pizzi
Elizabeth Weeks Tilney
Can M. Tiryaki
Juliana Chittick Tiryaki

2002
Noah K. Biklen
Joseph P. Ferrucci
Sarah Marie Lavery
Yansong Ma
Rashid Jamal Saxton
Suejin Sung
Victoria Partridge Walsh

2003
Andrew William Benner
Marcos Diaz Gonzalez
Li-Yu Hsu
Youngsoo Kwon
Dongyeop Lee

2004
Graham W. Banks
Valerie Anne Casey
Pu Chen
Spencer W. Luckey
James C. Nelson III
Adam Sokol
Damian D. Zunino

2005
Jennifer N. Carruthers
Ruth Shinenge Gyuse
Diala Salam Hanna
Brandon F. Pace
Noah Riley
Brett Dalton Spearman
Nicholas Martin Stoutt

2006
Eron Ashley
Angel Paolo Campos
Michael J. Grogan
Andrei Simon Harwell
Sean A. Khorsandi
David Nam

2007
Joseph D. Alguire
Brook G. Denison
Geoffrey R. Lawson
Heather L. Puurunen
Joseph M. Smith

2008
Elizabeth V. Baldwin Gray
Michael B. Crockett
Mark Charles Guberman
Whitney M. Kraus
Garrett T. Omoto
Leo Rowling Stevens IV
Shelley X. Zhang

2009
Lauren J Mishkind
Matthew A. Roman
Rebecca B. Winik

2010
Brett Patrick Appel
Nicholas A. Gilliland
Scott Brandon O'Daniel

2011
Patrick J. Delahoy
William Grandison Gridley
Lindsay N. Hochman
Eero Pekka Puurunen
Alexandra F. Taiker

2012
JohnTaylor Bachman
Amanda Marquit

2013
Antonia M. Devine
Ryan Salvatore
Paul C. Soper

2014
C. Chessin Gertler

*Deceased

Retrospecta 37
2013–2014

Published by the Yale School of Architecture
Dean Robert A.M. Stern

EDITOR-IN-CHIEF
Anthony Gagliardi

EDITORS
Dov Feinmesser
Jenny Kim
Andrew Sternad

GRAPHIC DESIGN
Yotam Hadar
Jiyoni Kim

EDITORIAL ASSISTANTS
Leah Abrams
Luke Anderson
Jessica Flore Angel
Jack Bian
Michelle Gonzalez
Kiana Hosseini
Anne Householder
Samantha Jaff
Nicolas Kemper
John Kleinschmidt
Clarissa Luwia
Richard Mandimika
Phillip Nakamura
Madelynn Ringo
Susan Wang
Melody Song
Winny Tan

DESIGN CONSULTANT
Pentagram, New York

YSOA PHOTOGRAPHERS
John Jacobson
Ivan Farr
Scott Parks
Dionysus Cho
Anne Ma
Jonathan Sun
Travel photos by respective studios

We would like to extend our most
sincere gratitude to:

Dean Robert A.M. Stern
Donna Wetmore
Jean Sielaff
John Jacobson
John Eberhart
Lillian Smith
Maria Huling
Marilyn Weiss
Michael Beirut, Pentagram, New York
Monica Robinson
Nina Rappaport
Patricia Mastrangelo
Richard Kaplan, Allied Printing
Richard DeFlumeri
Robert Liston
Robie-Lyn Harnois
Rosalie Bernardi
Rosemary Suggs Watts
Sheila Levrant de Bretteville

FORMER EDITORS
Jonathan Sun
Elena Baranes
Phillip Nakumura
Tyler Pertman

The faculty, staff, and students
of the Yale School of Architecture

We would also like to acknowledge the invaluable support of the Rutherford Trowbridge Memorial Publication Fund and the Paul Rudolph Publication Fund, established by Claire and Maurits Edersheim.

For more information and copies of this book.
Please write, call or visit us at:
Yale School of Architecture
180 York Street
New Haven, CT 06511
(203) 432-2288
www.architecture.yale.edu

Printed on Torraspapel CreatorSilk and International Paper Springhill Gray

Typeset in Founders Grotesk Text (Kris Sowersby, Klim Type Foundry, 2013), Foundry Gridnik (Wim Crouwel, 1960s / David Quay and Freda Sack, The Foundry, 2009) and Pitch (Kris Sowersby, Klim Type Foundry, 2012)

Printed and bound by Allied Printing Services, Manchester, CT.

ISBN 978-0-9898592-8-8

INDEX

Art & Architecture Building model: interim design scheme.
Yale Events and Activities Photographs,
Manuscripts and Archives, Yale University Library.